DEGAS AND THE BALLET
PICTURING MOVEMENT

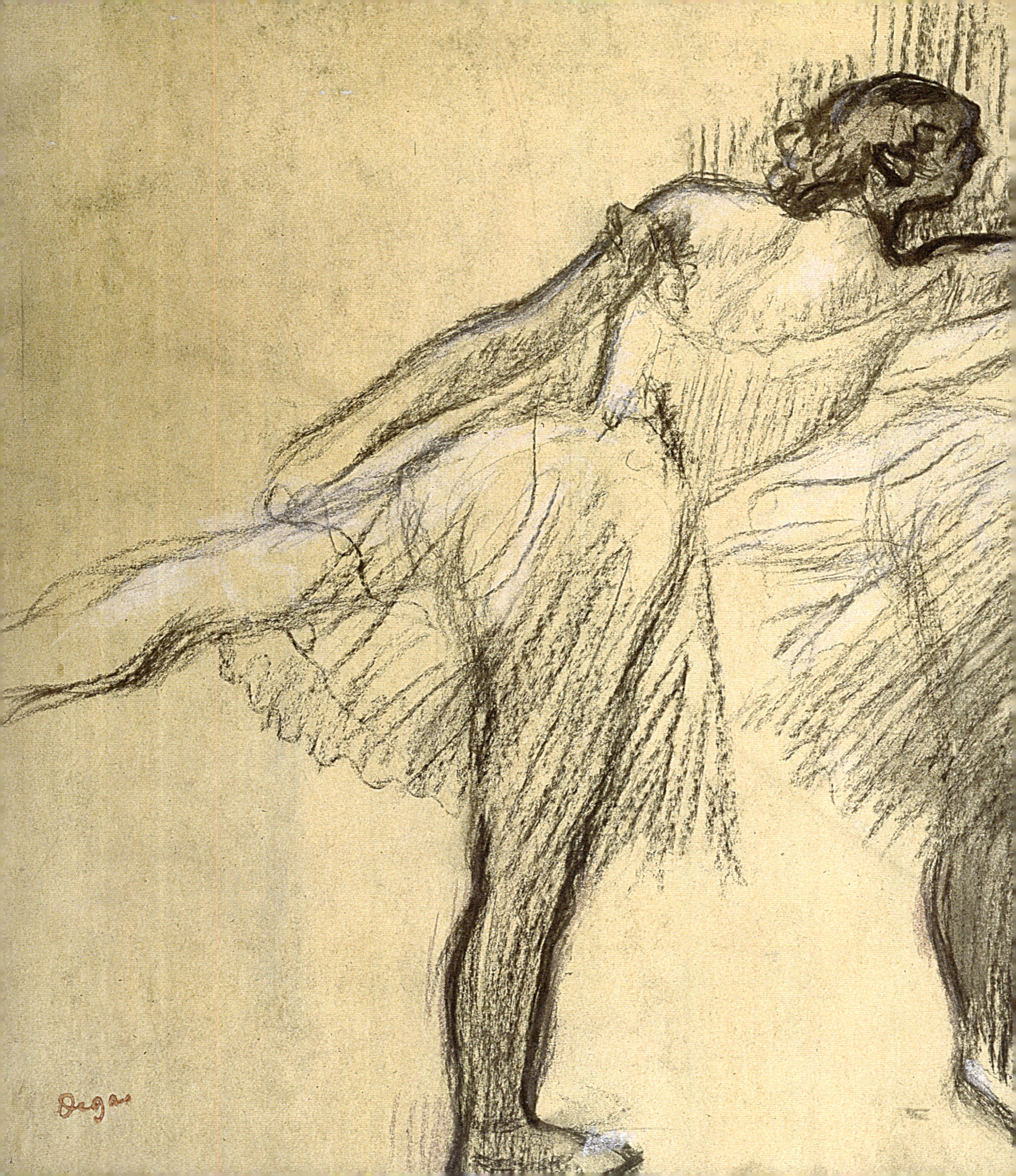
Degas

RICHARD KENDALL
JILL DEVONYAR

DEGAS AND THE BALLET

PICTURING MOVEMENT

ROYAL ACADEMY OF ARTS

This book is dedicated to Theodore Reff, teacher, colleague, friend

First published on the
occasion of the exhibition
'Degas and the Ballet:
Picturing Movement'

Royal Academy of Arts, London
17 September – 11 December 2011

Sponsored by

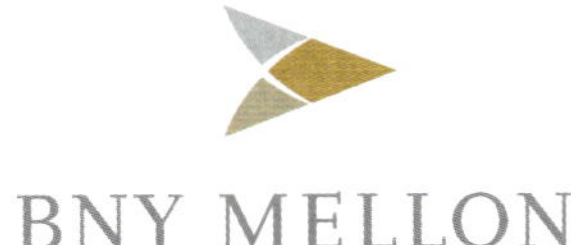

Supported by

region HOLDINGS

BLAVATNIK FAMILY FOUNDATION

The Royal Academy of Arts is grateful
to Her Majesty's Government for agreeing
to indemnify this exhibition under the
National Heritage Act 1980, and to the MLA,
for its help in arranging the indemnity.

Patron of the Exhibition
Darcey Bussell CBE

Exhibition Curators
Richard Kendall
Jill DeVonyar

Royal Academy of Arts
Ann Dumas

Exhibition Manager
Jane Knowles
Assisted by Philippa Hemsley

Photographic and Copyright Co-ordinator
Kitty Corbet Milward

CATALOGUE

Royal Academy Publications
Beatrice Gullström
Elizabeth Horne
Carola Krueger
Sophie Oliver
Peter Sawbridge
Nick Tite

Design
Kathrin Jacobsen

Colour origination
DawkinsColour

Printed in Italy
by Graphicom

British Library Cataloguing-in-Publication Data
A catalogue record for this book is available
from the British Library

ISBN 978-1-905711-69-7 (paperback)
ISBN 978-1-905711-68-0 (hardback)

Distributed outside the United States and Canada
by Thames & Hudson Ltd, London

Distributed in the United States and Canada
by Harry N. Abrams, Inc., New York

Note to the Reader
All works of art illustrated are
by (Hilaire Germain) Edgar Degas
(1834–1917) unless otherwise stated.

All dimensions are given in centimetres,
height before width (before depth).

Abbreviations are used in the endnotes
to indicate the following key sources:

BR   Brame and Reff 1984
J   Janis 1968
L   Lemoisne 1946–49
Nb. Reff 1985
R   Rewald 1944
RS   Reed and Shapiro 1984
T   Terrasse 1983

Full citations appear in the Bibliography
and Sources on pp. 264–70.

Illustrations
Pages 2–3: detail of cat. 106
Page 6: detail of cat. 1
Page 8: cat. 87
Page 10: detail of cat. 12
Page 13: detail of cat. 118
Page 14: detail of fig. 61
Page 17: detail of cat. 120
Page 18: detail of cat. 69
Pages 20–21: detail of cat. 7
Pages 68–69: detail of cat. 24
Pages 128–29: detail of cat. 55
Pages 184–85: detail of cat. 117

CONTENTS

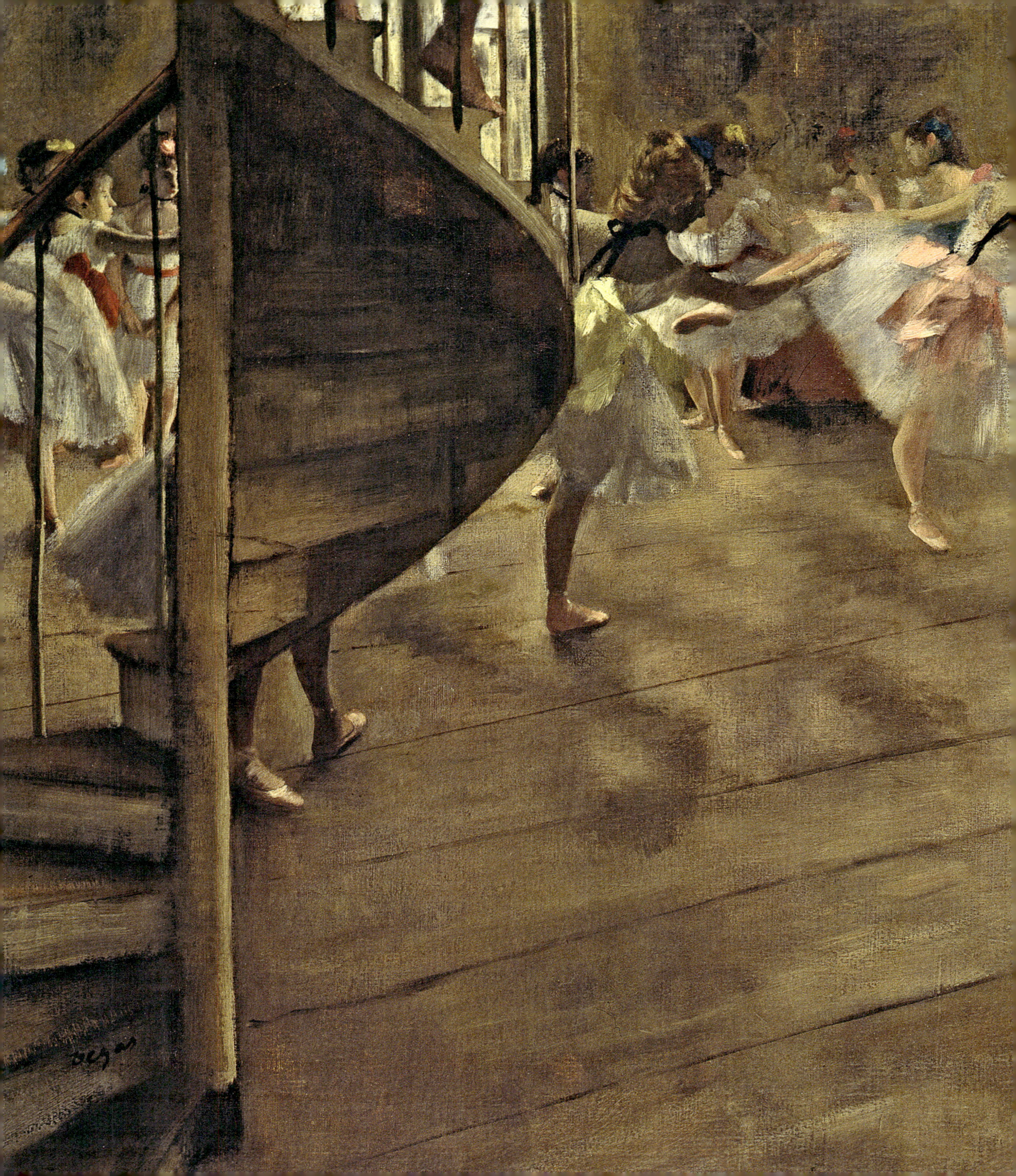

PRESIDENT'S FOREWORD

One of the greatest and best loved of nineteenth-century French artists, Degas is known above all as the painter of the dance. No artist before or since has explored the theme so extensively, so subtly and in such depth. Even in Degas's lifetime, his contemporaries sought explanations for his obsession, and his own cryptic observations offered few clues. The answer is surely that for him the most compelling of all artistic challenges was to capture the human figure in movement. In the ballet, he found the ideal subject, one that not only offered a complex and sophisticated range of movements but also accorded with his commitment to depicting modern life, a programme he shared with the Impressionist group, of which he was a leading figure.

The Royal Academy is proud to present 'Degas and the Ballet: Picturing Movement', the first exhibition devoted exclusively to Degas's dance subjects ever to be seen in London. The selection contains celebrated as well as little-known works in every genre that this daringly experimental artist explored – paintings, pastels, drawings, prints and sculpture – ranging from his first ballet pictures of the 1870s to the sumptuous pastels he created in the 1890s, at the end of his career. The exhibition is also the first to present Degas in a new light by examining his fascination with movement in the broader context of parallel advances in high-speed photography and the first films. Photographs by the pioneering stop-action photographer Eadweard Muybridge and the scientist Etienne-Jules Marey appear alongside samples of early films of the dance by the Lumière brothers and others. Degas acquired a camera himself in 1895, and some outstanding examples of his unique photographs, especially of dancers, are also to be found here, with his related pastels and drawings.

Richard Kendall, a leading authority on the artist, and Jill DeVonyar, a Degas scholar and former ballet teacher, have curated the exhibition with Ann Dumas of the Royal Academy. They are responsible for the careful selection and for having secured some ninety of Degas's great dance subjects as well as supporting documentary, photographic and film material. The four chapters of this catalogue represent Kendall's and DeVonyar's inspired vision for their exhibition and their years of research into connections between Degas's art and the photography and film of his day.

Ivor Heal has been responsible for the exhibition's beautiful design. All organisational matters have been expertly handled by Jane Knowles. Katia Pisvin and Philippa Hemsley have provided invaluable assistance throughout.

We express our most sincere thanks to all our lenders, public and private, who have so generously allowed us to part them from their works to make the exhibition possible.

The exhibition could not have been realised without the extremely generous support of BNY Mellon. In these challenging economic times we are very grateful to them for their sponsorship. We would also like to thank Region Holdings and the Blavatnik Family Foundation for their additional support, and we are delighted that Darcey Bussell CBE has agreed to be Patron of the exhibition.

Sir Nicholas Grimshaw CBE PRA

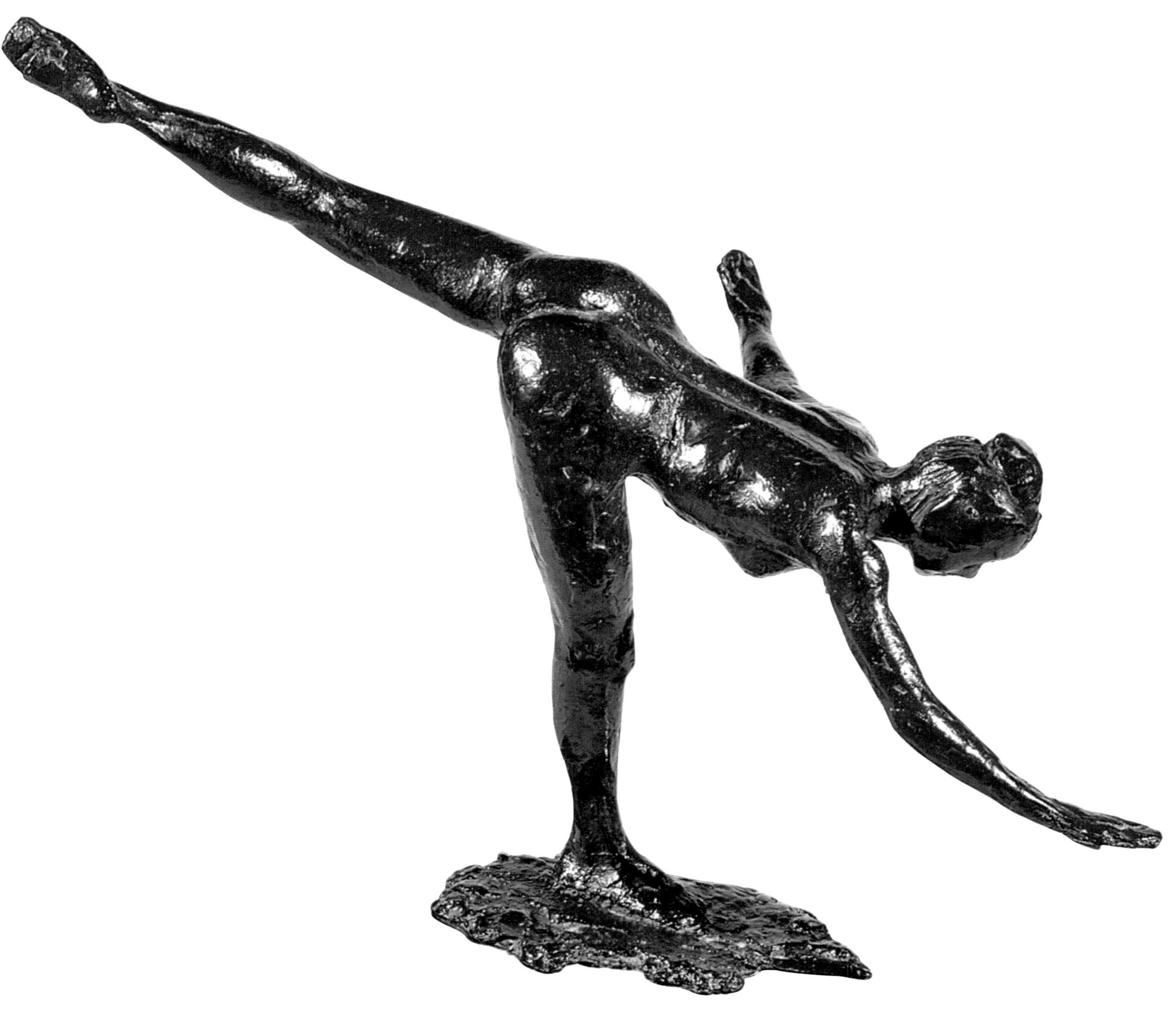

'They call me the painter of dancers, not understanding that for me the dance is a pretext for [...] rendering movement,' Edgar Degas once said. 'Degas and the Ballet: Picturing Movement' brings together many important and much-loved paintings, drawings, pastels and sculptures to provide a fascinating insight into the artist's approach to the visual challenges of expressing the figure in motion.

The work of Edgar Degas was a personal favourite of the art collector and philanthropist Paul Mellon, and the public's perception of Degas as a sculptor was heightened in 1956 after Mr Mellon bought the entire collection of the artist's original wax sculptures, later bequeathing them to galleries and museums in the United Kingdom, America and France for future generations to enjoy.

BNY Mellon's long-standing commitment to the arts as part of our global philanthropic endeavours, and in particular our valued and enduring partnership with the Royal Academy of Arts, has spanned many projects and remains a great source of pride to our organisation. The Royal Academy strives to engage with the broadest possible audience through its exhibitions, educational activities and publications, and its championing of public access and education reflects the key principles that inform BNY Mellon's international programme of arts sponsorship. It is therefore a particular privilege for us to support 'Degas and the Ballet: Picturing Movement'. We hope that you enjoy visiting this captivating exhibition.

Michael Cole-Fontayn
Chairman of Europe, Middle East and Africa, BNY Mellon

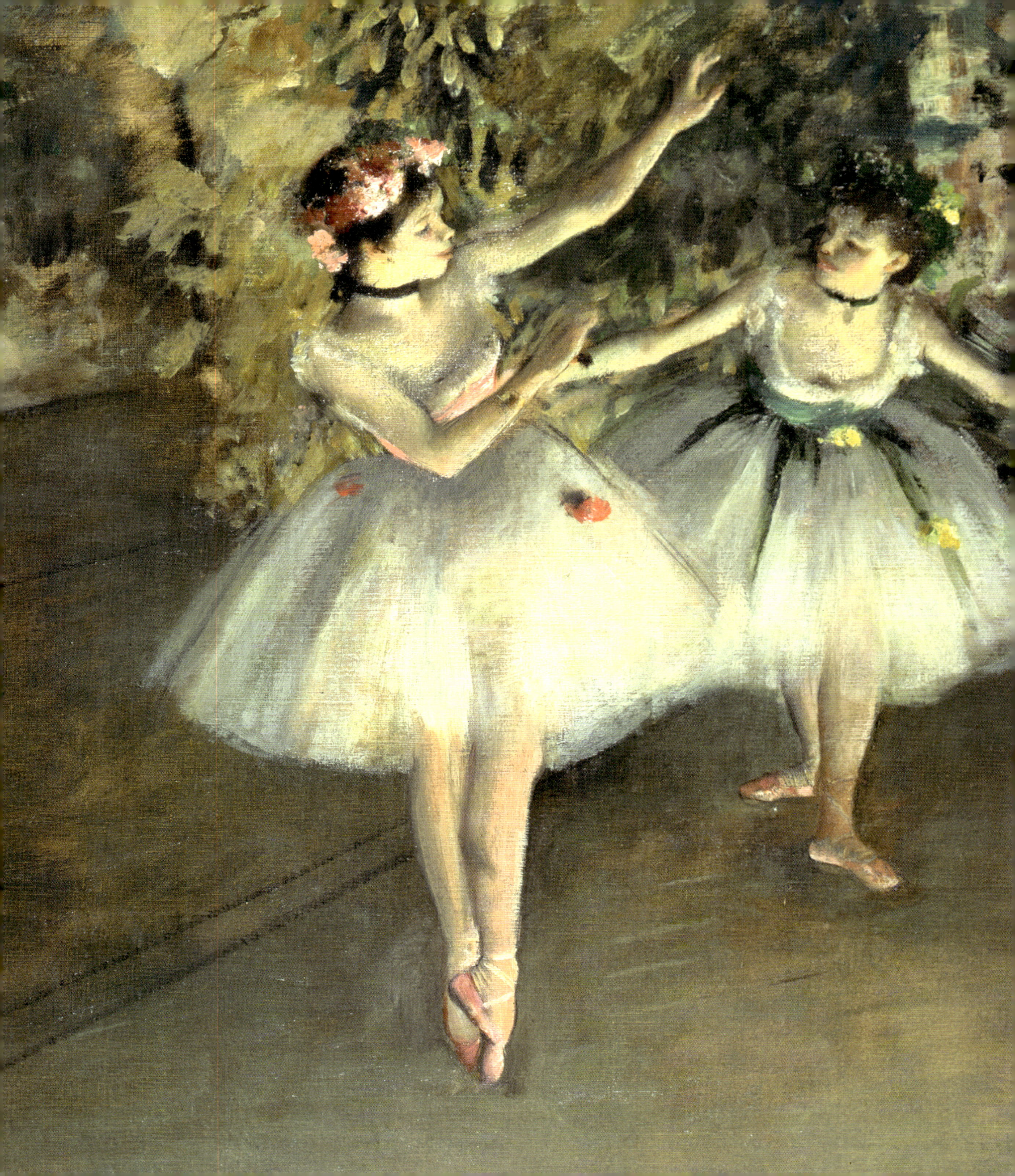

ACKNOWLEDGEMENTS

Richard Kendall and Jill DeVonyar are especially grateful to the following for their generous support and assistance: Joseph Baillio, Catherine Chevillot, Guy Cogeval, Peta Cook, Douglas Druick, Vivien Hamilton, Françoise Heilbrun, Theodore Reff, and Guy Wildenstein. They would particularly like to thank Harriet Stratis for her generous assistance and invaluable advice on Degas pastels. They would also like to thank the following for their kind co-operation, assistance and support: Hortense Anda-Bührle, Maria Antonova, Mathias Auclair, Graham Beal, Guy Bennett, Terri Boccia, William Brady, Rick Brettell, John Buchanan, Karen Bucky, Tobias Burg, Jay Clarke, Francesca Consagra, Juliane Cosandier, Alan Darr, Annette Dixon, Mark Evans, John Falconer, Peter Findlay, Matthew Gale, Thomas Galifot, Laura Giles, Ashley Givens, Lucas Gloor, Gloria Groom, Claire Guttinger, Dorothee Hansen, Colin Harding, Jefferson Harrison, Jodi Hauptman, Jan Howard, Nancy Ireson, Kimberley Jones, Muriel King, Sam Keller, Ulf Küster, Tom Lentz, Ellen McAdam, Suzanne McCullagh, Earle Mack, Michael Martin, Joan Michelman, Rebecca Michelman, Jane Munro, Maureen O'Brien, Steven Ongpin, Simon Ray, Christopher Riopelle, Anne Röver-Kann, Salvador Salort-Pons, Harriet Stratis, Marjorie Strauss, Joseph Strubel, Kristy Stubbs-French, Rachel Stuhlman, Jennifer Tonkovich, Gary Tinterow, Pierre Vidal, Stefan Wolohojian, Barnaby Wright, Sylvie Wurhmann.

The Royal Academy of Arts would like to thank the following for their assistance during the making of this exhibition and its catalogue: Giovanna Bertazzoni, W. M. Brady & Co., Melanie Clore, Peta Cook, Elizabeth Dixon, Amy-Rose Enskat, Evelyne Ferlay, Michael Findlay, Fine Art Museums of San Francisco (De Young Museum), Elizabeth Floyd, Alexandra Francis, Hannah Fuller, Graeme Gardiner, Thomas Gibson, Claudine Godts, Halcyon Gallery, Marie-Anne Krugier-Poniatowski, Tzila Krugier and Aviel Krugier, Galerie Krugier, Helen Loveday, Lord Macfarlane of Bearsden, Charles S. Moffett, David Norman, Odile Nouvel, Liberté Nuti, Alexey Petukhov, Caroline Porter, Simon Ray, Manuel Schmit, Kristy Stubbs Gallery, Aleksandra Todorovic, June Wallis, Ully Wille, Alon Zakain Fine Art.

INTRODUCTION

For better and for worse, Edgar Degas has become known to several generations as 'the painter of dancers'. From the beginning of his public career he exhibited pictures of ballerinas on stage and in their practice rooms that delighted some and horrified others. This was a highly original decision on his part, as well as a professionally demanding one. No previous artist in history had been so conspicuously identified with the ballet, which was at times dismissed as a minor or frivolous art that catered to voyeuristic tastes. For Degas, this reputation seems to have been an enticement, challenging him to confront a still-popular cultural form while aspiring to make radically new pastels, paintings and sculptures for his own times. As a leading member of the Impressionist group, he shared his colleagues' fascination with modern sights and sensations, from the vivacity of cities to the raucousness of street life, from fresh images of their surroundings offered by the photograph to the vividness of commercial illustration. While ballet overlapped with this contemporary world, it had another lingering significance. Seen as the descendant of a practice that reached back through the millennia, it also perpetuated the most timeless subject of the visual arts: the human body. Degas himself recognised this part of ballet's legacy and seems to have been inspired to maintain the tradition. Trained in the orthodox manner, he had learned to draw from living models and studied the great figurative works of the old masters. By choosing dance as his principal theme, he was able to stay loyal to the figure even as he articulated it in the down-to-earth terms of his age. As Degas was venturing into this territory for the first time, the poet and essayist Charles Baudelaire – whose definitions of 'modernity' influenced the Impressionist generation so profoundly – almost anticipated Degas's ballet compositions when he included these words in a short story: 'Dance is poetry with arms and legs, it is matter, gracious and terrible, animated, embellished by movement.'

Famously reluctant to speak about his art, in later life Degas would occasionally offer insights into his obsession with the ballet to friends and trusted admirers. Terse and sometimes oblique, these aphorisms are the closest thing we have to an artistic credo by this otherwise articulate individual. Such a memorable statement of this kind was offered to the American art collector Louisine Havemeyer, when in 1903 she visited the elderly Degas in the company of her friend Mary Cassatt. Louisine herself recalled asking him, 'Why, Monsieur, do you always do ballet dancers?' to which the artist replied, 'Because, Madame, it is all that is left us of the combined movements of the Greeks.' Another witness was the Irish novelist and critic George Moore, who remembered Degas saying that 'the dancer is nothing but a pretext for drawing'. Perhaps his most often cited remark on this subject, however, was another that emphasised the dynamic nature of the ballet. In a conversation recalled by an acquaintance who knew him

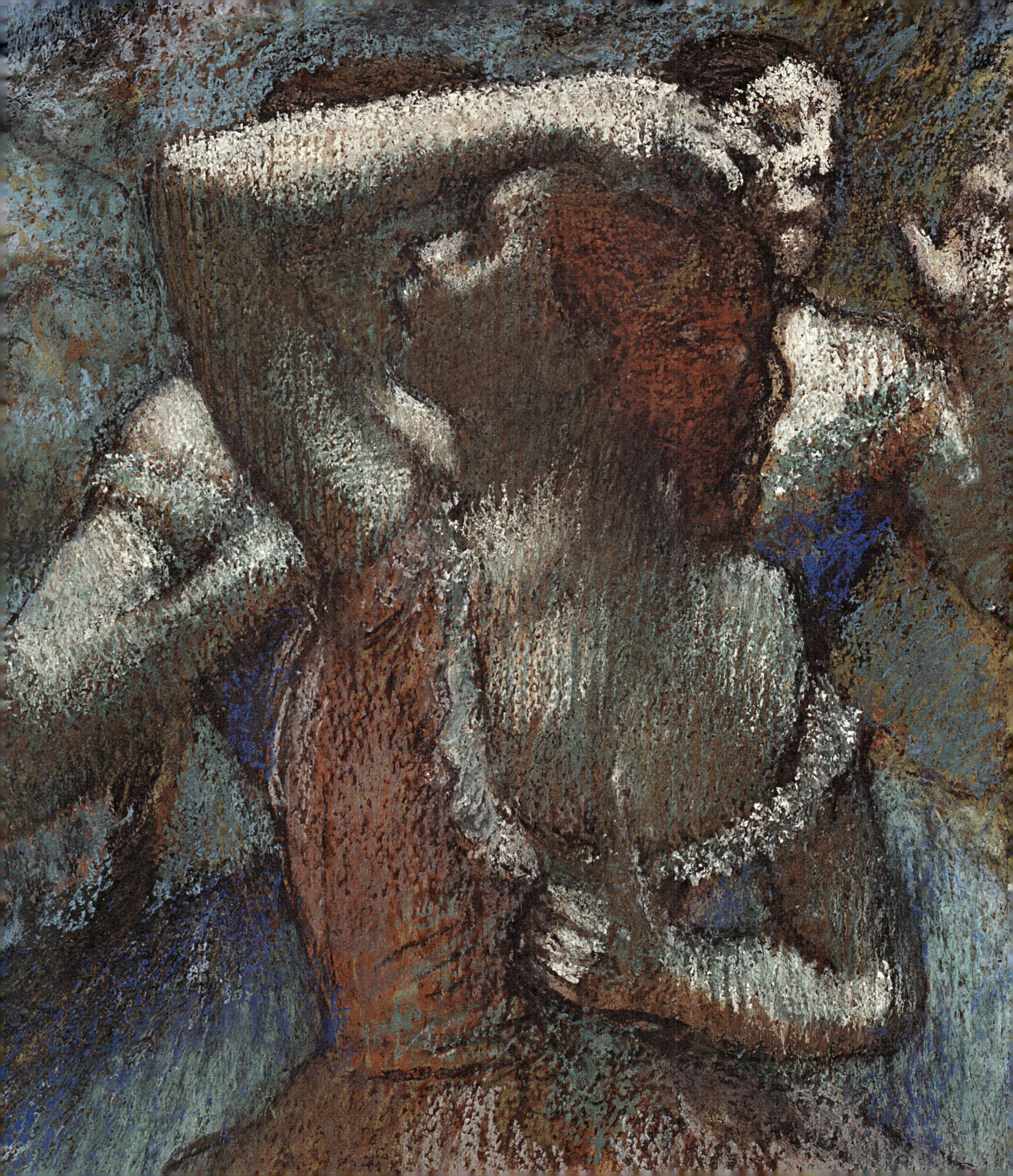

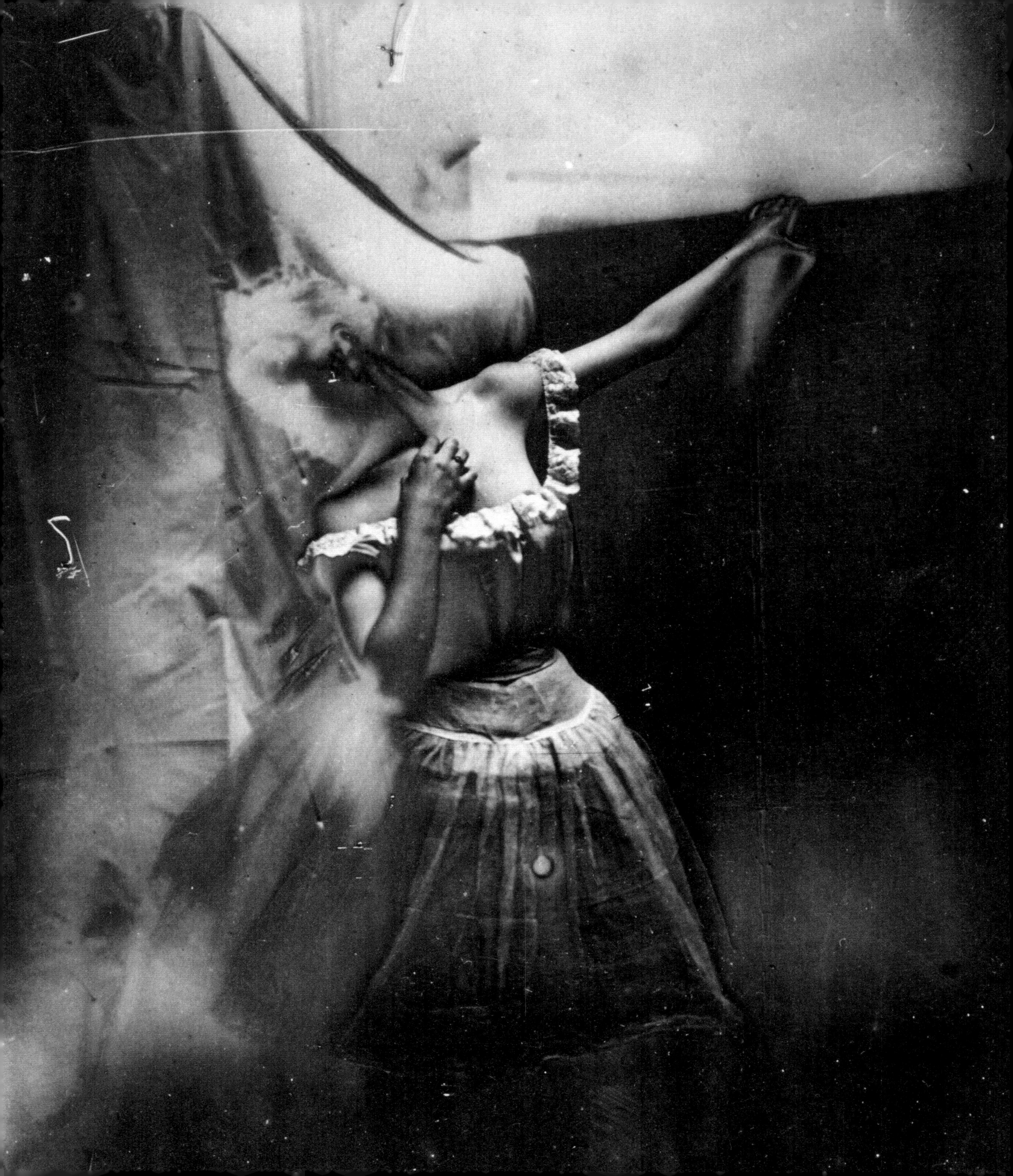

well in old age – the art dealer Ambroise Vollard – Degas is said to have observed: 'They call me the painter of dancers. They don't understand that for me the dancer was a pretext for painting pretty fabrics and rendering movement.'

The possibility that 'rendering movement' was a defining impulse behind Degas's ballet imagery has never been examined in depth or set in its wider context. In a fundamental sense, of course, this impulse reflected a concern of many of Degas's immediate predecessors and contemporaries, who found themselves in an increasingly fast-paced world and attempted to respond to it appropriately in their art. A thoughtful essay on this theme by Solange Vernois argues that the question of representing movement was 'at the heart of critical debates in the nineteenth century'.[1] For conservative factions, Vernois points out, energetic or wild movement in art could be regarded as unseemly, although more adventurous voices – such as those of Eugène Delacroix and Charles Baudelaire – took the opposite position, calling for 'Life, life at all costs, life everywhere!' and 'more imagination, thus more movement!'. Degas admired both these individuals, collecting hundreds of drawings by Delacroix and reading the works of Baudelaire as a young man. Like his two predecessors, Degas also spent most of his life in Paris, already one of the most progressive and energetic cities in the world. In 1876, at the time of the second Impressionist exhibition, 'The movement, and hustle and bustle of passers-by' on a Paris street was identified as an exemplary subject for modern painters by Degas's close friend Edmond Duranty. Soon afterwards, Degas himself imagined new approaches to art-making that were to be even more dynamic. In his notebook, he envisaged 'drawing things from above and below' and even tackling 'a series of arm movements of the dance, or of legs which wouldn't move, turning around them oneself...'

Intriguingly, the text by Vernois appears in a catalogue produced not by an art museum but a museum of science, the Musée Marey in the town of Beaune, birthplace of Etienne-Jules Marey. Among the most prominent French scientists of the late nineteenth century, Marey specialised in the subject of movement, studying the circulation of blood, the flight of birds and above all the actions of humans as they walked, ran and leapt. Like the more well-known Eadweard Muybridge, Marey made extensive use of photography to record his moving subjects and pioneered new apparatus that 'froze' minute actions in a thousandth of a second or even less. Symptomatic of their times was the fact that both men collaborated with the artistic as well as the scientific community, recognising common concerns and shared principles. Muybridge presented his photographic sequences to a group of painters and sculptors in Paris and Marey exhibited a range of projects that included his sculptures of flying birds and early attempts at filmmaking. Shortly before the first Impressionist show in 1874, Marey had published the widely read

Animal Mechanism in which he set out the principle that 'Motion is the most apparent characteristic of life'. An active populariser, he also spoke about his ideas in public and wrote articles for such illustrated magazines as *La Nature* and *Scientific American*. Like many of his artist-peers, Degas is known to have been aware of the work of both Muybridge and Marey, and of their association with high-speed photography. It is also clear that he responded to their images of movement, making drawings from photographs of horses and nudes by Muybridge and noting parallels between Marey's high-speed sequences of figures and his own wax sculptures of dancers. Part of his aim as a sculptor, Degas told a friend, was to capture 'movement in its exact truth'.

'Degas and the Ballet: Picturing Movement' follows several of these intertwined issues through the four decades or more of the artist's engagement with ballet. Some of his first pictures to capture the attention of collectors and critics were set at the Paris Opéra, home of the national ballet company. Almost shocking in their novelty, these works were hailed by some for their startling realism and damned by others for their unconventional compositions and 'distorted', even 'dislocated', representations of dancers' bodies. As we now know, Degas's pictures were based on scrupulous drawings made directly from young ballerina-models, often in his studio and less frequently at the Opéra itself. So precise, even analytical, did these studies seem that certain of his more astute admirers described them in scientific terms: one writer suggested that the artist had represented 'the exterior of the human animal' and 'the workings of its physiognomy', adding that Degas seemed 'haunted by the human figure in movement'. Another analogy occasionally used at this date linked Degas's art to the still relatively new medium of photography, an association he seemed to encourage by exhibiting a canvas with the title *Dancer Posing for a Photograph*. Ballerinas were already a heavily photographed profession, their calling cards – cartes de visite – and publicity shots selling by the thousands in a city obsessed by dance and by photography itself. In these years, Degas clearly made occasional use of such prints when working on certain of his pictures, while sometimes mocking the medium and its pretensions. Yet photography was already inescapable as a booming industry producing portraits of the obscure and the famous, and as a profession dedicated to bold experiments that promised to capture the world's vitality.

A largely unexplored factor in Degas's engagement with movement is the parallel development of the camera during these same years. The inability of early photographers to document figures in action, for example, may have prompted some of Degas's ambitious attempts to draw ballerinas hovering on pointe and occasionally leaping above the stage. Similarly, the growth of panoramic photography seems to have inspired the artist to experiment with new kinds of composition, in curiously wide exercise rooms where dancers are positioned in rhythmic or whimsical fashion. Innovative ways of looking and

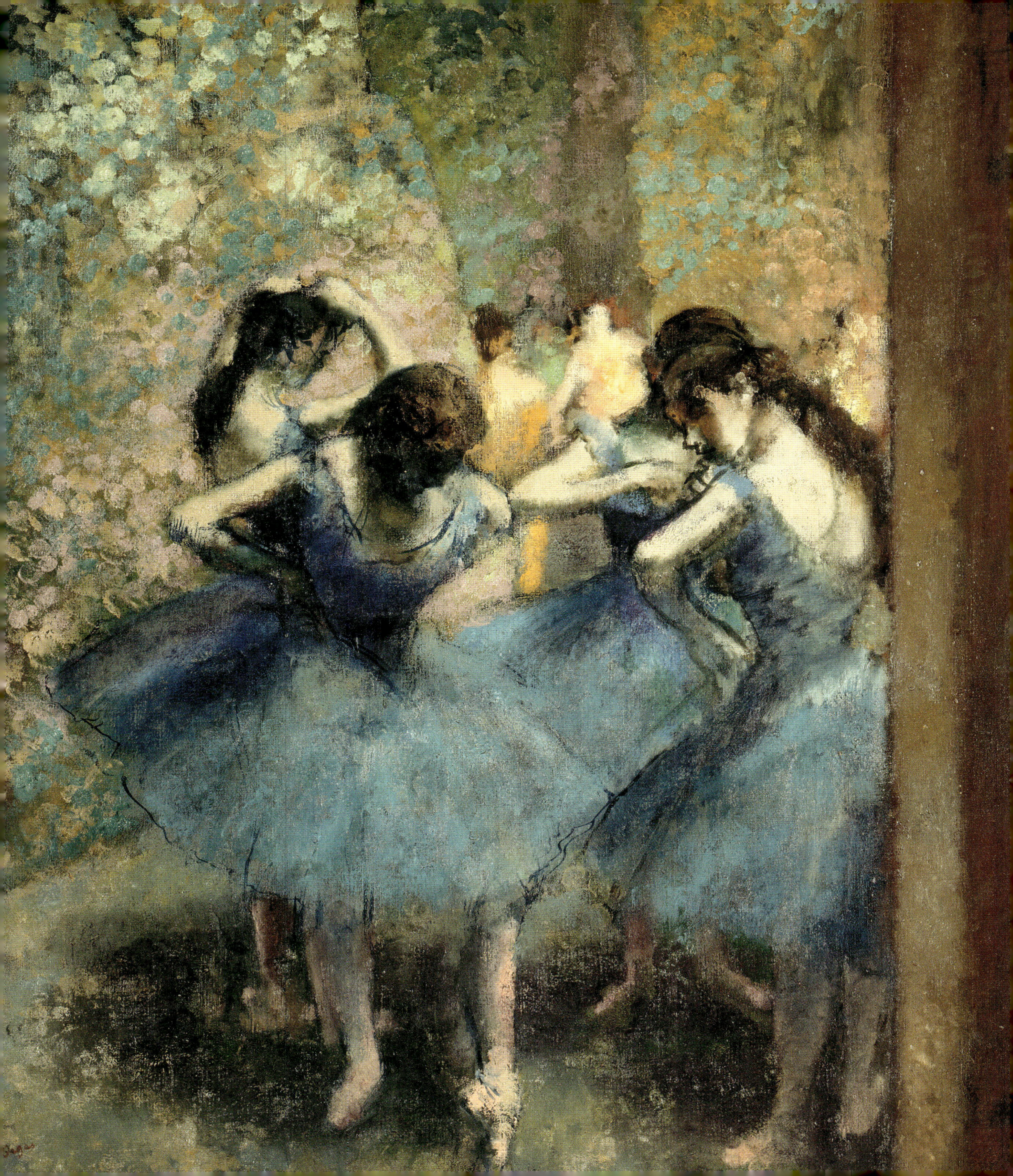

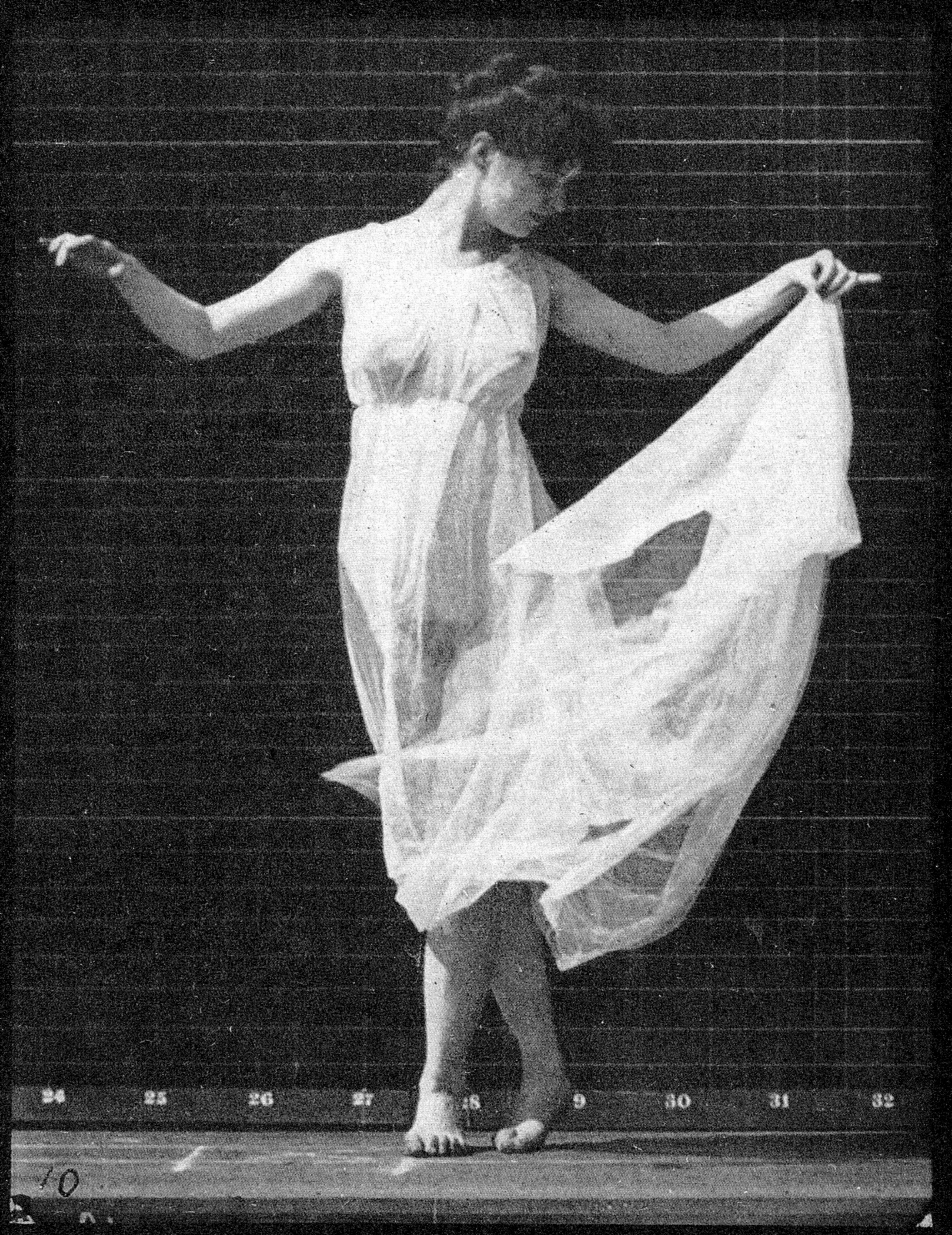

24 25 26 27 28 9 30 31 32
10

perceiving – again conceivably prompted by photographic precursors – may also lie behind his revolutionary *Little Dancer Aged Fourteen*, a figure that was studied from multiple points of view as if by a circular bank of cameras. Perhaps the most radical device to emerge from this dialogue, however, was the sequence in which two, three and sometimes more figures are shown moving in concert with each other as if in a single, unfolding action. Unquestionably informed to some degree by the work of Muybridge and Marey, this motif animated dozens of major drawings, pastels and paintings by Degas – and even certain groups of sculptures – from the *fin de siècle*. More than in his earlier years, colour now played a magisterial role in such works, its vibrancy contributing to a pervasive sense of energy as ballerinas stretch and perform, or merely arrange themselves around their colleagues.

The final chapter in this visual and conceptual saga began in 1895, when Degas acquired his first camera. Immediately fascinated by its potential for manipulating the chosen image, he took portraits by day and by night, and photographed a ballet dancer in several positions that soon began to appear in his pictures. Now more concerned with scenes in the wings than on stage, Degas also contrived groups of ballerinas who follow a common trajectory, rising from a bench or turning through space. Some of those who encountered such pictures marvelled at their new subtlety and power. Prominent among them was the young critic Gustave Geffroy, who wrote admiringly in 1894 of 'the rhythmic grace, the legs, the arms, the torso, the entire body in action' of one Degas dancer and described a picture as 'a passage of colour and form, a magnificent drawing in movement'. By a strange historical coincidence, 1895 was also the year that movement found a new expression in the world of photography, when the first films by the Lumière brothers were projected in central Paris. Degas's response to the medium is not recorded, but before long he was sharing at least one subject with the 'moving pictures'. Energetically embarking on a series of pastels of *Russian Dancers*, he may have been inspired by the same group of performers who were recorded by filmmakers such as Paul Nadar and the Lumières. Now less active himself, Degas gradually retreated from public life and often turned to his sculptures as his eyesight weakened. His passion for making photographs had been short-lived, but those around him continued to document the ageing artist with their cameras in both solemn and occasionally facetious moments. Around 1915, he was finally immortalised in the medium of the new century when the renowned director Sacha Guitry filmed him for a few seconds outside his apartment on the Boulevard de Clichy.

Richard Kendall and Jill DeVonyar

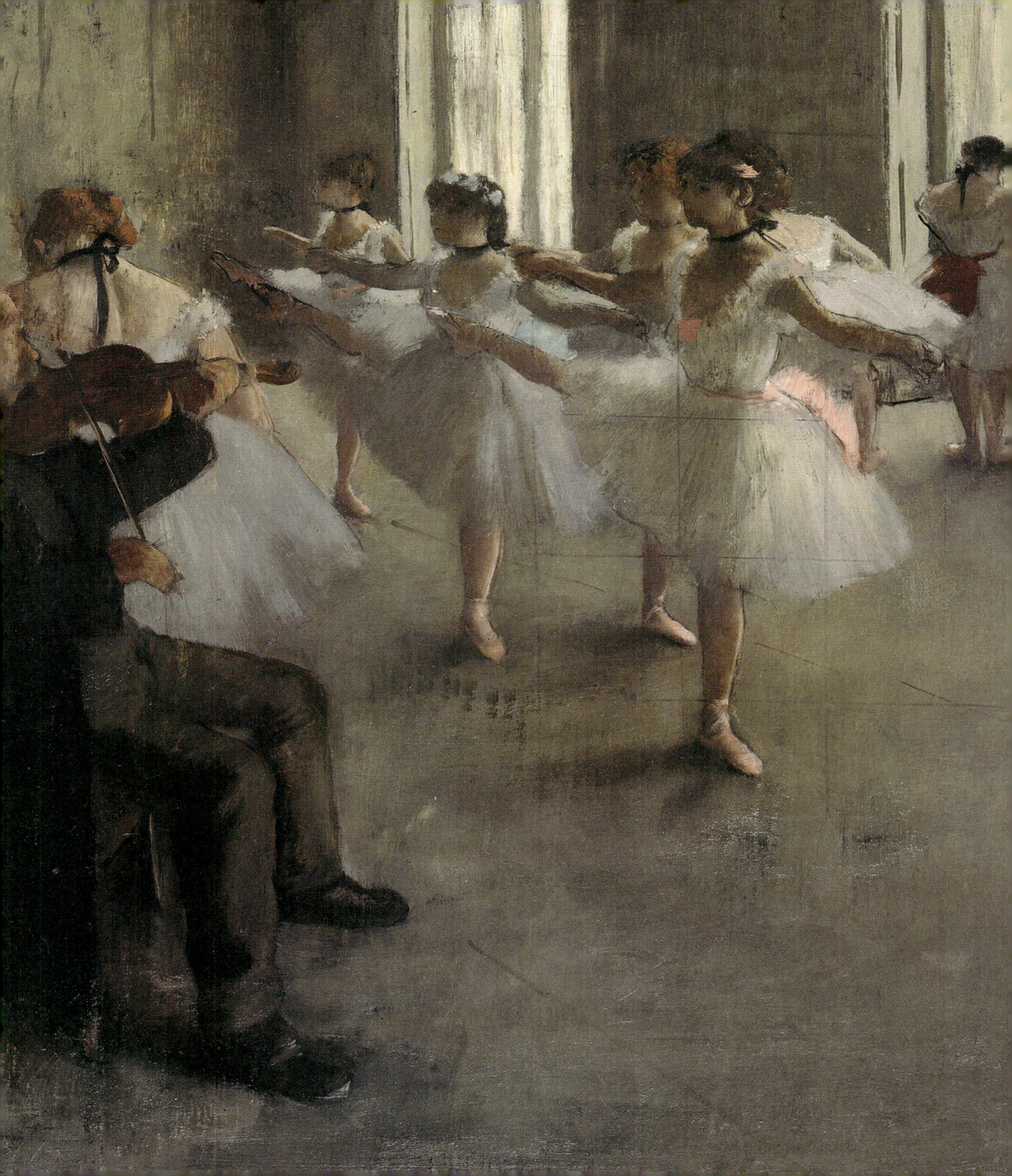

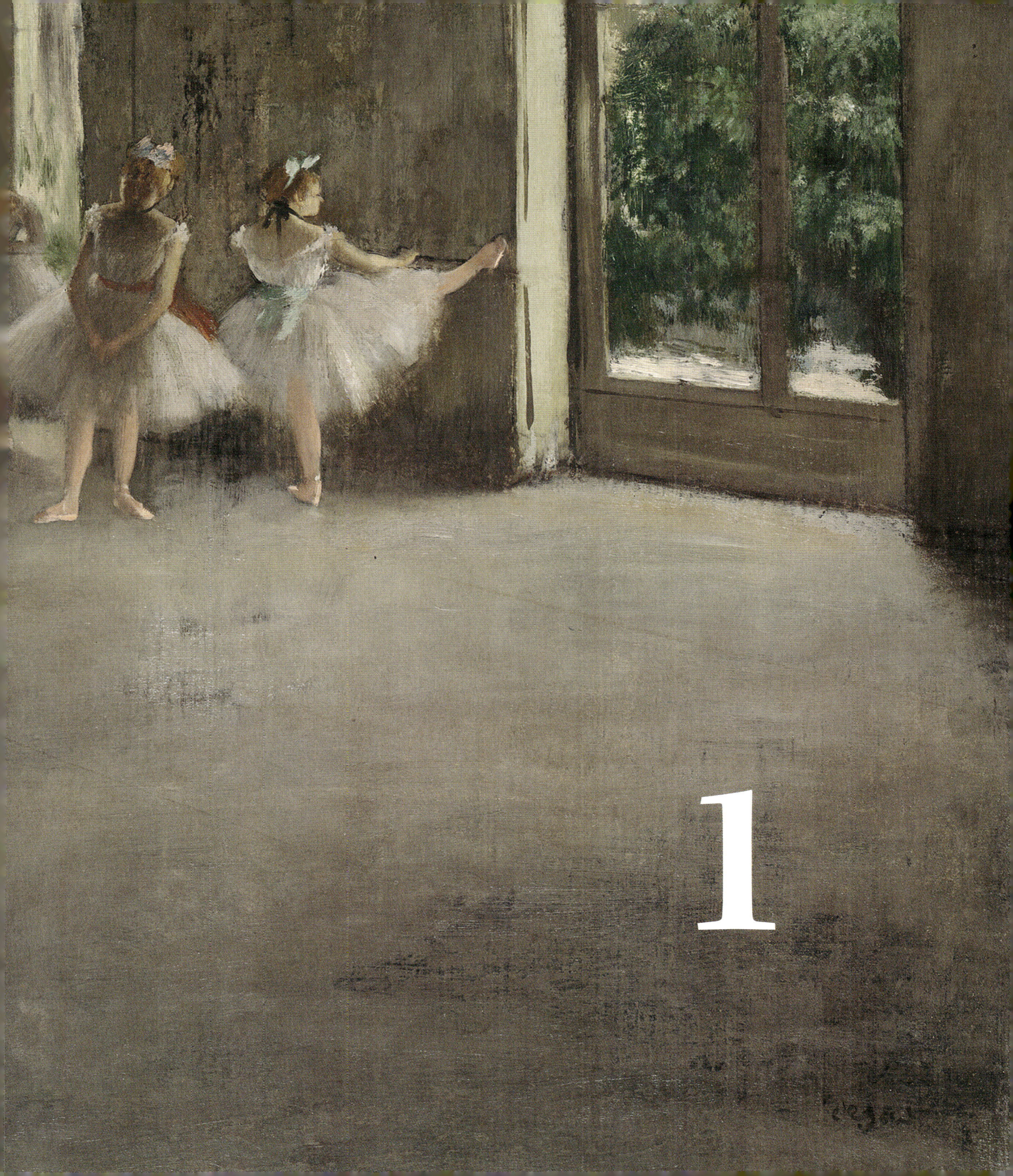

1

EARLY ENCOUNTERS WITH DANCE AND PHOTOGRAPHY

*Dance is poetry
with arms and
legs, it is matter,
gracious and terrible,
animated, embellished
by movement*

Charles Baudelaire[1]

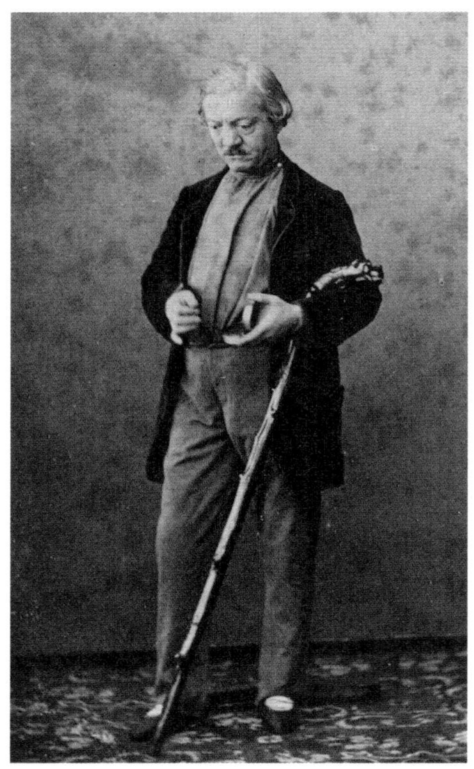

Fig. 1 *G. Bergamasco*, **Jules Perrot**, *c.* 1860.
Carte-de-visite photograph, 9 x 5 cm. Private collection

I n February 1874, after spending a day in 'the studio of a strange painter called Degas', the writer Edmond de Goncourt made notes in his journal about some pictures he had seen there.[2] One that he remembered in detail was said to feature a 'silhouette of dancers' legs coming down a little spiral staircase' and a 'striking patch of a tartan amidst all the puffy white clouds'. There is little doubt that he was referring to *The Rehearsal* (cat. 1), a magnificent oil painting on canvas that now belongs to the Burrell Collection in Glasgow. According to Goncourt, the 'graceful whirling movements' of the ballerinas in this picture had been 'captured from nature', a fact presumably passed on to him by the artist. Other contemporary accounts and documents tell us that during this same decade Degas frequently – even obsessively – observed such dancers at first hand, studying them in their classrooms and before the footlights, and recording the off-duty mannerisms that only an acute, patient eye would have noticed. In this fundamental sense *The Rehearsal* was a manifesto-like work, painted as Degas launched his career as an artist who was grounded in the day-to-day realities of ballet in the late nineteenth century. He was to spend the next two decades as a discreet observer, scrutinising the performances and back-stage gymnastics of the premier ballet company in Europe, that of the Paris Opéra. A man of his times, Degas became as fascinated by the dynamism of the corps de ballet as by their moments of poise and elegance, attempting to draw his dancer-models in mid-action and confronting a new medium that had also discovered the ballet: photography. Even *The Rehearsal* was touched by this radical invention, in a way that was both witty and conceptually provocative.

When he devised the innovative composition of *The Rehearsal*, Degas divided his canvas into several zones that each have a distinct character and tell us something different about the dancer's world. At right we find an area of repose where a seated dancer instinctively splays her legs to strengthen her inner thigh muscles, while her standing companion receives the attention of an older woman – wearing the 'tartan' mentioned in Goncourt's account – who fusses with the girl's tutu. Balancing this group at left is one of Degas's most audacious pictorial contrivances, from this or any other period: a partly truncated spiral staircase that is as wildly dynamic as the group of resting dancers is placid. Beyond them in the middle distance is the rehearsal itself, where a cluster of muslin-clad ballerinas in arabesque appears to advance from left to right and into the open space beyond. Finally, almost unnoticed in this bustling arena, a red-shirted ballet master stands at extreme right, implicitly bringing order to the proceedings and the visual equivalent of a full-stop to the momentum of his class. This was Jules Perrot (fig. 1), a veteran of the Romantic ballet who had long since retired from the stage but was still

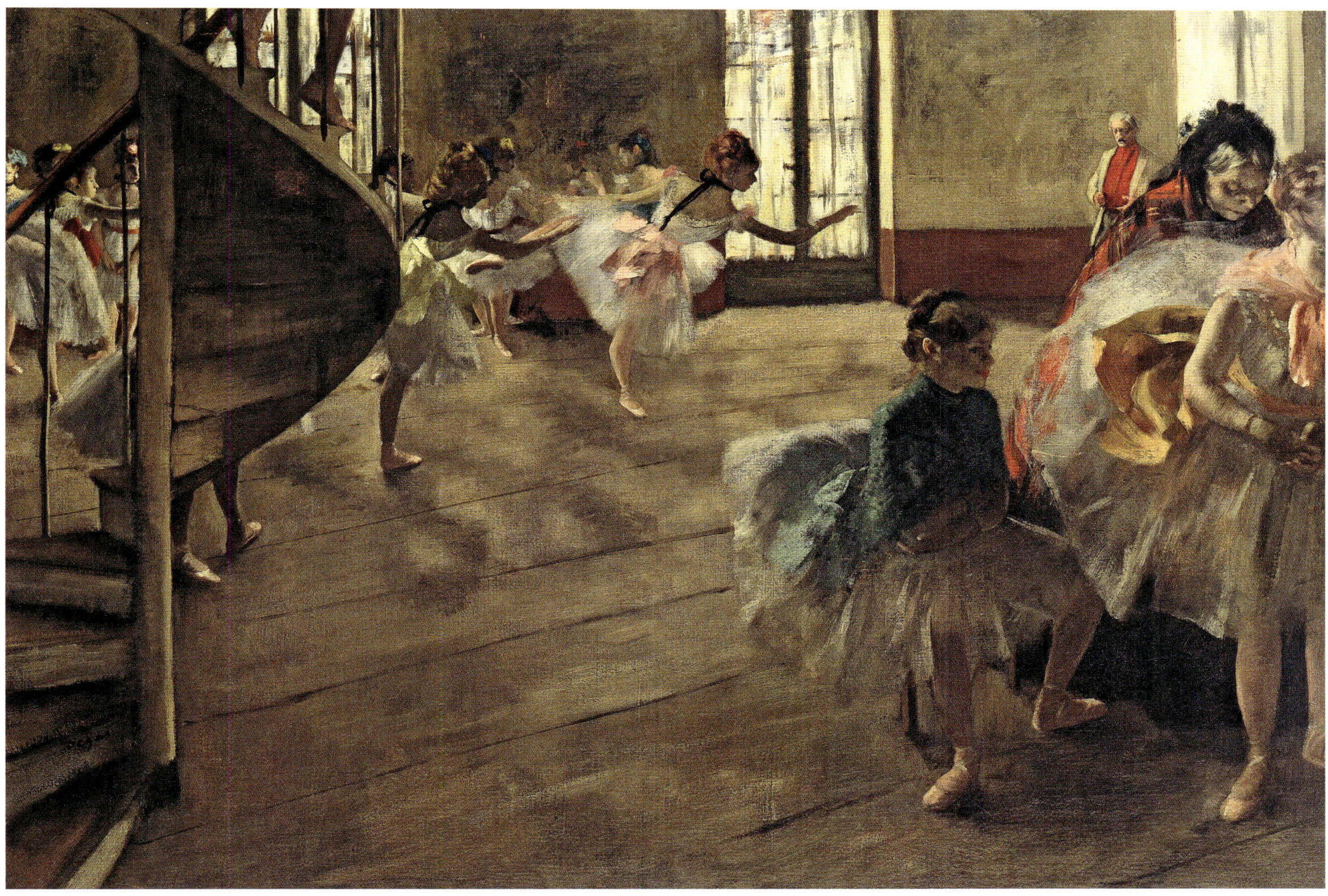

an iconic figure, representing the golden age of dancing during which the
Opéra company had achieved world renown. He was also a hardened
professional who knew at first hand the hours of punishing exercise and the
bleak surroundings of the dancer's practical existence. In *The Rehearsal* Degas
was notably frank about these factors, devoting much of the foreground to
a vista of bare boards that is only relieved at centre left by a subtle, shadowy
pattern; these 'figures of eight' were formed when the floor was dampened
with a watering-can to prevent the girls from slipping. Beyond are the grimy
classroom walls, their windows providing a hazy glimpse of the outside world
and pale natural light offering some relief from the austerity within.

Yet Perrot and Degas were surely attracted to such dreary spaces for the
same reason; from the endless hard work and repetitive daily routines there
would emerge what Goncourt rather inexpertly called the 'graceful whirling
movements and gestures' of ballet. A generation earlier, the young Charles
Baudelaire had described the phenomenon more eloquently in a short story
concerning a dancer, entitled 'La Fanfarlo': 'Dance is able to reveal everything
mysterious that music conceals, and it also has the merit of being human and
palpable,' he wrote; 'Dance is poetry with arms and legs, it is matter, gracious
and terrible, animated, embellished by movement.'[3] As he used the materials

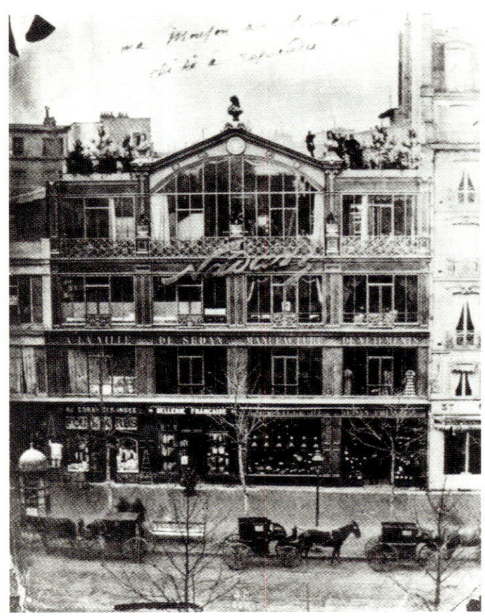

Fig. 2 *Nadar (Gaspard-Félix Tournachon),*
Studio of Nadar at 35 Boulevard des Capucines,
c. 1855. Photograph. Private collection

of his own craft, Degas was able to convey similarly complex ideas through the human forms and physical spaces represented in images such as *The Rehearsal*. The 'poetry of arms and legs' is most vividly captured in the horizontal rush of young women in arabesque – the only figures who are truly dancing – their elegantly poised limbs contrasted almost brutally with those of their foreground colleagues, who are nothing if not 'human and palpable'. The physicality of the models he represented in such pictures was acknowledged by Degas on a number of occasions. He later confessed to Walter Sickert that – as an artist – he may have 'too often considered woman as an animal' and told George Moore that the dancer was essentially 'a pretext for painting pretty materials and depicting movement'.[4] 'Matter, gracious and terrible' is everywhere in evidence in *The Rehearsal*, from the strong bodies of young dancers to the coarse structure of the room and the mechanical device of 'the little spiral staircase'. Degas was clearly delighted by the elegant, curving lines of this structure, introducing it into several other paintings over the years. Here it seems to whirl around the central axis, richly expressive of energy while creating a vertical thrust that is cleverly echoed in a pair of dancer's legs descending from the top.

When Goncourt visited his studio in early 1874, Degas was also much occupied with a group of little-known artists who were preparing to show their work in Paris. Within two months they had opened their first exhibition in the former studio of the celebrated photographer Gaspard-Félix Tournachon, known as Nadar, which was situated in the centre of the city on the Boulevard des Capucines (fig. 2). While some visitors welcomed this event and admired 'the intellectual honesty' of the participants, others mocked them as 'intransigents' who had offered 'an insult to the taste and the intelligence of the public'.[5] Now known throughout the world as the Impressionists, the group included painters who were principally concerned with the human figure, such

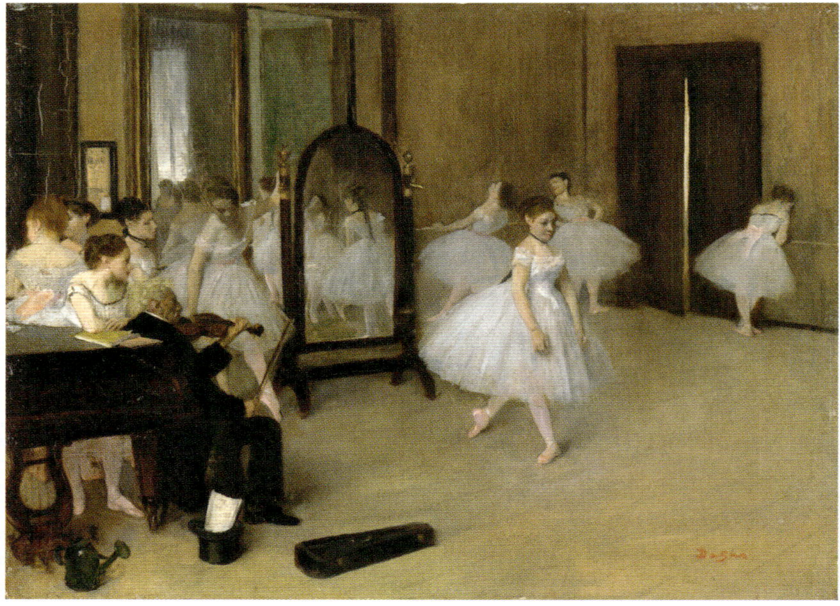

Fig. 3 **The Dancing Class**, probably 1871. Oil on panel, 19.7 x 27 cm. The Metropolitan Museum of Art, New York. H. O. Havemeyer Collection, Bequest of Mrs H. O. Havemeyer, 1929

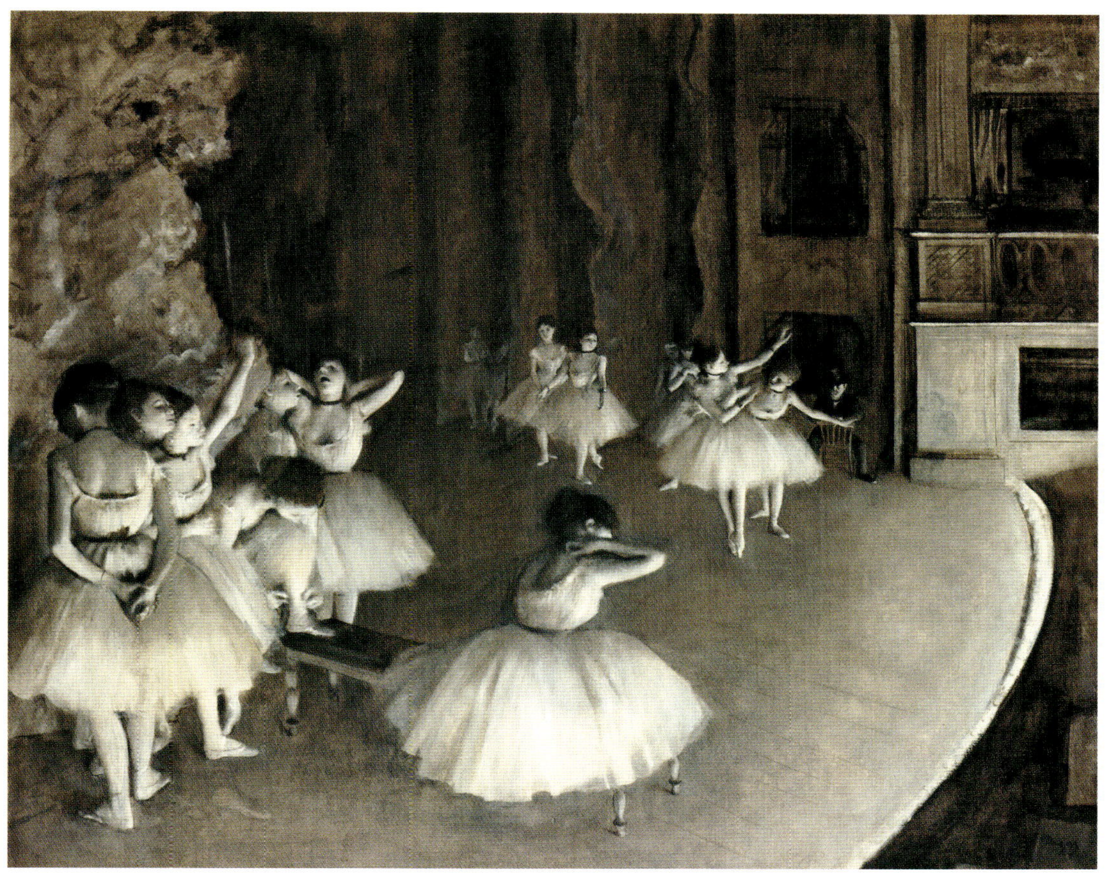

Fig. 4　**Ballet Rehearsal on Stage**, 1874. Oil on canvas,
65 x 81 cm. Musée d'Orsay, Paris

as Berthe Morisot, Pierre-Auguste Renoir and Degas himself, and the landscape
specialists Paul Cézanne, Claude Monet, Camille Pissarro and Alfred Sisley.
Degas had been among the most active proponents of this contentious project,
but his pictures were generally better received than those of his colleagues.
Following a pattern that would soon became familiar, he chose to exhibit the
broad range of his current subject-matter: listed in the catalogue were two
pictures of laundresses, three scenes of horse-racing and a single nude study,
alongside four works devoted to various aspects of the ballet. These included
a dance examination, a rehearsal on stage and a scene in the wings, as well as a
painting described simply as 'Dance Class', now known to be the near-miniature
oil on panel that hangs in the Metropolitan Museum of Art, New York (fig. 3).[6]
Conspicuously lacking was the Burrell Collection's *The Rehearsal,* perhaps
because the artist considered it still unfinished or was holding it in reserve for
one of the dealers and collectors who were already buying his work. Critical
response to Degas's submissions was overwhelmingly positive, with only one
dissenting voice suggesting that his *Ballet Rehearsal on Stage* (fig. 4) was 'very
strange'.[7] Others found this picture 'skilfully arranged' and Phillipe Burty, a
friend of the artist and critic for the prestigious *Gazette des Beaux-Arts,* asked in
his review if Degas himself might not become 'classic' in due course.[8] Burty went
further, arguing that no-one had previously made a 'portrait of the dancer, of the

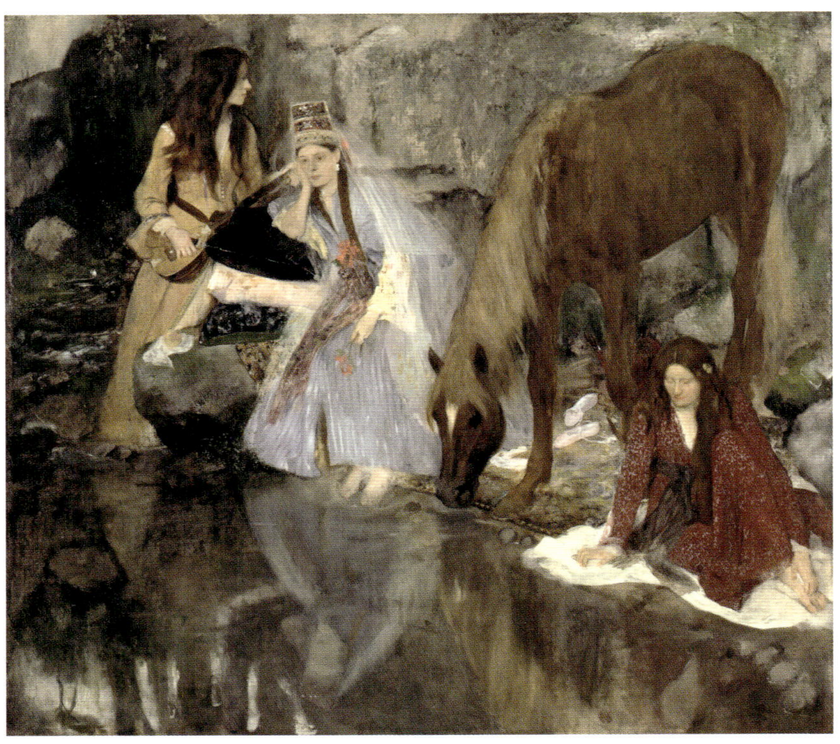

Fig. 5 **Mademoiselle Fiocre in the Ballet 'La Source'**, c. 1867–68.
Oil on canvas, 130.8 x 145.1 cm. Brooklyn Museum of Art, New York

coryphée, in gauze and in bone, the arms emaciated', and went on to admire one of Degas's 'most remarkable' works, the same monochrome painting *Ballet Rehearsal on Stage*, which Burty incorrectly described as 'a drawing'.[9] Summarising the views of several of his colleagues, the writer Jules Claretie announced that Degas's pictures were 'astonishing in their scrupulous truth'.[10]

Many of those who saw the exhibition agreed that Degas excelled as a draughtsman. He could draw the 'distortions of legs and the dislocations of the hips and feet that are required by the harsh exercise of the dance', noted Ernest Chesneau, another establishment voice; 'he draws in a fashion that is precise, exact, with no other prejudice than that of scrupulous fidelity'.[11] Visitors who knew Degas personally were probably aware that his training had been significantly different from that of his fellow-exhibitors. Encouraged by a father who was knowledgeable about the arts and loved eighteenth-century French painting, Degas had briefly attended the Ecole des Beaux-Arts in Paris before spending a full three years on self-directed study in Italy. Making hundreds of copies from works by the masters, from Giotto and Masaccio to Veronese and Michelangelo, he also drew nude models at the French Academy in Rome and developed the mastery of line and form that was later to impress his admirers. Settled back in Paris in 1859, Degas progressed slowly from pictures based on historical themes – the biblical Jephtha, the Babylonian Queen Semiramis – towards works more appropriate to a 'Painter of Modern Life', in Baudelaire's term.[12] In Degas's case, the search for a topical repertoire that would launch his career was slow and frustrating, but within a decade the transformation was complete. Now painting bold, questioning portraits of family and friends, and energetic scenes of the racetrack, he made works that looked like – and sometimes were – depictions of scenes by such contemporary novelists as Emile Zola, Gustave Flaubert and Edmond de Goncourt himself. In 1867 Degas's first known dance painting, *Mademoiselle Fiocre in the Ballet 'La Source'* (fig. 5), was shown at the vast official Salon in Paris where it was hardly noticed, though it earned a few words of praise in a review by Zola.[13] Brazenly representing the latest sensation at the Paris Opéra, Eugénie Fiocre, who was adored by many but described as 'without grace or talent' by one sceptic, this picture showed the young woman not dancing but posing languorously on stage in an exotic Middle-Eastern costume.[14] Based on numerous drawings that Degas appears to have made at first hand and perhaps from photographs, the picture was rooted in tradition but also seemed disconcertingly contemporary.

Degas soon became the first artist in history to specialise in the ballet, one of the dominant cultural modes in the French capital at this date. Among its other attractions, ballet allowed him to identify with modern metropolitan life in one of Europe's fastest-growing cities, where illustrated magazines, advertising and photography were already transforming the depiction of its glamour and squalor. Contrarily, a factor that was almost as important to Degas was the perennial challenge of pictorial compositions based on figures in interiors – here represented by ballet classrooms and stage scenes – which allowed him to maintain his dialogue with the great masters of the past ('O Giotto, let me see Paris, and you Paris, let me see Giotto', he wrote in his notebook).[15] Even such daring works as *The Rehearsal* have their roots in history: a figure by Andrea Mantegna has been seen behind one of his studies of Jules Perrot and the spiral staircase itself had antecedents in the seventeenth century.[16] The tension between these twin impulses tells us much about Degas and his unfolding career, which was further challenged by the conflicted nature of ballet itself. When admirers noted the 'scrupulous truth' of his dance scenes and proposed him as a 'classic' of the future, they were well aware that Degas's newly adopted theme had long provoked moral outrage. Trainee dancers at the Opéra could be chosen for their good looks as well as their aptitude on stage, and often came from poor homes where they struggled to survive on meagre pay. One notorious route to success was to catch the eye of wealthy male 'abonnés', regular subscribers who enjoyed privileged access behind the scenes and had been known to treat the corps de ballet as a 'seraglio' assembled for their benefit. It was these same adolescents and young women who appeared in such canvases as *The Rehearsal*, prompting innuendo from some critics and frank disgust from others in terms that were to persist throughout much of Degas's working life. His decision to adopt the dance was thus simultaneously audacious and shrewd, allowing him to assert himself as a major innovator who was in touch with current realities, even as he was tackling 'matter, gracious and terrible' in new kinds of visual poetry.

A much less familiar practice scene is *The Ballet Rehearsal* (cat. 2), executed in pastel three or four years after the Burrell painting. Choosing a similar backstage space in which a ballet class is underway, Degas now opted for a wide, frieze-like format that he was to return to and refine in a number of oil paintings over subsequent decades.[17] Reading this picture from left to right, we begin with the black-suited teacher and move to the chaotic group of ballerinas standing around and even *on* the grand piano. Probably showing

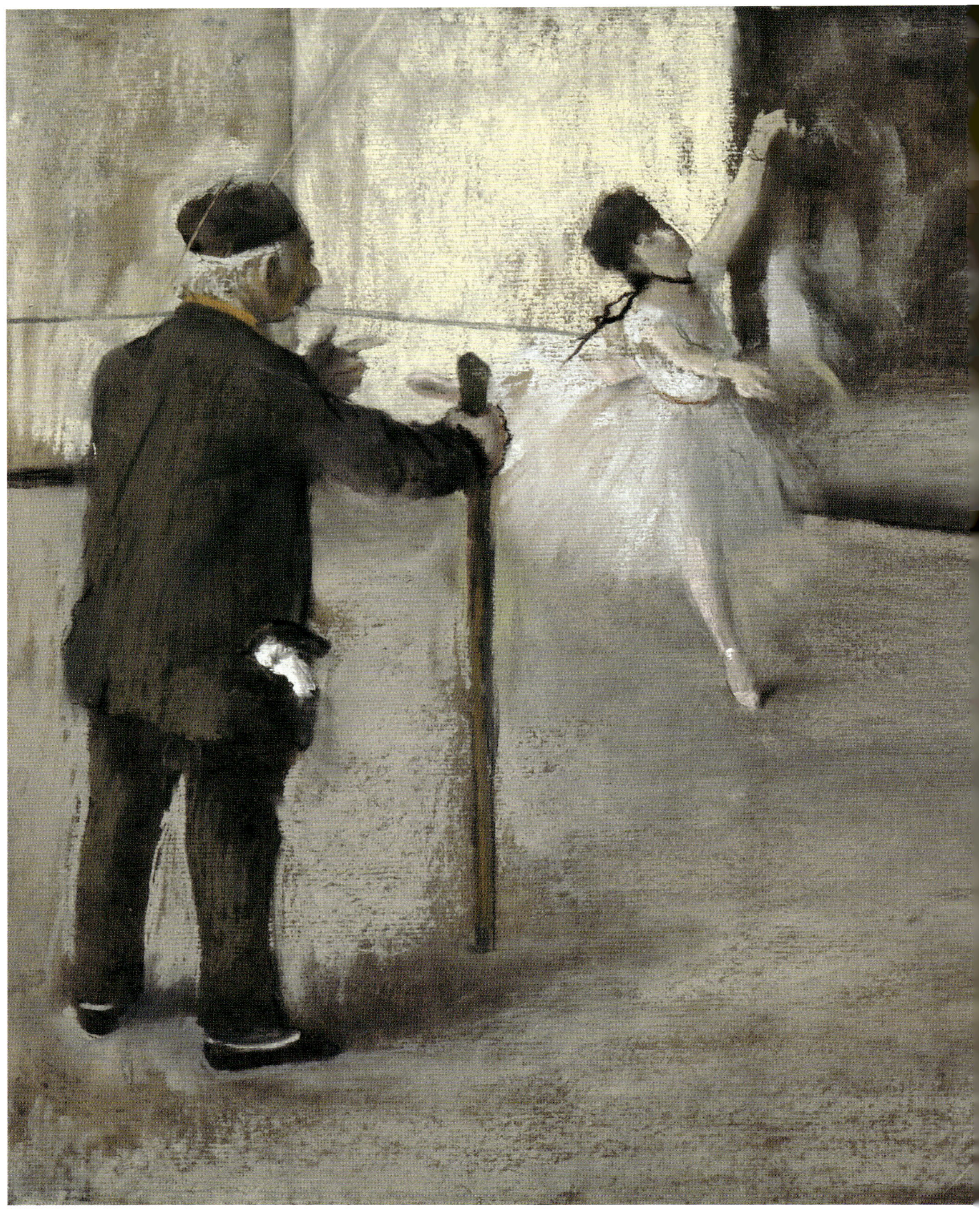

2

The Ballet Rehearsal
c. 1876–78
Pastel on board,
43 x 79 cm
Private collection

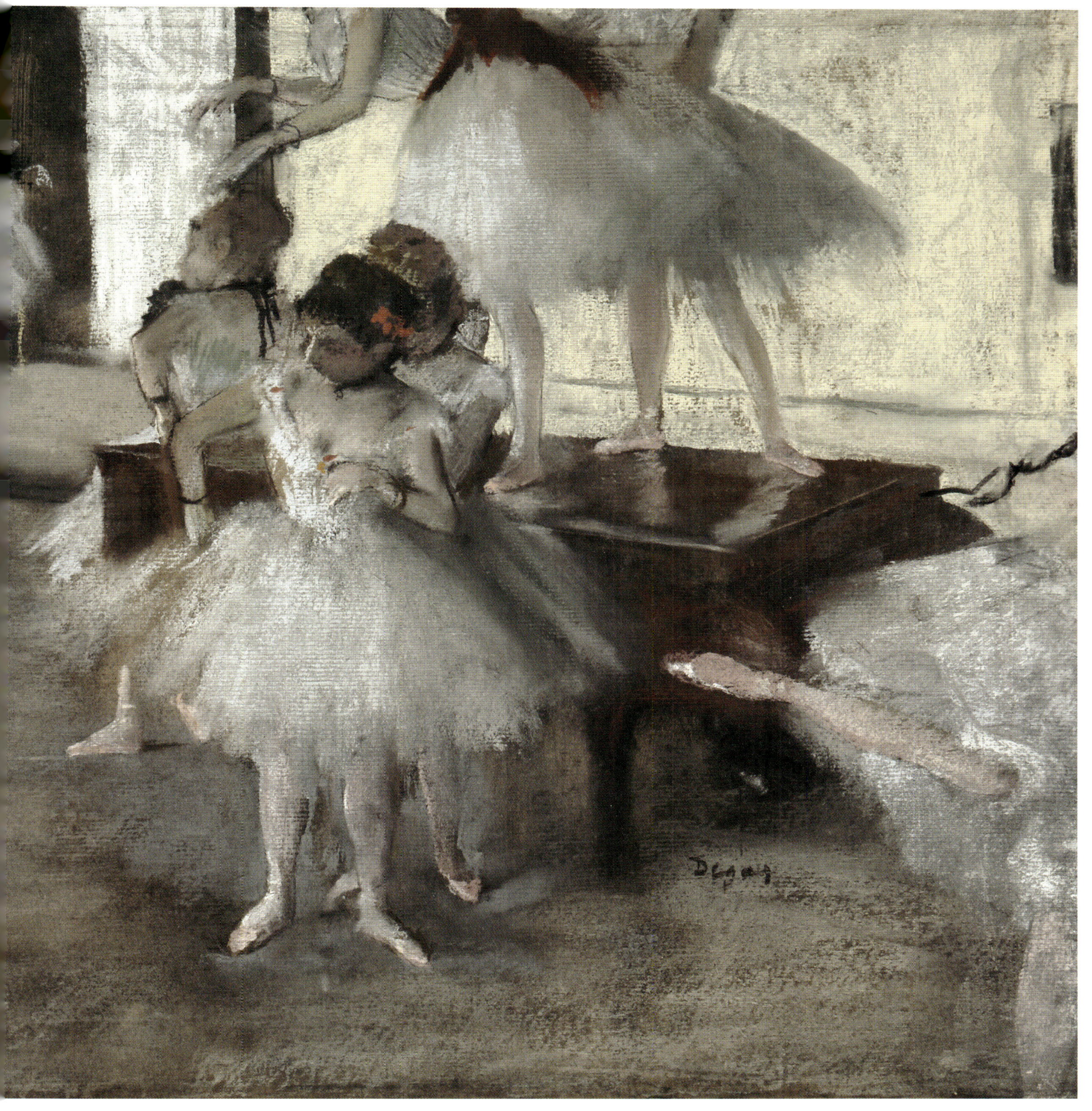

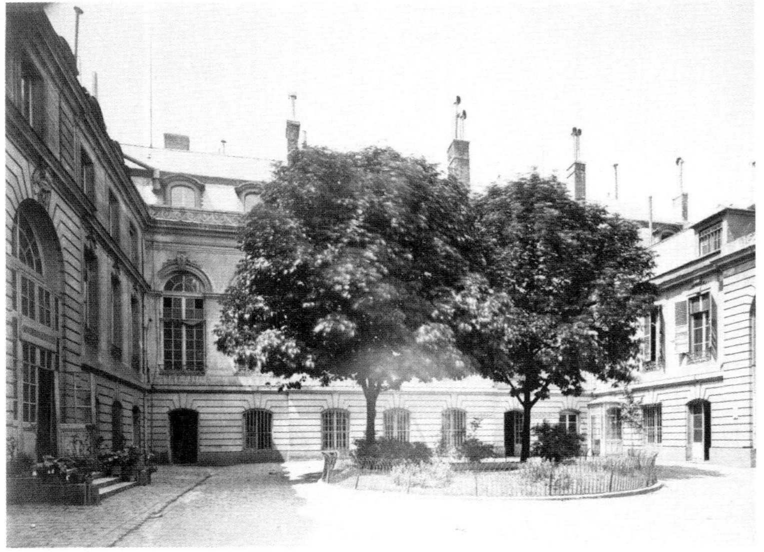

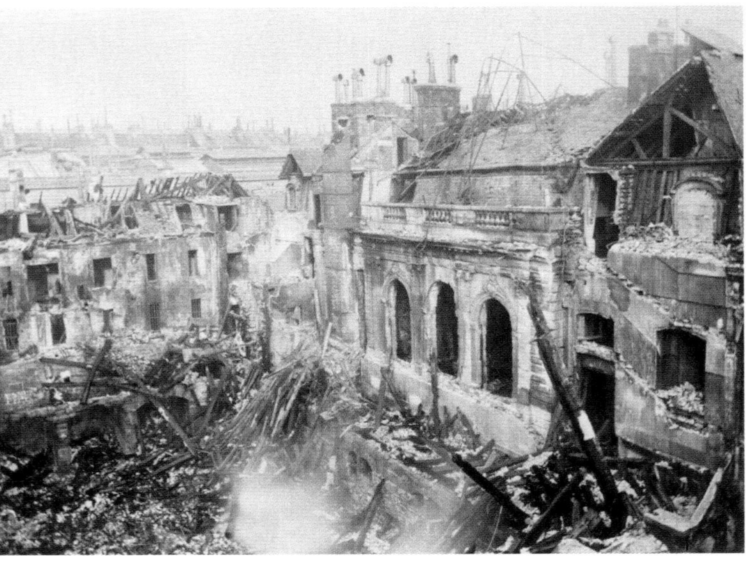

Fig. 6 *Louis-Amédée Mante*, Courtyard of the Hôtel de Choiseul Opera House on the Rue le Peletier, *c.* 1873. Photograph, 26.8 x 37.5 cm. Bibliothèque nationale de France, Paris. Bibliothèque de l'Opéra

Fig. 7 *Louis-Amédée Mante*, The Ruins of the Rue le Peletier Opera House, *c.* 1873. Photograph, 24 x 31 cm. Bibliothèque nationale de France, Paris. Bibliothèque de l'Opéra

Monsieur Pluque, who had a reputation for strict discipline, Degas mischievously suggests that he is blind to the antics of some pupils and preoccupied with a particular individual, the elegant young woman at upper left in 'attitude'.[18] The remaining dancers are presumably waiting for their turn or warming up for a lesson, but Degas has exploited this situation to introduce a note of human and visual mayhem into the room. While one figure stands as her costume is adjusted from behind, like her counterpart in *The Rehearsal*, two colleagues enjoy an anarchic moment on the piano and a third, at extreme right, almost disappears from view as she too executes a spectacular 'attitude'. Within the grid-like structure of this pale room, Degas seems to have assembled as many different types of physical activity as there are participants, from the statuesque, earthbound teacher to his almost weightless pupil who hovers on pointe, her pose echoed in the remarkable blur of pink stockings and white tulle at the right-hand edge. If at first glance the picture resembles a light-filled Dutch interior ('Fantin, Whistler and I, we were all on the same road, the road from Holland,' Degas later recalled), further scrutiny reveals a degree of informality that only an exceptionally confident artist of the 1870s would have dared to attempt.[19]

The Paris Opéra was a historic institution that had changed dramatically in recent years. In 1873 the old Opéra building on the Rue le Peletier disappeared in a catastrophic fire, to be replaced by Charles Garnier's modern structure that had been underway for a decade. The new building was soon opened with a fanfare and is still in use today. Like so many events of this period, the demise of the old building and the creation of the new are known to us more completely through the medium of photography. The discovery of some formerly unpublished prints of the old Opéra immediately before and after the fire has revealed more about the backstage spaces that Degas knew and painted (figs 6–7).[20] Taken by Degas's friend Louis-Amédée Mante, these images show such features as the distinctively shaped tall windows overlooking a courtyard that appear in his later ballet painting *The Rehearsal* (cat. 7), but not the humbler classroom depicted in *The Ballet Rehearsal*, which remains unlocated. These and other such photographs emphasise Degas's rootedness in the real spaces where the lives of the corps de ballet were played out, at a time when the camera had already become ubiquitous. Reflecting the pioneering role of the French capital in the history of the medium and its continuing claims to innovation, photography was everywhere visible in the streets and public places of Paris (fig. 3). Many hundreds of establishments offered city views, family portraits, cartes de visite and pictures of celebrities, among whom dancers were widely popular. Even dance teachers had their following; a daguerreotype of Jules Perrot (fig. 1) shows the former star in his characteristic outfit, with velvet jacket, dancing shoes and an ornate staff to beat time in the classroom. A comparison of this photograph with the corresponding figure in *The Rehearsal* leaves no doubt that Degas used the daguerreotype as he painted the miniature portrait. Yet this is no slavish copy; the artist used only the upper part of the body and reversed the tones of Perrot's outfit, so that his jacket is now light and his shirt deep red. The picture was taken in St Petersburg by the photographer Bergamasco during Perrot's long and successful employment as ballet master with the Imperial Theatre. Returning to France in 1861, Perrot longed for an engagement at the Opéra but was continually thwarted, appearing there only occasionally in the role of teacher. Although Degas is thought to have befriended him and painted his portrait somewhat later, there is no indication that they were close in the 1870s. The Bergamasco portrait, showing Perrot in ballet slippers and looking pensive, appears to have had some private significance for the artist, perhaps recalling the great days of ballet that survived only in legend. Paradoxically, therefore, this early and potentially significant evidence of Degas's use of a photograph in his art is immediately ambiguous; seeming to be factual, it represents a manipulation by the artist of the historical record.

The dancers who were drawn and painted by Degas came from a richly photographed generation, both as private individuals and as professionals. A decade earlier, the gifted 'étoile' from the Paris Opéra company, Marie Sanlaville, had begun to turn heads with her refined technique and dramatic gifts, evident in roles on the Opéra stage. Among them was a supporting part in *La Source*, the subject of Degas's 1867 Salon entry. Some years later she appeared in *L'Africaine*, an opera that inspired at least two works by the artist.[21] Sanlaville was well known to Degas and became the mistress of his friend Count Ludovic Lépic, who was also a landscape painter and an exhibitor in the 1874 and 1876 Impressionist exhibitions. A photograph of Sanlaville from the late 1860s shows her posed in a preparatory stance (cat. 3), wearing a 'rosebud' costume from the ballet interlude that at this time was included in performances of Mozart's *Don Juan*.[22] As it happens, Degas made an important painting – *Two Dancers on the Stage* (cat. 12) – that represents a moment from this interlude and even a similar costume, though without basing it on the Sanlaville print. Charming though she looks in her photograph, the briefest examination reveals that this was a studio shot, complete with time-worn scenery and ageing props that were unrelated to her current roles. Even more instructive is the just-discernible thread attached to her left wrist that helped to keep this raised arm steady while the photograph was taken. Such artificial, 'staged' images of current stars, which were once

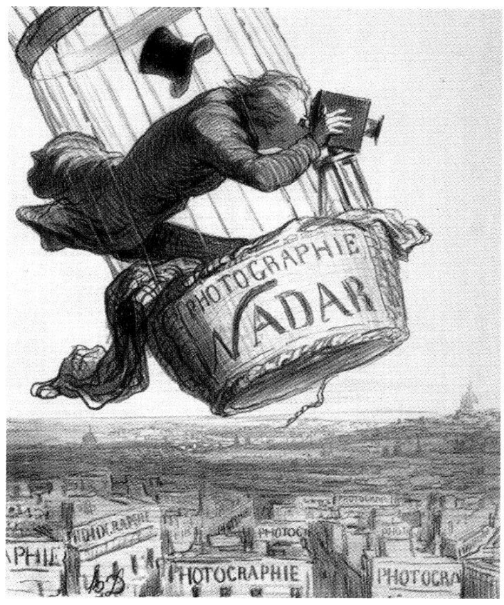

Fig. 8 *Honoré Daumier*, Nadar élévant la Photographie à la hauteur de l'Art (Nadar Raises Photography to an Art Form), 1862. Lithograph, 27.3 x 21.9 cm. Los Angeles County Museum of Art

3

**Portrait of Marie
Sanlaville in Costume
for Don Juan**
c. 1866–70
Carte de visite,
10.3 x 6.2 cm
Bibliothèque nationale de
France, Paris. Bibliothèque-
musée de l'Opéra

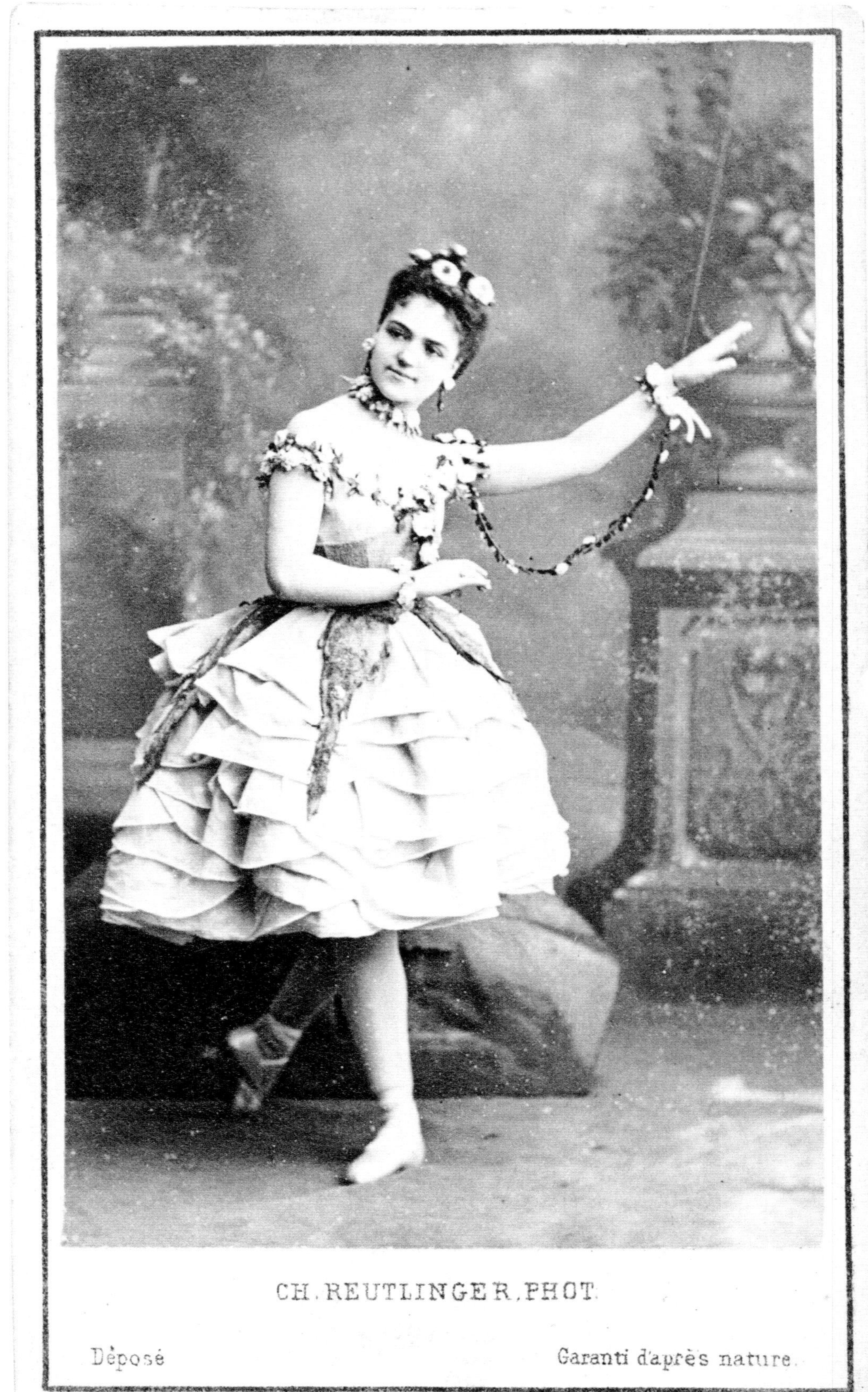

printed in their thousands, establish an important distinction in Degas's historical relationship with the medium. Setting aside the anomalous fact of the Perrot print, there is no evidence from any part of his career that Degas used conventional photographs of this kind as the basis for major pastels and paintings of dancers practising in class, waiting in the wings, or performing on stage. The case can be put even more strongly: perhaps the very limitations of commercial photography at this moment, as represented in the Sanlaville picture, contributed to Degas's sceptical response to prevailing modes of dance imagery and encouraged him to contrive new approaches to the subject. Seen in this way, *The Rehearsal* and *The Ballet Rehearsal* can be understood as determined attempts to advance beyond the photograph as it was popularly known in the 1870s. Degas would have been well aware that the 'frozen' legs on the stairs in the former work and the fluttering tulle at right in the latter were effects that would have defeated most contemporary cameras, as would any such interior views with moving figures. By drawing our attention to these features, Degas seems to distance himself, self-consciously and proudly, from the medium that was so widely admired, perhaps joining Baudelaire in his belief that photography had become 'art's most mortal enemy'.[23]

A comparative chronology of Degas's personal history and his known associations with the camera (pages 256–59) reveals that he was a child of the photographic age who matured with the medium up to and beyond the introduction of film. Born in 1834, just five years before the announcement of Daguerre's historic invention, Degas was photographed in his young adulthood for several cartes de visite (fig. 9) and was already familiar enough

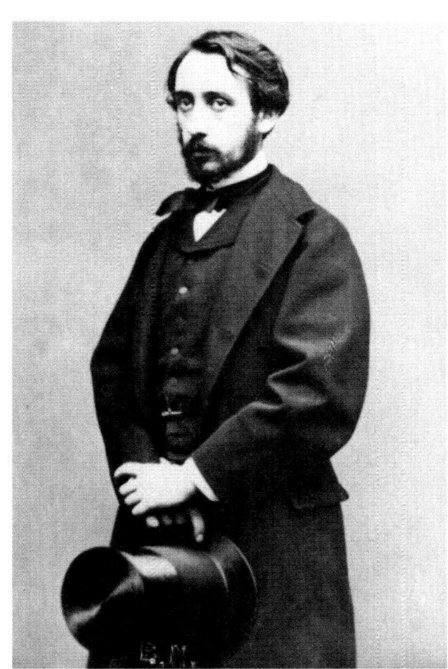

Fig. 9 *Unknown photographer*, Portrait of Edgar Degas, *c.* 1360 (?). Photograph. Bibliothèque nationale de France, Paris

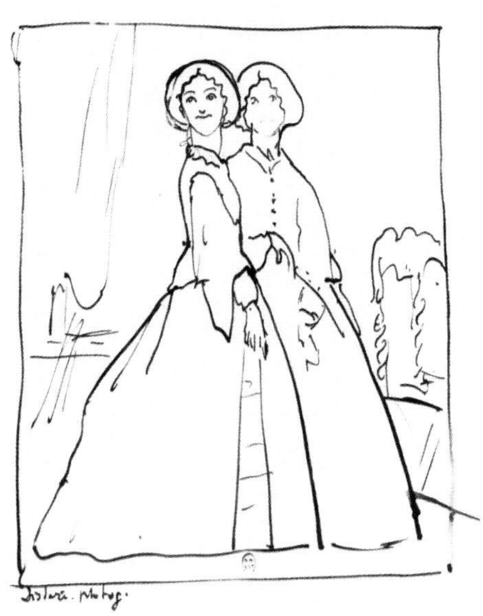

Fig. 10 Notebook 18, p. 31, showing a humorous drawing of a Disdéri photograph, *c.* 1861. Brown ink, 25.4 x 19.5 cm. Musée du Louvre, Paris, Cabinet des Estampes, inv. no. Dc 327 réserve

with their conventions to make fun of them: a crude drawing of two women in one of his sketchbooks used around 1860 is facetiously signed 'Disdéri photog.' (fig. 10), a reference to the hugely successful portrait photographer of that name.[24] André-Adolphe-Eugène Disdéri claimed to have invented the carte-de-visite format and certainly produced them on a massive scale, defining the middle classes in a new way but also perpetuating stock poses and unimaginative compositions.[25] In this same decade, however, Degas treated another Disdéri print with more respect, extracting the figure of the Princesse de Metternich from a joint portrait with her husband and using it as the basis for a small painting of his own.[26] In contrast to the flat monochrome of the original, Degas re-created the image with an exquisite palette of lemon yellow, gold and grey-green, and added a background of floral patterned wallpaper (fig. 11). He may also have exploited such ready-made photographic portraits – even works by Disdéri – when tackling the figure of Eugénie Fiocre for his 1867 Salon picture. Alongside his own numerous drawings of Fiocre, Degas would have had access to countless commercially available photographs that showed the young celebrity on stage and off; one little-known study of Fiocre was clearly based on a Disdéri shot of the young star in her role in *Néméa*.[27]

Other projects from this period reveal the artist's many and varied interactions with the new medium, from additional responses to cartes de visite to further attempts at harnessing the potential of photography in his professional life.[28] New studio portraits of Degas were certainly made in connection with his 1872 visit to relatives in New Orleans, recording his doleful stare at the camera as if he resented the entire operation.[29] While in Louisiana, the subject was still on Degas's mind: he wrote to the painter James Tissot in Paris, asking him 'Did you get my photographs?', and somewhat gnomically announced to another friend, the Danish artist Lorenz Fröhlich, 'Instantaneousness is photography, nothing more.'[30] Also during this period we find Degas consulting with his brother René to have photographs made of some of his paintings, conceivably resulting in the faded print that now belongs to the Musée d'Orsay (fig. 12).[31] New evidence that Degas distributed such photographs within the trade can be found in a text by Jules Claretie, written after a trip to England in 1876 to review current plays. Visiting the London gallery run by Charles Deschamps, who had begun to handle the artist's paintings, Claretie reports that he saw 'the almost unique collection of photographs of works by Monsieur Degas' and eulogised the qualities that were evident in them.[32] At around the same date Degas wrote cryptically to the baritone Jean-Baptiste Faure: 'Do not forget to remind Mérante about the photographs he offered me yesterday. I am eager to see them and to work out what I can make of this dancer's talent.'[33] It has been said that Degas also accumulated a collection of photographs by Adolphe Braun, the specialist in city views and monuments, but evidence for this has proved elusive.[34] Photographic material found in Degas's apartment after his death that has been associated with Braun seems more likely to have come from his brother-in-law Henri Fevre, an architect.[35]

Common to almost all these encounters with the camera in his early years was Degas's practical, even sceptical approach to much of the photography of his day. It could be useful to him in social exchanges, for recording pictures he wished to sell, and as an *aide-mémoire* when preparing for a painted portrait. Beyond this he felt free to mock the crude conventions

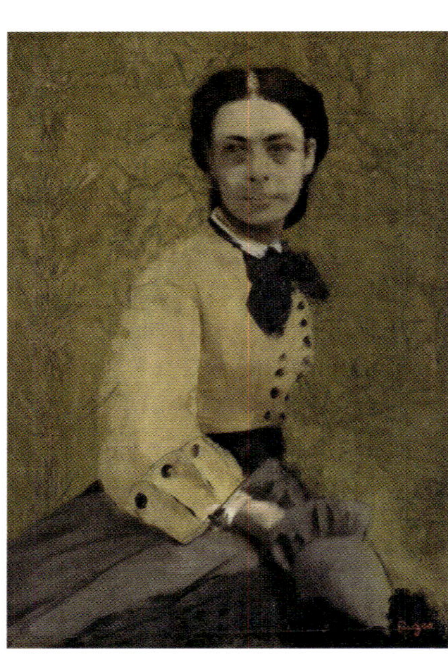

Fig. 11 **Princesse Pauline de Metternich**, *c.* 1865. Oil on canvas, 41 x 29 cm. National Gallery, London, inv. no. NG3337

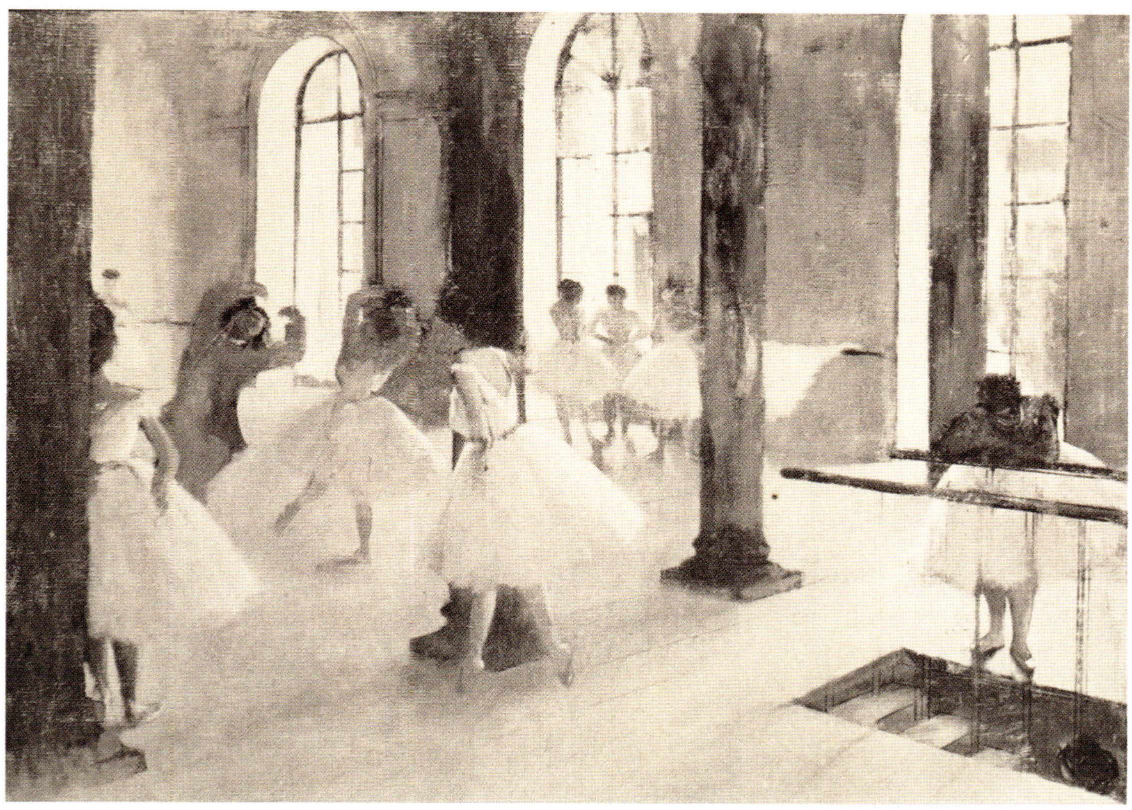

Fig. 12 *Unknown photographer*, 'Etudes de danseuses', tableau d'Edgar Degas, before 1917.
Silverprint, 14.5 x 22 cm. Musée d'Orsay, Paris, inv. no. PHO 1992 9 88. The painting that is the subject
of this photograph, *The Dance Rehearsal*, now belongs to the Phillips Collection, Washington DC.

of boulevard photographers and in certain circumstances – as with the
Metternich study – to transform them through the alchemy of art. Fascinating
in this latter case was his recognition that the original print had its own
distinct visual character, a monochrome identity that could be edited of
extraneous forms, transferred to canvas and given new life through his brushes
and colours. Even more intriguing was Degas's decision to soften many of the
elements in Disdéri's print while leaving others in sharp focus, manipulating
not just the physical appearance of the Princess but also her allure. Known as
a 'plain' woman in her day, she became in Degas's painting an elusive-seeming,
even seductive beauty. Created in unknown circumstances and left
undiscovered for a century, these two works and their connection appear to
be exceptional; few other painted compositions by the artist can be so closely
and confidently linked with a print by a professional photographer. Although
several other pictures have been compared to known photographs or more
generally to the idioms and technical accomplishments of the new medium,
Degas's *œuvre* – especially as a dance artist – was more typically informed by
or made in opposition to, rather than being dependent upon, the photograph.

Degas's calm, somewhat bemused accommodation with the photographic
industry is perfectly captured in his 1875 *Dancer Posing for a Photograph* (cat.
4).[36] Studios used by Parisian photographers, like those of painters, were often
found on the upper floor of buildings and typically had large windows to
provide a source of natural light. Nothing is known about the owner of the

4

**Dancer Posing
for a Photograph**
1875
Oil on canvas,
65 x 50 cm
The State Pushkin
Museum of Fine Arts,
Moscow

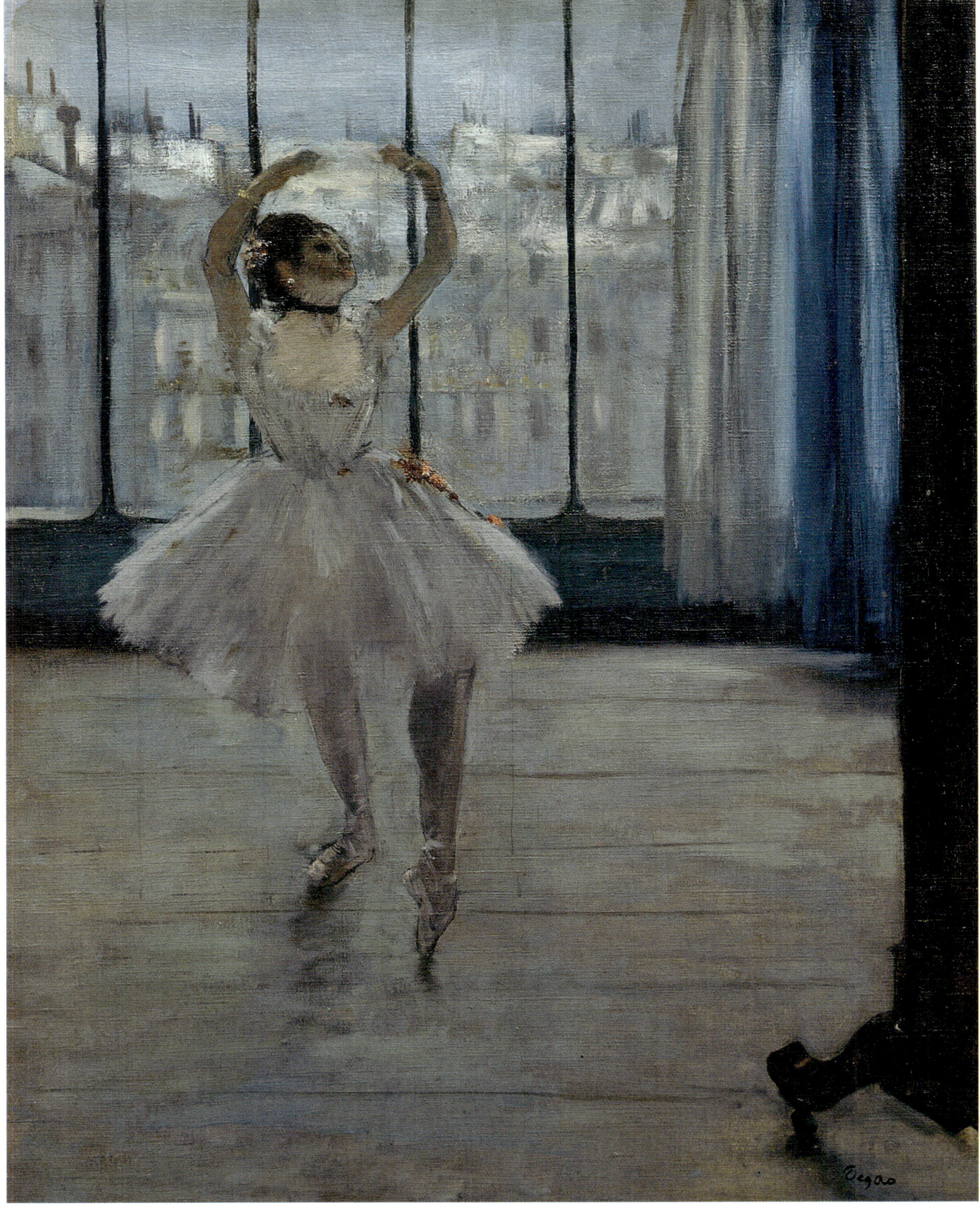

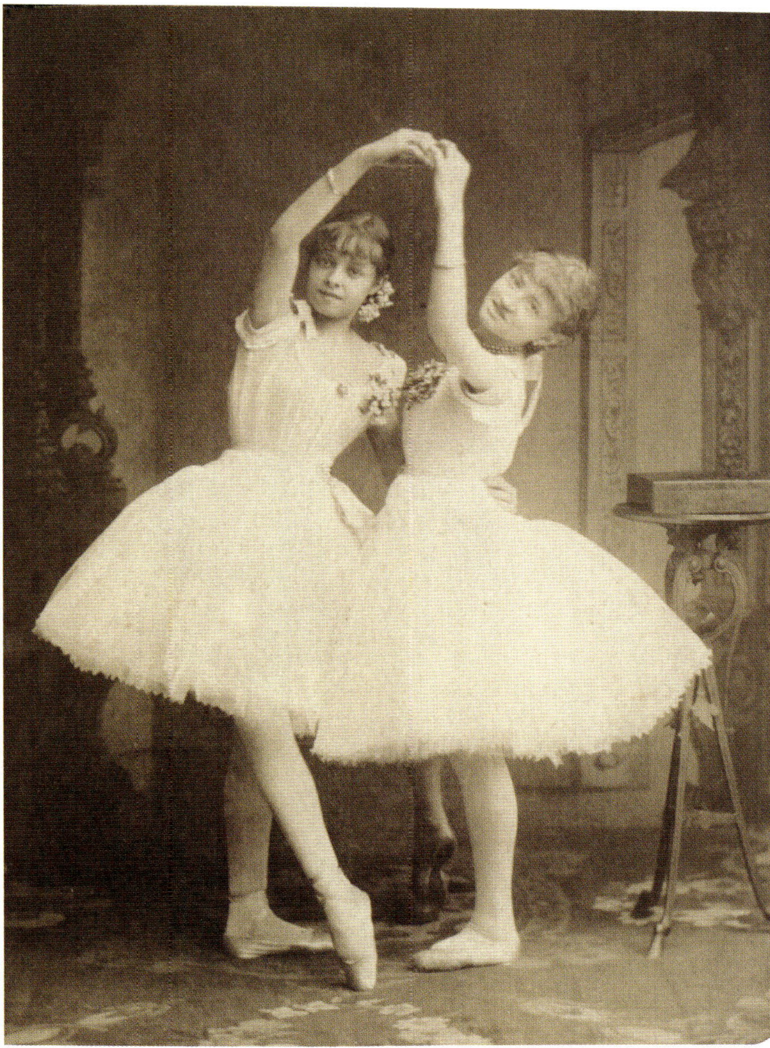

premises depicted, though by the mid-1870s Degas was certainly acquainted with
several professional photographers in the city: Nadar, whose glass-fronted, third-
and fourth-storey premises housed the 1874 Impressionist exhibition (fig. 2);
Louis-Amédée Mante, 'cellist in the Opéra orchestra, who took pictures of the
former Opéra building (figs 6–7) and became a pioneer of colour photography;
and a certain 'Bonnard photographe', drawn by Degas around this same date.[37]
Dancer Posing for a Photograph thus represents a confrontation between
camera and subject that was as familiar to the artist as it was to many of his
contemporaries. It also describes the highly artificial circumstances in which
much of the dance imagery of the day was created. Given these factors, Degas
may well have felt emboldened to introduce a tongue-in-cheek quality to his
canvas: this handsome scene of a dancer posing as if on stage could almost
represent the timeless beauty of ballet in the face of stark, modern interiors and
vulgar innovation. The freshness and self-containment of the young woman
also draw attention to the artificial set-ups and frozen postures of most cartes
de visite of such individuals, just as the vague view of Paris beyond was rooted
in a more plausible reality than that offered by most photographers. By
positioning his model against natural light, the artist emphasised a factor

vital to both professions, especially to photographers who still struggled with such interior compositions. Innovations in preceding decades, such as the wet collodion process and various systems for using colour, had pointed the way forward, but everyday photography still had major technical limitations. Although Degas's ballerina holds herself in a relatively stable pose, any movement she made would have registered as a blur on the photographer's camera. By contrast, when Degas executed his painting he had proceeded in a tried and tested fashion, making a careful drawing of the young woman that he then 'squared-up' for transfer to canvas.[38] In such situations, Degas might well have felt that he and his painter-colleagues still had the upper hand.

A commercially produced photograph of one of Degas's dancer-models, Melina Darde, offers another timely point of contact between the two disciplines (cat. 5). Standing at left with a companion, the young Melina holds the waist and the raised fingers of her colleague, giving them both greater stability in front of the camera. An approximate equivalent to Degas's *Dancer Posing for a Photograph*, this studio image has many of the charms that had made photography so popular throughout the French capital and beyond. Such prints were typically produced in large numbers for sale to a dancer's fans and admirers, then assembled in albums designed for this purpose and shown to friends and fellow-enthusiasts. Once again, the known identity of the model allows us to explore the options that a painter such as Degas still had at his disposal, even in an age that was already engulfed by photography. Around 1880 he made several pictures that included the figure of Melina Darde: one is the pastel *The Star: Dancer on Pointe*, now in the Norton Simon Museum (fig. 20), and a second is the oil painting in the Fogg Art Museum, Harvard, entitled *The Rehearsal* (cat. 7). In both works, Degas seems to have taken a quiet delight in giving a prominence to the trainee dancer that she is unlikely to have enjoyed at this date. For the former, he drew attention to this young novice with the Opéra company – which she joined around 1878 – by depicting her in a distinctive costume and a very visible role on stage.[39] Here Melina executes a difficult balance, an 'attitude en pointe', which could only have lasted for a mere second or two. Degas seems to exult in his ability as an artist to 'freeze' such a brief apparition, based on years of disciplined observation and on drawings made from a precisely directed dancer-model – Melina herself – in his studio. Few if any cameras could have come close to this precision in the late 1870s, and few photographers – or indeed artists – would have been confident in displaying the full length of her elegant young legs and even her undergarments. Such features would have been frankly scandalous in most contexts at this time, even at the Opéra, where those sitting near the stage or equipped with opera glasses might conceivably have glimpsed Melina in this way. Elsewhere, the market for suggestive and frankly pornographic photographs had long been established and continued to flourish, sometimes featuring ballerinas in compromising situations.

As Degas launched his project to introduce Melina Darde into *The Rehearsal*, he made an exquisite drawing of her that is now known as *Dancer (Battement in Second Position)* (cat. 6). Adding her name at right beside her tutu, Degas represented the teenager in one of the standard exercises of the dance class, the battement, in which the leg is rapidly raised and lowered a number of times to strengthen and stretch the muscles. Already proficient enough to have danced at the Théâtre Gaîté in Paris, Melina would have followed this

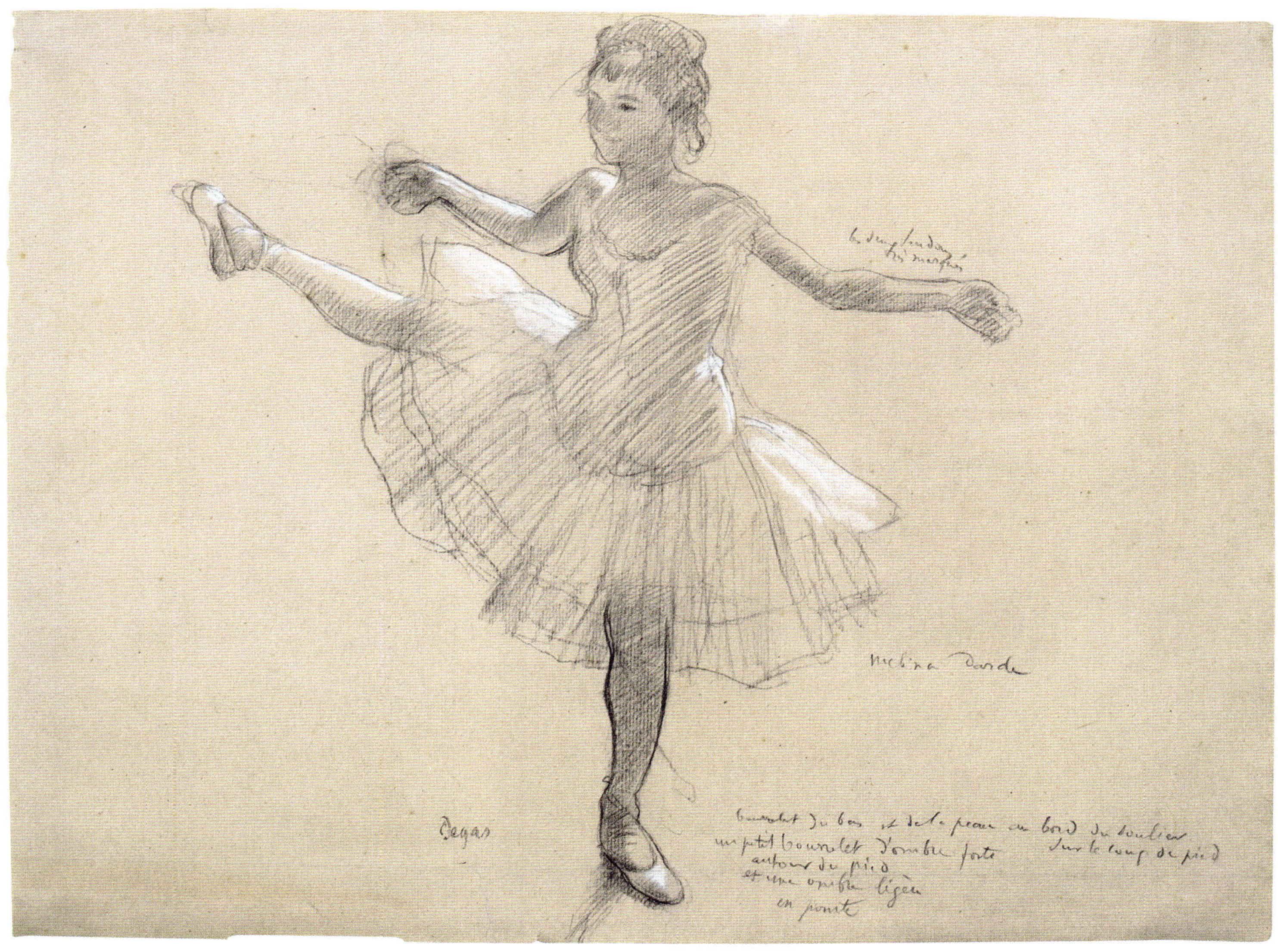

6

**Dancer
(Battement in
Second Position)**
1880
Charcoal heightened
with white on tan paper,
33 x 44.5 cm
Private collection,
Cambridge, Mass.

routine innumerable times; what she had *not* done by 1878 was to perform battements in the principal classroom at the old Opéra house, on the Rue le Peletier, which had been destroyed by fire five years earlier. Yet this is where Degas chose to situate Melina when he included her in his oil painting *The Rehearsal*, among colleagues in the high-ceilinged room with tall windows that is recognisable in photographs of the vanished building (figs 6–7). Calmly combining fiction with closely observed fact, the artist now absorbed his modern model into this historic setting. Compared to *The Star: Dancer on Pointe* or even *Dancer Posing for a Photograph*, the scene appears airy and sedate, the erect forms of the ballerinas echoing the vertical thrust of the architecture and their disciplined arms rhyming with its gently receding perspective. Degas went to great lengths to achieve plausibility in his implausible scene, studying the fall of light on muslin, hair and flesh, and the fine distinctions between one pair of arms or legs and another. Quietly dominating the room is the figure of a seated violinist at left, whose music reminds us that the girls are repetitively raising and lowering their limbs as we watch. In this otherwise still interior, whose antecedents can be found in both the Italian and Dutch traditions, a gentle

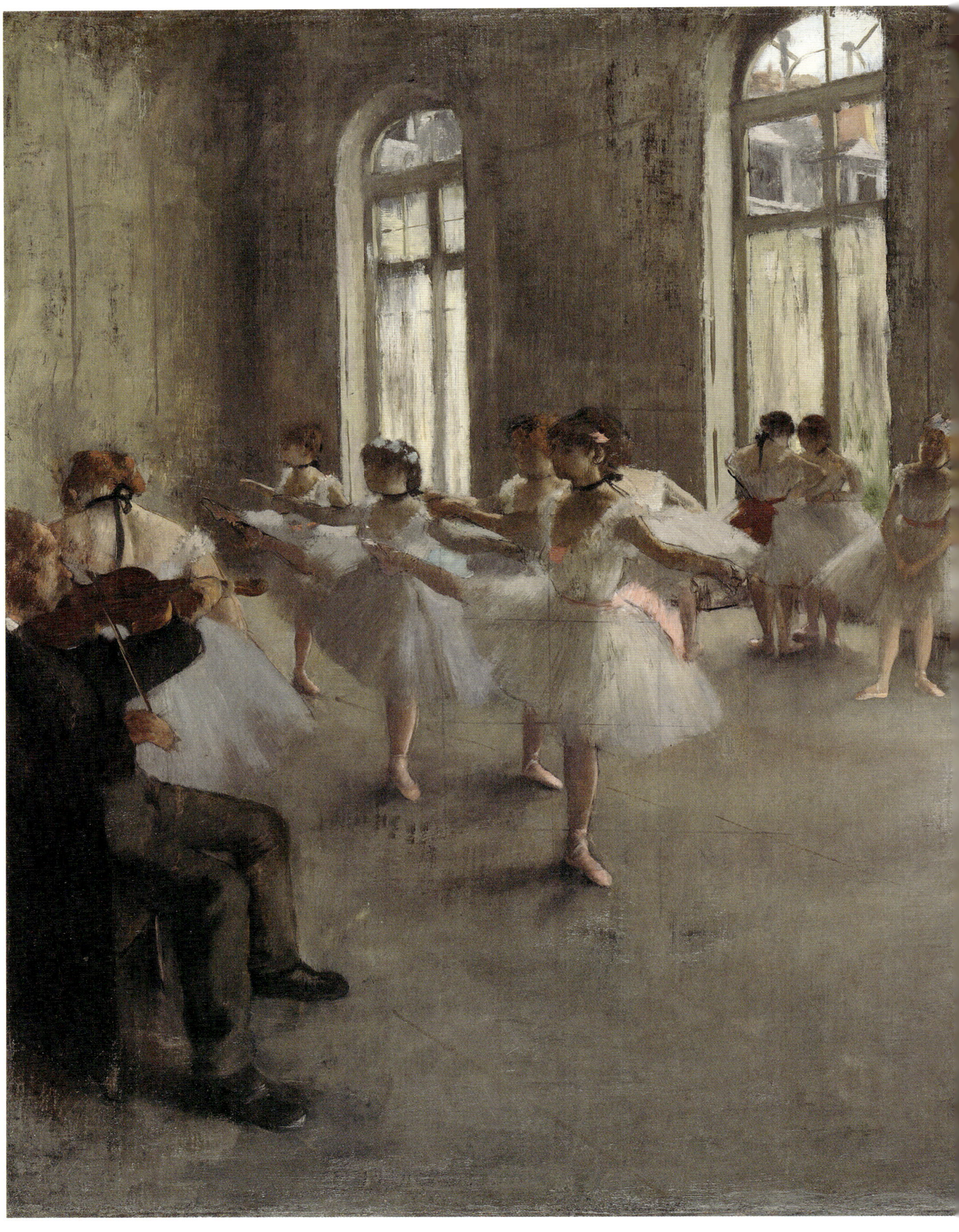

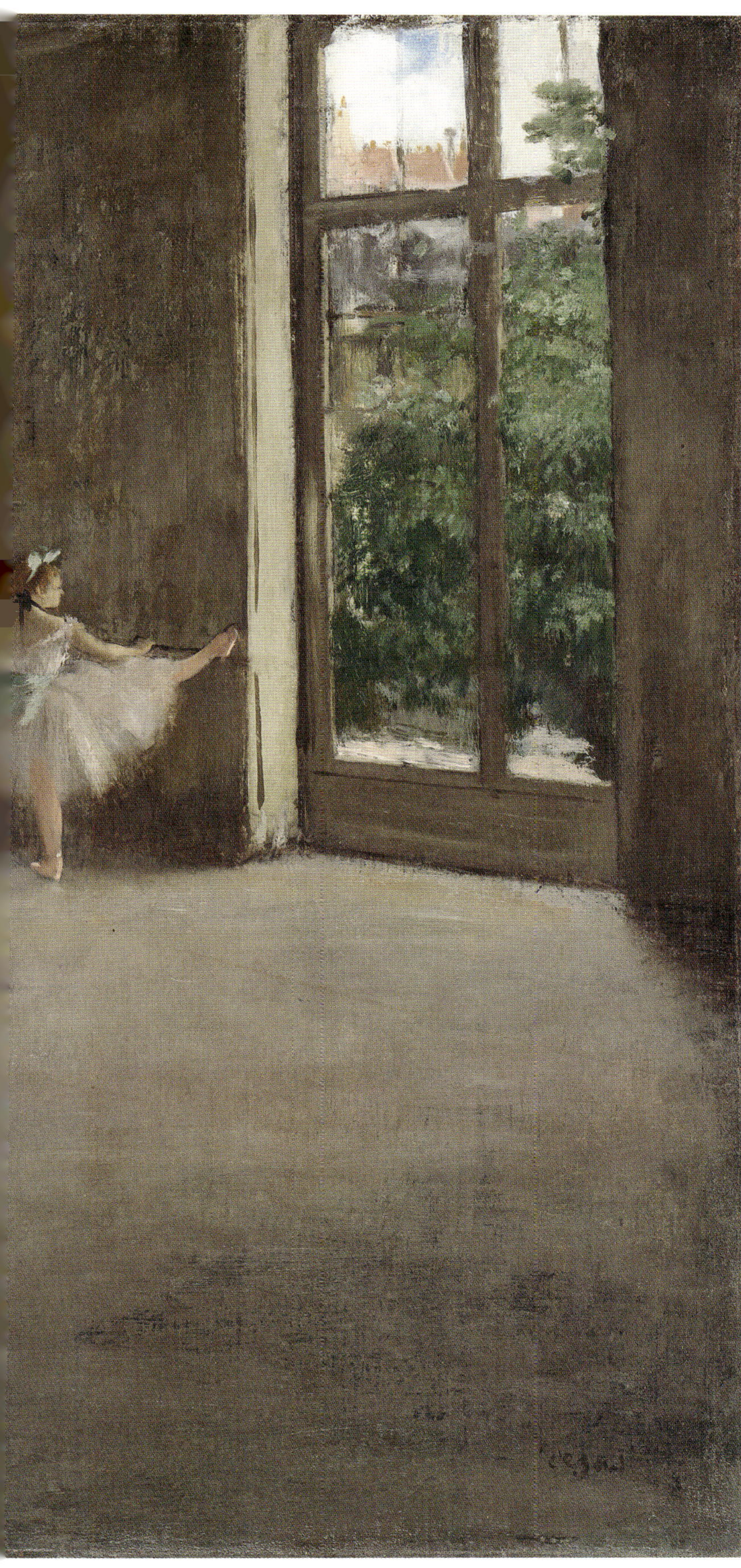

7

The Rehearsal
c. 1873–78
Oil on canvas, 45.7 x 60 cm
Harvard Art Museums/Fogg
Museum. Bequest from the
Collection of Maurice Wertheim,
Class of 1906

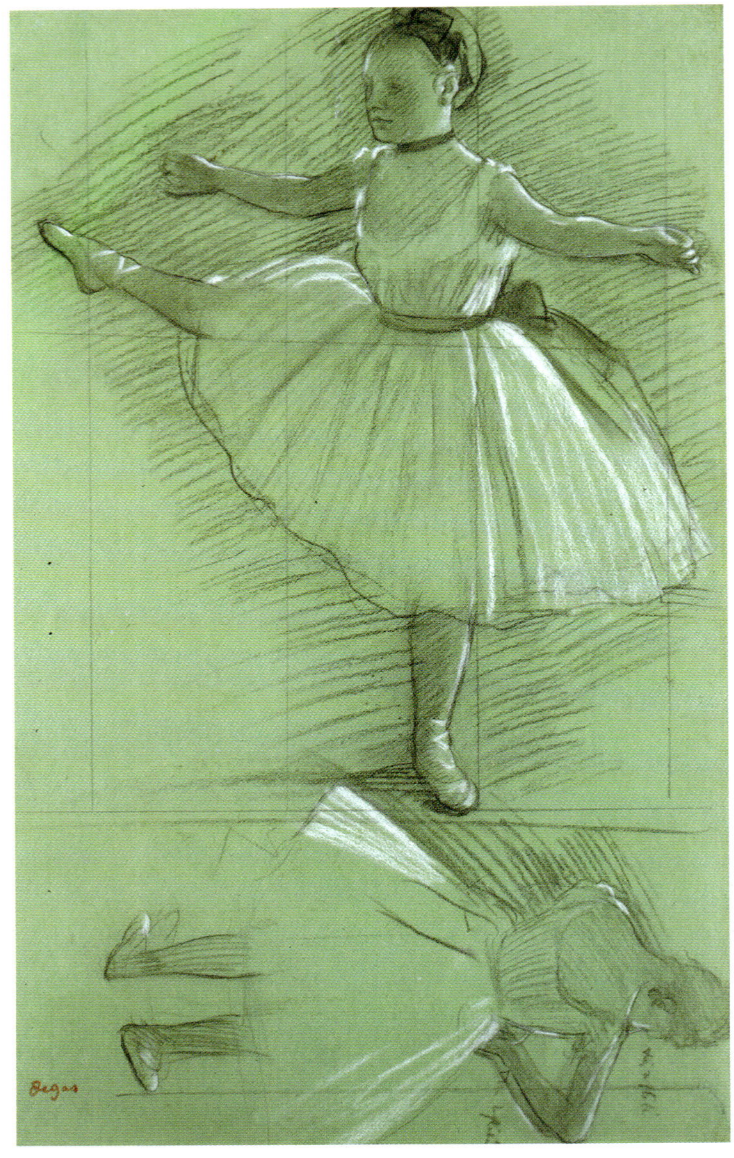

8

Two Studies of Dancers
c. 1873
Charcoal heightened
with white on green paper,
48 x 29.5 cm
Collection of Jan Krugier

wave of movement evokes a ritual that had been observed in this very space
for several generations.

Almost every dancer in *The Rehearsal* was first studied by Degas in one
or more drawings that he then carefully transferred to his canvas. This process
often involved superimposing a grid of lines on the drawn sheet that was
subsequently repeated on the picture surface, allowing the duplication of
the original forms and sometimes leaving ghostly rectilinear fragments within
the paint. Such an effect can be detected around the prominent Melina figure,
subliminally reminding viewers of the effort that the artist put into this work
and the precision at which he was aiming. Another sheet of this kind is *Two
Studies of Dancers* (cat. 8), for which Degas has chosen a rich green paper in
order to explore the light and shadow on his young model. Closely echoing
Melina Darde's pose in *Dancer (Battement in Second Position)*, the girl in
the larger study seems to have informed the individual to the left of Melina.
Almost reverting to his earlier classical manner, in his drawing Degas specified

the outlines of her body and tutu – again containing them within a grid for
ease of transfer to canvas – and added delicate highlights in white chalk.
Similar drawings have survived for such pictures as *The Rehearsal* from the
Burrell Collection, Glasgow, and *The Ballet Rehearsal*, again stressing Degas's
disciplined technique and his grounding in observed reality. From the early
1870s onwards, he not only studied dancers on stage and when possible in
class, but also paid some of these young women from the Opéra corps to
pose in his studio for pastels and paintings, and even for his first large-scale
sculpture, the *Little Dancer Aged Fourteen* (cat. 26). Few alternatives were open
to him at this time: illustrations in ballet manuals were rudimentary or non-
existent, as were authentic photographs of dancers at work.[40] It was not until
the 1890s that such pictures became available, when they could still be posed
by stiff, self-conscious individuals who performed for the benefit of the camera
(fig. 13). In this predicament an artist such as Degas was required to build up
his own reference collection of drawings that represented exercise positions
and movements executed on stage. Many hundreds of such studies were
accumulated by Degas over the years and retained until the end of his career,
the majority stored in portfolios for use in his studio but some occasionally
sold to collectors or given away to friends. A superb example of such a working
drawing is *Dancer at the Barre* (cat. 9), delicately draughted in pencil on white
paper and finely modified by the artist with minute erasures and further linear
touches. Again we sense the process of first-hand scrutiny as Degas posed his
model in a classroom or more likely in his studio. Relying on her professional
skills to maintain this extreme position, Degas was able to determine the
exact relationships between her limbs and the barre, for example, and the
fall of fabric in her skirt. Recalling the exceptional precision of one of Degas's
artist-heroes, Jean-Dominique Ingres, this sheet and others showing the same
exercise contributed to a small family of pictures in various media related
to this figure, from a modestly scaled pastel to some of the large, frieze-format
oil paintings.[41] Of unusual interest was Degas's decision to choose a work
closely related to *Dancer at the Barre* as a black-and-white illustration in
L'Impressioniste, a modest but innovative publication that accompanied

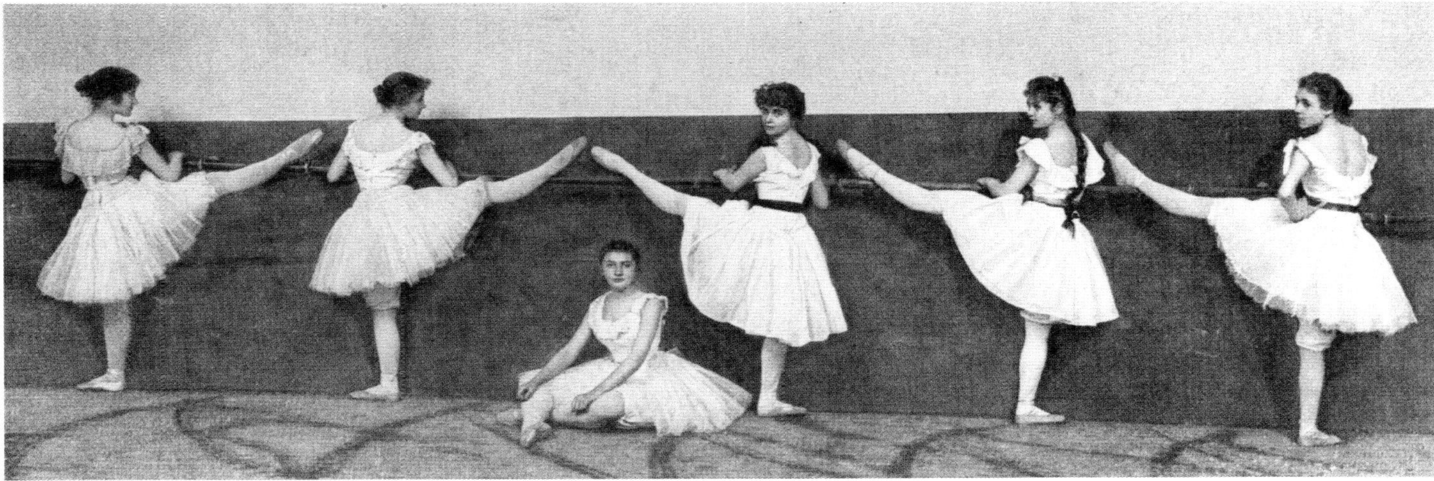

Fig. 13 *Unknown photographer*, Ballet students in a classroom
at the Paris Opéra, Le Figaro Illustré, 6, 59, February 1895

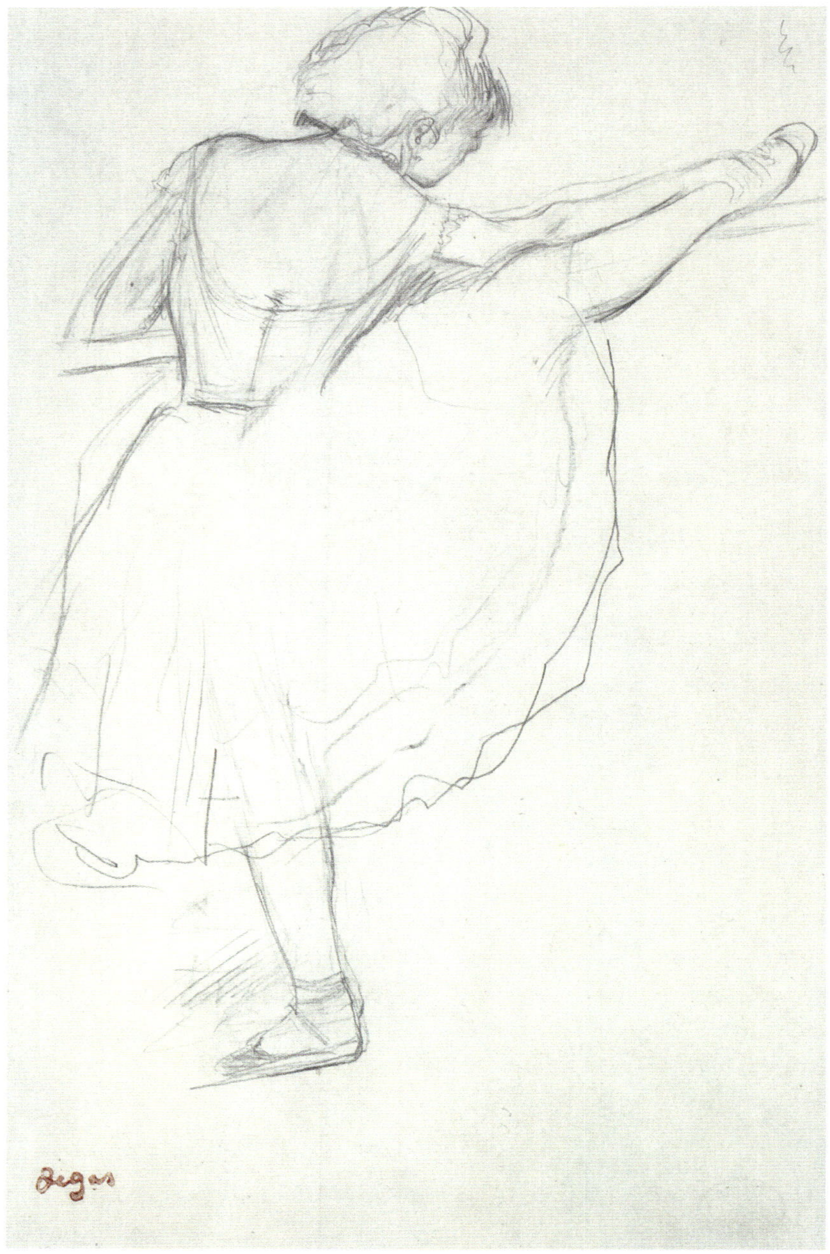

the group's third exhibition in 1877.[42] A contrasted approach to drawing
is represented by the vivacious *Study of Legs* (cat. 10), where separate sketches
have been artfully juxtaposed on a single sheet. Now emphasising a range
of classroom behaviours, Degas has drawn multiple feet and lower limbs
in a variety of positions that almost challenge coherence. Yet the clarity and
economy of his line triumphs, allowing us to discern some dancers' legs
at ease, others positioned for action or undergoing a routine stretch. Witty
and economical, this sheet recalls the mannered composition of certain
sketchbook pages made by artists from the Renaissance onwards, while still
reminding us of the informal nature of life backstage. Appropriately, the
drawing buzzes with nervous energy, encouraged by Degas's addition
of echoing lines around ankles, feet and calves.

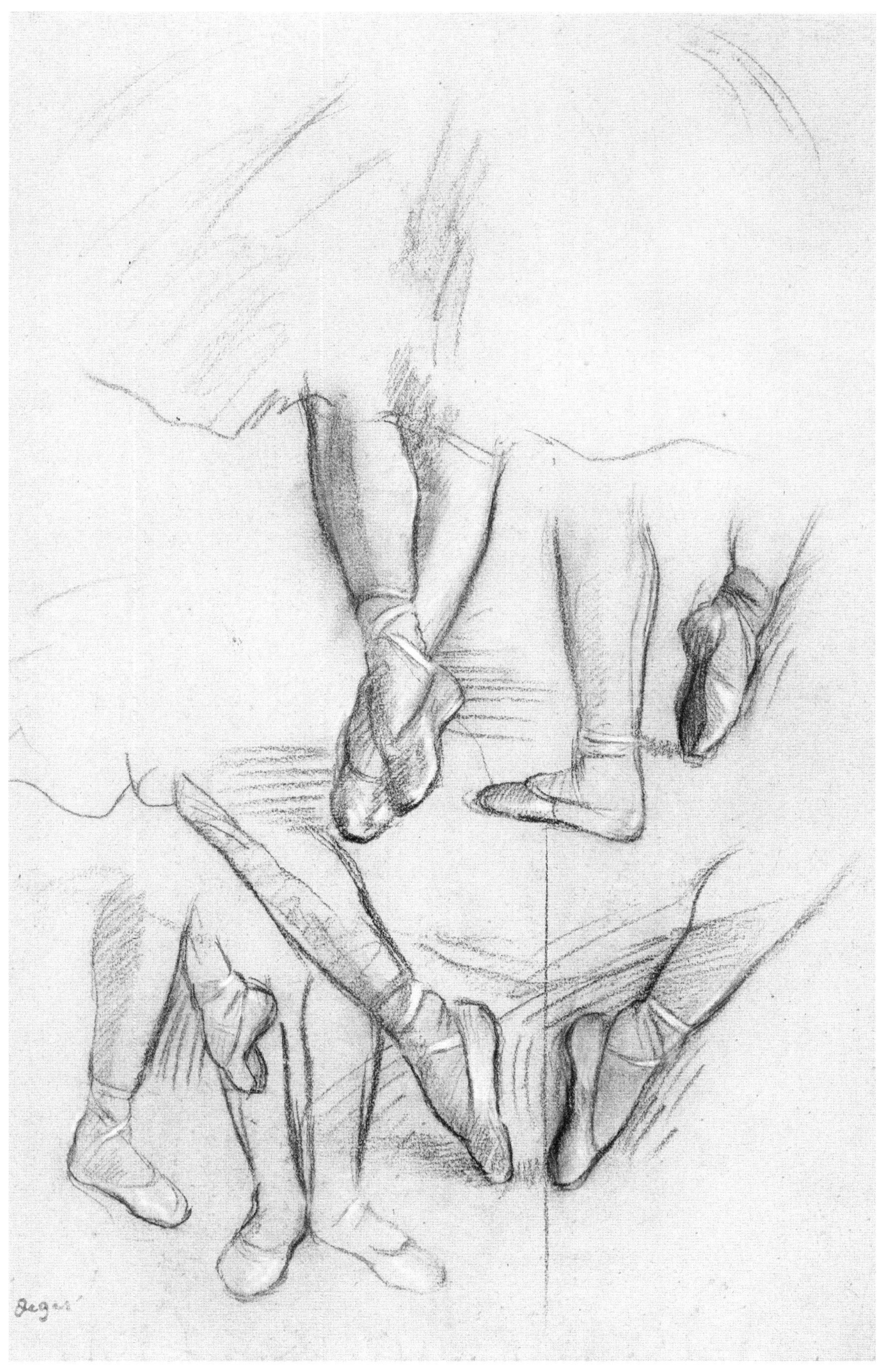

10

Study of Legs
c. 1873
Black chalk heightened
with white on blue paper,
46.5 x 30.7 cm
Private collection, New York,
courtesy of W. M. Brady & Co., Inc.

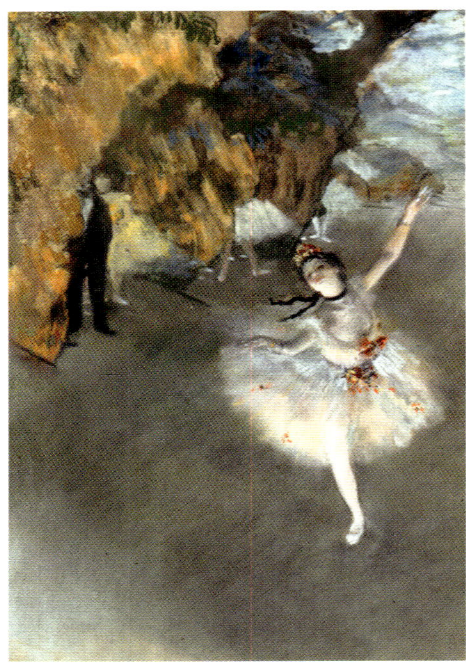

Fig. 14 *L'Etoile, or The Dancer on Stage*, *c.* 1876–77.
Pastel over monotype, 58 x 42 cm. Musée d'Orsay, Paris

THE DANCER IN MOVEMENT

During the memorable visit he made to Degas's studio in 1874, Edmond de Goncourt did not simply look at his pictures. The novelist noted that he also watched as Degas described the actions of ballerinas by 'mimicking a choreographic sequence'; it was 'very amusing', he observed, to see the artist 'high on his points, his arms rounded, mixing the aesthetics of a dance master with those of a painter'.[43] Degas's dancing skills are otherwise unknown, but the point of the presentation made for Goncourt's benefit was clear enough: the ballerinas in his works of art were almost all involved with movement of some kind, whether the stately routines shown in the Fogg Art Museum's *The Rehearsal* or the mischievous romping of the girls in *The Ballet Rehearsal*.

The much-cited statement that Degas's dance pictures were 'a pretext for depicting movement' too easily overlooks the delight that the artist clearly felt on his frequent visits to live performances at the Opéra, as well as his enjoyment of the animated company of dancers in classrooms and studios. This simple pleasure is wittily captured in a sketchbook used by Degas around 1877, in which he showed girls from the Opéra company exercising at the barre, rehearsing stage positions and gossiping with friends (fig. 15). The vitality of this page is given a further twist by evidence that it was drawn from memory, not at first hand, presumably recording an encounter that was still vivid in the artist's mind. The sketchbook was kept at the home of his friends the Halévy family, where Degas dined frequently and sometimes improvised drawings related to recent events or current projects. Ludovic Halévy, a novelist and man of the theatre, wrote a series of popular stories entitled *La Famille Cardinal* (1883), which described various adventures that included events backstage at the Paris Opéra. A substantial number of Degas's monotypes are related to these fast-moving tales of flirtation and intrigue, again allowing the artist to celebrate the dynamism of his subjects and experiment with suggestive shadows and fleeting forms.[44]

This preoccupation with the active and the transient was recognised by many of those who saw Degas's pictures at exhibitions held by the Impressionist group throughout the 1870s and into the following decade. In 1877, when *The Rehearsal* from Glasgow may finally have been seen in public, Degas's submissions were widely admired for their liveliness.[45] Claretie proclaimed of his display 'this is life itself'; a colleague noted that 'there is movement, life' in Degas's dance scenes, and a third critic went so far as to worry that one of the ballerinas – perhaps the figure in the now-famous pastel *L'Etoile, or The Dancer on Stage* (fig. 14) – was hurtling so fast down the stage that she would fall into the orchestra pit.[46] Underlying many of these responses was the belief that the vivacity of Degas's dance works captured 'a sentiment absolutely Parisian and modern': they expressed 'la vie parisienne', insisted Claretie.[47] For decades, the residents of the city had excoriated or celebrated the pace of life in the capital, just as its novelists, poets and artists had variously tackled the subject in words and pictures. Baudelaire famously made 'the fleeting beauty' of these urban surroundings into one of the themes of his essay *The Painter of Modern Life*, evoking the 'ebb and flow of movement, in the midst of the fugitive and the infinite' that clearly excited him as much as it had inspired the ostensible subject of the essay, the artist Constantin Guys.[48] The Impressionist group found their own spokesman in the novelist Edmond

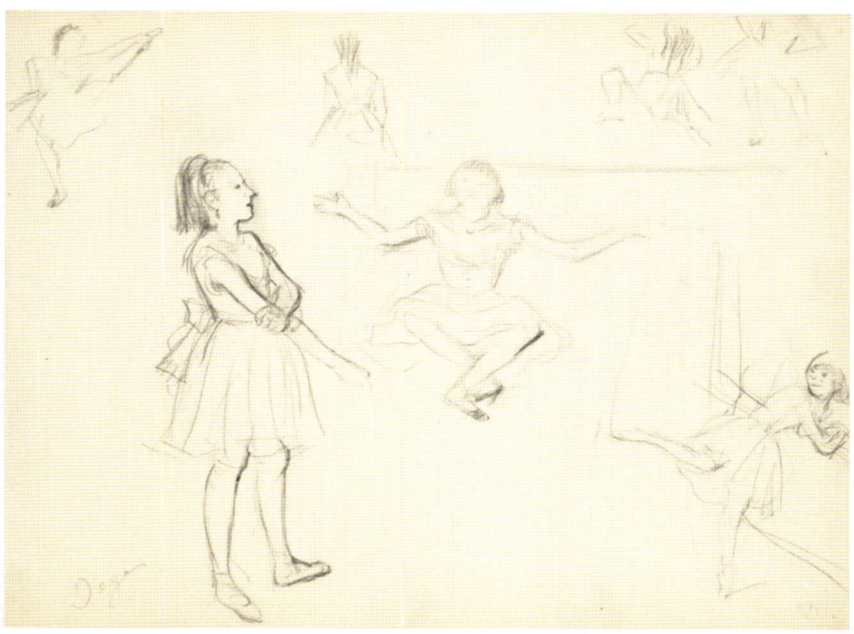

Fig. 15 **Notebook 28, p. 25, showing ballet dancers practising and resting**,
c. 1877. Graphite on paper, 24.8 x 33 cm. J. Paul Getty Museum, Los Angeles,
inv. no. 95.GD.35.12

Duranty, who appears to have collaborated with Degas on a seminal statement
of 1876 entitled *The New Painting*. Published at the time of the second group
show, Duranty's long text addressed the exhilarating subjects and themes that
were now being tackled by younger artists. While some of the 'new painters'
had attempted to render the 'trembling of leaves, the shimmer of water, and
the vibration of sun-drenched air', Duranty explained, others also aimed to
paint 'the walk, movement and hustle and bustle of passers-by' in their great
modern city.[49] The typical pedestrian. he argued, 'might be avoiding carriages
as he crosses the street or glancing at his watch as he hurries across the square.
When he is at rest, he will not be merely pausing or striking a meaningless
pose before the photographer's lens.' Even in this radical context, it seems,
the mobility of modern life could be set against the stasis of photography.

Many of these same sentiments were echoed in a notebook used by
Degas around this date to write down ideas for future pictures. On various
pages he imagined depicting 'smoke from locomotives, from tall factory
chimneys, from steamboats etc' and wrote of an 'infinite variety of subjects
in cafés, different tones of the glass globes reflected in the mirrors', while
instructing himself to 'do some arms or legs, or some backs … bare feet in the
act of dancing etc etc'.[50] Several motifs of this kind duly appeared in his work,
in black-and-white monotypes of brightly lit cabarets and bars, for example,
and in a tiny print of industrial smoke billowing across the sky.[51] Duranty's
'hustle and bustle of passers-by' also found expression in one of Degas's most
celebrated canvases of the period, a work that has often been discussed in
the context of photography. The painting, *La Place de la Concorde* (State
Hermitage Museum, St Petersburg), shows Marie Sanlaville's lover, Ludovic
Lépic, crossing the busy expanse with his daughters in a confusion of variously
directed bodies, an image that most photographers would have rejected as

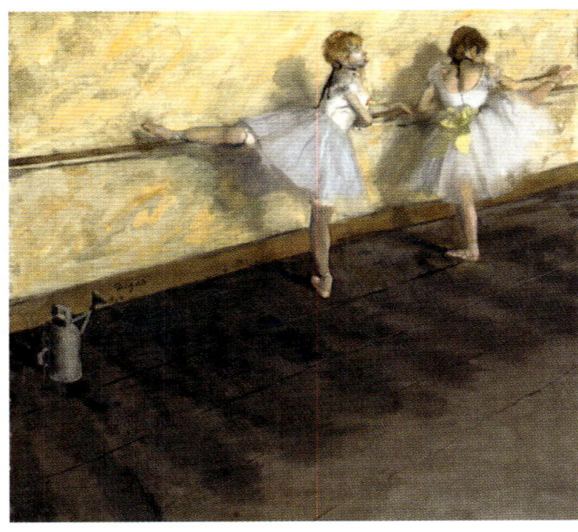

Fig. 16 **Dancers Practising at the Barre**, *c.* 1877.
Mixed media on canvas, 75.6 x 81.3 cm.
The Metropolitan Museum of Art, New York.
H. O. Havemeyer Collection, Bequest of Mrs H. O.
Havemeyer, 1929

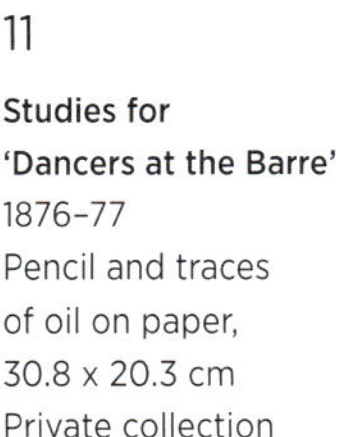

11

**Studies for
'Dancers at the Barre'**
1876–77
Pencil and traces
of oil on paper,
30.8 x 20.3 cm
Private collection

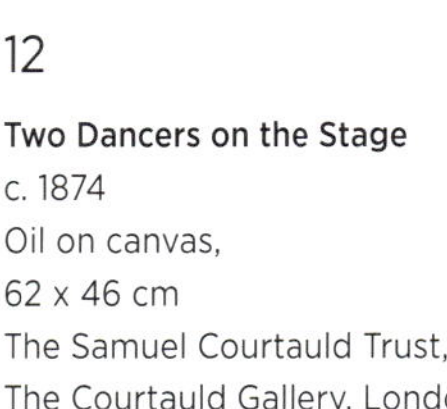

12

Two Dancers on the Stage
c. 1874
Oil on canvas,
62 x 46 cm
The Samuel Courtauld Trust,
The Courtauld Gallery, London

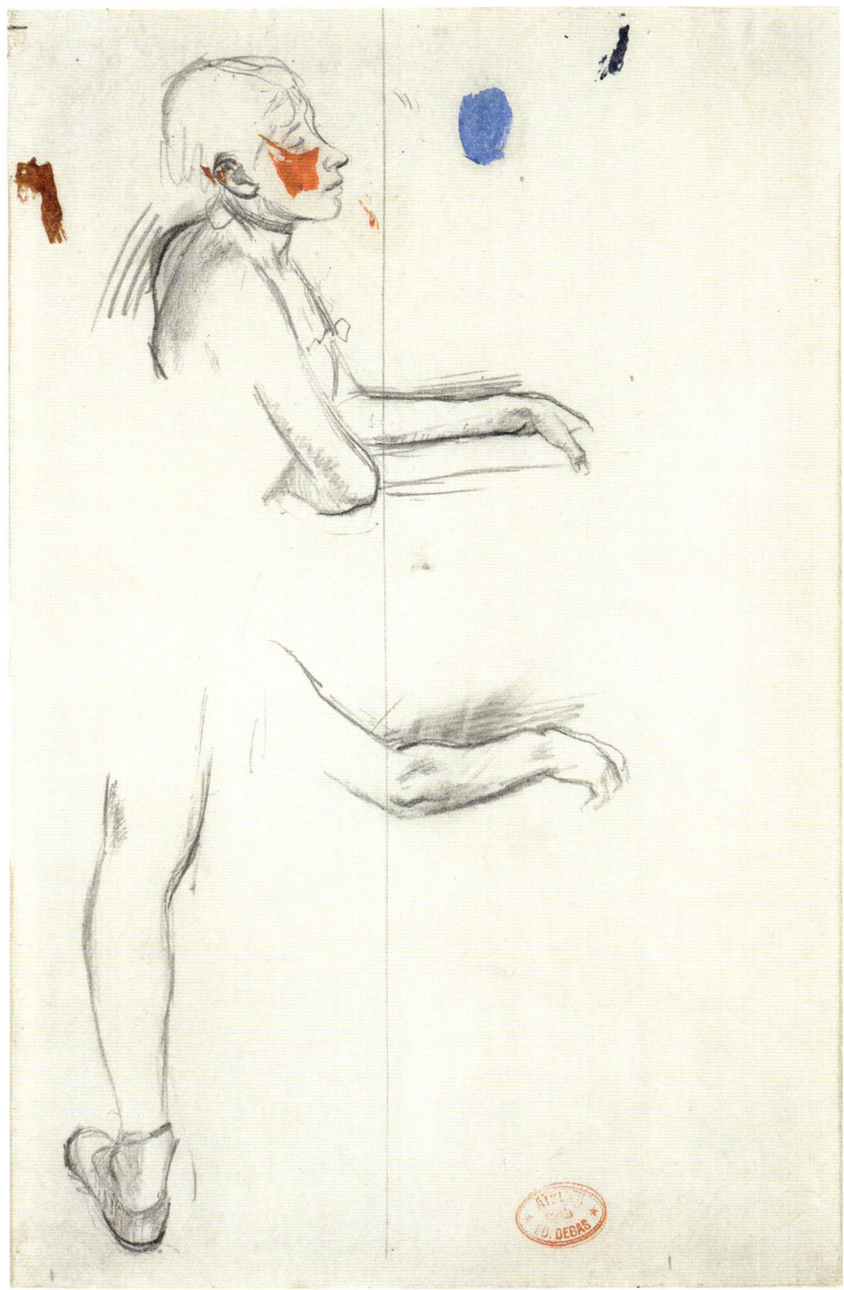

unseemly or regarded as a technical accident had it emerged from their cameras.[52] Amid the conflicting and sometimes wild claims that have been made about this composition, it should be noted that precisely such effects were being pursued by Degas in other aspects of his new urban imagery, such as the wilfully congested and blurred monotypes of figures moving in interiors and on the street.[53] Even Degas's more improvised drawings of dancers could have a surprisingly anarchic, multi-faceted quality, as he attempted to 'do some arms or legs, or some backs' in fresh and compelling ways. A particularly striking example is *Studies for 'Dancers at the Barre'* (cat. 11), in which the artist has uncharacteristically focused on disconnected parts of the young woman's body rather than the whole. In this scattering of sketches he seems

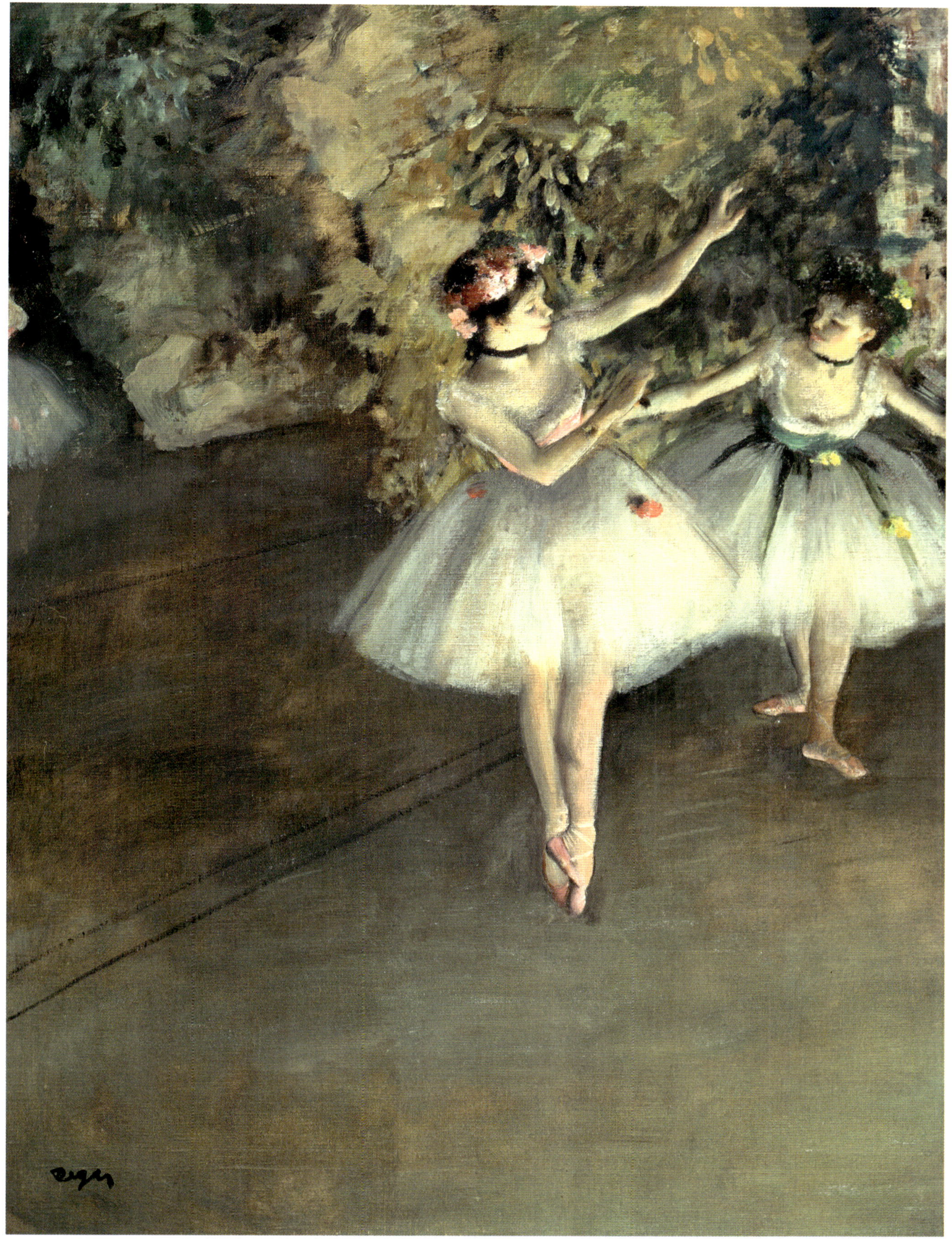

13

**Two Dancers in the Foyer
(Dancing School)**
c. 1873–75
Pastel and gouache
on paper,
29.8 x 21 cm
Private collection, courtesy
of the Halcyon Gallery, London

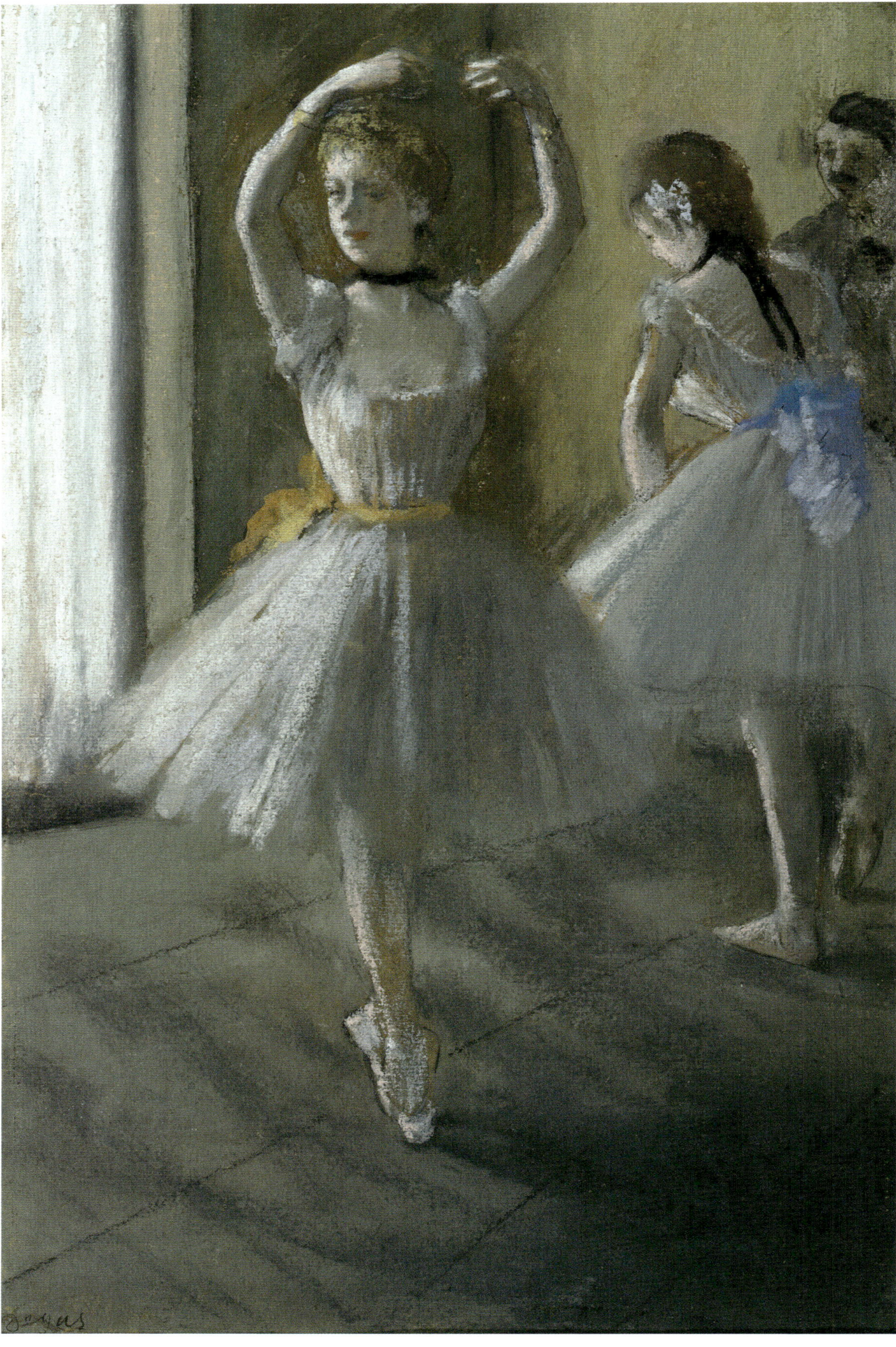

to have been determined to explore joints, selecting an ankle, two elbows and the junction of neck and shoulder blades belonging to a dancer who supports herself at the barre. Combining an almost surgical precision with an obvious delight in the girl's pert, upturned face, Degas also left several accidental splashes of colour on the sheet that reflect its casual use in the studio. Few studies exemplify so effectively Burty's 'coryphée, in gauze and in bone, the arms emaciated', which made up a true 'portrait of the dancer' for their self-consciously modern age. This drawing was used by Degas as he assembled information for an ambitious canvas of a classroom scene (fig. 16), a radically asymmetrical painting that was later given to another close friend, the industrial engineer and amateur painter Henri Rouart.[54]

A critical work that marks a broader transition from classroom to performance is the Courtauld's *Two Dancers on the Stage* (cat. 12), in which one superbly poised individual with an attendant by her side dominates the stage of the Paris Opéra. Crucial to the depicted scene is the fact that the star is in a position – 'en pointe' – that could only be sustained for an instant before she adjusted her equilibrium or moved on to a different step. Rather than representing movement itself, this subtle painting describes a tense interval between different phases of action, comparable to the moments when a gymnast is poised on a beam or an acrobat balanced on a wire. The subtlety of Degas's image emerges through a closer examination of the elements that he chose to introduce into – or just as significantly, omit from – this daring composition. Apart from the dancer's legs, the lower half of the picture is effectively empty, demanding the attention of the viewer to her athletic mastery as she hovers in space beneath the theatre lights. Especially finely observed are the left leg and foot, where much of her body weight is supported on the tips of her toes in a technical *tour de force* that had only been introduced into ballet a generation earlier. Making this detail the fulcrum of his design, Degas also noted the bulge in her shoe due to its light reinforcement for such extreme manœuvres, a nuance that presumably reflected Degas's first-hand study in the Opéra's classrooms and from models in his studio. So intrigued was he by this figure that it was repeated in several works, including *Ballet Rehearsal* (fig. 18) and *Ballet Rehearsal on Stage* (fig. 4).

The vividness of the Courtauld *Two Dancers on the Stage* contrasts with a more intimate variant of the subject in the small pastel entitled *Two Dancers in the Foyer (Dancing School)* (cat. 13). Here the artist represented a lesson or coaching session in which a confident young woman is positioned in 'sous-sous', though now with arms 'en couronne'. Sensuous, chalky marks evoke the textures of muslin, skin and the rough grey floorboards where darker patches show that is has again been watered to prevent slippage. In this secluded space the ballerina's action lacks the frisson and drama of the Courtauld painting, instead suggesting a tranquil moment among colleagues. A second dancer provides similar visual support to that of her counterpart in the larger work, although here she is clearly not dancing. Just visible behind her is a male figure in sombre clothes, perhaps an admirer or an abonné but conceivably the same dark-suited Pluque who appeared in *The Ballet Rehearsal*. Silhouetted against the shadowy room, we now feel that the principal dancer could hold her position almost indefinitely.

Presumably for practical reasons, few dancers of this era attempted to pose on pointe for the camera. Several years later, a rising star at the Opéra

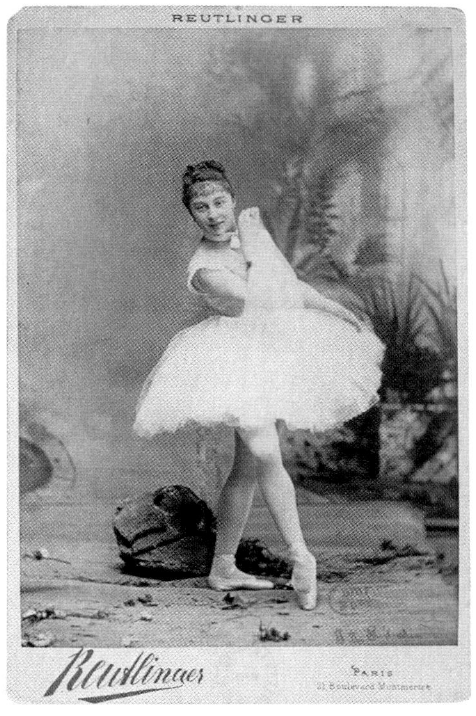

14

Reutlinger studio
Joséphine Chabot
Undated
Photograph, 13 x 9.5 cm
Bibliothèque nationale de
France, Paris. Bibliothèque-
musée de l'Opéra

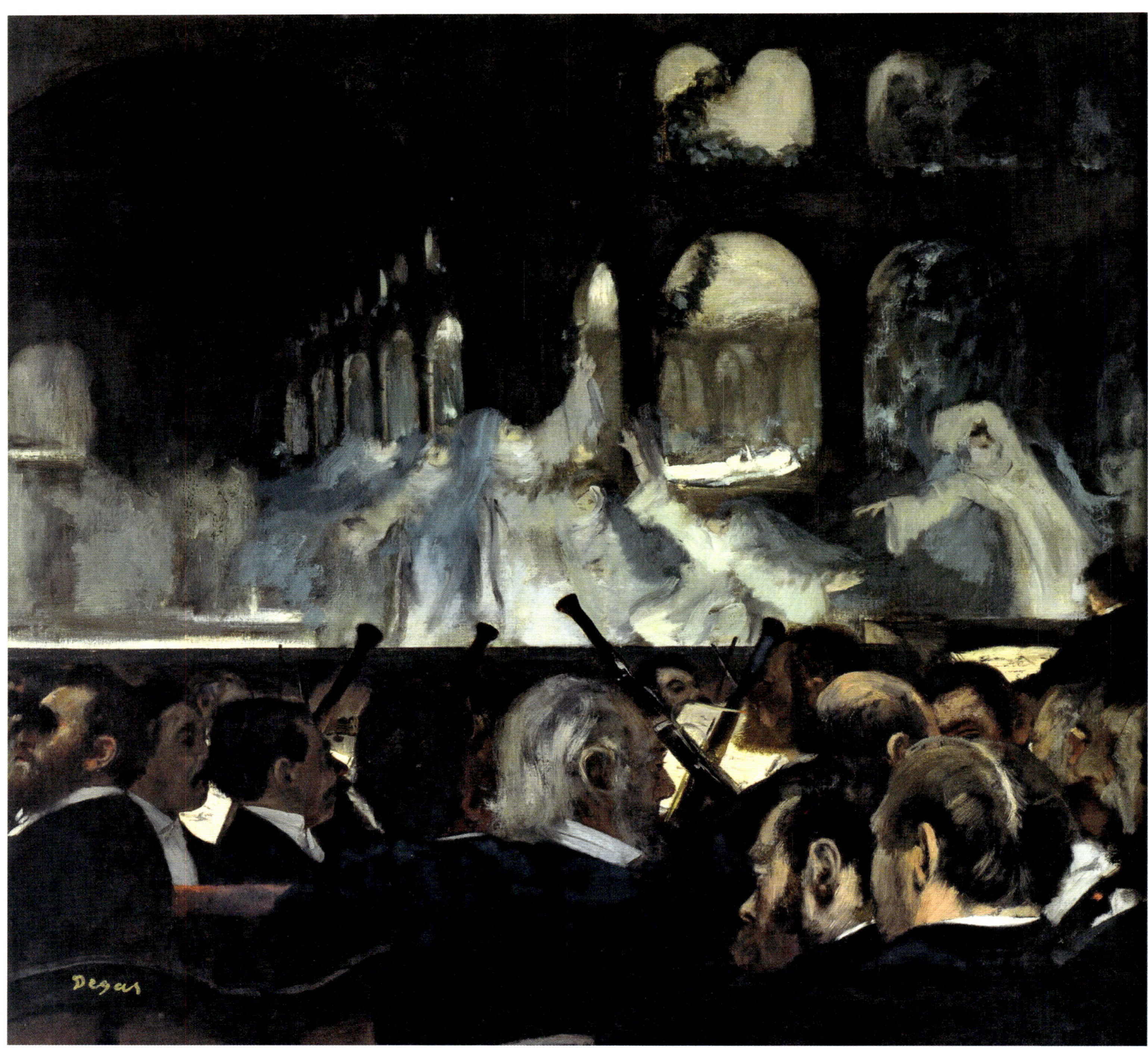

15
Ballet Scene from
Meyerbeer's Opera
'Robert le Diable'
1876
Oil on canvas,
76.6 x 81.3 cm
Victoria and Albert Museum,
London. Bequeathed by
Constantine Alexander Ionides

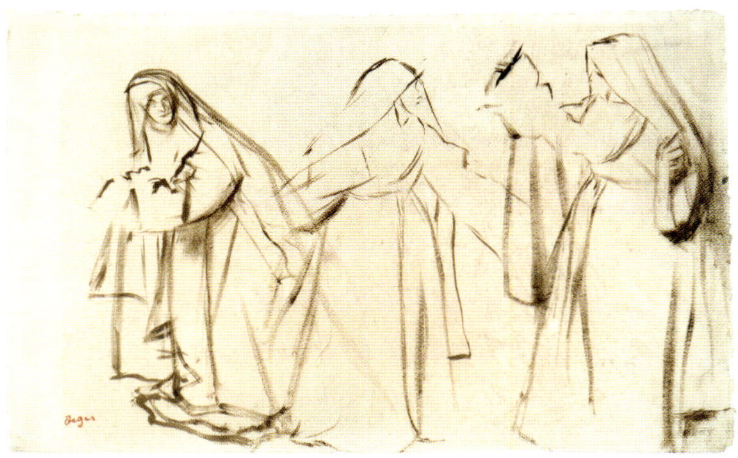

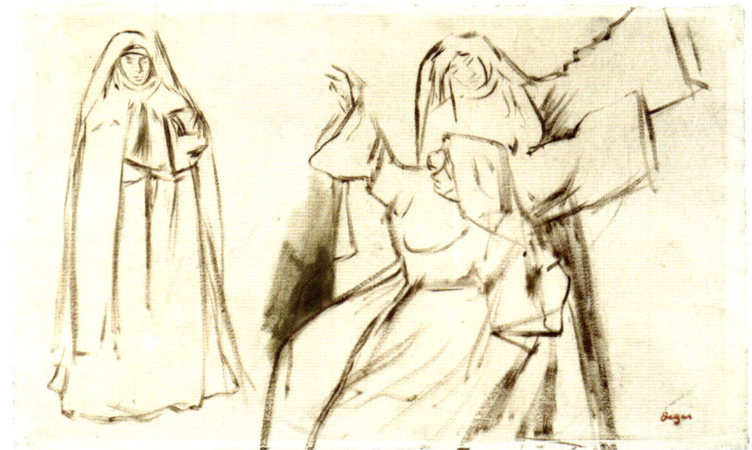

such as Joséphine Chabot chose to keep both feet on the ground when she was photographed by Reutlinger (cat. 14), although she otherwise presented herself in a lively, engaging manner as if she were on stage. Chabot was another member of the company whom Degas knew well: two letters of 1883 mention his meetings with this dancer and his efforts to promote her for advancement within the institution.[55] The artist's ability to gain admission to rehearsals was evidence of his own progress at the Opéra, where he had already become a partial subscriber and was thus entitled to see at least one performance a week. By 1885 Degas was an abonné himself, with the right to go backstage on performance nights and meet some of the cast in the Foyer de la Danse.[56] Throughout these years it is clear that he was becoming even more familiar with the Opéra repertoire and its employees, and bolder in his ambitions to represent them on paper and canvas. Ballet pictures were included on all but one of the occasions that Degas participated in the unfolding series of Impressionist exhibitions, now embracing views of dancers in the wings, pictures of a single star in the footlights (fig. 14), panoramas of the entire stage during a rehearsal (fig. 4) and numerous scenes of the classroom.[57] Of pointed significance was his addition of drawings to some of these shows, many of them studies of dancers that had been made in the course of creating his pastels and paintings, reminding admirers that his compositions were based on close contact with his subject-matter. Degas had long been spoken of as a specialist in the genre: as early as 1874, Ernest Chesneau had proposed that 'the foyer de la danse is his partiality'.[58]

Degas's self-confessed obsession with 'depicting movement' had emerged gradually and not always systematically. One of the mysteries that lingers from this story can be found in his large canvas entitled *Ballet Scene from Meyerbeer's Opera 'Robert le Diable'* (cat. 15).[59] Completed in 1876 but loosely based on an earlier work, this picture is among the most dynamic that Degas created in his entire career. Some light can be shed on the episode by an examination of both the painting's curious subject and its unusual origins. The composition is derived from an opera by Giacomo Meyerbeer that had been one of the cornerstones of the Paris Opéra's repertoire since its premiere in 1831. Considered a masterpiece of the Romantic imagination, the narrative was set to dramatic music and famed for the visual effects of certain scenes that unfolded as its bizarre plot advanced. Most celebrated was part of the

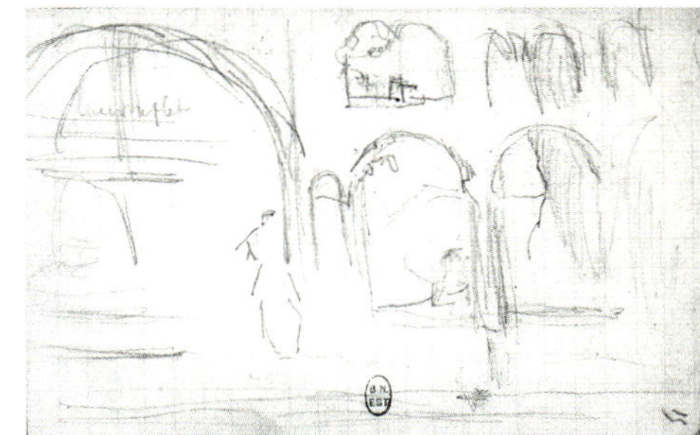

Fig. 17 **Notebook 24, p. 15, showing a drawing related to 'Robert le Diable'**, *c.* 1868–73. Pencil, 8 x 11.8 cm. Bibliothèque nationale de France, Paris, Dc 327 réserve

third act, which took place in a ruined convent lit by moonlight, where
dead nuns began to dance. This was not a decorous performance from the
traditional operatic or balletic repertoire but a wild, exotic display of unearthly
spirits who abandoned themselves to pagan behaviour denied to them in their
former existence. Deep shadows, a towering set of Romanesque arches
entangled with foliage, and a spot-lit tomb in the middle distance added to
the sense of delirium, which was mocked by some of the younger generation
but still drew crowds as late as the 1890s. Degas is known to have seen the
opera many times, including six visits between 1885 and 1892 when his name
appeared in the register of abonnés at the Opéra.[60] Further traces of his
presence at performances can be found in a pocket-size notebook he used
in the late 1870s, which also includes written notes on the spectacle and
small drawings that appear to have been made on the spot. These are mostly
concerned with the stage and the set itself, while one or two faint indications
of dancers may represent his first attempts to track their unconventional
actions (fig. 17).[61]

Ballet Scene from Meyerbeer's Opera 'Robert le Diable' was commissioned
by the most famous baritone of the day, Jean-Baptiste Faure, a prominent
patron of contemporary art and a friend and admirer of Meyerbeer. The
painting handed over to Faure in 1876 was something of a *tour de force*, even
by Degas's current standards of stage imagery. Dominated by theatrical gloom,
it presented several separate but complementary aspects of the Paris Opéra
that had helped to establish its reputation for excellence throughout the
world. In the lower section at right, the heads of several abonnés in the
front rows of the stalls summarised the importance to the institution of
businessmen and political figures of the day. Clearly portraits of specific
individuals, these partly conceal another male enclave, the orchestra, whose
members blow into their tubas and flourish their violin bows at the behest
of the conductor at extreme right. Across the footlights, Degas then conjured
an alternative world of make-believe, equally penumbrous but entirely
resistant to the social analysis applied to the auditorium. This change of milieu
is expressed through a fundamental shift in clarity, from the sharply detailed
cluster of subscribers in the foreground to the swaying, dissolving performers
on stage. Most unusually for this period in his art, Degas chose to blur the
contours and the subsidiary forms of most of the dancers, notably at left where
several nuns emerge from the shadowy cloister. The principal figures at centre
stage are the most carefully articulated, but even these are conjured from thick
paint that has been broadly applied – almost smeared – with large brushes.
Tellingly, the boundaries between one dancer and another are not always
clear and even the scenery seems to blend into these figures in places. For
Degas, accomplished draughtsman and pupil of the Florentine masters, this
was close to heresy, a departure underlined by his reluctance to revisit this
kind of technical adventure for another two decades.

A group of drawings related to the dancing nuns provides further insight
into Degas's struggle over *Ballet Scene from Meyerbeer's Opera 'Robert le Diable'*
(cats 16, 17). Carried out on paper in *essence*, a form of diluted oil paint that
he often favoured in these years, these studies represent various permutations
of nuns in full costume who almost all appear to be shown in the process of
moving. Impossible to execute during a performance and unlikely to have been
created purely from memory, these sheets may indicate that Degas had access

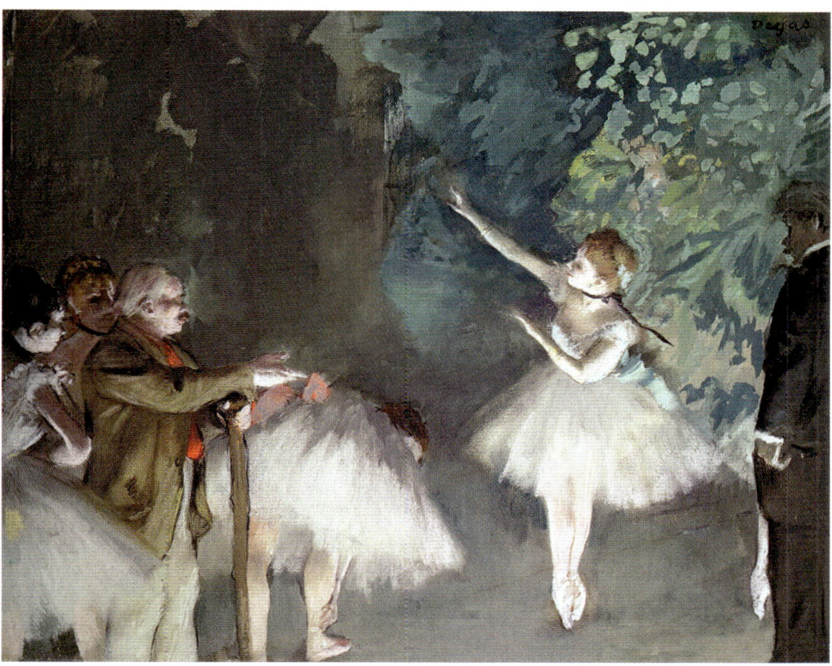

Fig. 18 **Ballet Rehearsal**, *c.* 1876. Gouache and pastel over monotype on laid
paper mounted on canvas, 55.2 x 68 cm. Nelson-Atkins Museum of Art, Kansas

to a dress rehearsal or to a cast member willing to pose for him. Whatever
their origin, they seem to present us with the clearest evidence yet
encountered of an attempt by the artist to document figures in live movement.
His sweeping brush strokes were clearly made in haste, with details such as
facial features perhaps added later to some but not all of the figures. Errors,
such as lines passing through an adjoining garment or an entire body, again
point to spontaneity, while links between individuals appear to anticipate –
without fully defining – the central group in the painting. It was on the canvas
itself that Degas's painterly instincts were given the greatest licence, as his
loaded brushes repeated the broad gestures on the preparatory sheets and
went even further, merging one hue into another and dissolving boundaries
between adjacent bodies. Several analogies for this technique suggest
themselves: one was the paint handling of Old Masters he is known to have
admired, from Venetian colourists such as Titian and Veronese to the virtuoso
practitioners of Holland, principally Rembrandt and Hals; a second was the
Japanese painting tradition, with its freely applied brushwork that was much
in vogue in Paris at this time. Degas was well aware of these precedents, but
may have been uneasy about invoking them at this moment in his career.
In their different ways, such techniques pointed backwards in history, to paint
handling and to assumptions about painting itself that his generation had
largely put behind them. It is hardly a coincidence that Degas chose not
to repeat this experiment in such a conspicuous way until his later years.

The end of this decade saw a number of startling advances in Degas's
dance art, among them moves towards the representation of figures who
were vividly active and sometimes airborne. By now a veteran of the genre,
he painted larger pictures that included the first of the novel 'frieze' canvases

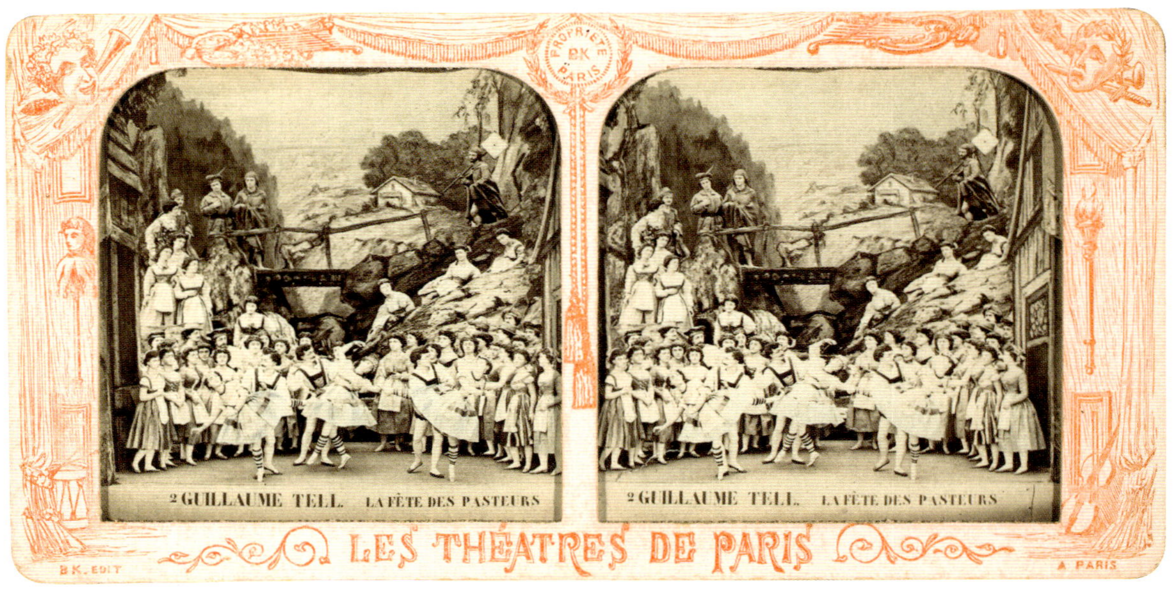

Fig. 19   *B. K.*, Guillaume Tell, La Fête des Pasteurs, from the series Les Théâtres de Paris, *c.* 1860.
Albumen stereographic tissue, approx. 8.8 x 17.6 cm. George Eastman House, Rochester, New York

of classrooms; exhibited ballet scenes in oil on canvas, pastel on paper, and water-based media on silk; and began work on the revolutionary – if entirely static – sculpture of the *Little Dancer Aged Fourteen*. Especially evident was his new-found confidence in depicting figures on stage, some perched hazardously on pointe, others dashing across the boards with colleagues and a few rare individuals leaping into space. Now in his mid-forties, Degas had already achieved a considerable reputation among collectors and dealers in Paris, as well as some admirers from abroad who began to acquire his dance works. It was probably on a visit to the French capital in 1877 that the wealthy Louisine Elder – later Havemeyer – from New York, guided by her friend Mary Cassatt, bought Degas's pastel known as *Ballet Rehearsal* (fig. 18), a brilliantly coloured masterpiece that shows Jules Perrot at left and at right a variant of the figure in the Courtauld's *Two Dancers on the Stage*, again shown precariously on pointe.[62] Henry Hill of Brighton was also accumulating ballet pictures and Sickert bought for himself *The Green Dancers* (Museo Thyssen-Bornemisza, Madrid), a close-up view of the stage from above with ballerinas captured in extreme acrobatic postures.[63] Never shy of repeating motifs or even large elements of existing compositions, Degas continued to be productive and materially secure while avoiding the press and working incessantly in his Montmartre studio, hoping – as he later said – to become 'illustrious but unknown'.[64]

The challenge of depicting full-costume, multi-figure stage scenes at the Paris Opéra was formidable, as Degas had learned with the two versions of *Ballet Scene from Meyerbeer's Opera 'Robert le Diable'*. Yet subjects of this kind had the added enticement of being manifestly beyond the capability of his photographer-colleagues and thus of particular appeal to a combative artist such as Degas. Stage lighting was still limited by modern standards and – coupled with the incessant movement of dancers – had the effect of putting live ballet performances beyond the reach of cameras for at least two decades.

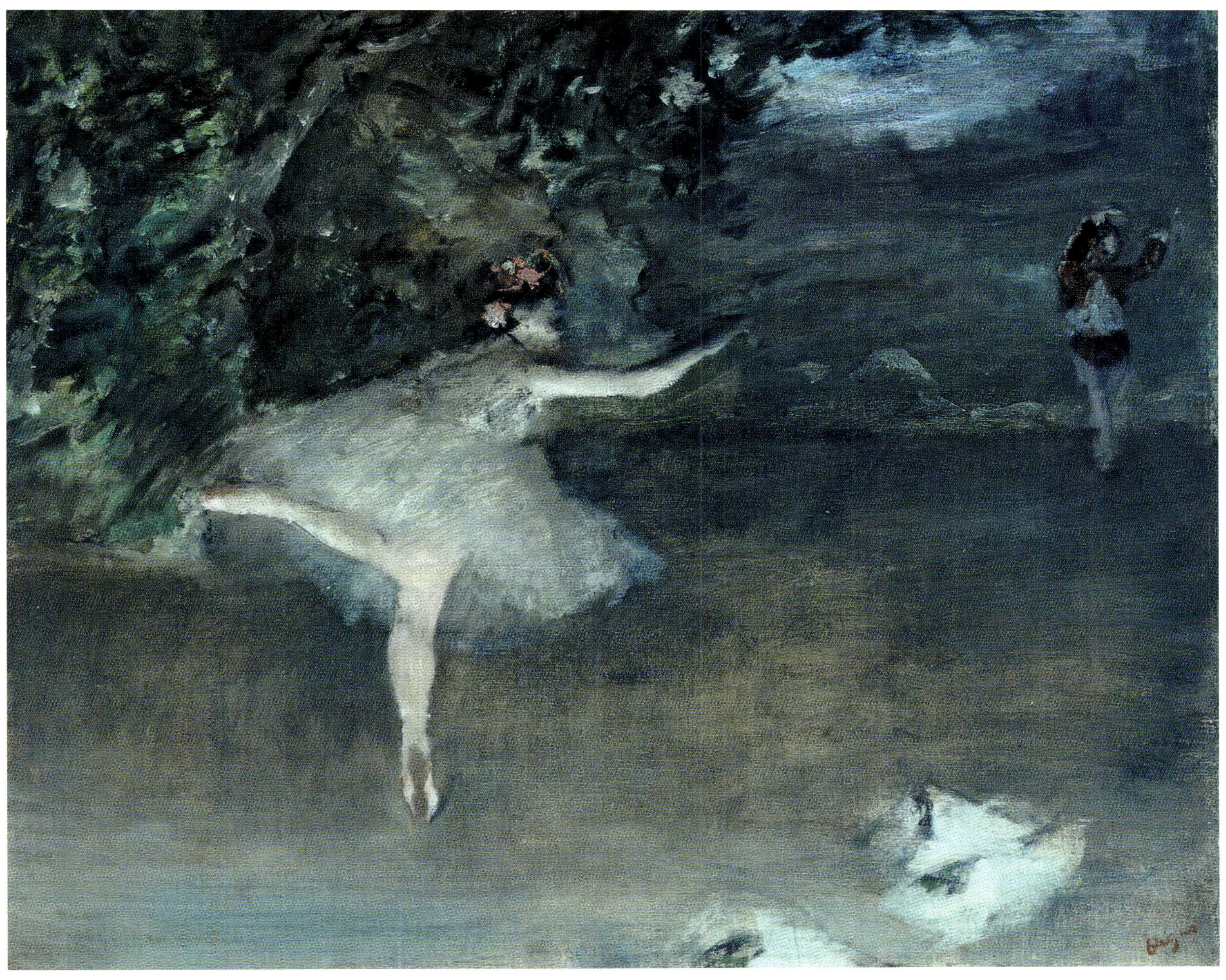

18

Dancer on Pointe
c. 1877–78
Oil on canvas,
43.2 x 61 cm
Collection of
Diane B. Wilsey

Photographs of Opéra productions made as late as the mid-1890s (cats 107, 108), while eerily appealing in their own way, showed the corps de ballet as grey blurs or streaks and were at best documents of stage sets. Degas's early attempts at painting the entire proscenium had been successful in their own terms, but only because he concentrated on scenes in which the majority of participants were static. In *Ballet Rehearsal on Stage* (fig. 4), for example, the work shown at the 1874 exhibition that was mistaken by Philippe Burty for a drawing, all but one of the dancers are in fixed, immobile positions. Oddly resembling a photograph, it was painted in monochrome as a first step towards engraving for reproduction, possibly in the *Illustrated London News*.[65] The problems of recording movement on a crowded stage had long taxed both artists and photographers, as stereographs from the 1860s demonstrate. Made to be seen through a special viewer that revealed the theatre stage

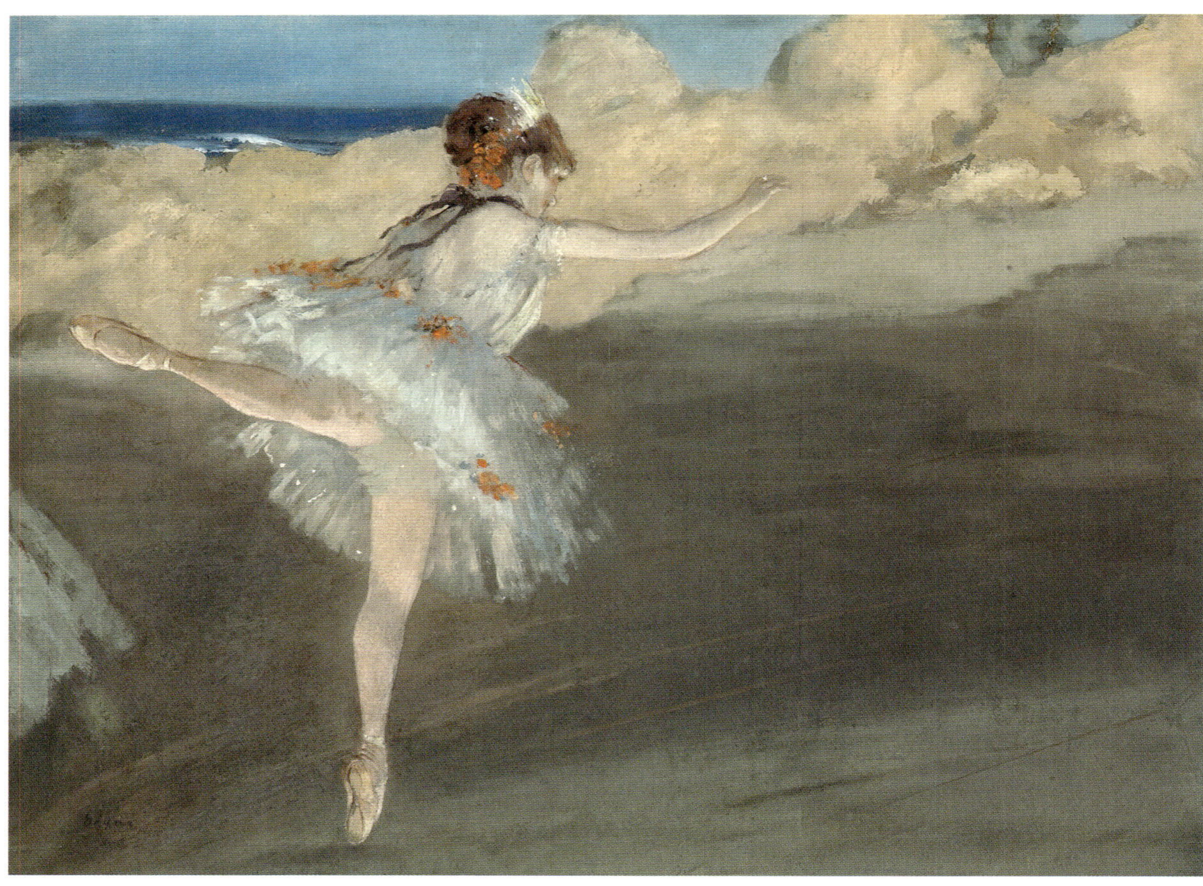

Fig. 20 **The Star: Dancer on Pointe**, *c.* 1878. Gouache and pastel on paper, 56.5 x 75.6 cm. Norton Simon Museum, Pasadena, inv. no. F.1969.40.P

in three dimensions, one of these stereographs (fig. 19) shows the cast of a performance of Rossini's opera *William Tell*. Charming though it seems today and thrilling though it may have been originally, these twinned pictures show the entire cast holding themselves absolutely still. It was only by ensuring that the participants 'froze' their poses throughout the exposure that such images could be made, in this case by a stereoscopic camera. Even the ballet dancers who participated in *William Tell* were required to support themselves in some way during this process, either by leaning on colleagues or – more remarkably – posing on their toes throughout.

In such a context, it is difficult not to see some of Degas's ballet pictures from the late 1870s as frankly defiant, both of such primitive forerunners in the theatre and of his photographer-peers. His oil painting *Dancer on Pointe* (cat. 18) is a case of this kind, despite its uncombative appearance. This delicate, atmospheric work seems to present the quintessential ballet experience that continued to attract audiences to the Paris Opéra and still delights their successors today. Against a wooded setting that might belong to a dozen different contemporary scenarios, a lone ballerina in a pale costume executes an arabesque. Around her is empty space, broken only at lower right by bouquets thrown from the auditorium and by a rare glimpse of a male dancer in the distance. Colour and effects of light and shade are generally subdued, while footlights project their pale radiance upwards towards the young woman. If most of these elements appear to be familiar, Degas's presentation of the principal figure is surely inspired. Rarely had a painted dancer seemed so evanescent, a cloud of tulle, pale flesh and pink flowers who hovers in space for a moment as she moves upstage towards the distant figure who beckons to her. With characteristic subtlety, the artist provided just enough visual support for her in the muted lines of the scenery, yet makes no secret of the extreme tenuousness of her position. In another instant she will advance, weightless but propelled by the momentum of her craft and the lure of her remote paramour.

Unmistakable even to the non-expert eye is the sense that Degas's painting represents an exceptionally brief moment of transition in mid-performance, one that could not possibly be sustained by the participants. As such it is a *tour de force* of draughtsmanship and audacious design, which allowed the artist to visit pictorial and conceptual territory that had remained largely unexplored in the naturalist context. Degas's means of arriving at such an image were still derived from his early training; a thrilling sheet of drawings (fig. 21) includes several studies of legs and a draft for the central ballerina, all made in rapid, economical lines as his model struggled to hold her position. Conveniently, her name was recorded on the sheet in a single word: 'Melina'.

Degas was sufficiently pleased with his invention to revisit it several times around this moment. In *The Star: Dancer on Pointe* (fig. 20), the figure of Melina Darde is almost the only evidence of life on a near-empty stage set showing a rock-strewn beach.[66] Isolated in this way she seems vulnerable, while retaining the intense energy and forward momentum of the ballerina in *Dancer on Pointe*. In both works, Degas took substantial liberties when establishing the viewpoint of the spectator, who by implication is exceptionally close to the action on stage. The full depth of the proscenium

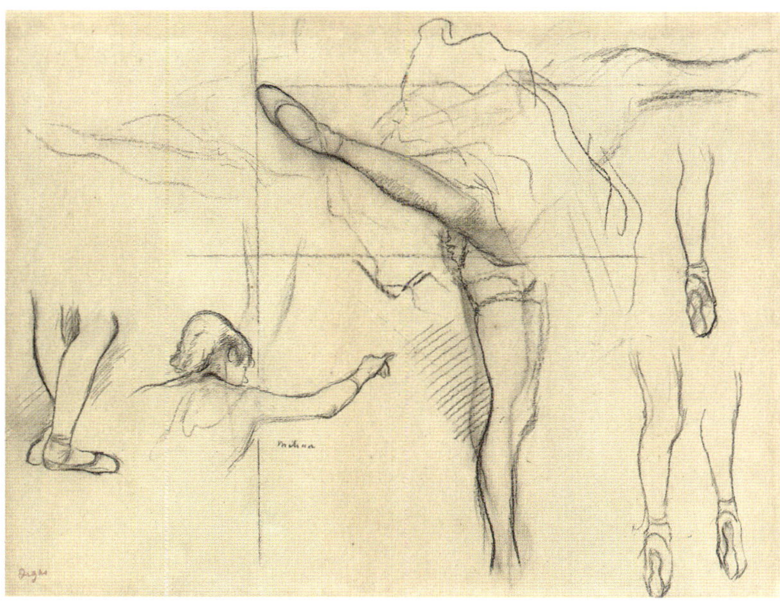

Fig. 21 **Dancer**, *c.* 1878. Charcoal on paper, 46 x 59 7 cm.
Private collection

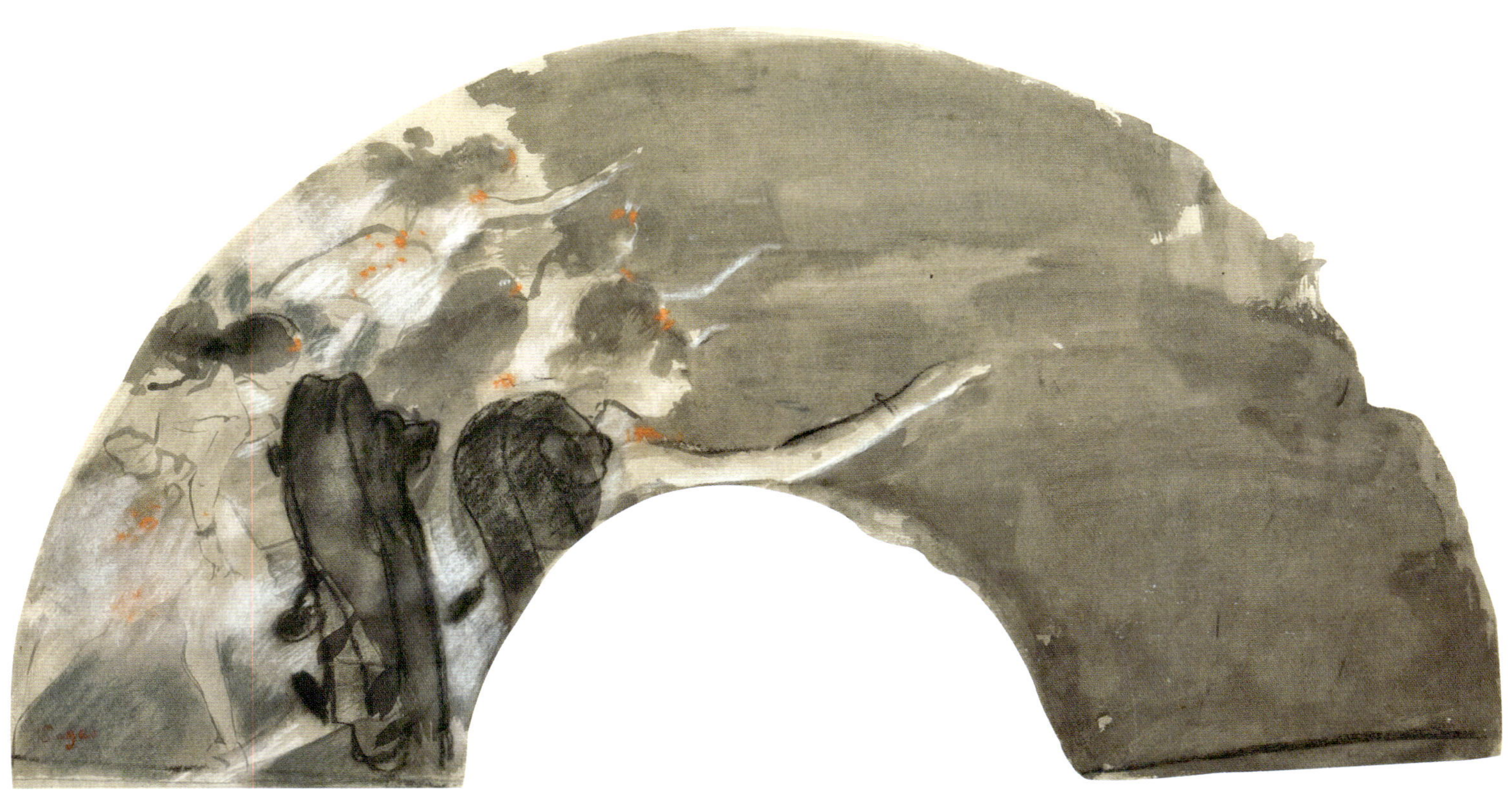

19

Dancers and Double Basses, Fan
c. 1879
Pastel, watercolour and graphite
on paper, 36 x 65 cm
Private collection, courtesy of
Kristy Stubbs Gallery, Dallas

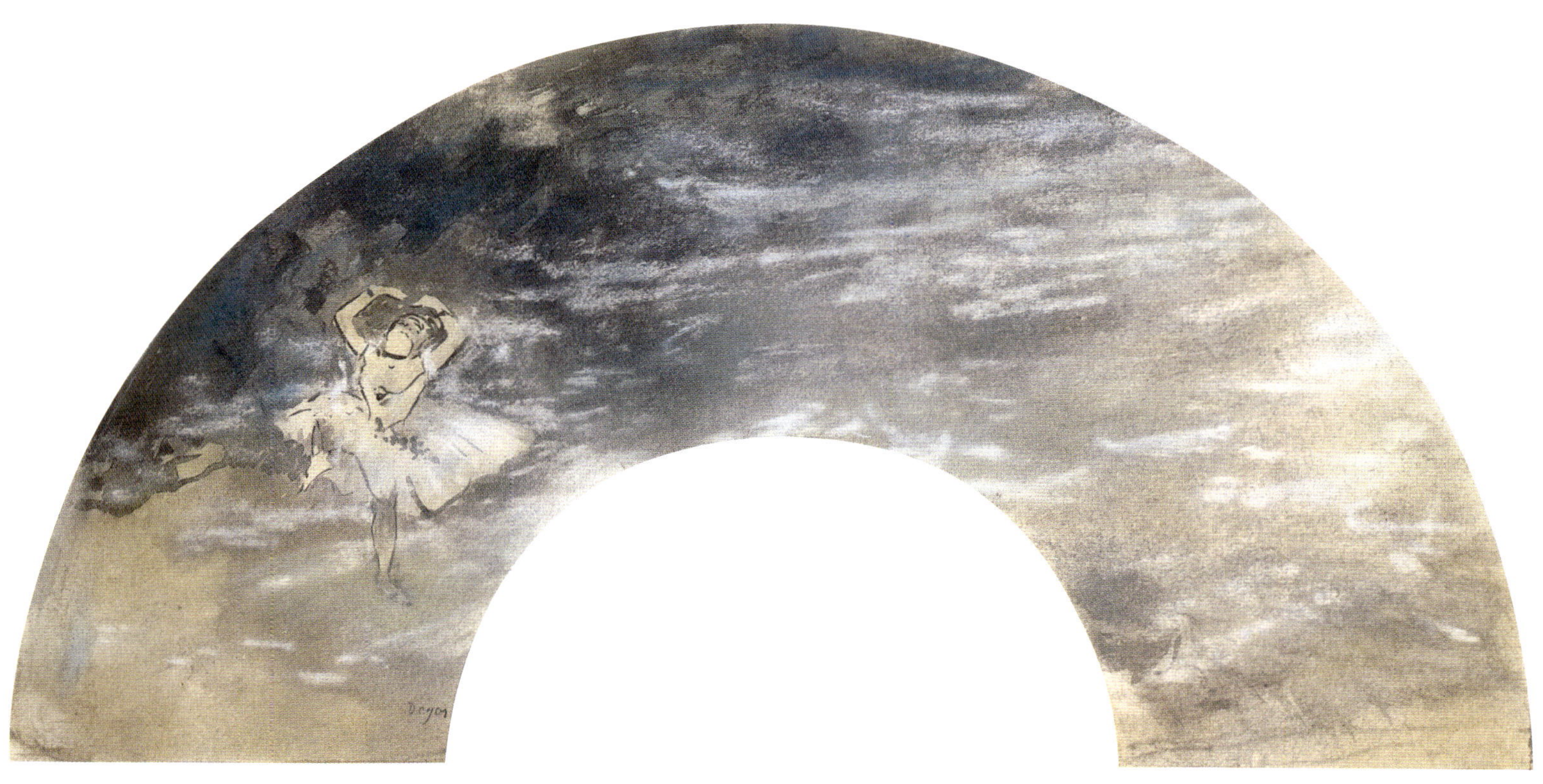

20

Dancer on Pointe
c. 1879
Gouache, Indian ink
and pastel on silk,
33.1 x 49.2 cm
Galerie Schmit, Paris

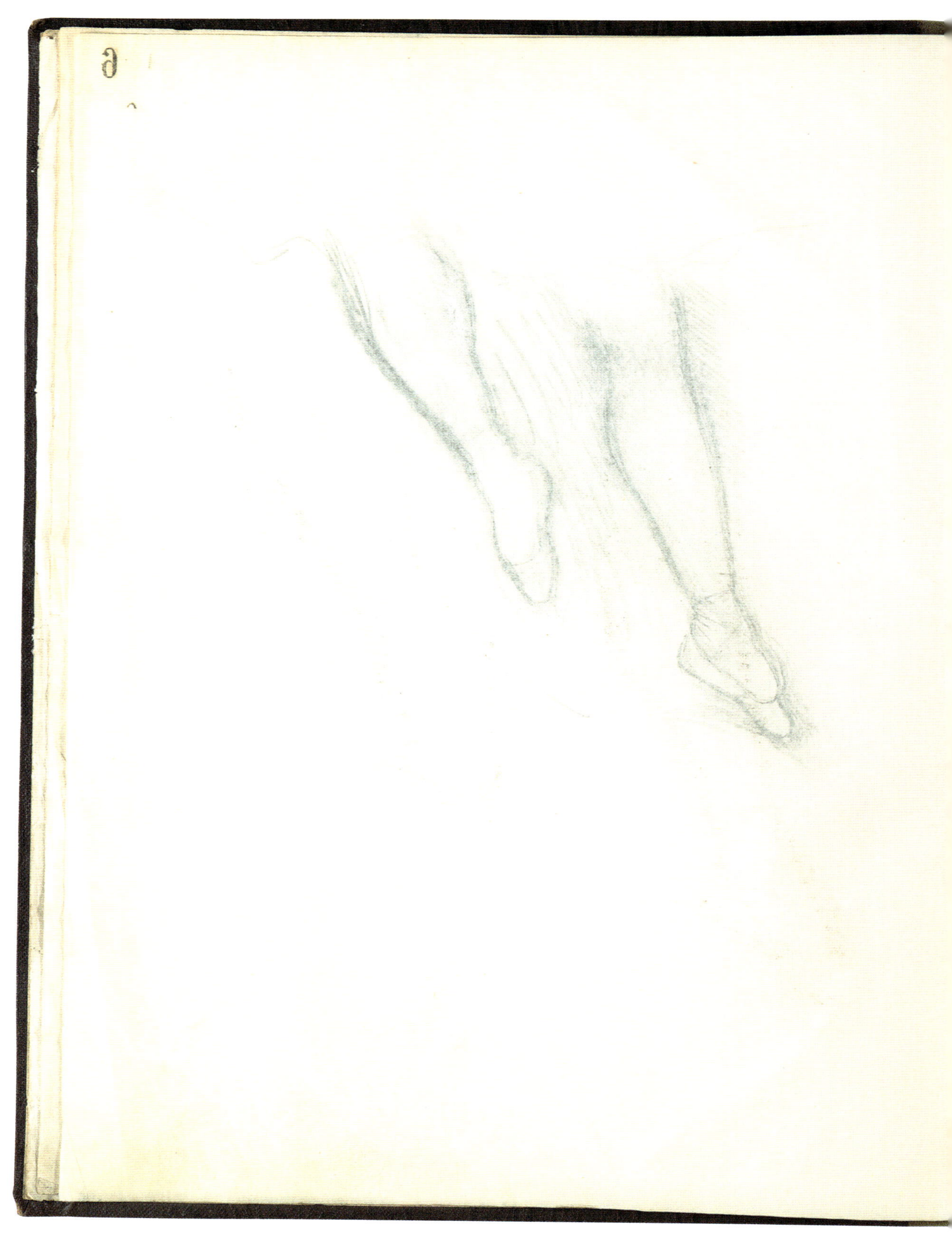

Fig. 22   **Notebook 36, p. 7, showing a ballet dancer's legs in a jump from
An Album of Forty-five Figure Studies**, 1882–85. Black chalk on eggshell paper,
26.8 x 21.9 cm. The Metropolitan Museum of Art, New York, inv. no. 1973.9

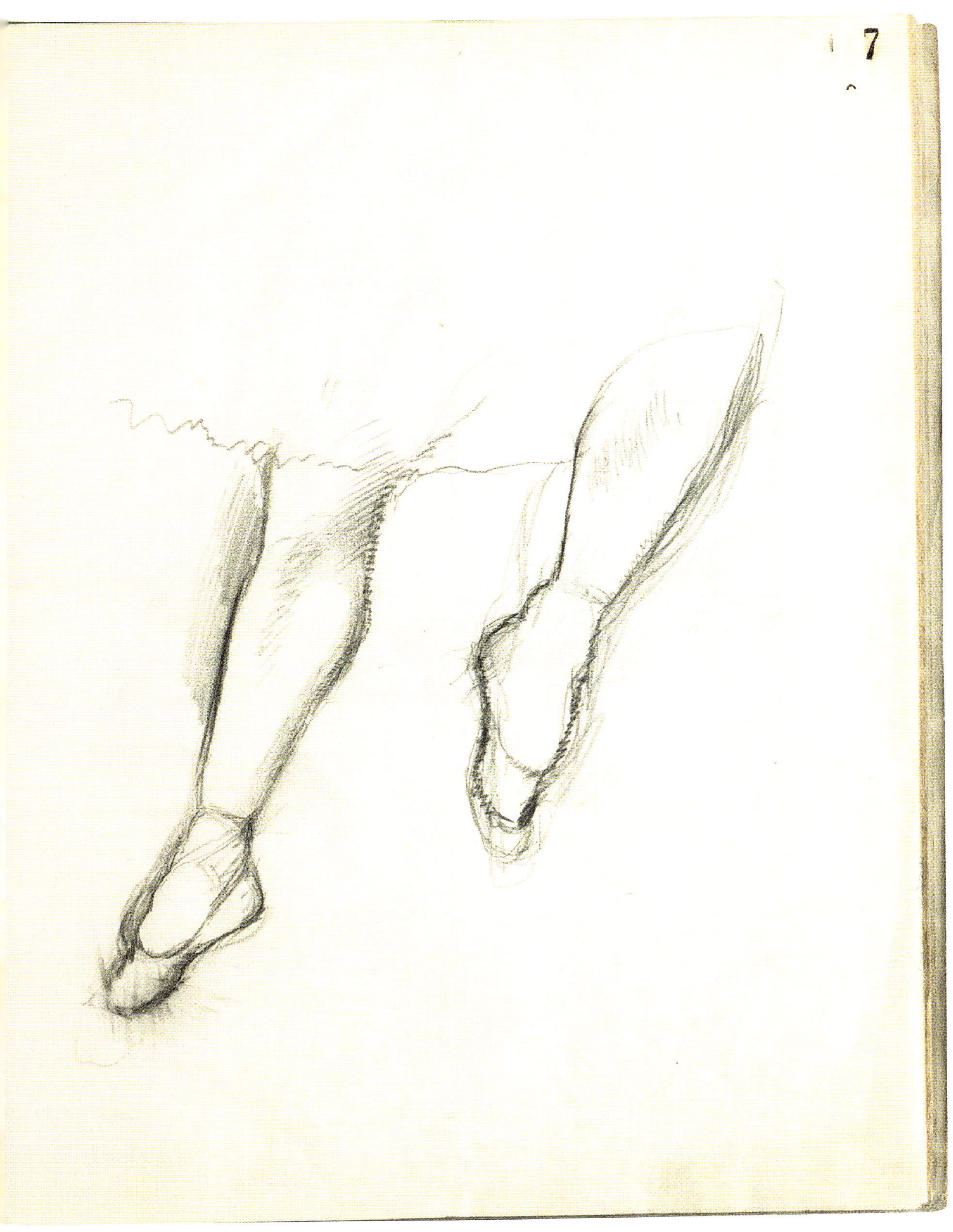

at the Opéra – which can still be experienced today – is considerable, indicating that the view in Degas's pastel could only have been achieved by an audience member with powerful opera glasses or a privileged visitor seated in a box beside the stage itself.[67] Degas experimented with many variations of this pictorial device during the 1870s, in pictures of performers seen from much higher seats in the building, as in his *L'Etoile, or The Dancer on Stage* (fig. 14). This was a period when concern over his own eyesight was growing, apparently heightening his awareness of perceptual and optical issues in ways that would sometimes find expression in his art.[68] In certain works, he experimented with differential focus, as if he were looking through a telescope or binoculars, or peering through the lens of a camera. Although these notions were rarely applied systematically, some of them seem to be evident in *Dancer on Pointe*, where areas of sharp detail and contrasting haziness subtly underscore the picture's impact. The distant scenery, for example, is almost entirely vague and featureless, like the backgrounds in many photographs that are focused on a human subject close to the lens. In other ballet pictures Degas became more confident in manipulating these factors, using them to create atmosphere, direct attention and sometimes to evoke the progress of dancers across a stage.

One format that lent itself surprisingly well to this challenge was the fan, a semicircular design intended to be framed and hung on the wall rather than used in a theatre. A popular challenge for artists of many kinds at this date, fan designs were also given special prominence at the fourth Impressionist exhibition held in 1879, when Degas listed four such works in the catalogue and Pissarro no less than eleven.[69] In characteristic fashion, Degas regarded the unusual curving form as one that was full of visual possibilities, producing some of the most asymmetrical, near-indecipherable compositions of his working life. The premise of each one that he exhibited was the same; the artist imagined himself high above the stage at the Opéra looking down on the action of a ballet from directly above. In some works, tiny dancer-figures skitter to and fro across bare boards, while in others vast expanses of colour evoke scenery flats that form mysteriously shaped rocks and trees, with glimpses of human action at their margins. A smaller group are based on views from the auditorium, such as *Dancers and Double Basses, Fan* (cat. 19), here with the double-bass head intervening between stage and audience, one of Degas's favourite features in his theatre and cabaret views. As in *Dancers in White*, lack of balance is near-complete, with at least five young ballerinas merging into one another as they appear to rush from one side of the stage to the other. Bleached by the theatre lights, these girls – like the star of Degas's painting *Dancer on Pointe* – seem translucent, their fleeting presences contrasted with the dark mass of the double bass. Subtle choices of media underlined this disparity; thin washes of ink and touches of colour for the dancers and heavier black chalk for the basses express in physical form the sensations unfolding in front of the audience. Another work of this asymmetrical type that is also near-abstract is *Dancer on Pointe* (cat. 20), which is dominated by a shimmering landscape of blues and silvers that might represent mist and sea. Here a tiny ballerina contrasts with the breadth of her fictive surroundings, her figure brilliantly evoked with a few touches of a paintbrush tip. Daringly balancing a featureless void against a soloist who holds the attention of the entire house, Degas shows her poised in mid-step,

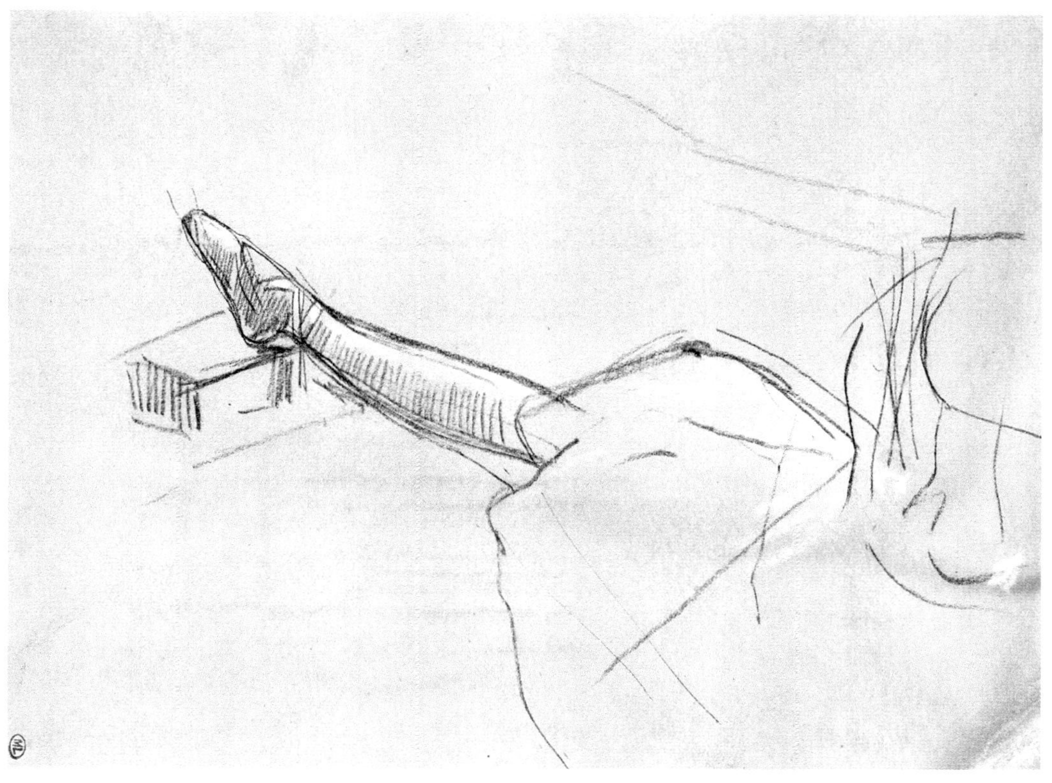

Fig. 23 **Study of a Dancer's Right Leg**, undated. Charcoal and white chalk on green paper,
21 x 31 cm. Musée du Louvre, Paris, Cabinet des Estampes, inv. no. RF 30016, recto

in a moment of brief equilibrium that captures something of the magic
of live performance.

The challenge of depicting a dancer in the air with both feet off the
ground was one that Degas had avoided until this moment. In several
small works made around 1880 he confronted the aerial step directly,
using first-hand observations stored in his mind over at least two decades
of ballet-watching and some brave attempts to capture such actions as they
were unfolding. In a sketchbook used between 1882 and 1885, several pages
are devoted to drawings of dancers' lower legs and feet, with some apparently
showing these limbs entirely off the ground (fig. 22). Here a *pas-de-chat* or *pas
battu* seems to be the subject, both of them quick jumps that involve bringing
the feet together in the air before the ballerina returns to the ground. Expert
draughtsman though he was, even Degas could not have drawn this step so
accurately and exquisitely in a few seconds. It seems reasonable to assume
that repeated scrutiny lay behind each drawing or even that the dancer agreed
to 'pose' in this position, perhaps seated on a bench or chair. A little-known
drawing reveals one such stratagem, when Degas chose to support a dancer's
leg on a table or similar surface as he drew the extended limb (fig. 23). The
difficulty of the artist's current task was well illustrated in the works on paper
that are related to his sketchbook studies. In *Three Ballet Dancers* (fig. 24), for
example, it is clear that the two young women at right have leapt into the air
and will shortly return to the stage, joining their colleague at left who might
might recently have completed the same action. We can only speculate

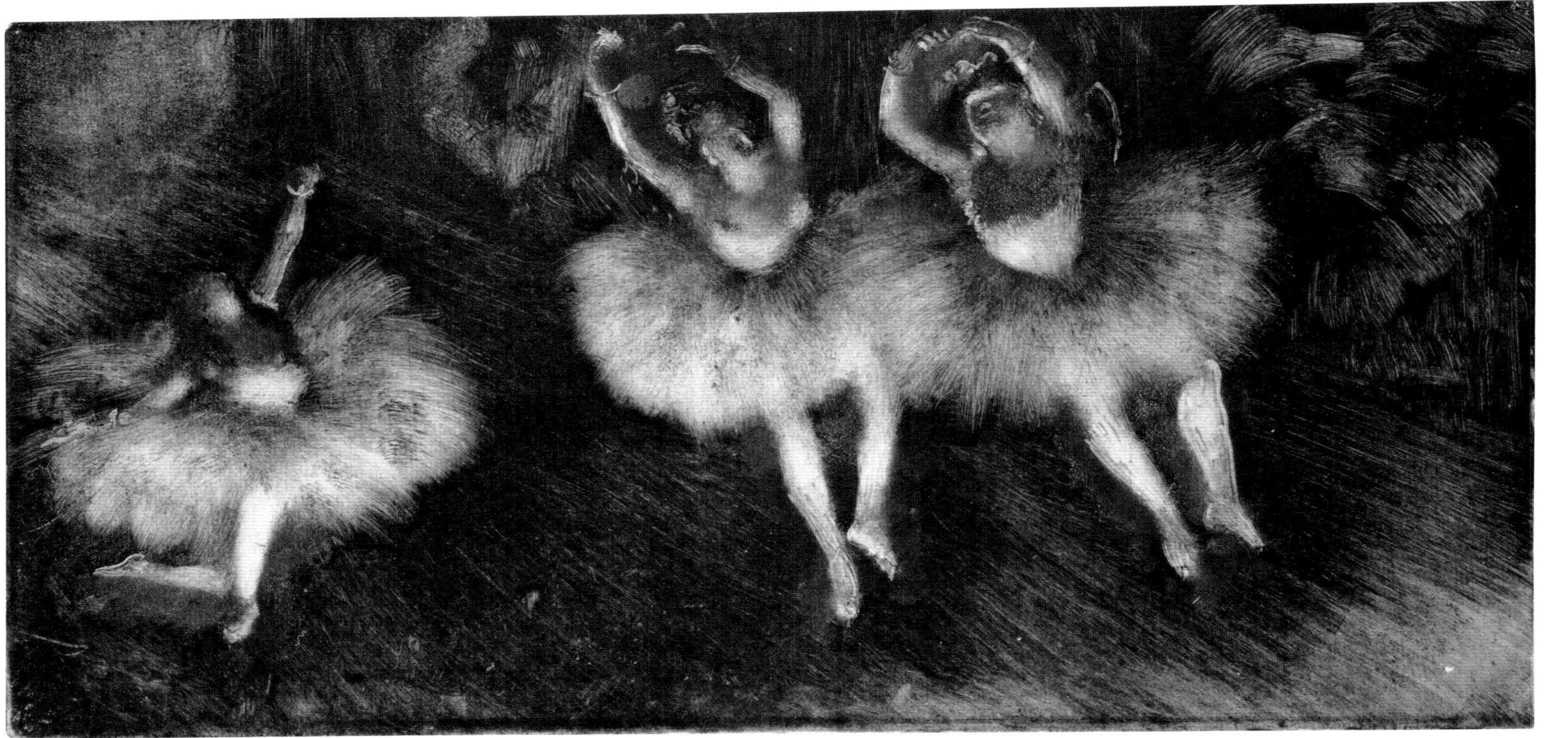

Fig. 24 **Three Ballet Dancers**, *c.* 1878. Monotype, 20 x 41.7 cm. Sterling and Francine Clark Art Institute, Williamstown, Mass., inv. no. CLK 339959

why Degas, having mastered these airborne feats so impressively, did not go further and make large pastels and paintings on the same theme. These were precisely the years when his contemporaries in science and in experimental photography were capturing the human body in rapid movement, a phenomenon explored in a later chapter.

Many small pictures of aerial dancers began life as black-and-white monotypes, a process that Degas had effectively invented in the mid-1870s. Monotype prints were made by applying black, greasy ink to the surface of a polished metal plate, then using brushes or sometimes fingers to add and subtract tone as a composition was created. This monochrome composition was printed by laying a sheet of paper on the inked image and applying pressure. Degas seems to have especially enjoyed the mobility of this medium, which lent itself to spontaneous effects of light and shadow, and a range of marks from the most precise lines to hazy, atmospheric blurs. Several writers have observed that his monotypes have a close affinity with photographs: they tend to be small, black-and-white images, and some were even executed on metal plates with the distinctive bevelled edges and makers' marks of plates that had been used by photographers.[70] This procedure and its wider echoes again add to the cumulative evidence of Degas's encounters with photographs and their producers throughout this decade and into the 1880s. As a printmaker he often worked with Camille Pissarro, telling him in a letter about the method for preparing a metal plate to be used in the aquatint process. This, he explained, involved spreading a liquid 'in the manner of photographers when they pour collodion onto their glass plates'.[71]

The implication, of course, was that both he and Pissarro knew about this procedure, even though neither was a photographer at the time. Four years later, Degas painted a portrait of another colleague in the Impressionist collective, Mary Cassatt, in which she leans forward and holds a group of black-and-white cards as if displaying them. While the significance of this composition has been disputed, the most probable explanation of the scene is that Cassatt was engaged in a well-known pastime of this era, showing cartes de visite to her friends.[72] Again involving a painter-colleague, Degas sent three photographs to Walter Sickert at an unspecified date during these years via their mutual acquaintance Ludovic Halévy, perhaps consisting of prints that had been made when they were all together in Dieppe in 1885.[73] On that well-documented occasion, the group had become acquainted with an English photographer named Walter Barnes, who was paid to record Degas as well as the entire party in elaborately posed tableaux. A subsequent letter to Halévy mentions Barnes and comments critically on the photographs, one of which – a pastiche of the famous *Apotheosis of Homer* by Ingres (Musée du Louvre, Paris) – was probably masterminded by Degas himself.[74] A connoisseur of the ironic, Degas surely relished this juxtaposition of the great neoclassical master of line with the near-banality of a holiday snapshot.

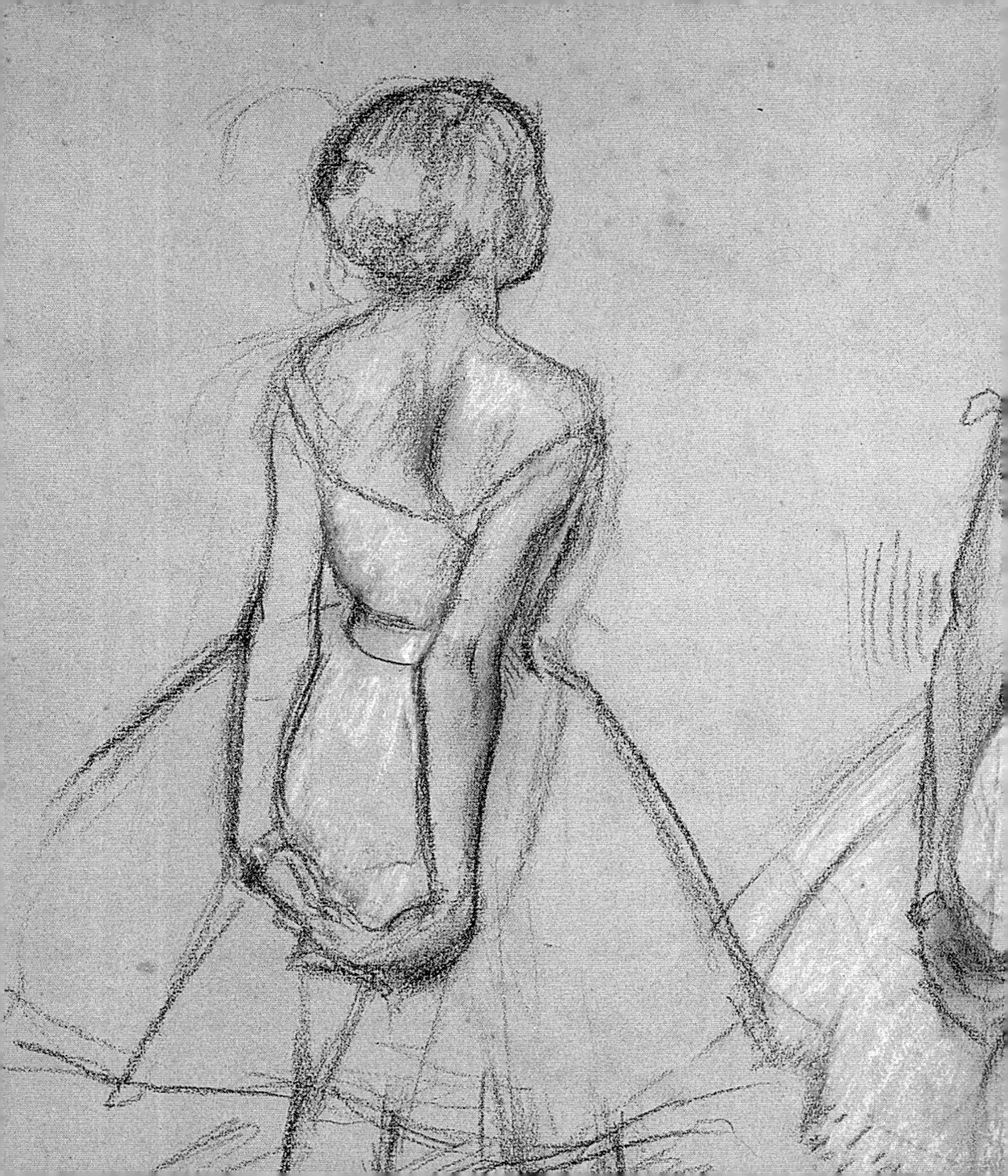

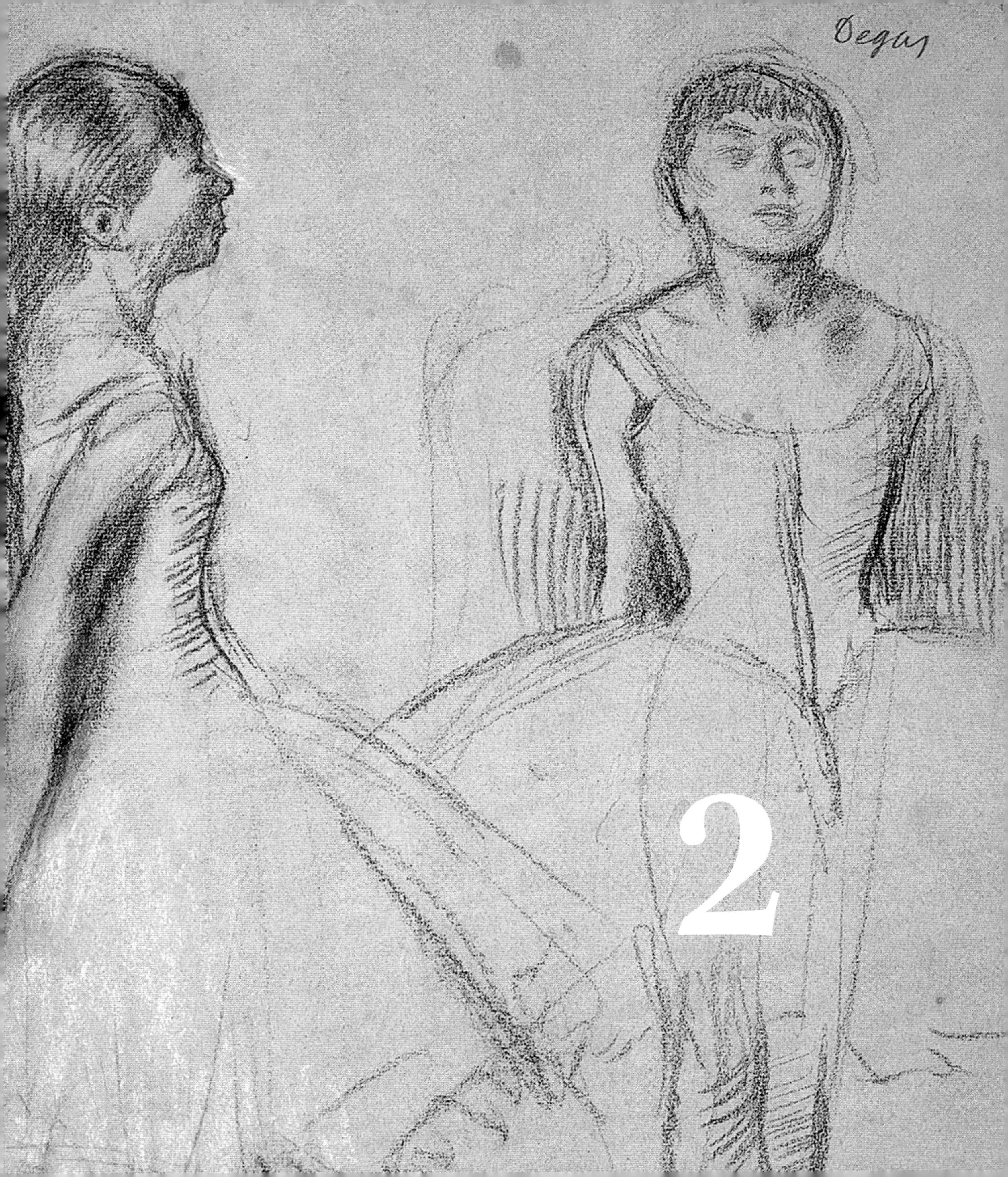

Degas
2

THE MOBILE VIEWER

*... make a suite [of drawings]
of a dancer's arm movements,
or of legs that don't move,
turning around them oneself ...*

Edgar Degas[1]

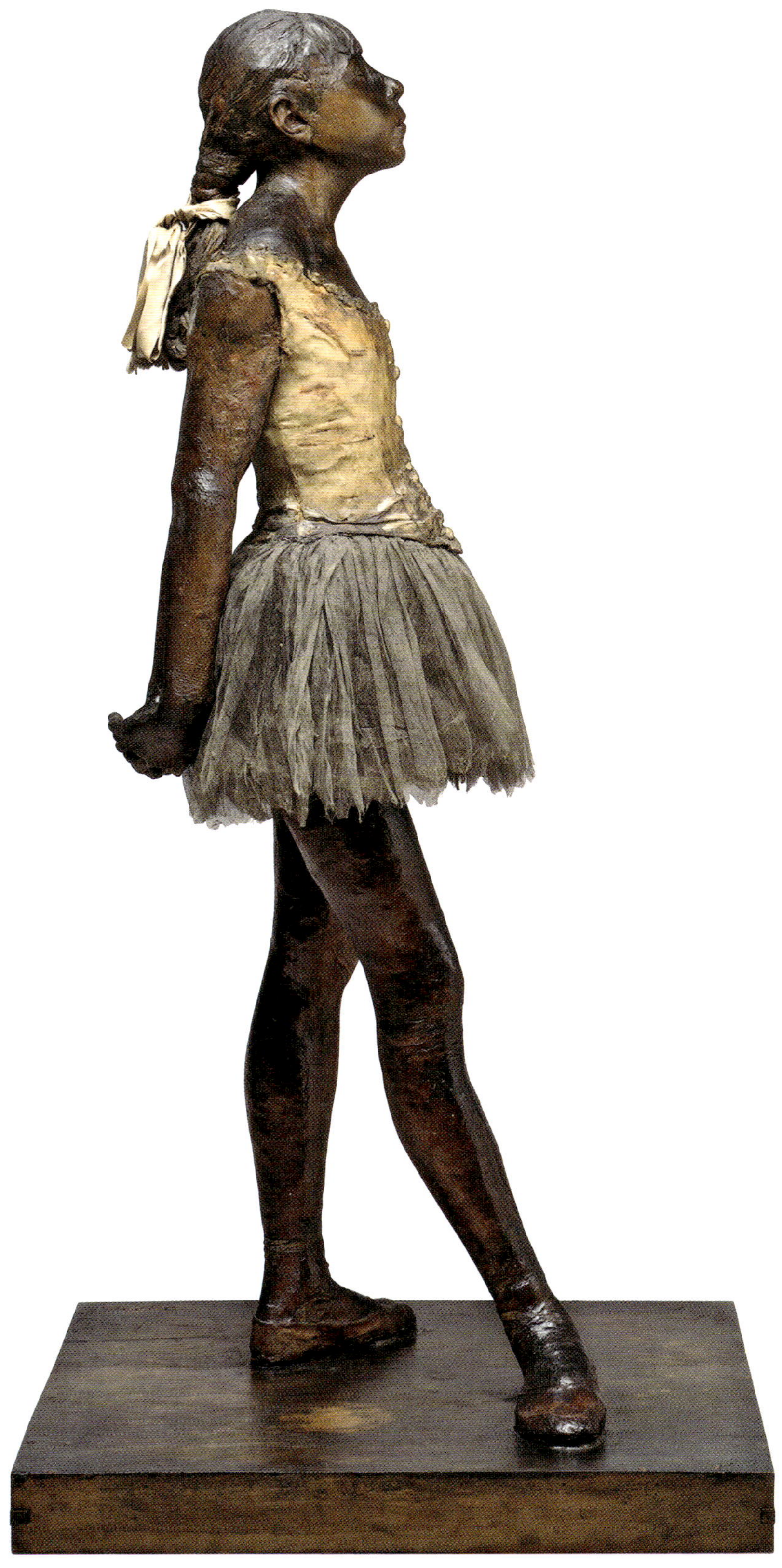

Fig. 25 **Little Dancer Aged Fourteen**, original wax,
1878–81. Yellow wax, hair, ribbon, linen bodice, satin
shoes, muslin tutu, wood base; overall (without base),
98.9 x 34.7 x 35.2 cm. National Gallery, Washington DC,
inv. no. 1999.80.28

When Degas was nearly thirty, his brother René sent news of the artist to their relations in New Orleans: 'Edgar is still working enormously hard, though he does not appear to be,' he wrote in a letter dated 22 April 1864: 'What is fermenting in that head is frightening.'[2] One of the issues 'fermenting' in Degas's head was surely what Baudelaire had recently defined as 'modernity': the shift from an art based on traditional themes to one that took its subjects from contemporary life and expressed the 'ephemeral, the fugitive, the contingent' qualities of the modern age.[3] A decade later, the launch of the first Impressionist exhibition revealed that Degas had risen to Baudelaire's challenge. Now a leading figure in the Parisian avant-garde, Degas was confidently painting his well-to-do peers at racecourses and studying immodestly attired laundresses at their grim labours, while gaining a reputation for his images of morally dubious ballerinas practising backstage. Yet his head was still busy with creative thinking, as revealed in notes he made in a current sketchbook:

> *For a studio project, set up tiers around the room in order to get accustomed to drawing things from below and above ... going up or down ... [draw] an entire figure, a piece of furniture, or an entire room ... Make a series of arm movements of the dance, or of legs that don't move, turning around them oneself, etc. Finally, study from all perspectives, a figure or an object, it doesn't matter which. One could use a mirror for this, so one doesn't have to move oneself.*[4]

In this chapter, two major initiatives that grew out of this moment of fervour will be explored: the drawings made by Degas for his iconic sculpture, the *Little Dancer Aged Fourteen* (fig. 25), and his extraordinary series of frieze-like oil paintings of ballet classrooms (cats 32, 33, 39, 40, 45 and possibly 46). Both of these ventures can be linked to the innovative schemes proposed in his sketchbook, and both entailed new ways of scrutinising and representing subjects such as dancers. For Degas, this also meant revisiting the traditional relationship between artist and model, and that between a spectator and a work of art. As his own directives suggest, he had become intrigued by the possibility of introducing an element of mobility into the artist's encounter with the visible world. In the case of the *Little Dancer* studies, Degas himself became the active observer – literally or notionally – by 'turning around' his model as he studied her or by rotating the young woman while he remained stationary. With the frieze paintings, it is the spectator's gaze that becomes the active constituent in the relationship, as he or she scans the canvas and with it the 'entire room' depicted by Degas. Although these two encounters are inevitably different in kind, they share a common outcome: the process of looking becomes a dynamic event involving the 'ephemeral' and the 'contingent', and perhaps even the 'fugitive', in Baudelaire's words. Informing both sequences of works was the medium of photography, as a precedent to be considered and explored – perhaps even surpassed – and as a spur to further invention.

Initial planning for the *Little Dancer Aged Fourteen* seems to have begun in the late 1870s and followed a pattern that was already characteristic of Degas's art in several respects, not least in its daring.[5] Degas was entirely untrained as a sculptor and still a relative beginner in the craft. His decision to depict a young ballerina at two-thirds life-size was thus bold by any standards. Perhaps for this reason, he decided to make an extensive series of drawings of the chosen model that were different in form and purpose from those he had typically created for his paintings and pastels. Nine such sheets have survived, all of them representing a dance student at the Paris Opéra school, Marie van Goethem, whose bleak background and short career have come to light in recent years.[6] Significant in understanding Degas's project is the evidence that she posed for him on several occasions and was apparently a patient subject. More revealing still was the artist's decision to draw her from multiple angles, clearly intending from the beginning to translate her figure into a sculpture, the largest he had ever attempted. Each sheet shows Marie from between one and five points of view; when all the drawings are considered together, it becomes evident that Degas made a total of twenty-six full or partial figure studies that portray her body from over twenty different points of view.

The ambition and scope of the *Little Dancer* enterprise and the determination with which Degas pursued it leave little doubt that the finished work was intended for public display, and perhaps as an announcement of his shifting ambitions. Modelled in wax and supported by a metal armature, the sculpture was finely detailed throughout and 'dressed' to appear as life-like as possible. As the sculpture neared completion, Degas clothed the girl's form in reduced-scale practice attire – involving a muslin skirt, lace-trimmed bodice and ballet slippers – and added a wig of real hair tied with a satin ribbon. When displayed at the sixth Impressionist exhibition in the spring of 1881, the sculpture prompted a heated and sustained debate between zealous detractors on one side and outspoken supporters on the other. Their responses can be broadly divided into three groups, each concerning a notable aspect of the *Little Dancer*: one focused on its shocking subject, another on the startling realism of the work, and a third on its innovative physical construction. Although depictions of various kinds of dancers dated back to ancient times, a frank representation in sculpted form of a ballerina from modern-day Paris was unprecedented. Also complicating matters was the fact that the individual chosen – thin, uncomely and dressed for the classroom rather than the stage – did not correspond with popular notions of the ballerina. Several critics made their displeasure known: 'Have you ever seen a model so horrible, so repulsive,' protested one reviewer; the girl was 'odiously ugly' and 'simply terrifying' according to others.[7] In the eyes of several she was implicitly immoral, a 'rat from the opera … learning her craft with all of her evil instincts and vicious inclinations', a girl who would inevitably become 'a woman whom diplomats will faun over one day'.[8]

A few visitors to the 1881 exhibition took the opposite view, claiming for example that the youngster's legs, 'conditioned by exercise', were 'admirable', and that she had a 'bright future' ahead of her.[9] Virtually all commentators acknowledged the degree of verisimilitude that Degas had achieved in his sculpture. Described as 'extraordinary' and 'unprecedented … in its excessiveness',

this quality was best evoked by the writer Joris-Karl Huysmans, who pronounced
that the ballerina seemed poised 'to walk off her pedestal'.[10] Many journalists
noted the 'real fabrics' that Degas had used and at least two were reminded
of life-like wax figures found in science museums.[11] For some, the realism of
Degas's sculpture was troublingly 'acute', and others noted parallels with the
'Realist' school of literature represented by Emile Zola.[12] The prominent critic
Paul Manz summarised many of these views when he asserted that the *Little
Dancer* was created by an 'observant artist' applying 'the supreme law of
naturalism', to produce a figure with 'a singular truth to movement in general'.[13]

The originality of Degas's sculpture was not merely rooted in his choice
of model or the unconventional materials used, but also in his fresh approach
to analysing the subject and translating it into three-dimensional form. Most
conspicuous was the artist's decision to draw Marie van Goethem repeatedly
and from multiple angles, a strategy that arguably had roots in practicality yet
is rarely encountered in the history of sculpture. Degas himself had not
employed this strategy in earlier attempts at modelling and was not to return
to it in later years. Indeed, his drawings of Marie far surpass in number any
comparable sheets executed for a single figure in any of his works of art. There
were several immediate reasons why such drawings would have helped him
to proceed. Unlike his earlier and much smaller statuettes of horses, the scale
of the *Little Dancer* required the building of an elaborate armature, which in
turn depended on a clear visualisation of the anticipated sculpture. Knowing
that Marie could only pose for a limited number of sessions, Degas's thorough
and detailed articulation of her body on paper would also have allowed him to
progress with his wax construction in her absence. But by making over twenty
studies of her body from different lateral points of view he went considerably
further, creating – in effect – a comprehensive account of her figure in the
round in a sequence of two-dimensional images.

Twenty-five years before the *Little Dancer* was begun, Degas had
scrutinised another subject from different points of view: a Hellenistic
sculpture in the Louvre, *The Borghese Gladiator* (fig. 26).[14] Drawing the
muscular body three times on a single sheet, he used a different scale for
each study and concentrated largely on the figure's back. While in this case
Degas himself moved around a finished work of art rather than a human
model, the seeds of his *Little Dancer* project may have been sown. The much
more recent sketchbook notes in which he envisaged drawing 'legs that don't
move, turning around them oneself' can be seen as another iteration of this
principle, and one that seems to have taken literal form in a sheet known
as *Five Studies of a Pair of Legs (Studies for the 'Little Dancer Aged Fourteen')*
(cat. 21). This drawing includes five sketches of Marie's lower limbs made from
contrasting viewpoints, all of them entirely consistent with a mobile viewer's
repeated observations of a stationary subject. The leg position in question,
known today as a 'casual fourth', is often adopted by ballerinas at rest and
corresponds precisely to the stance adopted by Marie van Goethem in Degas's
sculpture. Less extreme than the formal fourth position, which requires the
feet to be turned completely outwards and the body weight to be born equally
by both lower limbs, this 'casual fourth' was presumably chosen by Degas
for its innate stability and the ease with which it can be sustained over long
periods. Dedicating his drawing to the intricacies of this position, Degas paid
careful attention to the shape of his model's calf muscles, the long, flat face

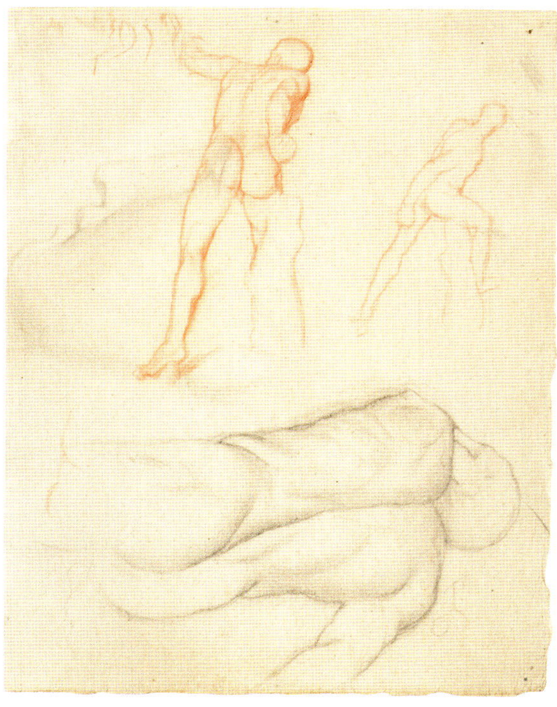

Fig. 26 **Copy after the 'The Borghese Gladiator'**,
c. 1854–56. Black and red chalk on paper, 31 x 24.1 cm.
Sterling and Francine Clark Art Institute, Williamstown,
inv. no. 1971.41

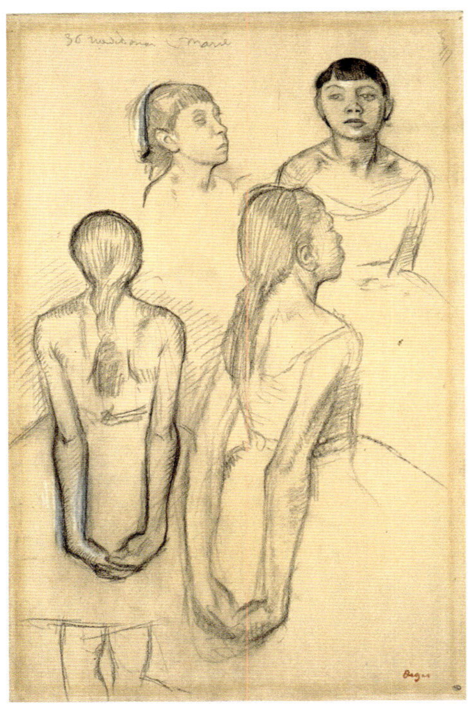

Fig. 27 **Four Studies of a Dancer**, *c.* 1878–81. Chalk and charcoal heightened with grey wash and white on buff paper, 49 x 31.7 cm. Musée d'Orsay, Paris, and Musée du Louvre, Paris, Cabinet des dessins, inv. no. RF 4646

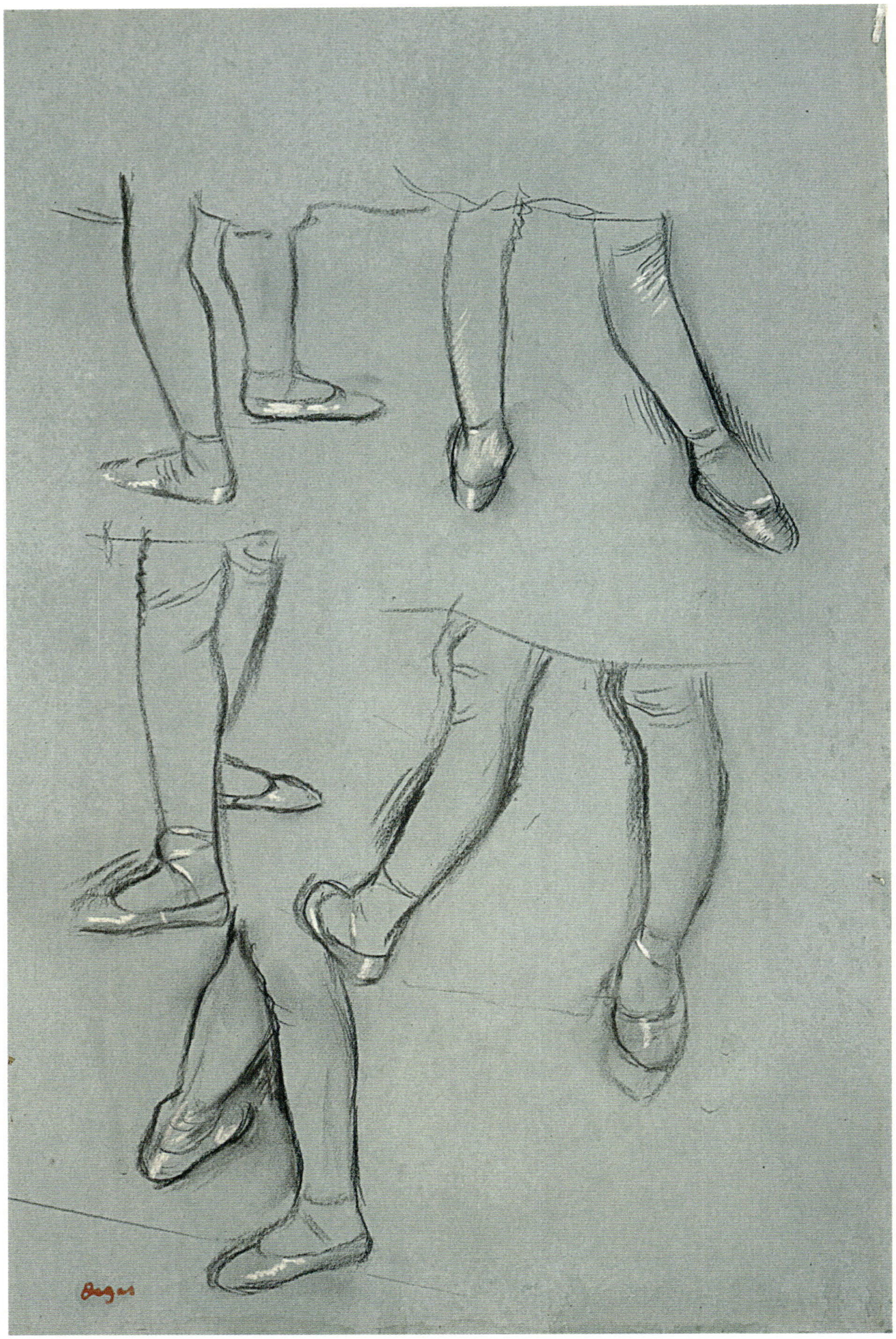

21

Five Studies for a Pair of Legs (Studies for the 'Little Dancer Aged Fourteen')
c. 1878–81
Pencil, charcoal and
pastel on green paper,
48.2 x 30.5 cm
Courtesy of Thomas
Gibson Fine Art Ltd

of her shins and the thinness of her ankles. *Five Studies of a Pair of Legs (Studies for the 'Little Dancer Aged Fourteen')* was a new kind of exercise for the artist, departing from Degas's normal practice of representing his subject from a single, fixed point of view. In this fundamental sense, it represented an inventive approach to the visible world and a challenging scheme for recording his cumulative observations of a three-dimensional form.

Another early application of this same principle was evidently *Four Studies of a Dancer* (fig. 27), on which Degas wrote down Marie's name and address at top left, perhaps suggesting that he had only recently met her.[15] Now in the collection of the Musée d'Orsay, this drawing was used to document her head and shoulders from several different angles, as if the artist had decided to acquaint himself with the somewhat dour personality in front of him. Also prominent in this sheet is Degas's attempt to come to terms with the complex position of her arms, a defining feature of the finished sculpture that Degas appears to have struggled with for some time. After experimenting in two drawn sheets with a pose in which Marie raises one arm to touch the opposite shoulder, he settled for the position we know today.[16] In this stance, his model stands with arms thrust firmly downwards behind her back and hands clasped, performing a once-common exercise intended to stretch the upper body and cultivate the regal carriage demanded of ballerinas.[17] Especially challenging in sculptural terms were the arms themselves, pulled in at the elbows and held slightly away from the body, presumably to allow space for the addition of a fabric tutu.

Both the Musée Orsay drawing (fig. 27) and *Five Studies of a Pair of Legs (Studies for the 'Little Dancer Aged Fourteen')* (cat. 21) raise the question of the specific course of action employed by Degas for drawing his model's physique in the round. One option implied by Degas's sketchbook statement was that Marie remained still while he moved around her. With *Five Studies of a Pair of Legs (Studies for the 'Little Dancer Aged Fourteen')*, this would have involved the artist drawing the first study of 'legs that didn't move' and then 'turning around them oneself' by advancing to a second point on an imaginary circumference around his model and adding another image to the same sheet. After three more moves of this kind with the model remaining stationary, Degas's vantage point would have been close to where he started. A second possibility presupposes that Degas himself remained stationary while Marie shifted her position each time a new drawing in the sequence was begun, though here the challenge of reconstructing her pose precisely on five occasions would have been considerable. A third strategy, which combines elements of the first and second, would have depended on a device frequently used by nineteenth-century sculptors: a floor-based wooden turntable large enough to support blocks of marble and clay or a posing model. A painting by an acquaintance of Degas, Jean-Léon Gérôme, shows just such a rotating platform in the latter's studio (fig. 28); smaller versions of this device were also available from suppliers, and it is known that Degas used one – probably a smaller variant mounted on a tripod – in later life.[18] His own suggestion that a mirror might be helpful in this process is less easy to comprehend: a single mirror placed behind the model would have merely reversed the image and a system of multiple mirrors would hardly have been practical.

Whatever procedure he followed, Degas had clearly embarked on a challenging trajectory that had implications not just for his drawing

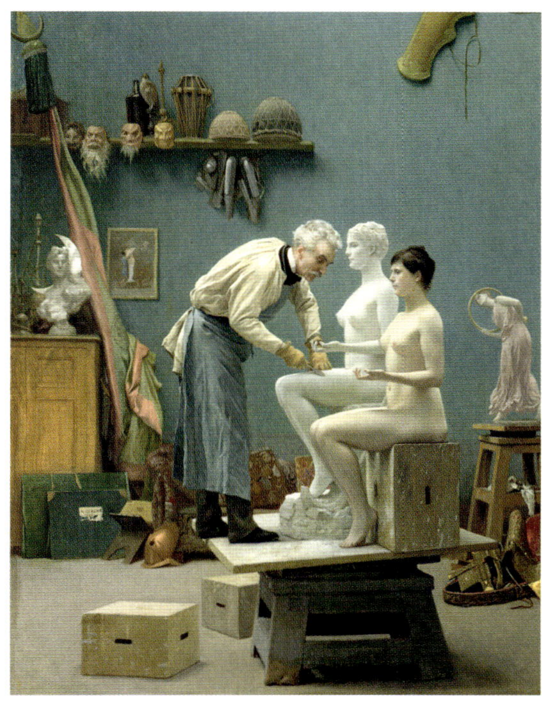

Fig. 28 *Jean-Léon Gérôme*, Working in Marble, or The Artist Sculpting Tanagra, 1890. Oil on canvas, 50.4 x 39.4 cm. The Dahesh Museum, New York, inv. no. 1995.104

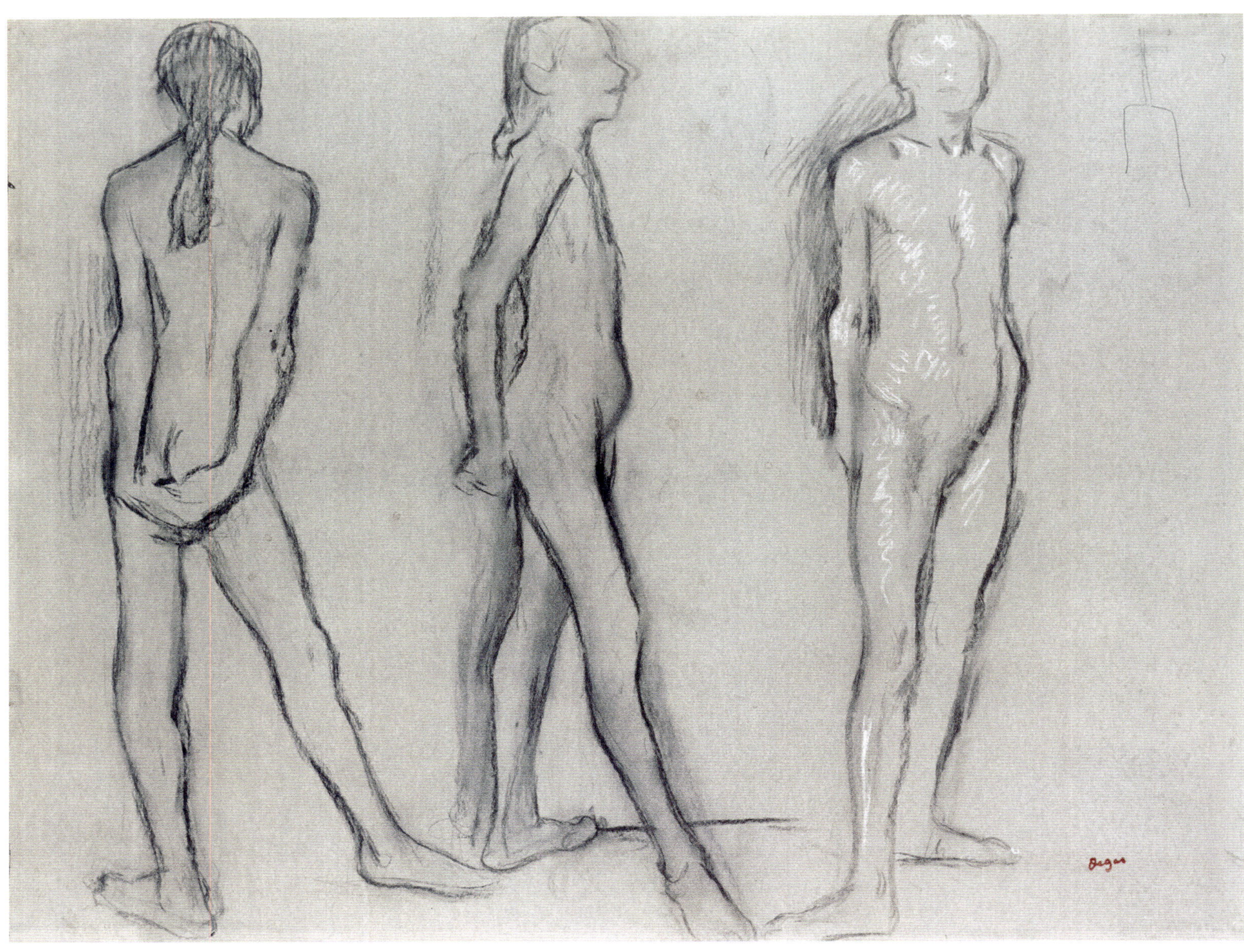

22

**Three Studies
of a Nude Dancer**
c. 1878–79
Charcoal heightened with
white chalk on grey wove paper,
47.7 x 62.3 cm
Private collection

and his projected sculpture, but also for his conceptualisation of the processes
involved. If he indeed relinquished his sedentary role as observer of the model,
he was abandoning a centuries-old relationship that reached back to his
revered masters of the Italian Renaissance. Also implicit in this novel approach
was the sense that his drawings might pass on the visual experience to those
who studied the resulting sheets: the mobile artist would thus invite the
viewer to share his revolution in space. Subsequent sheets seem to offer this
possibility more overtly and with greater confidence, notably two drawings
that show Marie unclothed. One of these, *Three Studies of a Nude Dancer*
(cat. 22) represents a striking sequence that depicts her from front, side
and back. Long and lanky, Marie appears to have possessed many attributes
common to pre-adolescent dancers: a lean yet developed musculature,
flexibility in the lower back and hips, and even a slight stomach bulge. As in
almost all the *Little Dancer* studies, Degas relied primarily on contour – drawn
with charcoal or black chalk – to evoke the shape of his model's body, here
softening some of these marks to reduce their severity and adding touches
of white to strengthen the description of a particular form. Unaccustomed to
drawing naked young women, Degas has nevertheless displayed considerable
sensitivity to the teenager's physique, while relentlessly pursuing his larger

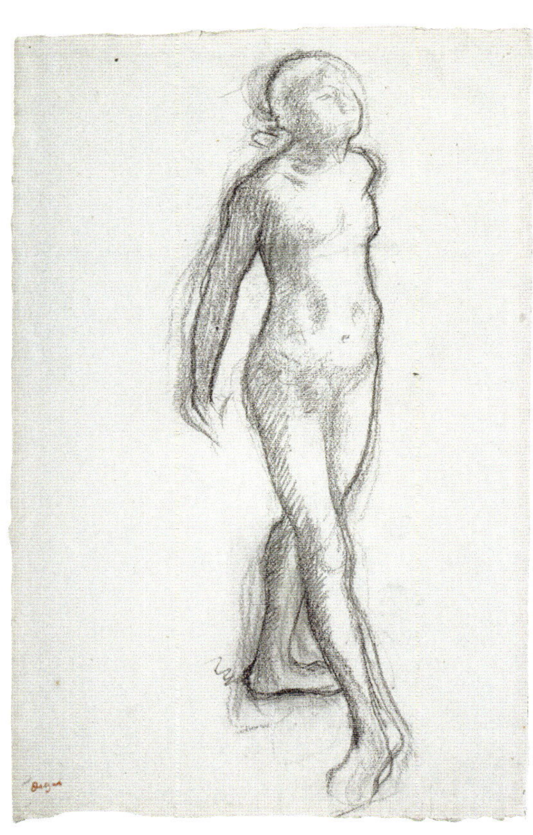

Fig. 29   **Study of a Nude Dancer**, *c.* 1878–81. Black chalk
and red charcoal on mauve-pink laid paper, 48.1 x 30.6 cm.
Nasjonalgalleriet, Oslo, inv. no. NG.K&H.B.15574

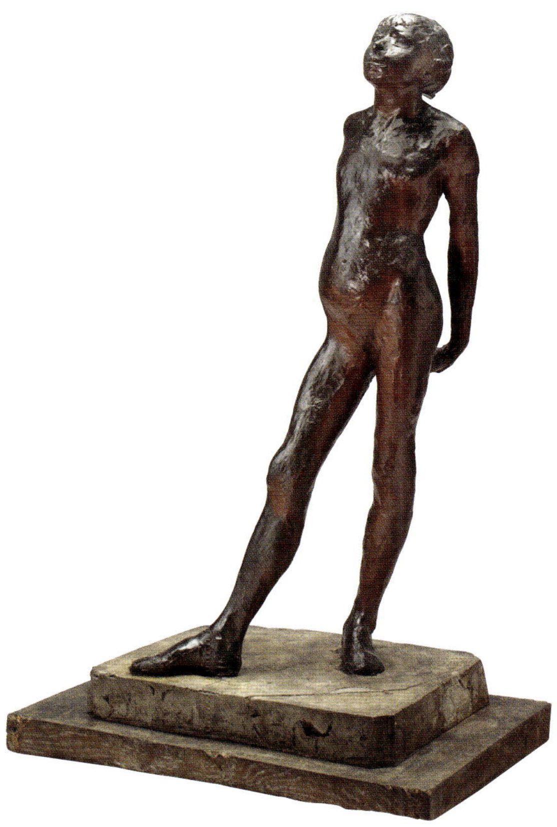

Fig. 30   **Study in the Nude of Little Dancer Aged Fourteen (Nude Little
Dancer)**, *c.* 1878–81. Red wax and plastiline; overall (without base),
69.5 x 29.3 x 30.3 cm. National Gallery, Washington DC, inv. no. 1985.64.46

23

**Three Studies of a Dancer
in Fourth Position**
c. 1878–81
Charcoal and pastel with
stumping and touches of brush
and black wash on greyish-tan
laid paper with blue fibres, laid
down on grey wove paper,
48 x 61.5 cm
The Art Institute of Chicago.
Bequest of Adele R. Levy

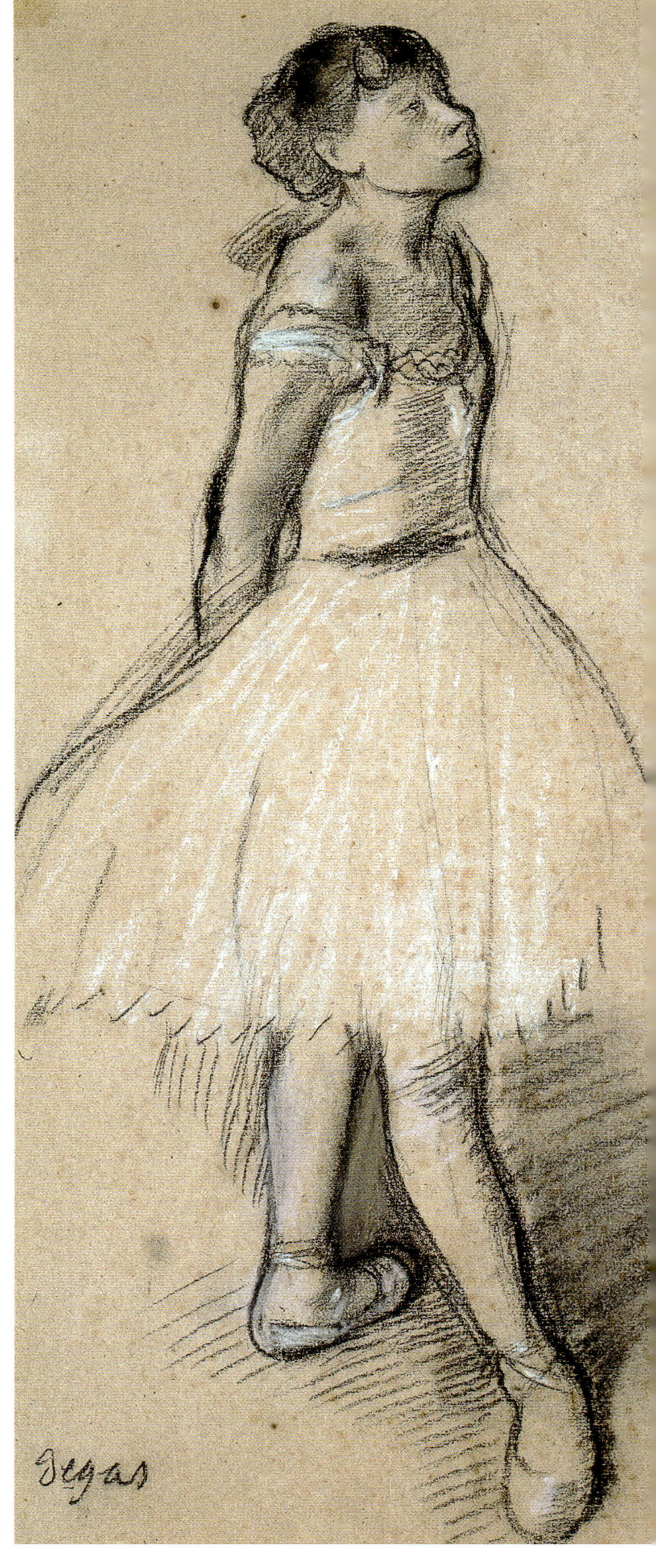

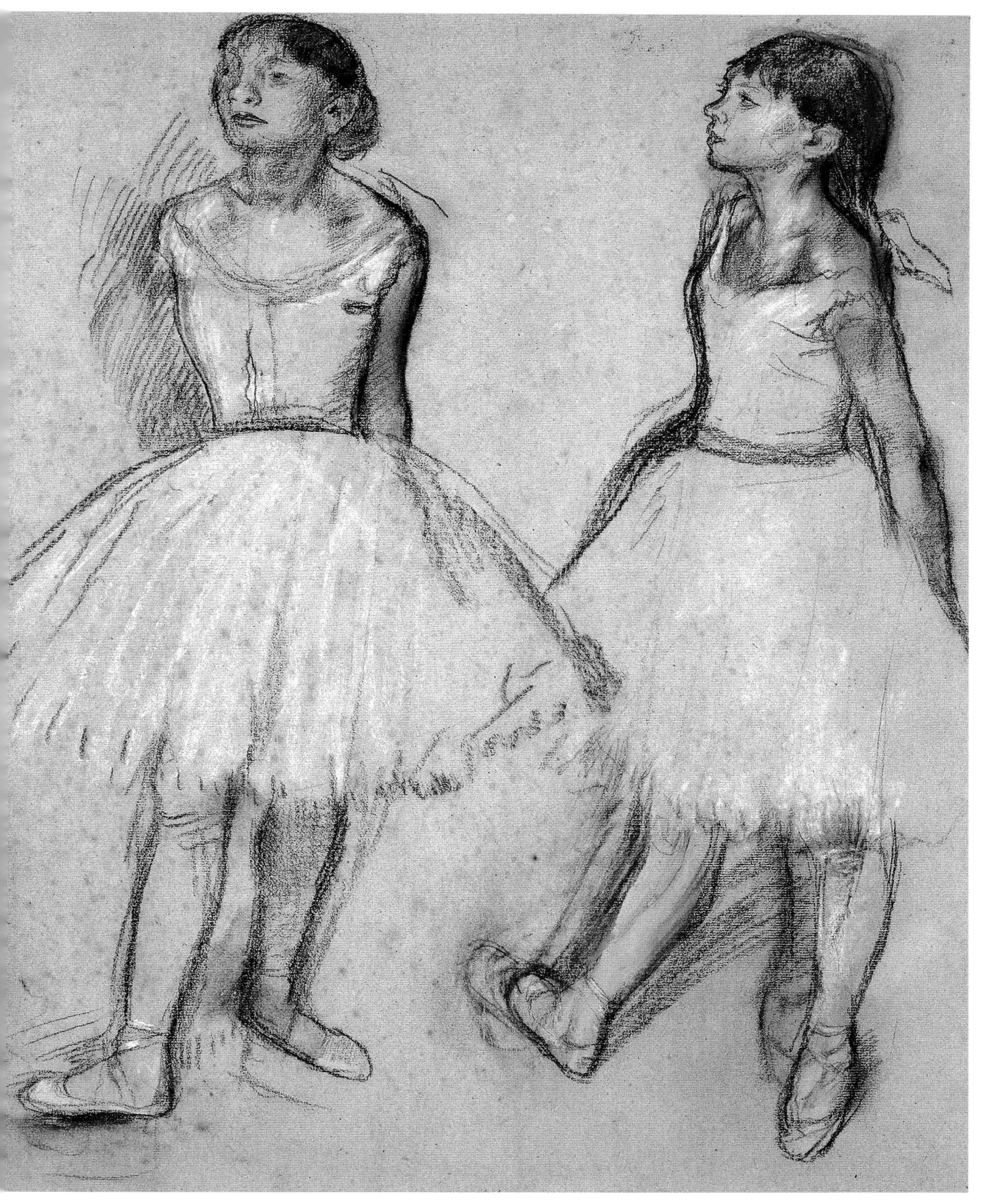

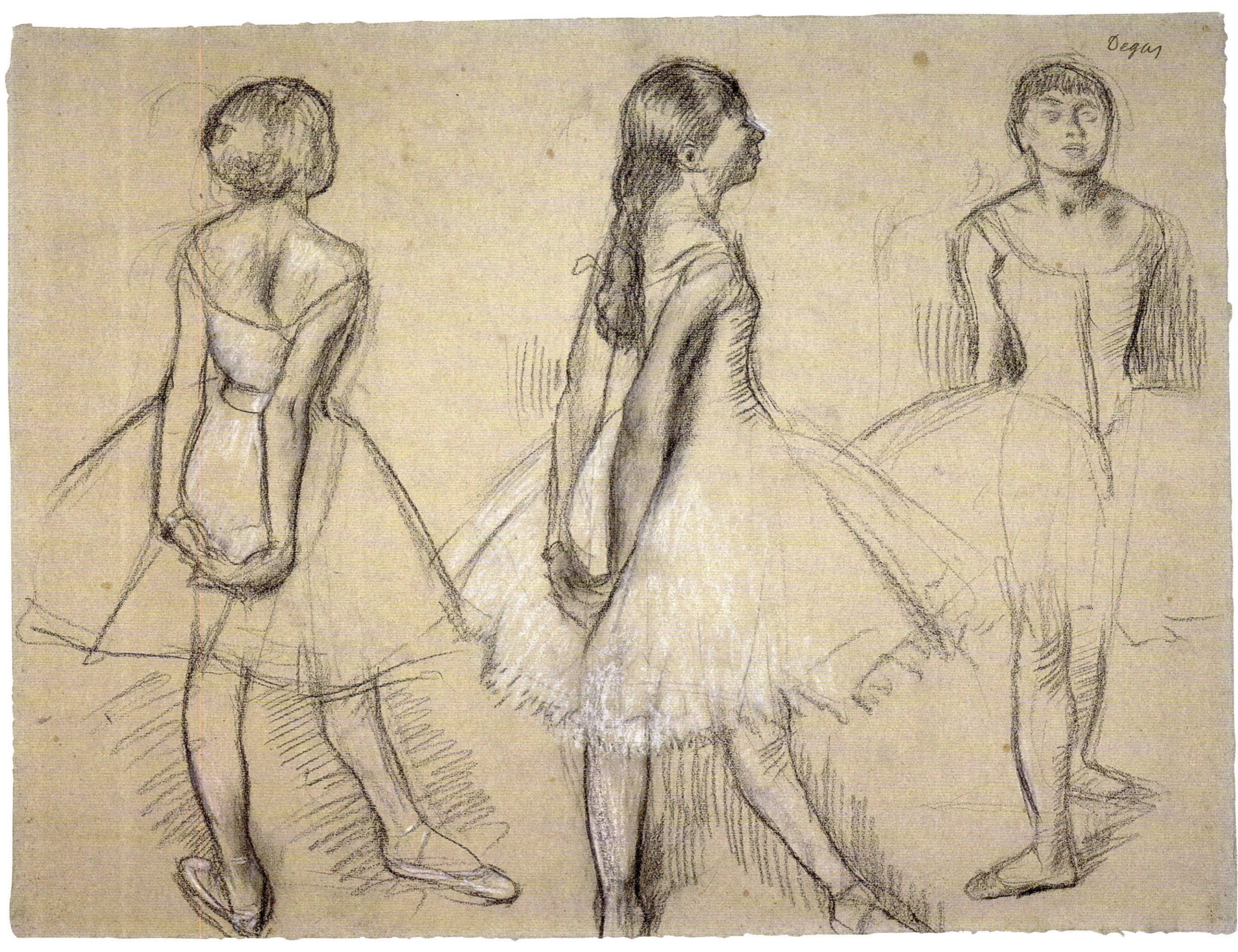

24

Three Studies of a Dancer
c. 1878–81
Black chalk heightened
with white on pink paper,
47 x 62.3 cm
The Pierpont Morgan Library,
New York. Gift of a foundation
in honour of Eugene and Clare
Thaw (2001.12)

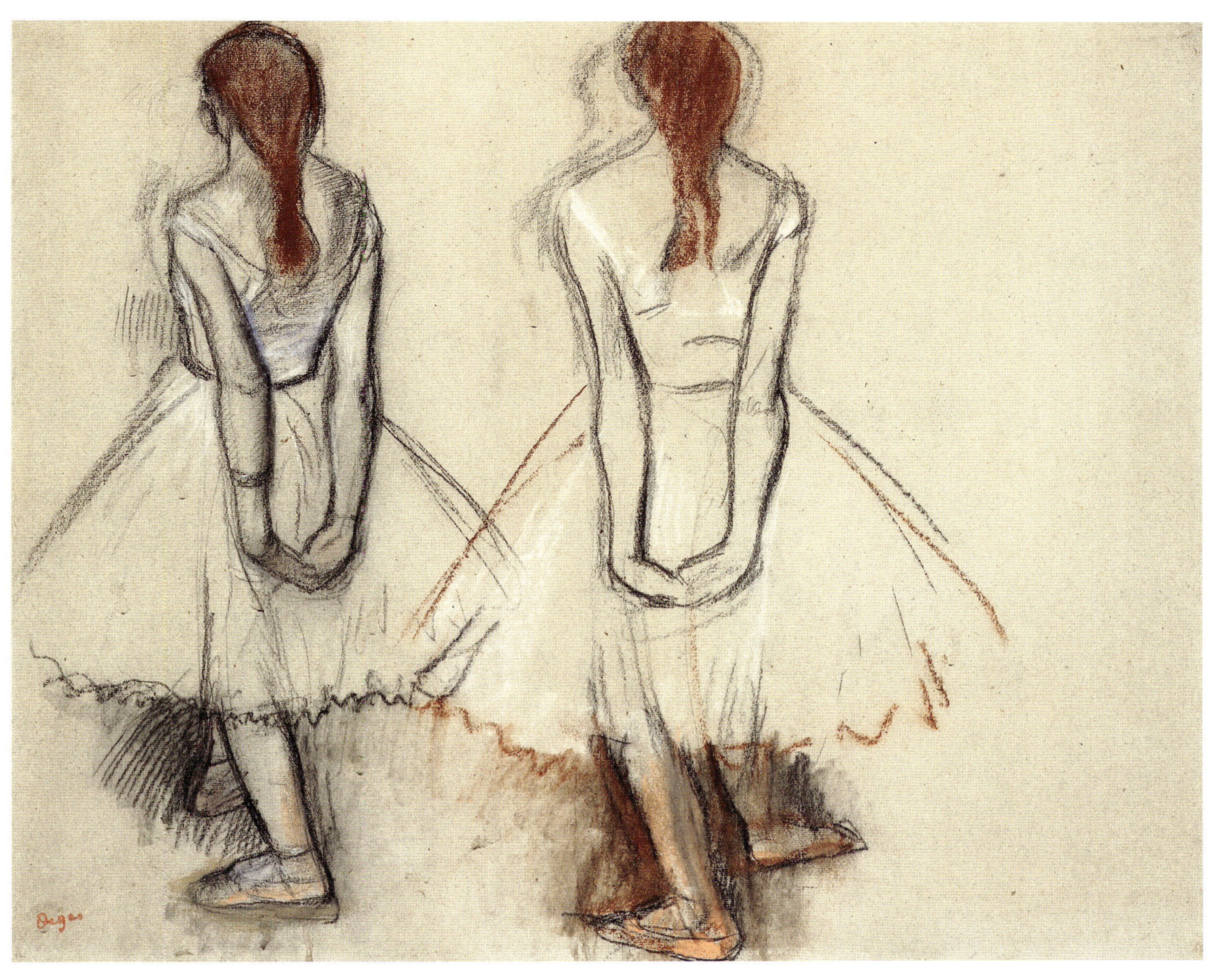

25

Two Studies of a Dancer
1878–79
Charcoal, pastel and wash
on paper,
47.2 x 58.5 cm
Private collection

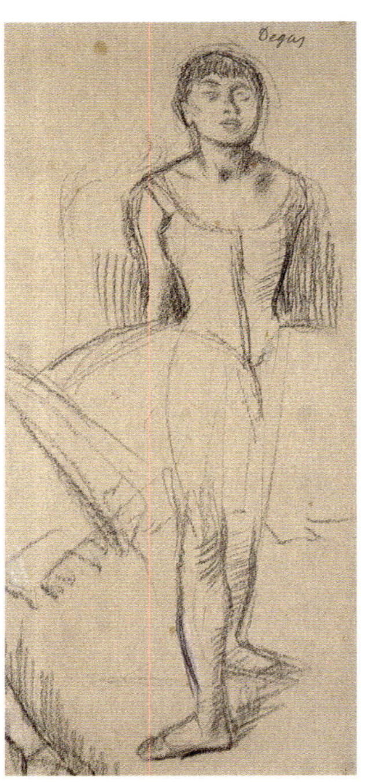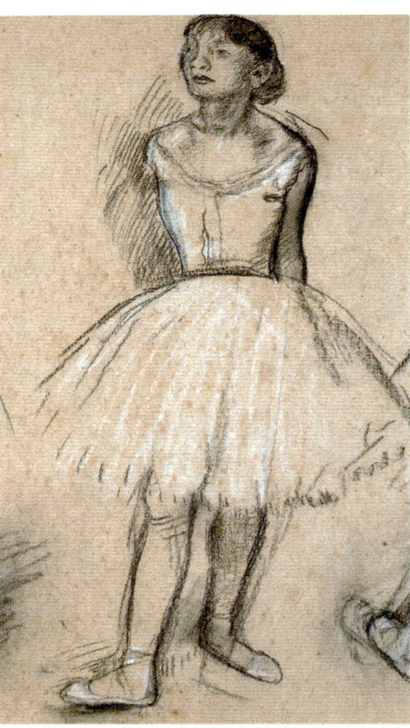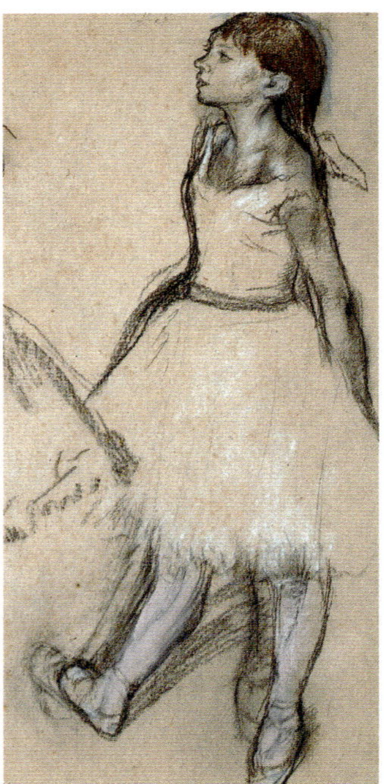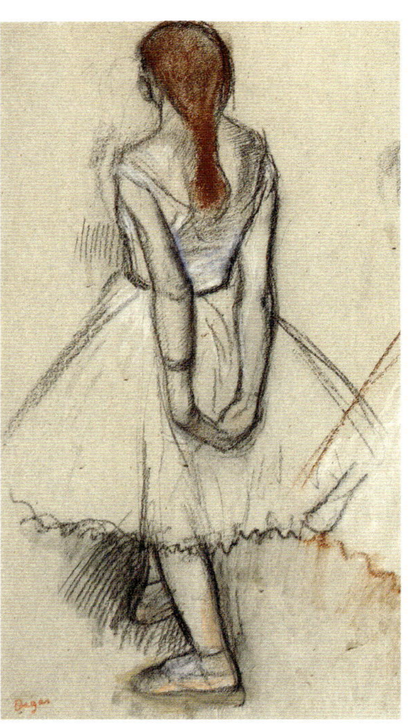

Fig. 31 **Composite image of eight figure studies for the Little Dancer Aged Fourteen**: from left to right N, Q, T, X, Z, D, F and I as indicated in the diagram overleaf (cat. 32)

concerns. This trio of similarly scaled images represents the model as if she has made two sequential turns to the right of approximately ninety degrees each. In this distinctive respect, *Three Studies of a Nude Dancer* is the only drawing in the group in which equidistant rotations succeed each other in a logical progression across the sheet. This sequence is augmented by another depiction of Marie undressed, now presented in three-quarter view (fig. 29) and situated approximately between the central and right-hand figures in *Three Studies of a Nude Dancer*. As with his drawings for the clothed model, when brought together these sheets would have been invaluable to Degas as he began to make a sculpted study of Marie in the nude (fig. 30). Much smaller than the *Little Dancer* itself, this maquette was nevertheless based on the same preliminary procedure: information gathered from Degas's three-dimensional survey of the model that had first been committed to paper now found itself embodied in a space-occupying form.

The most consistent account of Degas's perceptual and spatial attitude to the *Little Dancer Aged Fourteen* is found in a trio of drawings that show Marie van Goethem fully clothed, all of them rendered on virtually the same scale (cats 23–25).[19] Much discussed in the Degas literature in terms of their cultural significance, these images and their originality deserve further consideration as records of the artist's creativity.[20] The most developed among them is the arresting *Three Studies of a Dancer in Fourth Position* from the Art Institute of Chicago (cat. 23). Here a profile view faces left and its mirror image faces right, framing the central figure who gazes almost directly at us. As in the majority of drawings for the *Little Dancer*, the dominant forms of the model are defined by repeated contours, while restrained shading and occasional highlights enhance the articulation of her body. A curious detail here is that

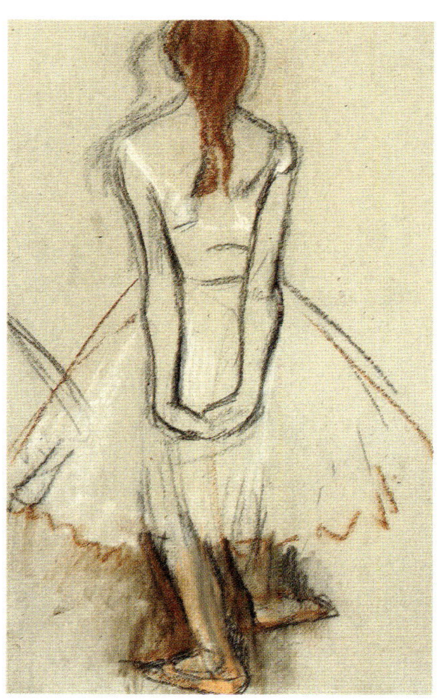 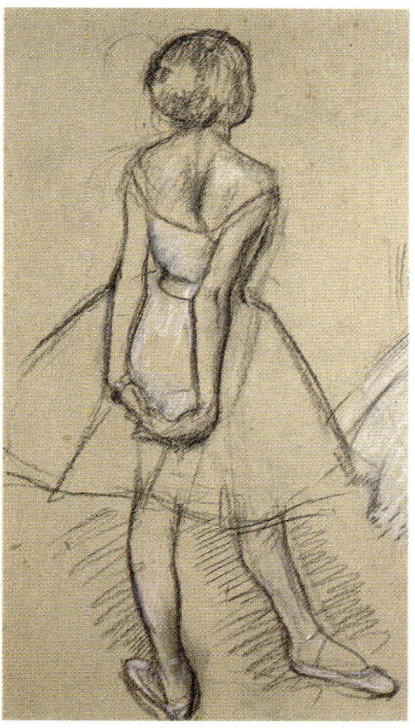 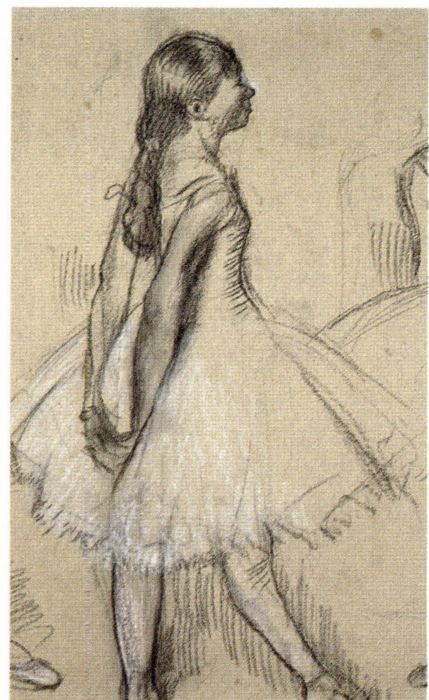 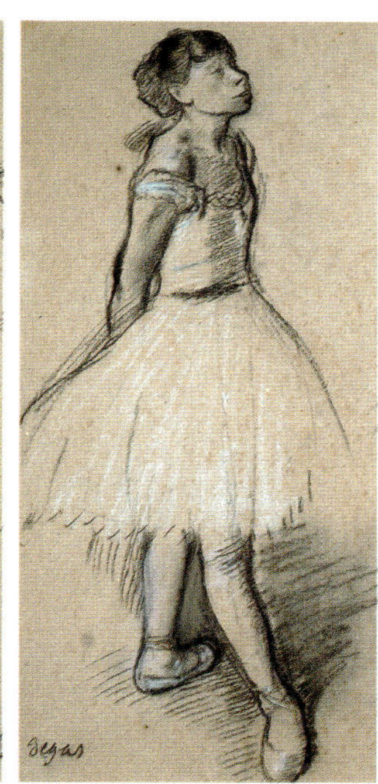

Marie's hair hangs down her back in the right-hand study but is held up
in a bun in the two others, possibly indicating that the sheet took more than
one studio visit for completion. This change in coiffure is also found in the
similarly titled and equally resonant *Three Studies of a Dancer* from the
collection of the Morgan Library (cat. 24). Here Degas resumed the inspection
of his subject in the round by supplementing the information recorded in the
Chicago sheet: the Morgan drawing fills 'gaps' in the first sequence and
effectively doubles the thoroughness of the artist's three-dimensional account
of Marie's stance. More is ascertained about the anatomical structure of her
back, for example, as well as the curiously taut position of her arms as they
press into the tutu and cause it to engulf her hands. Such details emphasise
Degas's close interrogation of his subject and his determination to create a
factual account in two dimensions of this young woman's figure and clothing.
The cycle continues with a third drawing that focuses exclusively on the
model's back (cat. 25). Studying two views of Marie that had not previously
been addressed, Degas returned to the challenge of her arms and drew them
from points of view that are only a few degrees apart. Signs of revision in this
vibrant sheet point to his enthusiastic and persistent engagement with the
challenge at hand. Notable is the summary indication of the girl's tutu, which
contrasts with the intense scrutiny of her legs and arms, and evidence of ever
more vigorous reworking elsewhere. Unique in this drawing is the suggestion
that water was used towards the lower edge to erase some of Degas's earlier
marks in order to clarify the lower limbs.

The collective significance of this suite of drawings for the *Little Dancer*
becomes dramatically evident when they are considered not as separate
sheets but as a continuous statement about a single entity. More precisely,
if each individual depiction of the clothed figure is extracted from its setting
and rearranged in a sequential progression, an almost continuous account
of Marie's figure results (fig. 31). Apparently proceeding towards this goal

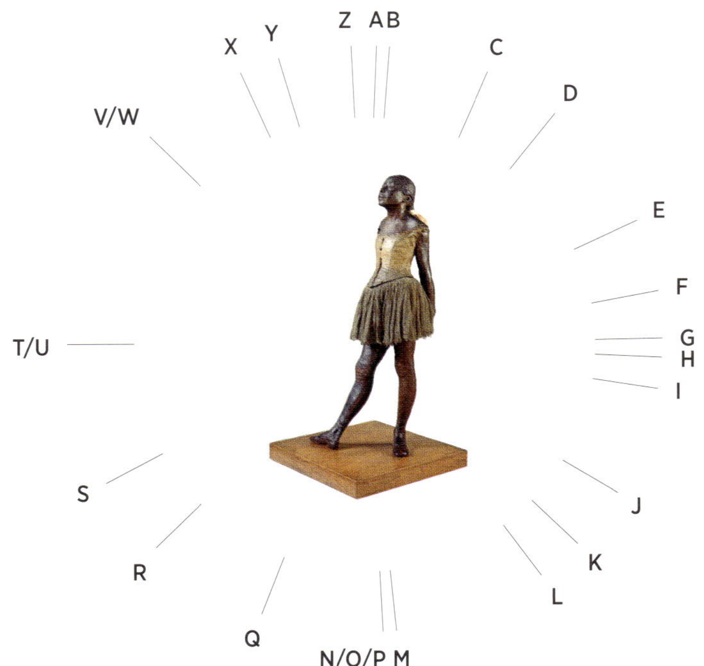

in a haphazard fashion, Degas nevertheless accumulated studies of his subject that broadly correspond to the primary points of a compass. The other drawings, such as those focusing on the model's legs or depicting her nude, provide additional views that enhance the 360-degree survey, leaving almost no principal angle unaccounted for (see fig. 32). Nothing in Degas's previous career prepares us for such comprehensiveness, which seems to point to an unusually clear, rational encapsulation of his sculpture in advance of its fabrication. Beyond the convenience of such a suite of drawings, the artist arrived at a sophisticated procedure for unifying many hours of patient scrutiny in a simple visual form. Comparable, perhaps, to the three-dimensional scanning process or laser analysis of our own day, Degas's creation of this apparently unprecedented set of drawings was a historic achievement in its own right, while distantly echoing certain developments in photography in the previous decade.

A further twist to the story of the making of the *Little Dancer Aged Fourteen* concerns the subsequent fate of Degas's wax sculpture. Remembered with great respect by some of those who saw it in 1881, the work was never again exhibited in the artist's lifetime or reproduced in any form. After his death, it soon attracted widespread attention when photographs were published and the wax was cast into bronze. Now 're-dressed' in modern tutus and adorned with fresh ribbons, these bronzes appeared over the years in at least thirty casts that continue to prompt controversy. The bronze in the Tate collection (cat. 26) is one of this extended family, exemplifying the process of replication that has made Degas's sculptures so well known and popular throughout the world. The original wax, meanwhile, is preserved in the National Gallery of Art in Washington, a unique object that has become much more familiar through the numerous bronze replicas. The attention to these bronzes, which are admired by millions from every conceivable angle, distantly echoes the obscure context in which Degas's *Little Dancer Aged Fourteen* was originally created.

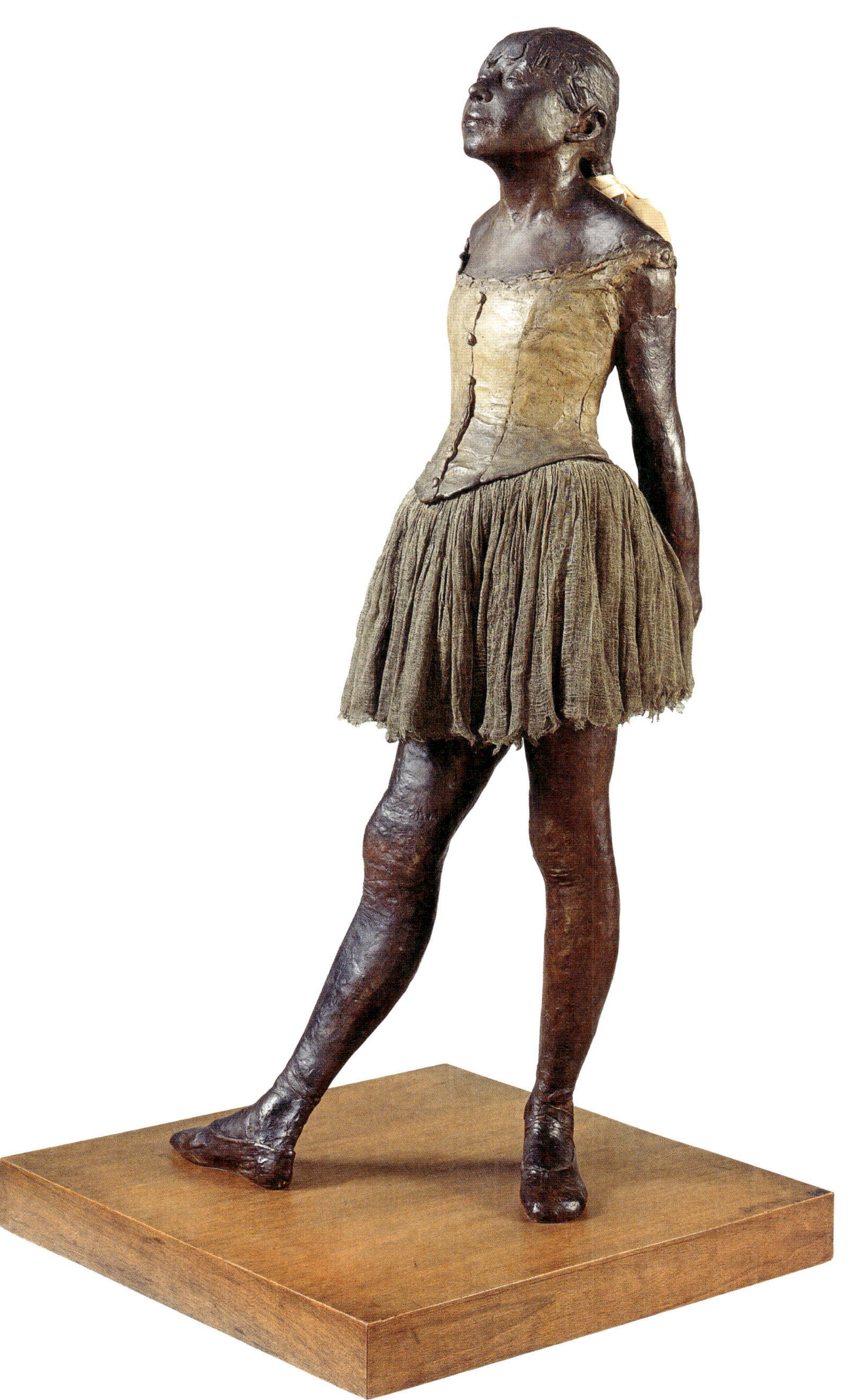

26

Little Dancer Aged Fourteen
1880–81, cast *c.* 1922
Painted bronze with
muslin and silk,
98.4 x 41.9 x 36.5 cm
Tate. Purchased with assistance
from The Art Fund, 1952

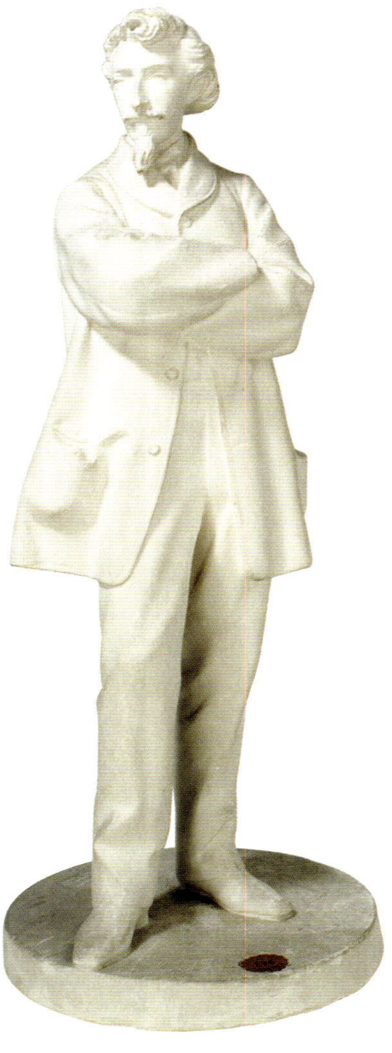

Fig. 33 *François Willème*, **Full-length self-portrait statuette**, *c.* 1865. Plaster statuette, height 37.5 cm, diameter 14.4 cm. George Eastman House, Rochester, New York

SCULPTURE, PHOTOGRAPHY AND SERIAL IMAGERY

Two decades before the *Little Dancer Aged Fourteen* appeared at the 1881 Impressionist exhibition, a strategy for representing a figure in the round that was strikingly similar to Degas's had been introduced by a now largely forgotten artist, François Willème. In Paris in the early 1860s, Willème created a sensation with a process known as photosculpture, which – according to one scientific commentator of the day – offered three-dimensional portraits of 'stunning exactitude'.[21] Other contemporaries spoke of the 'unprecedented fidelity of his work', while the writer Théophile Gautier claimed of one photosculpture that its resemblance 'in physiognomy and demeanour' to the sitter in question had 'struck him forcefully'.[22] Fundamental to Willème's technique was a novel application of the camera, by which a human subject was simultaneously photographed from twenty-four different angles. Once the photographs were processed, the information they provided was ingeniously transferred to a block of clay in a quasi-mechanical fashion that did not require the traditional expertise of a sculptor. Seen as an exemplary 'marriage' between art and engineering, photosculpture was regarded by its proponents as a unique expression of modernity: 'one of the most astonishing industries to which our époque has given birth', in the words of an enthusiastic journalist.[23]

As Willème prepared to launch his system in 1863, public interest was aroused by the conspicuously grand studio he erected on the Avenue de Wagram, in a fashionable area of central Paris. Surmounted by a glass cupola, the studio soon attracted large numbers of customers anxious to order depictions of themselves and their loved ones. On entering the building, Willème's clients passed through a long gallery where examples of his work were displayed, then ascended a staircase to the spacious, elegant rotunda above (fig. 34). The high walls below the cupola were divided into twenty-four vertical panels, each fitted with a console bearing a photosculpture. Beneath the photosculptures were barely detectable apertures in the wall, corresponding to a series of cameras that were directed at a platform in the centre of the room.[24] A portrait session began with the client adopting a seated or standing position on this platform directly below a plumb line hanging from the cupola. At the chosen moment, a cord connecting the mechanisms of all the cameras was pulled, activating them simultaneously and resulting in two dozen photographs taken from equidistant angles. All that was asked of the patron was this brief pose; remarkably, their completed photosculpture – usually made of plaster or fired clay – is said to have been delivered within a few days, while marble and bronzes versions inevitably took longer.[25]

Brilliant in its simplicity and challenging in its response to one of the most traditional arts, Willème's process in reality relied on a degree of manual intervention. Once the set of twenty-four photographs had been processed, the task of making the sculpture took place in a darkened chamber in the same building. This was equipped with a projector facing a screen of frosted glass, behind which was a table where a technician worked (fig. 35). Here a small rotating stand fitted with twenty-four equidistant stops supported the block of clay that represented the next stage in the procedure. By employing a pantograph – a simple device normally used by draughtsman to make enlarged or reduced copies of images on paper – the technician transferred the profile in the first photograph to his clay block by following its contours

on the screen (cat. 30).[26] When this step was completed, the stand bearing the
clay was moved to the next stop and the second photograph was inserted into
the projector. At a slight remove from the first contour, this second silhouette
was then transferred to the clay block. When these actions had been repeated
twenty-four times, the resulting sculpture was essentially an accumulation
of profiles that had now been realised in the round. Rough edges between the
carved lines then had to be smoothed and details more carefully articulated,
reportedly by a professional sculptor or by Willème himself.

Regrettably, very few of the photographs that Willème used to make the
sculptures in question have survived. An exception is a series of twenty-four
pictures showing a child seated on a bench, *Study for a Photosculpture, Sitting
Youth*, which is now in the collection of the George Eastman House, Rochester,
New York (cat. 27). Apparently taken in the Avenue de Wagram studio, these
prints illustrate the way that Willème's subjects were first documented in two
dimensions from a succession of angles before being translated into a three-
dimensional sculpture. More than thirty years ago, Janet Buerger briefly
mentioned a possible link between Willème's method and Degas's occasional
habit of making drawings from a single figure when preparing to create his
own sculptures.[27] Like Willème's, Degas's approach to the *Little Dancer* was
based on a series of two-dimensional images, in his case representing Marie
van Goethem. When subsidiary sheets are taken into account, Degas's twenty
or so surviving figure studies come close to Willème's set of twenty-four. From
their respective sequences both men proceeded to create a fully rounded form,
Willème through a semi-mechanised system and Degas by hand and eye alone.

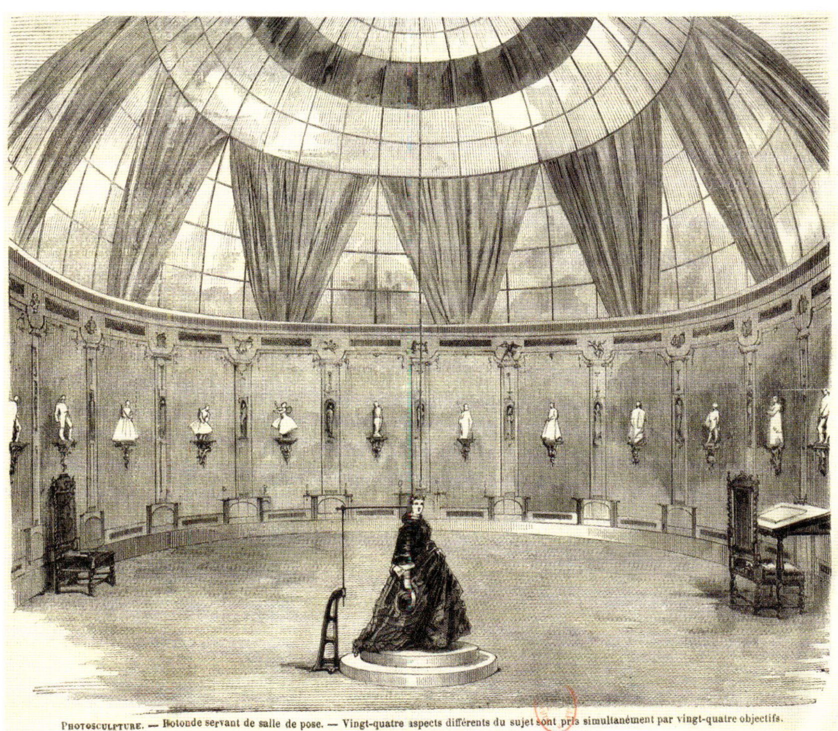

Fig. 34 *E. Morin (?)*, The rotunda of François Willème's studio, Le Monde illustré,
8, 31 December 1864, p. 428. Bibliothèque nationale de France, Paris

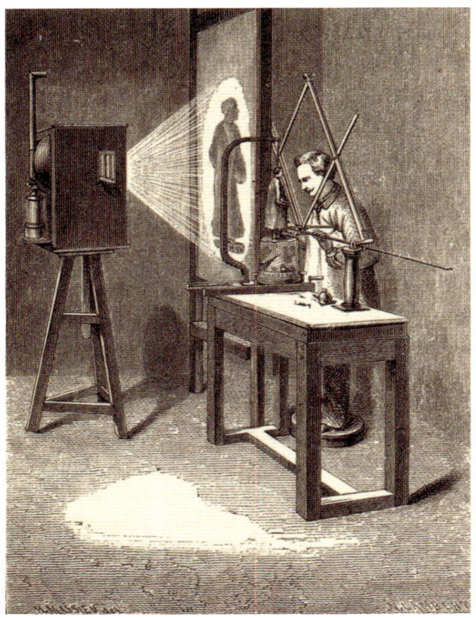

Fig. 35 **The darkened sculpting chamber in which François Willème's photosculptures were crafted.** Illustration by N. Lambert and H. Massieu, in Théophile Gautier, 'Photosculpture', extract from Moniteur universel, 4 January 1864, p. 7. Bibliothèque nationale de France, Paris

It seems highly likely that Degas, working on his *Little Dancer* some fifteen years later, knew of Willème's curious enterprise and may even have applied some of the latter's principles as he began the sculpture of the young ballerina. In addition Degas may have been aware that Willème himself had made sculptures of ballet dancers, some of which were exhibited in the grand entrance foyer of his premises (cat. 28). Willème was a vigorous and effective self-publicist, initially promoting his invention to the scientific community and encouraging subsequent articles in the popular press.[28] Between 1864 and 1866, for example, the widely read *Le Monde illustré* featured articles on photosculpture on several occasions, one of them (cat. 28) based on an illustrated essay by Théophile Gautier that was also printed as a brochure.[29] Even more conspicuous was the pavilion dedicated to Willème's photosculpture at the Exposition Universelle in 1867, an event that Degas is known to have attended.[30] A future editor-in-chief of the scientific journal *La Nature*, Henri de Parville, also addressed the subject of Willème's initiative in favourable terms, while the journal's founder, Gaston Tissandier, mentioned in 1874 that Willème's sculptures had been 'on view for a long time' at *La Maison Giroux*, the studio of a prominent photographer in the city.[31] Degas was active in Paris throughout this period, mixing with the fashionable and the obscure alike, appropriating images from illustrators and from photographers, and experimenting in his own studio with other novel techniques, materials and imaginative attitudes to the making of art. It was also in the 1860s that Degas seems to have taken his own first steps as a sculptor, creating at least two modest figures of horses that have been previously linked to such contemporary paintings as *Semiramis Building Babylon* and *Mlle Fiocre in the Ballet 'The Source'* (fig. 5).[32] Robert Soubieszek has argued that Rodin, too, became aware of Willème's procedure and applied it to some early works, making drawings of his subjects from multiple perspectives.[33]

Several surviving sculptures offer further insight into Willème's process and his significance for Degas's generation. *Bust of a Young Boy* (cat. 29) appears to be characteristic of the many thousands of portraits that resulted from the photosculpture process: modest in scale, unpretentious in appearance and largely uncomplicated in its factual presentation of the sitter's features and demeanour. Plausible as the representation of an individual, this bust nevertheless suggests a modest degree of idealisation. The boy's clothes seem almost too perfect in their arrangement and his solemnity speaks of incipient adulthood rather than youthful high spirits. All these characteristics are, however, entirely consistent with current modes in portrait photography and make it easy to understand why a three-dimensional extension of this practice in the form of photosculpture should have seemed so attractive to Willème's contemporaries. A second remarkable survivor is a finished portrait of Willème himself (fig. 33), which – like *Bust of a Young Boy* – was cast in plaster after the clay original made from its own photographic sequence. Here the sculptor-inventor presents himself as confident and relaxed, his casual jacket falling loosely about him with one pocket bulging. These features point to an important characteristic of Willème's approach to portraying his Parisian contemporaries. In principle, any clients willing to pay were free to choose their own postures and the outfits they wore in front of his cameras. While the process inevitably attracted the more affluent, some of Willème's sculptures disconcerted his critics by their frank contemporaneity; one argued that the

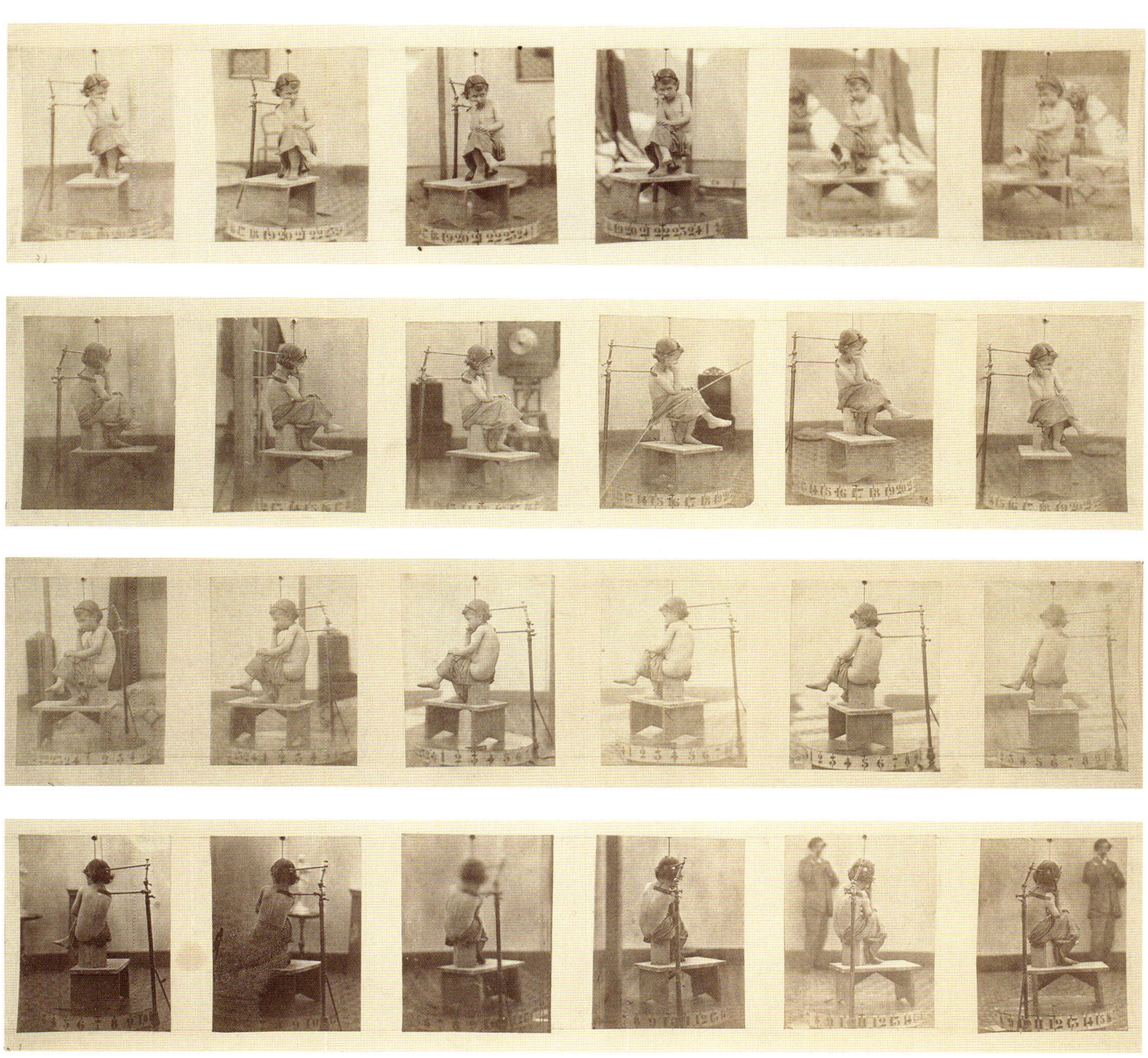

27

François Willème
**Study for a Photosculpture,
Sitting Youth**
c. 1865
Albumen print,
each 4.5 x 3.5 cm
Collection of George Eastman
House, Rochester, New York

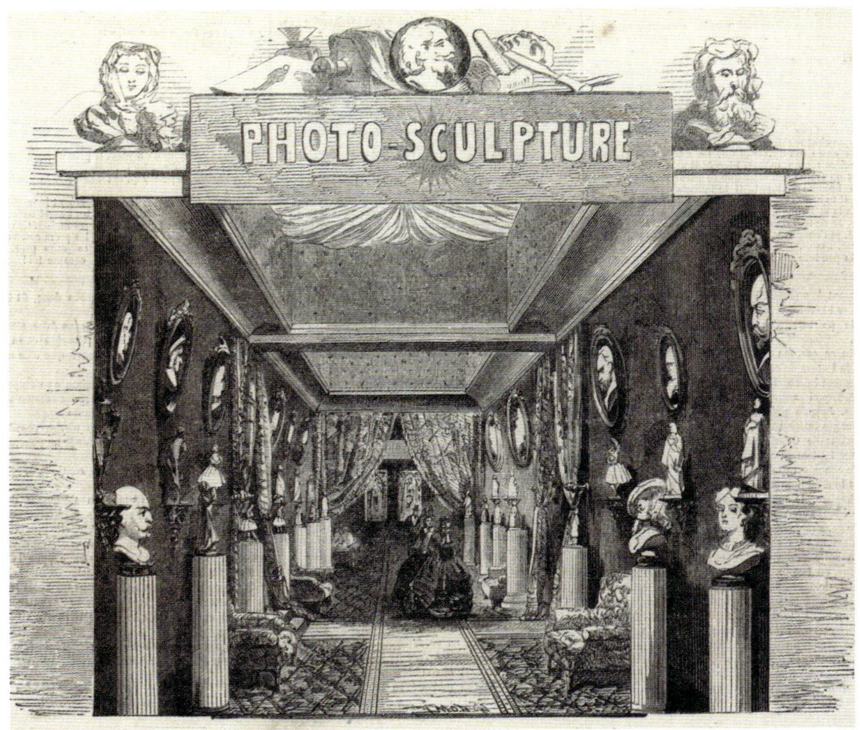

'popularisation of works of statuary' was a 'problem' that might be not be resolved.[34] Even an ardent supporter such as Tissandier expressed his doubts in later years. Accepting that Willème's figures could be 'exact', he conceded that 'from the point of view of art', they remained 'vulgar' and 'mediocre'; 'never will a man in a double-breasted frock coat or a women fortified with crinolines compete with the Apollo Belvedere'.[35] The latter observation is well exemplified in *Presumed Portrait of Comtesse Greffuhle* (cat. 30), a larger and much more elaborate photosculpture that is almost as concerned with the sitter's costume as with her physiognomy. This finely wrought figure was a superior product of Willème's studio, resulting from extended attention to detail and an unusually dramatic evocation of the model's presence. Here she might be making her appearance at a fashionable Parisian soirée or an elegant society ball, pausing to allow her *toilette* to be admired. Nevertheless this was a figure of present times, whose contemporaneity might again have offended the conservative critics of sculpture at this date. Though socially at the opposite extreme to Degas's *Little Dancer*, such an image of a woman 'fortified with crinolines' was still a potential threat to existing conventions and could have been subjected to a comparable – if more muted – chorus of disapproval if it had been exhibited in the grander contexts of the capital.

Photosculpture was already losing its appeal by the early 1870s, but it is clear that Willème's methods had become familiar throughout the Paris art world.[36] The ever-enterprising photographer Nadar, for example, seems to have enjoyed himself by making a group of successive self-portraits in the Willème manner, adapted for the equipment in his own premises on the Boulevard des Capucines (cat. 31). Seated in a swivel chair in front of a single stationary camera, Nadar turned in thirty-degree increments after each photograph was taken.[37] The result was a witty homage to Willème, whose

'Société Générale de Photosculpture de France' was also situated on the
Boulevard des Capucines from 1863 onwards, when Nadar's celebrated
photography studio was already established on the same boulevard.[38]
A famously restless and inquiring mind, Nadar was a close friend of near-
contemporaries such as Daumier and Baudelaire, following the former
as a political caricaturist and the latter as a poet and social commentator.
Most renowned for his experimental approach to photography, Nadar was also
notorious as an adventurer with a camera. The first in his profession to take
aerial photographs, from his own hot-air balloon suspended over Paris (fig. 8),
he also pioneered subterranean photography when he took pictures of
the catacombs beneath the city's streets. Principally remembered for his
uncluttered and expressive portraits of his peers, Nadar had an informal
style that contrasted with the manner of many of his rivals, including the
formidable Disdéri.

The alternative approaches of the two photographers are encapsulated
in a comparison between Nadar's *Twelve Self-portraits from Different Angles,
Study for a Photosculpture* and a superficially similar image by Disdéri, *Eugénie
Fiocre in the Ballet 'Néméa, ou l'Amour Vengé'* (fig. 36). This sheet of uncut cartes
de visite is characteristic of those that were mocked by Degas as a young man,
typically used to mass-produce photographs of society beauties and theatre
celebrities. Here the subject is the young star of the Paris Opéra who was
painted by Degas in 1867, Eugénie Fiocre, shown in costume in an artificial
setting as she re-enacts her role in a current production of the ballet *Néméa*.[39]
In this image, Fiocre as Cupid seems to be turning Willème's conceit on its
head: the teenage dancer is pretending to be a sculpture dramatically coming

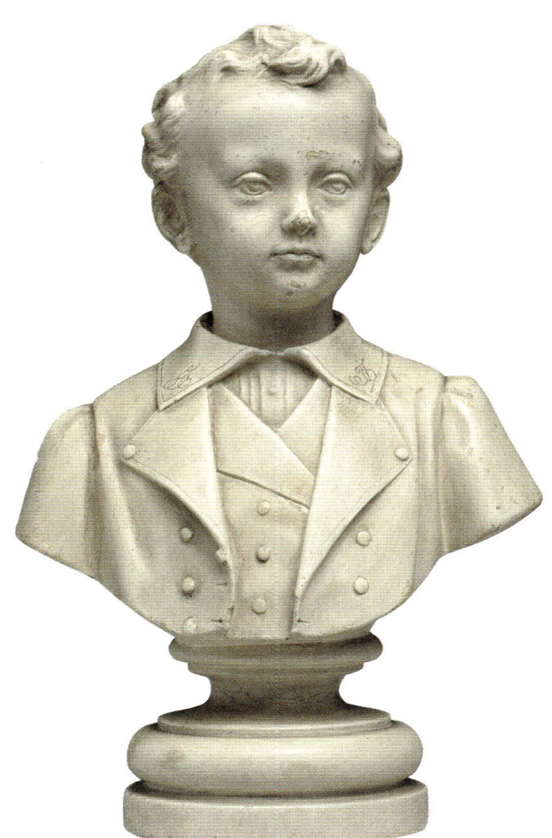

29

François Willème
Bust of a Young Boy
c. 1864–67
Plaster, 20 x 13.5 x 8.5 cm
Collection Gerard Levy, Paris

30

François Willème
**Presumed Portrait
of Comtesse Greffuhle**
c. 1863–68
Biscuit porcelain,
52 x 53 x 30 cm
Les Arts Décoratifs,
Musée des Arts
Décoratifs, Paris

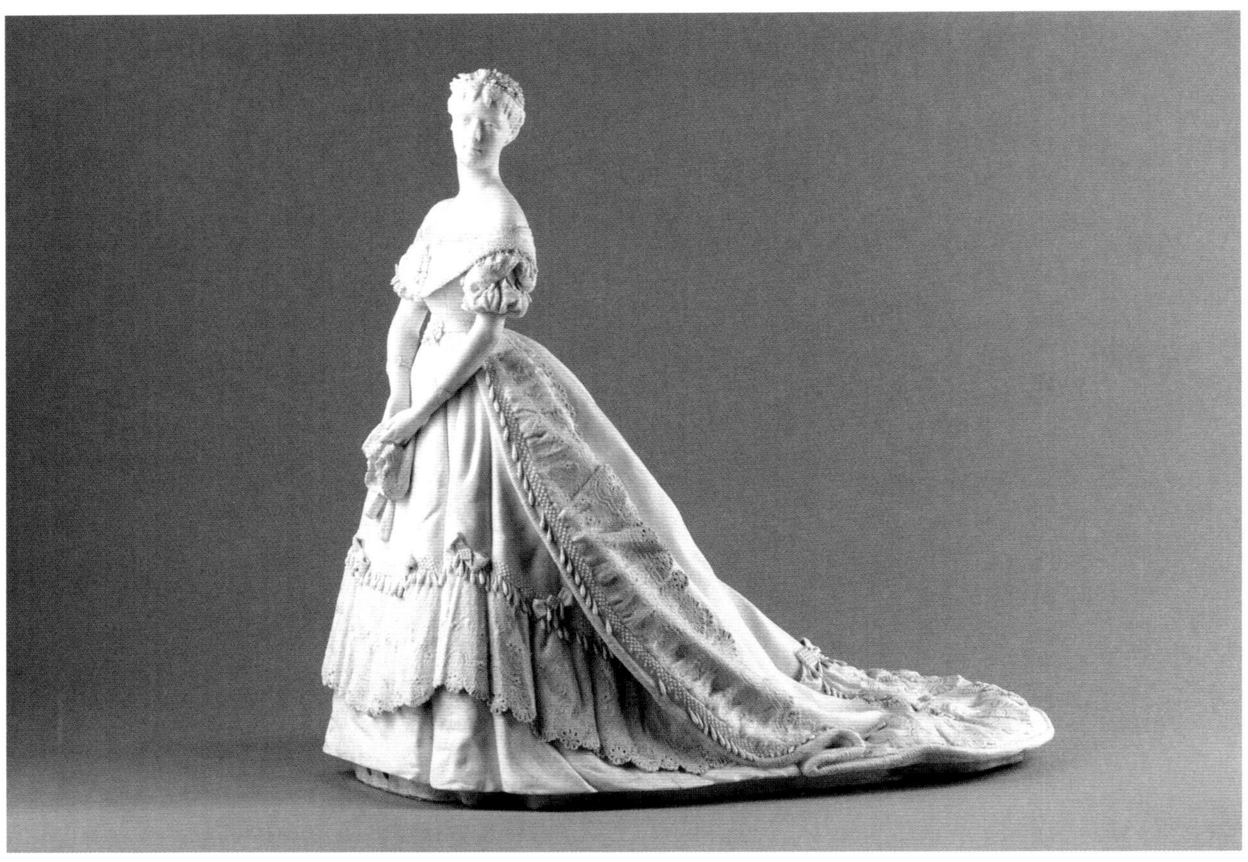

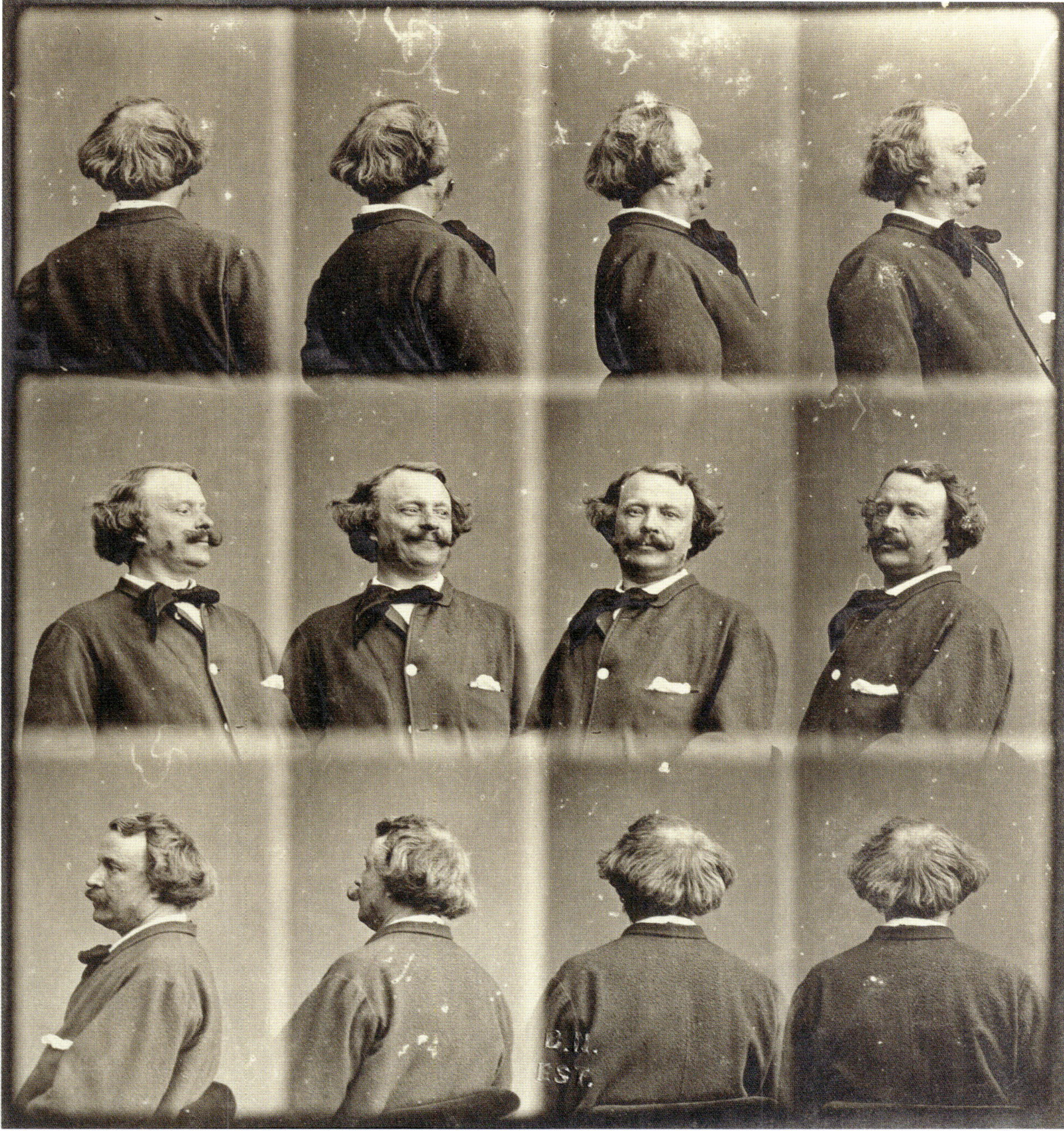

31

Nadar
**Twelve Self-portraits
from Different Angles,
Study for a Photosculpture**
After 1850
Photograph,
14.6 x 13.5 cm
Bibliothèque nationale
de France, Paris.
Département estampes
et photographies

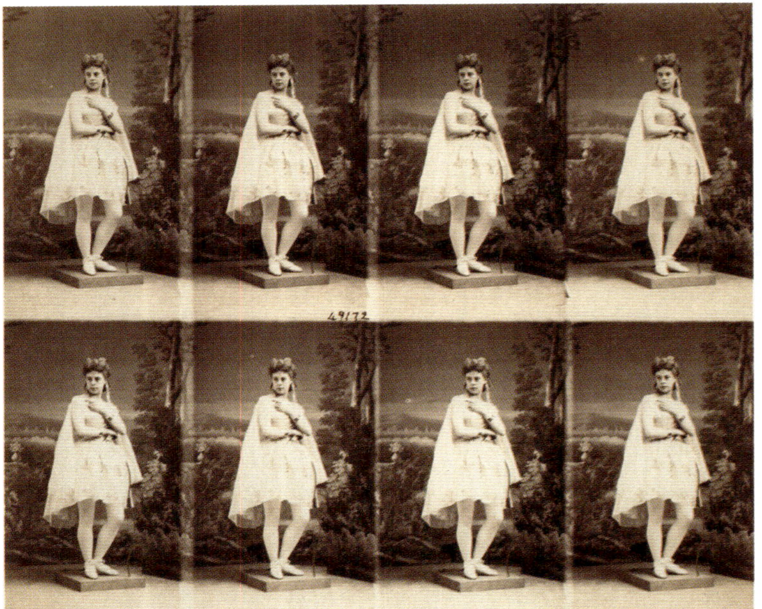

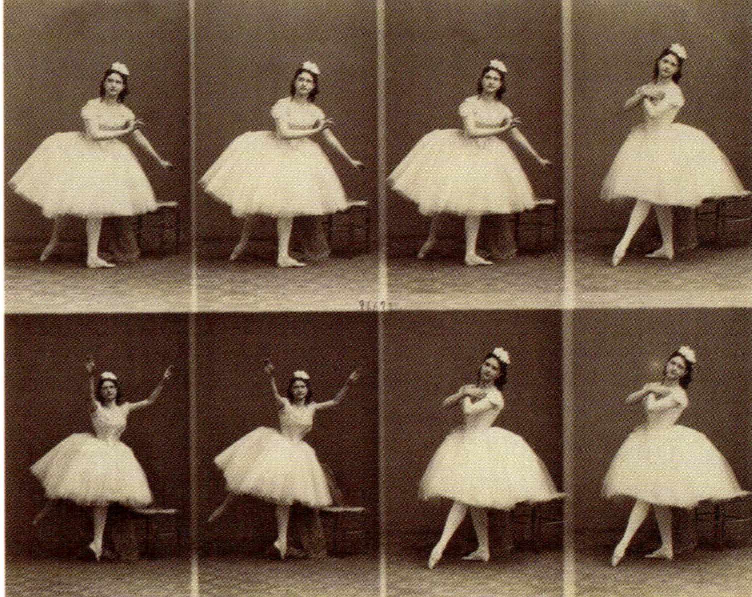

Fig. 36 *André-Adolphe-Eugène Disdéri*, Eugénie Fiocre in the Ballet 'Néméa, ou l'Amour Venge', July 1864 – February 1865. Albumen print, 6 x 10 cm. George Eastman House, Rochester, New York

Fig. 37 *André-Adolphe-Eugène Disdéri*, Marie Petipa, June–August 1862. Albumen print, 6 x 10 cm. George Eastman House, Rochester, New York

to life and her likeness has been photographed from a single point of view. Such photographs and other representations of dancers created a fascinating sub-genre that links the careers of Willème, Nadar, Disdéri and Degas himself, if only in their disparity. Willème was clearly proud of his small photosculptures of contemporary ballerinas, several of which can just be made out among his larger creations in one of the engravings that announced his new business in 1864 (cat. 28).[40] Nadar – or perhaps his assistants – also created portraits of dancers in relatively plain settings, while Disdéri undoubtedly led the field in the mass-production of 'staged' performance shots. Another sheet by Disdéri, for example, features Marie Petipa (fig. 37), a Russian ballerina who danced at the Paris Opéra during this period. Shown in three different poses, two of which were easily held for a period of time, Petipa would have needed some unseen form of support to maintain her balance in the third. In every case, the sculptor or photographer had to situate himself between extremes of realism and stylisation, between unique and multiple images, and between the exploratory and the predictable approach to visual representation. Paradoxically, Nadar and Degas were the only representatives of this group to make self-conscious reference to their predicament. Parody was implicit in many of Nadar's projects, while wit and profound innovation often went hand-in-hand in Degas's approach to drawing and painting, and to works such as the *Little Dancer*. Yet Degas seems not to have been counted among Nadar's numerous intimates and is said to have responded sarcastically to Nadar's claim that he too was an artist with the words: 'faux-artiste, faux-peintre, faux-tographe'.[41]

The Dance Lesson (cat. 32) is part of a series of pictures that belongs with the
most original and least understood inventions of Degas's career as a painter of
the ballet. Between the late 1870s and the turn of the century he made almost
a dozen such works, choosing a distinctive format that is more than twice as
wide as it is high.[42] Using canvases with near-identical dimensions and adding
a few similar-sized compositions in pastel on paper, Degas created these
'friezes' for reasons that remain unclear. Also common to the pictures in
question is their subject, a curiously shaped classroom in which ballerinas
exercise at the barre, await instruction or recover from their labours. The
consistent form of the friezes and their shared theme suggest that Degas
had a specific purpose in mind for them, or was perhaps following a still
unidentified historical model. It has been proposed, for example, that these
works represented schemes for modern mural paintings that were never
realised, perhaps recalling frescoes that Degas had seen and sometimes copied
as a young man in Italy.[43] As an adult he is known to have discussed ideas for
decorative projects, remarking on one occasion that 'it has been my lifelong
dream to paint on walls'.[44] Yet there is no evidence that Degas attempted to
secure such a commission for a public building or a private house, or executed
a scene of this kind on the large scale that would have been necessary for such
an installation. Revealing also was the fact that he continued to work on
the ballet friezes throughout his mature career and into old age, apparently
fascinated by their innate compositional challenges and their potential for
exploring the backstage lives of dancers.

From the beginning, Degas established most of the characteristic features
that were to persist throughout the series of frieze pictures. In *The Dance Lesson*,
which is generally accepted as the earliest of the group, an 'immense room' – in
Huysmans's words – that is unusually wide and shallow stretches from one side
of the painting to the other.[45] Dominating a large part of this space is a featureless
wall close to the viewer and at a slight angle to the picture plane, its proximity
oppressive beside the spaciousness elsewhere. At right several young dancers
bask in the distant sunlight, reflecting the air of lassitude and uncertainty that
pervades the entire scene. Here the girl in a red shawl at extreme left is clearly
weary, while the erect figure with a blue sash seems more statuesque than
animated. The half-dozen coryphées clustered at the window are similarly inert,
neither dancing nor exercising in the conventional sense. A notable feature of
The Dance Lesson – as in the later frieze compositions – is the artful positioning
of these young women across its broad expanse, subdividing the space and
articulating its essential rhythms.[46] Seen in this way, the ballerinas can be
understood as human markers in Degas's larger pictorial scheme or perhaps
notes on his musical stave: as our eyes sweep the composition from side to side,
then back again, we instinctively follow the procession of forms and intervals
that give the picture its understated life. Comparable qualities persist in
subsequent works from the series, such as *Dancers in the Green Room* (cat. 39)
and *Dancers in the Foyer* (cat. 40) from the turn of the century. Characteristic
in their rich colours and more expressive brushwork, these late paintings
nevertheless introduce only minor structural variations to the original prototype
and slightly larger groups of ballerinas in the immediate foreground. A less
common variant of the design reverses its principal forms, so that the foreground

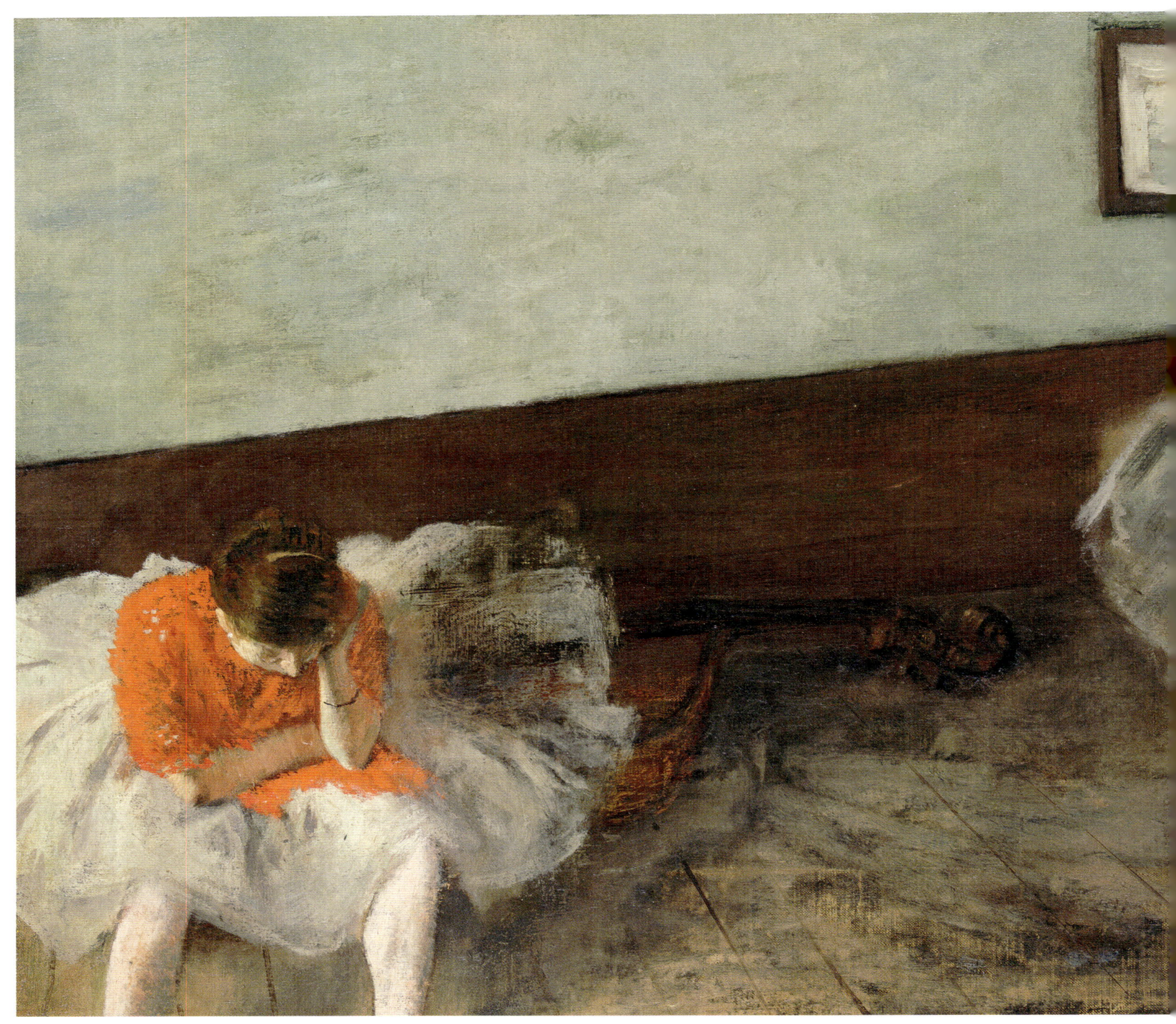

32

The Dance Lesson
c. 1879
Oil on canvas,
38 x 88 cm
National Gallery of Art,
Washington. Collection
of Mr and Mrs Paul Mellon,
1995.47.6

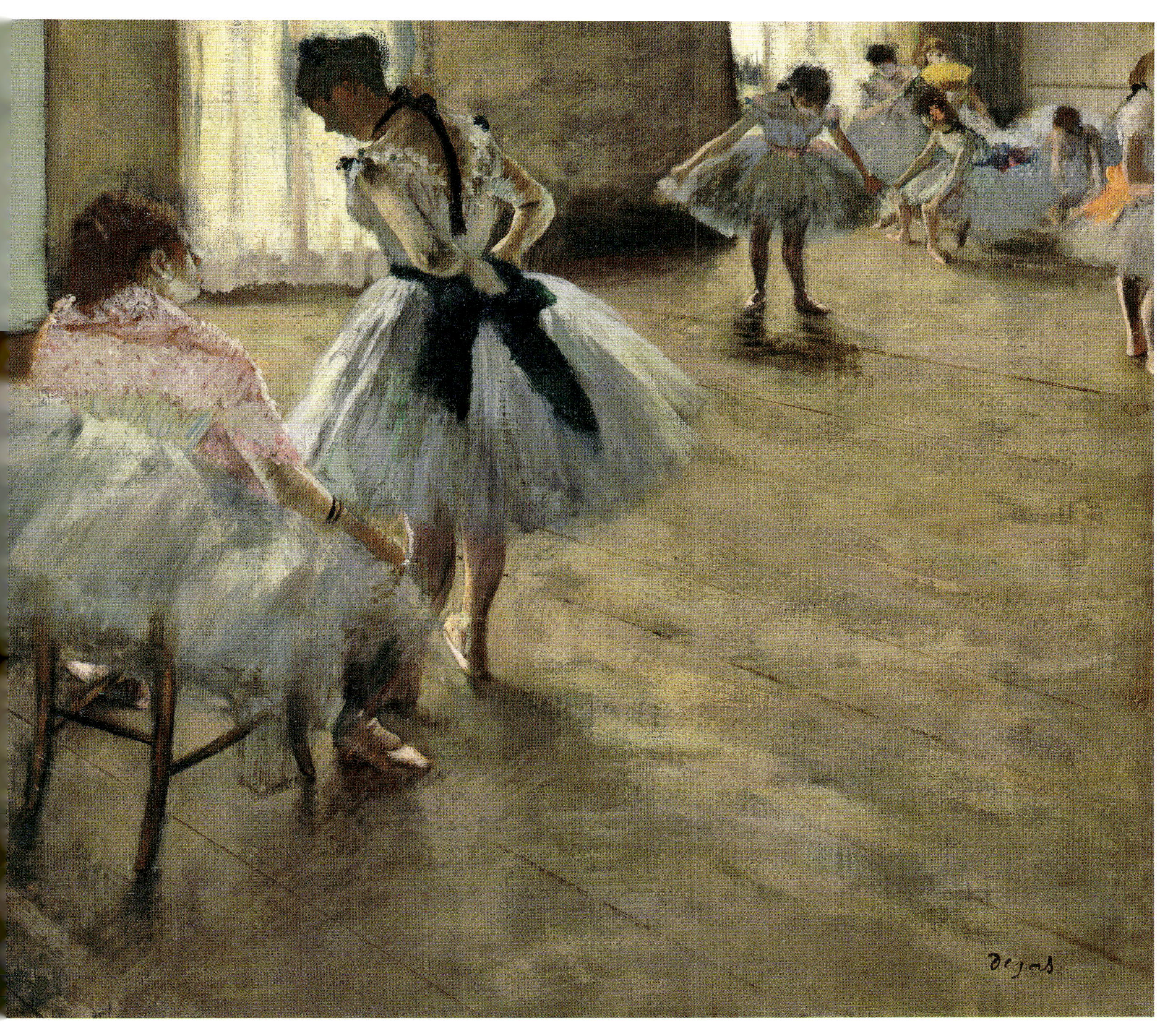

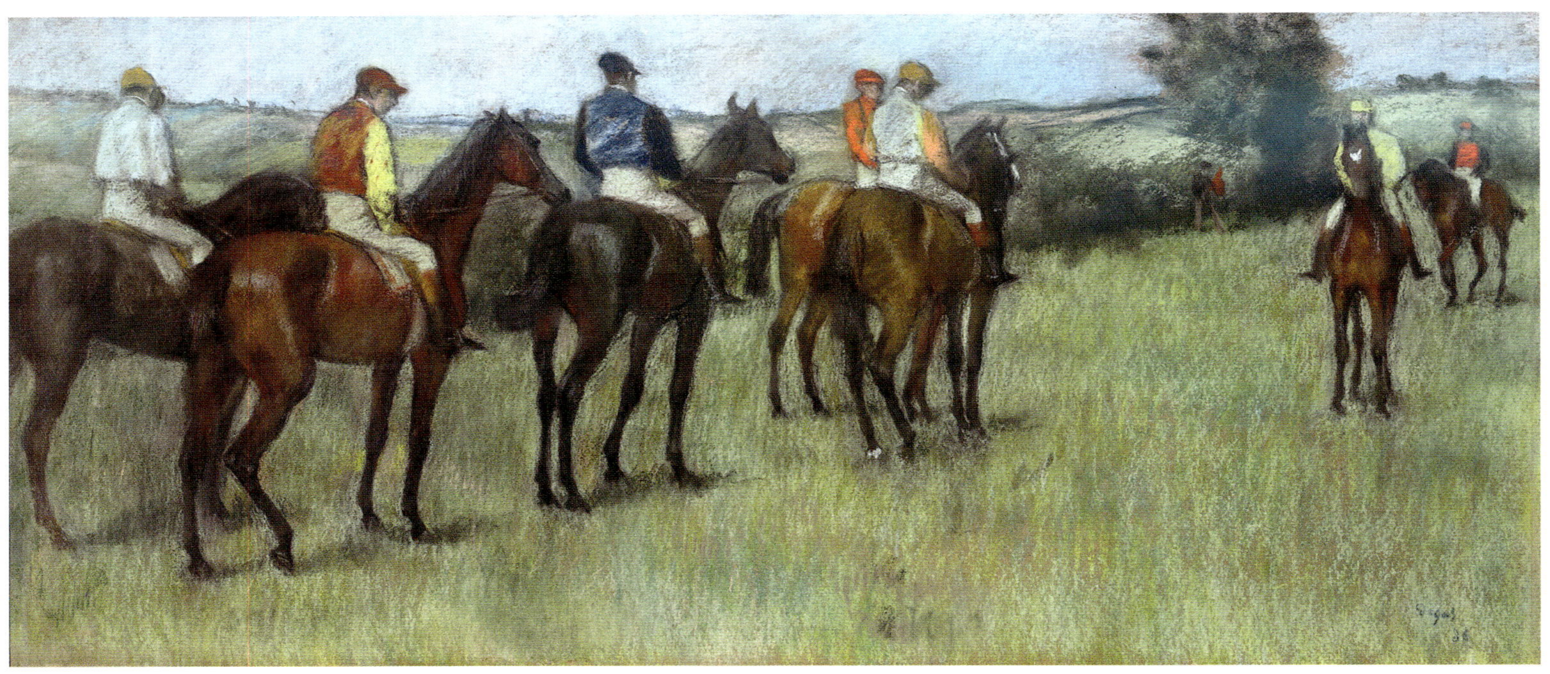

Fig. 38 **Jockeys**, 1886. Pastel on paper, 38.7 x 88.3 cm.
Alfred Atmore Pope Collection, Hill-Stead Museum,
Farmington, Connecticut, inv. no. 46-1-002

wall appears at right and the distant figures are found by a window at left. *Before the Ballet* (cat. 45) exemplifies this pattern and introduces a more purposeful air to the proceedings; here a group of dancers are practising at the barre as two of their companions adjust their costumes and ready themselves for action.

Each scene in the sequence of frieze pictures adds modest but significant nuances to the narrative, subtle shifts of light and shadow, and new combinations of hue and painterly touch. Yet all these works are inevitably dominated by the long, low format that Degas established from the start. For the viewer, this panorama-like design invites us to survey each painted room from side to side, as we would if stepping into any large space that was notably broad and shallow. Degas actively encouraged the scanning response in several ways, not least by seizing our attention with some feature or incident in the foreground, then leading our eyes to the farthest corner at left or right by means of perspective and the diminishing scale of the painted figures. Reflexively, we then look back across the breadth of the painting again, repeating our survey and becoming increasingly involved in Degas's subtly inflected design. Although the dancers themselves are largely inactive in their poses, the artist went to unusual lengths to animate them by inference. The dynamic engagement of the spectator with the painted classroom is largely responsible for this animation, a factor that unites the entire sequence of ballet friezes. It is also evident in another set of near-identical, frieze-like canvases and pastels that emerged alongside these dance pictures. Featuring racehorses parading across their exercise ground or lining up for the starter's flag (fig. 38), rather than ballerinas in class, these works employ similar diagonals that rise gently across the composition and similar contrasts between solitary and clustered horses and jockeys.[47] As in many of Degas's ballet and equestrian scenes in other formats, such devices generate energy within the picture as well as intervals of calm. Yet the case of the dance friezes remains exceptional, both as an obsessive, single-minded project that Degas followed across the decades and as a self-conscious cycle of variants on the ballet that presupposes the active scrutiny of the spectator.

New insight into these distinctive works can be found in a number of visual forms that were popular in Degas's day, all of them involving the scanning of horizontal scenes. Foremost among them were painted panoramas, which flourished in France and throughout Europe for much of the artist's lifetime. Large crowds queued to see re-creations of famous or exotic landscapes, historical and biblical narratives, military episodes such as 'The Siege of Paris' or 'The Battle of Champigny', and even more ambitious presentations that offered a 'Panorama of the History of the Century'.[48] Usually consisting of a circular building with a continuous scene painted on its inner wall – an early example was 123 feet in diameter – they also featured a viewing platform for the public at the centre (fig. 39).[49] Panoramas were renowned for the ingenuity of their visual effects and the vividness of the impression they created. Essential to their impact was the active participation of the audience, who were required to walk around the viewing platforms and gradually direct their attention to the unfolding painted drama. Some panoramas were partly based on photographs that had been projected onto continuous rolls of canvas mounted on the curving wall and subsequently painted, but all of them depended on skilled practitioners who could create a detailed and plausible illusion of reality.[50] The seriousness with which this phenomenon was regarded is reflected in the quality of the artists who chose to become involved. Louis Daguerre, the pioneer photographer, contributed to the beginnings of the genre by creating a simpler form known as a diorama; Charles Garnier,

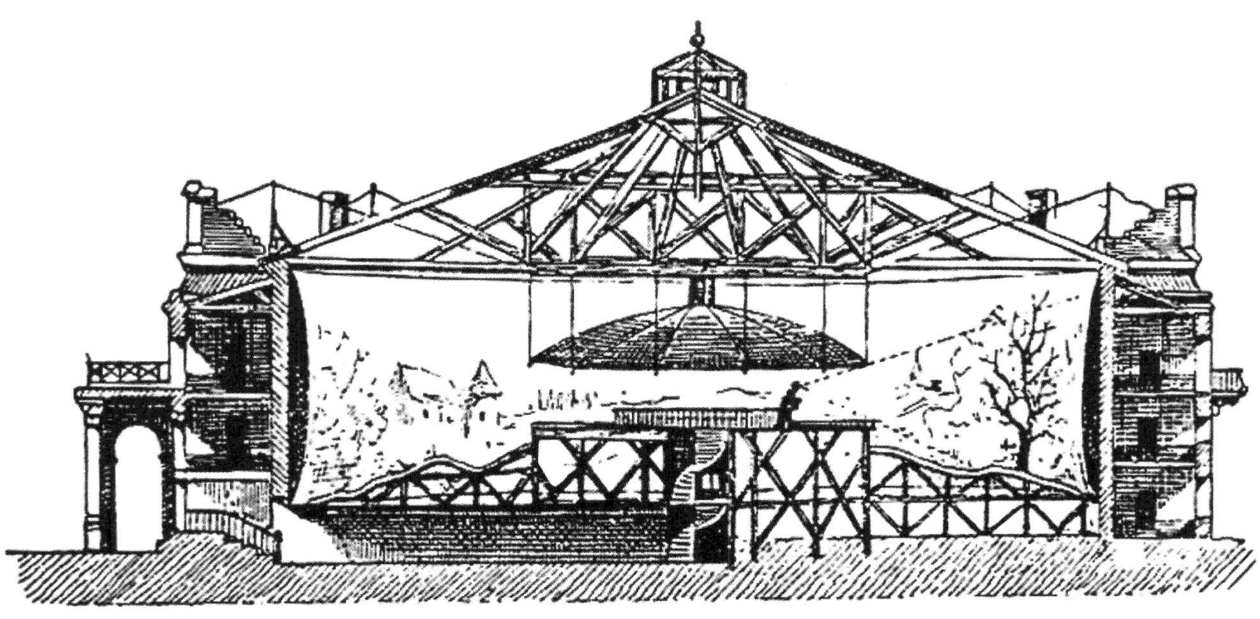

Fig. 39 *Artist unknown*, Engraving of a painted panorama, nineteenth century

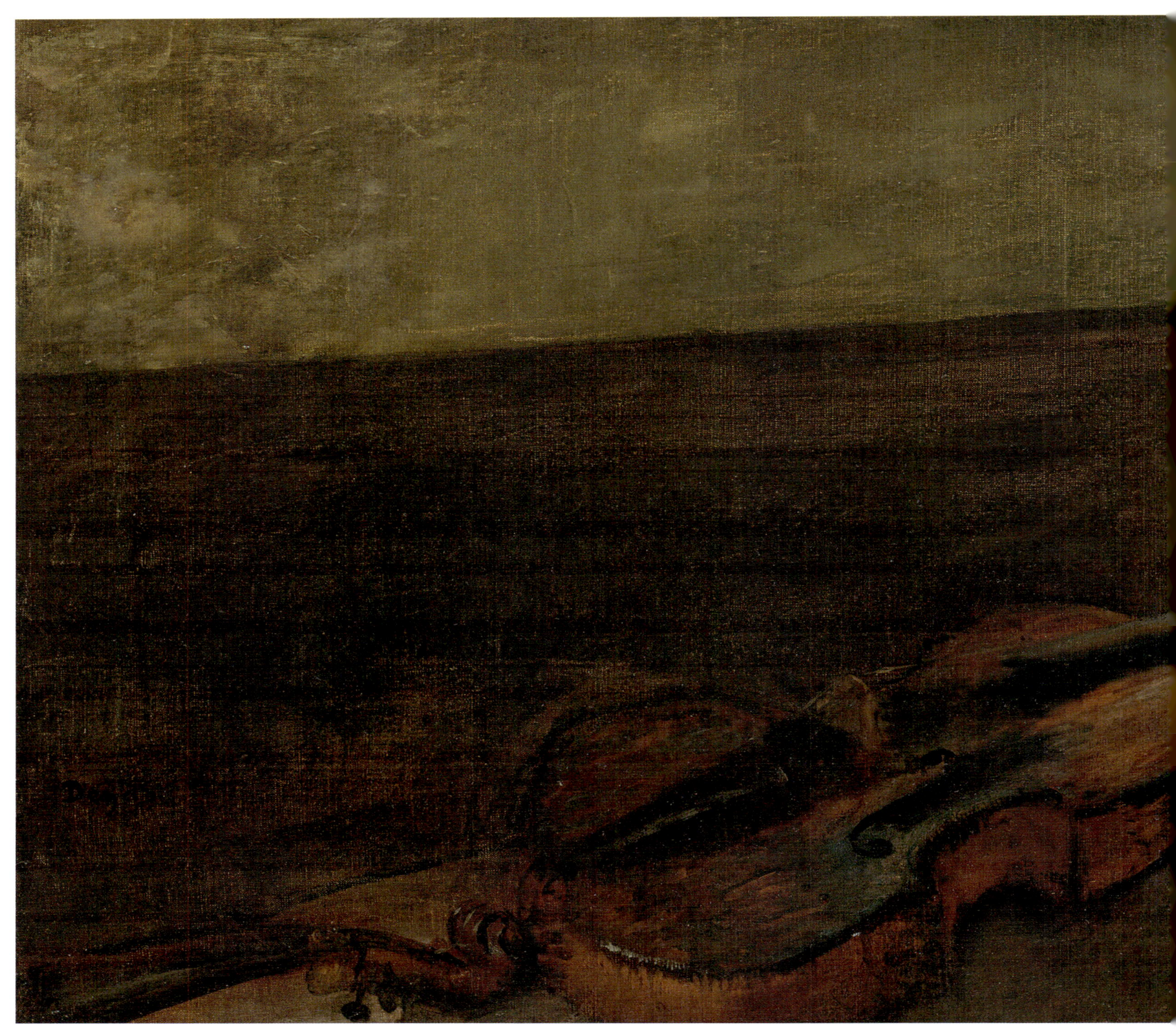

33

**Dancers in the Rehearsal Room
with a Double Bass**
c. 1882–85
Oil on canvas,
39.1 x 89.5 cm
Lent by the Metropolitan Museum
of Art, New York. H. O. Havemeyer
Collection, Bequest of Mrs H. O.
Havemeyer, 1929 (29.100.127)

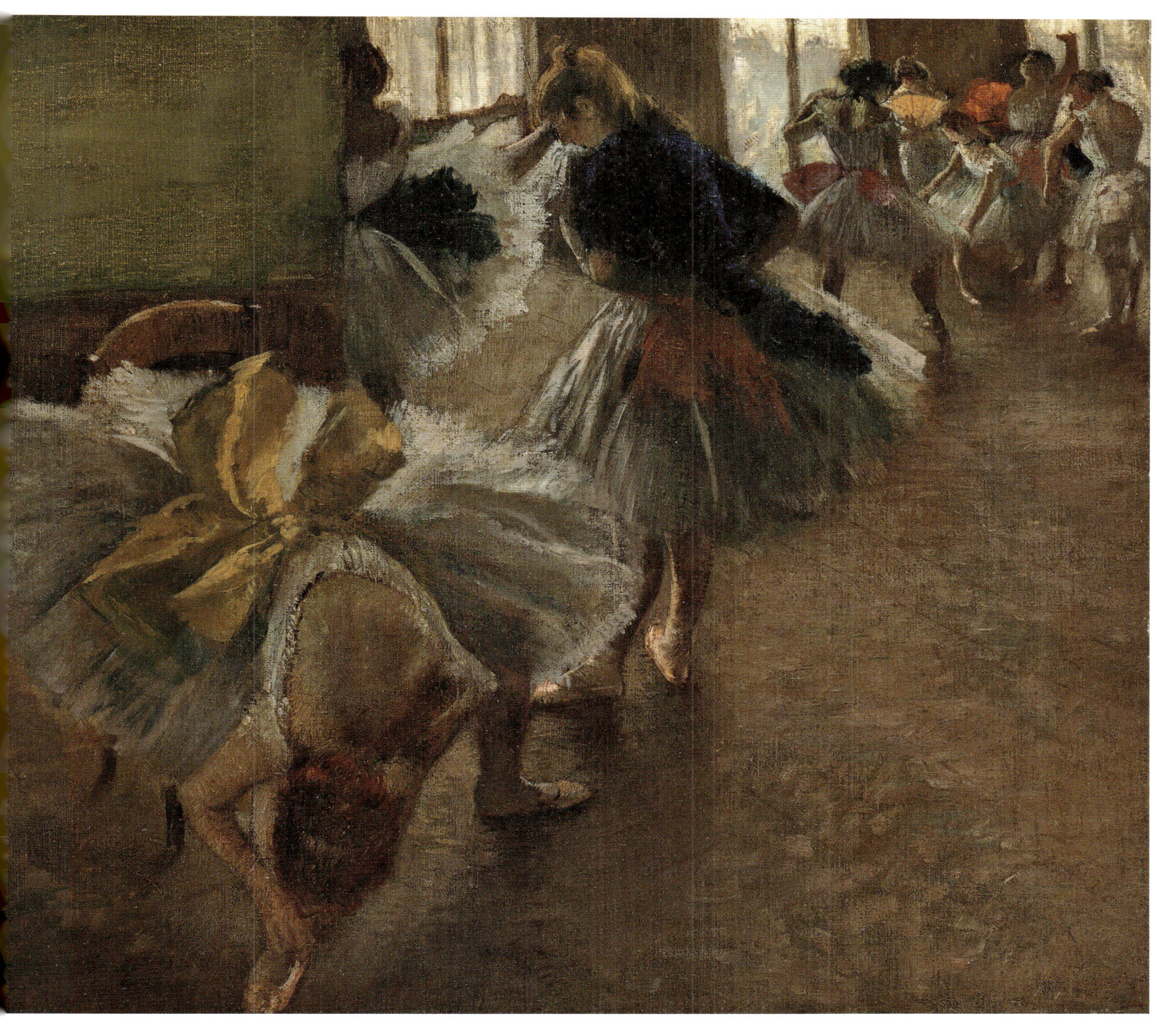

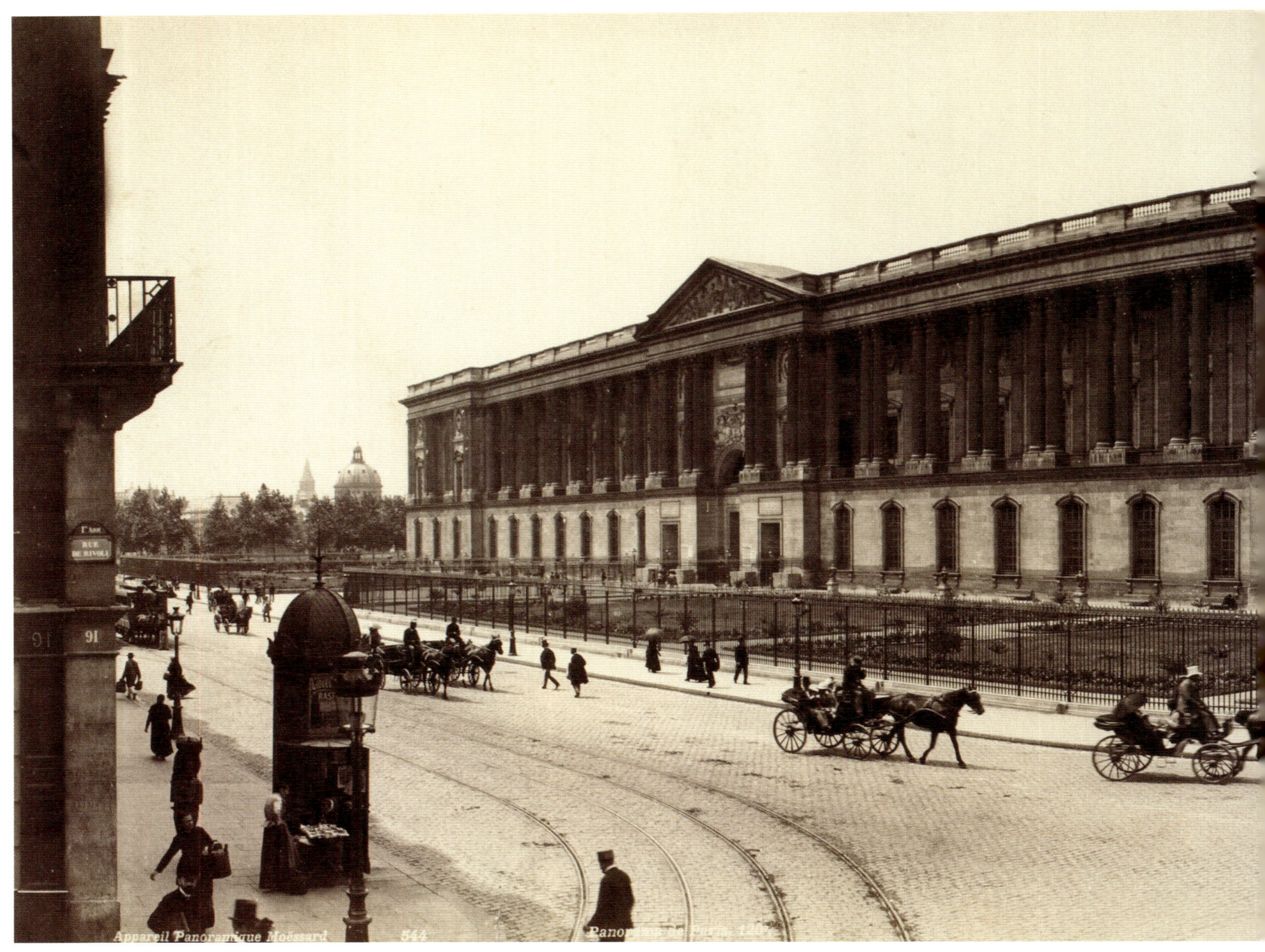

34

A. O. Champagne
**The Colonnade of the Louvre,
from the Rue de Rivoli**
1889
Albumen print,
20.3 x 55.5 cm
Collection of George Eastman
House, Rochester, New York

architect of the new Paris Opéra, designed a *Panorama Français* in 1880; Degas's friend, the military painter Edouard Detaille, worked on *The Battle of Champigny* in 1882; another of his acquaintances, Jean-Léon Gérôme, contributed to the genre, while two admirers of Degas's art, Henri Gervex and Alfred Stevens, created one of seven panoramas that featured at the 1889 Exposition Universelle.[51] Shared by most of these variants was the wide, horizontal composition that spectators followed from the beginning to the end of the narrative, bringing their own mobility to a visual experience that was otherwise essentially static. Although there is no evidence that Degas himself participated in this genre, his familiarity with many of its exponents increases the likelihood that – like great numbers of Parisians – he visited some of the panoramas in central locations in the city. An admirer of puppet shows, cabarets and the spectacular Expositions of these years, Degas was also

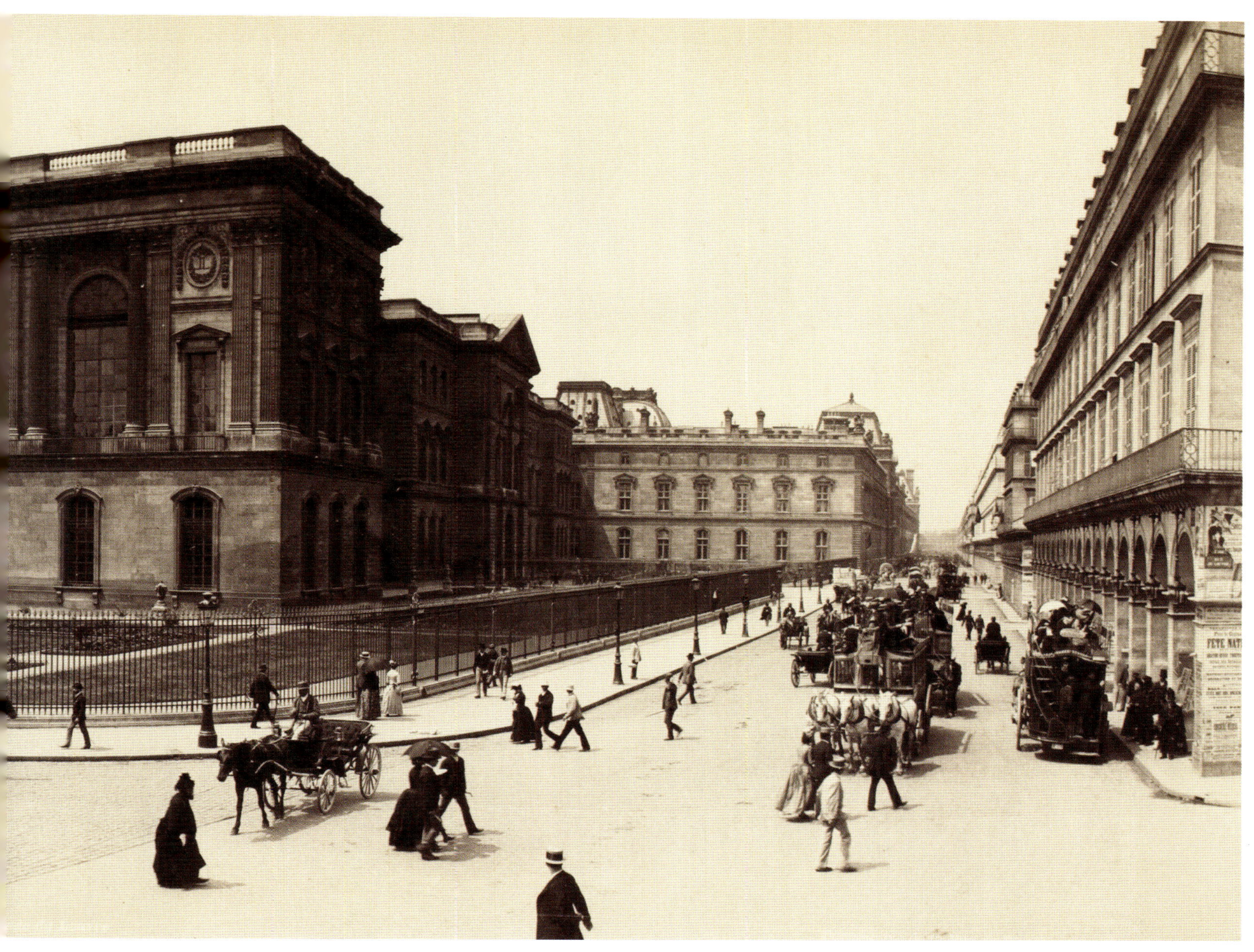

fascinated by the history of the Franco-Prussian war, a widely popular theme of the painted panorama in the 1870s.[52] Clearly aware of the format in its various manifestations, he seems to have echoed some of its features in the strictly contemporary experiments taking place in his studio.

Another invention of this same period that required a mobile gaze for a fixed visual presentation was the panoramic photograph, which also grew rapidly in popularity after its inception in the early nineteenth century. A fine example of the genre is *The Colonnade of the Louvre, from the Rue de Rivoli* (cat. 34), taken by the obscure A. O. Champagne in the centre of Paris at a site that is little changed today. Here the photographer has taken full advantage of his specialised panoramic camera to sweep across a wide expanse of streets and architecture, from the east-facing façade of the Louvre at left to a view plunging deep into the Rue de Rivoli at right. Prominent in the scene is a broad

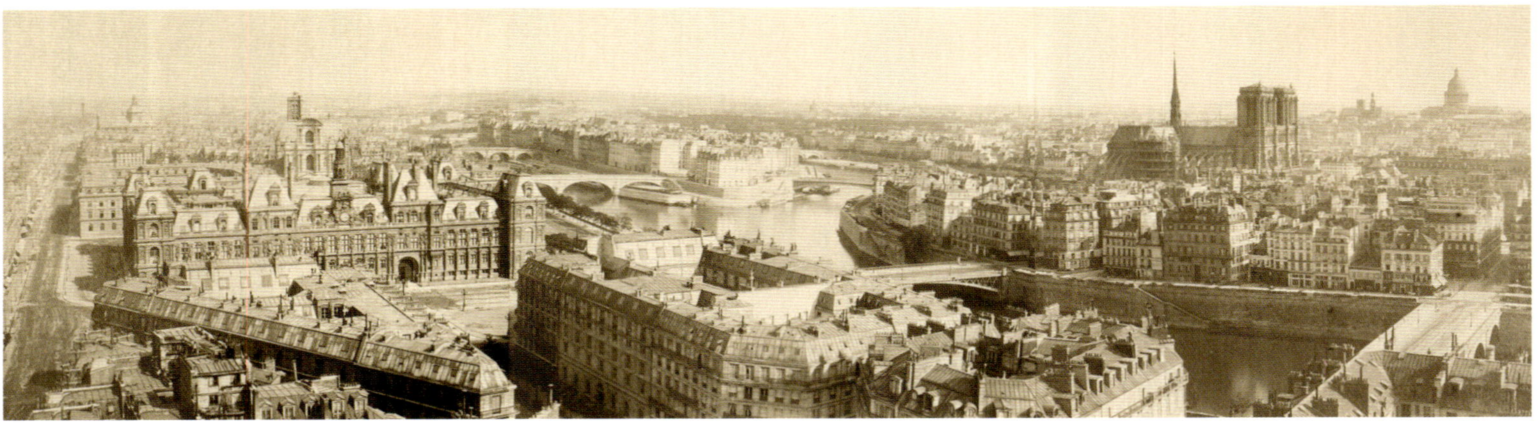

swath of relatively empty foreground that carries the viewer's attention from side to side and back again. As the eye moves, it follows the scattered human traffic as the populace advances on foot, in horse-drawn carriages and – at right – in the omnibuses that were already a feature of Parisian life. Just as forcefully as the painted panoramas on display in this same city, although on a much smaller scale, such photographs both insist on the engagement of viewers and partly orchestrate their visual response. Encouraging our participation in the horizontal sweep of the city and its day-to-day life, Champagne simultaneously blocked our progress into depth by emphasising the massive rectangular bulwark of the Louvre.

This photograph was one of many thousands of such scenes taken in these years and there is no reason to believe that Degas knew this particular work at first hand. A direct comparison with the spatial and compositional features of the artist's ballet frieze paintings, however, reveals his use of several visual conventions that are central to the impact of Champagne's print and many others like it. Though smaller overall, the wide horizontal print has similar proportions to those of Degas's canvases and also incorporates a discreet diagonal that runs from side to side. Both photograph and painting also show large areas of bare foreground with solitary figures 'cut' by the lower edge of the frame, while a largely uninflected, rectangular form occludes much of the middle distance in *The Colonnade of the Louvre, from the Rue de Rivoli* as it does in *The Dance Lesson*. Closely comparable, too, is the dependence of both images on a perspective 'rush' into depth at right, challenging the flatness of the picture surface but kept within strict bounds. This device carries our eyes steeply upwards, towards a cluster of distant pedestrians in one case and ballet dancers in the other. Yet the most important structural elements are again those that encourage us to 'scan' the two depicted spaces, much as an onlooker might do if actually present at this intersection on the Rue de Rivoli or when standing in the curiously proportioned classroom used by the Opéra ballet.

A further analogy between Degas's approach to his frieze paintings and the work of photographers such as Champagne emerges from an examination of the panoramic cameras used to make such pictures. Most often directed at broad landscape vistas or cityscapes, cameras of this type were built to capture a wider angle of view than that currently achievable with standard lenses. From the 1840s onwards, various mechanical systems had been developed

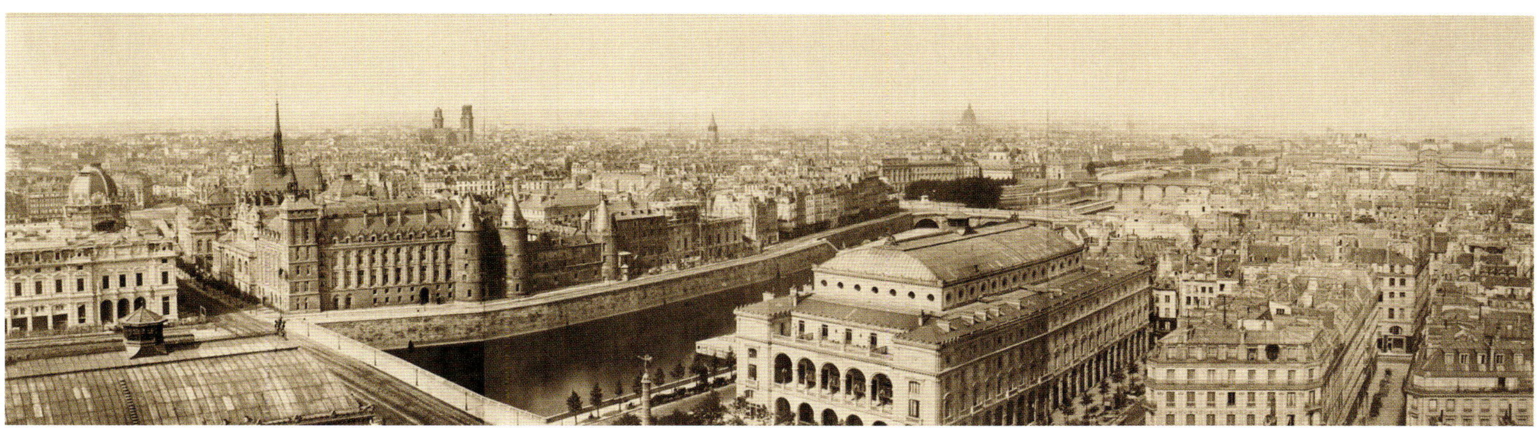

to achieve this end: one of them swung the lens itself from side to side
in relation to the fixed camera body; another turned the entire camera
in front of the chosen subject; and other alternatives were designed to pass
the lens horizontally across a single photographic plate of frieze-like
proportions. The widely adopted Pantascopic camera, invented in 1862
but still in use decades later (cat. 37), relied on a clockwork device to
achieve the latter effect, photographing a field of 110 degrees on a glass
surface prepared with a collodion solution. A camera of this kind was used
for a series of landscape views by Adolphe Braun, who was more famous for
his photographs of city views and works of art, some of which Degas is said
to have owned.[53] Other models were able to achieve up to 360-degree coverage
of the chosen site, creating a continuous photographic 'frieze' that was
analogous to the painted panorama. Uniting all these methods was the
principle of systematic scanning at the chosen location, with the panoramic
camera imitating the action of a human eye as it turned mechanically to
inspect its distant subject. Such an approach was implicit in the photograph
by Champagne and in certain more inventive panoramas of Paris that shed
further light on Degas's long, low paintings and pastels of ballet classrooms.

When Degas was still around thirty years old, another little-documented
photographer named A. Gueuvin carried his panoramic equipment to the
top of the Tour Saint-Jacques in Paris, about half a mile east of the site of
Champagne's print. On a brilliantly sunny day, Gueuvin looked south and
across the rooftops of the city in the direction of the cathedral of Nôtre-Dame,
titling the resulting print *Panorama of Paris from the Tour Saint-Jacques,
Facing East* (cat. 35). A second such shot was taken from the same site and
presumably on the same day, again benefiting from the bright sunlight
to produce a high degree of detail in both shadowed and illuminated areas
of his photograph (cat. 36). In contrast to Champagne's near-street-level view
of the city, Gueuvin seemed to delight in this extraordinary sight of central
Paris from above and the dizzying sensation of his bird's-eye view. Far from
mere documentation, these inventive images aspired to offer the public some
novel experiences of the capital, showing rooftops and courtyards that were
normally invisible at ground level and relishing the broad expanse of the city
spread out before them. More adventurous still was a panoramic photograph
taken two decades later by Etienne Neurdein at a site that was especially well
known to Degas: the busy multiple intersection in front of Charles Garnier's

36

A. Gueuvin
**Panorama of Paris from
the Tour Saint-Jacques,
Facing West**
c. 1864
Albumen print from wet
collodion on glass negatives,
25.4 x 76.2 cm
Victoria and Albert Museum,
London. Transferred from
the British Museum

37

*John R. Johnson
and John A. Harrison*
**Pantascopic panoramic camera
(no. 74) with plate holder**
1862
Wood and brass, 22 x 32 x 21 cm
National Media Museum,
Bradford. By courtesy
of the Board of Trustees
of the Science Museum

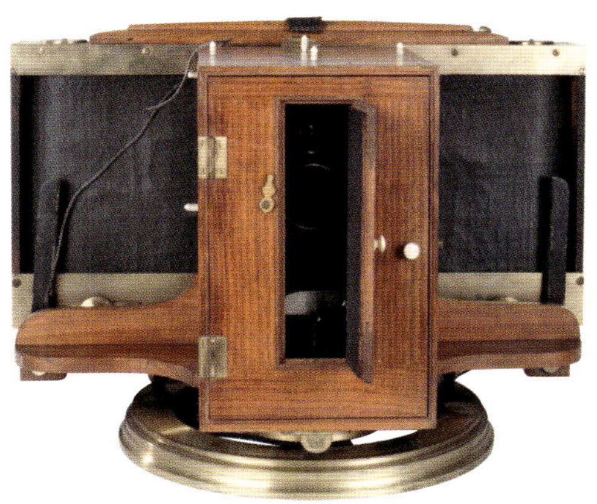

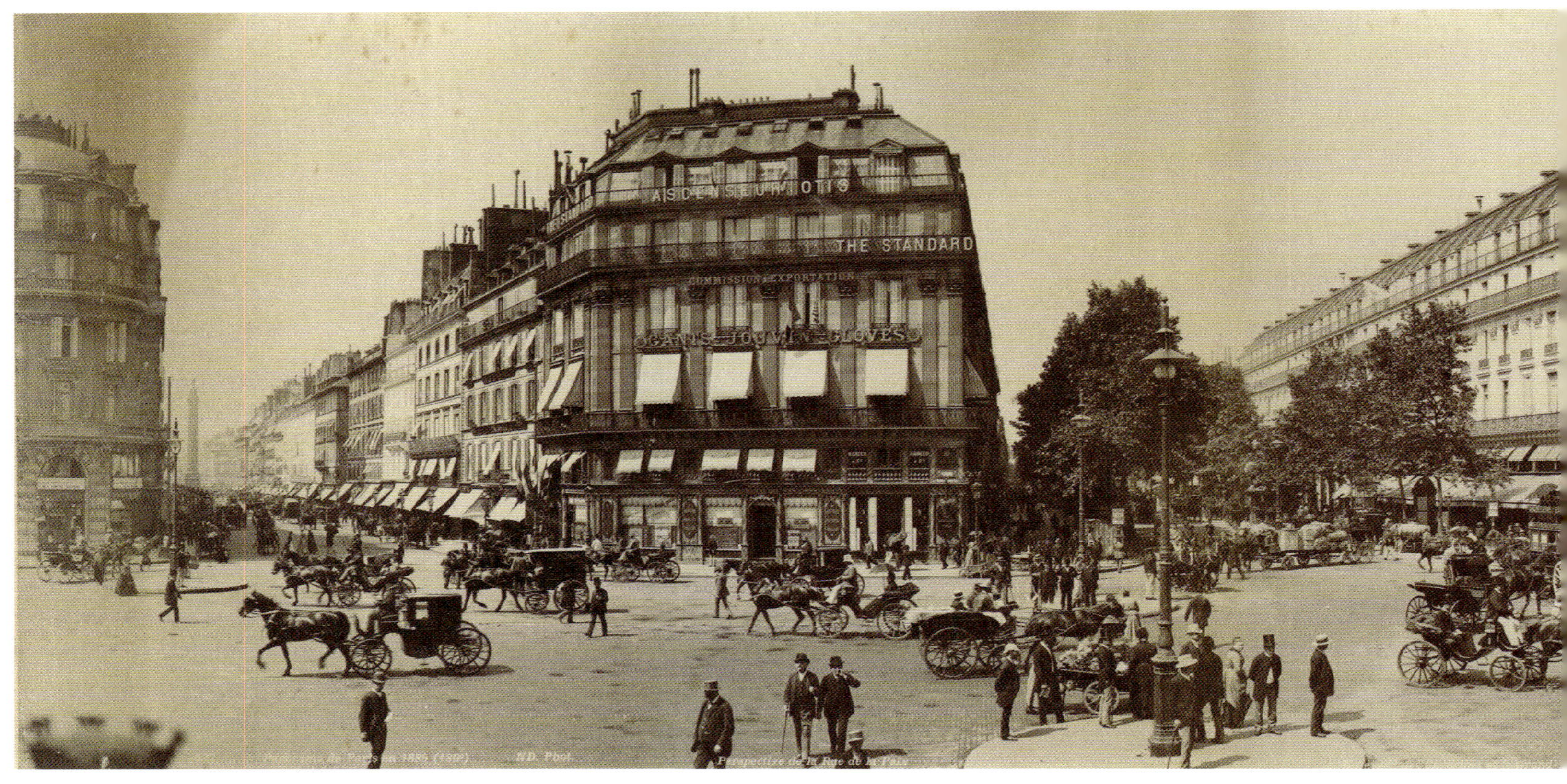

38

Etienne Neurdein
**Panorama of the Rue de la Paix
and the Garnier Opera House**
1889
Photograph on archival board,
23 x 86 cm
Thomas G. Yanul, USA

Paris Opéra (cat. 38). Here Neurdein adopted a position on the corner between the Boulevard des Capucines and the Place de l'Opéra, looking out from a first- or second-floor window.[54] Using a Moessard panoramic camera with a 150-degree sweep, he was able to 'flatten' almost three sides of the square into a single image as if it were a continuous row of buildings in the same plane. Unlike the panoramas of both Champagne and Gueuvin, Neurdein's view of the Place de l'Opéra is a self-conscious distortion of reality as experienced by the human eye, stimulating our imaginations and encouraging us to ponder the limits of everyday vision. Neurdein and his brother achieved considerable recognition for their audacious views of Paris and other cities in Europe, earning gold medals at several exhibitions in the last decade of the century.[55] At a time when Paris was swamped by photographers of all kinds, including those making panoramas, Gueuvin and Champagne seem to have largely disappeared from the record, remembered as innovative but apparently transient practitioners.

At this point in his career, as we have seen, Degas delighted in depicting his chosen subjects in ways that took the viewer beyond conventional visual experience. Reminding himself in the late 1870s to 'get used to drawings things from above and below', he added in the same notebook that 'neither monuments nor houses have ever been drawn from below, close-up as they appear when you walk down the street'.[56] This self-consciousness about ways of seeing the world was a persistent theme in Degas's art during these years, expressed in unusual vantage points, vertiginous angles of view and compositions that encouraged a challenging engagement with the observer's surroundings. His frieze paintings of dancers emerged at precisely this point,

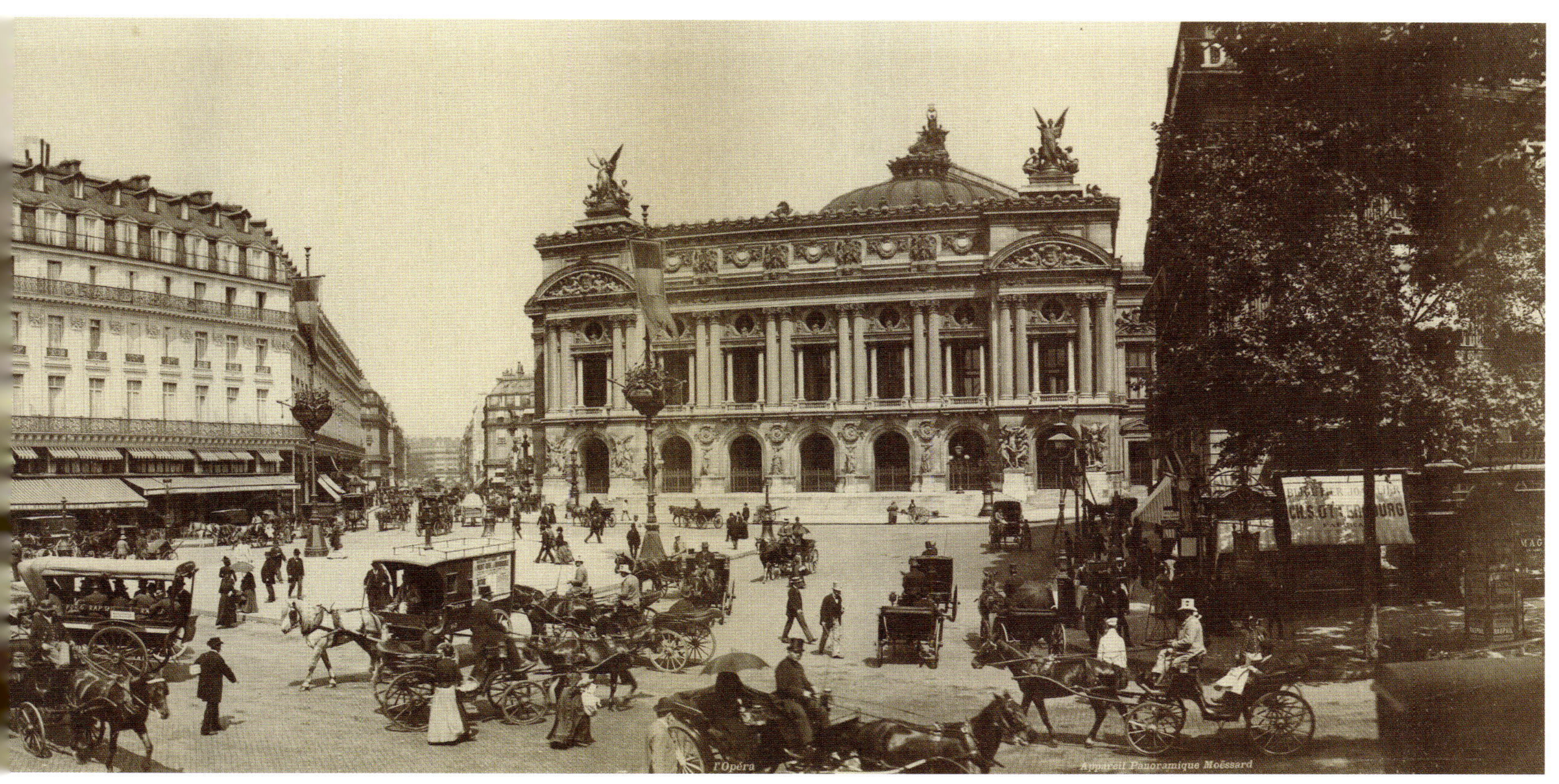

their novel shapes announcing a fresh approach to the modern urban
environment and some of their features inviting his contemporaries to rethink
their own relationships with works of art. The technique of 'cropping', for
example, draws attention to the arbitrary nature of views constructed by
painters and photographers alike. In *The Dance Lesson* (cat. 32) the severed
legs of the girl at left remind us that we can see only part of a larger scene,
as if the picture frame is a window or viewfinder through which we are
looking. The bisected figure in the distance at extreme right in Degas's
painting offers a second reminder of this fact, while contributing to the
broader thrust that unites his composition along a diagonal axis. Subtly
underlining this axis is the line that marks the colour shift on the foreground
wall, where Degas mutely reinforced the angled thrust that echoes throughout
the painted classroom. Within this overall scheme each dancer asserts her
modest dynamism, frozen in the act of turning around, rising or descending,
in an ingenious series of postures that ends with the almost formless ensemble
in the distance. With understated skill, Degas also encourages the viewer's
gaze to cross and re-cross the room from side to side, bringing life to the
scattered ballerinas who might otherwise seem merely distracted by inertia
or weariness.

A similar logic is taken further in *Dancers in the Rehearsal Room with
a Double Bass* (cat. 33). Now autumnal or even wintry in its shadowy palette,
this canvas is again constructed around a thrust of momentum from the
lower-left corner towards a window at upper right. Far from concealing his
intentions, Degas has made the two-toned intervening wall even wider and
deeper, underlining its effect with a massively prominent double bass that

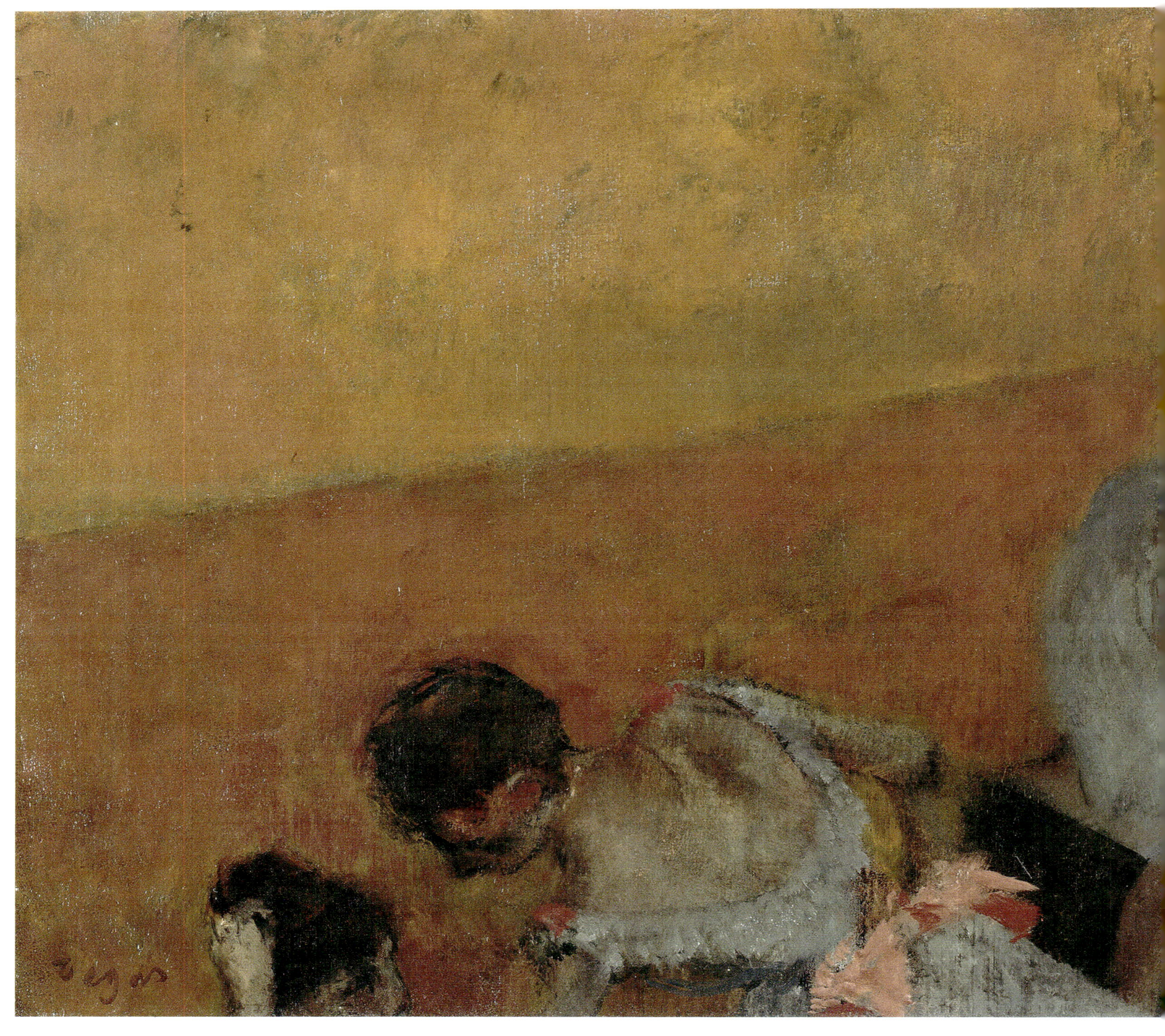

Fig. 40 **Dancers Climbing a Staircase**, 1886–90. Oil on canvas,
39 x 89.5 cm. Musée d'Orsay, Paris, inv. no. RF 1979

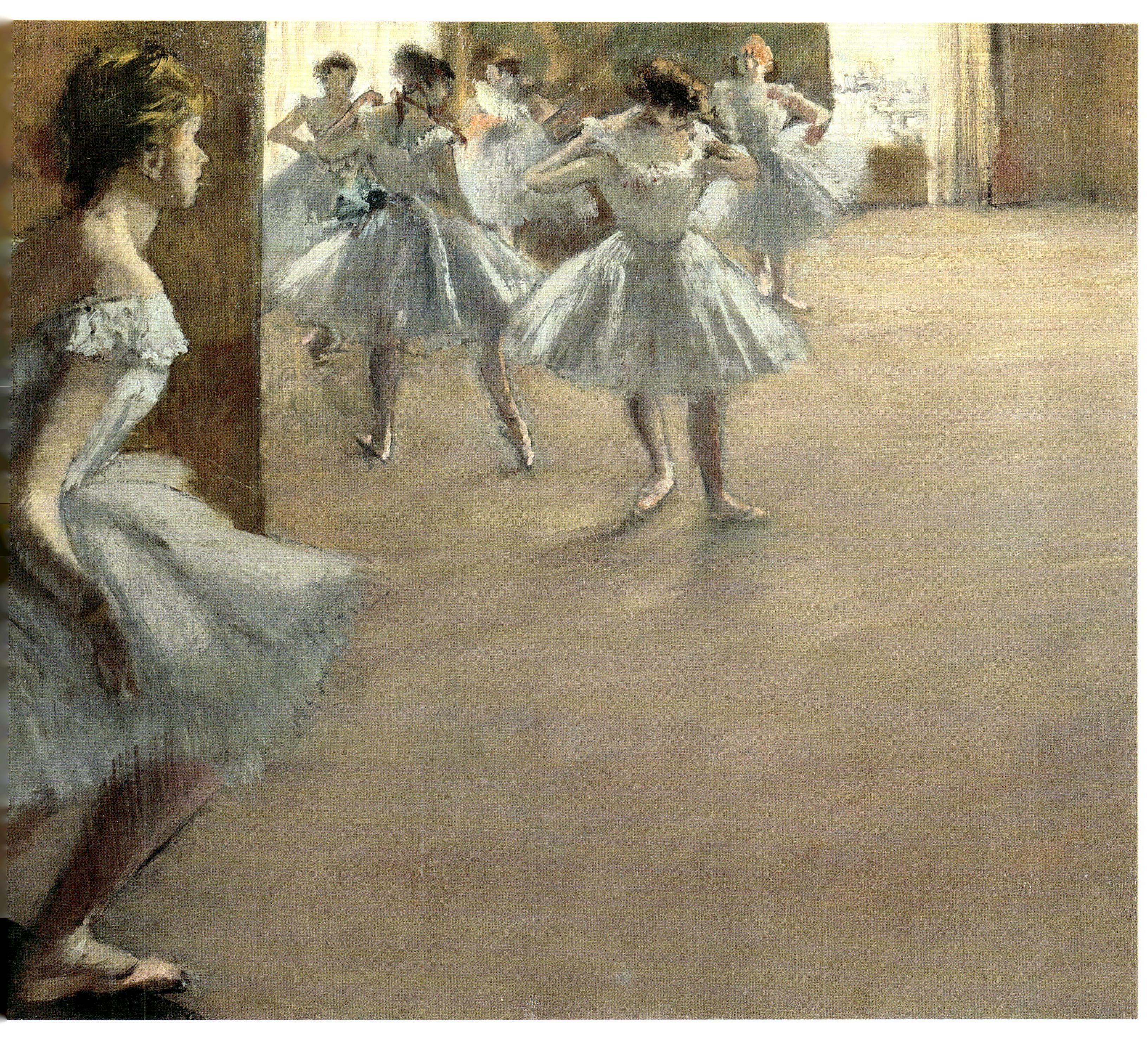

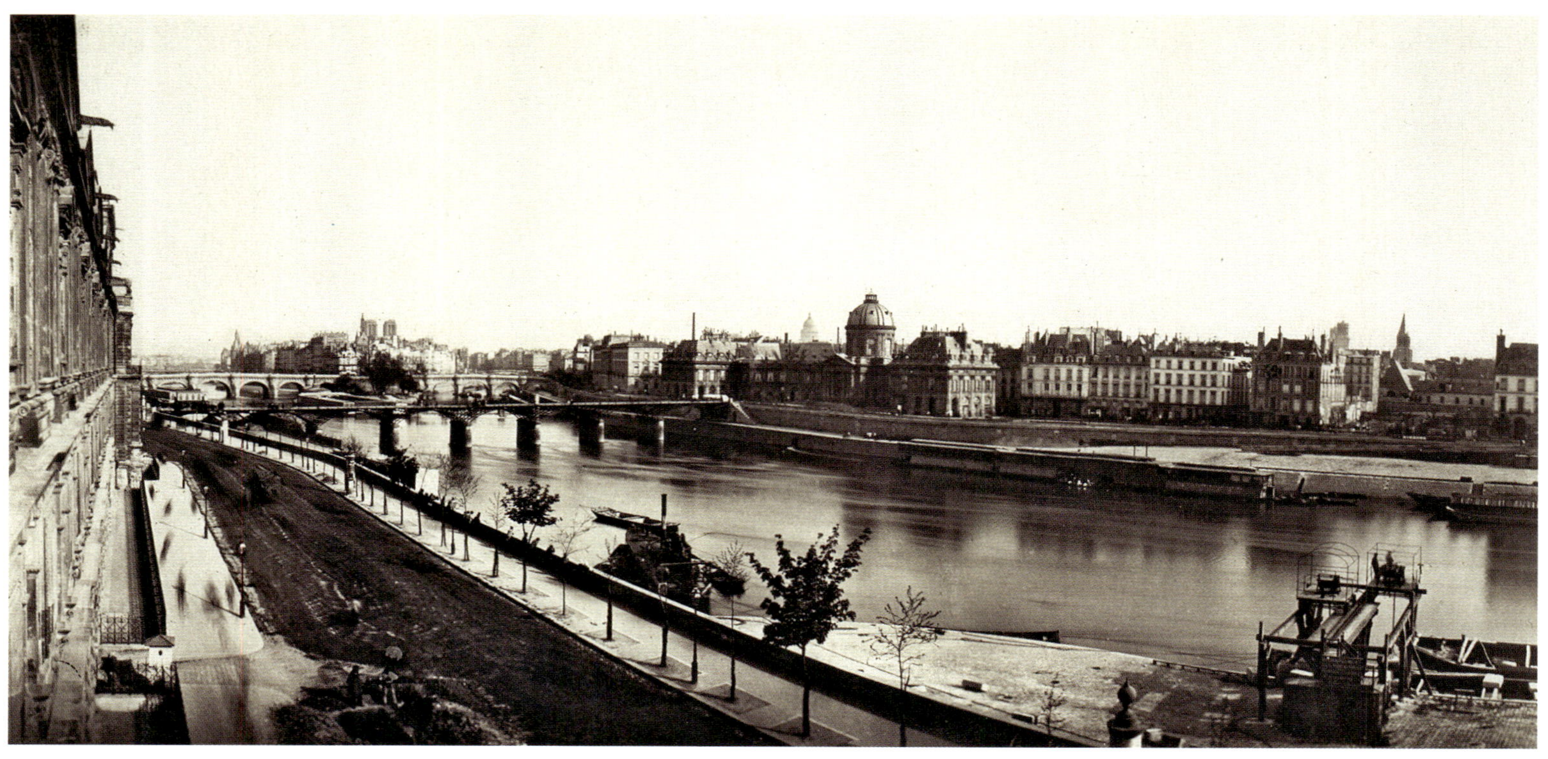

Fig. 41 *Baldus*, Paris, Panorama taken from the Carrousel, undated. Silver print on albumen paper, 13.3 x 28.2 cm. Bibliothèque nationale de France, Paris

amplifies the picture's diagonal design. Here the dancers themselves have also become more active, bending and stretching in the foreground and evidently preparing for an imminent class in the far corner. Where *The Dance Lesson* was sedate, almost soporific in its atmosphere, *Dancers in the Rehearsal Room with a Double Bass* bustles with activity and purposefulness. Again comparison with Champagne's panorama of Paris is difficult to resist, notably in the emphatic mass of Degas's wall where the Louvre played this role in the photograph and in the thrust into depth at right. An even more dynamic print by the celebrated Edouard-Denis Baldus reminds us of the visual vocabulary that was shared by panoramic photographs and the artist's frieze pictures. Baldus specialised in sweeping views of architecture and wide rural or urban spaces, the latter exemplified in his *Paris, Panorama taken from the Carrousel* (fig. 41). Now the viewer is situated close to the south flank of the Louvre, while the Seine and the Left Bank stretch out across the composition. Almost all the lines defining the principal structures in the photograph converge towards a point at extreme left, emphasising the diagonal momentum of the river and the just-perceptible pedestrians walking beside the Louvre. Anticipating Degas's painting is the vibrancy of Baldus's scene, as well as its containment within a rational system that is both energising and harmonious.

As the series of panoramic canvases progressed, Degas's appetite for inventive variants around his central theme seemed to increase. In *Dancers Climbing a Staircase* from the late 1880s (fig. 40), he brazenly invented a foreground staircase that appeared in neither earlier nor later frieze pictures. The result of this sleight of hand is dramatic, propelling the central ballerina upwards into the classroom where she is about to join her colleagues in the middle distance. Behind her, two companions appear less focused on their task even as they unwittingly contribute to the angled flow of figures from lower left to upper right. Still present, however, are the two-toned wall and the windows beside which the class is congregating, the windows' diminished scale reminding us of the extent of this long, narrow chamber. *Before the Ballet* (cat. 45) reverses this compositional scheme and relies less on ingenious structures and tricks of perspective, perhaps reflecting Degas's greater confidence and a more mature mastery of his means. Even the angled wall has lost some of its importance, now largely obscured by the seated dancers in the foreground and reduced to a richly textured single tone. In its place, the artist subtly linked foreground and background along the diagonal line of a raised leg at centre. More subtle too is the role of colour in this sumptuously painted canvas, in which a copper green at right gradually blends into subdued rose and brown passages in the far corner, creating a kind of chromatic momentum. Also given greater emphasis are the four subsidiary dancers at the barre, who are not only visibly exercising but providing a counterweight to their colleagues at right. This manipulation of his pictorial design becomes even clearer as we move from picture to picture in the frieze cycle, while Degas's physical handling of paint and colour follows a parallel trajectory toward his distinctive late style.

Degas's seemingly endless fascination with the panoramic dance scene is exemplified in several works that reached fruition in the 1890s. In both *Dancers in the Green Room* (cat. 39) and *The Rehearsal Room* (cat. 40) he remained as faithful as ever to his basic compositional conceit, luring our attention from one margin of the canvas to the other and thus animating his gathered human cast. With the former, many components of earlier works point to specific links with the past, notably the conspicuous dancer with a dark sash – who first appeared around 1879, in *The Dance Lesson* (cat. 32) – and the angled bass in *Dancers in the Rehearsal Room with a Double Bass* from the Metropolitan Museum of Art (cat. 33). Again with both later works, close study of the canvases and X-ray analysis has established that Degas began painting them in the 1870s and then returned to make extensive revisions of colour, texture and composition almost twenty years later. A rare demonstration of such literal continuity in the work of an artist of Degas's generation, this process also suggests an evolution through time that underlines his continuing engagement with both the series principle and the friezes themselves. Especially eloquent in the latter is the shift in facture from early to late versions. In *Dancers in the Green Room* from the Detroit Institute of Art, smouldering ochre-browns and dense brushwork recall the artist's growing obsession with predecessors such as Veronese, Titian and Rembrandt, while in the Bührle Collection's *The Rehearsal Room* rich, gestural flourishes of paint suggest the openly expressive modes of some of Degas's younger colleagues at the *fin de siècle*. The briefest comparison with an early work in the series, such as *The Dance Lesson*, reminds us forcefully of the distance the artist has travelled, from near-miniature precision to a breadth of touch that would have been unthinkable in the 1870s. All these qualities also have the effect of enlivening the human actors in question, as if they had been sketched at speed or captured by a camera that was unable to focus in the available light. Like the blurred pedestrians in Baldus's *Paris, Panorama from the Carrousel*, Degas's figures seem more – not less – energised by their imperfect finish.

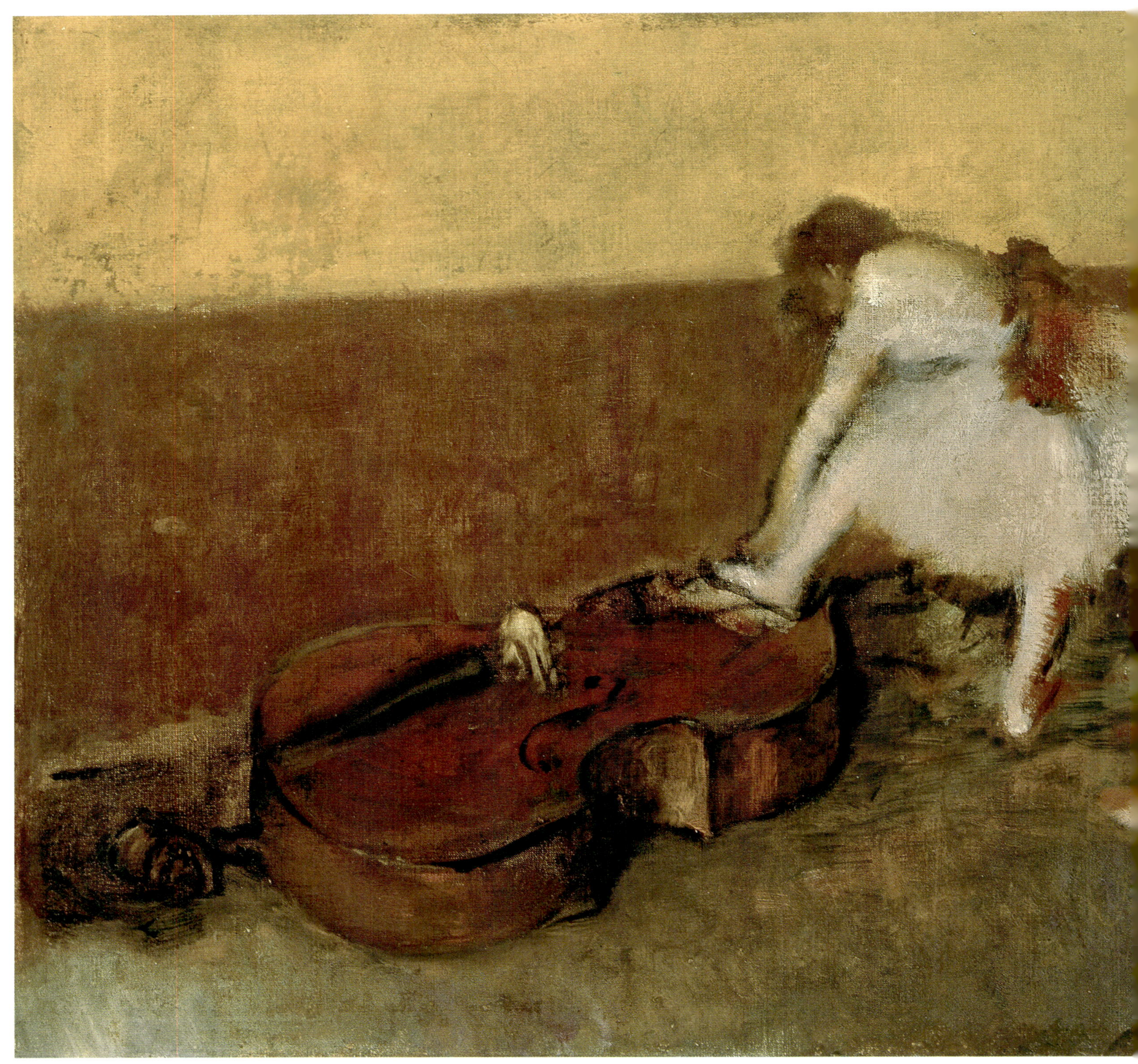

39

Dancers in the Green Room
c. 1880–94
Oil on canvas, 41.3 x 87.6 cm
Detroit Institute of Arts.
City of Detroit Purchase

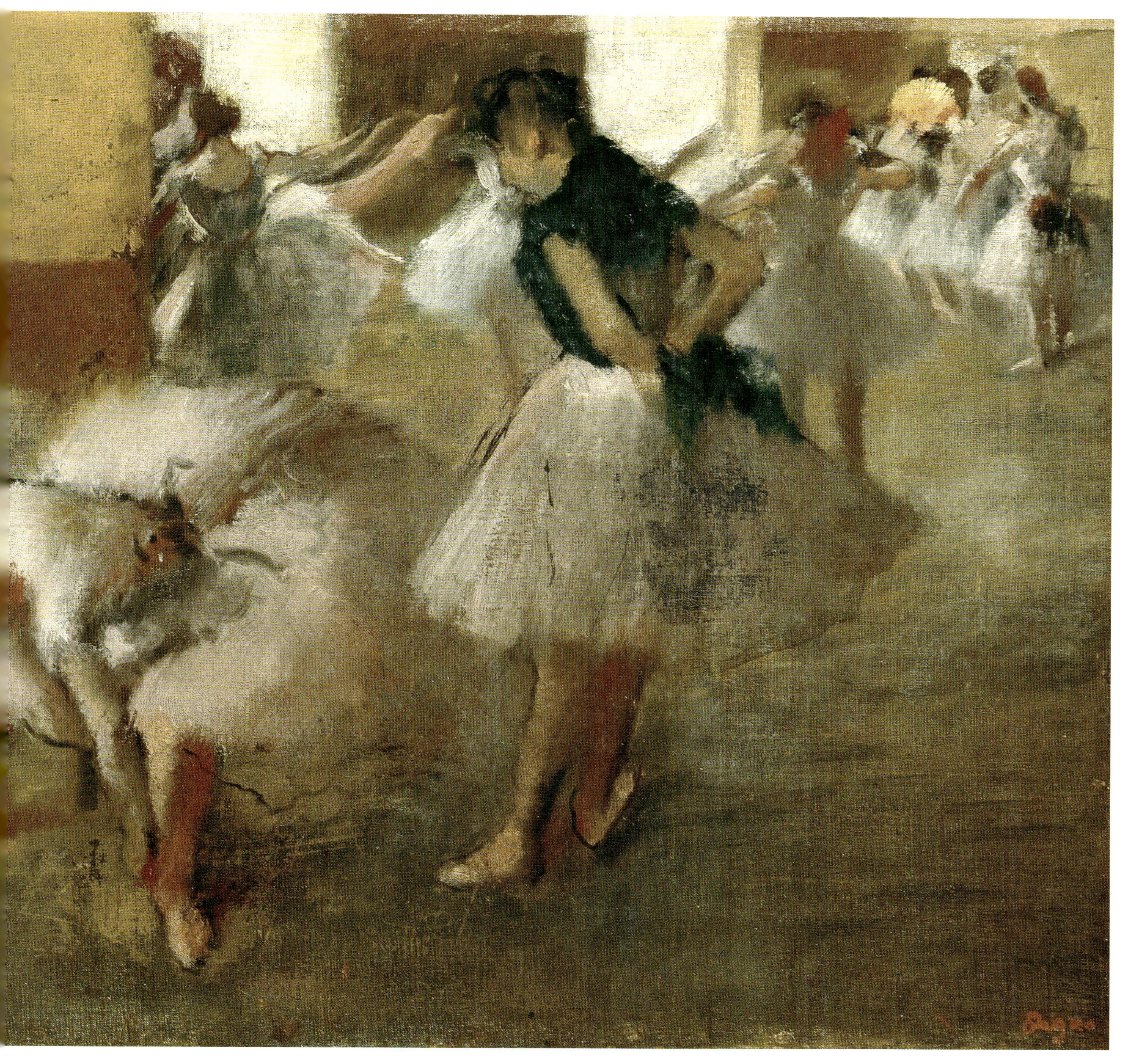

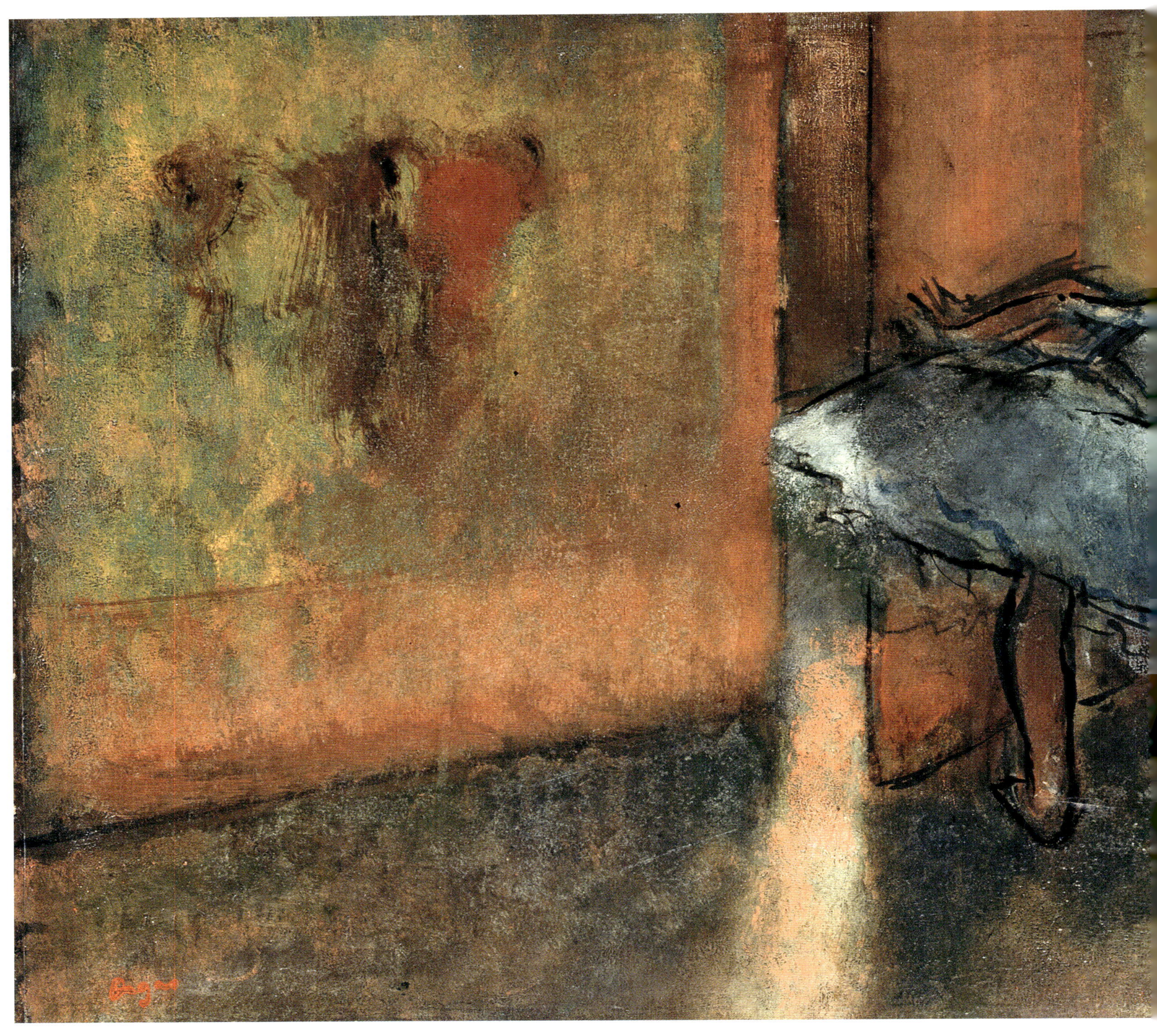

40

Dancers in the Foyer
c. 1889–1905
Oil on canvas, 41.5 x 92 cm
Foundation E. G. Bührle
Collection, Zurich

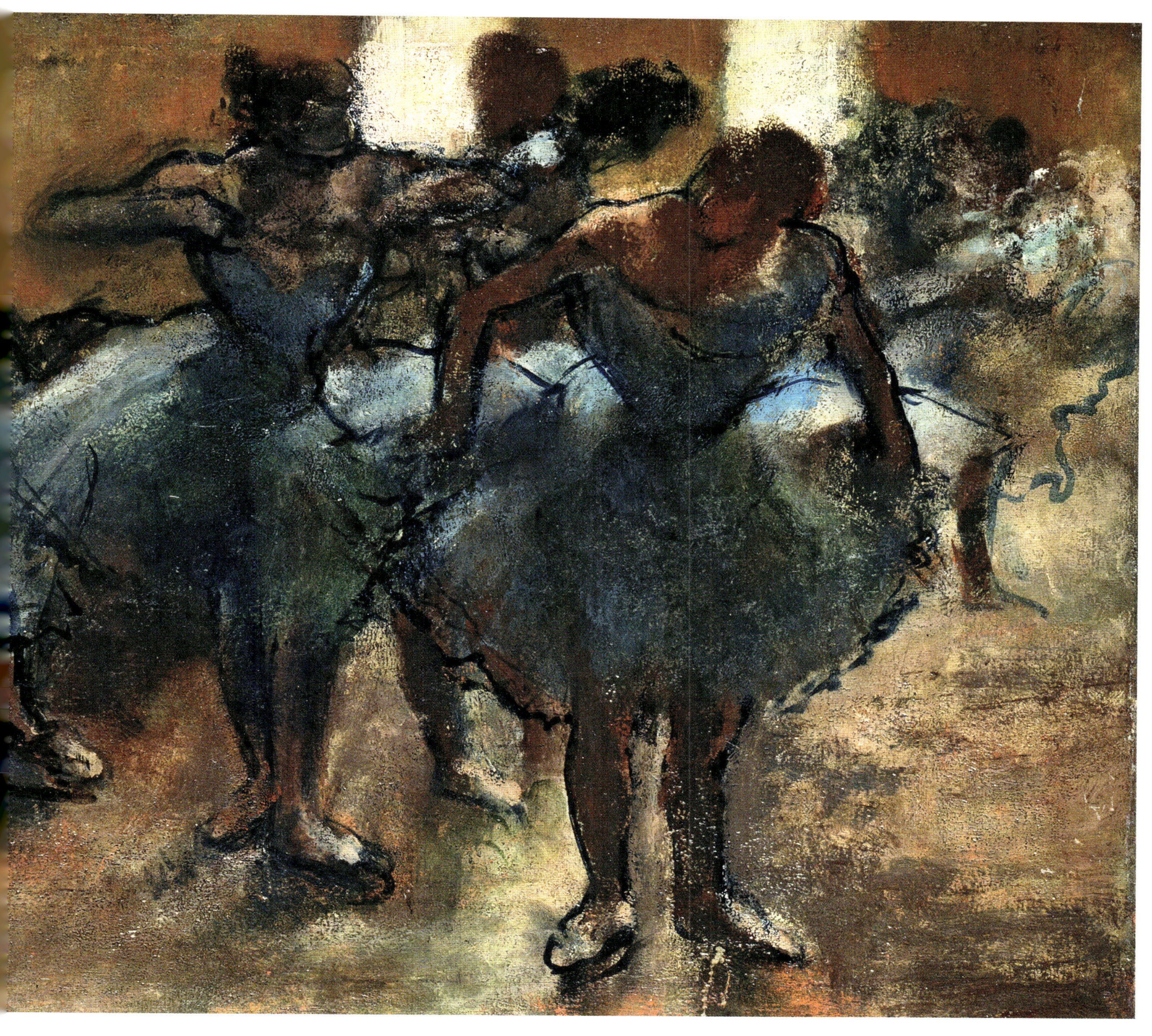

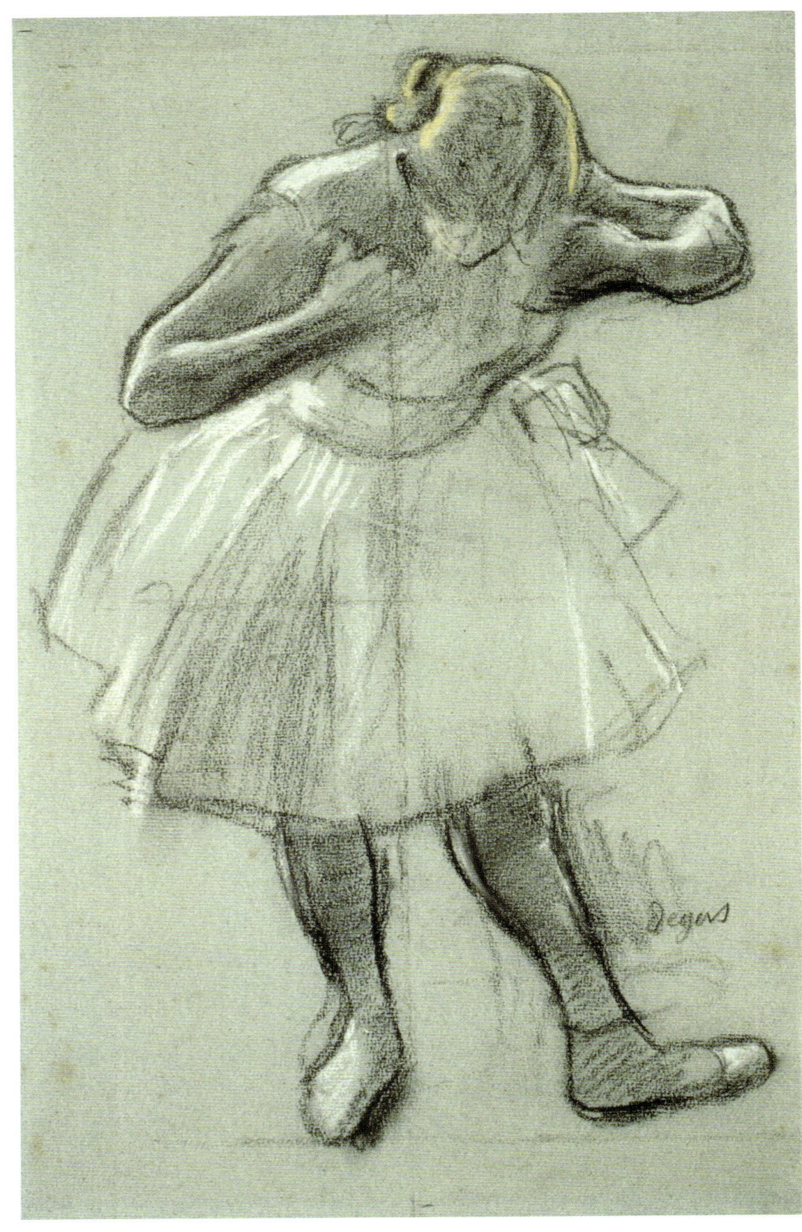

41

Dancer Bending Forward
1874–79
Charcoal with stumping,
heightened with white and
yellow pastel with stumping,
on blue laid paper ruled
with charcoal,
46 x 30 cm
The Art Institute of Chicago.
Mr and Mrs Martin A. Ryerson
Collection

These two late canvases, like the entire cycle of frieze paintings, were still painstakingly built up from drawings that Degas accumulated during sessions with dancers posed in his studio or at the Opéra itself. Scores of sheets of this kind survive today, offering us further insight into the repetitive processes that ran through his two-decade-long cycle of pictures. One group of such drawings represents the figure of a ballerina facing to our right who raises her arms and appears to be adjusting her shoulder-straps. *Dancer Bending Forward* (cat. 41) from the Art Institute of Chicago is an unusually large study of this kind that has been linked to the Musée d'Orsay's *Dancers Climbing a Staircase*.[57] This individual stands to right of centre in the painting, her left leg advanced and head tilted downwards slightly to her right. Broadly and rapidly executed in charcoal in the drawing, the figure speaks of an early encounter with a model as Degas's exploration of this pose was in its preliminary stages. Already

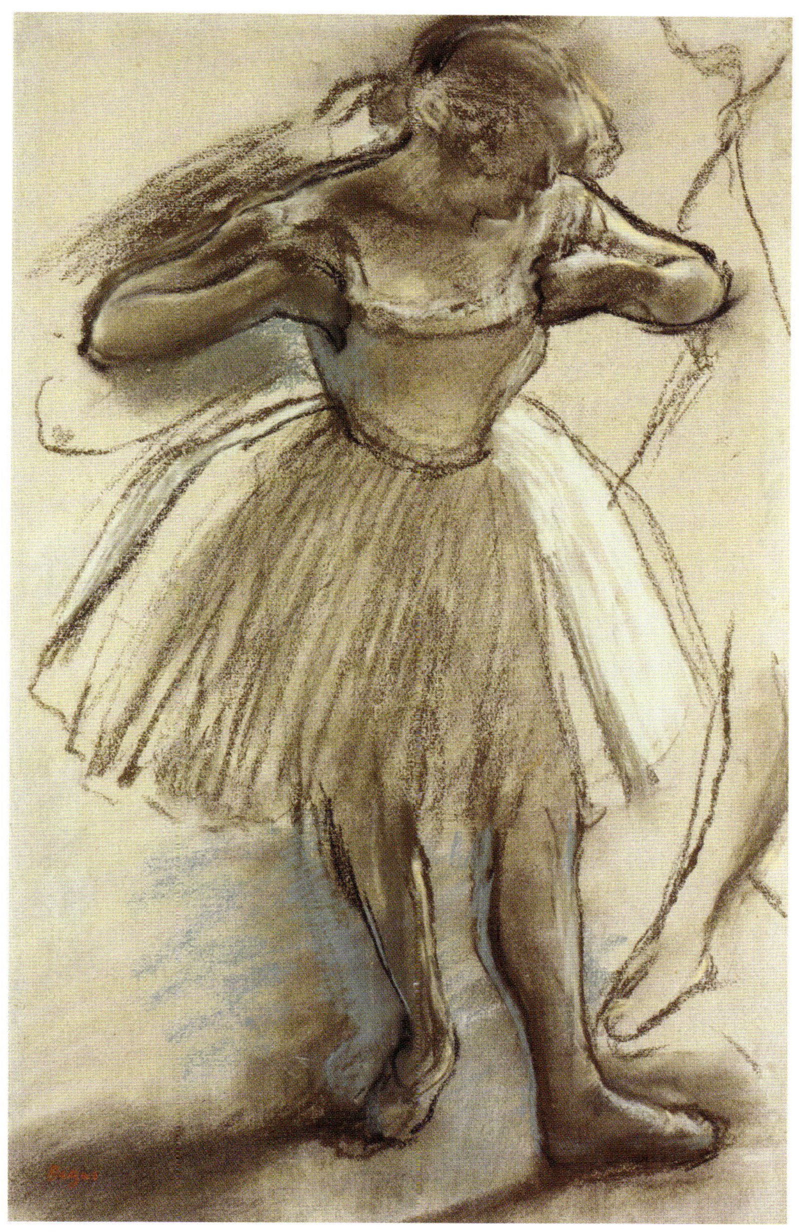

anticipating the sunlight flooding into the classroom from the background
windows, the artist has highlighted her body and costume at several points
in white chalk or pastel. An even more developed sheet returns to the same
challenge. Entitled *Ballet Girl* (cat. 42) and owned by the Rhode Island School
of Design, this magnificent study records further refinements to Degas's
conception. Multiple modifications have been made to the position of the
dancer's limbs and head – the latter now turned to the left – while her overall
stance appears to be finally resolved. Touches of pale pastel were again added
as the figure was further defined in this complex process, covering earlier
statements of her physique on the same sheet and developing a sense of her
bodily volume. One side effect of Degas's approach is that the young woman
in this sheet seems to be moving, his accumulated silhouettes hinting at before
and after positions of her body in the gradual development of the image.

42

Ballet Girl
c. 1886–88
Pastel on blue paper
(now faded),
45.7 x 26.5 cm
Museum of Art, Rhode Island
School of Design, Providence.
Gift of Mrs Gustav Radeke

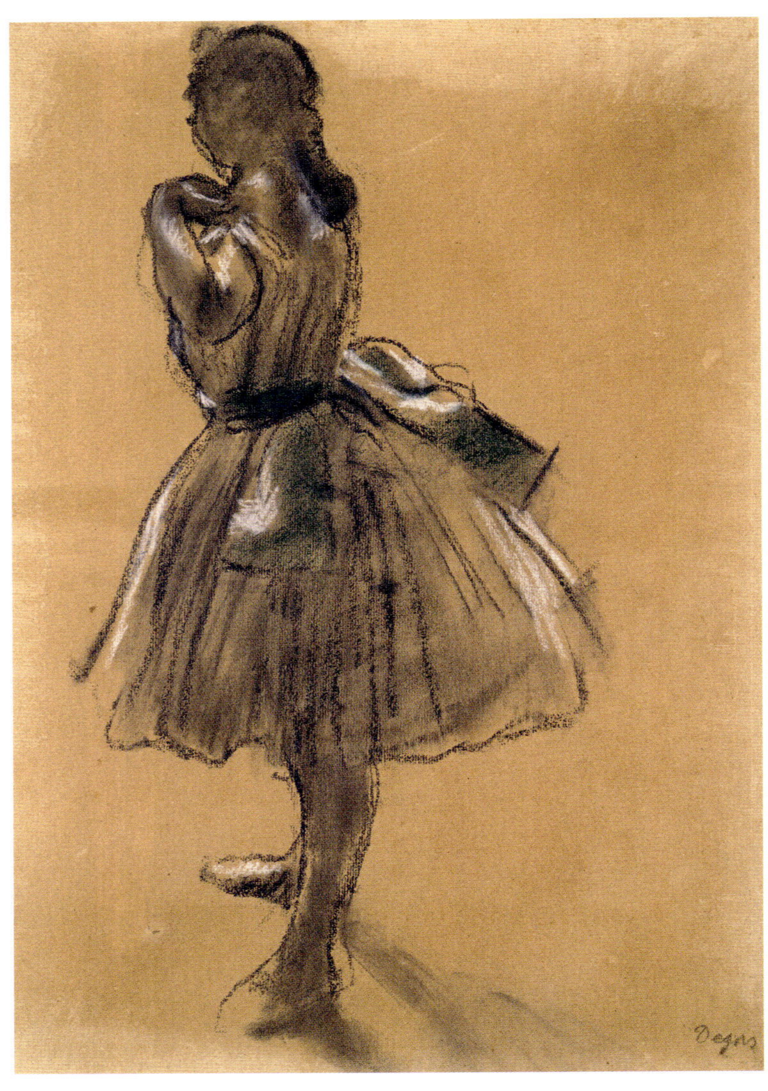

43

**Dancer Adjusting
Her Dress**
c. 1885
Charcoal heightened
with pastel on paper,
61.5 x 46.3 cm
Portland Art Museum,
Oregon. Bequest of
Winslow B. Ayer

The suggestion of movement is further extended in *Dancer Adjusting Her Dress* (cat. 43), where a model with a now-familiar physique stands sideways to the picture plane but here looks towards the left. Boldly summarising this statuesque individual in broad sweeps of line, Degas has either asked the girl to turn on a central axis or has himself moved around her as if completing his spatial tour. The sense that we have been thoroughly introduced to this distinctive pose is palpable, as is the implication that the artist – as with his approach to the *Little Dancer Aged Fourteen* – had resolved to record her somewhat more broadly and in an ever more animated fashion in three dimensions. Using the assembled sheets in the same way that he evidently used the drawings of Marie van Goethem, Degas could plausibly have drafted a wax sculpture of the girl with raised arms from these graphic accounts. A strikingly similar model appears in the more complex study known as *Dancers* (cat. 44), in which the artist drew her several times and added secondary sketches of variant poses and somewhat more elevated arms. Pushing beyond the Rhode Island pastel in a technical sense, this figure seems vibrant with energy, almost suggesting several young women advancing

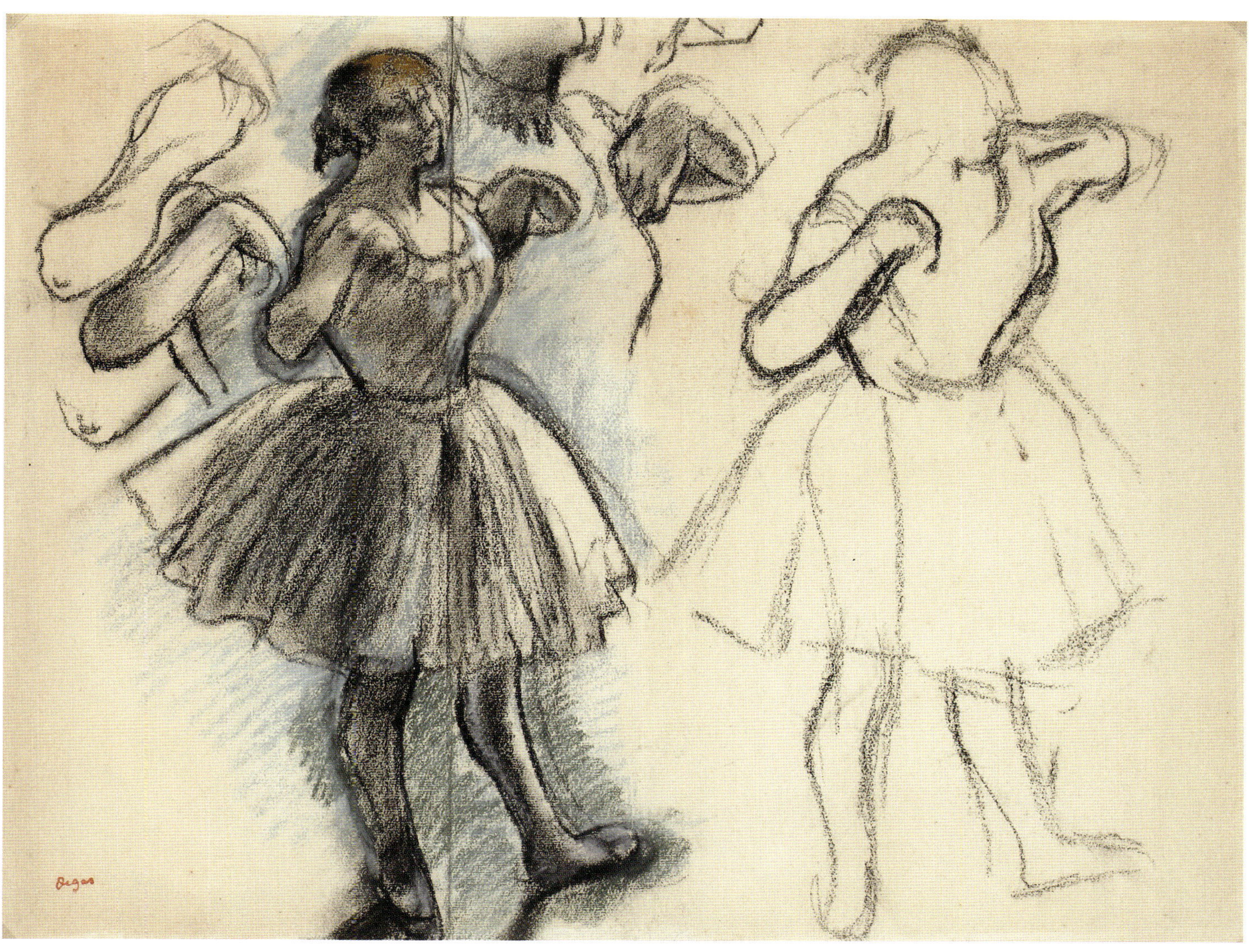

across the classroom in unison. This was presumably part of Degas's intention, although something of his career-long alertness to the definitively active lives of dancers is also embedded in the sheet. Possibly evident, too, is Degas's awareness of the sequential photography of Etienne-Jules Marey and Eadweard Muybridge, where new modes of energising the depicted body were suggested to artists and photographers alike.

A pose comparable to – but not identical with – that in *Dancers* appears at the centre of the Bührle Foundation's *Dancers in the Foyer* (cat. 40), a significantly later canvas in which a descendant of *Ballet Girl* is shown more frontally. Especially instructive here is the richly worked surface of the painting itself, evoking the way in which Degas's brushes have been used not merely to establish areas of colour but also to 'draw' hundreds of fine, dark strokes both under and over his swathes of golds, ochres and greens. This progress from drawing to painting then back again is vividly illuminated in the remarkable charcoal study *Three Dancers in Tights* (cat. 47), a composition that may broadly echo an earlier stage in the evolution of the foreground group in the Bührle canvas. With firmly stated contours and extensive internal

44

Dancers
c. 1885
Charcoal and pastel
on paper,
47 x 62 cm
Private collection

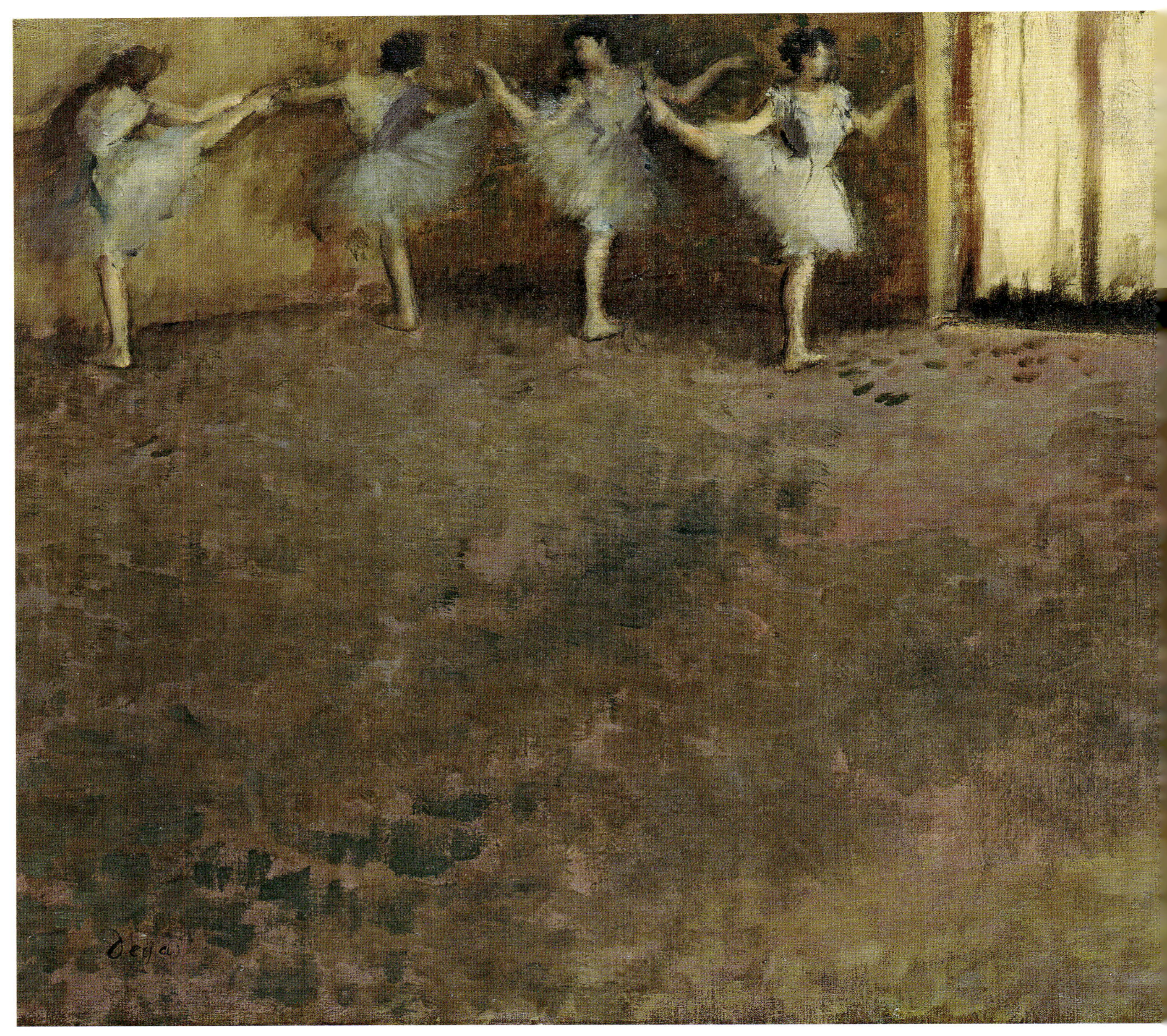

45

Before the Ballet
c. 1890–92
Oil on canvas,
40 x 89 cm
National Gallery of Art,
Washington. Widener
Collection, 1942.9.19

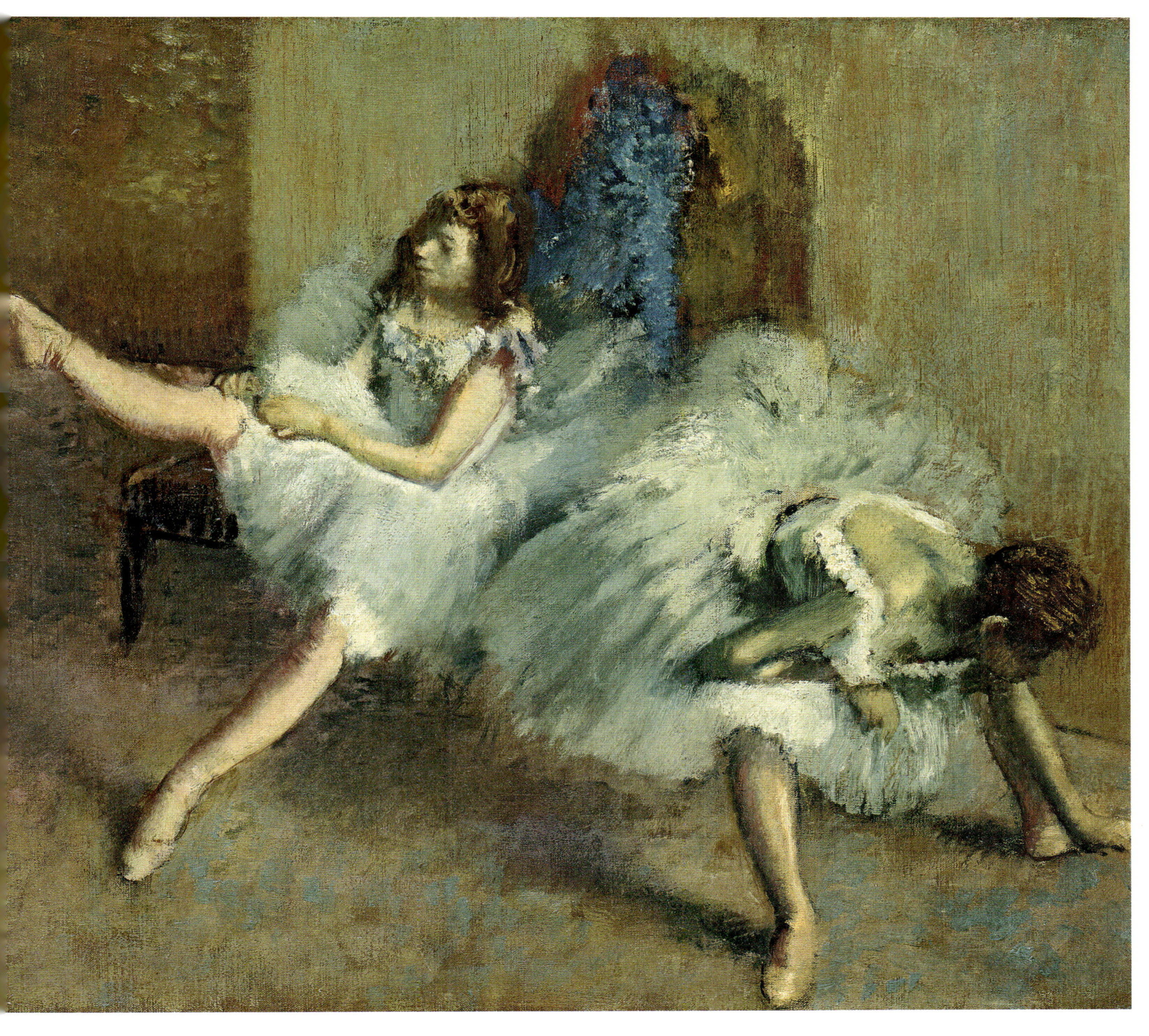

46

The Rehearsal Room
c. 1905
Charcoal and pastel on tracing
paper mounted on wove paper,
46.4 x 101.6 cm
Lent by the Toledo Museum
of Art. Gift of Mrs C. Lockhart
McKelvy

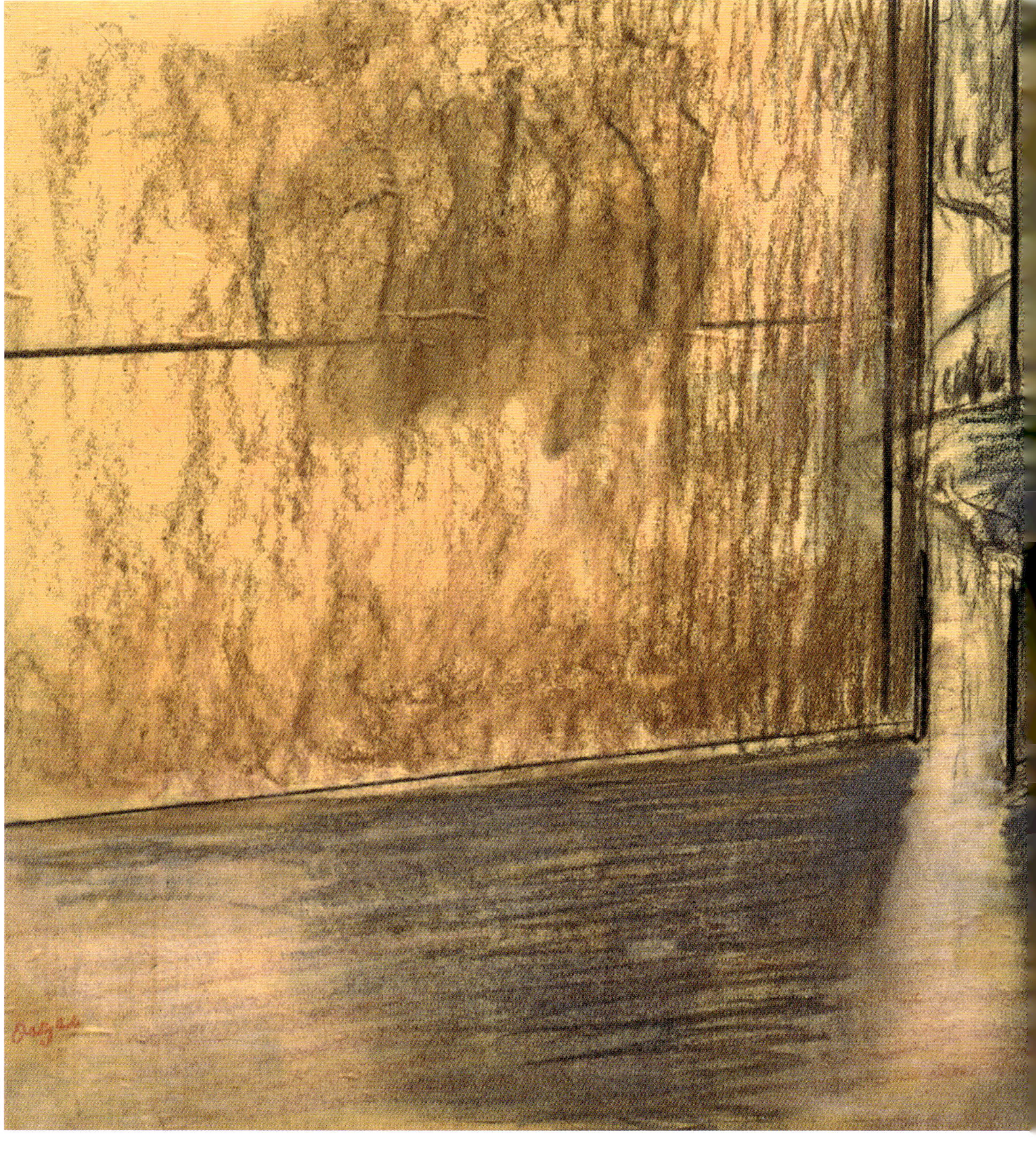

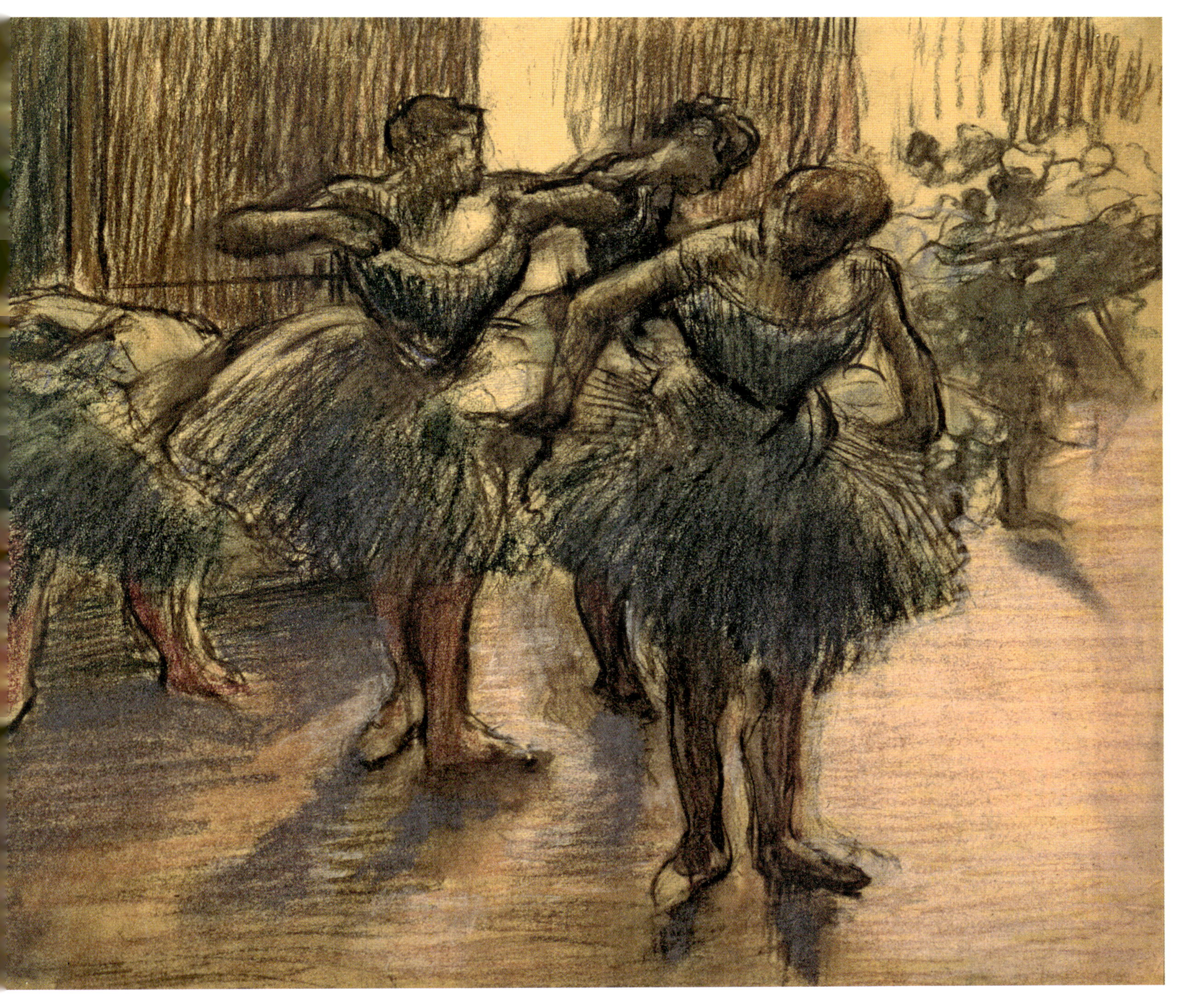

Three Dancers in Tights
c. 1892–95
Charcoal on tracing paper,
laid down, with traces
of blue paint on the
right-hand figures,
47.7 x 38.5 cm
Collection of Jean Bonna,
Geneva

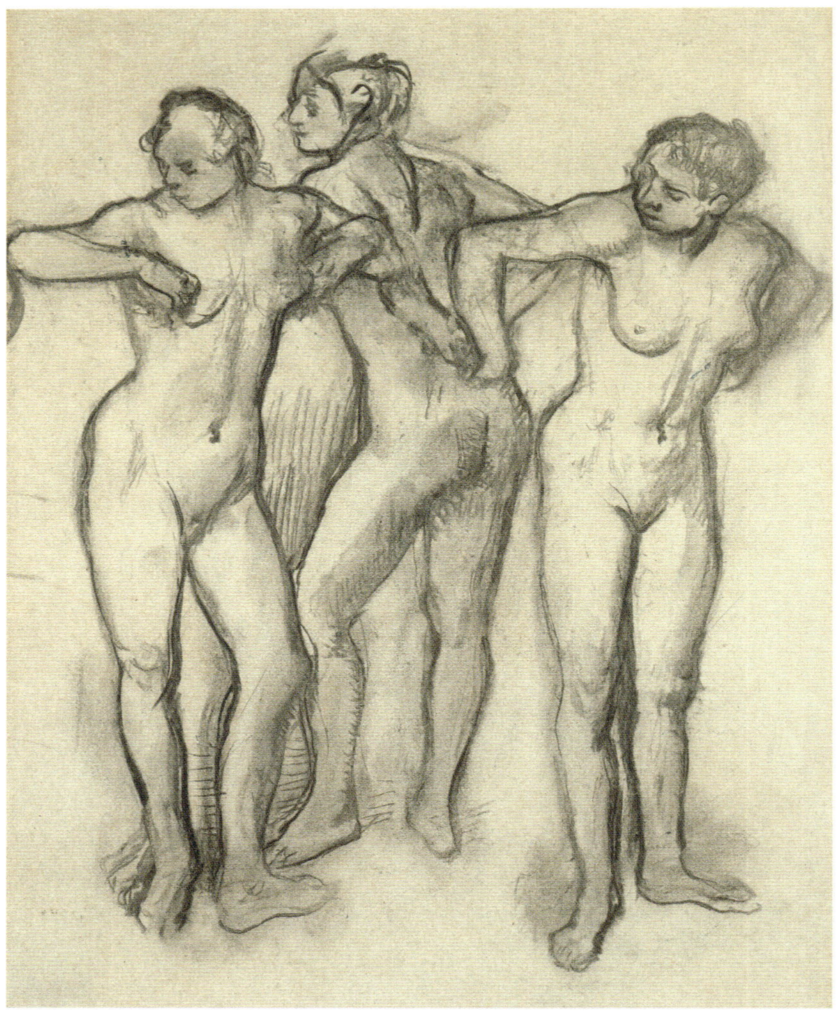

modelling, these athletic figures have a refinement that gradually gave way
to the breadth of representation that dominates the later friezes, such as
Dancers in the Foyer. Distantly recalling his training as a young draughtsman,
Three Dancers in Tights reminds us of the artist's continuing mastery of line
and form in later life. It also exemplifies Degas's capacity for simultaneously
reaching back to the classical tradition and forward to a more reflective time
when he could explain that his muscular, athletic ballerinas were 'a pretext
for depicting movement'.

At the turn of the century and even beyond, Degas was still capable of
introducing startling new possibilities into his frieze series, notably several
that revisited the relationship between drawing and dynamic composition.
In a fascinating hybrid form that appears around this date, a group of works
in charcoal and pastel on paper – made on the same scale as his frieze
canvases – allowed him to suggest rapidly captured ballerina-figures in their
shadowy exercise spaces with a distinctive graphic urgency. Again consulting
studies of individual ballerinas that might be used in more than one work,
Degas typically re-created such figures afresh as he proceeded and instilled
them with new vibrancy. The scintillating *The Rehearsal Room* (cat. 46), for
example, bristles with energy, from the busily self-absorbed women adjusting

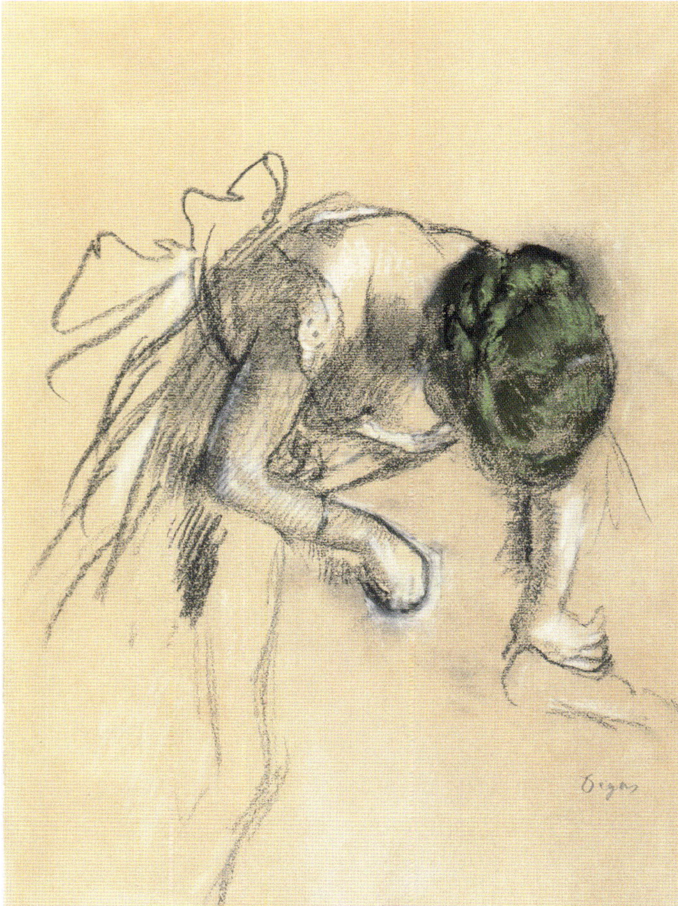

themselves before class begins to the vigorously textured walls and floor that
surround them. This broad handling is nevertheless carefully controlled: the
finely delineated structure of the classroom itself reminds us of the deliberation
with which the artist devised such compositions, as well as their probable
origin in a specific practice room known to him. Striking also is the role of the
blank wall at left, which occupies almost half the rectangle and seems to exist
purely to emphasise the left–right trajectory of our gaze. Closely echoing
Dancers in the Foyer (cat. 40) in oil on canvas from the Bührle Foundation,
the Toledo pastel may have been preparatory to it or perhaps simply conceived
as a parallel creation. Vividly evident in this pairing is the interplay between
expressive line, contrasted colour and energetic mass, uniting the figures and
allowing the artist to articulate the muscular individuals who posed for him
within the visual architecture of his pictures. Far from the serenity of the stage,
these individuals flex their broad shoulders and adjust their massive skirts,
almost merging into a single energetic organism. Comparable in its vigour but
original in another sense is the extraordinary *Frieze of Dancers* (fig. 42), one
of Degas's greatest – if most oblique – tributes to balletic animation. Made in
uncertain circumstances, this canvas is perhaps best understood as a homage
to the renowned frescoes that Degas had seen as a young man in Italy, here

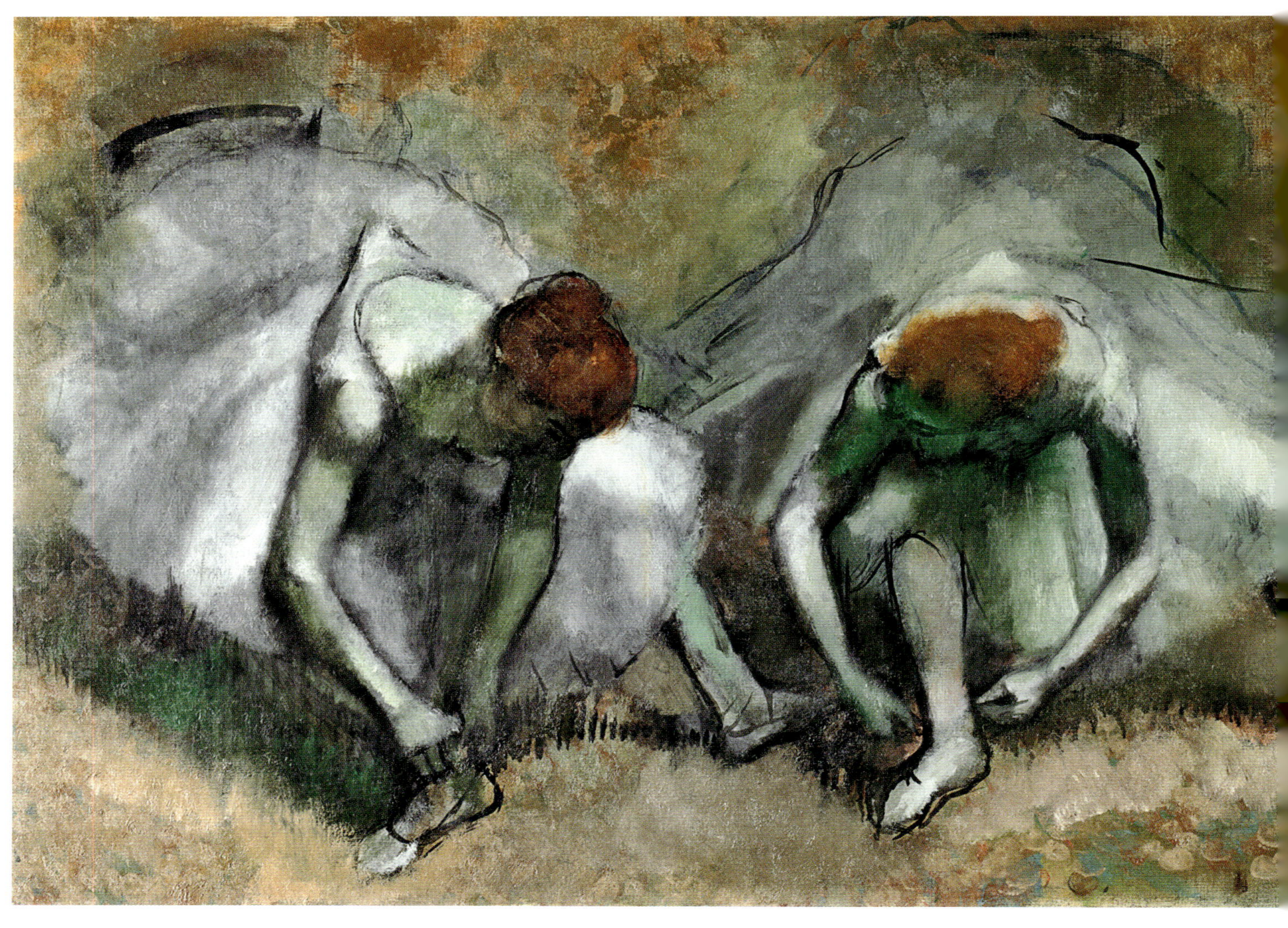

Fig. 42 **Frieze of Dancers**, *c.* 1895, Oil on fabric, 70 x 200.5 cm.
The Cleveland Museum of Art, Gift of the Hanna Fund, 1946.83

transposed to the more pedestrian world of *fin-de-siècle* Paris. In contrast
to most homages of this kind, however, *Frieze of Dancers* impresses us with
its simplicity; a single figure is shown four times, as if the artist had adopted
a succession of viewpoints while moving around his posed model. Recalling
the intricate process by which the *Little Dancer Aged Fourteen* was made, this
painting invites us to follow Degas's progress in our imaginations, reliving his
encounter with a restless young woman and adopting the role of the roving
film camera so beloved of modern movie-makers. In another sense, the model
in *Frieze of Dancers* underlines Degas's loyalty to certain thematic devices
throughout much of his career. Variants of a seated ballerina resting in a
classroom, for example, had appeared in several of his earlier frieze pictures
and survived into his last. Why this attachment to a relatively minor figure?
As so often, such an actor played several roles in the broader drama, from a
quietly poignant reminder of ballet's demands on the human body to a vital
component in the dynamism of the larger composition. In this second sense,

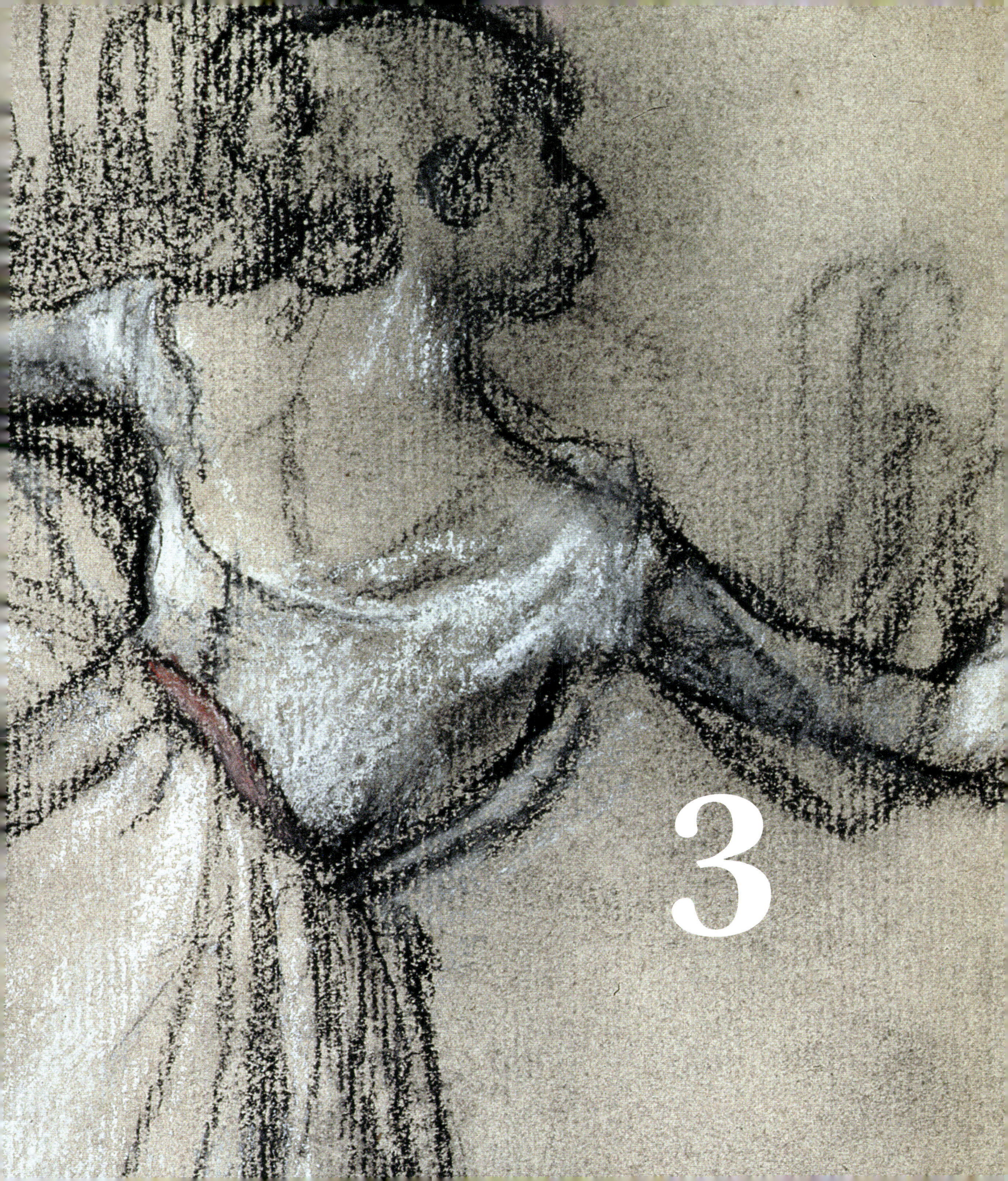
3

THE HUMAN ANIMAL

*...Do the same subject
over again, ten times,
a hundred times.
Nothing in art must
seem to be chance...
not even movement*

Edgar Degas, 1881[1]

By the mid-1880s, Degas had become an artist with a national – and increasingly, international – reputation, as well as a highly distinctive repertoire of subject-matter. The ballet was widely recognised as his signature theme, although some admirers were already suggesting that it had a significance beyond the delights of performances at the Paris Opéra. At the time of the fifth Impressionist exhibition, Joris-Karl Huysmans wrote an extended appreciation of Degas's art that was partly focused on his canvas known as *The Dance Lesson* (cat. 32).[2] 'What truth! What life!' he exclaimed of this picture, arguing that it revealed the 'perspicacity of an analyst both cruel and subtle'; Degas's 'observation is so precise', he noted, that 'a physiologist could make a curious study of the organism' of each of these aspiring ballerinas.[3] Summarising the dance works in the exhibition, Huysmans asserted that Degas's eye was 'curiously haunted and preoccupied by the figure in movement'.[4]

The larger sense that Degas's art was based on rigorous, first-hand examination of the world around him was by now a persistent critical trope: one writer praised the artist's 'scrupulous study' of his models, another admired his 'rare truthfulness,' and Huysmans himself noted the 'absolute reality' of Degas's depictions of dancers and other subjects.[5] It was again Huysmans who took these ideas further than his colleagues and instinctively related them to the wider preoccupations of their age. In a favourable comparison with his literary heroes, the Goncourt brothers, Huysmans claimed that Degas was alone among his artist-contemporaries in capturing 'the most ephemeral sensations, the most fugitive of refinements and nuances'.[6] In yet another vivid phrase, Huysmans declared that Degas had chosen to represent 'the exterior of the human animal, in the environment in which it operates, to show the movements, the positions, the gestures, the workings of its physiognomy'.[7]

This extraordinary and apparently intuitive account of Degas was offered by one of the most original minds of the younger generation and still remains a useful corrective in our own times. Huysmans appears to have had little personal contact with Degas, even as he acquired pictures by the artist for his own collection and continued to eulogise him in print for a number of years.[8] All the more remarkable, therefore, is the fact that Huysmans sensed larger purposes behind these ballet pictures, purposes that Degas himself was to acknowledge to varying extents on subsequent occasions. In separate conversations, as we have seen, Degas is said to have told George Moore that 'the dancer is only a pretext for drawing' and insisted to Walter Sickert that he may have 'too often considered woman as an animal'.[9] Degas's later remark to Louisine Havemeyer that 'depicting movement' was the true object of his ballet pastels and paintings was made more than two decades after Huysmans's review, but it again suggests the complexity of the artist's motivation and its links with issues beyond the immediate world of contemporary art.

49

Little Girl Practising at the Barre
c. 1878–80
Black chalk and graphite,
heightened with white chalk
on pink laid paper
31 x 29.3 cm
Lent by the Metropolitan
Museum of Art, New York.
H. O. Havemeyer Collection.
Bequest of Mrs H. O. Havemeyer,
1929 (29.100.943)

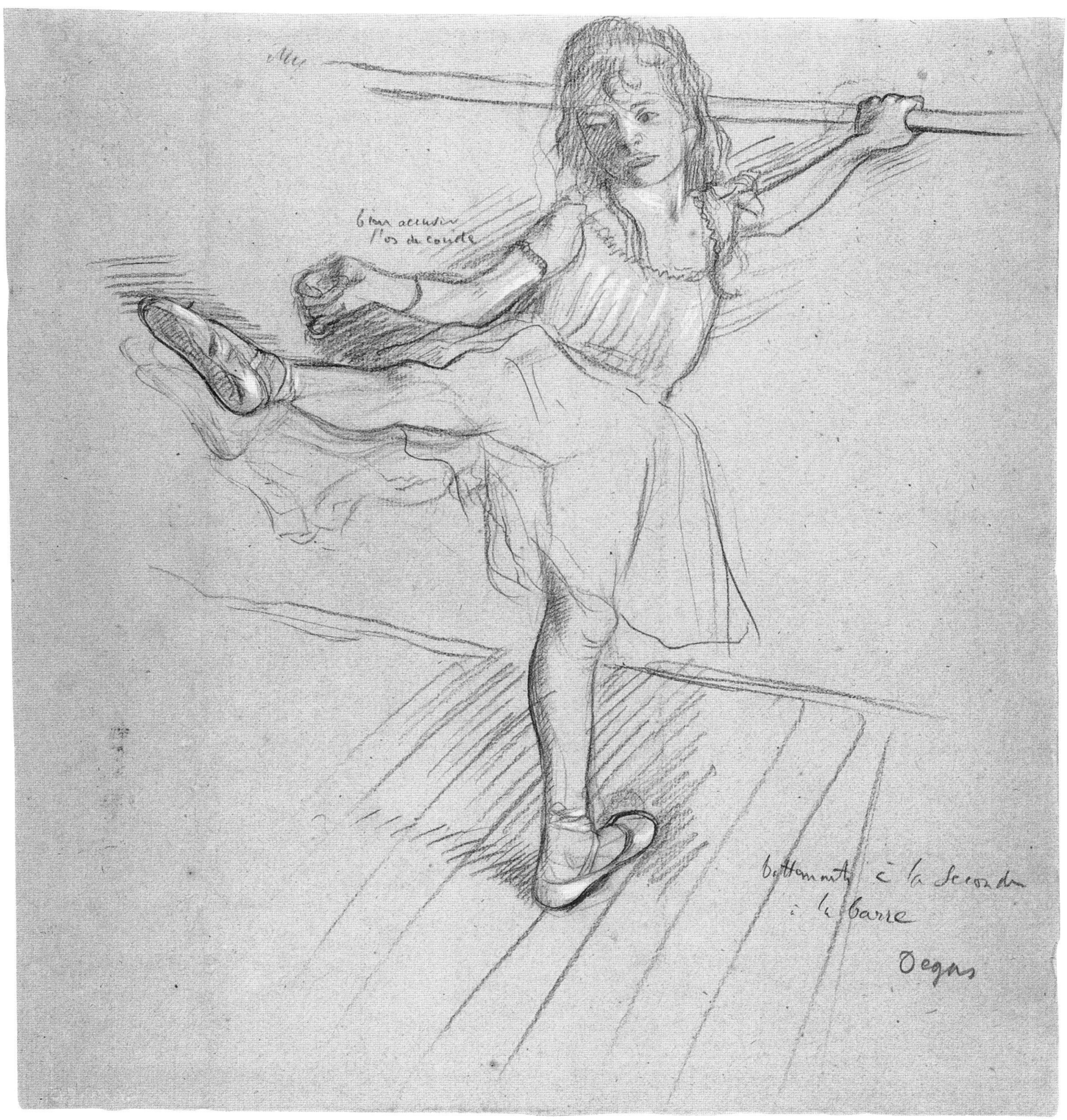

bien accuser
l'os du coude
battements à la seconde
à la barre
Degas

In exploring this little-studied territory today, we can take advantage of a rich trove of material that was known only in part or not at all to those outside Degas's immediate circle. This includes details of his public and private involvement with the world of the Opéra and its personnel, day-by-day accounts of Degas's attendance at dance performances, and recollections of his acquaintance with Opéra ballet teachers, musicians and the dancers themselves. Better understood, too, are the circumstances in which his ballet pictures were conceived and executed, the identity of his models, and even the rooms in which they trained and rehearsed. Spanning the most refined spectacle at one extreme and the mechanics of the classroom and studio at the other, this substantial body of evidence contrasts with more limited accounts of Degas's specific interests in matters beyond the arts, such as those hinted at by Huysmans. Here again, modern research has begun to open up the subject of Degas's broader intellectual milieu, elucidating his political views, his literary tastes and skills, his passion for music and his alertness to science and technical innovation: in effect, 'the artist's mind'.[10] Personally, Degas emerges as both a well-educated and well-read individual, enjoying the company of friends who were poets and librettists, novelists and engineers, composers and administrators, while cultivating his own curiosity about such topics as the history of physiognomy and the latest innovations in photography.

A small drawing that was probably made by Degas before the 1880 exhibition reveals something of this enquiring mind at work. In *Little Girl Practising at the Barre* (cat. 49), his attention was almost entirely focused on the young pupil herself, with just a few lines indicating her relationship to the surrounding space. As he proceeded, Degas used gentle strokes of black chalk to draft her torso, head and limbs, followed by crisper, darker lines as the girl's definitive form emerged. Degas's 'singular exactitude' – in Huysmans's phrase – was soon evident in the meticulous rendering of body positions that are unique to the ballet, such as the dancer's diminutive left foot turned sharply out in its miniature satin shoe and the right foot 'pointed' to continue the line of her raised leg. Less satisfactory, perhaps, is the young model's over-large head and rather shapeless torso, which is barely articulated in the waist and shoulders; Degas may have been unused to drawing children in these circumstances. But the implication that he intended to learn from this experience, or anticipated the making of a more developed pastel or oil painting that would feature the same young dancer, is supported by a number of factors. Above the right arm a note reads 'bien accuser l'os du coude' ('emphasise the elbow bone') and near his signature Degas wrote the technical term for the girl's actions; 'battements à la seconde à la barre'. No finished picture of this model seems to have been attempted, however, though he drew several other child-ballerinas around the same date and added these sheets to his portfolios, which already represented a personal archive to be consulted as further challenges presented themselves. In time these studies were joined by hundreds of others, eventually recording dancers of all ages and in widely varying positions, the majority of whom did not appear in his completed compositions. Had Huysmans been aware of these assembled studies, he would surely have been further inclined to admire the 'analytical perspicacity' of this artist who was always 'haunted by the human figure in movement'.

Two characteristics of *Little Girl Practising at the Barre* and scores of comparable studies take us beyond the charming particularity of Degas's young ballerinas. Everything about this drawing tells us that it was created at first hand, from 'life', as Degas worked directly and rapidly in front of his delicate model. We are also made vividly aware that the young dancer was actually moving while Degas was drawing her, at least for some of the time. 'Battements' are defined as a series of rapid, disciplined upward 'kicks' that form part of a ballerina's daily exercise, intended to stretch and strengthen the body. While Degas must have watched the child demonstrate this procedure, it seems unlikely that she was in continuous movement as he attempted to draw her. It is equally clear that she could not have held her right leg rigidly in this position beyond a few seconds when he began to draw; the effort of remaining motionless in such a pose might have defeated a seasoned adult. The extreme exertion involved in this session – as well as the shifting dynamic between artist and model – has surely left its traces in Degas's clustered lines and multiple contours around the limb in question, where we sense both the tremulousness of the girl and his struggle with the self-imposed task. On a miniature scale, *Little Girl Practising at the Barre* thus encapsulates one of the principal challenges that Degas faced as a dance artist: to record in fixed strokes of chalk and charcoal, pastel and paint, a subject that was ultimately defined by its transience. In this drawing and others of an even more ambitious kind, he pursued a goal that he knew to be ultimately unattainable, grasping at what Huysmans called 'the most ephemeral sensations, the most fugitive refinements and nuances'. Caught up in the rush of events and an endlessly shifting and dissolving panorama of bodies and limbs as he attempted to draw dancers in mid-movement, Degas found his skills – and the nature of drawing itself – taxed to their limits. In the relatively modest case of *Little Girl Practising at the Barre*, he was probably able to achieve some control over the outcome by drawing the model in circumstances of his own choosing. Patient training of his eye and modifications to his working practices must also have contributed to the artist's readiness for such an enterprise, but the self-contradictory nature of his ambition remained.

More than a decade of such activity had now left behind a mass of annotated drawings, letters and other documents that sporadically recorded Degas's use of dancer-models, from virtual beginners to major *étoiles*. At a time when the Opéra classrooms were out of bounds to all but the most privileged or well connected, he clearly relied for the most part on dancers who posed for him in his studio or elsewhere on a frequent basis. Around 1867, for example, it had been the sensational Eugènie Fiocre, the young star of such Opéra productions as *La Source* and *Néméa*; several years later Degas added the name of the obscure Joséphine Gaujelin to a drawing (fig. 43); in 1878 the adolescent Melina Darde featured in another analysis of 'battements à la seconde' (cat. 6); and an obscure member of the Opéra corps, Marie van Goethem, was recorded in nearly a dozen drawings for the *Little Dancer Aged Fourteen* (cat. 26).[11] Over subsequent years Degas carried out such first-hand studies of individuals even more often. but was less inclined to add names to the sheet. Yet the artist's technical ambitions as documented in these drawings became noticeably more extreme, especially with respect to the athletic activities of the young women. Choosing to heighten the exertions of his subjects, not just in a single leg but also in the arms and ultimately the entire body, Degas would sometimes blur their features or reduce their faces to a simple formula, as if the dancers' identities were now less relevant to his

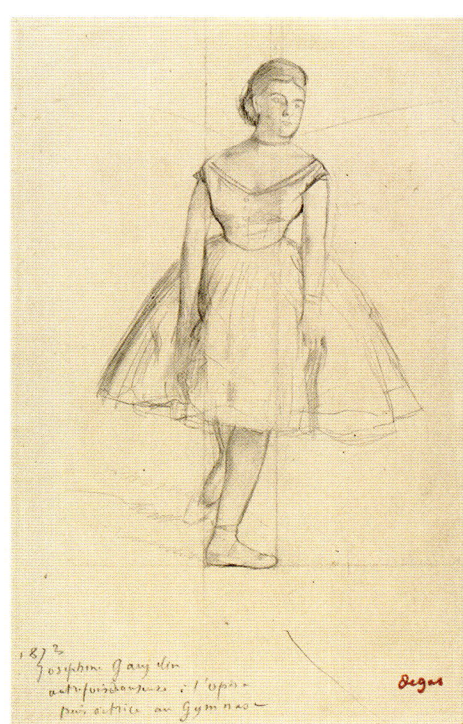

Fig. 43 **Joséphine Gaujelin**, 1873. Pencil and black chalk on paper, 30.7 x 19.7 cm. Museum Boijmans Van Beuningen, Rotterdam, inv. no. FII 169

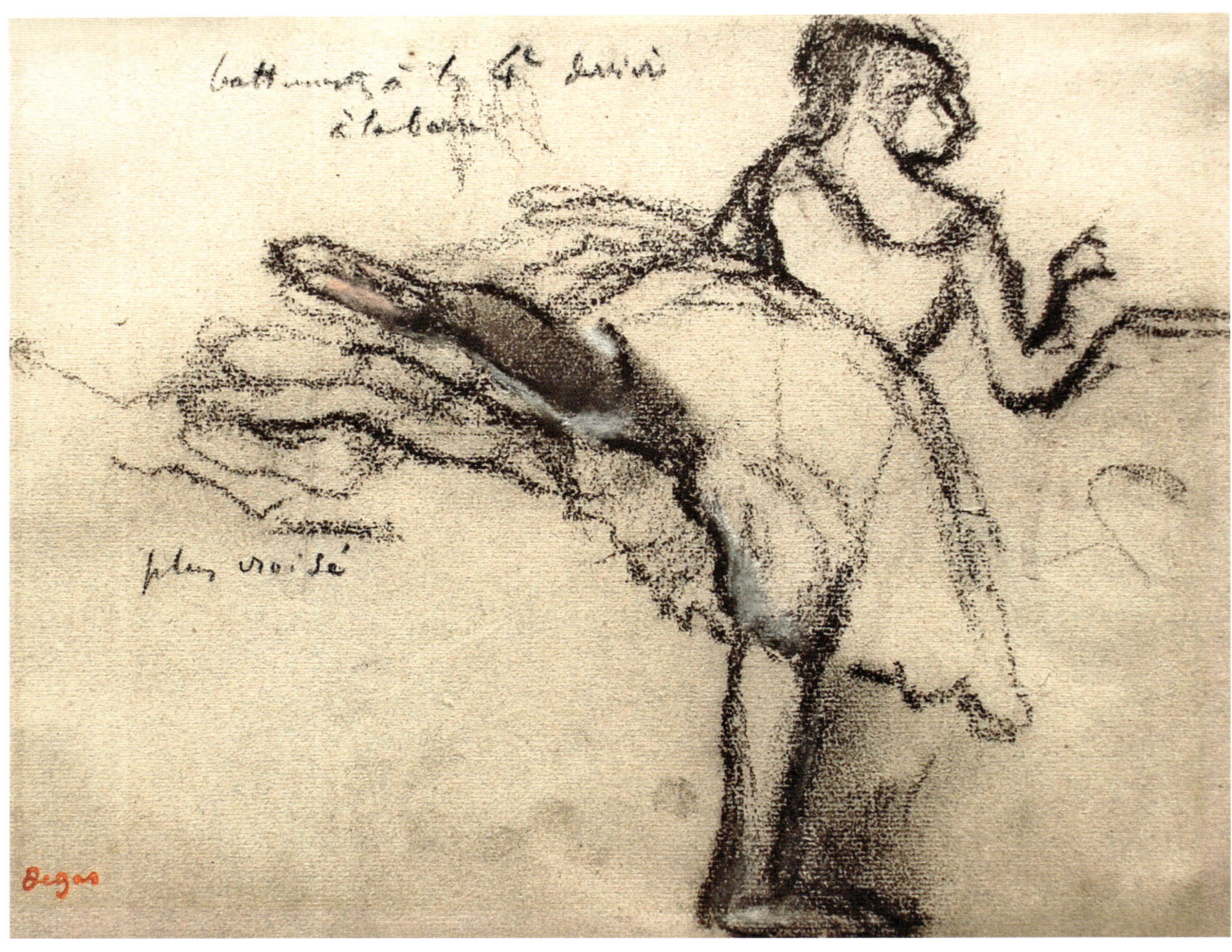

50

Dancer at the Barre
c. 1880–85
Charcoal (?) heightened with
white and pink pastel on paper,
c. 22.9 x 32.4 cm
Collection of the Flint Institute
of Arts, Flint, Michigan

artistic concerns. No longer a mere chronicler of children at the barre or of individual Opéra ballerinas in the wings or classroom, Degas effectively acknowledged that his dancers had become a 'pretext for depicting movement'.

A telling feature of many such drawings is the multiple contour, in which the artist first outlined a limb, shoulder or other form and then outlined it again one or more times, often close to his previous mark. Such echoing lines are visible throughout *Little Girl Practising at the Barre*, most clearly in the web of chalk strokes around the child's raised leg. There are several ways to understand this proliferation of lines: they may represent attempts by the artist to make a quick, imperfect draft from an unfamiliar individual who was unaccustomed to holding still; they might also indicate an accumulation of positions that this leg had actually occupied during Degas's drawing session; a third option, which is the most radical in artistic terms, is that he consciously attempted to evoke the instability of the limb as it wavered

during his observation of the model. While this conundrum is inherently
unsolvable in *Little Girl Practising at the Barre*, it takes on considerable
significance in the larger graphic *œuvre* that Degas dedicated to dancers in
action. Among numerous drawings that might be used for comparison, *Dancer
at the Barre* (cat. 50) offers another variation on the theme of 'battements'.
Undated but probably executed in the mid-1880s, this sheet is based on a
model who was clearly a mature teenager or young woman, with a physique
that had been disciplined through sustained practice in the Opéra classrooms.
Standing firmly on her right leg and holding the barre in the approved fashion,
she is shown executing a series of battements – vertical kicks that here rapidly
raised her back leg into the air and returned it to the floor. Degas has spelled
out with some care the location of the raised limb at its highest point, but also
indicated more summarily three or more adjacent positions that it had already
passed through. The result is a series of echoing lines that become firmer as
they ascend, creating an effect that resembles sympathetically vibrating waves
or ripples on water.

Dancer at the Barre and many drawings of a similar kind are intriguing
in themselves but also problematic in a larger sense. Given Degas's famously
accomplished draughtsmanship and what Huysmans called 'the perspicacity
of an analyst', there is surely no question of these multiple lines indicating
hesitation or misjudgement of his subject. The contrast between the energetic
passage around the model's leg and the tranquil character of her body, the
latter expressed in firm, simple contours, appears to discriminate pointedly
between these two areas and their relative dynamism. Revealing too is the fact
that more than half the sheet is devoted to the left leg and its vibrant activity,
effectively making these elements into the central subject of Degas's
composition. The essence of the dancer, such drawings tell us, is not just her
technical prowess or the mysterious geometry of her body, but the ability to
move her limbs through space in an expressive yet fundamentally disciplined
manner. As he struggled to acknowledge this fact in his art, Degas appears
to have simultaneously pushed at the limits of his craft and at the frontiers
of familiar conceptual territory. One development that evidently grew out
of these concerns was the creation of pairs and trios of drawings that – when

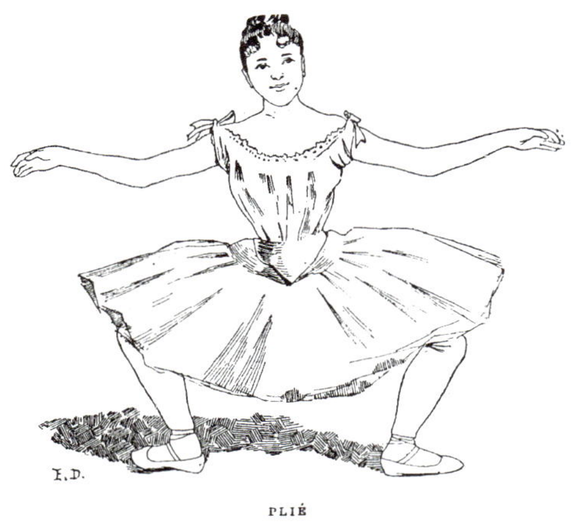

Fig. 44 *E. Dousdebès*, 'Plié in Second Position', from
Berthe Bernay, La Danse au théâtre, Paris, 1890, p. 134

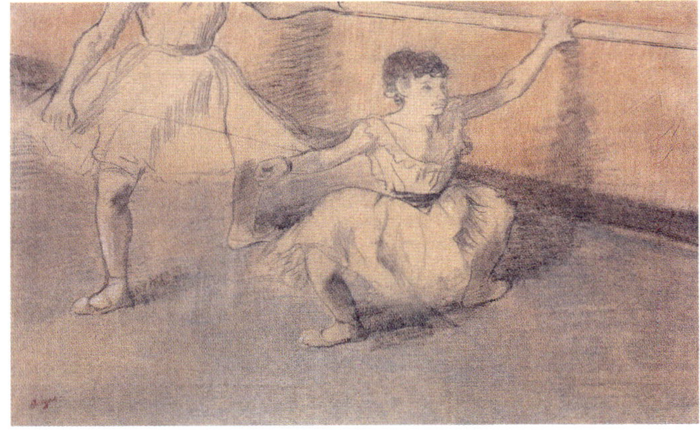

Fig. 45 **Dancers in Plié at the Barre**, *c.* 1885.
Pastel on paper, 32 x 52 cm. Private collection

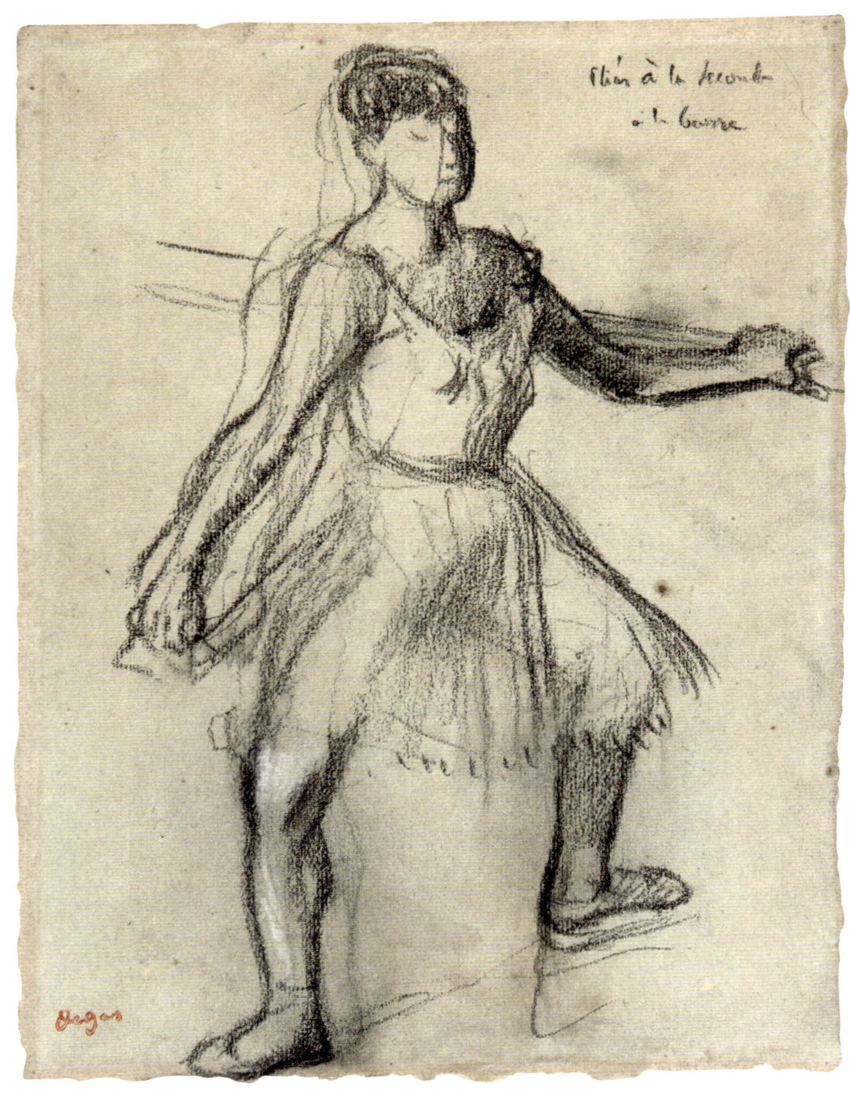

51

**Plié in Second Position
at the Barre**
c. 1880–85
Black and white prepared
chalk on pink modern laid
paper, faded to off-white,
30.8 x 23.4 cm
Harvard Art Museums/Fogg
Museum. *Bequest of Richard
B. Sisson and through the
generosity of Anthony and
Celeste Meier*

seen together – show a single dancer in successive phases of an unfolding action. In *Plié in Second Position at the Barre* (cat. 51), for example, Degas depicted another standard exercise, the plié, which formed part of everyday classroom routine at the Paris Opéra in the nineteenth century as it still does today. With one hand on the barre and legs well apart, the dancer executing such a plié is required to lower her body by bending her knees and then straighten up, a procedure that is typically repeated several times; an illustration of the period shows the plié at the lowest point of its descent (fig. 44). This process is normally continuous, but a well-trained subject would be able to hold the position in mid-elevation long enough for the artist to begin his drawing and then return to it as required. As in many rapidly executed sheets of this type, Degas's black chalk lines tend towards the broad and energetic, with lighter marks indicating his first attempts to articulate a bodily form, and firmer, darker contours eventually defining the more crucial elements. Here the haste required – or the artist's relative inexperience with this position – produced a strikingly free rendering, again accompanied by multiple outlines in certain passages and their characteristic suggestion

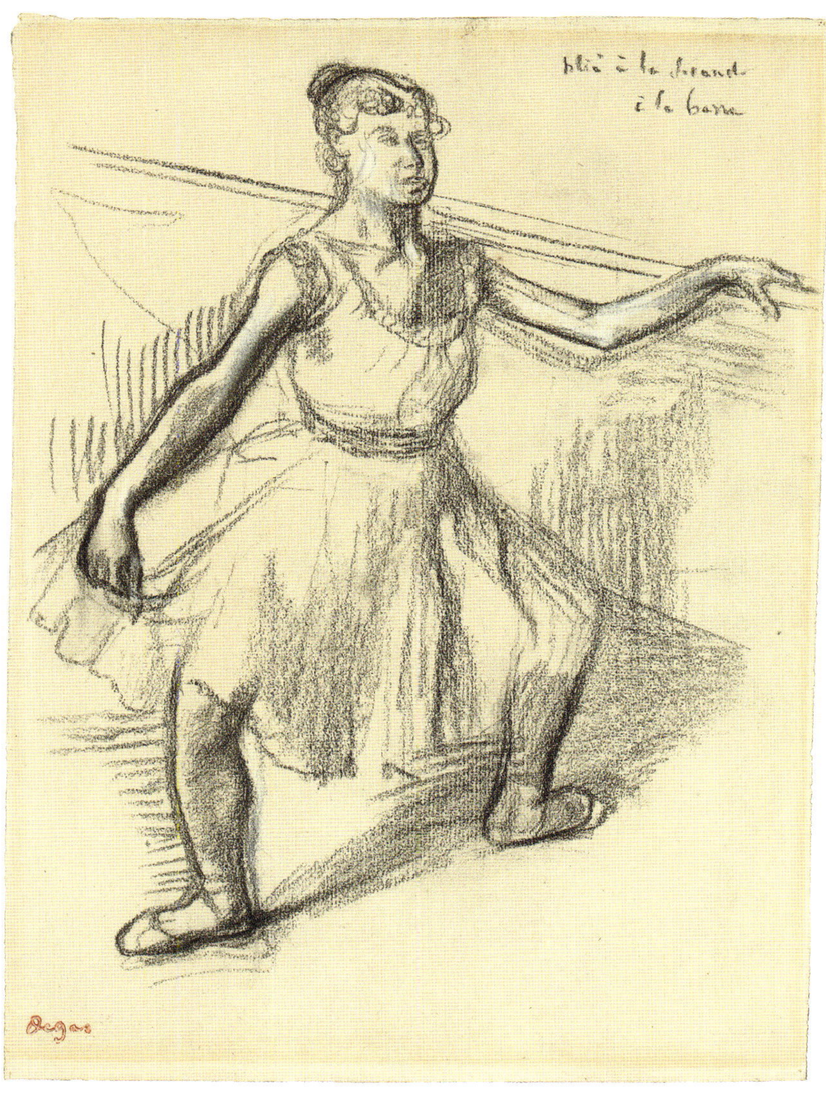

of movement. When making what appears to be a second drawing of this same long-limbed individual, *Study of a Dancer* (cat. 52), Degas drew her body with greater precision but again emphasised the structure of arms and legs at the expense of areas such as the face. Most tellingly, this sheet shows the dancer slightly lower in her trajectory than in *Plié in Second Position at the Barre*, as if glimpsed at a different stage of the exercise represented in the earlier study. When placed side by side, the two drawings are less suggestive of fixed positions than phases in the same movement, or even – to the twenty-first-century eye – a photographic sequence or two frames from a film.

The reason for making such twinned drawings was never spelled out by Degas himself, although their explicit association with movement is confirmed in a finished pastel that incorporates *Study of a Dancer*, a composition that specifically evokes the up-and-down trajectory of the plié (fig. 45).[12] Other studies of this kind became more adventurous and technically taxing, as Degas turned from barre exercises to the range of steps that formed an essential part of every dancer's 'centre-floor' repertoire. These included such graceful actions as the arabesque and the port-de-bras, but also the conspicuously dynamic

52

Study of a Dancer
c. 1880–85
Charcoal heightened
with pastel on paper,
31.7 x 23.8 cm
Private collection

137

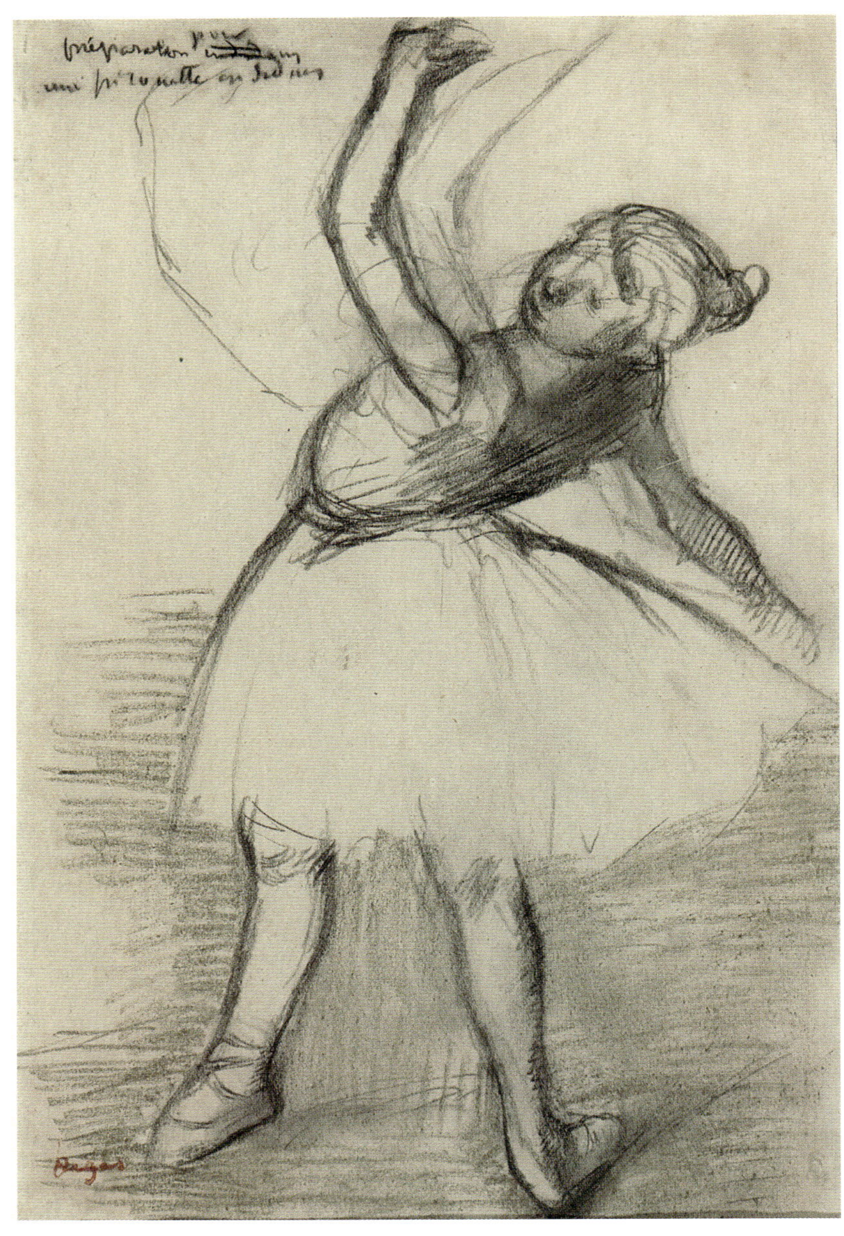

53

**Preparation for
an Inside Pirouette**
c. 1880–85
Charcoal and black
crayon on paper,
33.6 x 22.7 cm
National Museum, Belgrade

pirouette and pas-de-chat, which involve spinning and jumping into the air according to rigorously prescribed conventions. Testing the dancer's training and physique to their limits, these manoeuvres also challenged the artist's powers of observation and split-second analysis in new ways. In *Preparation for an Inside Pirouette* (cat. 53), for example, the dancer is shown in the midst of a sweeping, circular movement with the upper body, her supple spine allowing her to lean backwards while one arm makes a sweeping arc through space. Fascinatingly, there is once again evidence on the sheet itself that Degas watched and drew this model as she moved: several prior positions of the left arm remain lightly indicated on the paper, evoking the passage of this limb through space while she was under observation. *Dancer (Préparation en dedans)* (cat. 54) goes even further in challenging traditional modes of representation and suggests the demands placed on the artist in such

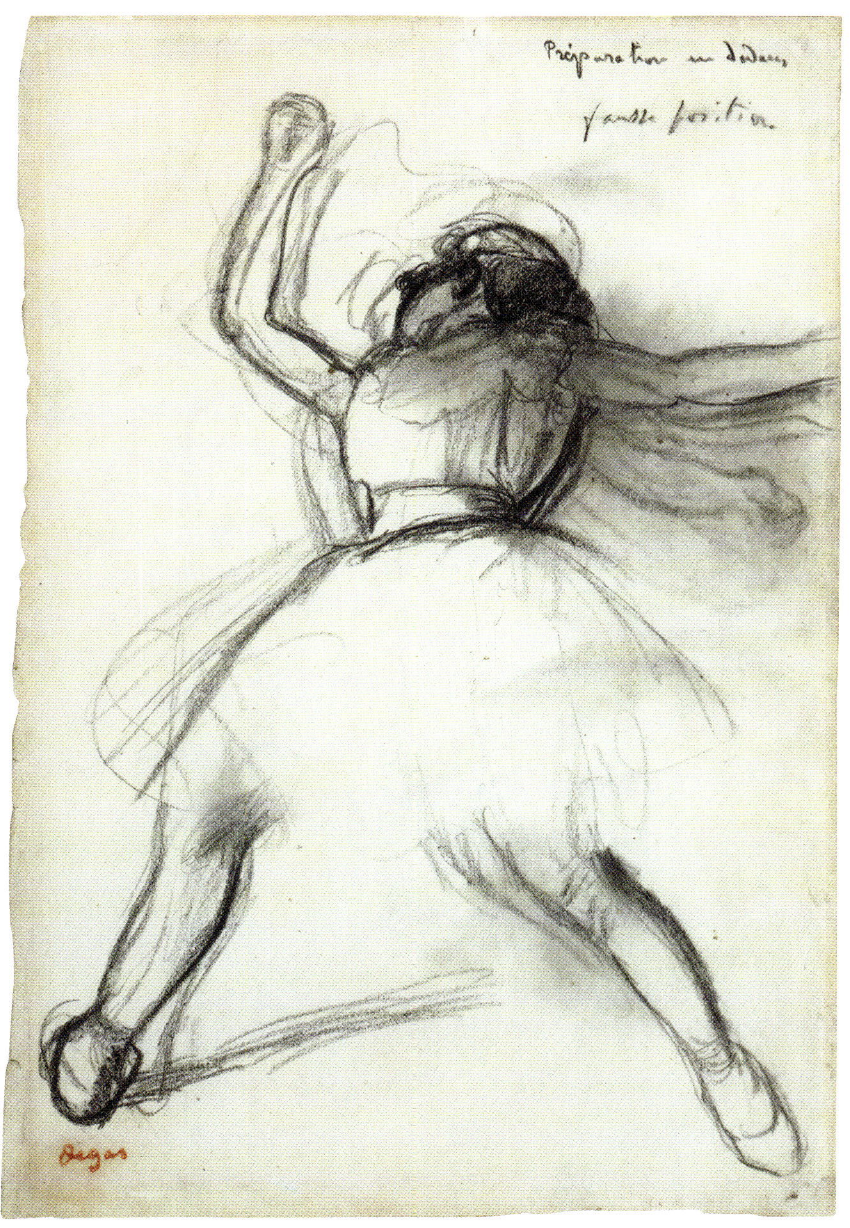

circumstances. Here Degas portrayed the young woman as she built up
momentum in order to galvanise a turn or jump that will spin her around
and away from us towards the right, a series of events lasting just a few
seconds. Practical considerations, therefore, place this drawing in an even
more extreme category than those previously discussed: the definitively
unstable position in *Dancer (Préparation en dedans)* could not have been
maintained artificially for the benefit of the artist and was not easily
reconstituted at will. Yet as multiple contours around legs and torso
reveal, the model appears to have repeated the action for Degas a number
of times, while he struggled to draw the virtually undrawable.

The extremity of the tasks he now set himself challenged the foundations
of Degas's draughtsmanship. If the subtlety of his vision seemed to increase,
his willingness to sacrifice the refinement of line for which he had been

54

Dancer (Préparation
en dedans)
c. 1880–85
Charcoal with stumping
on buff paper,
33.6 x 22.7 cm
Trinity House

139

55

Dancer at the Barre
c. 1885
Charcoal with pastel
and white chalk on paper,
31.1 x 23.5 cm
Fred Jones Jr Museum of Art,
The University of Oklahoma,
Norman. Aaron M. and Clara
Weitzenhoffer Collection, 2000

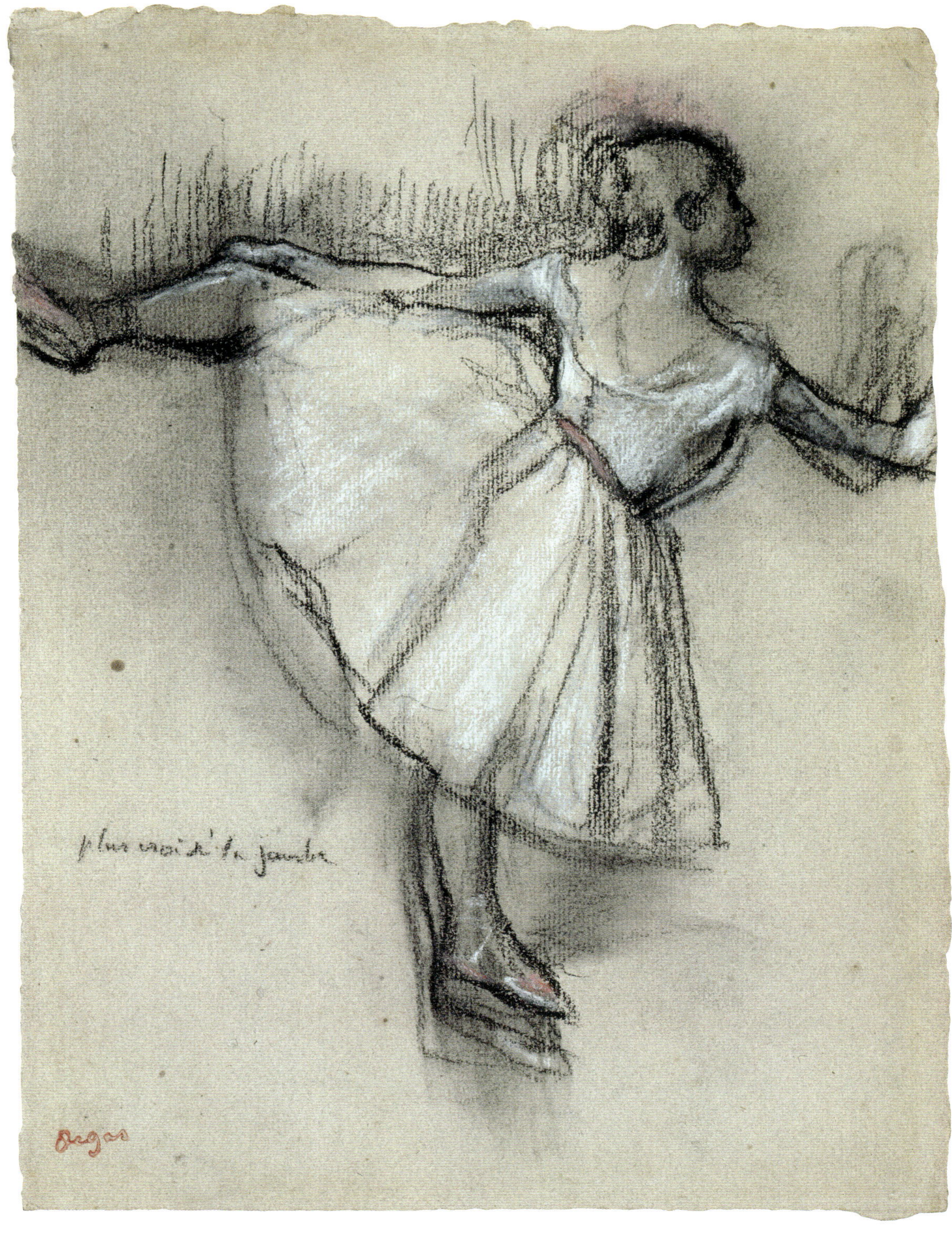

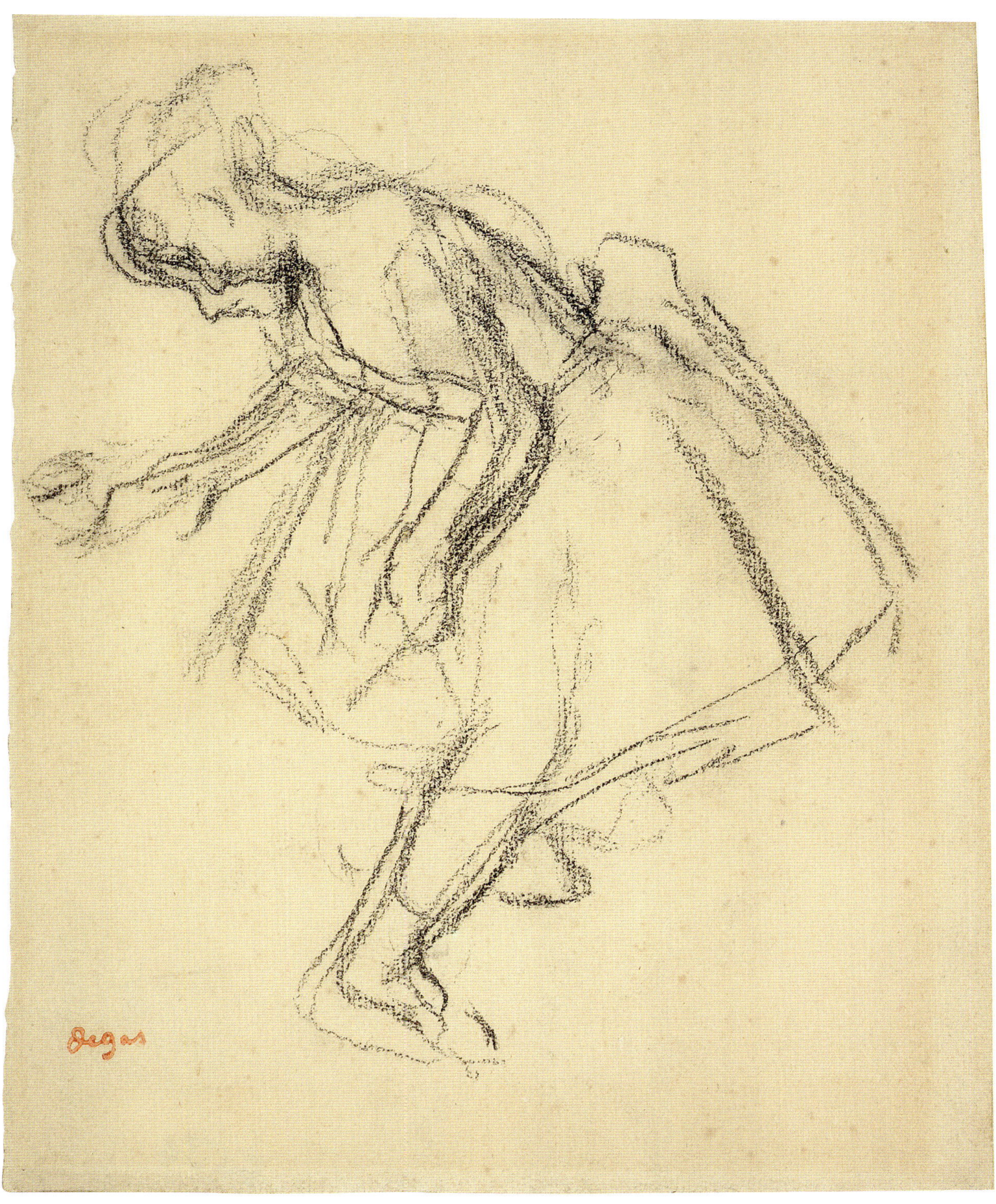

Study of a Dancer
1878–79
Charcoal on paper,
27.9 x 23 cm
Private collection

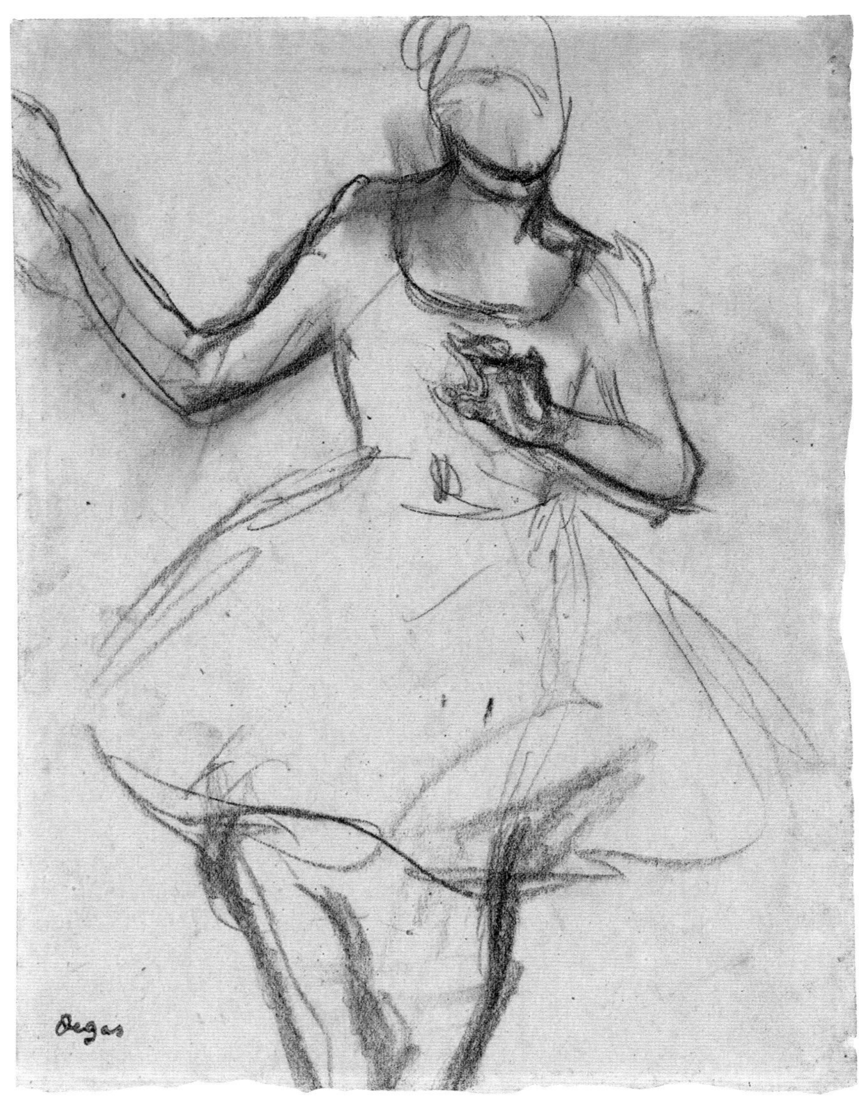

admired for so long could sometimes be startling. In *Dancer at the Barre* (cat. 55), the sense of vigorous engagement with a model who was posing imperfectly is almost inescapable; every part of her body appears to be moving, as Degas struggled to define the positions of her feet, right arm and upper torso. Whether practising this stretch of her left leg at the barre or in centre floor, this girl embodies a kind of nervous vibrancy rather than repose, a quality that Degas was nonetheless determined to record on paper. The similar-sized drawing *Dancer Seen from Behind* (cat. 58) might have been the work of a couple of minutes, so vividly has the artist captured this coryphée in mid-step. Especially focusing on her lower leg movements, he developed these limbs in heavy silhouette and added just a touch of colour, perhaps unable to detain her for a more complete session. Several such drawings are approximately nine inches high, raising the possibility that they come from a sketchbook or pad that he could use discreetly during a dance class held at the Opéra or elsewhere. Two similarly scaled pages were taken up by a pair of separate works that are both known as *Study of a Dancer*, in each case representing steps that might appear on stage. The slightly squarer

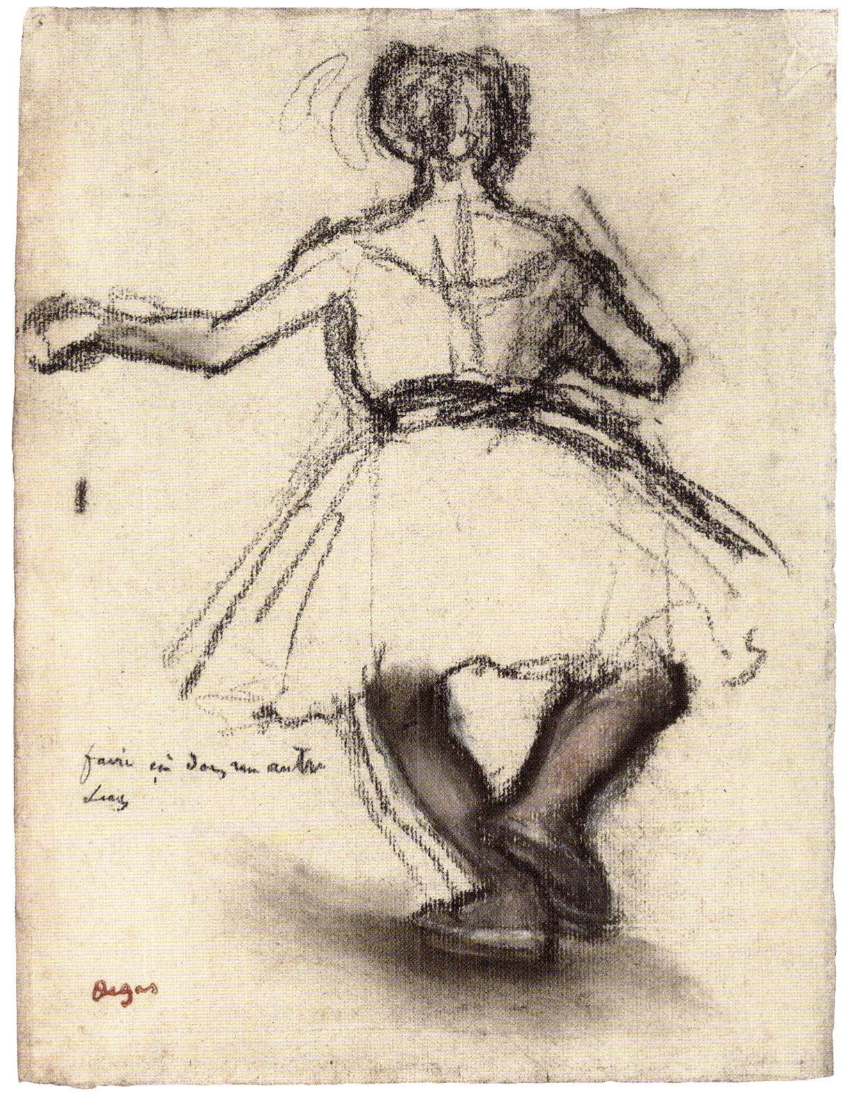

58

Dancer Seen from Behind
c. 1885
Pastel and charcoal
on pink paper,
31 x 23.5 cm
Private collection

sheet (cat. 56) shows an unfolding upper-body movement that recalls a *révérence*, the last exercise performed during class. This wonderfully fluent drawing must have been executed in a matter of seconds, so economical are his lines and so plausible the sense of a dancer's sweeping action, perhaps made as she salutes her teacher. Most energetic of all is the second *Study of a Dancer* (cat. 57), in which the flow of the artist's looping marks seems to be in sympathy with the grace and buoyancy of the ballerina. Almost crude by conventional standards, this vivacious sheet points forward to the *fin-de-siècle* line studies of Rodin, when he was confronted by such models as dancers from Thailand. Arguably more potent still is a comparison between *Study of a Dancer* and the drawings of Matisse, where line takes on a life of its own, irrespective of the dance genre under consideration.

A small but significant feature of many studies of this kind is Degas's own annotation on the sheet in question, typically recording the name of the step or pose represented, such as 'à la cinquième' (fig. 46). Using the terminology of classical ballet and echoing the captions that accompanied illustrations in dance manuals (fig. 47), Degas's notes reinforced the formality

**Study of a Ballet Dancer,
Pas de Bourrée**
c. 1880–85
Brown conté crayon and
pink chalk on paper,
34.3 x 22.8 cm
Snite Museum of Art,
University of Notre Dame,
Indiana. Gift of Mr John
D. Reilly, 1963

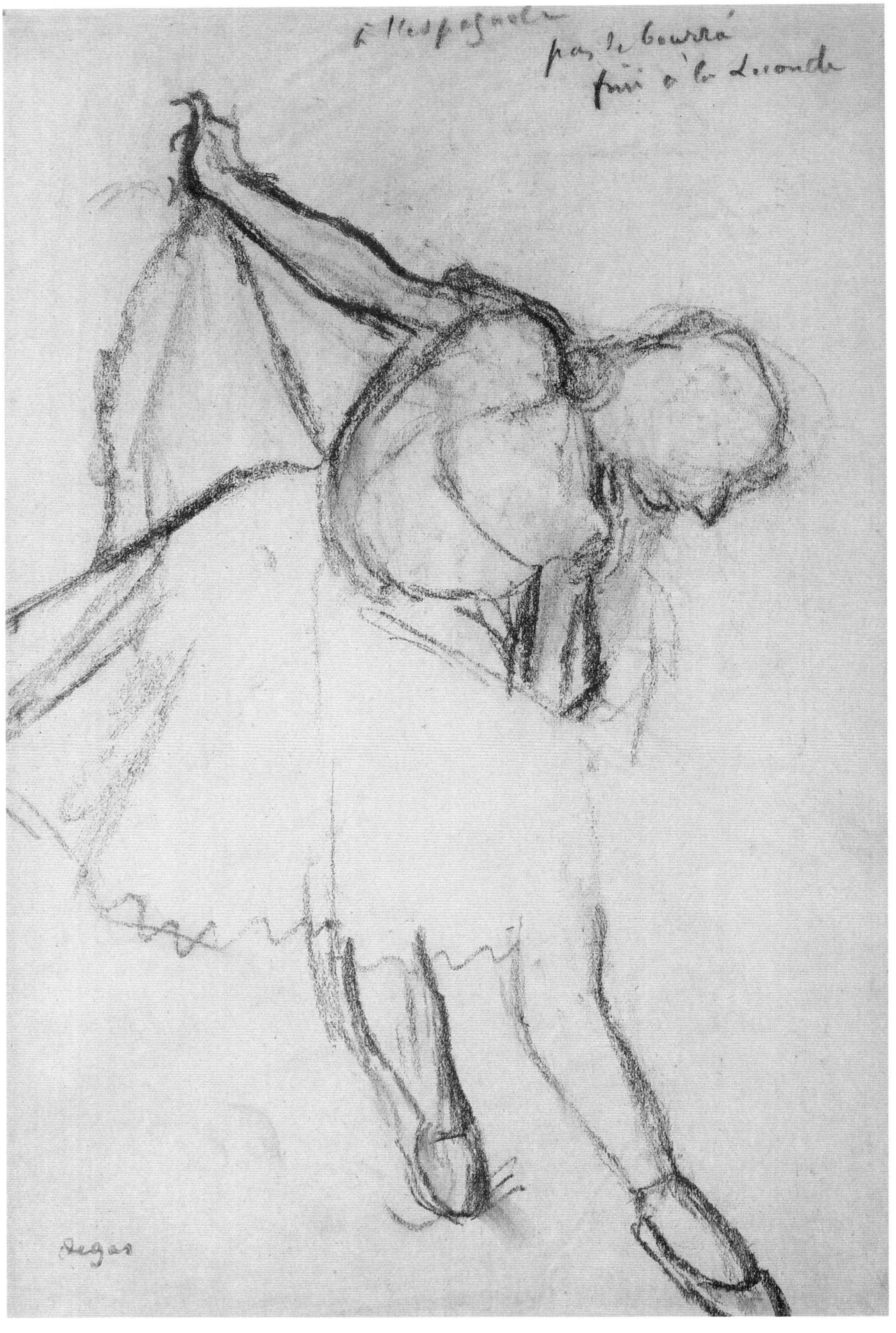

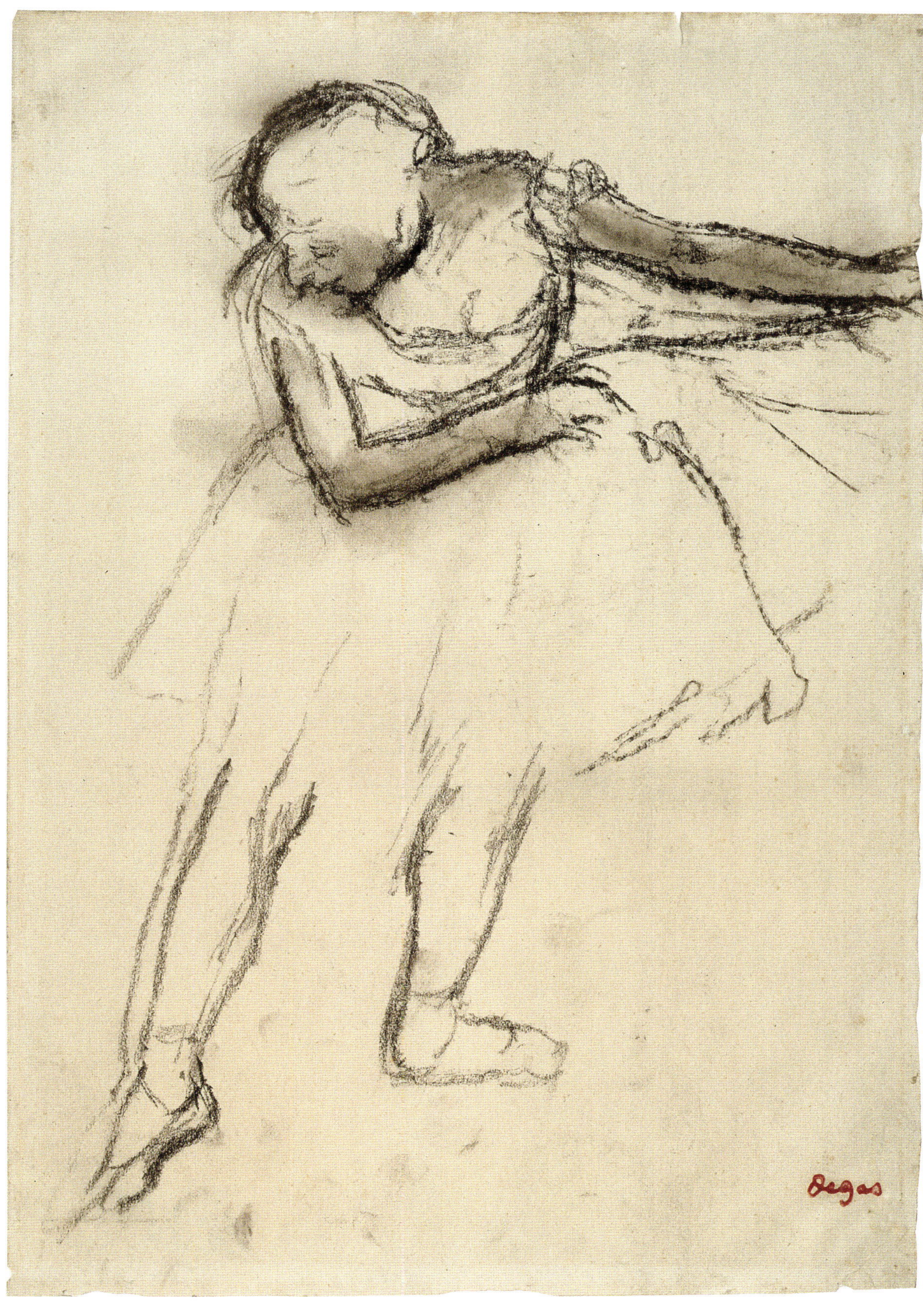

60

Dancer Executing a Pas de Bourrée in the Spanish Style
c. 1880–85
Dark brown chalk on paper,
32.9 x 23.1 cm
Museum Boijmans Van
Beuningen, Rotterdam, inv. no.
FII 131 (PK) (Koenigs Collection)

of his classroom project and hinted at its larger role in his art. Sometimes included are less canonical remarks, among them overheard comments about an individual dancer's technique or the artist's observations on his own drawing, the former clearly documenting his presence in the ballet class as opposed to his private studio.[13] Amassing detailed first-hand knowledge in this way, Degas introduced a systematic element into his practice that currently had implications beyond the visual arts. As Huysmans suggested, a persuasive analogy could be found among certain novelists of the period who, like Degas, described the 'the exterior of the human animal, in the environment in which it operates, to show the movements, the positions, the gestures, the workings of its physiognomy'. Gustave Flaubert's obsession with gathering circumstantial detail for his novels and his ambition to write 'scientific' studies of the age, and Emile Zola's determined list-making and 'research' into character and location, both offer parallels with Degas's practice, a fact seemingly acknowledged in the artist's reading habits.[14] Like these writers, Degas also insisted on the detachment of his procedures. 'No art was less spontaneous than mine,' he told George Moore, and in later years discussed 'the science of art' with the young polymath Paul Valéry; 'he would say that a picture was the result of "a series of operations"', Valéry reported.[15]

Degas's complicity in certain of his own dance experiments becomes apparent when other – arguably even more ambitious – classroom drawings are examined. *Study of a Ballet Dancer, Pas de Bourrée* (cat. 59), for example, shows a standard balletic exercise performed with un-classical bravura. As the inscription indicates, the young woman is executing a 'pas de bourrée', a transitional step that here involves some flourishes in the Spanish manner. Not satisfied with this single view, however, when making *Dancer Executing a Pas de Bourrée in the Spanish Style* (cat. 60) the artist drew the same rather sharp-faced individual from the opposite side and in virtually the same position. In both drawings, summary marks and multiple lines again suggest Degas's and the dancer's haste, while in a third and fourth sketch of a similar position he added a frontal and another lateral glimpse of the model to the group.[16] Two explanations of this unusual quartet are possible. One is that the dancer repeated her movement four times and at four different angles relative to the artist, as he remained stationary; the other envisages Degas himself

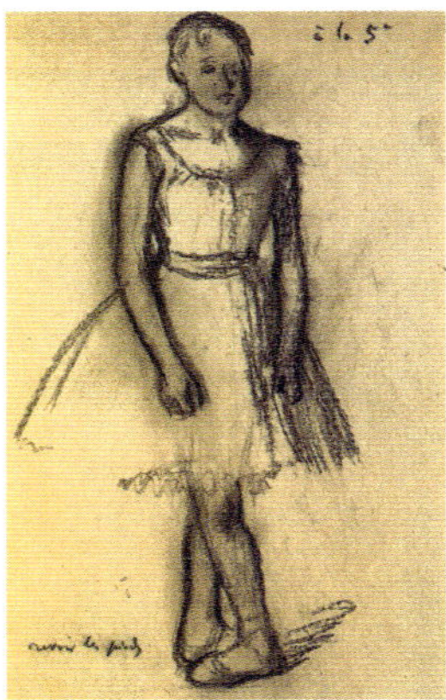

Fig. 46 **Dancer in Fifth Position**, *c.* 1885. Charcoal on light brown paper, 35.5 x 22.5 cm. Private collection

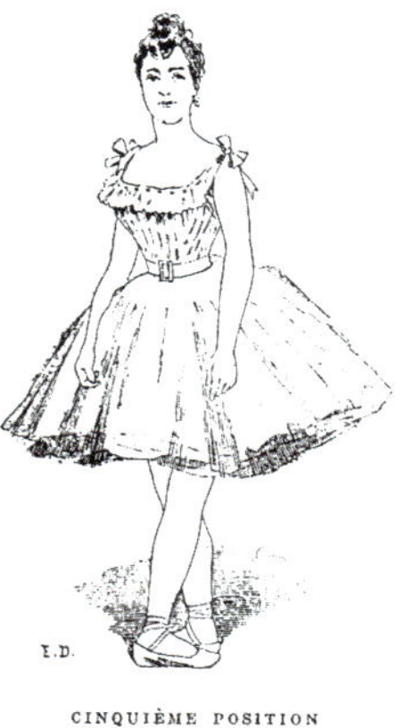

Fig. 47 ***E. Dousdebès***, **'Cinquième Position',** **from Berthe Bernay, La Danse au théâtre,** Paris, 1890, p. 134

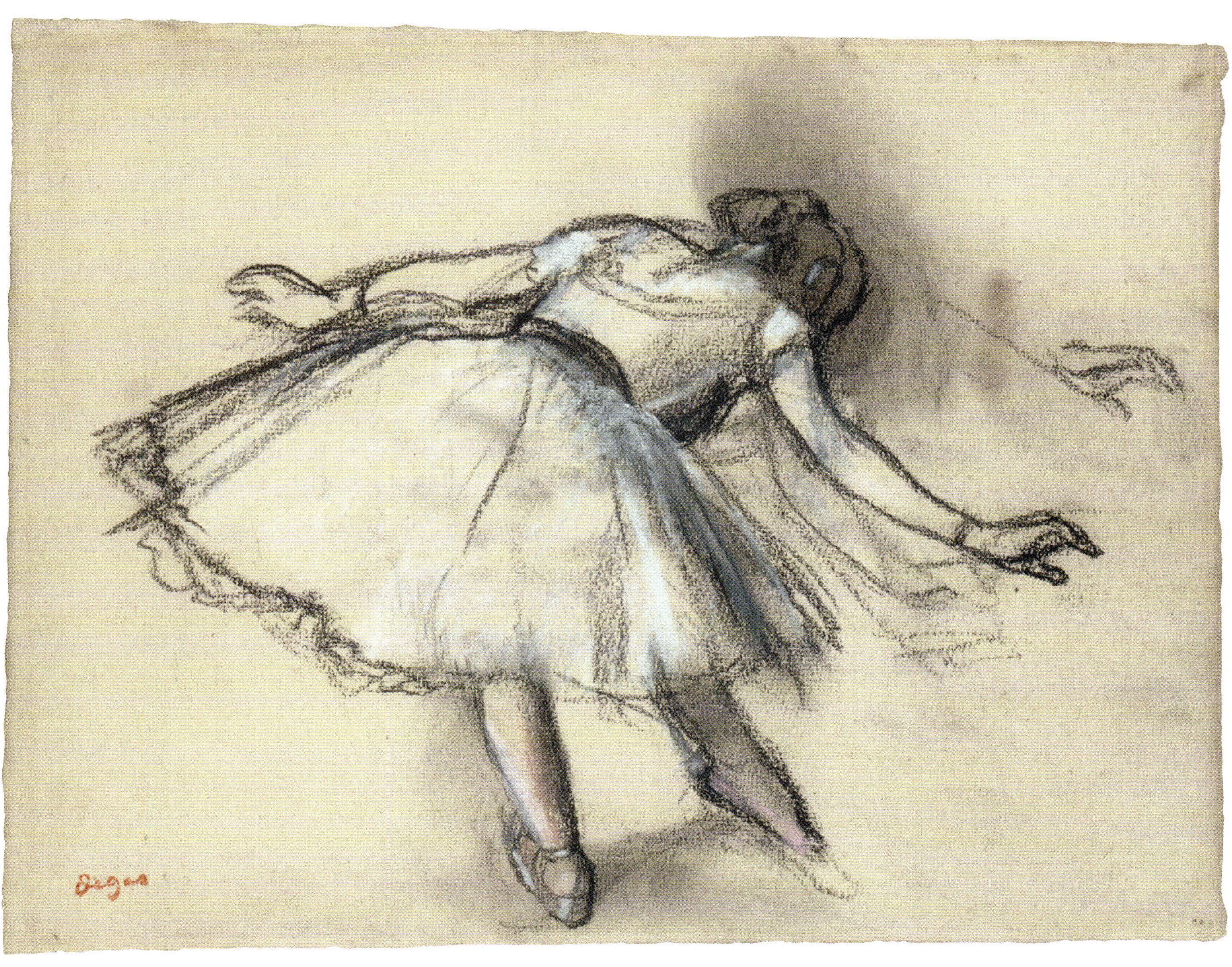

moving around *her*, as he had done when drawing Marie van Goethem, while
his new model repeatedly performed a 'pas de bourrée' for his benefit. In either
case, this challengingly mobile relationship between artist and human subject
gives additional meaning to his declared passion for 'depicting movement',
and invites us to question other clusters of drawings made during these years.
The exquisitely observed *Dancer Executing a Port de Bras* (cat. 61), for example,
shows many characteristics already discussed in the present context: the
figure is manifestly caught in mid-action, here gracefully bending forward;
repeated contours around her body and dress suggest Degas's haste in drawing
a shifting position or the ballerina's own vacillation; and one limb – the right
arm – was drawn repeatedly and is easily understood to be in motion. Less
expected is the existence of another drawing of this step that plausibly
represents the same model, who again wears a dark sash.[17] As with the
previous trio, this pair reveals the figure from alternative angles and
collectively proposes an ambitious, multiple perception of a single model.
Whether it was she who rotated around Degas or the artist who circled around
her, the codes and assumptions that had governed such drawing practices
over the centuries were clearly under assault.

61

Dancer Executing a Port de Bras
c. 1880–85
Black chalk and pastel on paper,
24.7 x 32 cm
Private collection

Hailed in 1880 as 'a pupil of the great Florentines' by Charles Ephrussi, editor of the *Gazette des Beaux-Arts*, Degas had learned as a young man to draw in the traditional manner.[19] Making drawn and painted copies in the Louvre and during his travels in Italy, he also became well versed in the history of art and in earlier, more academic ways of representing the body in action. Stylised animation of this kind was typically presented to art students through class exercises and engravings (fig. 48), and was exploited by the young Degas in his ambitious canvases on classical and biblical themes.[20] Many painters of his generation still maintained these time-honoured modes, using such devices as an echoing sequence of limbs or other forms in their scenes of battle, athletic events and moments of personal drama. In Degas's early maturity, however, he joined his Impressionist colleagues in departing from these conventions and from the mannered narratives that often resulted. Insisting on a radical re-engagement with the visible world in all its aspects, the group sought to depict not just the quotidian events of their age but also its characteristic dynamism. Several subjects associated with Degas illustrate the challenges that this approach entailed. As a painter of horses since the 1860s, for example, he took pains to study thoroughbreds in action at the Bois de Boulogne in Paris and elsewhere, and gradually abandoned the clichés that had governed their representation for centuries.[21] A similar impetus lay behind his studies of pedestrians on Paris streets, where 'the hustle and bustle of passers-by' described by Edmond Duranty was translated into fragmentary figures on canvas and near-indecipherable silhouettes on monotype plates.[22]

As he tackled the energetic world of the ballet during these same years, Degas was similarly obliged to question an existing repertoire of representational modes, though admittedly with a weaker precedent that was dominated by popular illustration and caricature.[23] In all these contexts, the technical limitations of photography made the medium almost irrelevant to Degas's ambitions, which required him to scrutinise his energetic subjects on stage and in class as directly and freshly as he was able. Huysmans and others were quick to note these strategies, which involved setting aside the weightless nymphs of the past and their fairy-like choreography and replacing them with studies of modern young athletes in the disciplined actions of the dance studio. The characteristic detachment of his vision, which led Degas to record the 'physiognomies' of the Opéra ballerinas with 'the perspicacity of an analyst', had been widely sensed. Some sympathetic critics now went further, making a direct comparison between Degas and certain Impressionists on the one hand with modern scientists on the other: one of his colleagues was likened to an 'engineer' and another to a 'chemist', while the entire group were seen to be 'working in their own laboratory'.[24]

Degas's occasional engagement with technical and scientific issues has begun to attract scholarly attention in recent decades.[25] These interests may have dated back to his schooldays at the Lycée Louis-le-Grand in Paris, where introductory classes in the sciences formed part of the rigorous curriculum for some pupils.[26] Even more significant were his close friendships with fellow students from these years that were maintained into adult life, notably with the successful engineer, Henri Rouart, and the specialist in electric power and

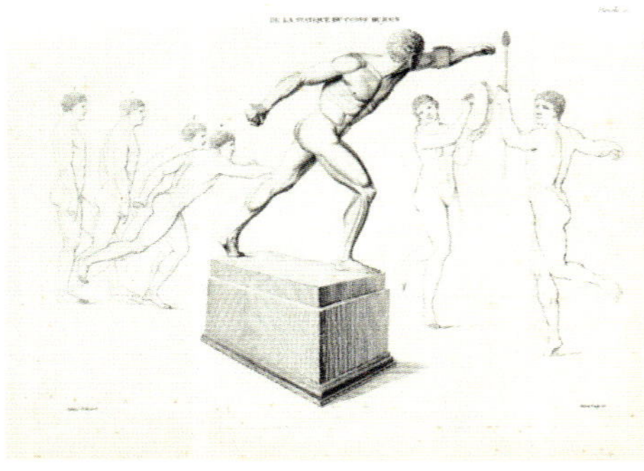

Fig. 48   From *Jean-Gaalbert Salvage*, Anatomie du Gladiateur Combattant, Applicable aux Beaux Arts ou Traité des os, des muscles, du mécanisme des mouvements, des proportions et des caractères du corps humain, Paris, 1812. Royal Academy of Arts, London

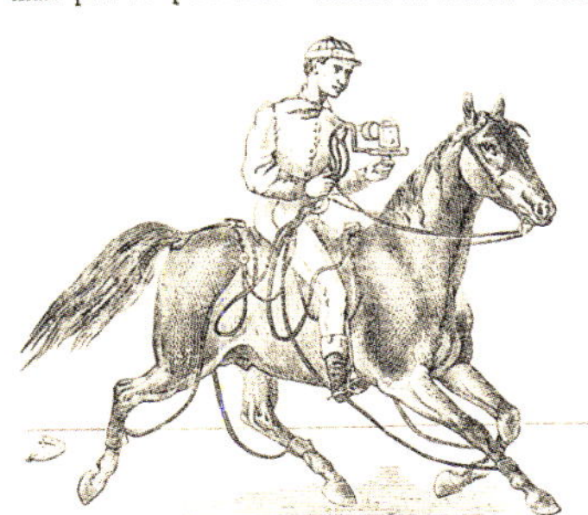

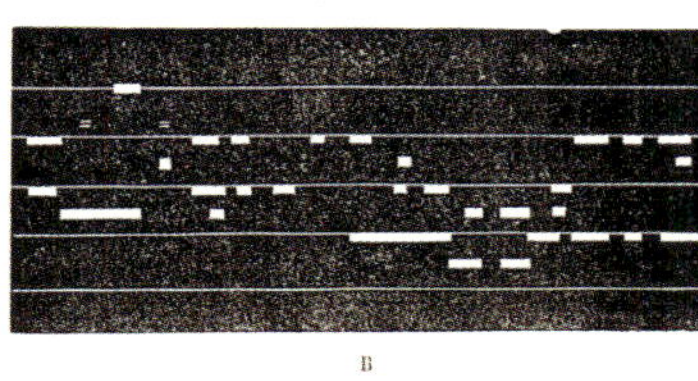

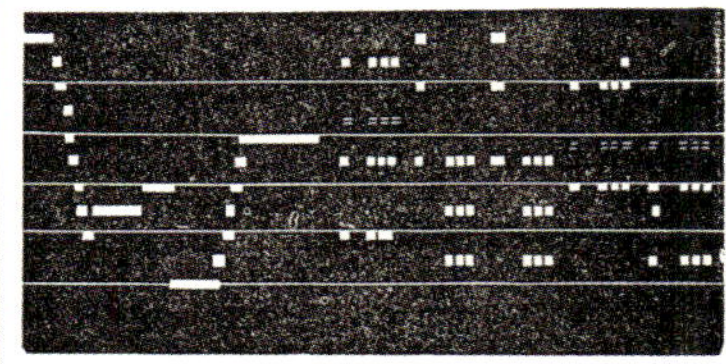

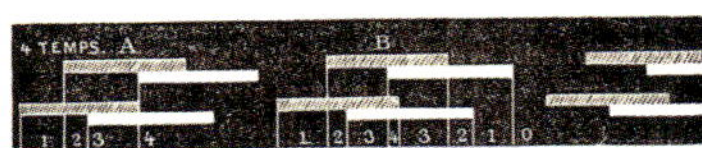

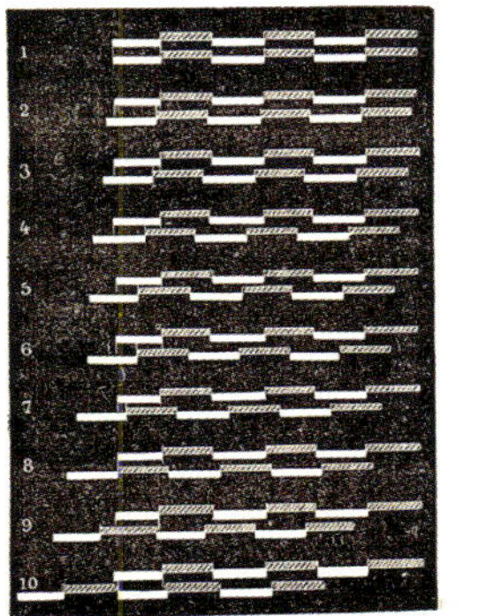

The reproduced page of *La Nature*:

MOTEURS ANIMÉS

EXPÉRIENCES DE PHYSIOLOGIE GRAPHIQUE[1]

(Suite et fin. — Voy. p. 273.)

III. *Des allures du cheval*. — Tout le monde sait reconnaître si un cheval marche, trotte ou galope; mais peu de personnes seraient en mesure d'indi-

Fig. 1. — Appareil enregistreur des allures du cheval.

quer le rythme et l'ordre de succession des mouvements des membres aux différentes allures. Ces mouvements, en effet, se succèdent avec trop de ra-

Fig. 2. — Tableau synoptique des différentes allures du cheval d'après les auteurs classiques.—1, *amble*; 5, *pas*; 8, *trot*, etc.

pidité pour que nos yeux puissent les suivre. L'oreille est plus apte que l'œil à percevoir ces rythmes et c'est elle qui nous renseigne d'ordinaire sur l'al-

[1] Conférence faite pendant la session de Paris de l'*Association française pour l'avancement des sciences* le 29 août 1878.

(6ᵉ année. — 2ᵉ semestre.)

lure d'un cheval. Lorsqu'à chaque révolution du pas on entend deux battues, il s'agit de l'*amble* ou du *trot*; trois battues inégalement espacées correspondent au *galop*; enfin, quatre battues signalent l'allure du *pas*.

Mais ces allures peuvent être plus ou moins irrégulières, altérées, boiteuses; de plus, l'animal, pas-

Fig. 3. — Notations de deux airs, A et B, exécutés sur le clavier d'un harmonium.

sant d'une allure à l'autre en un temps très-court, comment pourra-t-on saisir la manière dont se fait le passage? Ces questions sont d'une grande importance pour l'écuyer ou le vétérinaire qui ont fait de grands efforts pour les résoudre.

Ainsi que je le disais tout à l'heure, l'oreille

Galop à 3 temps. — A, indications des 3 temps. — B, indications du nombre des pieds qui forment l'appui du corps à chaque instant du galop à 3 temps.

Galop à 4 temps.
Fig. 4. — Notations du galop à 3 et à 4 temps.

juge mieux que la vue les rythmes de mouvements successifs; mais pour saisir la production de ces battues rythmées à deux, à trois ou à quatre temps, il faut savoir à quel pied attribuer chacun de ces bruits. D'ingénieux expérimentateurs ont appliqué aux quatre pieds du cheval des sonnettes de timbres différents formant entre elles l'accord parfait.

19

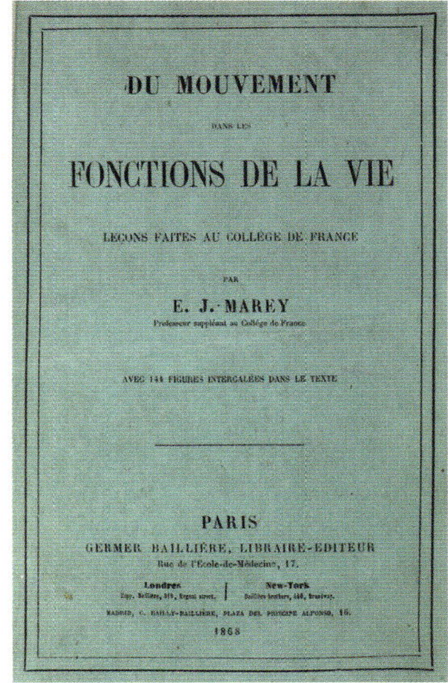

machinery, Alfred Niaudet.[27] In his thirties, Degas became absorbed by the science of physiognomy, citing in his notebooks the influential theorist Johann Caspar Lavater, and tackling Charles Darwin's recently published *Expression of the Emotions in Man and the Animals*.[28] His curiosity was symptomatic of a growing involvement with the sciences among the French populace at large, expressed in proliferating botanical and zoological gardens in Paris and elsewhere, in spectacular exhibitions of mechanical and technical wonders, public lectures by prominent scholars, and a boom in scientific publications both esoteric and popular. It was perhaps through Niaudet, a frequent contributor to its pages, that Degas first encountered the widely read science magazine *La Nature*, a richly illustrated bi-monthly founded in 1873 and published by Victor Masson. *La Nature* provided detailed information for the general reader

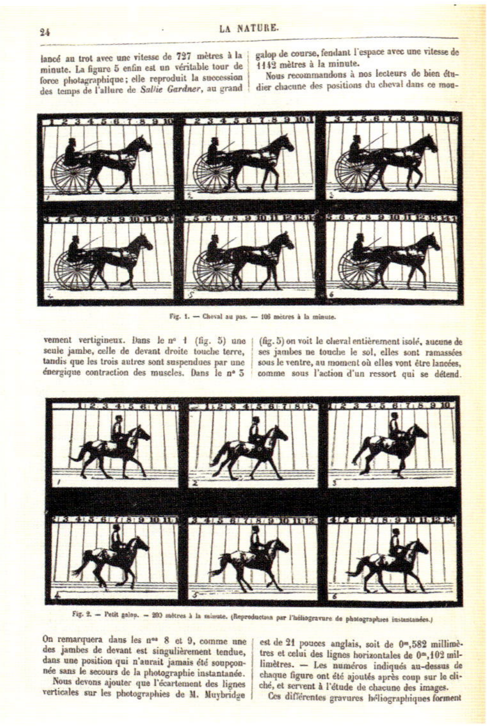

lancé au trot avec une vitesse de 727 mètres à la minute. La figure 5 enfin est un véritable tour de force photographique; elle reproduit la succession des temps de l'allure de *Sallie Gardner*, au grand galop de course, fendant l'espace avec une vitesse de 1142 mètres à la minute.

Nous recommandons à nos lecteurs de bien étudier chacune des positions du cheval dans ce mou-

Fig. 1. — Cheval au pas. — 106 mètres à la minute.

vement vertigineux. Dans le n° 1 (fig. 5) une seule jambe, celle de devant droite touche terre, tandis que les trois autres sont suspendues par une énergique contraction des muscles. Dans le n° 3 (fig. 5) on voit le cheval entièrement isolé, aucune de ses jambes ne touche le sol, elles sont ramassées sous le ventre, au moment où elles vont être lancées, comme sous l'action d'un ressort qui se détend.

Fig. 2. — Petit galop. — 260 mètres à la minute. (Reproduction par l'héliogravure de photographies instantanées.)

On remarquera dans les n°s 8 et 9, comme une des jambes de devant est singulièrement tendue, dans une position qui n'aurait jamais été soupçonnée sans le secours de la photographie instantanée.

Nous devons ajouter que l'écartement des lignes verticales sur les photographies de M. Muybridge est de 21 pouces anglais, soit de 0m,582 millimètres et celui des lignes horizontales de 0m,102 millimètres. — Les numéros indiqués au-dessus de chaque figure ont été ajoutés après coup sur le cliché, et servent à l'étude de chacune des images.

Ces différentes gravures héliographiques forment

64

Gaston Tissandier
'Les Allures du Cheval',
La Nature, 289
14 December 1878
Journal, 30 x 21 cm
The British Library, London

on a wide variety of scientific topics, from advances in astronomy and ethnography to news about devices that exploited steam and electricity, and such occupations as amateur photography and bird-watching. While much of this material was presumably outside Degas's concerns, the publication is known to have caught his attention on at least one occasion.

A sketchbook used by Degas in the late 1870s includes a note that reads 'Journal: La Nature, Victor Masson (année 1878)'.[29] Between September and December of that year, two timely but independent articles devoted to the study of movement appeared in Masson's *La Nature*: one – published in two parts – dealt with recent work by the eminent French scientist Etienne-Jules Marey (cat. 62, fig. 50), the other with the English photographer Eadweard Muybridge (cat. 64). Both texts addressed their themes in the context of the moving horse, although each referred to procedures that were already being applied to human subjects. Degas was presumably attracted to such material initially through his interest in drawing and painting horses, but also as an artist currently tackling the dynamic figure in various ways. The first article to appear was written by Marey himself, a Professor at the Collège de France and a prominent member of the Parisian scientific establishment, who for more than a decade had been publishing books and over a hundred articles on movement-related topics.[30] After boldly asserting in 1873 that 'Motion is the most apparent characteristic of life,' Marey pursued his pioneering research into the rhythms of the human heart, the patterns of limbs in motion, the flight of birds and many similar issues.[31] One of his self-confessed challenges was to represent his findings in visual form. For readers of *La Nature* in 1878, Marey described the 'graphic method' used in certain of his experiments, here involving a hand-held apparatus that translated a horse's characteristic steps – such as the walk, trot and gallop – into pulses of compressed air and registered them in coded form on paper. The resulting sequences of monochrome 'bars' printed beneath the illustrations of horses and their riders, Marey explained, recorded movements that occurred 'more rapidly than our eyes are able to follow them' and allowed a precise analysis of each of the horse's varied gaits.[32]

Published two months later, the second article in *La Nature* (cat. 64) concerned Muybridge and was signed by the editor, Gaston Tissandier, who later reproduced a letter he had received from Marey who wished to contact Muybridge at the latter's current base in San Francisco.[33] Tissandier's summary of Muybridge's recent achievement took up less than a page of text, but was accompanied by reproductions of five remarkable 'series of photographs' of horses and their riders that were soon to become world-famous. Previously admired in the United States as a photographer of the landscape, Muybridge had begun to acquire a reputation for his horse studies while remaining virtually unknown in Europe. In the mid-1870s, he developed a system of 'instantaneous photography' in the open air that could capture not just the 'walk' and 'trot', but also a horse at full gallop. Partly prompted by a wider controversy over the position of a horse's legs at such moments, this project depended on increased shutter speeds and an ingenious system of multiple cameras that were arranged alongside the moving animal. Muybridge's success in photographing rapid movement proved to be a landmark for his new technology and also for the study of many phenomena that had been beyond the range of photographic equipment. His achievement with horses and the attention it attracted soon inspired him to begin his own documentation of humans and of other creatures in motion, eventually resulting in his monumental eleven-volume publication of 1887, *Animal Locomotion*.

Nothing is recorded about Degas's immediate response to the Marey and Muybridge articles in *La Nature*, though he later made a number of drawings of both equine and human subjects from *Animal Locomotion* and may even have acquired his own copy of the publication.[34] Given Muybridge's obscurity in France in 1878, however, Tissandier's article may have represented Degas's first encounter with the photographer's work. As Muybridge's own scrapbook of newspaper and magazine cuttings reveals, coverage of his activities in the English and French press grew rapidly from this moment, reaching a new pitch when he crossed the Atlantic to lecture in London and Paris in 1881.[35] During this same year Muybridge produced his first book, *The Attitudes of Animals in Motion*, available in a very small edition and illustrated with pasted-in photographs of his outdoor apparatus for taking photographs and numerous prints of recent studies of movement (cats 65.1–2). These included remarkable but relatively crude images of men walking, jumping and engaged in a range of athletic exercises, some of which resurfaced in his subsequent public presentations and pointed the way forward for Muybridge's career. An ambitious entrepreneur and a flamboyant performer, Muybridge was soon addressing European audiences at the grandest level, from leading scholars and other luminaries to representatives of the British royal family. In 1882 he gave several talks in London, including a memorable occasion on 16 March when he spoke at the Royal Academy, which was 'filled to overflowing by a thoroughly appreciative body of spectators'.[36]

The case of the already much-published Marey and his reputation in Europe is fundamentally different (cat. 63; fig. 49). Marey was a distinguished figure in his field and in 1878 his work may have been known to Degas for several years. Much of the material that formed the basis of Marey's essay in *La Nature*, for example, had appeared in 1873 in a widely circulated book with the resonant title, *La Machine animale: locomotion terrestre et aérienne* (cat. 66), which soon appeared in translation as *Animal Mechanism: A Treatise on Terrestrial and Aerial Locomotion*.[37] Profusely illustrated and aimed at a broad

65.1

Eadweard Muybridge
'Athlete Running', plate 95
of The Attitudes
of Animals in Motion
1881
Albumen print,
23.5 x 31.5 cm
Royal Academy of Arts, London

65.2

Eadweard Muybridge
'Athlete, Backwards Somersault',
plate 104 of The Attitudes
of Animals in Motion
1881
Albumen print,
23.5 x 31.5 cm
Royal Academy of Arts, London

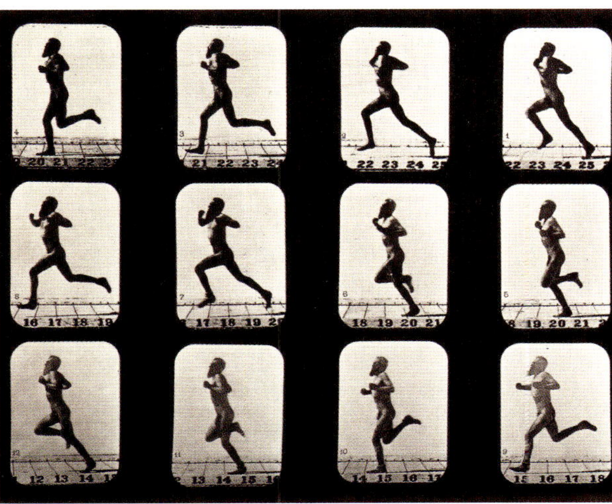

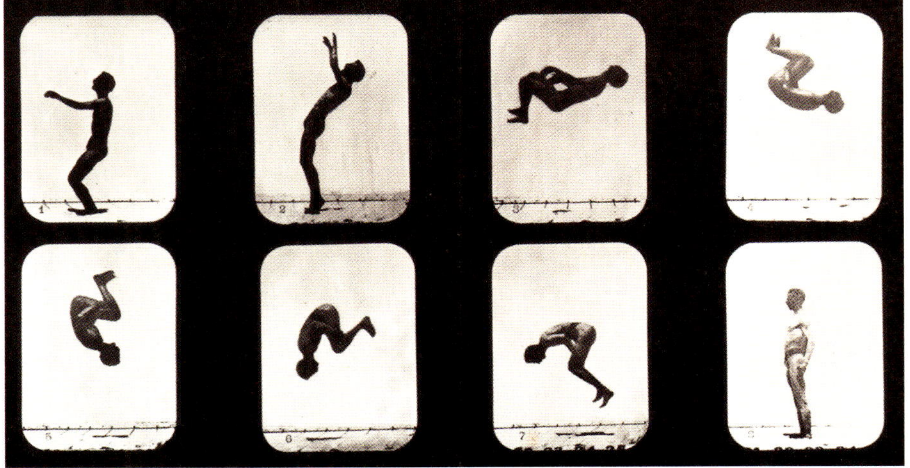

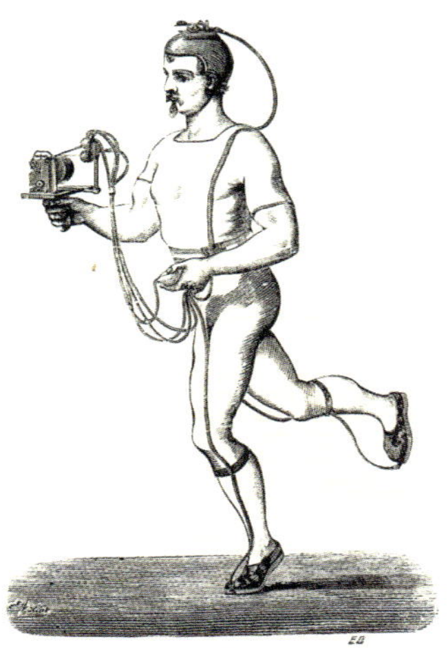

66

Etienne-Jules Marey
La Machine animale: locomotion
terrestre et aérienne
1873
Book, 21.5 x 14.5 x 2.8 cm
The British Library, London

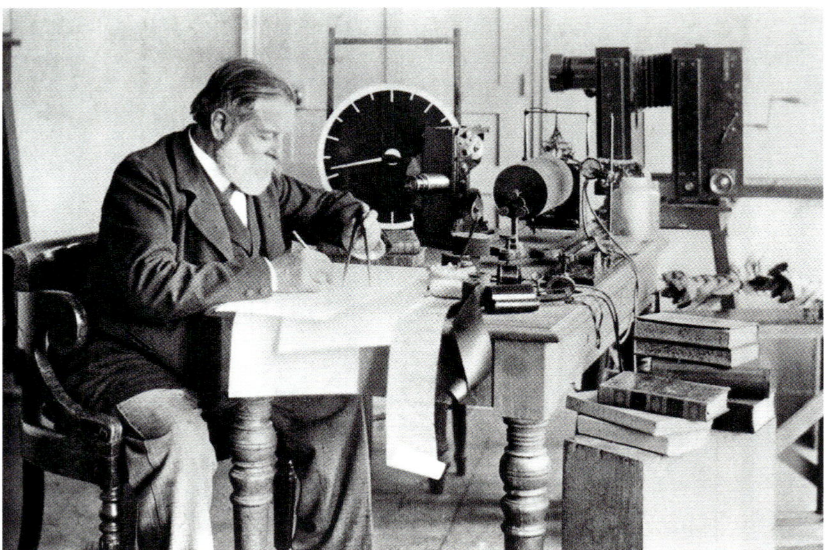

Fig. 49 *Unknown photographer,* Etienne-Jules Marey Seated in His Laboratory,
date unknown

readership rather than the specialists who studied his research papers in professional journals, this volume was among many initiatives that broadcast Marey's erudition in France and beyond. Earlier in the decade, the book had reached Leland Stanford, Muybridge's supporter in San Francisco, and helped persuade him to underwrite the latter's photographic experiments.[38] Persisting over the years with his lectures at scholarly gatherings and for the interested citizens of Paris, Marey regularly released the findings of his laboratory and in 1881 established an ambitious research centre, the 'Station Physiologique', that was financed by the city. A man of wide and colourful interests, Marey was also an accomplished pianist and a gifted amateur artist who made drawings and sculptures in the course of his various studies.[39] Ballet and dance were also part of his wide-ranging expertise: he spoke at the Sorbonne on 'the laws of ancient and modern dance' and later supervised photographs of ballet steps for an important historical volume on the subject.[40] Directly and indirectly influencing several colleagues at the Ecole des Beaux-Arts in Paris, Marey insisted that 'science and art meet in the search for truth'.[41]

More than is generally realised, a substantial feature of both Marey and Muybridge's articles and publications was the emphasis they placed on the visual arts. Near the beginning of Marey's text in *La Nature*, for example, he explained that – like a scientist – 'The artist, in attempting a representation of the horse' also 'seeks to translate its bearing with greater and greater fidelity'.[42] Several pages and no less than nine engravings were then devoted to 'the artistic representation of the horse and animals', with reference to sculptures and reliefs from ancient Assyria to the Renaissance (fig. 50). Critical of some of these examples but approving of others, Marey reminded his readers that 'nothing could replace the patient study which provided the painter or sculptor with a scientific knowledge of the forms and appearance that the limbs adopted in their different positions'.[43] Implicitly addressing members of Degas's generation who depicted the horse, Marey added: 'if the painter or sculptor wishes to animate his work … he must have an exact understanding of its various gaits.' Tissandier, too, echoed this theme when he explained in *La Nature* that the 'instantaneous photographs' of Muybridge would 'interest the physiologist … as much as the painter.'[44] Still based in the United States, Muybridge had also chosen to embrace the visual arts in a number of ways. By 1879, he was actively collaborating with the prominent realist painter Thomas Eakins on the correct placement of horses' legs in one of Eakins's current paintings and appears to have inspired the artist to make his own highly innovative photographs of the human body in action.[45] Muybridge, too, is said to have used reproductions of historic works of art in his lectures at this date and was already imagining a wider influence for his ideas. 'In his enthusiasm,' *The Californian* announced in August 1880, the photographer now predicted 'a great revolution, not only as regards the rearing and training of horses for speed, but in the matter of their representation on canvas'.[46]

The complex and suggestive links between art, science and the depiction of movement represented by Marey and Muybridge finally coincided when the two men met in Paris in the autumn of 1881. On 26 September, Muybridge was invited to address a gathering at Marey's home where – according to journalists present – two hundred guests included the renowned German physicist Herman Helmholtz, the fashionable Parisian photographer Nadar, and Gaston Tissandier, editor of *La Nature*.[47] A brief report of the event in *La Nature* summarised Muybridge's presentation to his French audience of 'new photographic marvels', which included pictures of humans, horses and other animals based on his distinctive early series of multiple photographs, such as those included in *The Attitudes of Animals in Motion*.[48] Muybridge also demonstrated his latest apparatus, the zoöpraxiscope (cat. 68), a handsome brass, wood-mounted projector that passed a beam of electric light through a rotating glass disc (see cat. 67). The sequential images on these discs allowed him to project a similar range of creatures onto a screen, re-creating their distinctive movements to the amazement and delight of those present. Two months later Muybridge again lectured in Paris, now moving from scientific to artistic territory and the grander surroundings of a successful painter's studio, that of the famed creator of equestrian battle scenes, Ernest Meissonier. From the detailed newspaper and magazine accounts that followed the 26 November occasion, it seems that Muybridge repeated his previous performance and again highlighted the significance of his animated 'projections', some of which are said to have been twenty feet high.[49] It is also clear that he was showing not just horses, dogs and birds in mid-action, but a range of human subjects such as 'men in the act of wrestling, running, jumping and other athletic exercises'.[50] Photographs of all these activities had been included in *The Attitudes of Animals in Motion*, but examination of the surviving slides and glass discs shows that Muybridge's displays were not strictly photographic. Although each image had begun as one of his serial photographs, most were 'strengthened' in crucial areas and some appear to have been entirely 'painted' in black and white or colour. Nevertheless, the impact of these projected pictures on those present in November 1881 was again dramatic. Writing of this most 'extraordinary of spectacles,' even the conservative art critic, Albert Wolff, echoed Muybridge's words by acknowledging in *Le Figaro* that it represented an 'artistic revolution'.[51]

Muybridge suddenly became 'one of the topics of Parisian conversation', according to a contemporary account, yet frustratingly

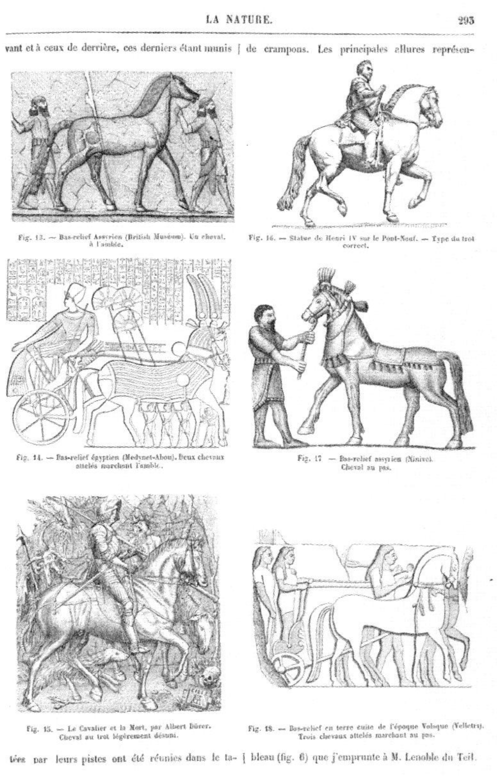

Fig. 50 *Etienne-Jules Marey*, 'Moteurs animés', La Nature, 279, 5 October 1878 (cat. 62), p. 293. Natural History Museum, London

67

Eadweard Muybridge
**Athletes Running (White
and Black Running Race)**
1893
Zoöpraxiscope disc, glass,
diameter 30.48 cm
Loaned by kind permission of
Kingston Museum and Heritage

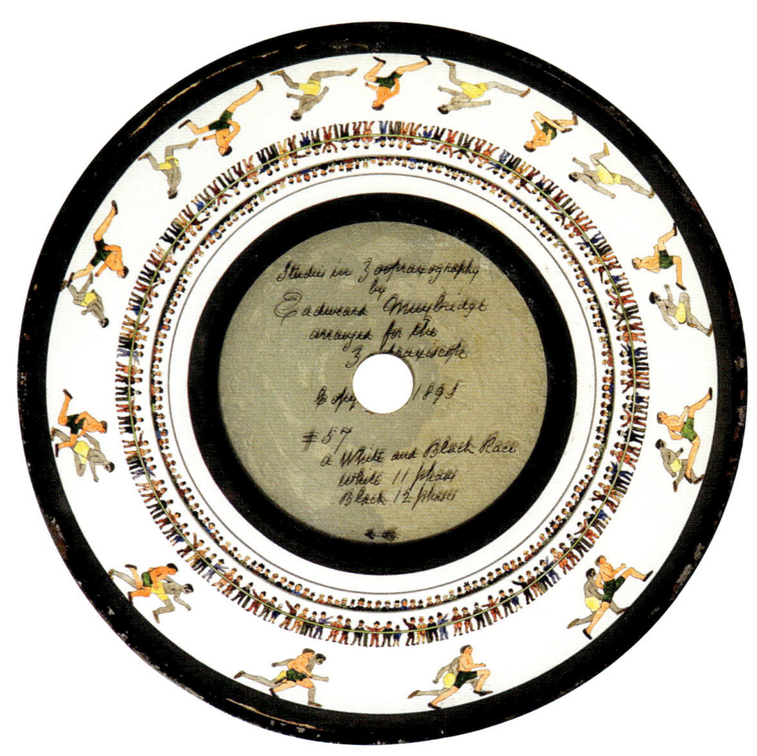

68

Eadweard Muybridge
Zoöpraxiscope
c. 1879
Wood, photographic lens,
metal, 58.8 x 27.5 x 143.5 cm
Loaned by kind permission of
Kingston Museum and Heritage

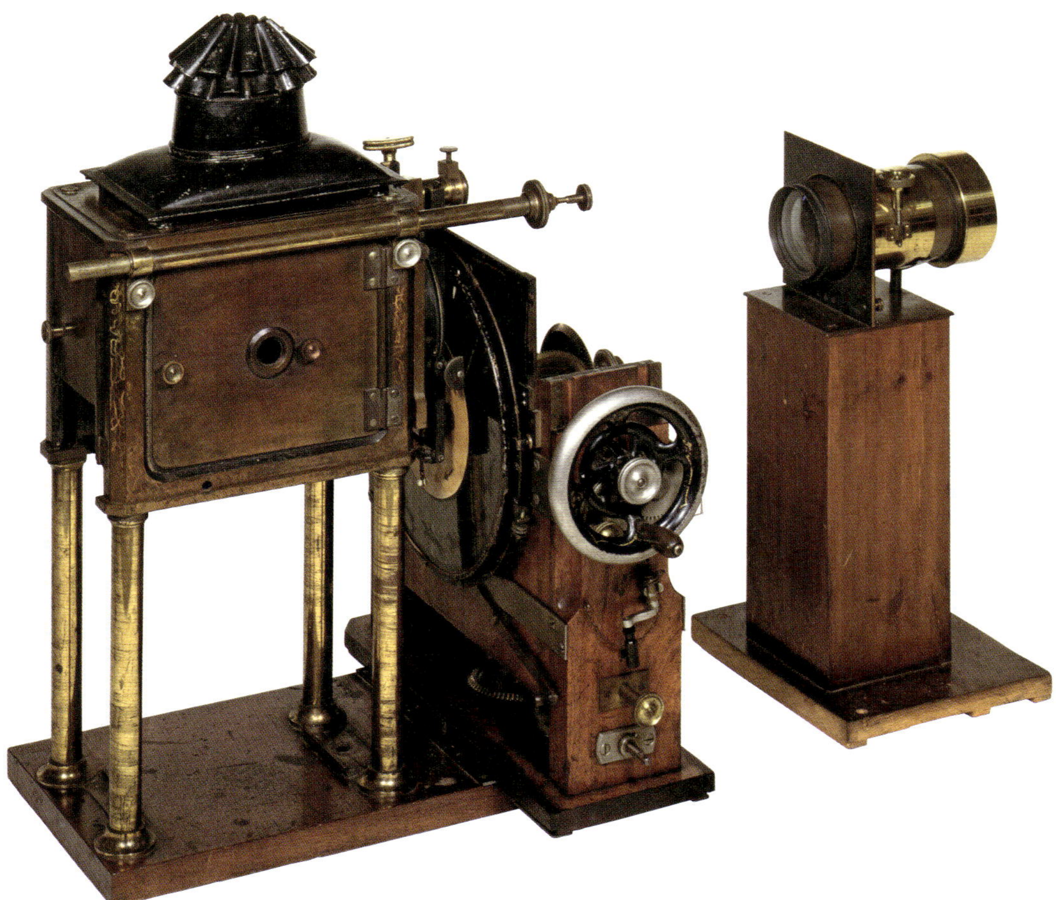

few details survive of his impact on the city's artistic community.[52] A collaboration on a book devoted to the horse was proposed by Muybridge, Marey and Meissonier, but this failed to materialise, and it later emerged that Meissonier had decided to revise several of his paintings of horses in response to Muybridge's discoveries.[53] Some sense of the occasion and its interest for the art world can be gained from various accounts of those present in the gathering at Meissonier's studio, which is said to have included 'the most eminent artists, scientists and literati of Paris'.[54] Among them, we are told, were such prominent painters as Léon Bonnat, Alexandre Cabanel, Edouard Detaille and Jean-Léon Gérôme, the latter a frequent user of conventional photographs in his work; the successful sculptors Eugène Guillaume and Alexandre Falguière; and the novelist Alexandre Dumas.[55] Also identified by the press in the largely anonymous throng were twenty or so less garlanded colleagues of Meissonier's, though all represented the conservative world of Parisian high culture. Beyond this familiar coterie we are left to speculate about the attendance or otherwise of those with a more marginal status, notably members of the Impressionist group to which Degas belonged. There were certainly more points of contact at this date between these two factions than is often assumed, several of which could have resulted in invitations to Muybridge's talk or subsequent information about its contents. After his own conventional beginnings, Degas had maintained a number of friendships with artists outside Impressionist circles and would sometimes acknowledge their achievement. Meissonier himself was a good case in point, the object of Degas's frank admiration on different occasions as both a painter and a sculptor of horses.[56] Bonnat and Degas were personally closer; fellow-students of drawing when they were in Rome as young men, Degas long retained an affection for Bonnat and even exchanged self-portraits with him in later years.[57] Gérôme and Detaille were also among Degas's social acquaintances, and Nadar and Degas had known each other since at least the time of the 1874 Impressionist exhibition, held in the photographer's vacated studio.[58]

Degas would clearly have been no stranger in the company gathered together by Meissonier in 1881, which also happened to include one of his leading admirers in the French press. Besides Wolff, the only other art critic known to have attended was Jules Claretie, novelist and contributor to *Le Temps*. Claretie had praised Degas's work at all six of the Impressionist exhibitions to date, announcing just a few months before Muybridge's talk that the artist possessed 'infinite spirit and infinite talent'.[59] Although Claretie showed limited patience with most of Degas's colleagues, he was a long-standing advocate for Degas as an outstanding exponent of 'realism'. Often celebrating his pictures of ballet dancers, Claretie typically emphasised their 'scrupulous truth', a view echoed in April 1881 when he first saw Degas's *Little Dancer Aged Fourteen*.[60] It is instructive to find that Claretie's vocabulary was mirrored in the language of many of those who currently admired Muybridge's photographs and projections. One such writer noted that the galloping horse he had seen projected at Meissonier's studio was 'an exact image' of this animal in reality and Wolff insisted that Muybridge's demonstration had been 'prodigious in truth'.[61] During the Meissonier soirée, Marey himself compared the zoöpraxiscope images of birds in flight to works by Japanese painters, proposing that these scenes would now allow European artists 'to paint the truth' as effectively as their Asian counterparts.[62] Other voices took up this refrain, recalling how the photographed subjects had 'traversed the screen ... as if the living animal were moving' or claiming to have experienced the human models 'as we see them in the street'.[63]

This uneasy confluence of language and imagery in the 1880s tells us much about the circumstances in which Degas's project as the 'painter of dancers' continued to unfold. Then, as now, such easily used notions as 'realism' and 'truth' were at best approximate and subject to continual redefinition, taking on subtly different resonances within journalism and literature, painting and sculpture, photography and science. For centuries, works of art had been admired for their portrayal of 'real' people and events, as successive generations advanced in skill and in their mastery of such disciplines as anatomy and perspective. Special esteem was often granted to those artists who evoked movement on canvas or in marble, again linked to the assumption that perfect mastery in this technique would evolve over time. In 1878, when Marey reported his discoveries about the horse in action, he clearly took it for granted that they would contribute to this larger endeavour and that contemporary painters would 'faithfully translate' his newly demonstrable facts into their pictures. Meissonier's decision to 'correct' the positions of certain horses seems consistent with this view, though paradoxically he was now mocked by some of the younger generation for his obsessively detailed, sentimental scenes of events that he could never have witnessed.[64]

Marey, Muybridge and many of their admirers were effectively attached to a simplistic notion of perceptual realism in the arts, one that had long been rejected by more radical practitioners in the city. Prominent among these were the group associated with Impressionism, who had specifically turned their backs on the trompe-l'oeil precision and historical subterfuge of Meissonier, Detaille and others.[65] In its place, immediacy of perception and sensation was celebrated, often involving sacrifice of detail in the cause of evoking contemporary experience. While this view is now widely understood, Degas's own identification with the group often confounded his admirers as well as his detractors. When Claretie recognised the 'naturalism' of Degas's *Little Dancer Aged Fourteen* in 1881, he was clearly uneasy with the sculpture's modern subject even as he approved of the work's startlingly 'real' appearance. Other critics found themselves similarly confused: one claimed that Degas's dancer-figure had 'the truth of pantomime'; another compared its 'realism' to that of Zola's insalubrious novels; and a third suggested that the sculpture belonged in 'a museum of zoology, anthropology, physiology'.[66]

Untroubled by such debates in the contemporary art world and encouraged by his reception in Europe, Muybridge returned to America where he threw himself into the development of his latest photographic projects. Now based at the University of Pennsylvania, he launched an ambitious scheme to photograph hundreds of men, women and children, and an array of creatures from the Philadelphia zoo, publishing them in his historic *Animal Locomotion*. In this eleven-volume book he aspired to create 'a logical and progressive atlas of human and animal movement' that would be appropriate to late nineteenth-century culture.[67] Muybridge's distinctive mode was the multi-part photographic sequence, consisting of between twelve and thirty-six images arranged in horizontal registers that recorded a single movement lasting just a few seconds (cats 69–71). In most cases, three cameras arranged

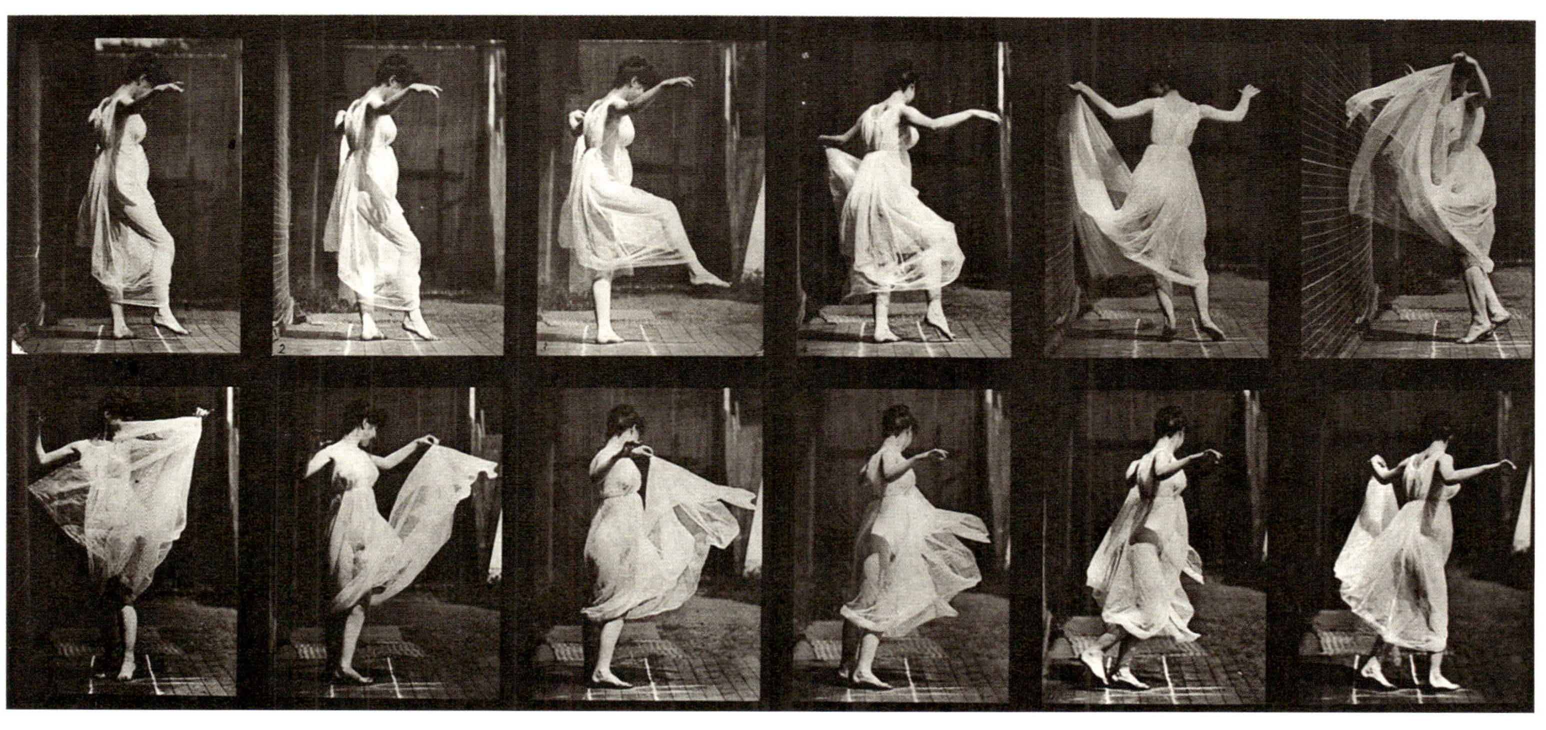

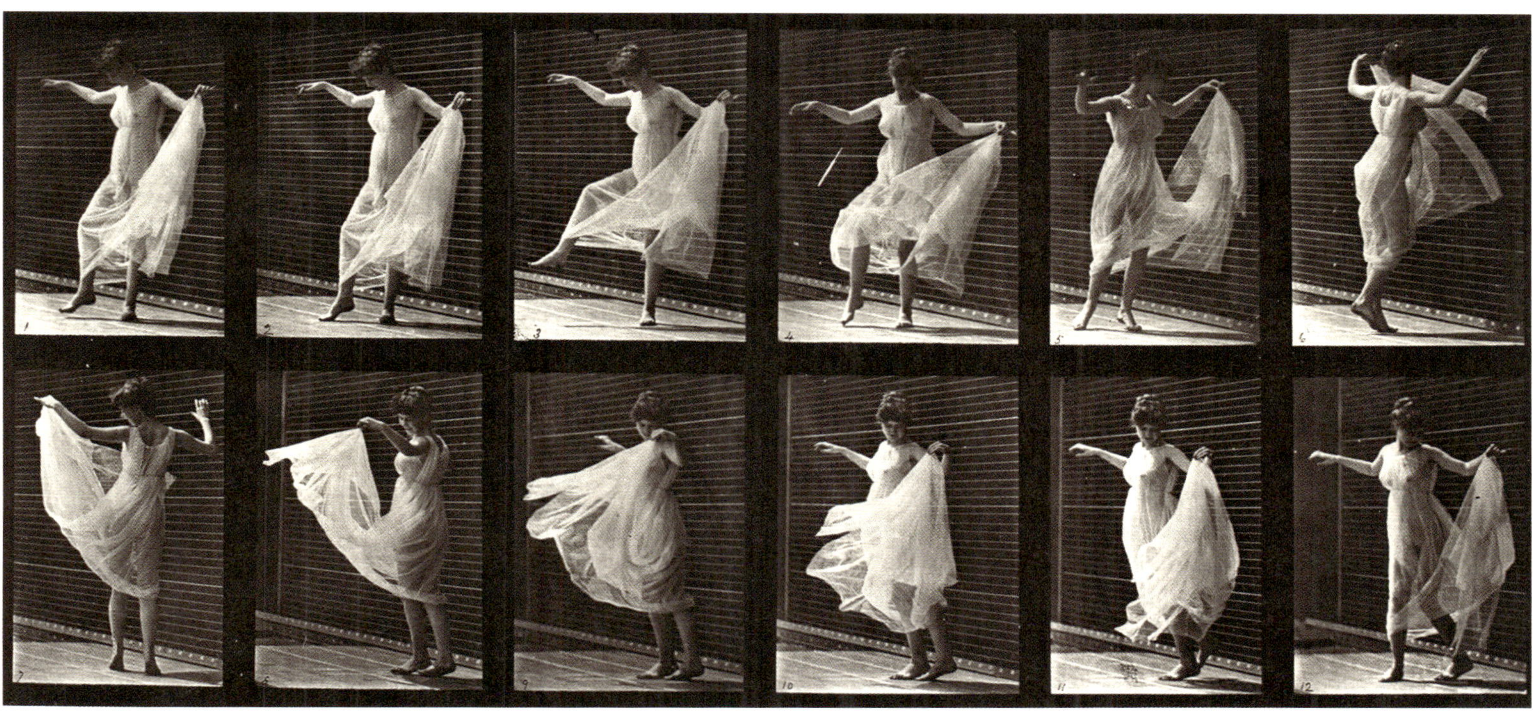

and relaxing, moving slowly and sometimes at speeds that challenged
his equipment. As many subsequent critics have pointed out, however,
Muybridge was neither trained in science nor inclined to extreme rigour.
Along with magnificent panoramas of athletes and depictions of ordinary
citizens in commonplace activities, he included such oddities as two women
waltzing together in the nude, a man pushing a lawn roller and a child
watering a plant.[68]

Publication of *Animal Locomotion* took place in 1887, when Muybridge
undertook further lectures and promotional events that eventually brought
him back to Europe. Tireless as ever, in 1889 he spoke in a succession of British
cities, including Newcastle, Bristol, Leeds, Liverpool, Bath, Ipswich, Glasgow,
Birmingham, Dundee and Belfast.[69] In May he was again in London, where
a presentation was delivered at the Royal Institution and recorded in a striking
portrait in the *Illustrated London News* (fig. 51). Two lectures were apparently
given at the Royal Academy, documented in a series of brief letters that are
still in the Academy's archives (cat. 72). According to this correspondence,
Muybridge's subject was '*Animal Locomotion* in its relation to design in art',
in which he endeavoured to condense his usual course of four lectures while
omitting as little important matter as possible.[70] Another letter records
a request from Lawrence Alma-Tadema to invite Muybridge to talk to Royal
Academy students about his work and a briefer note acknowledges his
receipt of a cheque for services rendered.[71]

MOVEMENT IN THREE DIMENSIONS: DEGAS'S SCULPTURES OF THE DANCE

Unknown to most of Degas's contemporaries was the presence in his studio
of a substantial group of sculptures, all but one of them unexhibited. After
experimenting with modestly scaled wax studies of horses in his early years,
he had increasingly turned to the subject of dancers, the majority representing
naked rather than clothed models and considerably smaller than life size.[72]
The *Little Dancer Aged Fourteen* of 1881 had been an important departure
from his practice in its scale and the use of 'real' accessories, but other
statuettes also incorporated unconventional materials – such as clay and
plastilene – as well as fabric and commonplace objects. Distinctive in almost
all his three-dimensional studies of dancers was their implied animation,
which ranged from the disciplined exertions of the classroom to vivid
arabesques and lively Spanish dance steps associated with the stage. This
extended series of works was in many ways analogous to Degas's reference
collection of drawings of ballerinas, ranging over almost every aspect of their
bodily exertion. Like the drawings, the sculptures were principally made for
his private edification, representing a means to an end rather than a group of
finished objects to be shown in public or sold. Comparable, too, was the sheer
obsessiveness of the artist's approach to this private task, expressed in certain
poses that were repeated with only minor variations and in his focus on
minute nuances of position and gesture, anatomy and musculature. Created
in the context of art, these works can nevertheless be understood as Degas's
own interrogations of observed phenomena, representing accumulated
research materials to be preserved in his studio-laboratory for further
consultation. Over the years a significant number were incorporated into

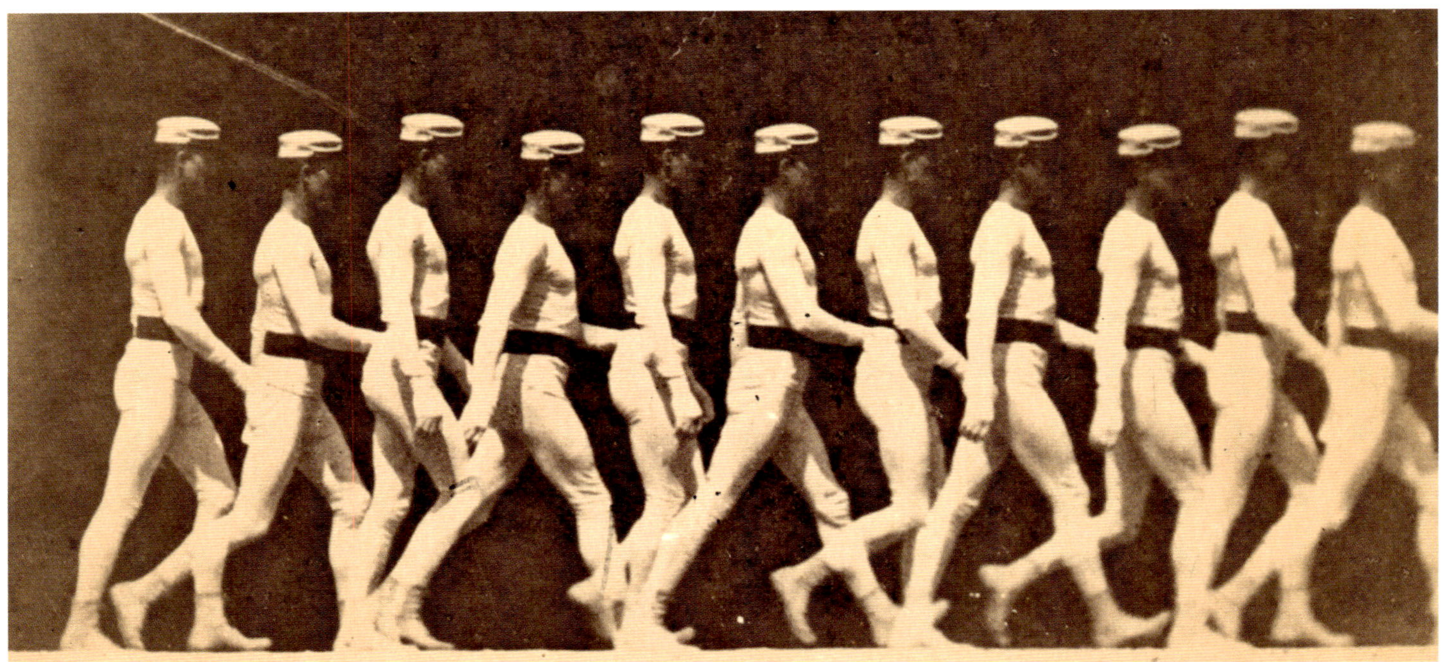

73
Etienne-Jules Marey
'Analyse de la marche',
from Marey 1886,
Station Physiologique II;
Locomotion Humaine
1886
Chronophotograph pasted
into album, 26.5 x 24 x 8 cm
Collège de France, Paris

74
Chronophotographe
fixed-plate camera
1883
Wood, photographic lens,
metal, 57 x 54 x 35.5 cm
National Media Museum,
Bradford. By courtesy of
the Board of Trustees of
the Science Museum

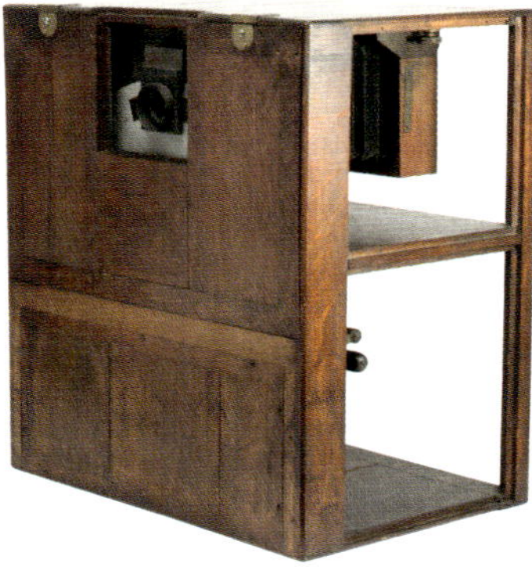

the artist's pictures, and used as 'models' in the creation of other works, where they were typically 'dressed' for their new roles.[73]

Almost half the sculptures retrieved from Degas's premises after his death were devoted to the ballet; presumably there were more among the wax and clay figures considered beyond repair and destroyed by his executors.[74] Seen by just a few friends and rarely mentioned in his lifetime, they also lacked the critical assessment that had grown up around his pastels and paintings. In 1897, however, the artist set aside his customary reserve and talked candidly about his sculpture to an acquaintance, the journalist François Thiébault-Sisson, who later published an account of their conversation. After explaining that he had started out as a sculptor of horses, Degas reminded his companion that in those days 'Marey had not yet invented the device which made it possible to decompose the movements – imperceptible to the human eye – of a bird in flight, of a galloping or trotting horse'.[75] Noting that Meissonier himself had once been obliged to study horses on the streets, Degas continued, 'I wanted to do at least as well as Meissonier but I did not restrict myself to sketches ... I realised that to achieve exactitude so perfect in the representation of animals that a feeling of life is conveyed, one had to go into three dimensions.' Explaining that 'the same is true of renditions of the human form, especially of the human form in motion', he suggested that Thiébault-Sisson himself might 'Draw a dancing figure; with a little skill you should be able to create an illusion for a short time. But however painstakingly you study your adaptation, you will achieve nothing more than an insubstantial silhouette, lacking all notion of mass and volume and devoid of precision.' In conclusion, Degas added that as a sculptor he wished to express 'movement in its exact truth'.

Degas's familiarity with Marey's work in 1897 is consistent with the wide renown that the scientist had achieved by this date, most recently as a pioneer in such fields as manned flight and early film. His former colleague and rival

Eadweard Muybridge, by contrast, had long since come to realise that 'he did not have the background, training, instruments or knowledge' to compete with Marey; by the early 1880s 'scientific interest in his own work all but vanished', to cite Marta Braun.[76] But it was undoubtedly Muybridge who had first prompted Marey to take up photography as a medium for serious research. As early as 1882, Marey used a 'photographic gun' of his own invention to record the 'bird in mid-flight' mentioned by Degas and had worked on a variety of related experiments with human and animal subjects at his Station Physiologique. Here Marey began making photographs of men running and horses trotting, using cameras built to his own specification that were capable of exposures of at least one thousandth of a second. The crucial distinction between his process and Muybridge's was that Marey was able to create a single negative on a small glass plate that simultaneously showed all the phases of the action in question (cat. 73). Not only did this save the considerable labour of assembling a grid of separate images, as Muybridge was obliged to do in his preparations for *Animal Locomotion*, but it also removed the elements of irregularity and occasional manipulation that have been identified in the Englishman's work; he sometimes inserted individual images in the wrong order, for example, or 'borrowed' one from another sequence when an exposure failed. Marey's superior procedure required the building of several unique cameras, one of which now belongs to the National Media Museum, Bradford. This *chronophotographe*, or fixed-plate camera (cat. 74), reveals Marey's ingenious use of a rotating slotted disc to make the rapid exposures required for his minutely detailed studies of figures in action. The resulting chronophotographs – as Marey called them – combined extraordinarily fine detail with unexpected visual drama, as well as a mesmerising sense that the passage of time had finally been captured in one frame.

Marey was characteristically eager to show his chronophotographs and explain their significance to the wider world. Lectures to learned bodies in Paris, some of them open to the public, continued to accompany his research papers and he was as active as ever in publishing his work. In 1882 examples of his first photographs of flying birds appeared in *La Nature* and several other professional journals, while an early sequence showing the phases of a running figure featured as a wood engraving in *Scientific American* (fig. 52).[77] By 1884 his articles had also been accepted by numerous specialist and

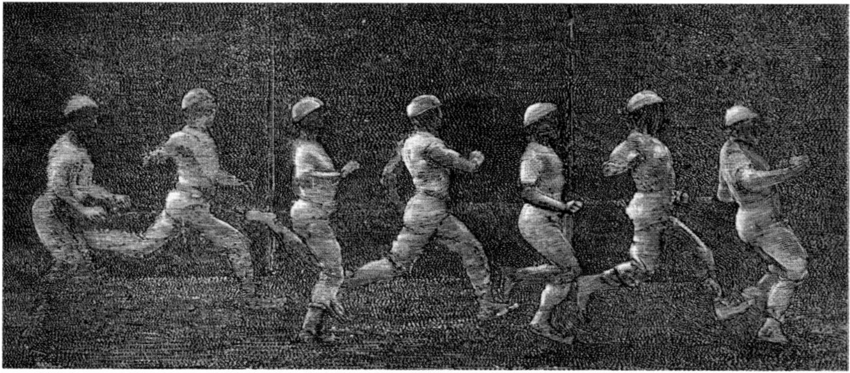

Fig. 52 *Etienne-Jules Marey*, Wood engraving of the phases of a running figure, in Scientific American, 9 September 1882, p. 167. The British Library, London

produire les images des pieds et rendraient celles-ci confuses.

Cette piste est surélevée de 20 centimètres environ au-dessus du terrain environnant, et tout le long de ce relief règne une planche sur laquelle sont peintes des divisions alternativement blanches et noires, ayant chacune une longueur de 1ᵐ,50. Cette règle divisée se peint dans les photographies et sert à mesurer les longueurs parcourues entre deux images successives, à apprécier la taille du sujet, l'amplitude de ses réactions, l'étendue des déplacements de chaque partie de son corps.

Pour connaître la vitesse des mouvements il faut mesurer les temps employés à parcourir les différents chemins. Or si le rouage qui fait tourner le disque avait toujours la même vitesse, si le nombre des fenêtres était le même pour toutes les expériences on n'aurait qu'à déterminer une fois pour toutes l'intervalle de temps qui s'écoule entre deux images et l'on aurait du premier coup l'expression de la vitesse. En effet si les éclairements successifs sont séparés par 1/10 de seconde et si l'intervalle des images, mesuré d'après l'échelle des longueurs, est de 0ᵐ,50, il est clair que dans une seconde, 5 mètres ont été parcourus. Mais la vitesse du disque varie suivant la nature des expériences, il faut donc la contrôler. On pourrait obtenir ce contrôle au moyen d'un chronographe inscripteur indiquant l'intervalle de temps qui s'écoule entre les différents tours du disque pendant la durée de l'expérience; mais cette méthode donnerait deux sortes d'indications indépendantes : celle des espaces sur la plaque photographique, celle des temps sur un cylindre tournant. Il nous a semblé préférable de recueillir sur la plaque elle-même l'indication du temps qui s'écoule entre les images successives. Ce résultat fut obtenu de la manière suivante.

Il suffit, pour connaître la fréquence des rotations du disque, de photographier successivement la position d'un corps animé d'une vitesse uniforme et connue. La figure 1, montre, au-dessus de la tête du marcheur, l'appareil qui sert à cet usage et que nous appellerons *chronographe photographique*. C'est un cadran de velours noir sur lequel des clous brillants, disposés en couronne, partagent la circonférence en un certain nombre de parties égales. Une aiguille brillante tourne continuellement au-devant de ce cadran, avec une vitesse d'un tour par seconde.

Il est clair que si le disque de l'appareil photographique ne faisait qu'un tour par seconde, on n'aurait qu'une image de l'aiguille sur le cadran. Si le disque fait 6 tours par seconde, on aura 6 images, etc. Quand la vitesse du disque est uniforme, les images sont également espacées sur le cadran. Les divisions de celui-ci permettent d'estimer aisément la fraction de seconde correspondant à l'intervalle des images.

L'emploi de cette méthode se comprendra mieux si l'on considère une de ses applications. La figure 2

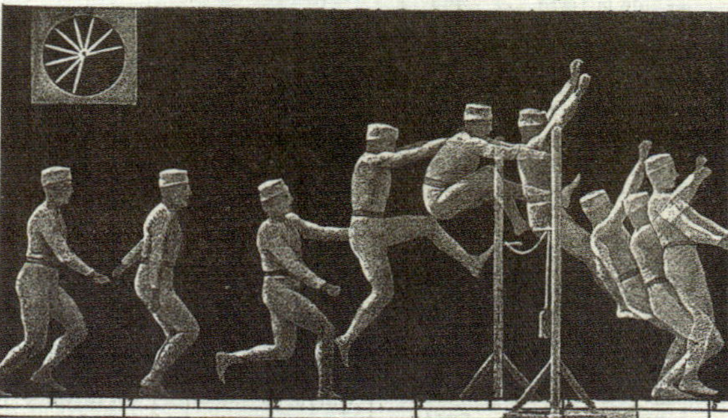

Fig. 1. — Écran noir devant lequel passe un homme vêtu de blanc dont on photographie les attitudes successives. — Mire pour estimer les espaces parcourus. — Chronographe pour mesurer les temps employés à les parcourir.

Fig. 2. — Sauteur franchissant un obstacle. Reproduction par l'héliogravure d'une photographie instantanée de l'auteur.

représente un sauteur qui franchit un obstacle. La série des photographies commence au moment où le sauteur prend son élan par une course préalable ; elle finit lorsque le saut est accompli et que la chute sur le sol a éteint en partie la vitesse de chute.

Analysons cette figure : nous y voyons que le sauteur est représenté 9 fois, c'est-à-dire que 9 rotations du disque se sont produites pendant la durée de l'expérience ; chaque rotation ramenant la fenêtre du disque en face de l'objectif, a laissé arriver la lumière pendant un court instant, ce qui a suffi, chaque fois, pour donner une image. Ces images successives se sont produites en des lieux différents de la plaque, parce que le sauteur occupait lui-même des positions différentes au-devant de l'écran lorsque chacun des éclairements s'est produit. L'espace parcouru, soit sur terre, soit en l'air, pendant l'intervalle de deux images se mesure aisément au moyen des divisions de la règle placées en bas de la figure. On voit que cet intervalle n'est pas toujours le même et que

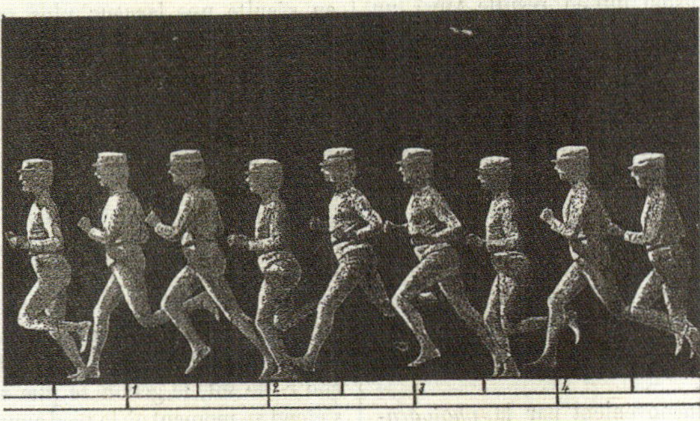

Fig. 3. — Un homme qui court. Reproduction par l'héliogravure d'une photographie instantanée de l'auteur

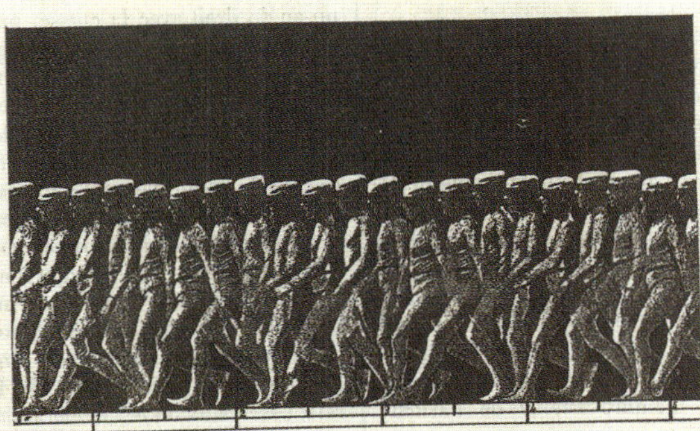

Fig. 4. — Un homme qui marche. Photographie instantanée.

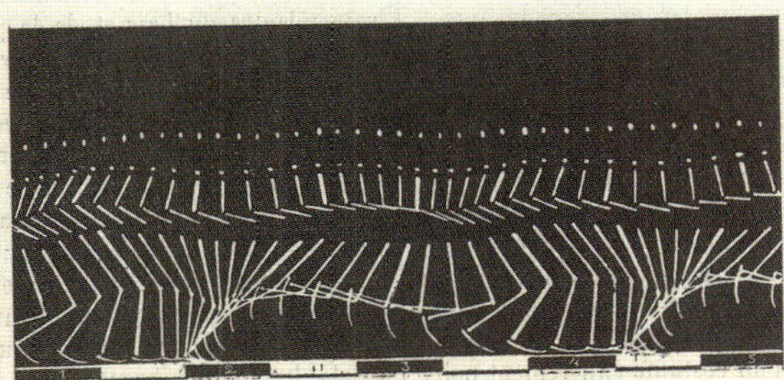

Fig. 5. — Photographie instantanée des bandes de métal brillant appliquées le long de la jambe et du bras d'un coureur.

si nous supposons que des intervalles de temps égaux aient séparé les images successives, la plus grande vitesse avait lieu dans la course qui précède le saut, qu'un ralentissement s'est produit pendant que le sauteur était en l'air ; enfin que ce ralentissement s'est encore augmenté après la chute, la vitesse se perdant en partie au moment où le corps retombe sur le sol.

Pour savoir si les images se sont produites à des intervalles de temps égaux, et pour connaître la durée de ces intervalles, il faut consulter le cadran du chronographe ; on y voit que l'aiguille lumineuse y est représentée autant de fois qu'il y a eu d'éclairements, c'est-à-dire 9 fois. Que l'intervalle des éclairements était constant, car les images de l'aiguille dont la rotation était uniforme forment entre elles des angles égaux. Enfin, la valeur absolue des intervalles de temps qui séparent les éclairements est exprimée par l'angle que font entre elles les images de l'aiguille sur le cadran. Cet angle est d'environ 36°, ce qui montre que l'intervalle de temps entre les éclairements successifs est de un dixième de seconde.

De ces mesures de temps et d'espace, on déduit aisément la vitesse du sauteur aux différentes phases de l'expérience.

Cette vitesse était de 7 mètres par seconde pendant la course préalable ; elle était de 5 pendant la suspension ; elle est tombée à 3ᵐ,50 après la chute.

Photographies partielles. — Lorsqu'on prend sur la même plaque une série de photographies représentant les attitudes successives d'un ani-

popular periodicals, one including a chronophotograph of a high jump that was printed in the *Revue Scientifique*.[78] Although these efforts undoubtedly spread his fame in Paris and elsewhere, a more private glimpse of Marey's activities can be found in the manuscript albums he compiled during these same years, which are today preserved at the Collège de France. Documenting his activities at the Station Physiologique from 1882 onwards, they variously contain original photographic prints of athletes in action and views of scientific apparatus and facilities; copies of articles that emerged from his current research; and handwritten notes and captions. One volume is devoted to the 'Materials and Techniques' that were then in use and includes views of buildings, cameras and Marey's photographic 'gun'. Pasted into a second album are several sequences of prints dated 1883, among them early examples of his 'geometric chronophotographs'. As two specimens reveal (cat. 76), the model depicted had been dressed in a black costume with white lines marking his limbs and torso, allowing Marey to photograph an 'abstract' version of the man's movement and study the precise trajectory of his body. A third volume extended the documentation of the Station Physiologique, both visual and textual, in remarkable photographs such as those recording successive images of a seagull in flight (cat. 77). Also present in these albums were early traces of Marey's fascination with figures 'en relief', works in sculpture that had literally begun to extend his own research into a new dimension.[79] One text, for example, noted his recent presentation of 'a series of figures in relief of a flying bird' and anticipated using the same sculptural method to represent 'the movements of man and animals in their successive phases'; characteristically, Marey added that

76

Etienne-Jules Marey
**Geometric chronophotographs
pasted into album**
1883
Album, 23.5 x 30 x 4.5 cm
Collège de France, Paris

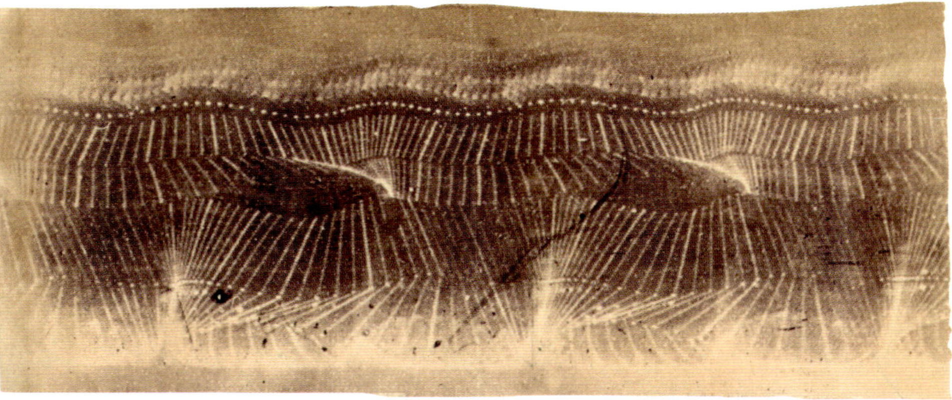

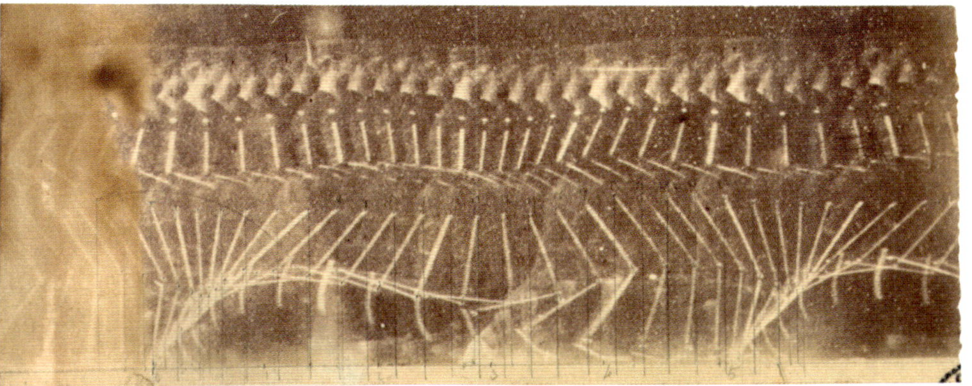

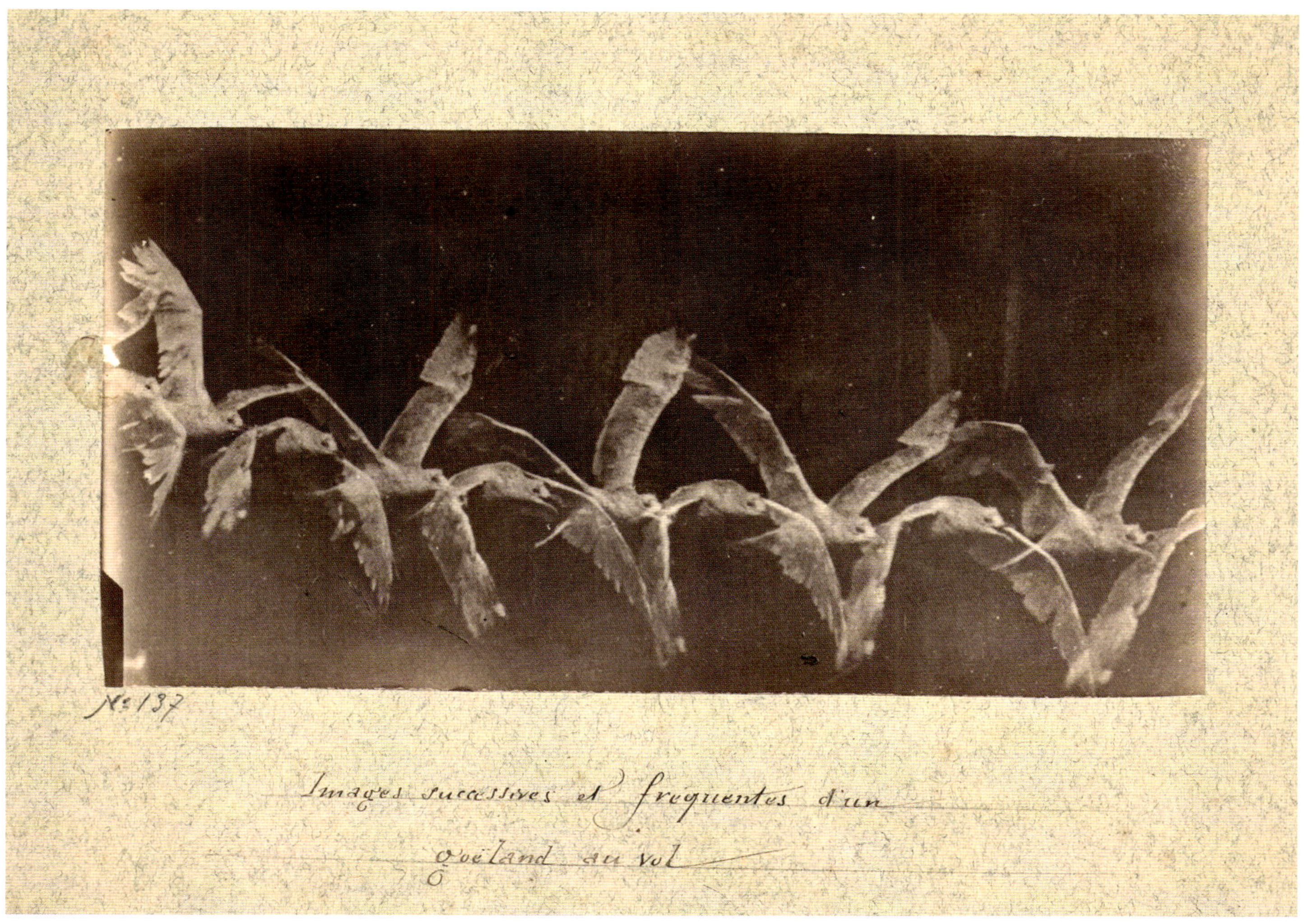

77

Etienne-Jules Marey
'Images successives et fréquentes
d'un goëland au vol', from Marey
1882–86, Station Physiologique;
Méthodes, Installations et
Instruments
1882–86
Chronophotograph pasted into
album, 26.5 x 24 x 8 cm
Collège de France, Paris

such projects would be useful 'to the Arts as they would be to Science'. Discussed at greater length in the next chapter, this unexpected step still deserves to be more widely recognised.

It was against the background of Muybridge's recent lectures in Paris and Marey's widely broadcast experiments at the Station Physiologique that Degas's studies of dancers unfolded during the 1880s. His clearest and most direct response to Muybridge occurred at the end of this decade, when the artist made several drawings from photographs in *Animal Locomotion* and even used the publication as he worked on his sculptures of horses. Most frequently discussed is *Horse and Jockey* (fig. 53), in which Degas used red chalk to make a loose transcription of a single frame from Muybridge's 'Annie G. in Canter' (fig. 54), a set of twelve instantaneous photographs of a racehorse and jockey.[80] Other such transcriptions from equine subjects have been added to this list more recently, notably by Shelley Sturman in her remarkably detailed study of a set of bronze casts from Degas's sculptures.[81] Almost unnoticed, however, has been his interest in Muybridge's photo-sequences of naked or lightly clothed women, inspiring several drawings of figures that in turn provided the basis for a number of substantial pastels.[82] What is now beyond doubt is that Degas had access to *Animal Locomotion* and was both

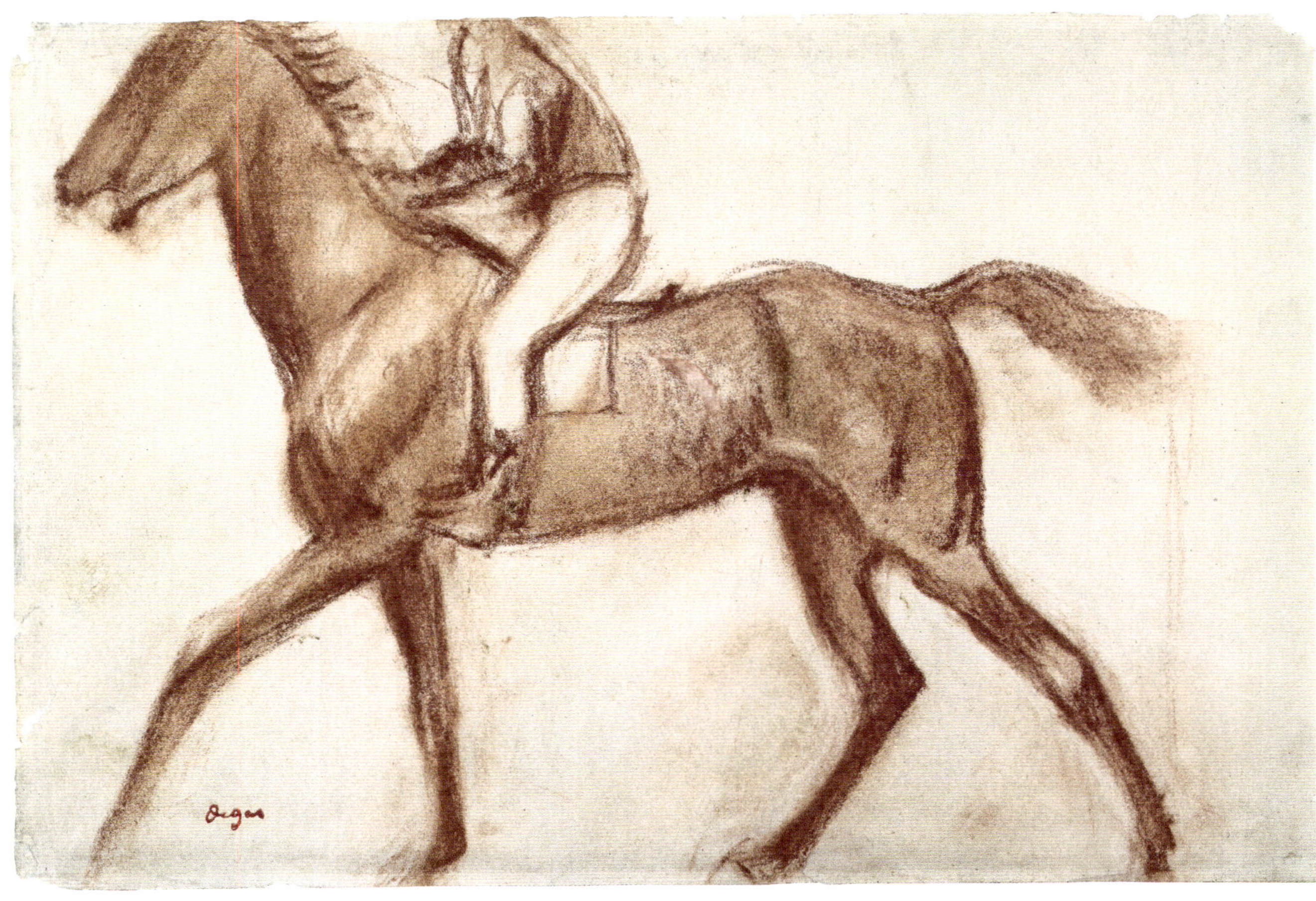

Fig. 53 **Horse and Jockey**, *c.* 1888. Chalk on paper, 28.3 x 41.8 cm.
Museum Boijmans Van Beuningen, Rotterdam, inv. no. FII 22

stimulated by its imagery of arrested movement and inclined to embrace
its radical approach to 'the human animal'.

It had presumably become clear to Degas at an earlier date, however, that
the very public involvement of Marey and Muybridge with the study of figures
in action had some parallels with his own concerns as draughtsman, painter
and sculptor. Coincidentally, all three men had chosen to study the horse in the
formative stages of their investigations, yet soon focused on the human body as
their principal subject. Uniting their approaches in a more fundamental sense
was a concern with the minute physiological inflections of each animal or
figure as it progressed through space. Aspiring to record and comprehend such
elusive actions, which are 'imperceptible to the human eye', in Degas's reported
words, each of them devised strategies that reduced these events to a series
of 'frozen' moments, whether in a sequence of drawings or in rapid exposures
on a photographic plate. Beside the meticulous procedures of Marey and even
the more improvised methods of Muybridge, Degas's pursuits in the studio
inevitably seem haphazard. Never a systematic individual, his remarks to
Thiébault-Sisson and his demonstrable interest in Muybridge nonetheless
indicate his awareness of an affinity between them and a sense that he could
learn from their work. Yet almost perversely Degas chose not to become directly
involved in photography for another decade, despite its increasing availability

to the amateur and its ubiquity in his world. Especially suggestive – yet largely
unexamined – is the resonance between Degas's activities as a sculptor and
those of Marey, whose explorations of the medium unfolded during this same
decade. A fascinating case of parallel developments in disciplines that are often
thought to be worlds apart, this phenomenon still awaits a thorough study
that acknowledges the separate contributions of artist and scientist. As the
pioneering museum director Pontus Hulten noted in 1977: 'Degas interested
himself in an intuitive fashion in that which was for Marey the object of
scientific study. With the former, an anxiety, an irrational vision which is that
of every artist. With the latter, a prescience of the real, and the truth.'[83]

When talking with Thiébault-Sisson, Degas explained that his sculptures
of horses had helped to give 'a feeling of life' to the equestrian pastels and
paintings he was currently working on. The wax figures of ballerinas that soon
joined them evidently played a similar role, helping Degas to compose his
pictures of ballet classes and performances in the seclusion of his studio, while
still embodying the vitality of the models who had posed for him. The nudity
of their subjects, however, placed these figures in a somewhat different
category. In practical and historical terms, they linked the artist with the
disciplines of observation and delineation learned in his youthful life classes,
and through them with the classical tradition that would continue to haunt
his work until the end. Yet in the context of art at the *fin de siècle*, such works
might also evoke intimacy as well as athleticism, the subjectivity of the
creative process and something of the objectivity of science, as Degas strove
to 'achieve exactitude' and represent 'movement in its exact truth'. It is less
surprising to find that both Marey and Muybridge used nude or minimally clad
figures in much of their photography, in order to clarify the action of limbs and
muscles that would otherwise be concealed. The effect with Degas's dancer
sculptures is of course similar, allowing the artist to spell out the forms of hips,

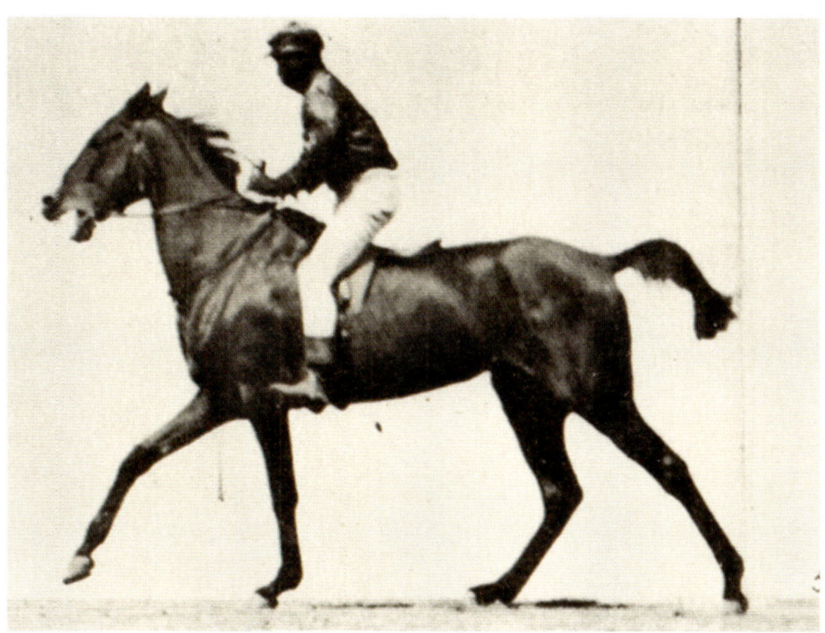

Fig. 54 *Eadweard Muybridge*, 'Annie G. in Canter', plate 621 of Animal Locomotion, 1887.
Collotype, 49.5 x 61 cm. George Eastman House, Rochester, New York

backs and shoulders that were largely covered by costumes on stage, and to pay attention to the nuances of muscular activity and the physical strains placed on the ballerina. As observers, we become conscious of the extremity of certain positions and the fact that many of them could not be held rigidly for more than a few seconds, even by a strong, seasoned ballerina. The sense of arrested motion or actual precariousness is also a central factor in many of these works, linked to our awareness that such positions were both preceded and followed by closely analogous bodily conformations. Recalling the multiple 'stages' in Degas's sequences of drawings of clothed dancers, such as those executing a plié (cats 51, 52), some of the waxes based on related steps can also suggest phases in a single movement when seen together.

With the inevitable exception of the *Little Dancer Aged Fourteen*, even Degas's most earthbound sculptures of ballerinas are energised by the implicit dynamism of their subject. The elegant, restrained *Dancer Ready to Dance, Right Foot Forward* (cat. 79), for example, shows one such figure in a characteristic exercise – the 'tendu' – that was part of daily classroom routine. Poised and seemingly still, in reality this dancer would be engaged in the process of

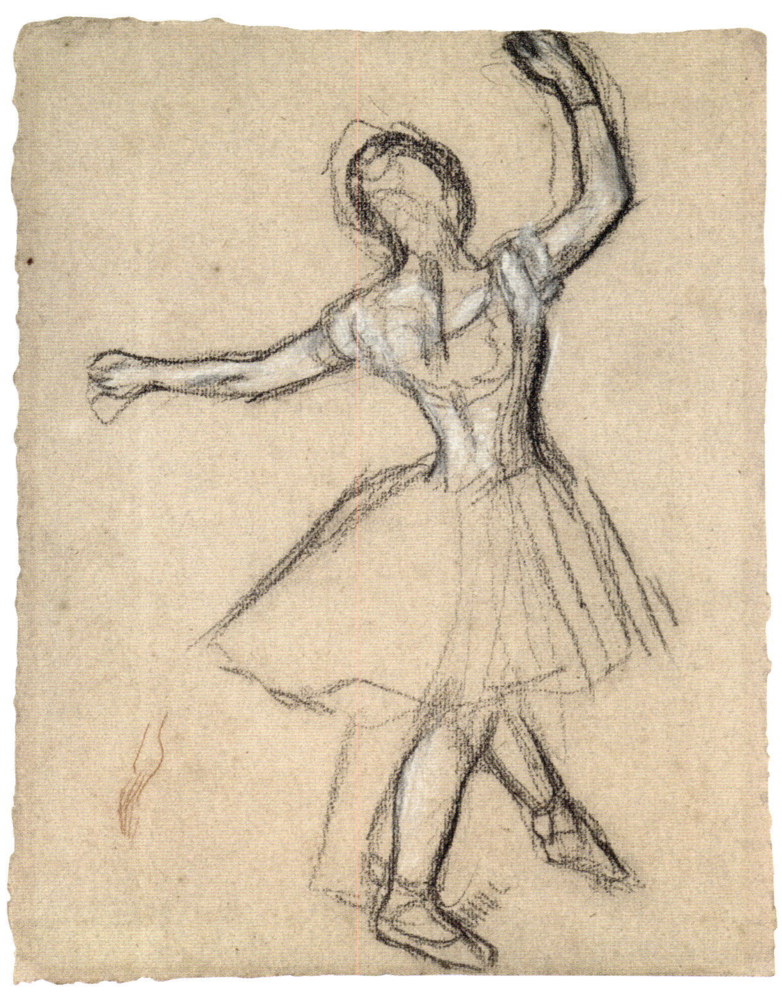

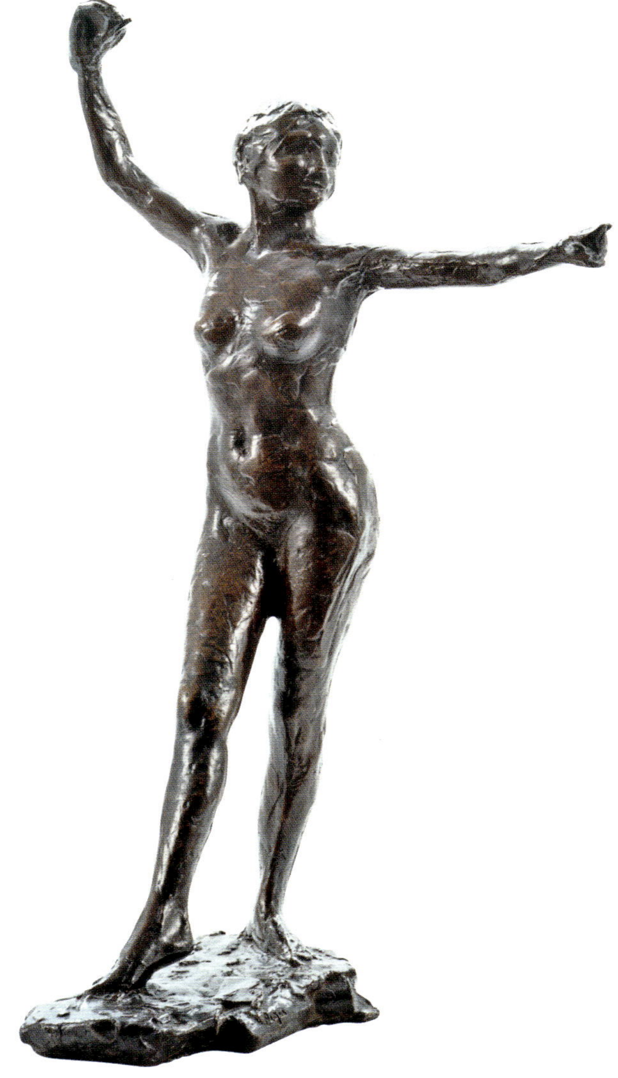

extending or retracting her right leg in order to exercise certain leg muscles. A vigorous drawing of the same step, now seen from behind (cat. 78), introduces us to a slimmer, more energetic individual who wears a practice costume. Revealing here are the charcoal lines made by Degas as he hastily recorded the girl's transient positions: multiple contours around head, arms and legs appear to evoke her movements, again contrasting with the more sedate *Dancer Ready to Dance, Right Foot Forward*. The closely comparable but more energetic *Dancer Moving Forward, Arms Raised, Right Leg Forward* (cat. 80) leaves no doubt that this individual is shown in mid-step, apparently transferring her weight from one leg to another in an action known as 'temps lié'. Performed both in class and on stage, this fleeting movement has been skilfully captured in the forms of the bronze, based on Degas's original wax, one of the largest and most imposing of his surviving sculptures. The partly fractured volumes and fissured legs and feet in this work reflect the damaged condition of many such waxes when they were discovered at the end of the artist's life. Lending some of his sculptures a curiously archaic appearance, they also remind us that ballet was routinely cited in Degas's era as the descendant of ancient Greek dance.

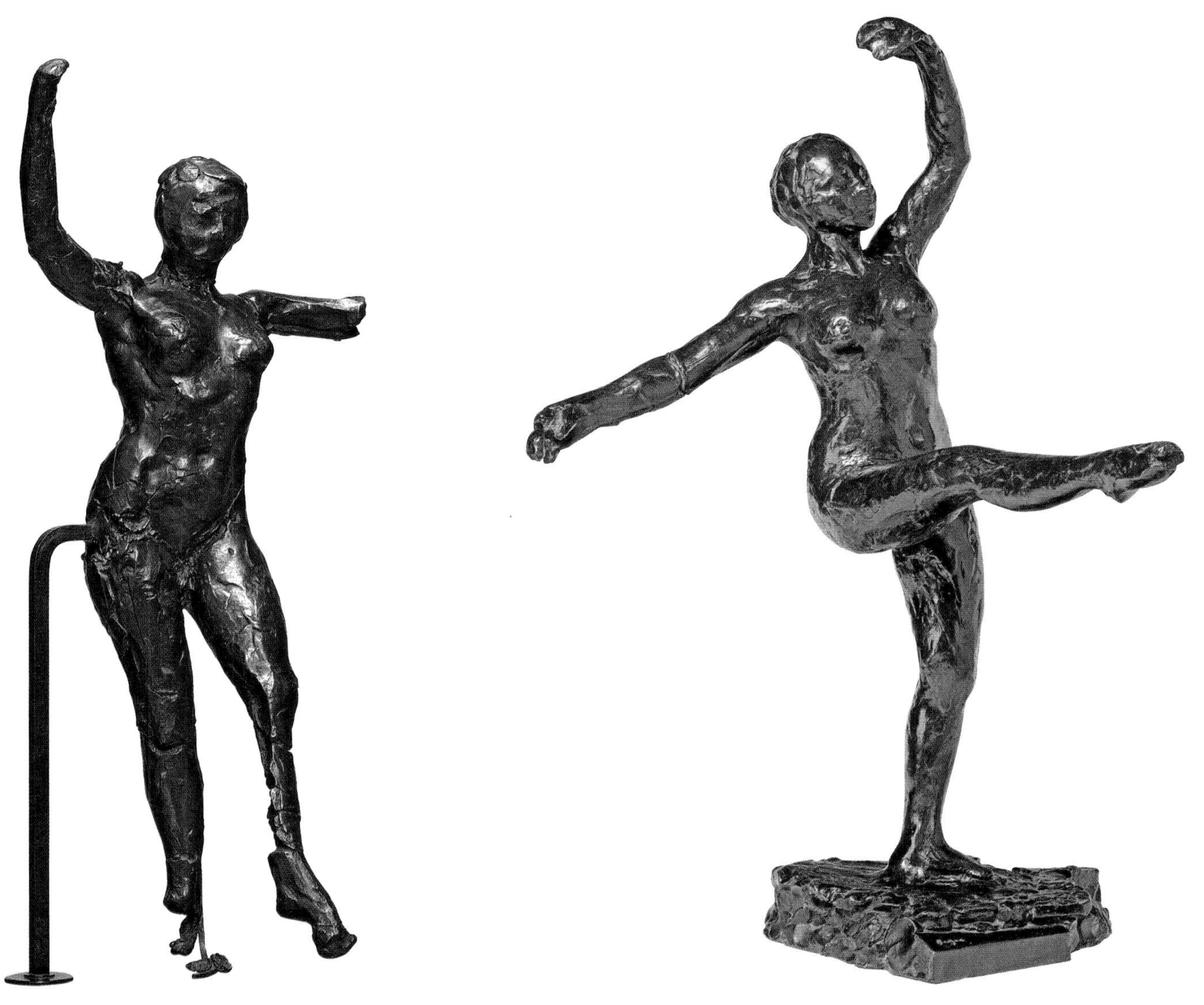

82

Dancer with Bouquets
1890–1900
Oil on canvas, 180 x 151 cm
Chrysler Museum of Art,
Norfolk, Virginia.
Gift of Walter P. Chrysler Jr
in memory of Della Viola
Chrysler Jr

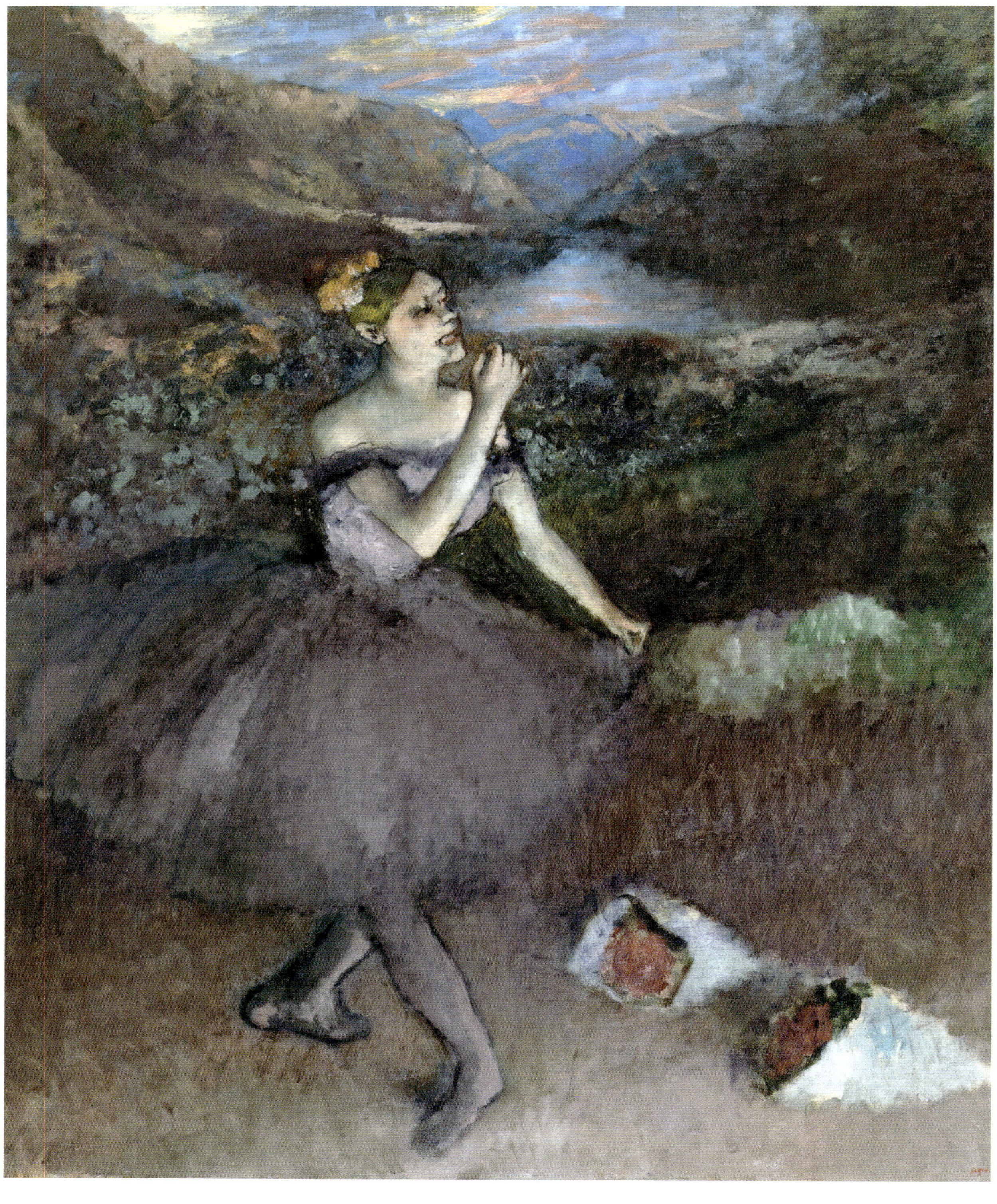

Made from a wax that was better preserved, *Dancer Fourth Position Front on the Left Leg* (cat. 81) shows a step that was rarely depicted by Degas, although it was found in the classroom as well as in performance. Movement is now more evident throughout the model's body, with one lower limb raised and her opposing arm held high, as she executes a 'battement en avant' or 'développé en avant'. The latter involves a slow and elegant leg extension that would surely have challenged both Degas's human subject as he worked from this pose and the artist's own ability to capture such an unstable form. The bronze *Dancer Bowing, First Study* (cat. 84) is unquestionably related to the stage rather than the routines of daily exercise. Despite being represented in the nude, this figure is shown as if advancing towards the theatre footlights, bearing most of her weight on the left leg and formally saluting an imaginary audience. A scene of precisely this kind is found in the remarkable oil painting *Dancer with Bouquets* (cat. 82), one of many dramatic examples of a confluence between Degas's two- and three-dimensional creations. Degas made several

83

Dressed Dancer at Rest, Hands Behind Her Back, Right Leg Forward
Original wax, *c.* 1895
Bronze, 42.9 x 22.2 x 25.4 cm
Private collection

84

Dancer Bowing, First Study
c. 1882–95
Bronze, 22.2 x 11.8 x 16.8 cm
Musée d'Orsay, Paris. Acquired through the generosity of the artist's heirs and the Hébrard family, 1931

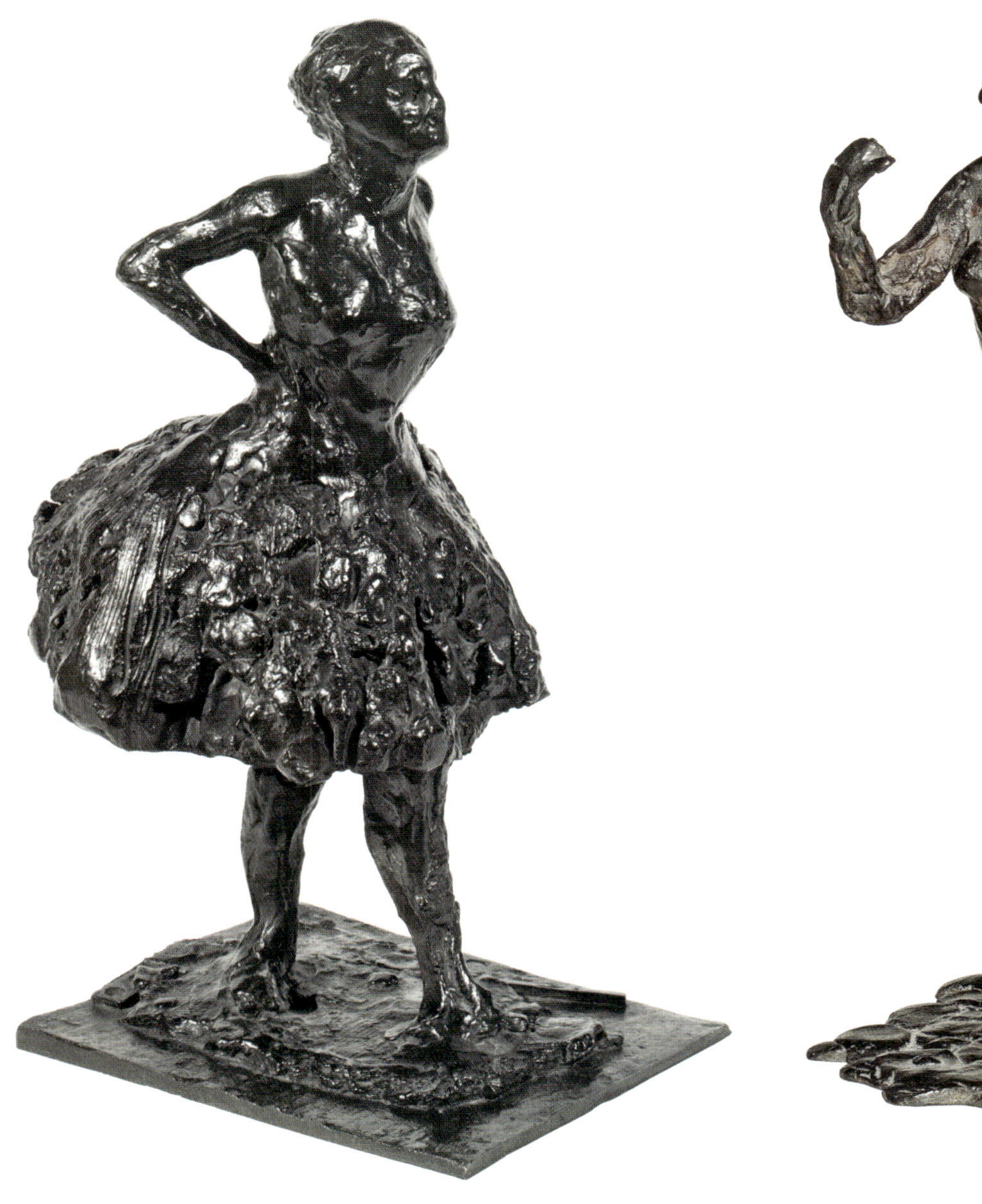

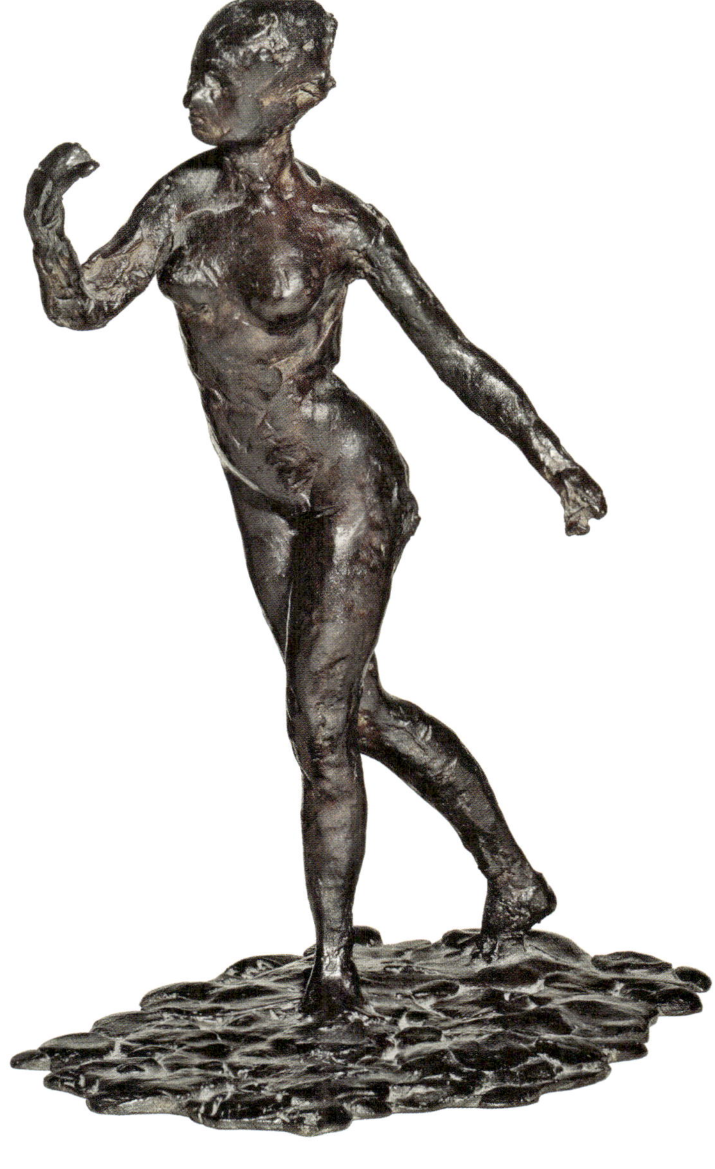

drawings for the vividly lit human subject of this canvas, while his statement to Thiébault-Sisson reminds us that such a figure might also have been informed by the sculpture *Dancer Bowing, First Study*. Unlike a human model, his wax was always available for consultation and could be studied at will from any angle, helping to elucidate the dramatically disposed overlapping limbs that contribute to the picture's extraordinary energy. Equally evident in *Dancer with Bouquets* is the potency of Degas's colour in these years, here used to bring the subject in her lilac outfit startlingly to life against a green, blue and pink stage landscape. Most unusually, a second sculpture distinctly echoes the principal subject of this work, even repeating the motif of the dominant tutu. In *Dressed Dancer at Rest: Hands Behind Her Back, Right Leg Forward* (cat. 83), Degas portrayed a ballerina in the act of stretching her shoulders and arms to relieve the pressures of rehearsal or performance. In common with the star of *Dancer with Bouquets*, the body of this figure seems almost dominated by her majestic costume, which is charmingly weightless in the painting yet evocative of something more solemn in the bronze. Where the diaphanous confection worn by the woman on stage seems expressive of her animation, the massive-seeming outfit of the sculpted figure speaks of inertia, even exhaustion.

The most compelling parallel between Degas's sculptures and contemporary photographs of figures in movement is that based on his three large arabesque studies, all of them made on approximately the same scale.

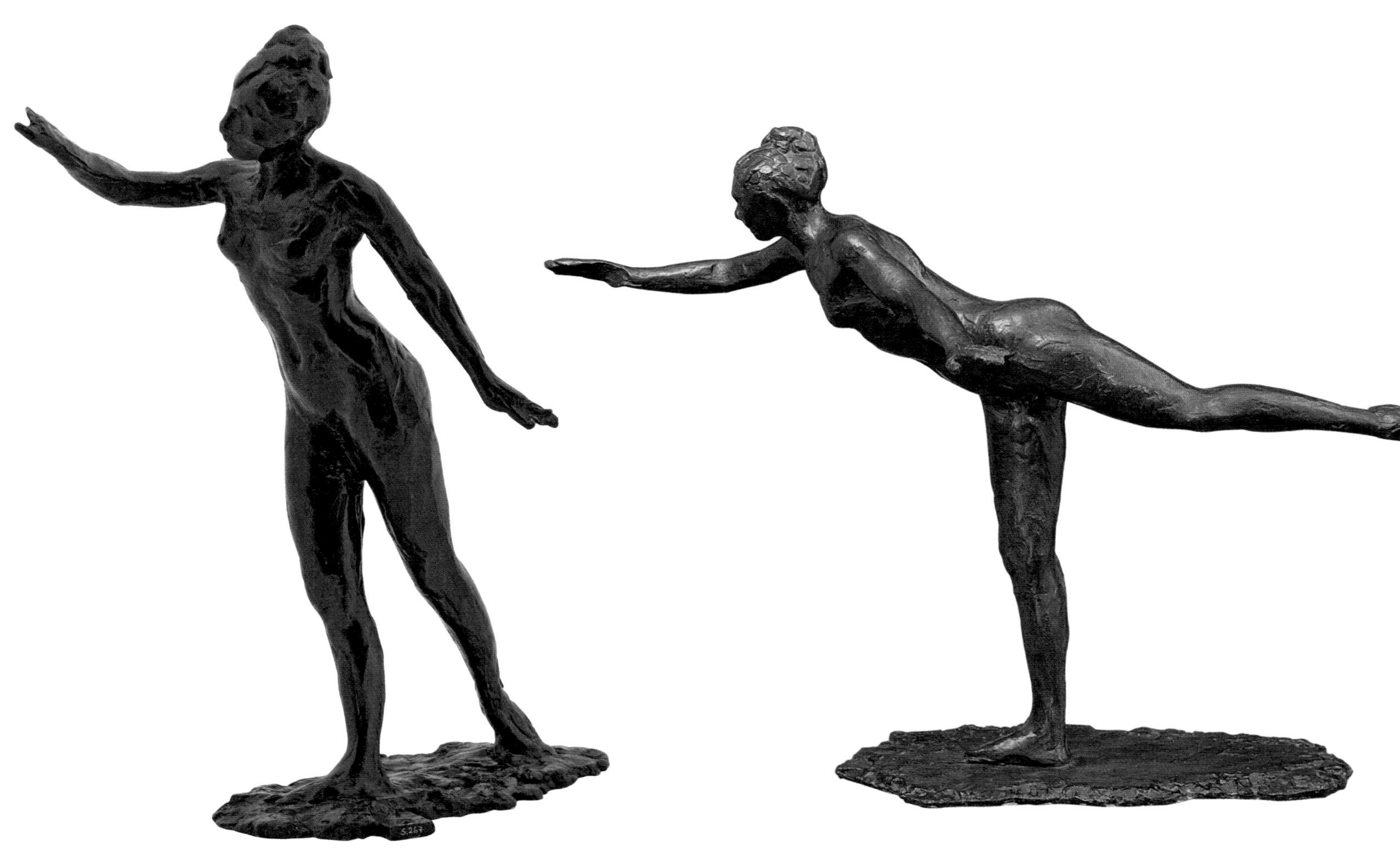

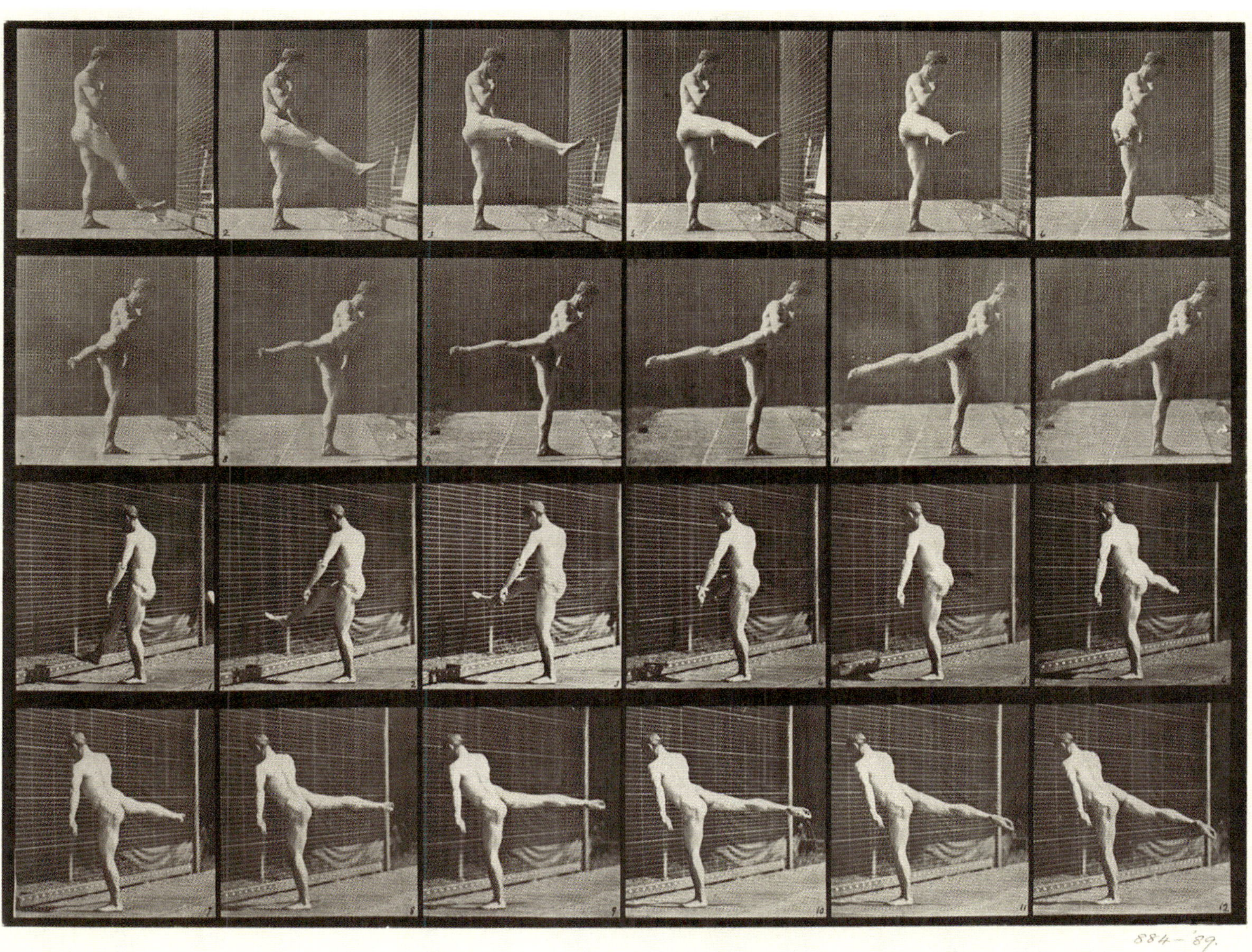

884 - 89.

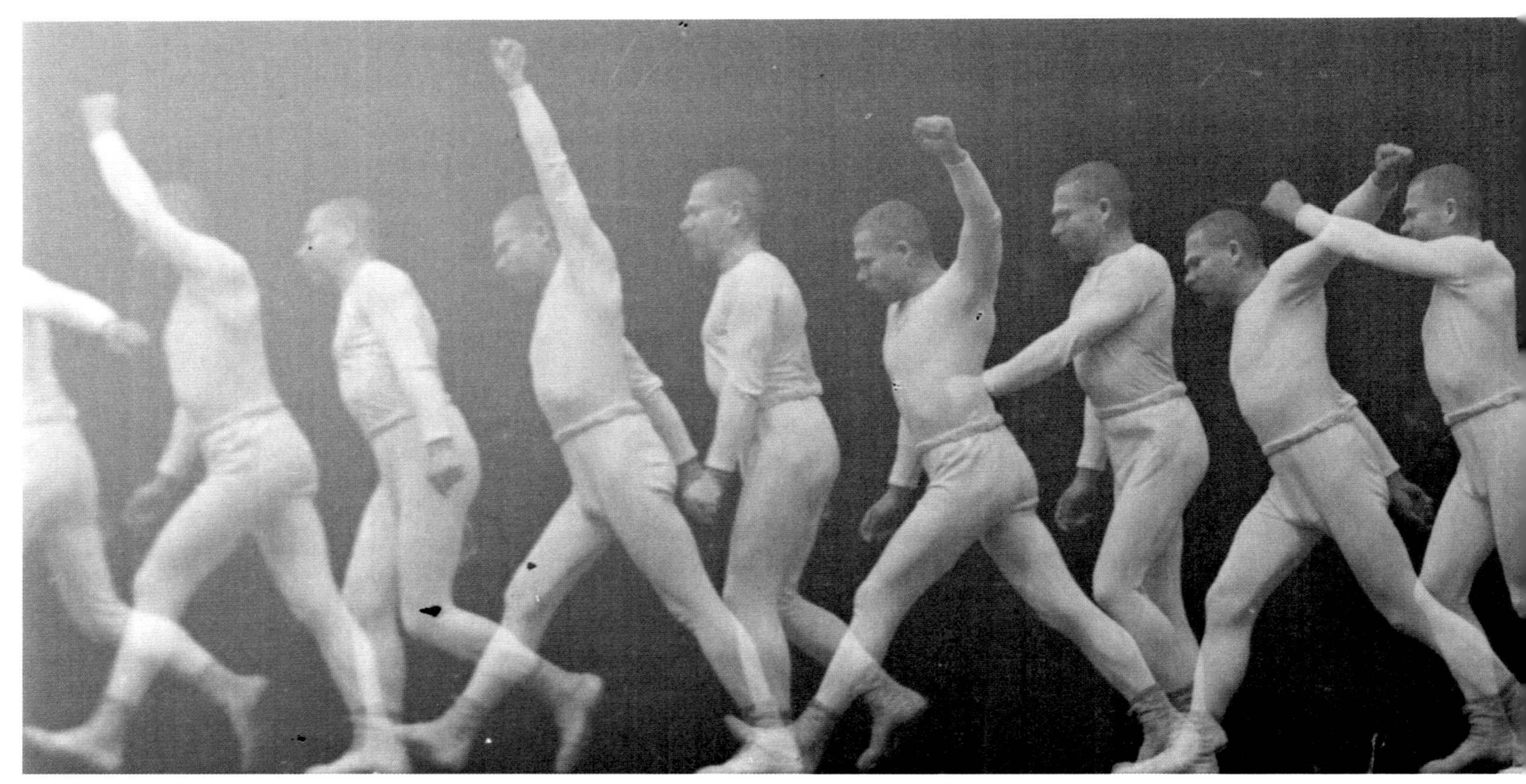

Fig. 55 *Etienne-Jules Marey,* Marche avec balancement
du bras droit, chronophotographie, sujet Sandoz, *c.* 1890.
Photograph. Collège de France, Paris, inv. no. BIUM P287

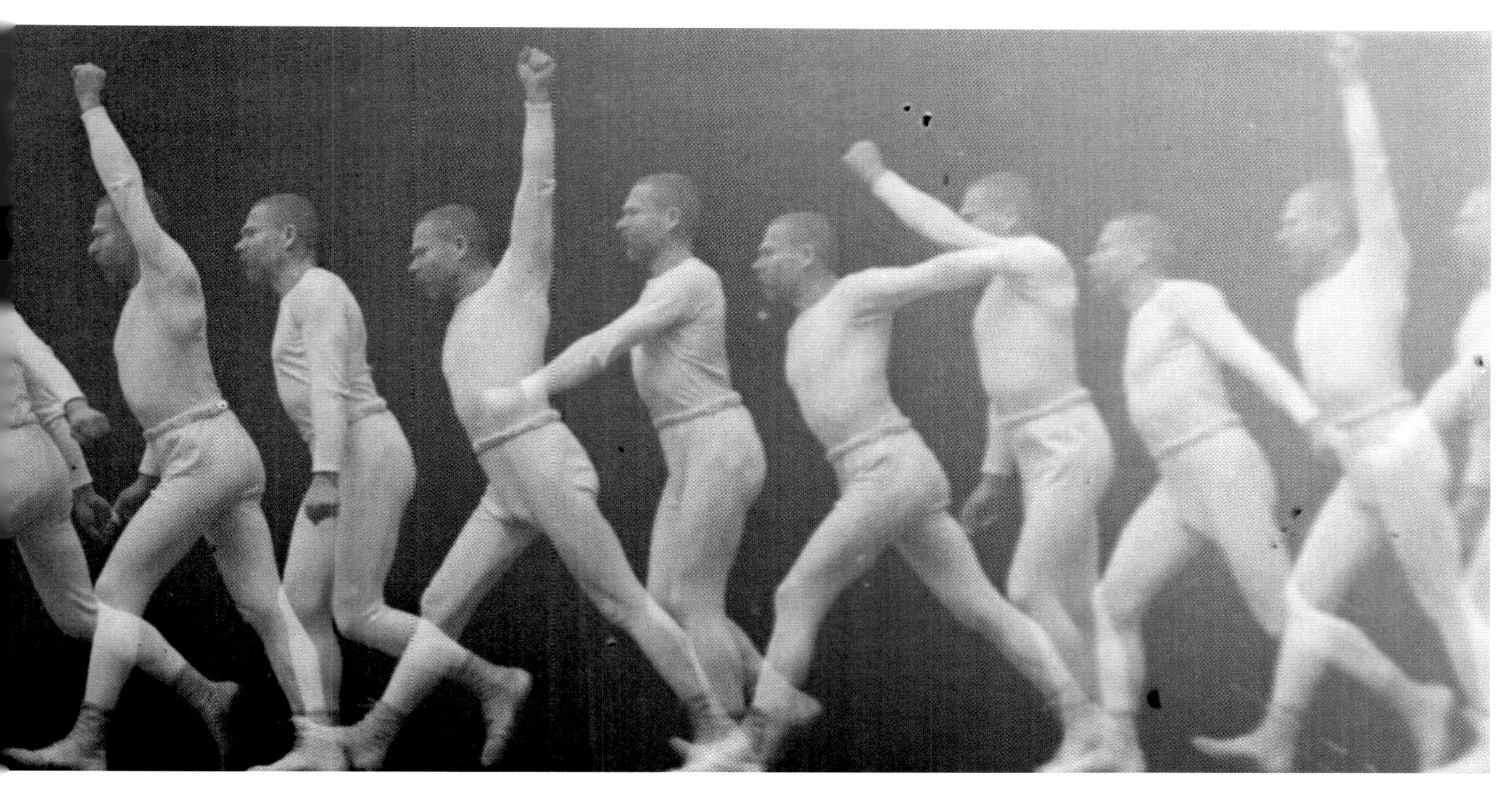

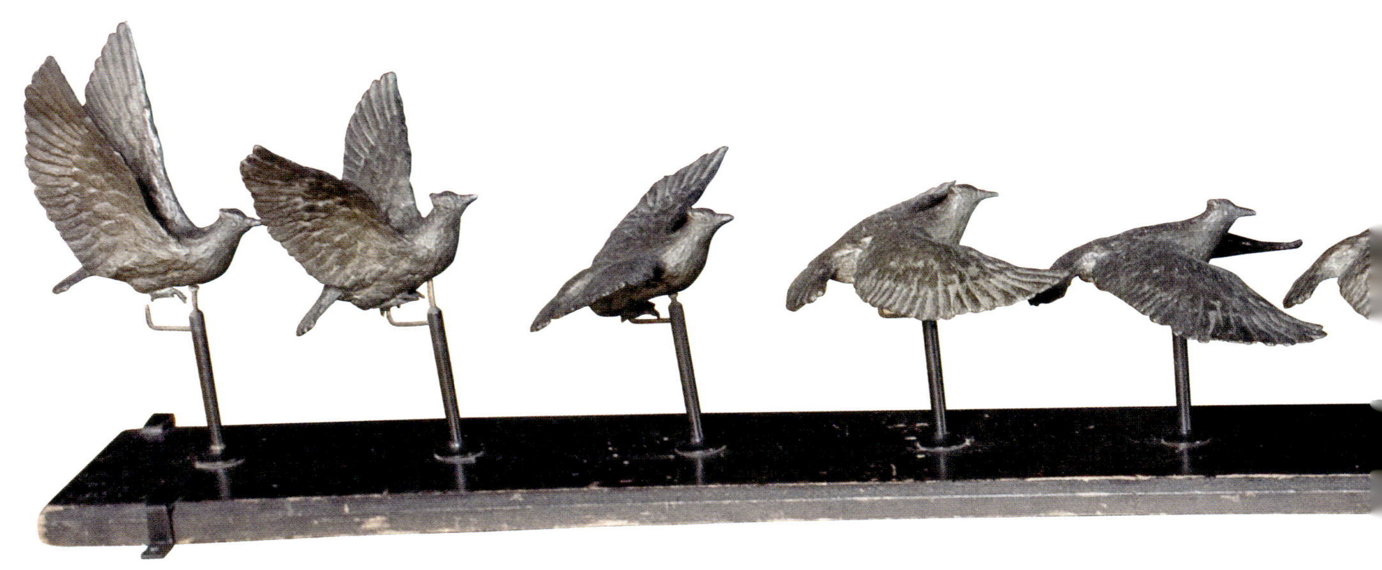

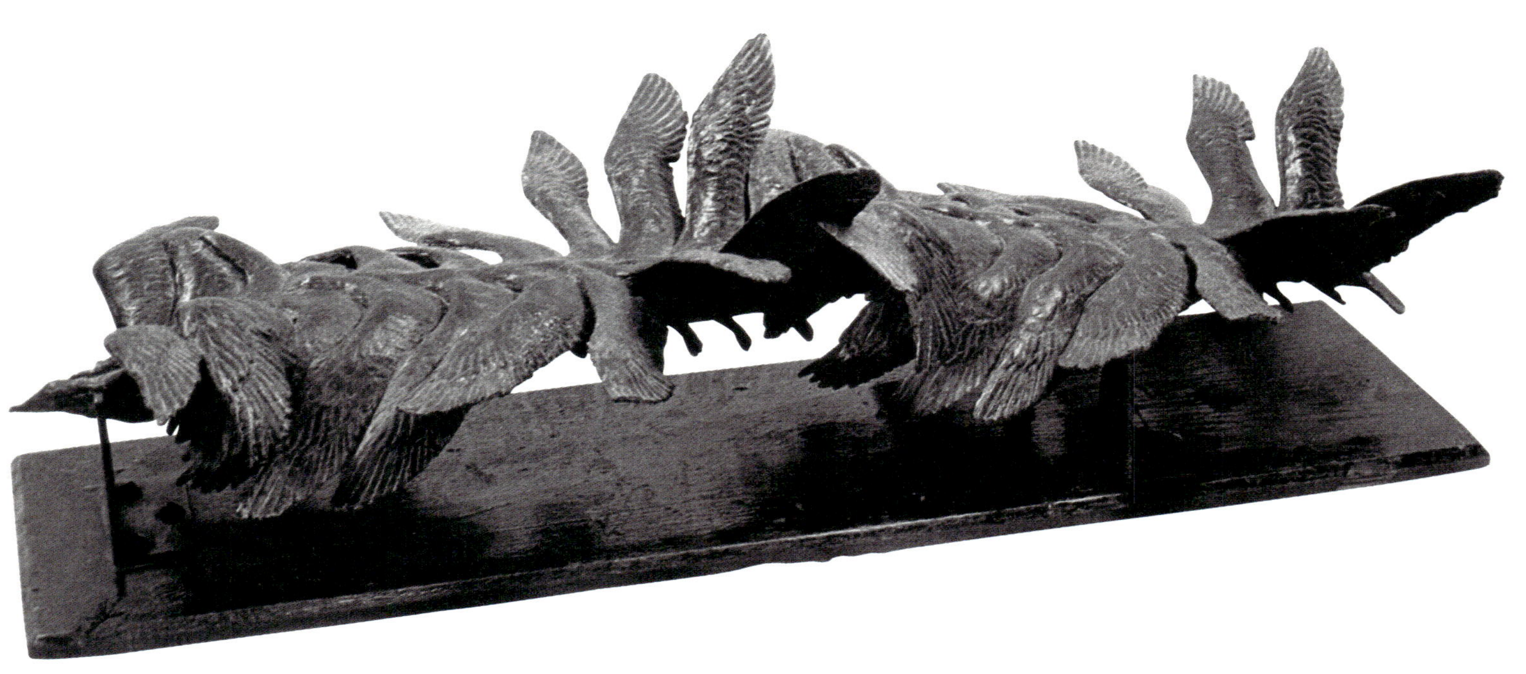

91

Etienne-Jules Marey
Flight of a Gull
1887
Bronze, 16.5 x 58.5 x 25.7 cm
Dépôt du Collège de France,
Musée Marey, Beaune

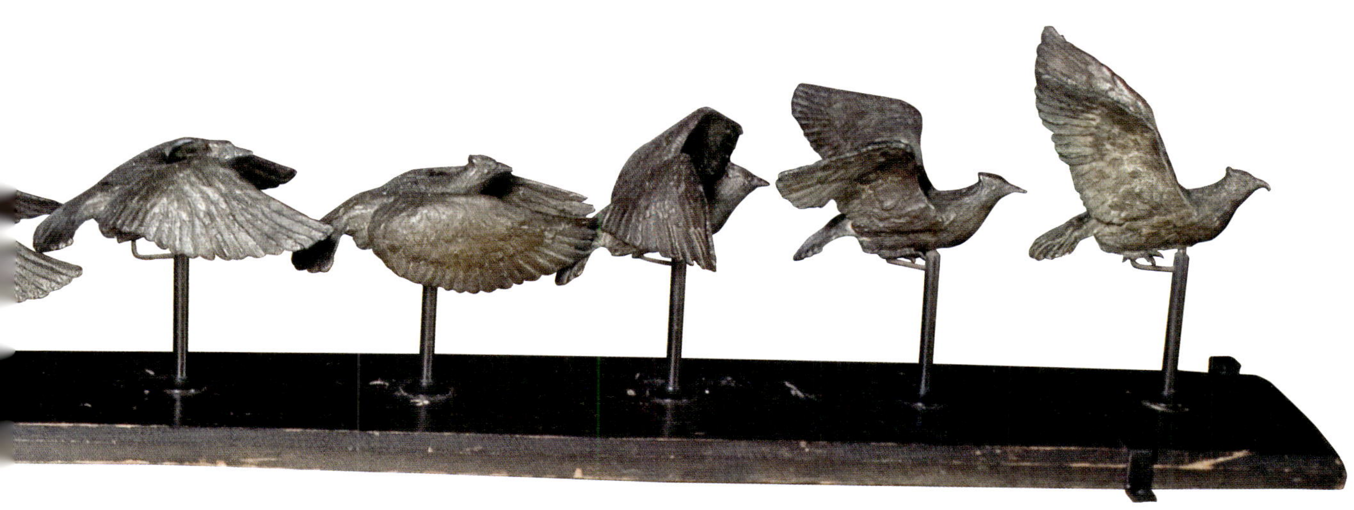

originals as substitute 'models' when making a number of pastel compositions, some of which encourage the viewer to see the depicted figures in a cohesive lateral movement (cat. 106).[85]

An unexpected and previously unnoticed parallel between Degas's linked sculptures and the new modes of photography can be found in two plates from Muybridge's 1887 *Animal Locomotion*. Both titled *First Ballet Action* (cats 88–89), these plates show an impressively trained male dancer executing a *grande ronde de jambe en l'air*, a continuous movement that here culminates with the raised leg in arabesque.[86] By the time Degas's series of arabesque sculptures was made, several reproductions of Marey's chronophotographs of moving figures had been published in *La Nature*, *Scientific American* and other journals.[87] Appearing as early as 1882, the image of a running man had many of the essential features of Degas's sculptural sequence, not least the lateral rhythm of the rising and falling limbs. A chronophotograph of a more acrobatic white-clad figure, *Man Walking and Swinging Arm*, made around 1890 (fig. 55), is even closer to Degas's energetic group in the dramatic display of extended arms and legs, and the play of silhouetted forms. Parallels between the scientist's photographs and Degas's arabesque series acquire further resonance when set beside the sculptures that Marey himself had already begun making as part of his research at the Station Physiologique. First envisaged in 1886, Marey's pioneering creations were based on high-speed photographs of seagulls and pigeons taken simultaneously by three cameras that recorded the birds along three axes.[88] Also using his own drawings and those made by his assistant, Georges Demenÿ, Marey developed these images into three-dimensional, slightly less than life-size forms that were first cast in plaster and subsequently – with the help of a Neapolitan sculptor – rendered in bronze.[89] The initial sets consisted of individual birds mounted separately and arranged in a sequence (cat. 90), one of which was shown in Paris in 1887 and 'created a sensation in scientific circles' in the words of Georges Didi-Huberman.[90] A further display of Marey's sculptures became part of a larger event at the 1889 Exposition Universelle, when the presentation of a wide range of his activities again attracted

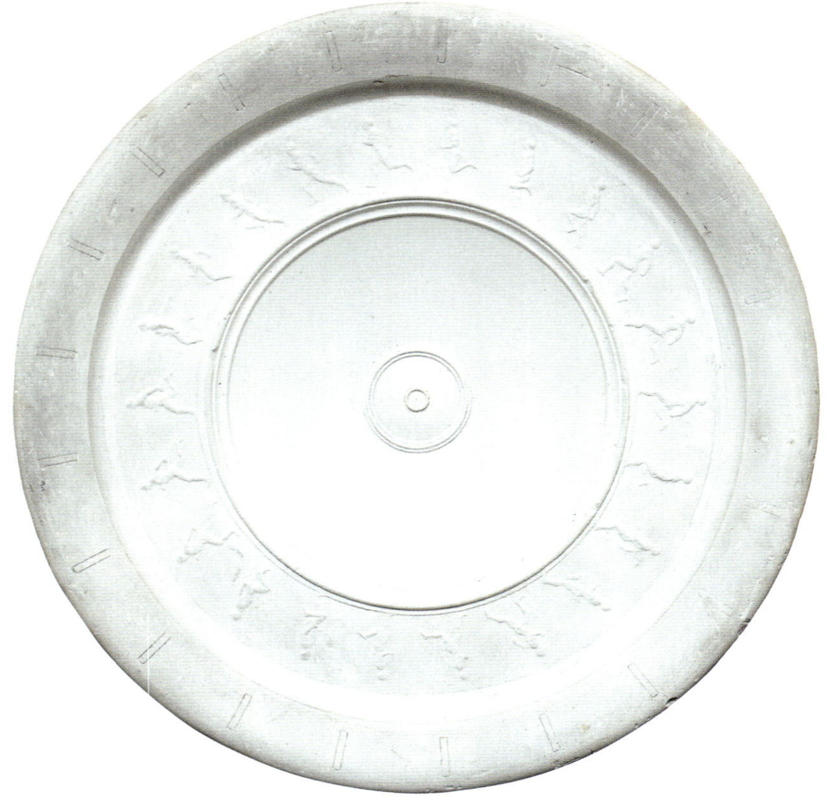

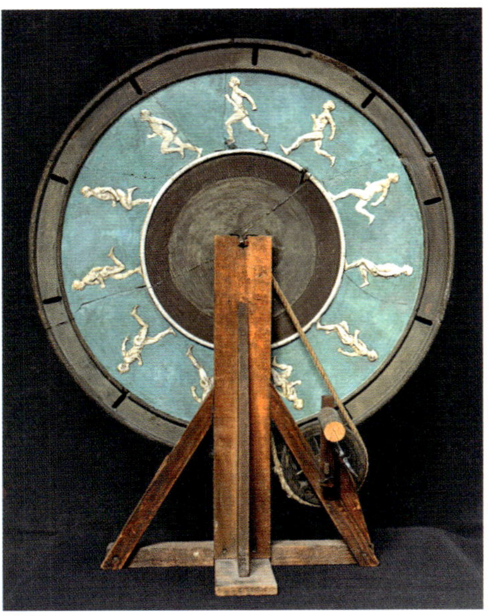

Fig. 56 *Paul Richer*, **The Runner**, *c.* 1895. Phénakistiscope, mixed media, 70 x 45 x 15 cm. Ecole des Beaux-Arts, Paris

considerable attention.[91] Addressing birds in flight rather than human subjects in action, Marey's sculptures nevertheless tackled a theme directly comparable with that in Degas's wax sequence, aspiring to 'embody' movement and the passage of time rather than represent it in two dimensions. By compressing the spaces between images of the individual birds and 'merging' their bodies in a single sculpture (cat. 91), Marey was able to emphasise the dynamic rise and fall of wings and their forward momentum as almost abstract entities. A parallel development in the same year was the creation by Marey of a new kind of zoetrope, in which three-dimensional models of a single seagull in different phases of flight were made to spin around a central axis, creating a remarkable sense of the living bird in action when seen at close quarters.[92]

Marey's ambitions to use sculpture to depict 'the movements of man' seem not to have come to fruition, but others soon took up the challenge, not least his friend Paul Richer. Richer had originally trained as a doctor and studied with Jean-Martin Charcot, eventually becoming Professor of Anatomy at the Ecole des Beaux-Arts, where Degas's own career had begun.[93] In 1895 Richer created the intriguing *The Runner* (cat. 92), a mould for a bronze disc that produced the illusion of movement when rotated in a device that he called a *phénakistiscope* (fig. 56).[94] Richer also experimented with making plaster figures in a variety of poses that represented extreme actions, such as his startlingly dynamic *French Boxing, Direct Kick* (cat. 93). This figure – which has a striking resemblance to certain of Degas's sculptures, notably *Dancer Fourth Position Front on the Left Leg* (cat. 81) – shows a young man involved in a necessarily short-lived movement associated with boxing that went even further than Degas's waxes in representing a split-second action. The project was realised more ambitiously at the turn of the century, when Richer created the complex three-dimensional group known as *The Race, Group of Three Runners* (cat. 94). Though presented as a realistic scene, this vigorous work combines three positions of a single figure in a way that directly echoes the photographs of Muybridge, Marey and their followers, who were numerous by this date. The degree of precision in *The Race, Group of Three Runners*, however, is still essentially paradoxical, representing each of the runners' movements very plausibly while 'freezing' them as a human tableau. Tantalisingly, such activities at the Eccle des Beaux-Arts – which is situated immediately across the Seine from the Louvre – appear to have unfolded independently of Degas's own sculptural and photographic researches in his Montmartre studio. Still refusing to exhibit his wax figures or have them cast in bronze, he occasionally showed his latest production to a visiting friend or fellow-artist and entertained them with ideas about such figures in movement.[95] An occasional visible presence in the city, Degas also visited the Louvre in the company of colleagues and young admirers, but there is no evidence that he knew of Richer's ingenious and provocative experiments taking place nearby.[96]

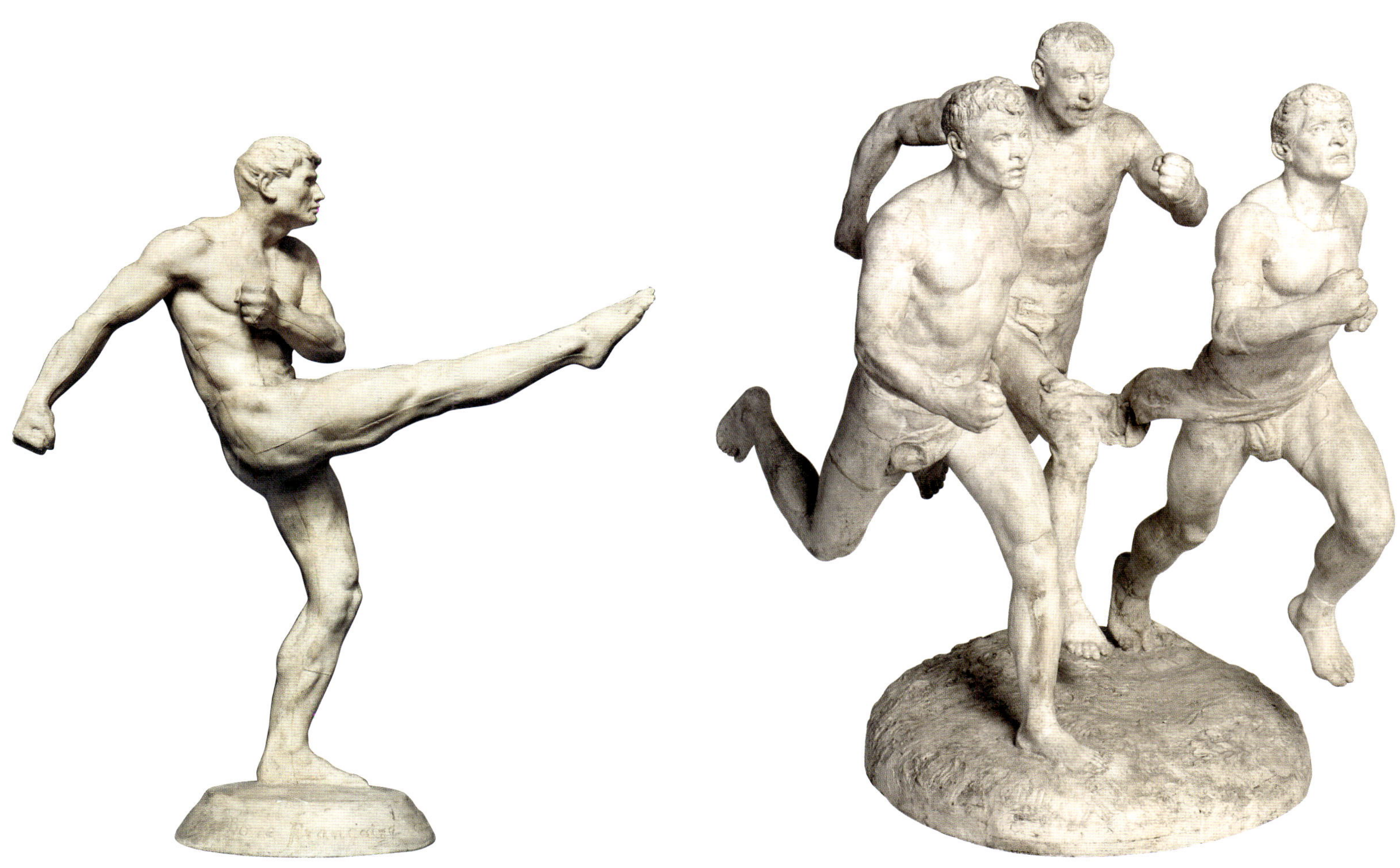

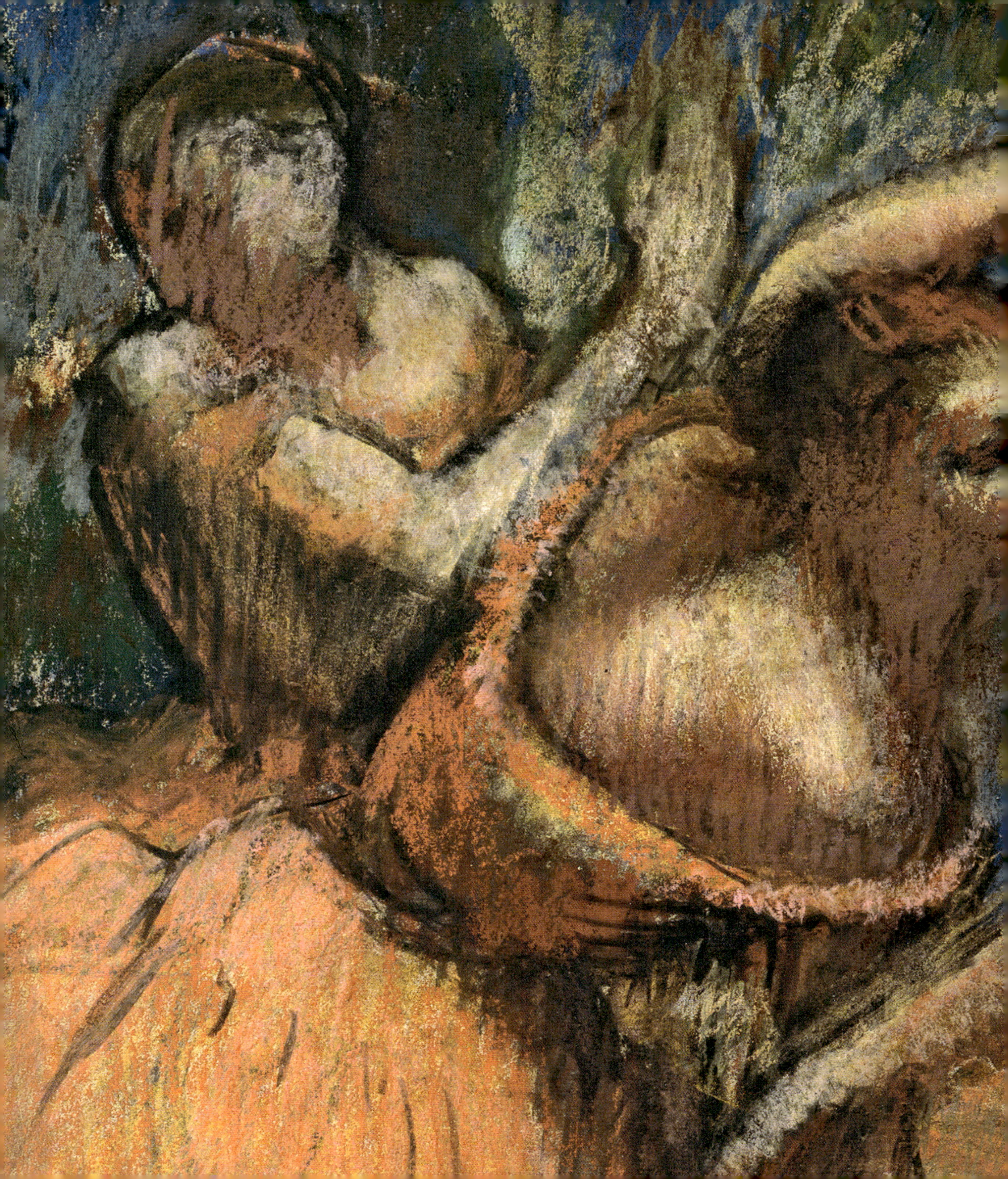

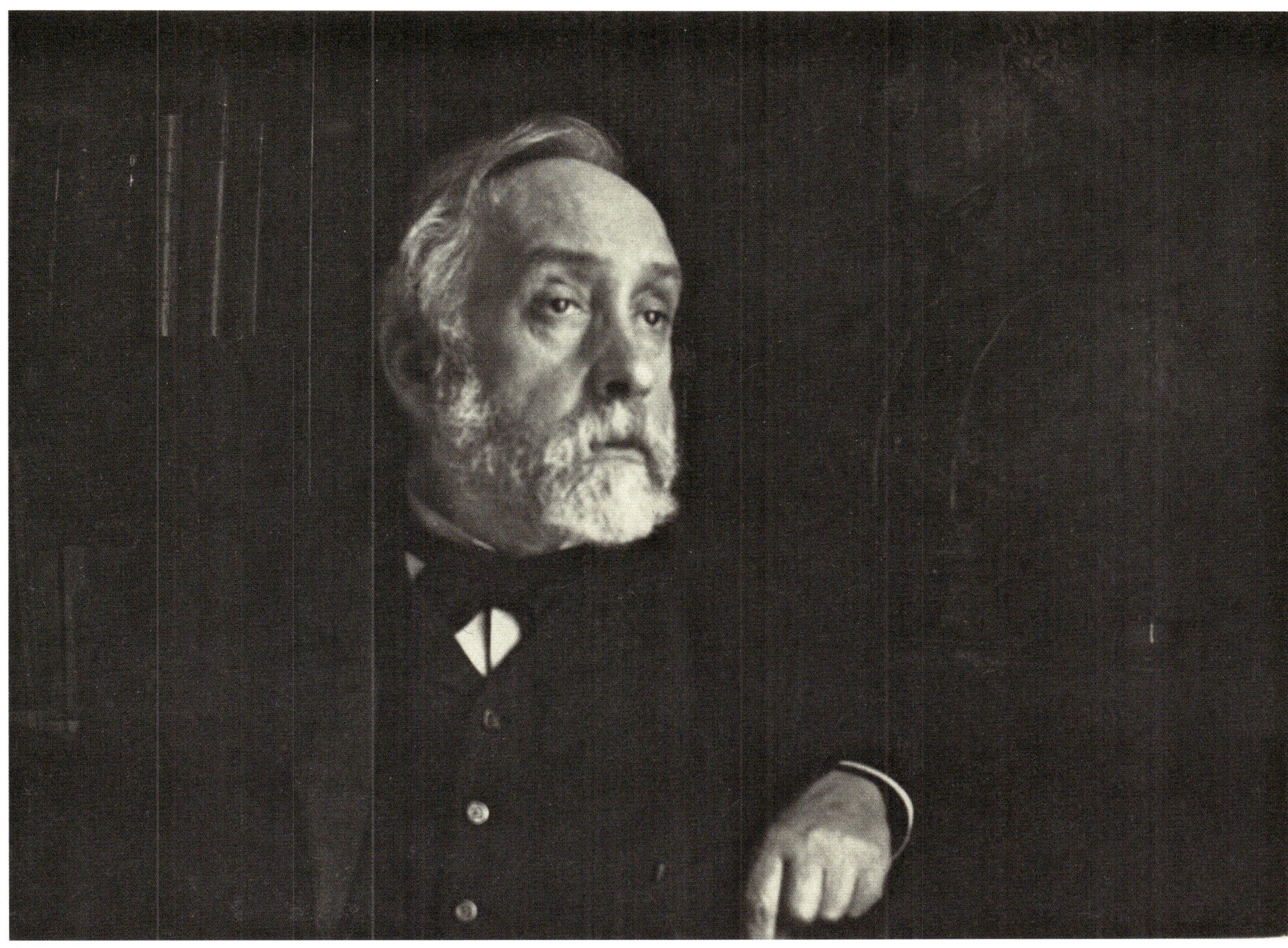

Fig. 57 **Self-portrait in Library (Portrait Bust in Background)**, 1895.
Gelatin silver print, 18.3 x 24.3 cm. Musée d'Orsay, Paris

following in the footsteps of many of the artist's friends in Paris. In the
previous decade the society hostess Hortense Howland had photographed
Degas and their mutual acquaintances at ease in her garden, and the Halévy
clan were known to engage in enthusiastic photographic projects.[4] It was
formerly said that Louise Halévy, Ludovic's wife and a close friend of Degas,
was so skilful in the darkroom that the artist entrusted some of his processing
and enlargement tasks to her, though this view is now questioned.[5] The family
of the artist Henry Lerolle, also intimates of Degas, similarly acquired expertise
in the medium and compiled albums of their own photographs, recording
their leisure pursuits, family gatherings and occasional moments of private
spectacle (cat. 111).[6] Degas's own brother, René De Gas, had been involved with
the medium as a young man and acquired one of the new models in the 1890s,
taking pictures that have sometimes been confused with the artist's own.[7]

The confident tone of Degas's letter to Marguerite was clearly that of a
recent convert to amateur photography, if one who still struggled occasionally:
'Yesterday I tried a portrait,' he told Marguerite on the same occasion, adding

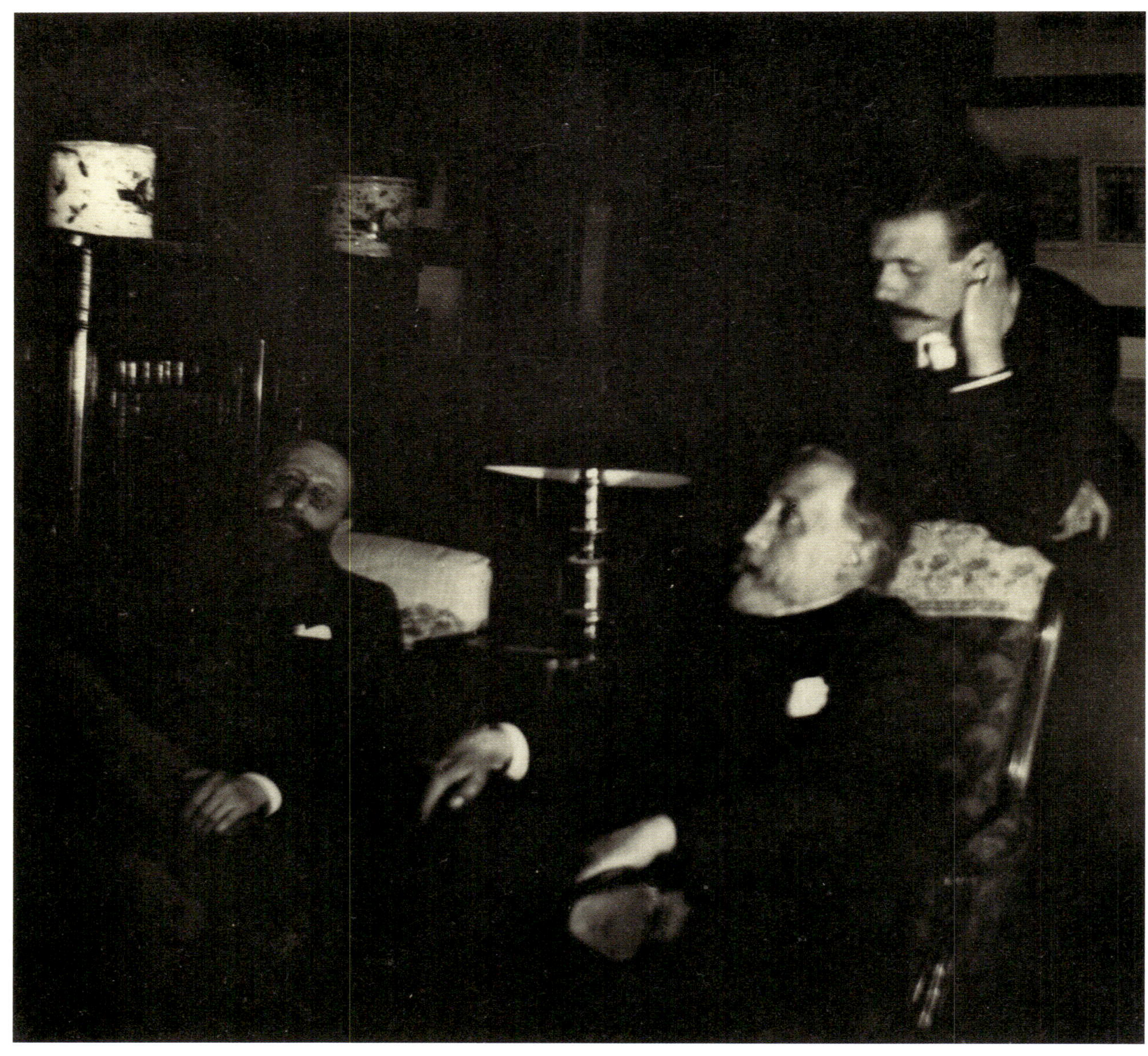

95

Jules Taschereau, Edgar Degas
and Jacques-Emile Blanche
December 1895
Enlarged silver gelatin print
from glass negative,
23.1 x 24.8 cm
Sterling and Francine Clark
Art Institute, Williamstown,
Massachusetts

that 'an accident with my small camera ... spoiled everything.' He was writing from the Auvergne in central France, where a health cure recommended by his doctor had allowed him to spend time with his newly adopted hobby. Other correspondence during these same weeks revealed his new-found enthusiasm for the medium and a characteristic passion for experiment and innovation. A sequence of short notes written to Guillaume Tasset, a colour merchant in Montmartre who had branched out into photographic supplies, reveals that Degas was sending the products of his own cameras back to Paris for prints and enlargements to be made. Tasset was asked about manipulating tonal effects and cropping compositions, and instructed to send the latest panchromatic plates for him to try.[8] More outlandish efforts were also mentioned, including Degas's attempts to photograph reflections on a wall and take pictures at night, baffling those around him. 'They probably thought I was crazy,' he later acknowledged.[9] When announcing his eventual return to Paris in a letter to Ludovic Halévy, Degas was clearly undaunted: 'One fine

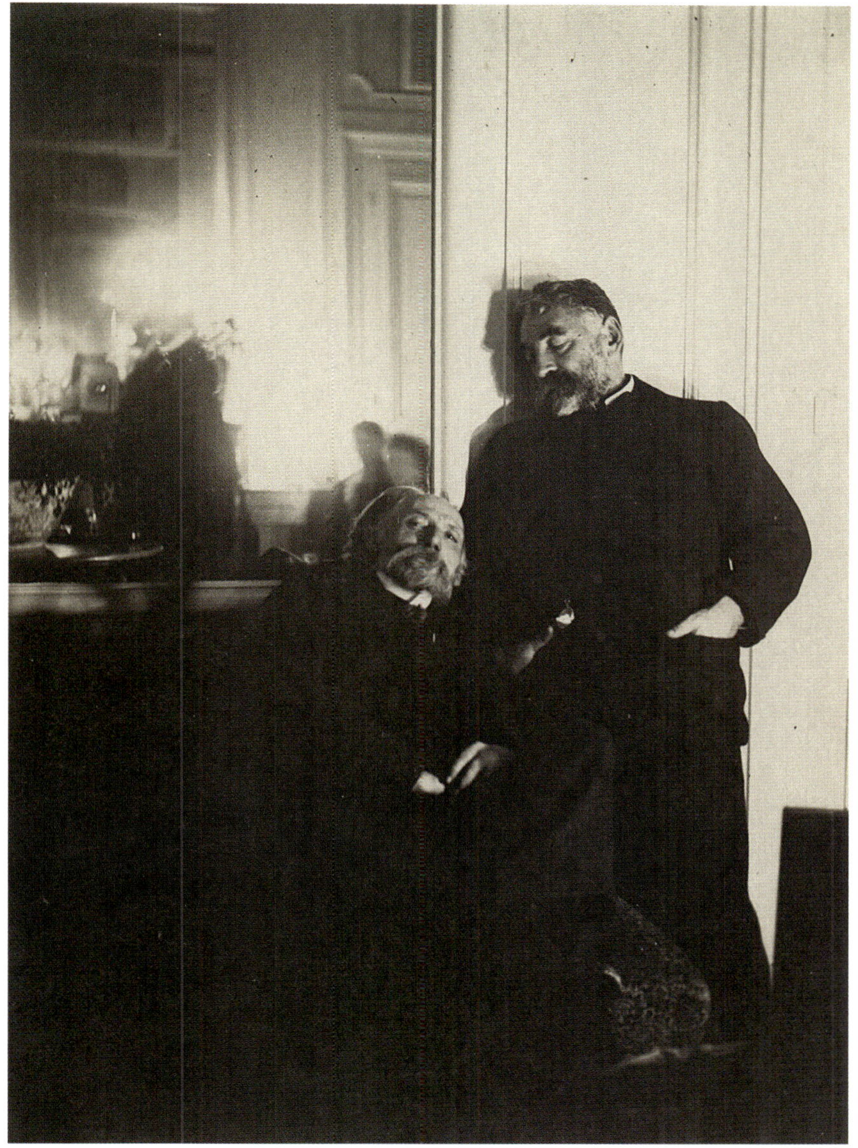

day I shall burst in on you, with my camera in my hand,' he wrote
in late September.[10]

    Degas's technical antics in the capital soon became notorious in his social
circle; it was claimed that Stéphane Mallarmé and Pierre-Auguste Renoir had
been subjected to a 'fearful quarter hour of immobility' when he made a portrait
of them both indoors, resulting in 'the finest likeness of Mallarmé that I have
ever seen', according to Paul Valéry (cat. 96).[11] Ludovic's son, Daniel Halévy, noted
of Degas: 'As his days are full he takes photographs in the evening. "Daylight"
he says "is too easy. What I want is difficult – the atmosphere of lamps and
of moonlight."'[12] On 29 December 1895 Degas put these ideas into practice,
commandeering a family party after dinner and arranging to make a complex
group portrait. 'We had to obey Degas's fierce will, his artist's ferocity,' Daniel
recalled, as 'he moved lamps, changed the reflectors,' and tried to light the legs
of his subjects 'by putting a lamp on the floor … The pose was held for two
minutes – and then repeated. We shall see the photographs tonight or tomorrow

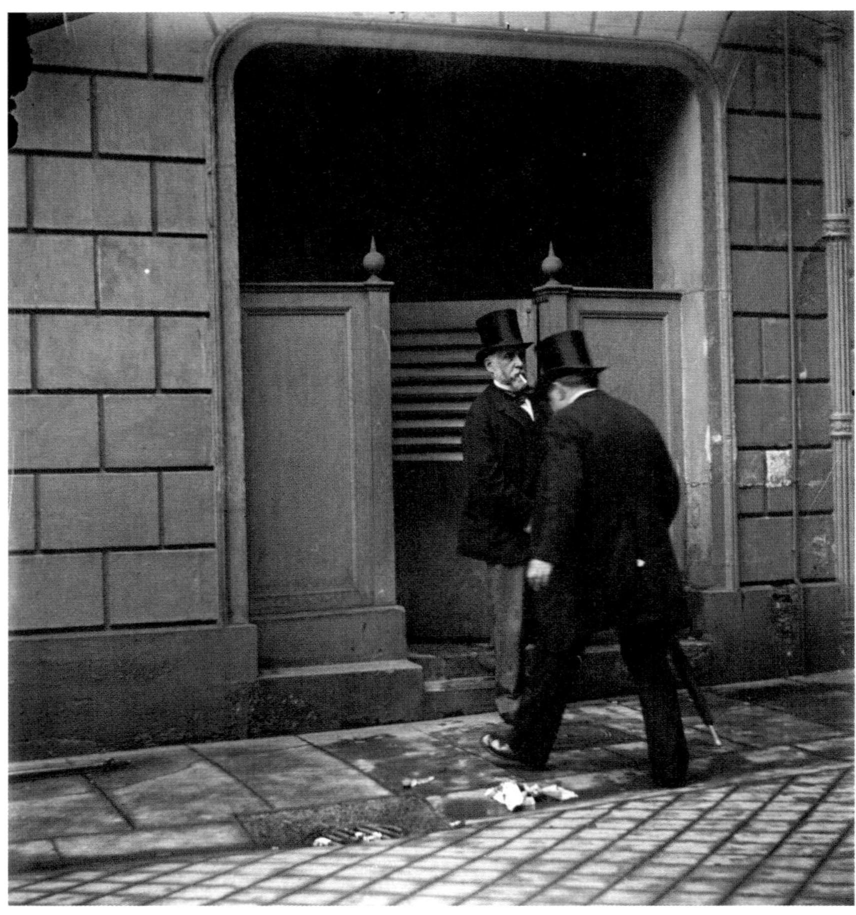

Fig. 58 *Giuseppe Primoli*, Degas Leaving a Public Convenience near the Boulevard du Conservatoire ('Vespasienne'), 25/26 July 1889. Silver gelatin print, 9 x 8 cm. Fondazione Primoli, Rome

morning, I think.'[13] In making the gently atmospheric *Jules Taschereau, Edgar Degas and Jacques-Emile Blanche* (cat. 95), Degas submitted to his own procedure, first arranging two friends in positions that could be comfortably sustained and then inserting himself into the foreground at the last moment. Wilfully plunging most of the room into deep shadow and cropping legs and arms, he also contrived to put the middle distance in focus while softening the forms of his human subjects. Here he achieved the understated, artful balance of so many of his paintings, while conjuring up a scene of after-dinner masculine intimacy that is strangely endearing. Surviving today in what appears to be its original frame, this print may have been chosen for display by the artist or one of his sitters.

Unorthodox though some of Degas's exploits in the medium undoubtedly were, they belong with the profusion of amateur and professional photographic activities that were now seamlessly woven into the lives of the artist and his contemporaries. The dismissive or facetious attitudes he had displayed towards the photograph as a younger man were also less evident, along with his discomfort in the presence of cameras. During this same period, for example, Degas frequently allowed himself to be photographed in situations that ranged from the formal to the entertaining and even the bizarre. The inspired Italian snap-shooter Giuseppe Primoli captured him emerging from a public *pissoir* (fig. 58) and on a crowded street watching the theatrical celebrity Réjane pass by, and friends occasionally recorded him at ease in their gardens or on holiday.[14] During a memorable trip through Burgundy by horse and carriage in 1890, Degas was photographed on several occasions by the camera of Charles de Meixmoron and perhaps that of Albert Bartholomé, his companion on the journey. De Meixmoron was a proselytiser for both amateur photography and outdoor painting, and seems to have persuaded the holidaymaker Degas to participate in both: a little-known photograph by De Meixmoron from this occasion shows Degas – an outspoken opponent of 'pleinairisme' – calmly painting in a field.[15] Other informal shots by an anonymous acquaintance reveal him in high spirits outside the country home of his friend Paul Valpinçon's family (fig. 78) and a more poised composition taken by René De Gas shows the artist with one of his young nieces.[16] In yet other casual contexts, Degas is seen at ease in his own apartment in photographs that were presumably arranged by himself, and extravagantly relaxed in the presence of the elegant Lerolle sisters.[17]

Surrounded by professionals and competent amateurs, Degas himself remained technically unreliable as a photographer but willing to compete with his peers in sheer energy and inventiveness. At least one of his cameras – he ordered a second while staying in the Auvergne – is thought to have been a recent model from Kodak that could accommodate both glass plates and the revolutionary new roll film.[18] Purchased from Tasset et Lhote in Montmartre, whose premises were close to his studio, this apparatus was soon pushed to its limits by an artist who took an almost perverse delight in rule-breaking. Errors of many kinds occurred, destroying some of his carefully devised compositions and resulting in double exposures that nevertheless fascinated Degas enough for him to keep them.[19] Typically preferring to work indoors by artificial light, he tested the patience of his models but again retained a number of blurred portraits that evidently pleased him. Certain of these approaches seem distinctly radical, even obtuse, but they were arguably consistent with the anarchic experiments in his studio during the same period, when images made of pastel, charcoal and oil paint evolved in ways that defy most attempts at decipherment. Characteristic of both activities was the mixture of technical innovation with methods that were already long outmoded. In his Kodak camera, for example, he chose to expose his pictures on glass rather than the more up-to-date flexible film, yet insisted on ordering the latest panchromatic glass plates made by the Lumière company – announced in the specialist press just two months earlier – that could reproduce an unprecedented range of tonal values.[20] His undoubted successes as a photographer emerged despite – or perhaps because of – these self-imposed limitations and were dominated by a series of bold, subtly inflected portraits of acquaintances from the worlds of art, literature and music, and many unforgettable images of himself in solitude (fig. 57). A number of prints are known to have been lost, but of the approximately sixty original photographs that have been catalogued by Malcolm Daniel, some surviving in multiple examples, the majority are portrait studies of some kind.[21] Works in other categories include the pictures of dancers and female nudes that have become widely celebrated, as well as experiments in landscape and whimsical groups of figures outdoors. Miscellaneous though they seem, this modest group of photographs includes a number ranked with the finest of their kind from the late nineteenth century.

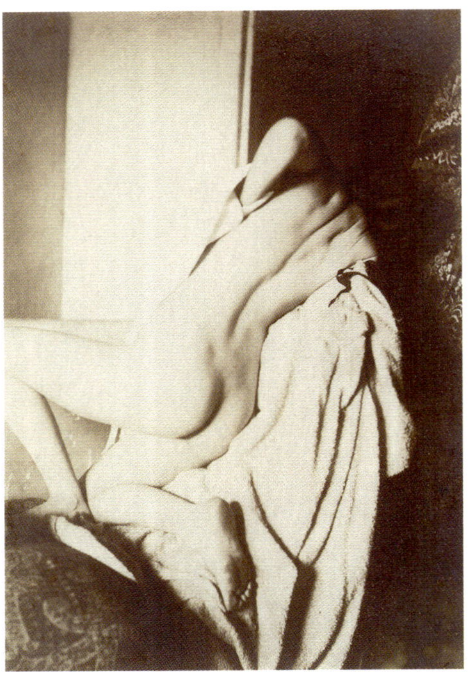

Fig. 59 **After the Bath, Woman Drying Her Back**, 1896.
Gelatin silverprint, 16.5 x 12 cm. J. Paul Getty Museum,
Los Angeles, inv. no. 84.XM.495.2

Like almost every other aspect of Degas's circuitous, lifelong relationship with photography, his adventures with a camera were fraught with paradox. As a young artist in the 1870s, he had dismissed the still-novel medium – or perhaps its claims to artistic status – by announcing somewhat obscurely that 'instantaneousness is photography, nothing more', yet two decades later he chose to throw himself into photography like an excited adolescent. Intensely preoccupied by colour in his studio during these same months, when pastels such as the rainbow-hued *Russian Dancers* were on his easel (cats 112–14), Degas the photographer wilfully adopted the bleak language of black, white and grey in his studies of those around him. Perhaps most surprisingly of all, the artist who had been obsessed for three decades by the human figure in movement now accepted the dictates of a camera shutter that 'froze' everything it encountered. That Degas thrived on contradiction was confirmed by several of his colleagues in later life; Camille Pissarro memorably suggested that the politically conservative Degas was 'an anarchist in art' and Walter Sickert reported his remark that 'One gives the idea of the truth by means of the false.'[22] The young Valéry remembered Degas saying that 'painting isn't so difficult when you don't know ... but when you do ... it's quite a different matter!' and recalled his pleasure in a critic's claim that he was 'continually uncertain about proportions'.[23] To this list we might add the image of a self-taught photographer who delighted in both innovation and redundant practices, pushing at the boundaries of the craft and yet never fully mastering it.

Degas's brief career as a photographer barely registered outside his immediate circle. A modest display of prints was assembled for a short time in January 1896, on the walls of Tasset et Lhote, but the event went unnoticed in the press.[24] References to photography in his correspondence also dwindled from this date onwards; one letter written during the year noted the re-photographing of 'the little Ingres', and his photographs of dancers and female nudes may also have been made at this time, although documentation remains sparse.[25] A few subsequent records indicate that other pictures were attempted, among them a portrait of a little girl made around 1901 that was dated by the subject herself.[26] Extraordinary though it may already seem, Degas's engagement with photography becomes even more baffling when we discover that it effectively ended within a year. A variety of extraneous factors no doubt contributed to this move, most prominently the failing eyesight that had troubled him for decades and now threatened to engulf his life. 'Everything is long for a blind man, who wants to pretend that he can see,' Degas wrote around 1896 on a sheet of Tasset et Lhote notepaper.[27] It is also conceivable that attempts to integrate his photography with the making of art frustrated or disillusioned him, perhaps reviving his scepticism about the medium in earlier decades.

The mystery has only deepened in our own times through the gradual discovery that some of Degas's photographs are directly related to major pastels and paintings from the late 1890s. The most widely discussed case is probably that of *After the Bath* (fig. 59), a majestic, almost shocking composition that appears to have inspired several works on paper and canvas around 1896. Known only in a single monochrome print that may have been made by Degas or another photographer under his direction, this image was unquestionably linked in some way to the remarkable oil painting with the

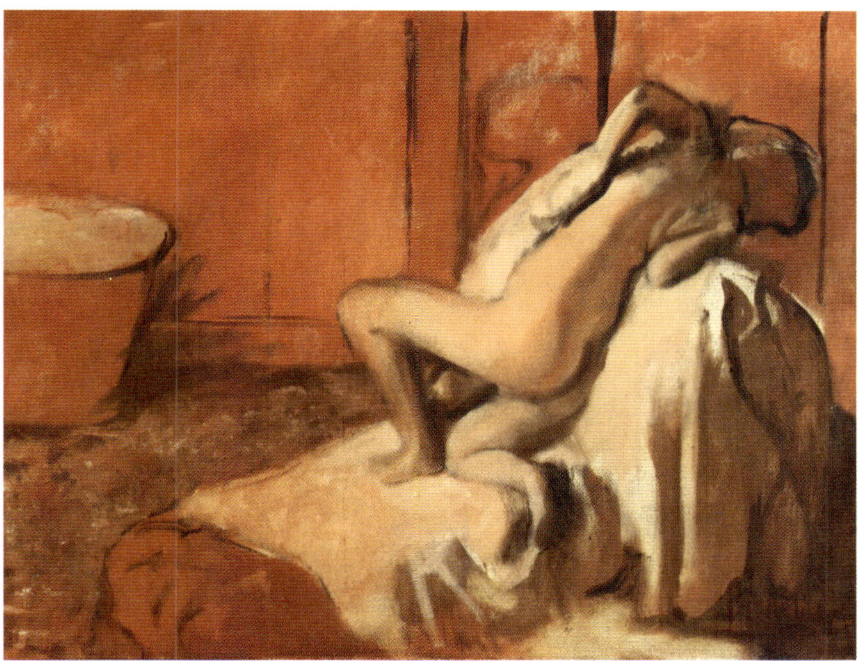

Fig. 60 **After the Bath (Woman Drying Herself)**, *c.* 1896.
Oil on canvas, 89.5 x 116.8 cm. Philadelphia Museum of Art

same title (fig. 60). Here there can be no doubt of Degas's direct embrace
of photography as an integral part of his creative process, even as the starting
point for a series of career-defining pictures. The three glass plates depicting
ballet dancers (figs 62–64) given to the Bibliothèque nationale by René De Gas
are technically dissimilar from the reclining nude, yet again relate closely
to a group of works executed by Degas in these same years.[28] 'Standard,
commercially available gelatin dry plates' were used in this case, subsequently
acquiring a range of fiery orange and red tones that are said to be the result
of darkroom manipulation prior to printing (fig. 61).[29] Based on a single model
who is wearing a practice outfit, not a stage costume, these three images were
presumably contrived by the artist with specific ends in mind. Representing
a front, back and side view of the young woman, they are otherwise united in
several telling respects. Each photograph shows the dancer in self-absorbed
mode, stretching an arm or shoulder, or adjusting her costume. These actions
might all be found in a classroom or dressing room, but are arguably more
appropriate to the theatre wings, a favourite site of Degas's later dance art
that allowed him to create freely and beyond the constraints of formal
choreography. Consistent with this context is the bright light coming from
above in all three photographs and the hint of nervous attention to her
appearance and deportment shown by the model. Most significant in the
larger context, perhaps, is the fact that all three ballerina-figures are not
exercising or dancing, but are clearly posing and therefore stationary.

A subtle drawing in charcoal that is undoubtedly related to the model
in the first of these photographs unexpectedly presents her naked (cat. 97).
Distantly recalling Degas's academic training, *Half-length Nude Girl, Left Arm
Uplifted* was evidently used to distil the essence of the young woman's pose

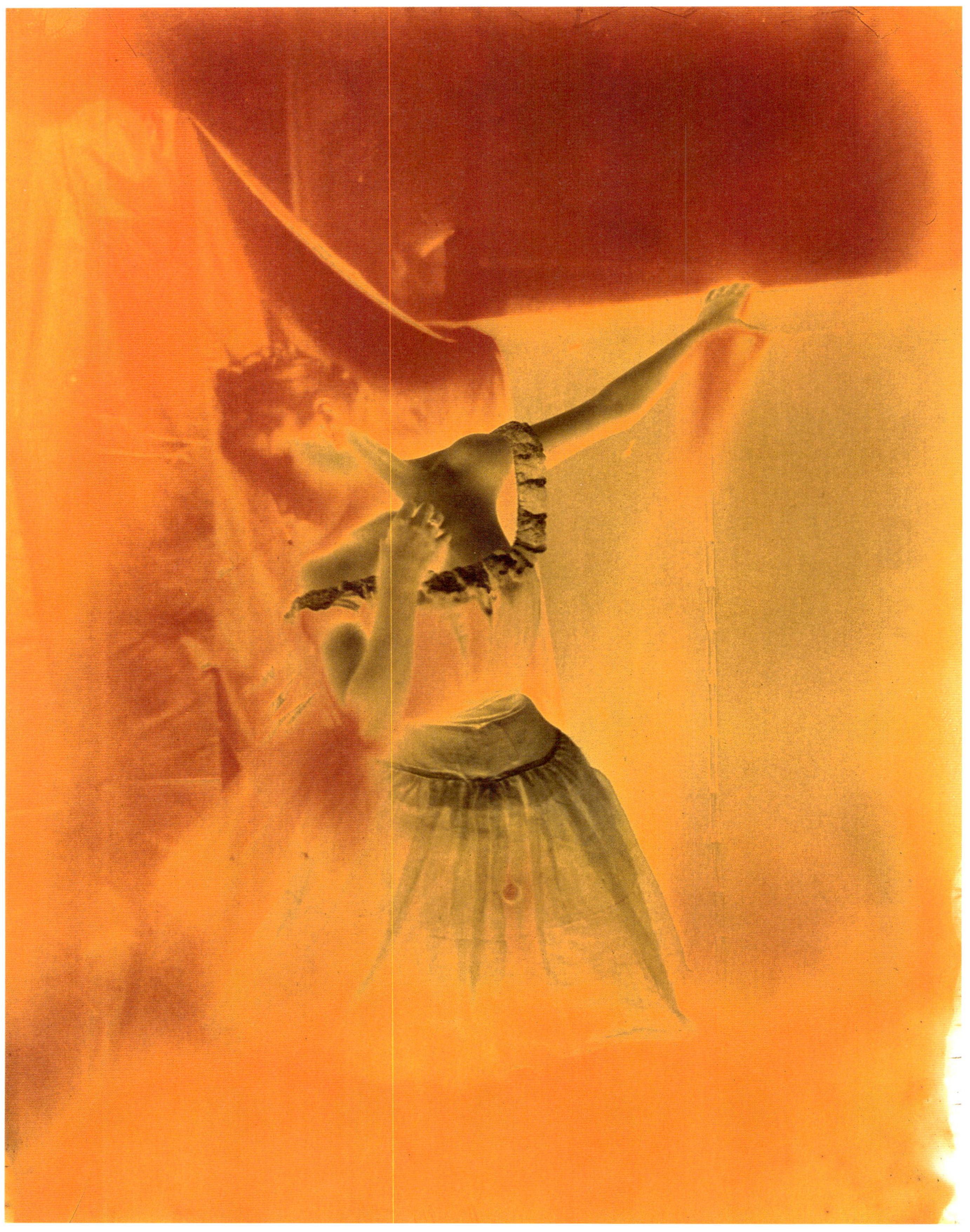

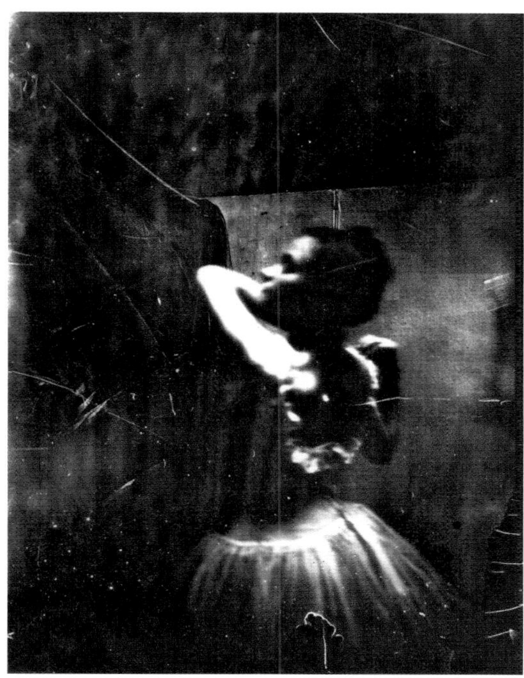

Fig. 62 **Dancer Adjusting Her Shoulder Strap**. Modern print from gelatin dry plate negative, 18 x 13 cm. Bibliothèque nationale de France, Paris

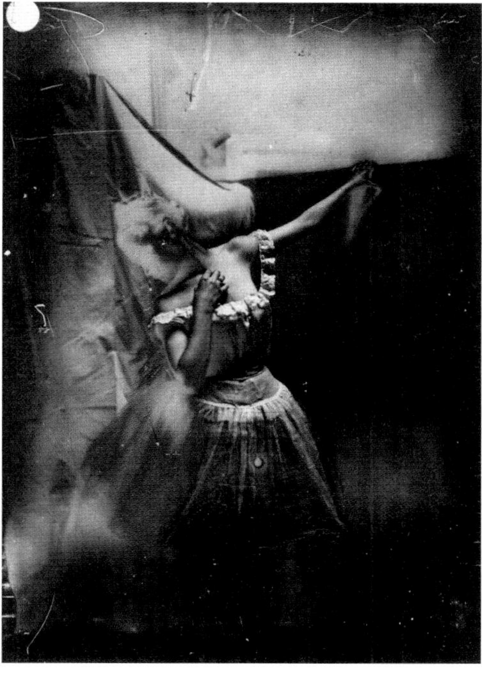

Fig. 63 **Dancer (Arm Outstretched)**. Modern print from gelatin dry plate negative, 18 x 13 cm. Bibliothèque nationale de France, Paris

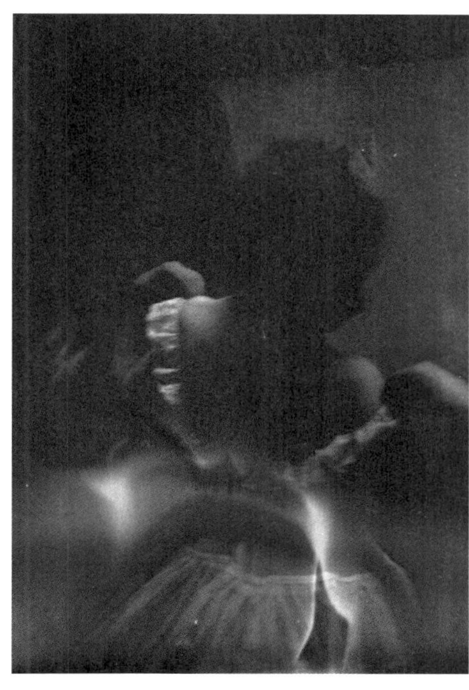

Fig. 64 **Dancer Adjusting Her Two Shoulder Straps**. Modern print from gelatin dry plate negative, 18 x 13 cm. Bibliothèque nationale de France, Paris

Fig. 61 **Dancer (Arm Outstretched)**, late 1895 or 1896. Gelatin dry plate negative. Bibliothèque nationale de France, Paris

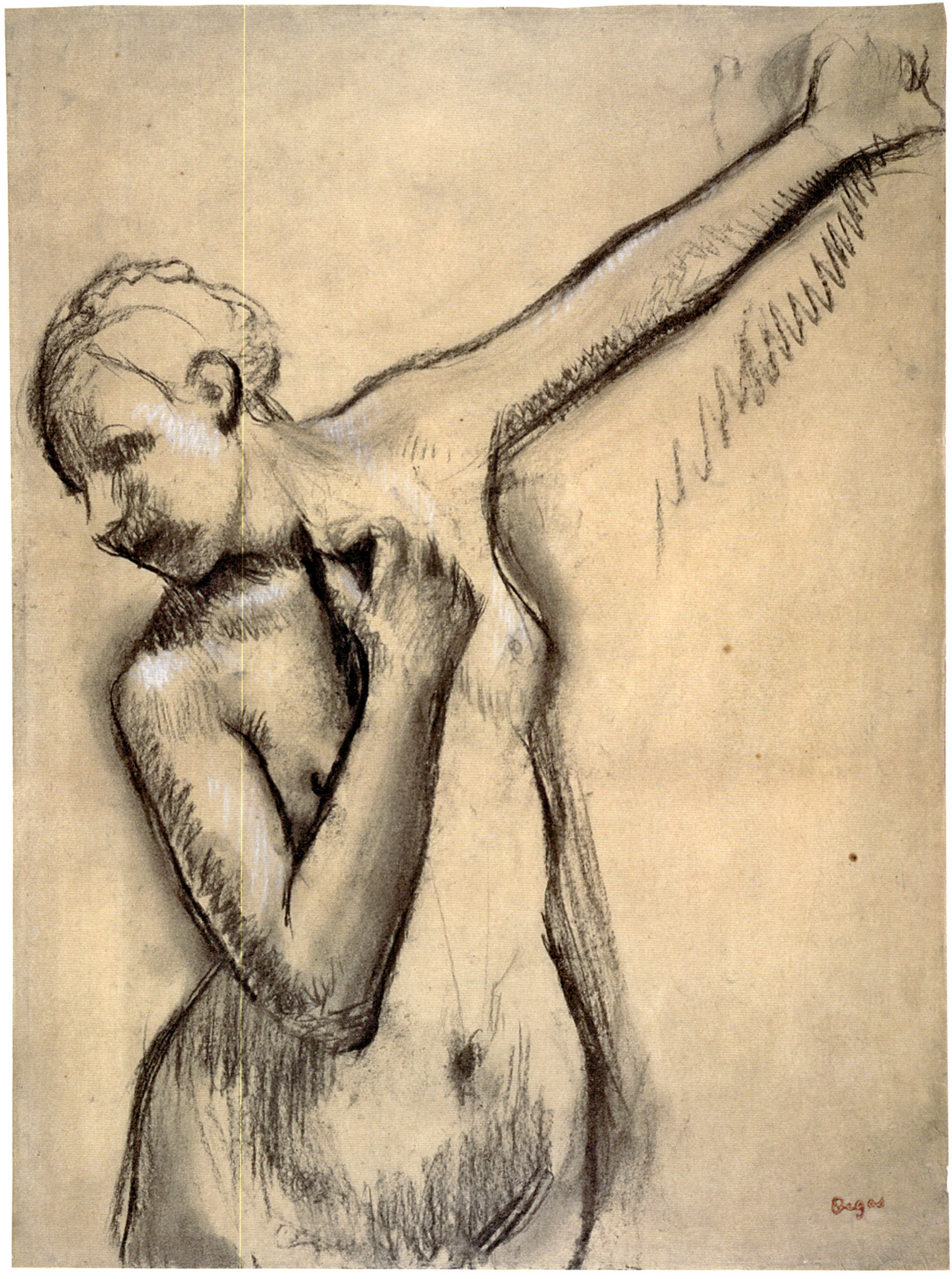
Degas

for projects that may have already been underway. The pose reappeared in
a number of important compositions set in the wings, principally in pastel but
occasionally in oil paint on canvas. Compared to the photographed ballerina,
the dancer with her left arm extended in Degas's drawing seems elegantly
statuesque, evoking ancient figures in marble or the forms of a classical relief.
She also stands quite still, divested of even the modest dynamism apparent
in her photographed alter ego. Preserved by the artist in his portfolios and
presumably consulted as required, this delicate study emphasises his
willingness to depart on occasion in radical and surprising ways from his
own photograph-based imagery. A more direct response to the photographs
is exemplified in *Blue Dancers* (fig. 65), in which all three of Degas's images
of the young woman have been integrated into a stage setting. Now dressed
in the tutus with frilled edging that the original model wore, each of these
individuals can be directly linked to one of the celebrated photographs.

When Degas contrived yet another picture featuring the photographed
ballerina, *Study of Dancers* (fig. 66), the single figure in *Half-length Nude Girl,
Left Arm Uplifted* survived only as a pale fragment at upper left, displaced
by three conspicuously more energised colleagues who have burst into the
composition. Here their diagonally opposed limbs seem to scuttle upwards
from the left-hand corner, then across and deep into the pictorial void, an
effect accentuated by Degas's decision to depict them from a high vantage
point. Fascinatingly, all these individuals relate directly or indirectly to the

97

**Half-length Nude Girl,
Left Arm Uplifted**
c. 1898
Charcoal heightened
with white on tracing paper,
53.9 x 38.8 cm
Lent by the Syndics of the
Fitzwilliam Museum, Cambridge.
Bequeathed by Andrew S. F.
Gow through the National Art
Collections Fund

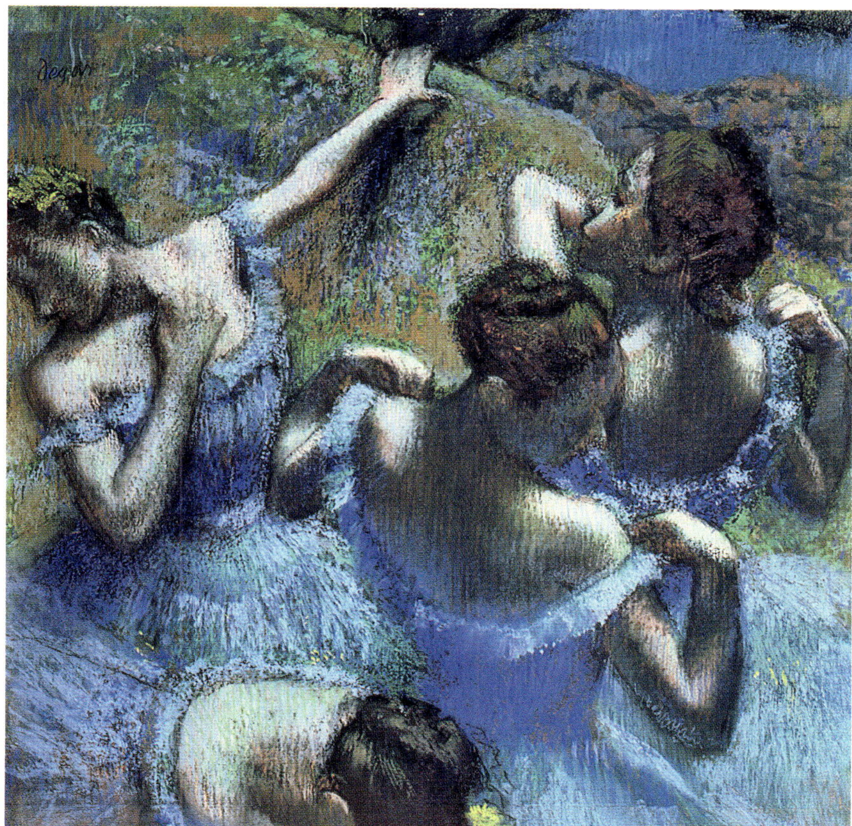

Fig. 65 **Blue Dancers**, *c.* 1899. Pastel on paper,
65 x 65 cm. Pushkin Museum, Moscow

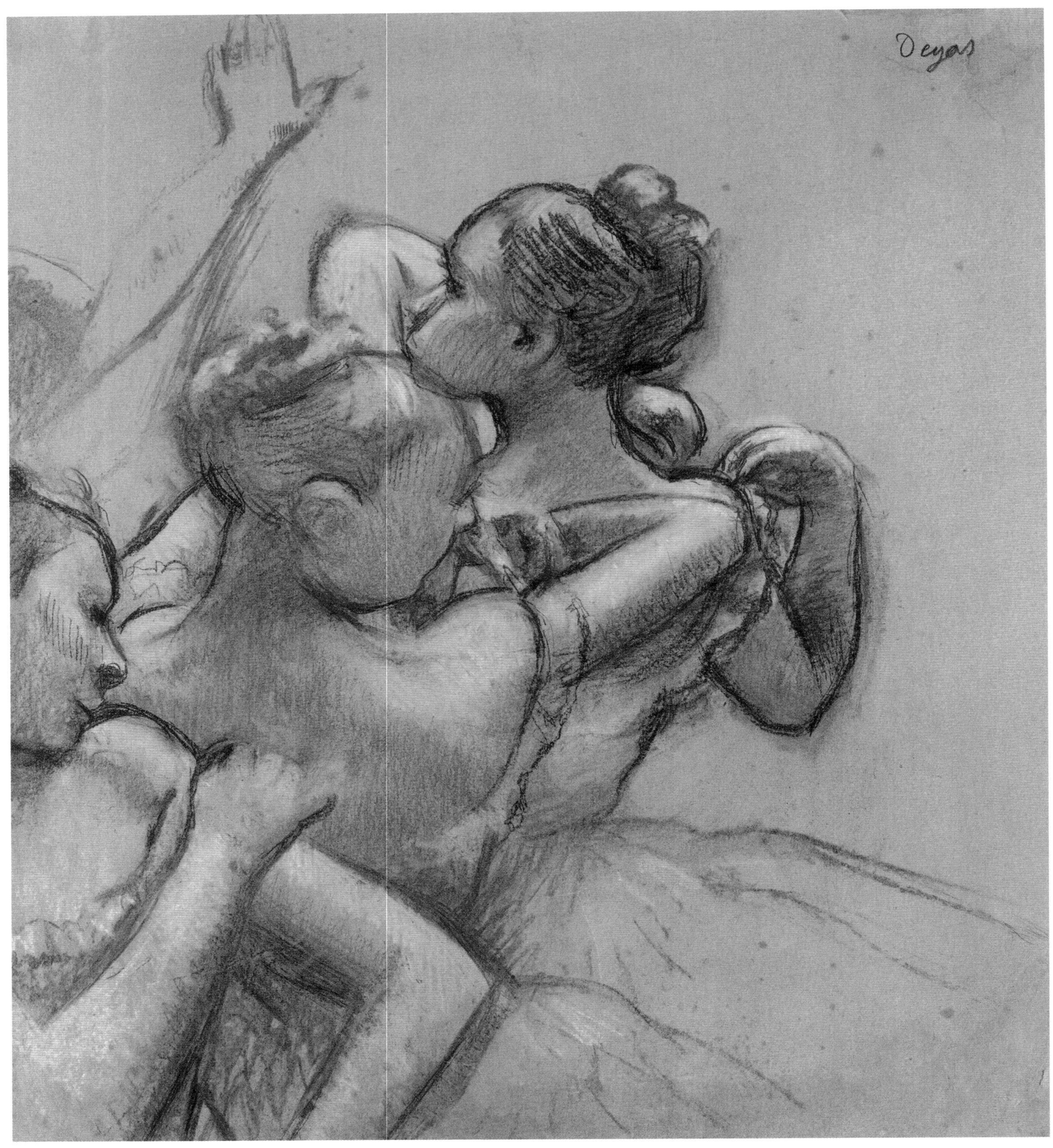

Fig. 66 **Study of Dancers**, 1895–1900. Black, red and white chalk on
tracing paper on card, 52.3 x 49.1 cm. Kunsthalle Bremen, 606-1950/5

198

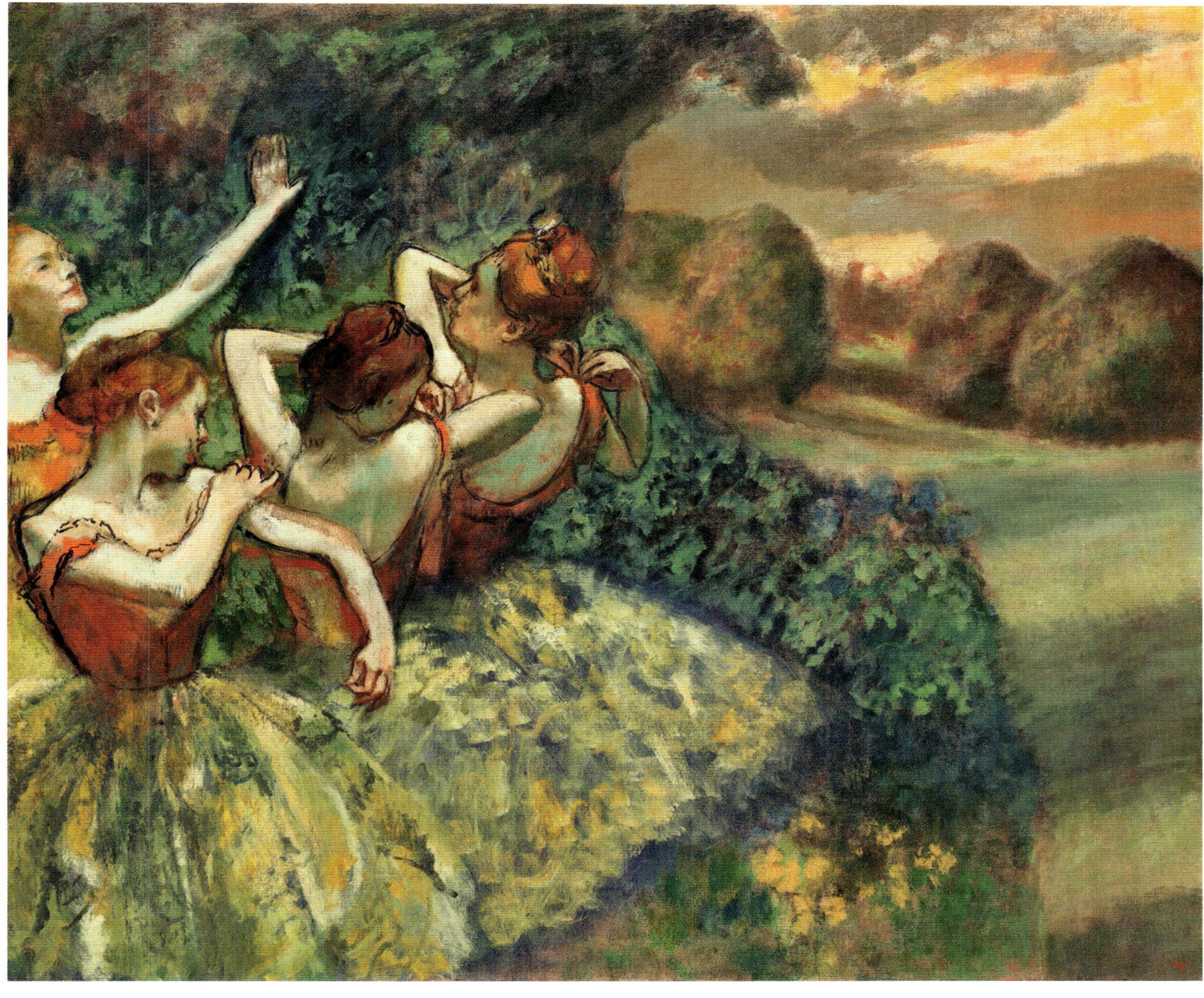

Fig. 67 **Four Dancers**, *c.* 1899. Oil on canvas, 151.1 x 180.2 cm. National
Gallery of Art, Washington DC. Chester Dale Collection, inv. no. 1963.10.122

trio of dancer photographs, yet their nervous energy in the new scene again
seems to be an invention of the artist. Whereas the photographed figures were
effectively still, these overlapping and fragmented ballerinas demand to be seen
as animated personalities in unfolding physical relationships with themselves
and their surroundings. *Study of Dancers* was made in preparation for one
of the grandest, most ambitious oil paintings of Degas's career, *Four Dancers*
(fig. 67), in which richly applied oranges, blues and mineral greens added further
vitality to the scene. In this monumental picture the women are shown beside
a section of scenery preparing to go on stage, self-consciously adjusting their
attire before stepping into the footlights. Understated though they are, both
canvas and drawing are emphatically concerned with energy, not with stasis.

Degas the amateur photographer would have been well aware that the technology available to him in 1895, though infinitely more accommodating than that of previous generations, was still inadequate for his needs as an artist of movement. However successfully he fixed his models on camera, the exposure times required by his apparatus precluded the capture of their casual actions. It was only in the subsequent manipulations of his studio, when Degas transformed and reinvented his ballerina-figures in line and colour, that he could energise their bodies and settings. In the multi-figure *Study of Dancers* and the painting associated with it he achieved precisely that, apparently encouraged by new modes of visual representation that were now current outside the confines of the arts. By this date the work of Muybridge, Marey and their followers was widely known and already influential in a number of fields. For Degas, the repeated figures in successive positions in Muybridge's photographs and the evolving bodily masses in the chronophotographs of Marey must have been a revelation. His awareness of these advances is surely signalled in the most explicit fashion in *Study of Dancers*, in which the overlapping forms of the three women irresistibly suggest the qualities of instantaneous photography. A detail from one of Marey's photographs (fig. 68) shows just such a conflation

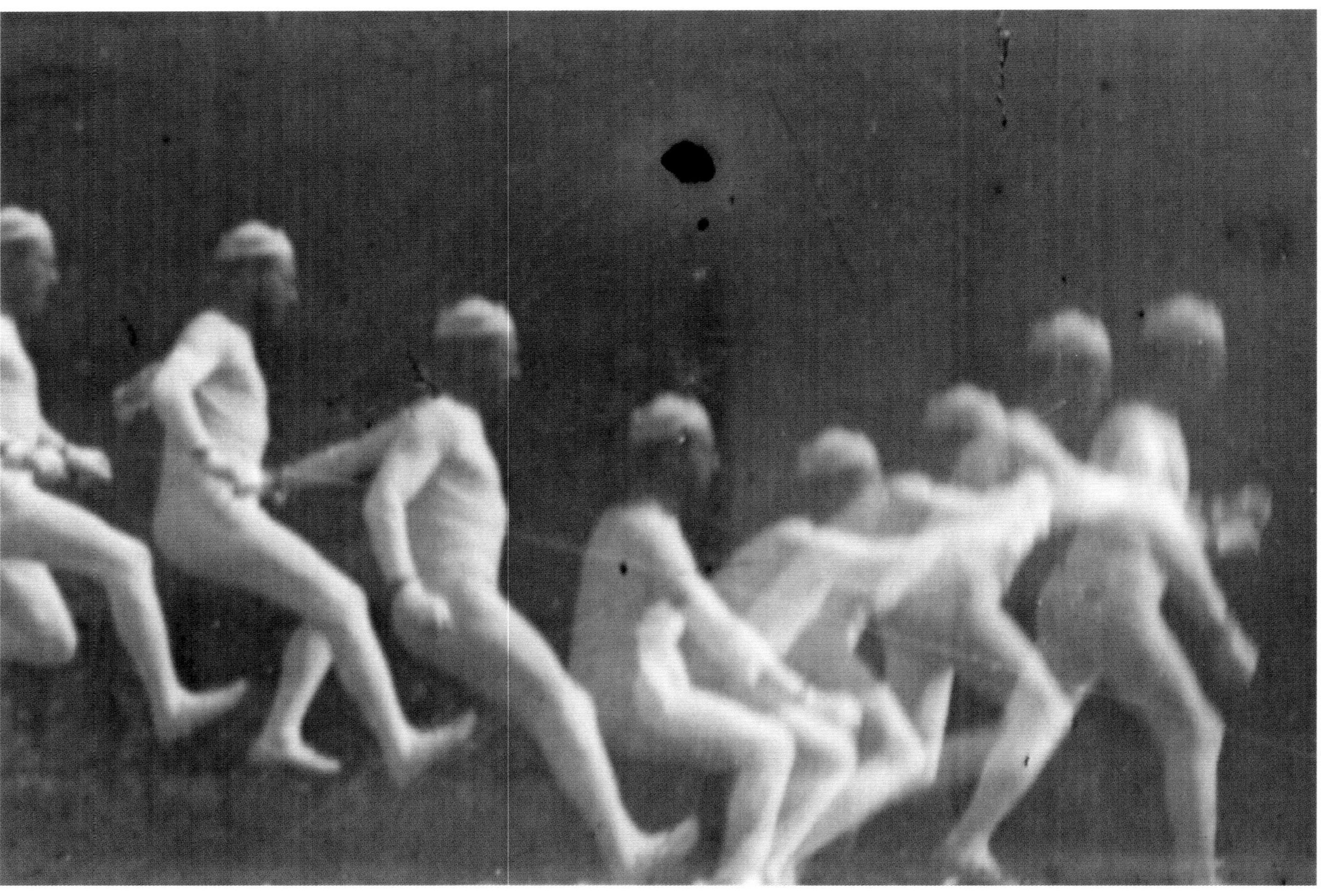

Fig. 68 *Etienne-Jules Marey*, Saut de l'homme en blanc, 1882–89 (detail).
Chronophotograph, 9 x 12 cm. Collège de France, Paris

mesures qu'on doit prendre sur une image à dimensions réduites il faut faire une série de calculs pour avoir la longueur réelle des objets représentés, il est désirable de trouver le moyen de supprimer ces opérations un peu longues. On y arrive en agrandissant l'image, au moyen de la lanterne à projection, jusqu'à ce qu'elle ait ses dimensions réelles, c'est-à-dire jusqu'à ce que l'échelle métrique présente exactement un mètre de longueur sur l'écran. Dès lors toutes les dimensions de l'image peuvent être directement mesurées.

Les épures que donne la Chronophotographie contiennent donc les deux notions nécessaires pour connaître un mouvement : celle d'espace et celle de temps. Toutefois ces deux notions qu'il fallait concilier sont, dans une certaine mesure, incompatibles entre elles, de telle sorte que, pour les obtenir toutes deux, on est souvent obligé de recourir à certains artifices, ainsi qu'on va le voir.

Influence de la surface couverte par l'objet en mouve-

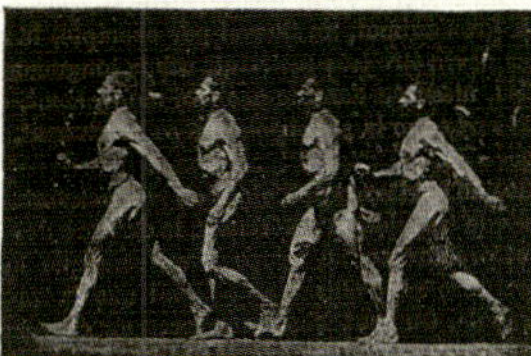

Fig. 39. — Un Homme qui marche : Chronophotographie sur plaque fixe.

ment. — Pour une même vitesse de translation, si l'objet étudié couvre peu de surface dans le sens du mouvement, on en peut recueillir un grand nombre d'images sans qu'elles se confondent en se superposant : c'est le cas du projectile que nous considérions tout à l'heure. La notion de temps est

Fig. 69 *Etienne-Jules Marey*, Le Mouvement, Paris, 1894, p. 57

des cas cependant, au moyen de certains artifices, on échappe à cet inconvénient.

Le moyen le plus naturel consiste à réduire artificiellement la surface du corps étudié. On rend invisibles, en les noircissant, les parties qu'il n'est pas indispensable de représenter dans l'image, et l'on rend lumineuses au contraire celles dont on veut connaître le mouvement. C'est ainsi qu'un Homme vêtu de velours noir (fig. 43), et portant sur les membres des galons et des points brillants, ne donne, dans l'image, que des lignes géométriques sur lesquelles pourtant se reconnaissent aisément les attitudes des différents segments des membres.

Dans l'épure que l'on obtient ainsi (fig. 44), le nombre des

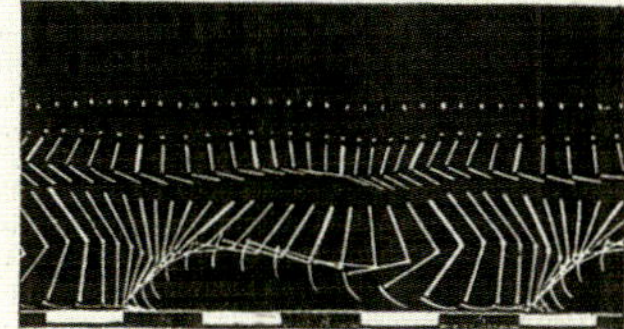

Fig. 44. — Images d'un coureur réduite à des lignes brillantes qui représentent l'attitude de ses membres (Chronophotographie géométrique).

images peut être considérable et la notion de temps très complète, tandis que celle d'espace a été volontairement restreinte au strict nécessaire.

Chronophotographie stéréoscopique. — On a vu au chapitre II comment on obtient les images stéréoscopiques des figures engendrées dans l'espace par le mouvement de lignes droites ou courbes. Ces images étaient discontinues, c'est-à-dire formées au moyen d'ouvertures intermittentes de l'objectif; cela avait pour but de mieux faire comprendre

Fig. 70 *Etienne-Jules Marey*, Le Mouvement, Paris, 1894, p. 61

simultanés des attitudes des ailes et du corps d'un Oiseau à

Fig. 124. — Statuette faite d'après des épreuves chronophotographiques.

certains instants de son vol. Et nous désirions vivement qu'un artiste voulût bien consacrer son talent à représenter

Fig. 71 *Etienne-Jules Marey*, Le Mouvement, Paris, 1894, p. 172

---

of bodily masses, where multiple exposures of a single rising figure almost fuse into a single image. Marey's work in particular had become more broadly familiar in France in the intervening years, thanks to his steady production of articles and books, presentations at the Collège de France and elsewhere, and the appearance of his photographs and sculptures in exhibitions such as the 1889 Exposition Universelle. Still publishing in *La Nature* and *Scientific American*, Marey also began to direct his texts and illustrations at the photographic community through such periodicals as *L'Amateur Photographe* and *Paris Photographe*; in 1892, his book *La Photographie du mouvement* appeared, followed two years later by a second volume, entitled simply *Le Mouvement*.[30]

Marey used the opportunity of the 1894 *Le Mouvement* to summarise two decades of research into the principal enquiry of his career, seemingly with the student or general reader in mind. Extensively illustrated, his opening chapters briefly addressed the subjects of 'Time', 'Space' and 'Movement', arguing that an understanding of the latter phenomenon necessarily involved the former two. Ranging widely over his more recent experiments with photographing the actions of birds, fish and other life forms, and the historic 'filming' of a breaking wave, Marey also reintroduced material from his 1878 article in *La Nature*. Brief acknowledgement of Muybridge's contribution to their shared subject was made, with illustrations of his instantaneous photographs of horses but including no reference to the later *Animal Locomotion*.[31] One chapter examined chronophotography with the fixed-plate camera that Marey himself had designed, an example of which survives in the collection of the National Media Museum, Bradford (cat. 74). This ingenious apparatus depended on a rotating disc in front of the lens that allowed a brief exposure to be made every tenth

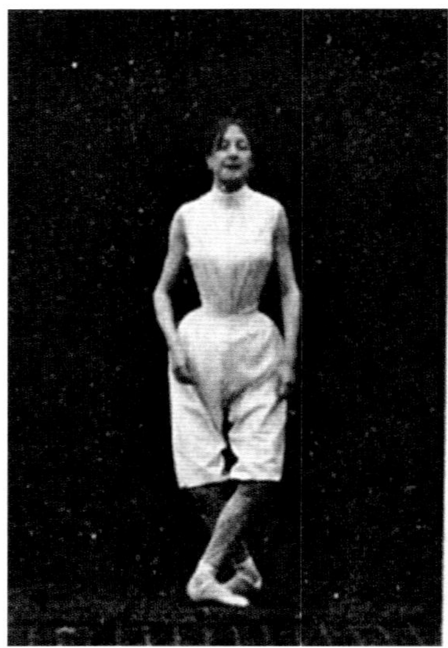
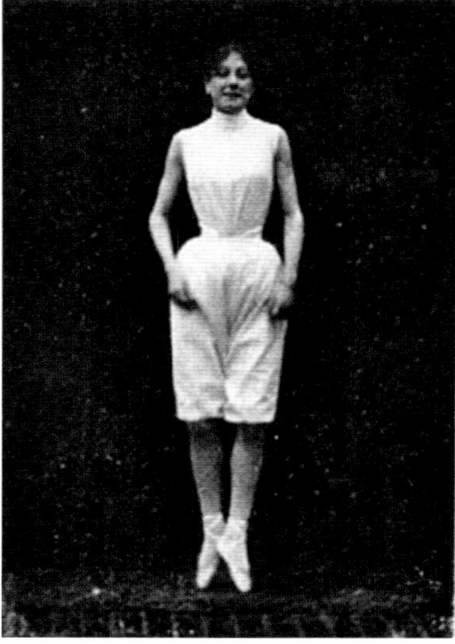
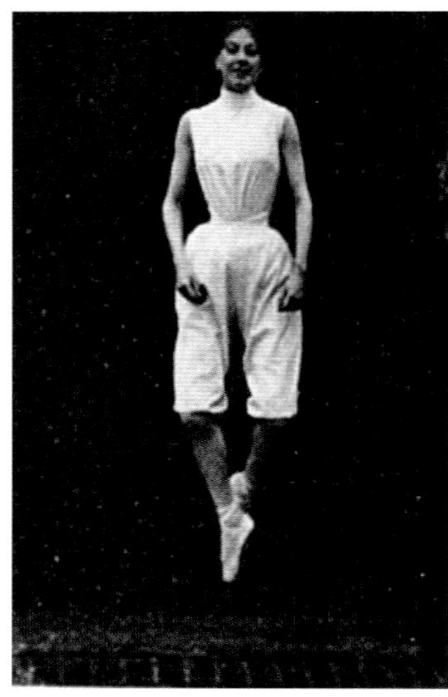

of a second, recording the moving subject on a single glass plate. In Marey's 1894 book a selection of chronophotographs produced with this type of camera surveyed men walking and running, as well as the 'geometric' rendering of movement that reduced such actions to patterns of straight and angled lines (fig. 70). As in 1878, Marey again emphasised the importance of his latest studies for contemporary painting and sculpture. In a chapter entitled 'Locomotion de l'homme au point de vue artistique', he argued that 'instantaneous photography' had already exercised a 'perceptible influence on the arts', allowing painters and sculptors to determine 'the attitudes of man and animals in their most rapid movements'.[32] His illustrations included a painted Greek vase and a modern sculpture representing a naked male runner, the latter created with Marey's help by Georges Engrand (fig. 71).

Le Mouvement also referred explicitly to the dance, recording Marey's contribution to a historically based book on dancing in antiquity that was currently being prepared by Maurice Emmanuel. Approached by Emmanuel to apply instantaneous photography to this subject, Marey had used his camera to record the rhythmic flow of a dancer's 'Greek' costume and 'all the model's phases of movement'.[33] When the profusely illustrated book appeared in 1896, accompanied by an article in the *Gazette des Beaux-Arts* written by Emmanuel himself, both publications revealed that Marey and his assistant Georges Demenÿ had also photographed ballerinas of their own day to accompany parts of Emmanuel's text.[34] One such individual was shown executing a jumping movement know as 'entrechat quatre' (cat. 98) and a lively sequence of 'battements' (fig. 72), and another demonstrating an ancient Greek dance (fig. 73). All these steps, Emmanuel announced in the book's preface, had been personally supervised by Joseph Hansen, 'Maître de Ballets à l'Opéra'.[35] Representing a fascinating practical conjunction of science and ballet in the late nineteenth century, this project also emphasised a shared conceptual understanding within these disciplines that reverberated in the wider world. In both his book and article, Emmanuel stressed that the 'movements of the body are the essence of dance, just as sounds are the essence of music'.[36]

Little serious attention has been paid to the photography of dancers by Muybridge and Marey. Characteristically, Muybridge's response was both

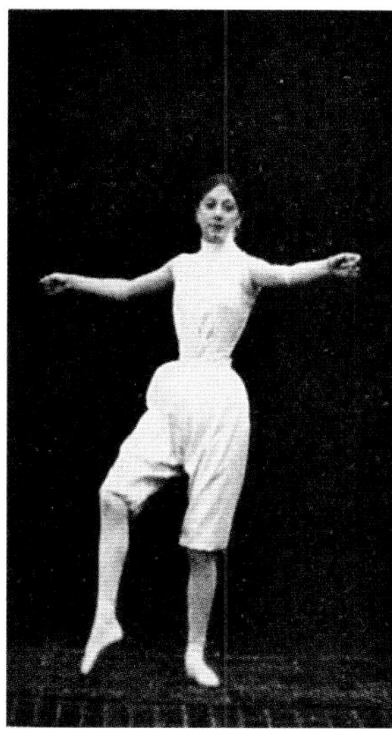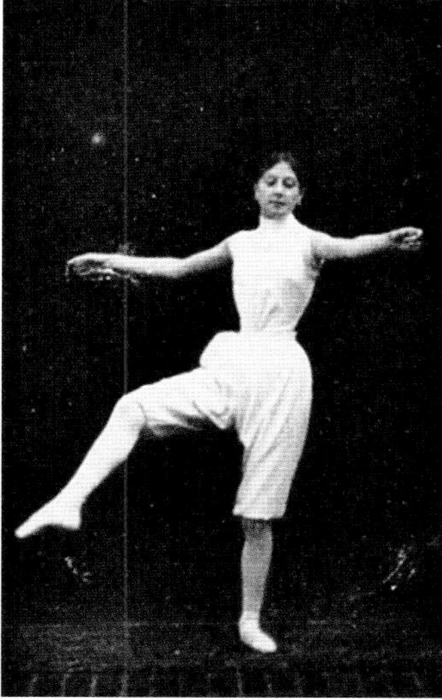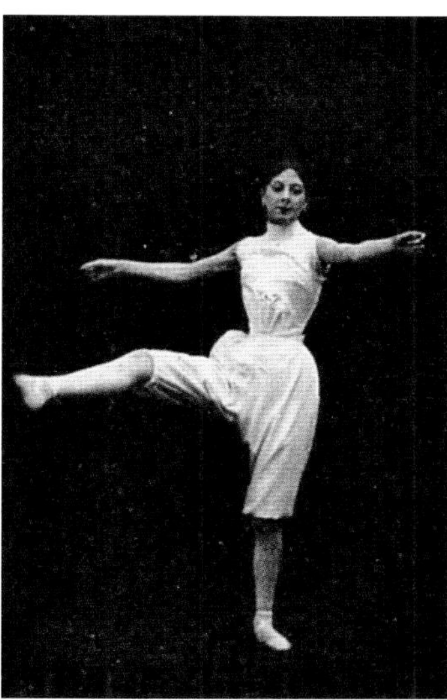

Fig. 72 *Maurice Emmanuel*, La Danse grecque antique d'après les monuments figurés, Paris, 1896, plate II: 'Analyse chronophotographique d'un grand battement, à la quatrième ouverte' by Georges Demenÿ

more extensive and less rigorously conceived, appearing over the years in photographs on glass, zoöpraxiscope discs and other forms, with such titles as *Dancing (Fancy)*, *Woman*, *Fan Dance*, *Grecian Girl Dancing* and even *A Couple Waltzing*.[37] Discs and slides with images of this kind were used in Muybridge's public presentations from the 1870s onwards, when they may have prompted some of the protests against 'exhibiting semi-nude figures' on such occasions.[38] Of greater significance are ten plates in *Animal Locomotion*, eight of which depict a dancing female figure, presumably posed by 'the première danseuse of a Philadelphia theatre', the 'danseuse from New York', or one of the 'female art students and artist's models' who are said to have worked for Muybridge.[39] Whatever the skills and profession of the young woman displayed, the resulting photographs show her performing improvised or casual dances that are unrelated to traditional ballet, as is suggested by her vaguely 'Greek' costume (cats 69–71). The exception to this group, as we have seen, is a pair of plates from the same publication that are both entitled 'First Ballet Action' (cats 88, 89), based on a muscular male figure who has clearly been trained in ballet technique.[40] Degas presumably had an opportunity to see Muybridge's photographs of dancers when using *Animal Locomotion* to make his drawings of horses and of female nudes, though no direct traces of their influence on his art have been identified. The resemblance between 'First Ballet Action' and Degas's sculptures of ballerinas in arabesque is, however, distinctly compelling (cats 85–87, 104), conceivably due to a shared source in the historic classroom repertoire. Similarly, the photo-sequences of 'Greek' dancing taken by Marey for Emmanuel's publications may succeed rather than anticipate the artist's pronounced interest in this subject in late life. Speaking often of 'the movement of the Greeks' and its importance for ballet tradition, the ageing Degas somewhat uncharacteristically introduced explicit references to this theme in certain pictures of the 1890s, from glimpses of antique temples to scantily clad dancer-acolytes.[41]

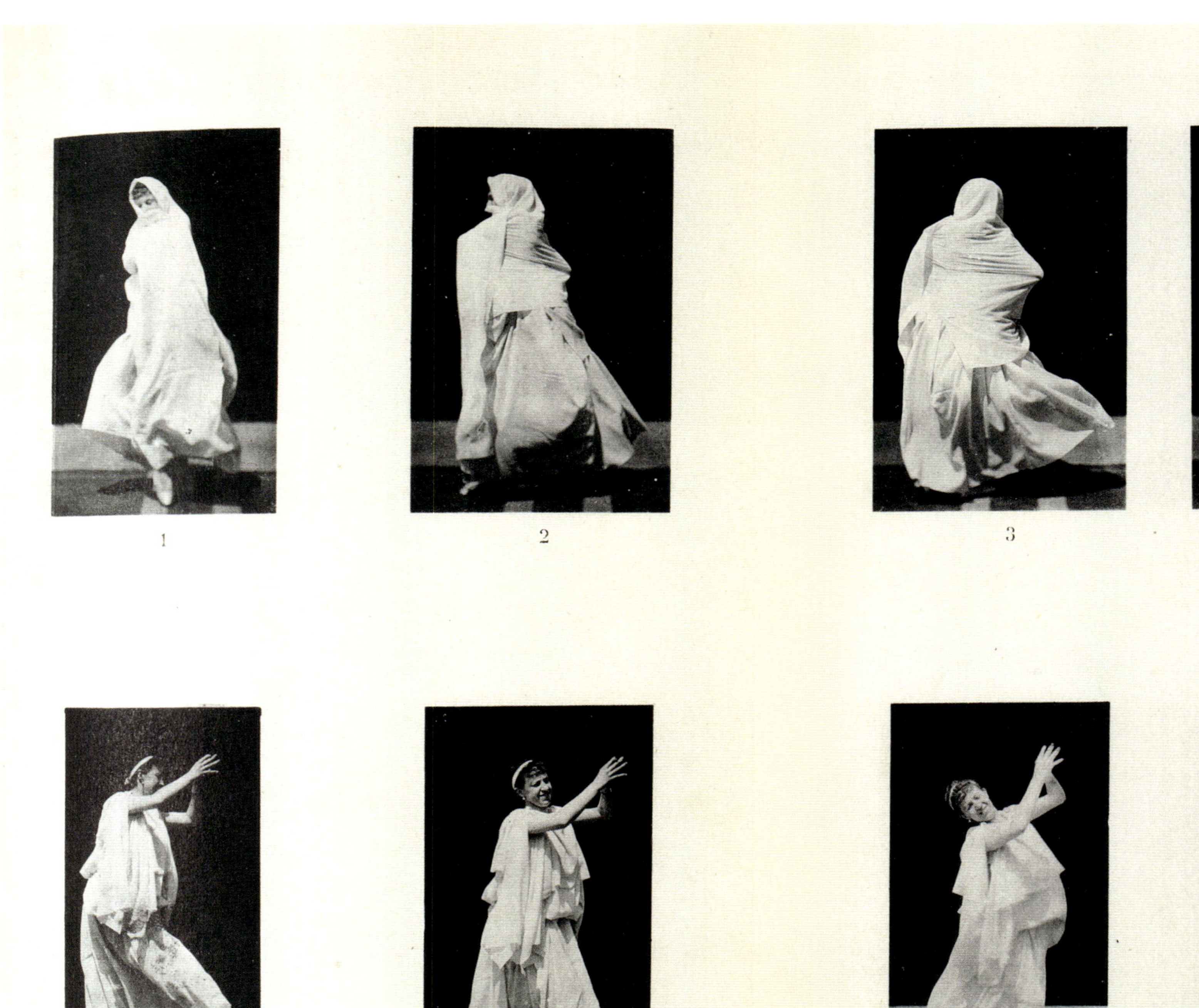

Fig. 73 *Maurice Emmanuel*, La Danse grecque antique d'après les monuments figurés, Paris, 1896, plate V: 'Images empruntées à diverses analyses chronophotographiques' by Etienne-Jules Marey

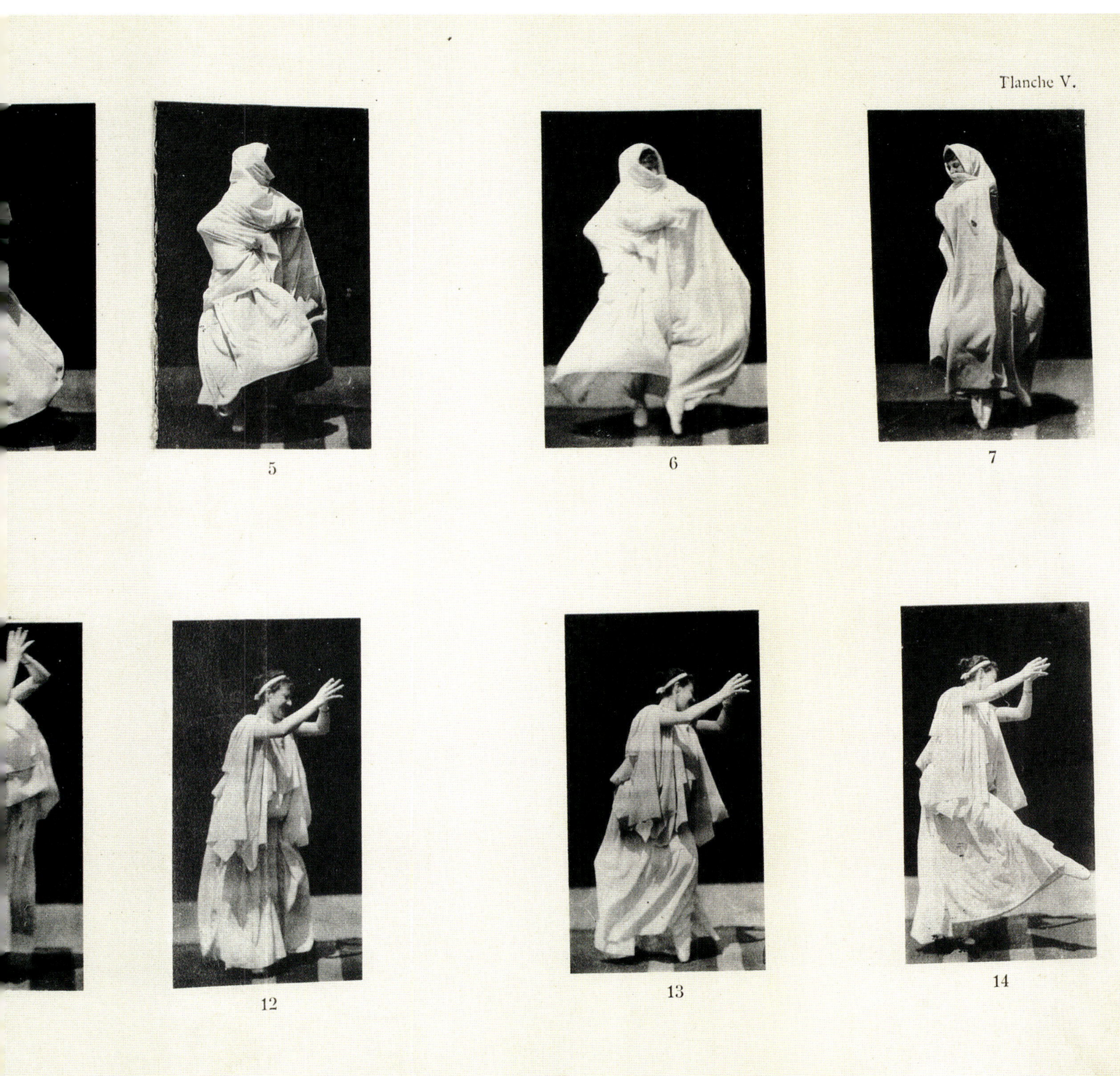

5

6

7

12

13

14

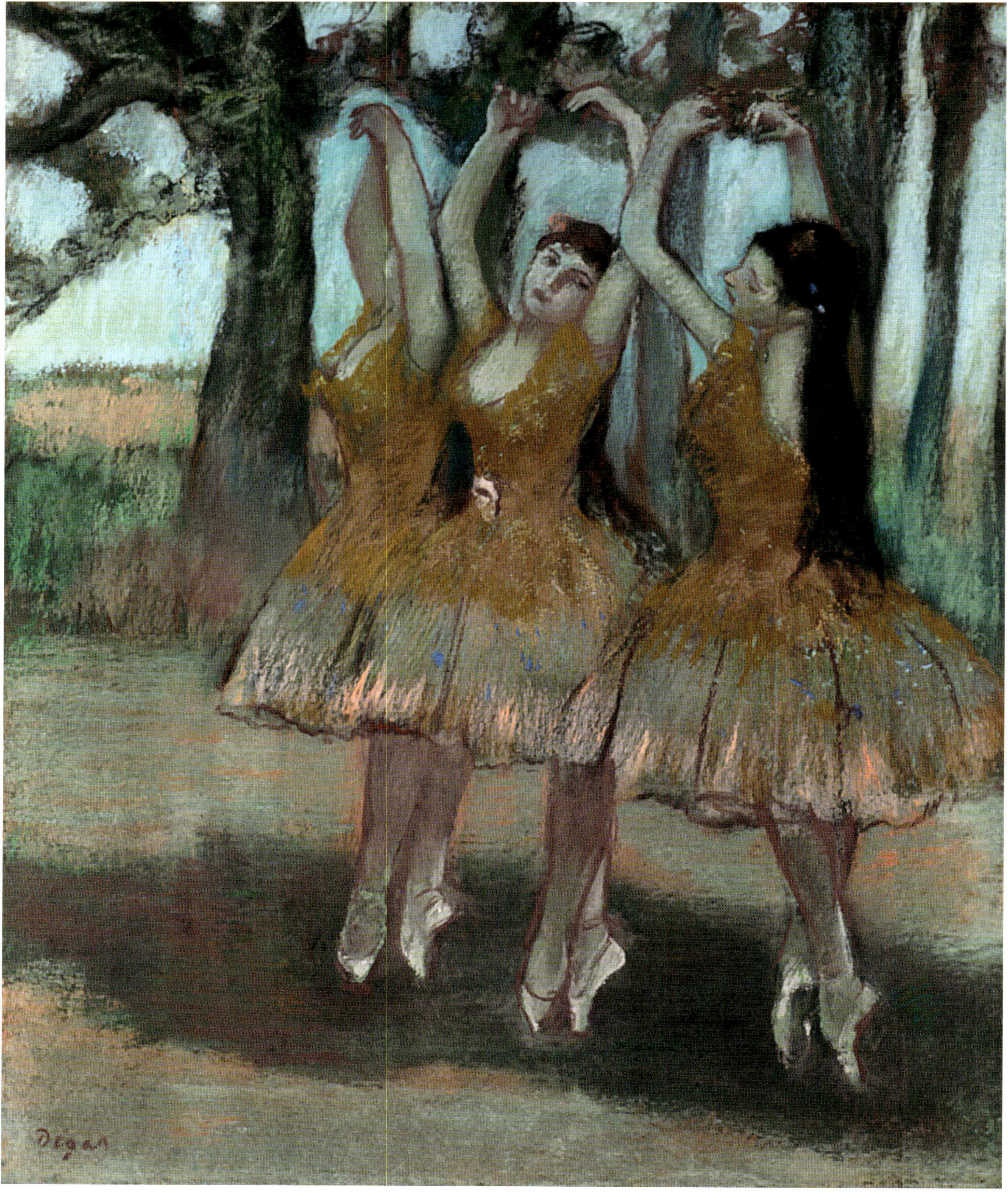

Some of the images of dancers made by Muybridge and Marey towards the end of the century were consonant with and perhaps influential upon Degas's achievement, just as the precedence of the two men as photographers of human movement surely retained its significance for the aging artist. A majestic pastel such as *The Greek Dance* (cat. 99) might almost be a gentle reprimand to Muybridge's *Fancy Dancing* series, re-asserting the seriousness of ballet's roots in the past and the continuing relevance of the classical tradition in the present. These elegant ballerinas on point were probably performing in one of the many Greek-themed scenarios that appeared on the Opéra stage in this decade. Three productions of this kind are documented: *Salammbô*, which premiered in 1892; *Déidamé*, opening the following year; and *Sylvia*, a ballet first mounted in 1876 that was reprised in 1892.[42] Yet Degas's picture could never be mistaken for a mere illustration of such an event. Instead he chose to evoke the subtle rhythms within and around this group of highly trained dancers, as they move in sympathy with one another. Deep shadow gives prominence to their pale feet and emphasises the delicacy of the manœuvre they undertake, as they appear to turn weightlessly like beings from another realm. Even the line of trees behind them acts as a foil for their tremulousness, its emphatic verticals emphasising the curving, supple movements of the dancers' bodies in the foreground. A striking feature of *The Greek Dance* is the closely similar size and body type of the three young women, echoed in their improbably identical long, dark tresses. The invitation to perceive this group as a representation of a single figure traversing the stage from right to left, rotating slightly as she advances and in places almost blurring into a single form, is surely irresistible. At this fundamental level, the pastel seems closer to Marey's chronophotographs than to Muybridge's subdivided grids of athletes in action. Yet Paul Valéry, who first became acquainted with Degas in this decade, argued eloquently if obliquely for a rapport between the French artist and the work of the English photographer. Muybridge's sequences, Valéry proposed,

> *showed how inventive the eye is, or rather how much the sight elaborates on the data it gives us as the positive and impersonal result of observation. Between the state of vision as mere patches of colour and as things or objects, a whole series of mysterious operations takes place, reducing to order as best it can the incoherence of raw perceptions, resolving contradictions, bringing to bear judgements formed since early infancy, imposing continuity, connection, and the systems of change which we group under the labels of space, time, matter and movement.*[43]

This final phrase, which is again startlingly reminiscent of Marey in *Le Mouvement*, seems increasingly applicable to Degas's art as he approached the *fin de siècle. Three Dancers in Violet Tutus* (cat. 100), made in the second half of the decade, broadly reprises the scale and format of *The Greek Dance* and again relies on the repeated motif of a dancer lifting her arms above her head. Yet these figures are clearly earthbound, shown gently but firmly moving across the stage into open space at left.[44] Even more than in the earlier work, the performers are now indistinguishable from each other, inviting us to perceive them as part of a Marey-like progression of a single model in front of his fixed-plate camera. The rich ultramarine-purples of their skirts seem to flow from dancer to dancer, much as the pale costumes and skin tones

99

The Greek Dance
c. 1887–92
Pastel on joined paper
laid down on board,
58 x 49 cm
On loan from The Honorable
Earle I. Mack Collection, USA

100

Three Dancers in Violet Tutus
c. 1895–98
Pastel on paper laid
down on board,
73.2 x 49 cm
Private collection

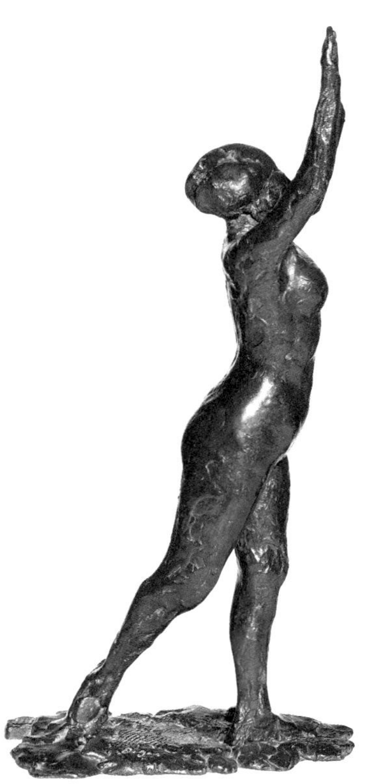

Fig. 74 **Dancer Moving Forward, Arms Raised,
First Study**, *c.* 1881–85. Bronze, 35.7 x 15.6 x 17
cm. Musée d'Orsay, Paris

of Marey's athletes can blend into a single, slightly blurred tone. Pictorial vibrancy is also common to both types of composition, created through reverberating lines in arms, legs and torsos, even in the physical qualities of the pictures themselves. Some of Degas's pastel marks were applied in repeated, informally parallel lines that 'rhyme' with the contours of the dancers and their costumes, just as Marey – for scientific purposes – would impose repeated curves on the figures in his 'geometric' renderings of movement. In *Three Dancers in Violet Tutus*, this almost unnoticed resonance within the fabric of the scene is enhanced at a chromatic level, by the visual interactions of warm and cool hues – orange and blue, rich purple and yellow-green – and even the granular nature of pastel itself. Successive applications of this chalky material followed by the use of fixative can create a richly varied texture, like a miniature landscape of colour with peaks and troughs of shifting hues. Seen from a slight distance, their surfaces become energised, even restless, a quality that the artist seems to have specifically encouraged in his late work.[45]

Present in Degas's studio when he made *Three Dancers in Violet Tutus* was his wax sculpture *Dancer Moving Forward, Arms Raised, First Study*, from which a posthumous bronze was made (fig. 74). Embodying the dialogue between two and three dimensions that characterised much of his career, the juxtaposition of these two works also reflected the artist's immediate practical circumstances, where two- and three-dimensional creations emerged in close proximity. Generally dated to the end of the previous decade, the wax figure may have helped him to develop the pastel when a human model was not available. The bodily conformation of the sculpture certainly anticipated the repeated poses in *Three Dancers in Violet Tutus*, even though the modelled individual is heavier in build than the slender coryphées in the picture. It was around this date that Degas had his memorable conversation with Thiébault-Sisson, explaining how such exercises had contributed to his attempts to capture 'movement in its exact truth'. The muscular forms of his sculpted dancer, who is represented naked, embody this aspiration, flowing sensuously and naturally, and contributing to a buoyancy that seems to lift her forwards and upwards with a persuasive sense of mobility.

Many such sculptures were scattered through Degas's studio, where he continued to work on them intermittently towards the end of the century and even beyond. To the frustration of his many admirers, Degas refused to have any of them cast into plaster or bronze for commercial distribution. When the young dealer Ambroise Vollard proposed to Degas that such casts be made, he protested angrily that he 'wouldn't take a bucket of gold' for the pleasure he derived from remodelling and revising his wax and clay figures.[46] Vollard was one of a select group of acquaintances who were occasionally allowed into the studio and also among those who later wrote down their reminiscences of the artist at work. Occupying the top floor of Degas's house on the Rue Victor Massé in Montmartre, the studio was described by Valéry – another privileged visitor – as 'a long attic room, with a wide bay window (not very clean) where light and dust mingled gaily. The room was pell-mell – with a basin, a dull zinc bathtub, stale bathrobes, a danseuse modelled in wax with a real gauze tutu in a glass case, and easels loaded with charcoal sketches of flat-nosed, twisted models.'[47] Other witnesses described 'tables covered with lumps of clay and unfinished waxes' or recalled seeing the decayed figure of the *Little Dancer Aged Fourteen* lying 'in pieces'; 'how faded the gauze was

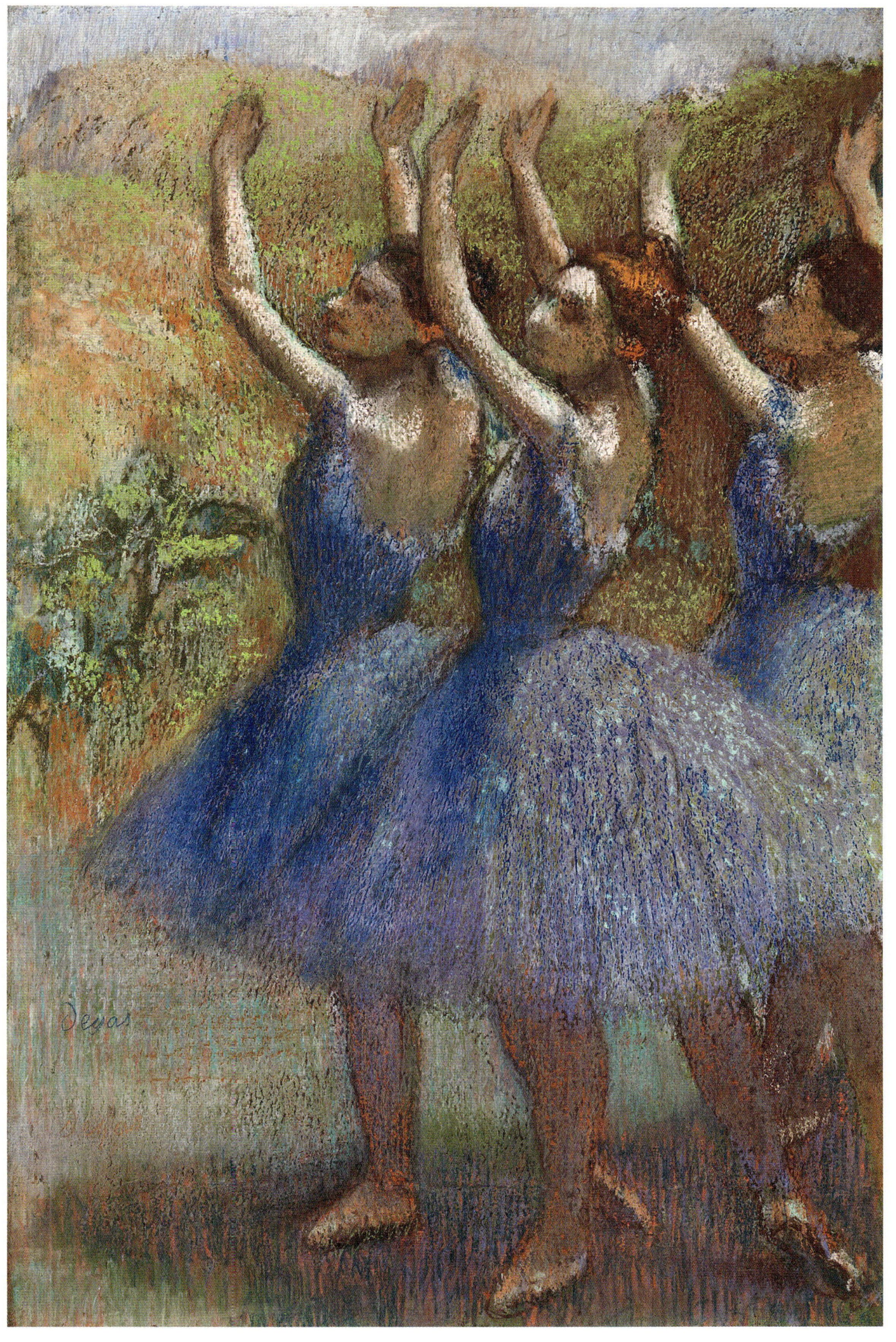

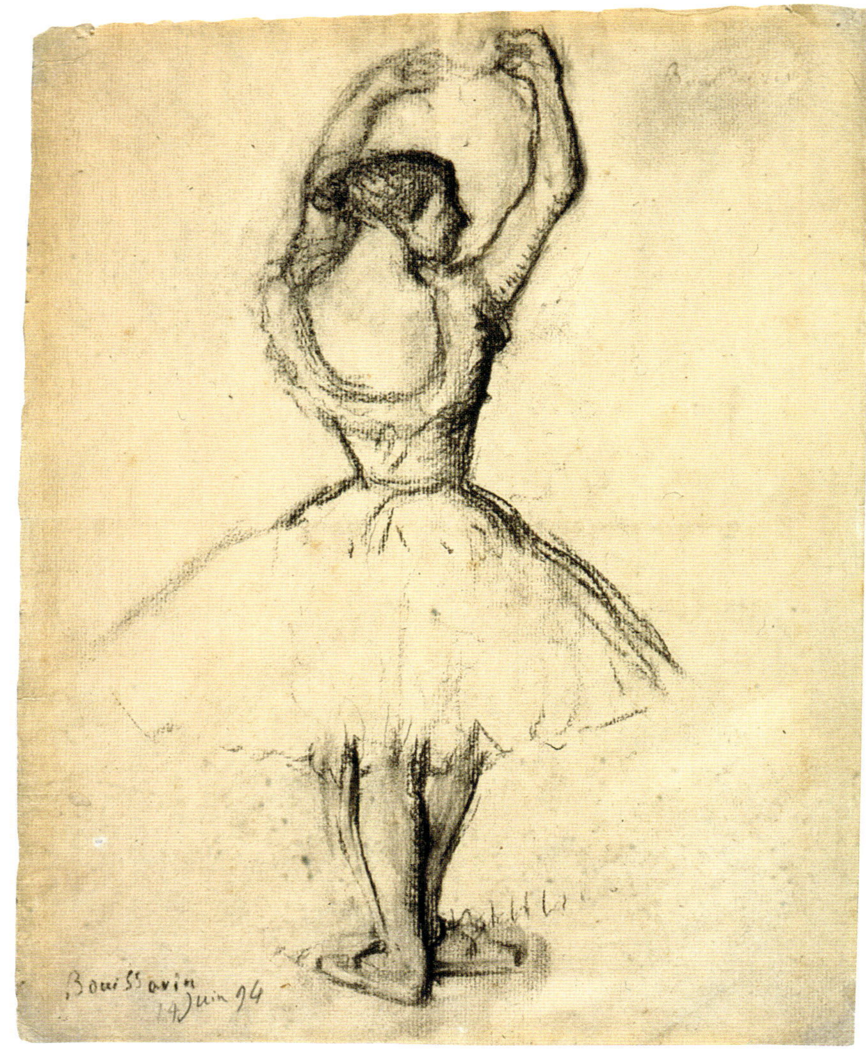

Fig. 75 **Dancer with Arms Raised, Seen from the Back**, 1894.
Charcoal on paper, 31 x 24.5 cm. National Museum, Belgrade

and how woolly the dark hair appeared,' recalled Louisine Havemeyer
of her visit in 1903.[48]

Despite rumours to the contrary, then and now, it is clear that Degas
worked stubbornly and productively in his studio into the beginning of the
twentieth century; in a letter of 1907 he wrote 'here am I back again at
drawing and pastel', and in March 1910, he told the same correspondent
'I do not finish with my damned sculpture'.[49] Selling occasional pictures
through the Durand-Ruel gallery and sometimes through other dealers
such as Vollard, he resisted the idea of solo exhibitions and preferred
to accumulate drawings, pastels, paintings and sculptures as part of his
continuing, unfinished creative process. Turning repeatedly to certain poses –
a nude wiping her back, a dancer standing in the wings – he would produce
sequences of works that varied little in composition but allowed him to
explore minute shifts of pose and gesture, and newly expressive combinations
of form and colour. The ballet dancer and the nude now dominated his *œuvre*,

while other subjects that had once brought him fame – cabarets and cafés, racecourse meetings, and portraits of topical figures – had long since fallen away. As the volume of critical commentary faded, some writers stayed loyal and younger figures came forward, understanding that Degas's art was evolving slowly – like that of Monet in Giverny and Cézanne in Aix-en-Provence – and at the same time becoming radically new. In 1894 Théodore Duret, senior critic and former champion of Edouard Manet, had written a thoughtful article in the *Art Journal* that attempted to summarise Degas's developing *œuvre*. After dutiful remarks about his academic beginnings and his early respect for the masters, Duret emphasised the central role of drawing, 'the whole basis of his art'.[50] Referring to the theme of the ballet dancer, he argued that Degas's earlier genre pictures of 'slim and elegant beings in graceful motion' had been gradually overtaken by 'something infinitely more powerful', conveying 'a world of meaning to which at first they were strangers'; 'he gives their form the movement of female athletes'.[51] Although reluctant to abandon entirely the notion of Degas 'the painter of modern life', Duret grasped the seriousness of his accumulated body of work as 'one of the most powerful, the most complex, and the most wholly instinct with vitality amongst that of the masters of the nineteenth century'.[52]

Duret was never personally close to Degas, so he would have known little about the curious working routines of the artist as he grew older. Visitors to the Rue Victor Massé studio continued to note the coming and going of models and the artist's dependence on them for many of his projects. As with his first pictures of the ballet from the 1870s, Degas still made studies from figures poised as if in class or on stage, sometimes adding their names and even the date to the sheet in question. In June 1894, for example, an obscure ballerina at the Opéra known simply as Mlle Boussavin stood for several drawings (fig. 75) and duly appeared in one of Degas's most 'Greek' ballet pictures from this moment.[53] The artist Suzanne Valadon also posed for Degas during these years, probably for his scenes of bathers, gaining his friendship and respect for her own 'beautiful drawings'.[54] A somewhat fictionalised series of recollections, entitled 'Degas et son modèle', was published after the artist's death and offered further details about the disorder of the 'attic room' and its coldness in winter, and the artist's benevolent if eccentric behaviour towards the young women who still modelled for his pictures and sculptures.[55] The drawings made from these individuals show how consistent Degas was in his attention to the living body, recalling sheets made decades earlier when he first educated himself in the ways of the dance. In the superbly vibrant *Study of a Dancer in Tights* (cat. 102), he examined this anonymous individual from both front and back, using a supple line that shows no sign of feebleness or decline. Unconcerned with details, Degas emphasised the rhythmic flow of her limbs and torso, which might almost have been moving as his drawing progressed. Repeated contours left unerased add to this sense of movement as they had done in comparable studies in the 1870s and 1880s, while here a finger or perhaps a cloth produced soft areas of tone that suggest volume. By combining rear and frontal views on the same sheet, Degas yet again expressed his interest in the three-dimensional body as a living whole and hinted at a mobile relationship between artist and subject. Either the model changed positions as he was drawing or Degas moved to a different vantage point halfway through the session, but the result was another record of mutual dynamism.

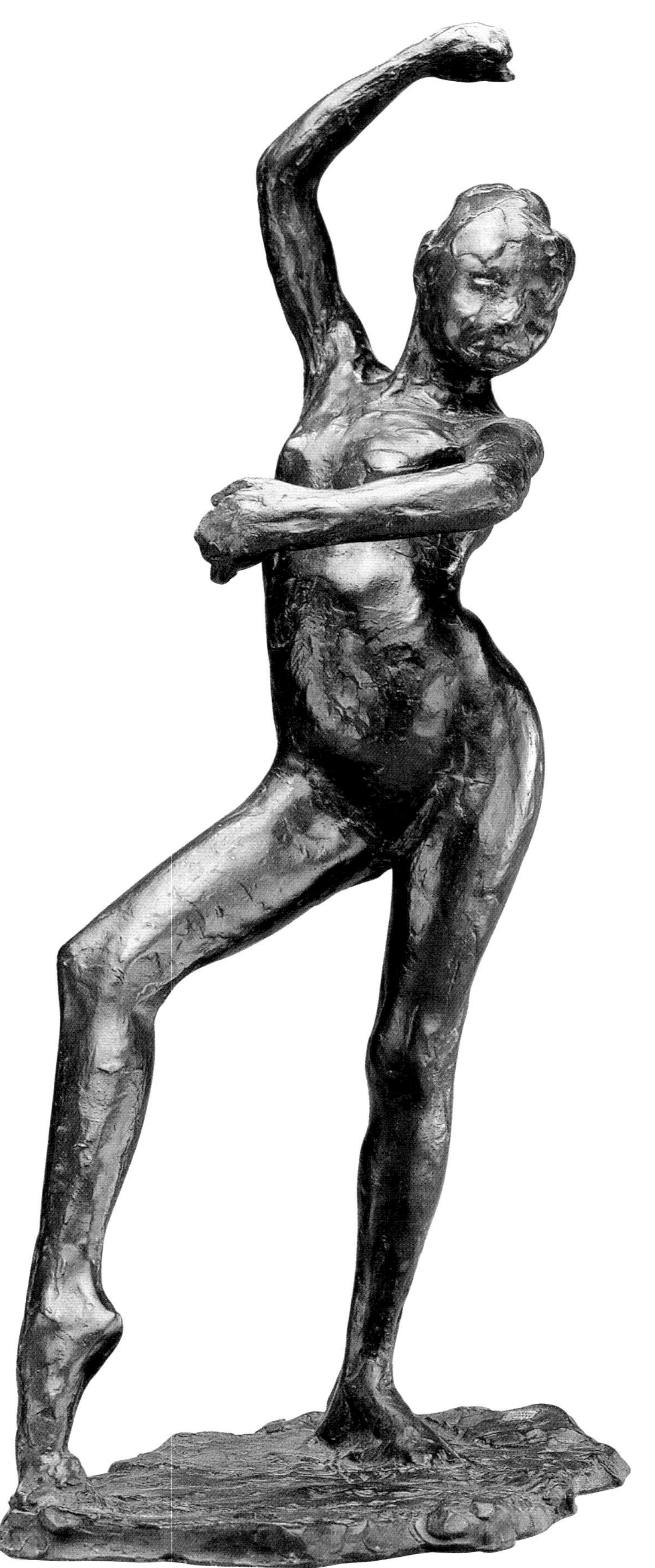

101

Spanish Dancer
1919–22
Bronze with black patina,
43.2 x 17.1 x 21.9 cm
Detroit Institute of Arts.
Gift of Robert H. Tannahill

102

Study of a Dancer in Tights
c. 1900
Black crayon on paper,
60 x 45.5 cm
National Museum, Belgrade

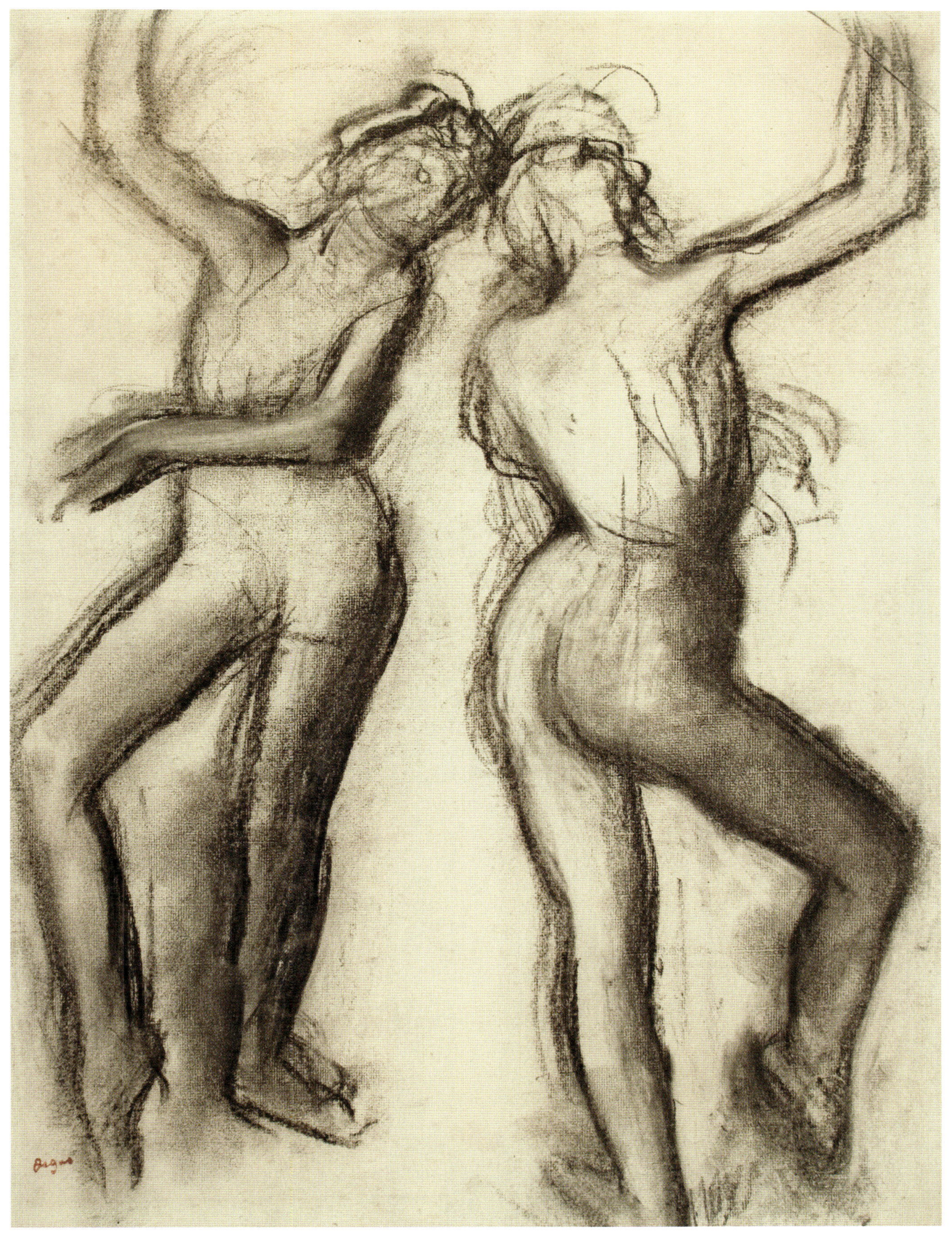

As with his drawings for the *Little Dancer Aged Fourteen*, the multiple viewpoints in *Study of a Dancer in Tights* suggest that Degas was considering this lithe, animated figure as the subject of a possible sculpture. The distinctively angled hips, raised right foot and counterposed arms relate the model's position to Spanish – or possibly Italian – folk dance, a subject he explored over the years in three waxes and several drawings and pastels.[56] The earliest example, *Spanish Dancer* (cat. 101), was made in the previous decade, its sinuous surfaces and delicately articulated forms placing it among the artist's more finished works in three dimensions. Degas's own satisfaction with this variant was signalled by his uncharacteristic decision to cast it in plaster around the turn of the century, a step taken with only two other sculptures from his entire *œuvre*.[57] This trio of plasters were also the only such works to be displayed in the apartment situated below his studio, a set of formal rooms in which he lived and sometimes entertained guests. Perhaps stimulated by daily contact with the plaster *Spanish Dancer*, Degas undertook a second version that was left in a much more unfinished state, with marks of his sculpture tools clearly visible in its wax surface.[58] A third sculpture, *Dancer with Tambourine*, also relates to this theme but appears to have suffered somewhat during the artist's later years, when many of his wax and clay models were neglected or abandoned. Common to all three figures, however, is a sense of lithe, almost serpentine exertion as the portrayed dancer moves her body in a stylised, flamboyant manner. It was perhaps this flamboyance that brought Degas back to study the same position several times, determined to animate his inert materials and not just 'depict' movement, but embody it in the sinuous forms and flowing surfaces of these statuettes.

In the early 1890s, after years of near-obsessive devotion to the ballets mounted at the Paris Opéra – which he had sometimes attended three or four times a week – Degas seems to have gradually retreated from this venerable institution. Now he relied more often on memories, the drawings he had accumulated and his first-hand scrutiny of the dancers who came to Montmartre to pose for him. If his creativity became somewhat more hermetic, it lost none of its intensity and may even have been liberated from what remained of the social documentary project of the early Impressionist years. A remarkable work that survives from around 1900, *Group of Dancers* (cat. 103), brings together several of the evolving patterns in Degas's late career as an artist of the dance. Unsigned and unexhibited in his lifetime, this is one of many pictures that were stored among his possessions and first seen at the sales following his death in 1917. Like the slightly earlier drawing derived from his own photographs, *Study of Dancers* (fig. 66), this larger sheet has been ingeniously contrived from a number of elements that can be found in other studies of the period. Initially based on posed models who were clearly naked, this group of ballerinas is again set in an indeterminate space on stage that is neither public nor wholly private. Once more the dancers stretch or attend to their outfits, their bodies and limbs overlapping in patterns of restlessness. Even more than in the preceding sheet, Degas has emphasised the internal rhythms that energise and unify the group as a whole, here using charcoal lines that he has drawn and redrawn several times as the picture advanced. Distantly recalling the wave-like patterns of the dancing nuns in his *Ballet Scene from Meyerbeer's Opera 'Robert le Diable'* and its accompanying studies (cats 15–17), *Group of Dancers* takes Degas's preoccupation into new territory.

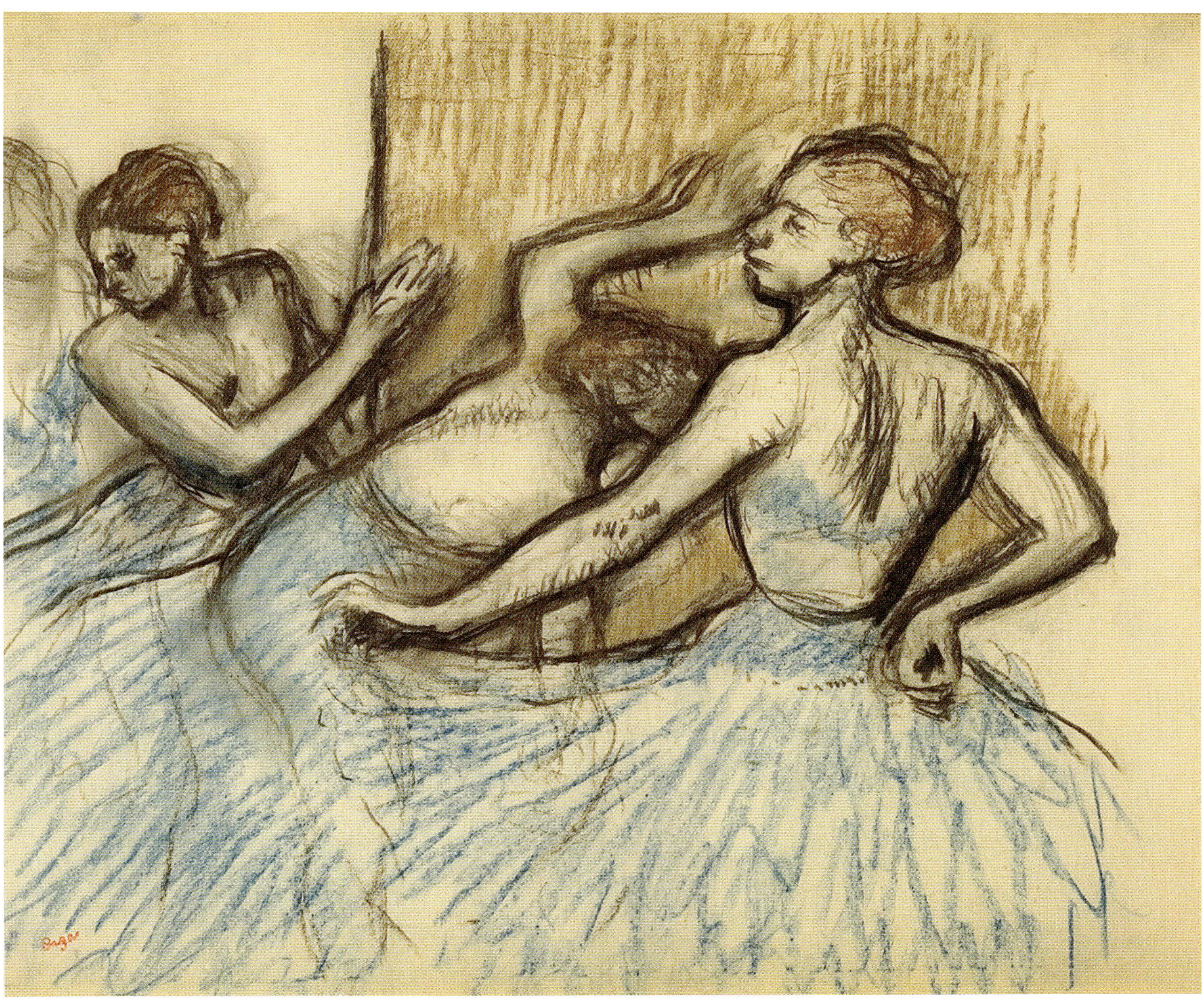

103

Group of Dancers
c. 1900
Charcoal and pastel on paper
laid down on board,
57.2 x 69.5 cm
Private collection, courtesy
of the Halcyon Gallery, London

Now a long way from Duret's earlier notion of dancers as 'slim and elegant beings in graceful motion', this powerful work seems to belong to the age of Matisse's wildly animated *La Danse* of 1909.

Degas's preoccupation with the idea of movement, not just with its depiction, is vividly suggested in an event recalled by Walter Sickert. The two men had met in the 1880s and remained in contact for some years, their friendship and mutual respect reflected in time spent by Sickert in Degas's secluded apartment and studio. On one of his last visits, 'in the early nineties', Sickert remembered that Degas took him to see a variant of his 'arabesque' sculptures: 'he showed me a little statuette of a dancer he had on the stocks, and – it was night – he held a candle up, and turned the statuette to show me the succession of shadows cast by its silhouettes on a white sheet'.[59] Crude though this demonstration must have been, the remarkable shadow-play of a dancer apparently in movement again linked Degas with the nineteenth-

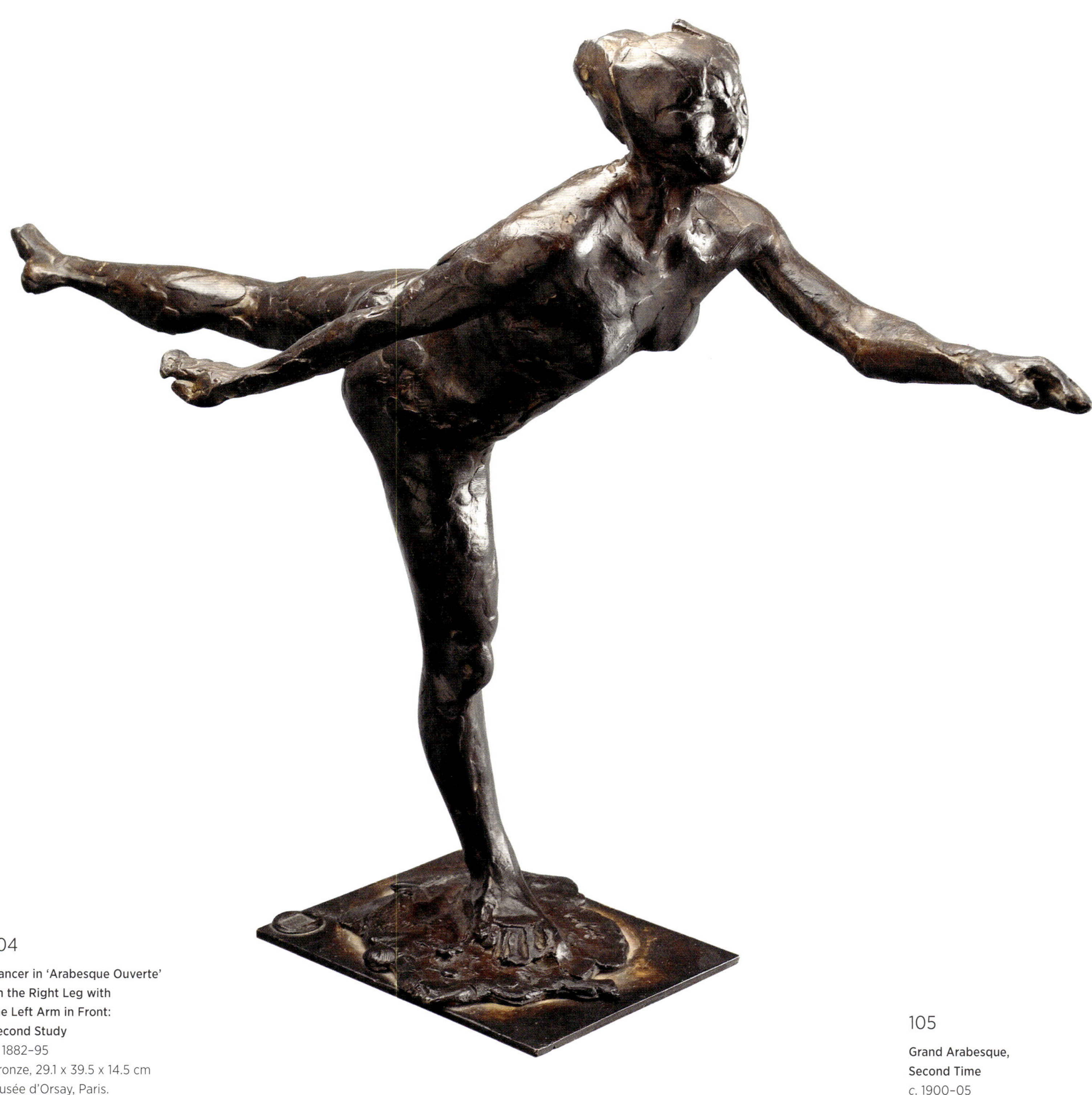

104

**Dancer in 'Arabesque Ouverte'
on the Right Leg with
the Left Arm in Front:
Second Study**
c. 1882–95
Bronze, 29.1 x 39.5 x 14.5 cm
Musée d'Orsay, Paris.
Acquired through the
generosity of the artist's heirs
and the Hébrard family, 1931

105

**Grand Arabesque,
Second Time**
c. 1900–05
Charcoal on tracing paper,
50.8 x 43.2 cm
Private collection

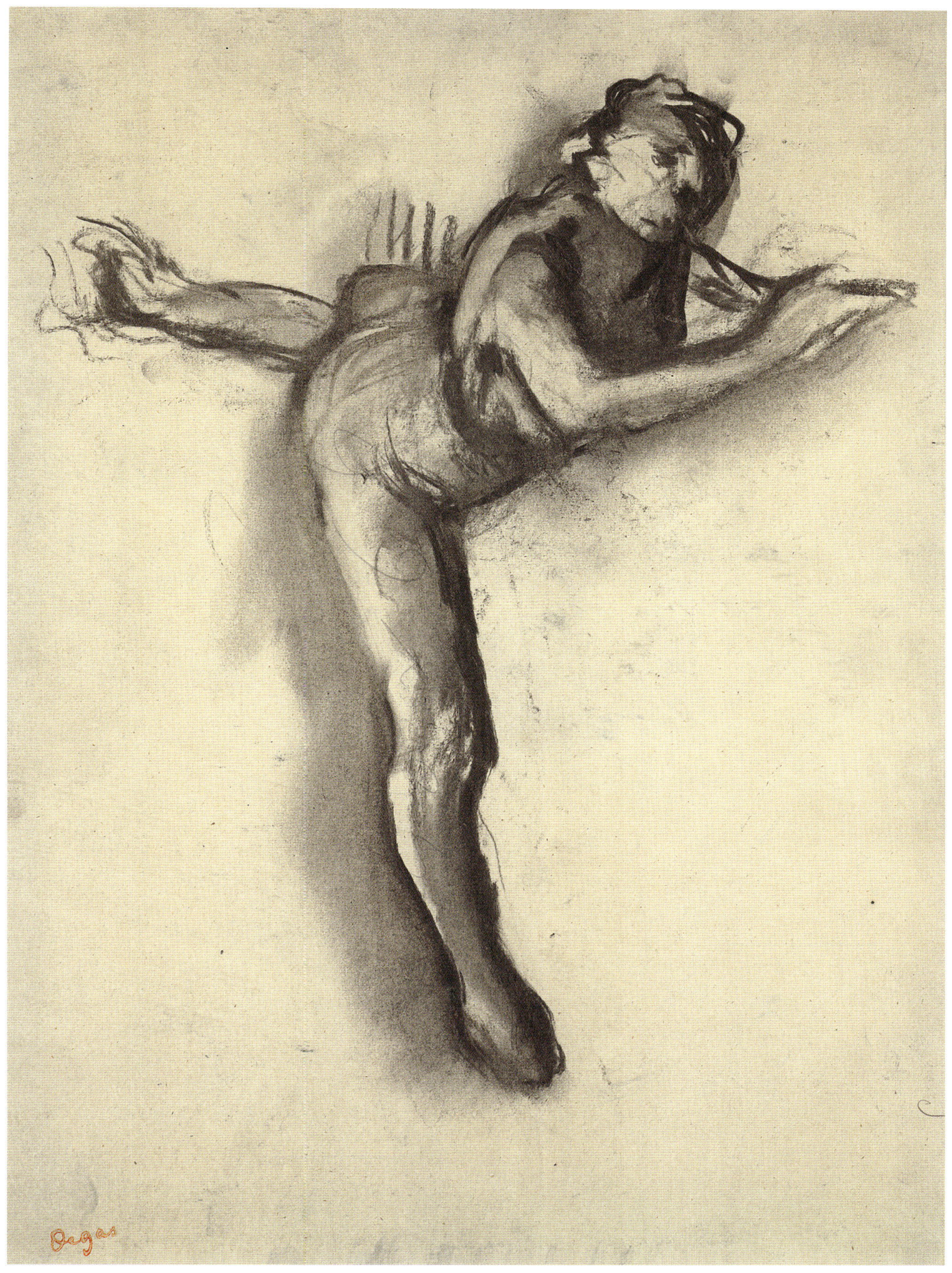

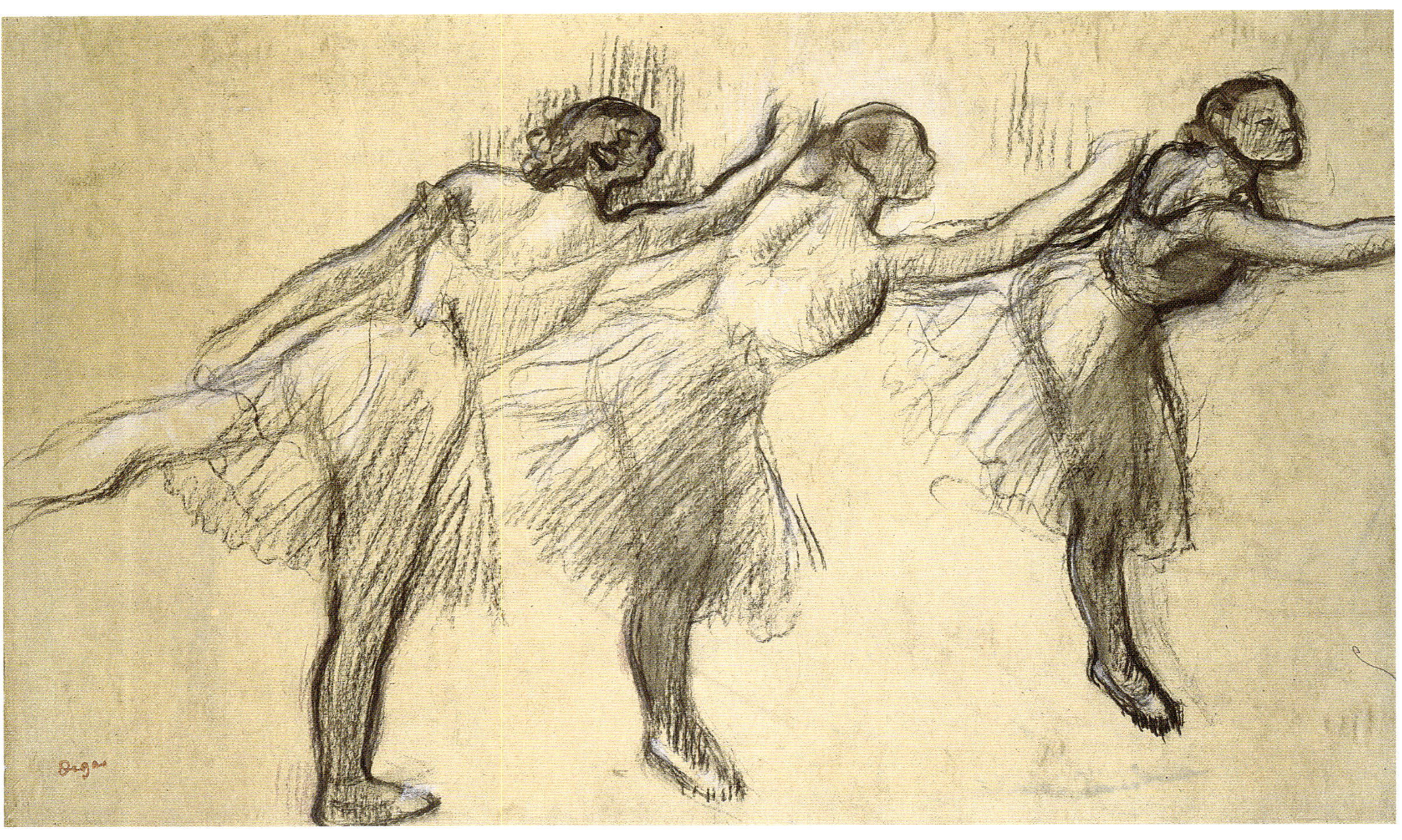

106

Three Studies of a Ballerina
c. 1900–05
Charcoal rubbed and
touched with pink and
brown pastels on thin,
yellowish oiled paper,
laid down on stiff paper,
39 x 63.8 cm
The Ashmolean Museum,
Oxford. Bequeathed by
Mrs W. F. R. Weldon, 1937

century passion for visual spectacles of all kinds, from painted and photographed panoramas to proto-filmic devices such as Muybridge's zoöpraxiscope and Marey's sculptural zoetrope. It also draws attention to a curiously circular relationship between some of Degas's more innovative images of the dance. When he sculpted the figure of a dancer in arabesque, his ballerina-model held a pose that would normally be only part of an extended series of movements. In the finished work used in the performance for Sickert's benefit, represented by the original wax and the later bronze *Dancer in 'Arabesque Ouverte' on the Right Leg with the Left Arm in Front: Second Study* (cat. 104), her form was definitively fixed, even though Degas knew that the position was inherently unstable and sustained with great difficulty. During the spectacle created for Sickert, the artist now delighted in bringing the dancer back to life. This Pygmalion-like moment and its suggestive flow between the animated and the inert, the real and the unreal and then back again, haunts many similar projects concerned with the ballet that Degas pursued at the turn of the century. Based on either a living model or perhaps the same sculpture that entertained Sickert, the charcoal drawing *Grand Arabesque, Second Time* (cat. 105) is exceptionally plausible in its suggestion of transience. Heavy contours around the lower leg and parts of the upper torso remind us of the sheer mass of the human body, while almost entirely erased marks elsewhere evoke our fleeting perceptions of figures and other objects seen in passing. Less anatomically precise than the drawings that

Degas made in the 1870s and 1880s, this superb sheet nevertheless seems to describe his subject with immense authority, confronting us with the experience of being present when the living dancer was expertly posing.

A more ambitious extension of this motif is the charcoal and pastel *Three Studies of a Ballerina* (cat. 106), another undated work that probably belongs in the new century. Almost certainly exploiting a single model – human or sculpted – as he drew three linked figures in arabesque, Degas positioned them across the sheet in a continuous flow of limbs and tutus. Scanning the scene from left to right, we become aware that the artist has slightly turned the second two figures on their axis with respect to their neighbours, introducing a further dimension to their progress through space. Such drawings were typically made by Degas in preparation for more elaborated pictures in pastel or oil, when colour became an additional factor in their visual dynamism. Partly with this process of replication in mind, he had long since adopted the practice of drawing on tracing paper, which allowed compositions to be transferred to another surface and even reversed as necessary. Over time Degas seems to have preferred the neutral texture and practical convenience of this unusual material over standard types of paper, arranging for many of his drawings on tracing paper to be stuck down on card by his *colleur*, Monsieur Lézin, so that he could then develop them with pastel.[60] The group of ballerinas in *Three Studies of a Ballerina* has an unusually rich history in this regard, having first appeared in less emphatic terms in the background of the Burrell Collection's oil painting *The Rehearsal* (cat. 1) in 1874. Two works in pastel then gave the same trio of figures more prominence in the 1880s, and finally a richly brushed canvas – possibly reworked by Degas himself – appeared towards the end of his active career with this group still intact.[61] The process of repetition within a single image is thus extended to a larger sequence of pictures that reverberates across the years, bringing 'continuity, connection' – in Valéry's words – to Degas's half-century as a dance artist.

DEGAS IN THE AGE OF FILM

Historians of early film have emphasised the origins of the medium in more primitive forms, reaching back to the seventeenth century and embracing children's toys, shadow projections and lantern slides with moving parts. By the 1870s modifications involving photography had been made to such devices as the zoetrope – a revolving drum with sequential images on the inside, glimpsed through a series of slits – but despite their ingenuity they went little beyond parlour entertainment. This apparatus was invoked soon after Muybridge's photographs of a horse in movement appeared in *La Nature* in 1878, when the magazine *L'Illustration* advertised reproductions of his pictures arranged on a strip that could be viewed in a zoetrope.[62] A more effective presentation of this same material was soon achieved by Muybridge himself in his zoöpraxiscope displays, which created a proto-cinematic experience for his often large audiences. Despite claims by those present that these flickering images of their contemporaries appeared 'as we see them in the street', the somewhat coarse and partly hand-painted projections still fell short of verisimilitude. The potential of photography to record animated subjects was recognised by both Muybridge and Marey, who are today

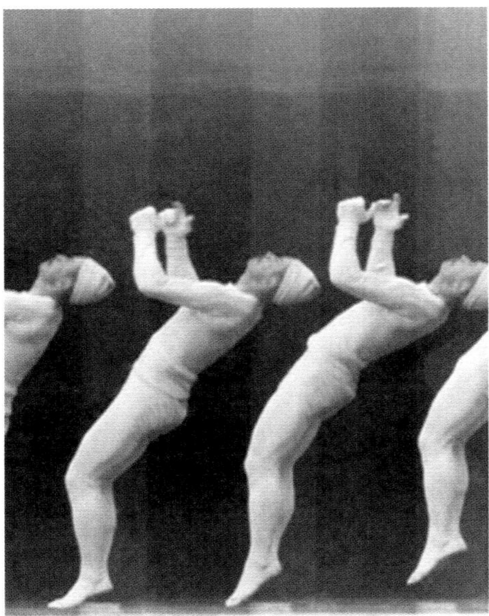

Fig. 76 *Etienne-Jules Marey and Georges Demenÿ*,
Saut périlleux, 'Filmes chronophotographiques
(Men in Movement)', 1890–1904. Film still.
Cinémathèque française, Paris

counted among the leading pioneers of film. With very different backgrounds and professional priorities, both men explored the use of multiple photographic images to study and later to project moving figures. Marey had been intrigued for more than a decade by such 'toys' as the phénakistoscope and the zoetrope. In his 1874 *Animal Mechanism*, for example, he suggested that by using a device of this kind and 'representing faithfully the successive attitudes of the body during walking, running, etc, we might reproduce the appearance of the different kinds of progression employed by man'.[63] The next step taken by Muybridge in a similar direction a decade later was greatly to improve the quality of his photographic sequences in the pages of *Animal Locomotion*, a visually compelling achievement that was seen by Thomas Edison and led to a meeting between the two men the following year.[64] Already an internationally famous inventor, Edison was further inspired by Muybridge's photographs to pursue a form of mass entertainment that would involve both sound and moving pictures.

By a curious historical coincidence, the invention that finally enabled Marey to make the first true films emerged around the same moment and from the same source – George Eastman's Kodak – that had allowed Degas to become a successful amateur photographer. The system of chronophotography developed by Marey in the 1880s had already resulted in multiple images of a moving figure on a single glass plate, rather than the successive plates used by Muybridge. As a scientist with no desire 'to reproduce what the eye could already see' for its own sake, Marta Braun explains, Marey was driven to create his pioneering films by a wish 'to analyse movement in real time'.[65] In 1888 he publicly announced his technique for making 'a series of images on a long band of sensitised paper' – in Marey's words – achieved by 'rapid stoppages at the moment of pose' in the manner that soon became fundamental to cinematography. But paper had its practical drawbacks and it was not until the early 1890s, when Kodak introduced celluloid film on a large scale, that Marey could begin reliable filming at his Station Physiologique and at other locations. Before this final breakthrough had occurred, however, Marey included his new camera and samples of film in a display at the Paris Exposition Universelle of 1889, alongside his selection of chronophotographs, sculptures of birds and a range of other materials. Attracting considerable professional attention, not least from the visiting Edison, Marey's display was seen by vast numbers of visitors to the exhibition, probably including Degas himself. The artist had reportedly been offered rooms to show his own pictures at this prestigious event, but declined in his habitual fashion whenever approached by officialdom, yet in August 1889 he wrote to a friend urging him to see one of the spectacular technical exhibits.[66] Unconcerned by the rush to produce the first viably projected films, Marey continued to refine his equipment and apply it to strictly technical pursuits. Through the 1890s and the early twentieth century, he made hundreds of short black-and-white films of athletes in action, animals jumping and trotting, and such curiosities as a human subject speaking noiselessly. Most memorable, perhaps, are the naked or neutrally clad figures who walk, sprint and perform somersaults (fig. 76), some of them bringing vividly to mind the acrobatic female models who appear as dancers or bathers in Degas's art during these same years. Marey himself showed no interest in filming the dance, but a startling number of pioneering commercial cinematographers did choose to do precisely that.

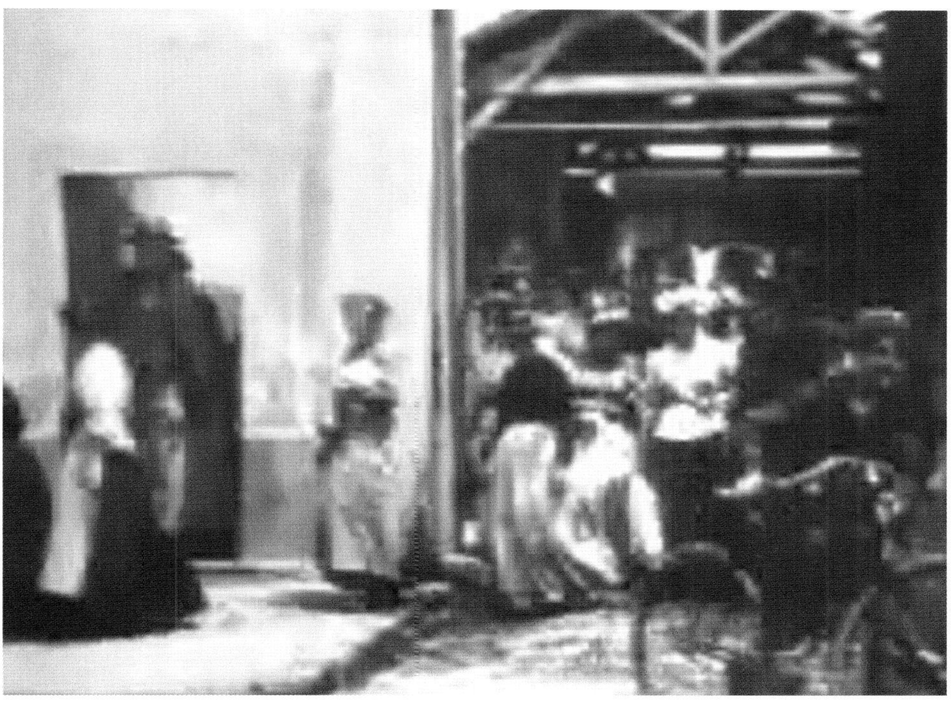

Fig. 77 *Louis Lumière*, **Sortie d'usine**, 26 May 1895.
Film still (Lumière catalogue, no. 91–1)

Films by the Lumière brothers were first shown to private gatherings in the course of 1895, followed by the historic public launch of the new medium in late December. This took place at the Grand Café in the centre of Paris before an audience that – according to an anonymous eyewitness – consisted of 'scholars, professors and photographers'.[67] The programme of short films depicted a seaside bathing scene, a family gathering and other commonplace events and situations, as well as a now-famous sequence of a busy street in Lyons (fig. 77) The same writer was thrilled by this latter spectacle, 'with all its movement of trams, carriages and pedestrians', declaring that the entire presentation offered 'an illusion of real life'. Another commentator claimed that 'it is life itself, it is movement taken from life', and even announced that 'death has ceased to be absolute'.[68] For Degas and his colleagues, reports of this occasion and the Lumières' invention itself might well have brought back memories of their own earlier careers. The Grand Café was situated on the Boulevard des Capucines, adjacent to the former site of Nadar's studio where the first Impressionist exhibition was held in 1874. Any sense of nostalgia they felt may also have extended to the subjects chosen by Auguste and Louis Lumière; bustling streets, bathing parties and family groups had featured widely in the Impressionist repertoire in the early years, not least in Degas's own pictures.[69] The Grand Café itself was also close to the Paris Opéra, the implicit or explicit setting for much of Degas's dance *œuvre* over three decades.

Representing a return to their past and a dramatic reinvention of their once-shocking iconography, the 1895 films would have seemed curiously familiar to the Impressionist generation, as would some of the language used to herald the new medium. Two decades earlier, Edmond Duranty – reputedly

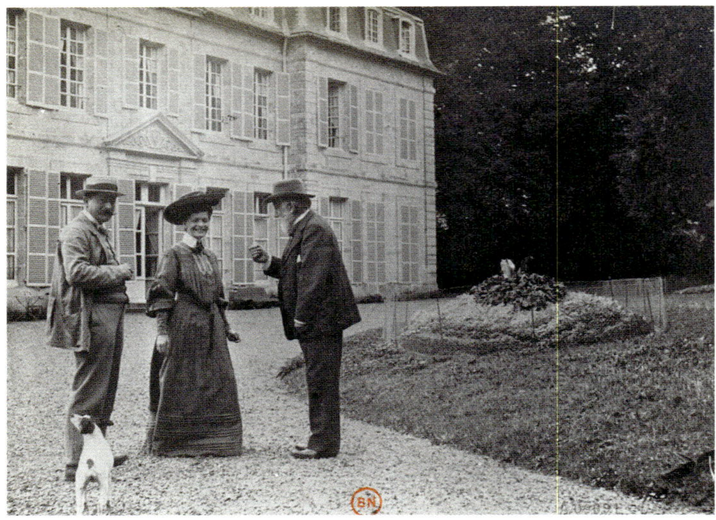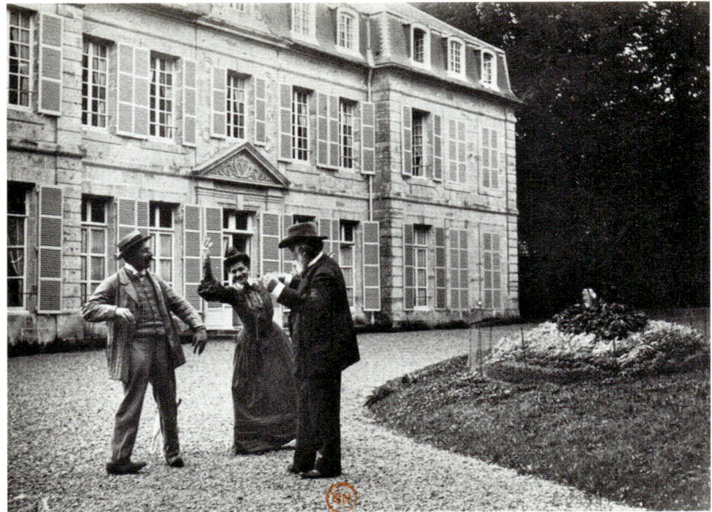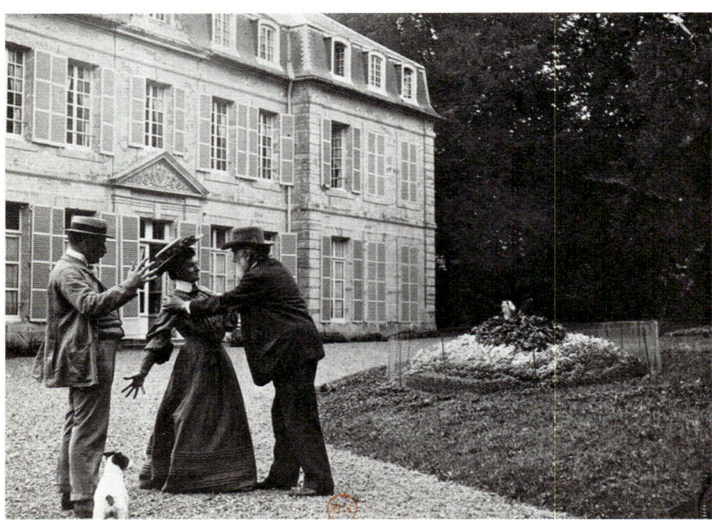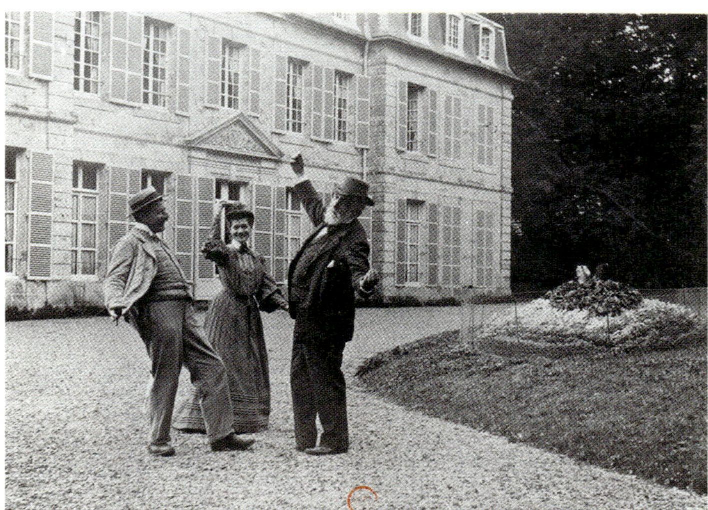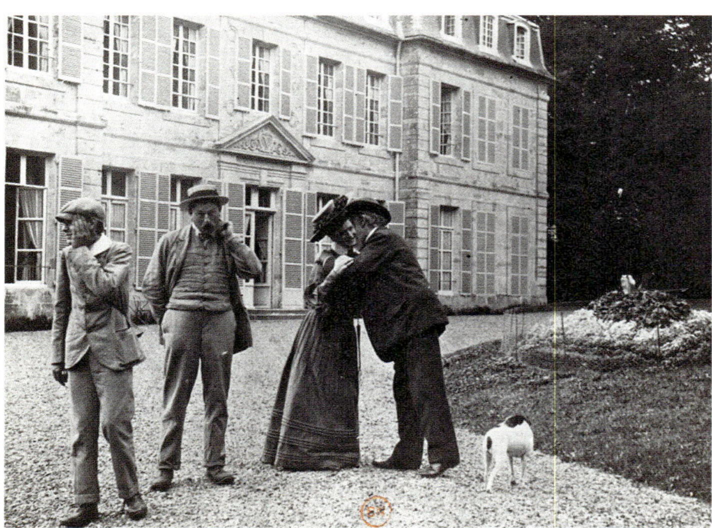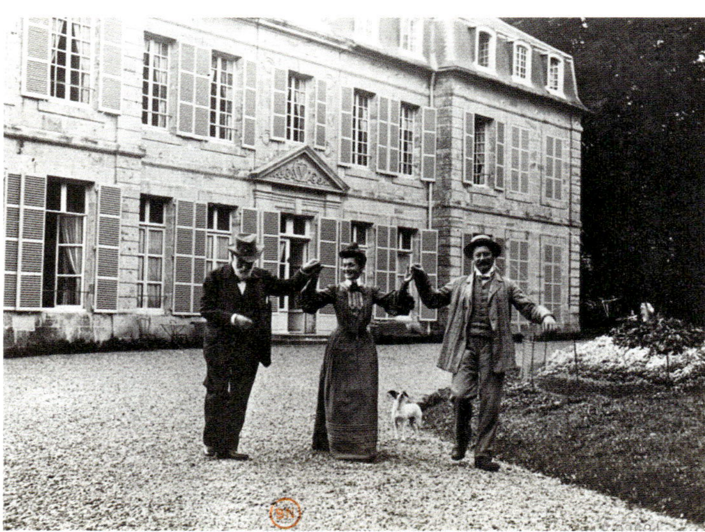

Fig. 78 *Unknown photographer*, Series of six photographs of Degas with friends at Ménil-Hubert. Bibliothèque nationale de France, Paris

with Degas's assistance – had proposed that young painters should engage
with modern city life, with 'merchants' and 'family scenes', 'the movement,
and the hustle and bustle of passers-by'.[70] This rhetoric had already been
echoed when Muybridge's zoöpraxiscope was displayed in Paris in 1881
and now reappeared – almost word for word – in responses to the Lumière
brothers' films. Remarkably, one of the leading chroniclers of Parisian culture
over these decades was present on all three occasions: the longstanding
admirer of Degas's art, Jules Claretie. Like Duranty before him, Claretie now
admired the Lumières' filmed portrayal of 'the hectic haste' of modern life
and wrote of the 'sensation of absolute truth' that he experienced at the Grand
Café, before proposing that these 'animated charcoal drawings' should have
colour and sound added to them.[71] Claretie also envisaged new kinds of
animated battle scenes by the painter Detaille, as well as elaborately filmed
dramas and operas, with 'their gestures, their extras and their movement
of crowds, their décor, their music, their choirs'.[72]

As a lifelong habitué of Parisian cafés, cabarets and theatres, Degas
would inevitably have been aware of the new spectacle in the city where
it was soon to become ubiquitous. Almost immediately after the 1895 debut,
films were shown in other temporary premises and within months the first
designated 'salles de projection' sprang up in Paris and around the country.
Two episodes from Degas's personal life illustrate the way that the medium
rapidly permeated French culture, innocently and otherwise. The first
concerns his longstanding friends the Valpinçon family, whose château
at Ménil-Hubert in Normandy was often used by Degas as a retreat from
his cares in Paris. Here the sometimes solemn city-dweller would unwind
in congenial company, giving good-humoured 'dancing lessons' to their
married daughter, Hortense Fourchy, and 'amusing himself with amateur
performances, charades etc. organised for his own benefit'.[73] On one undated
occasion in the 1890s the party improvised 'a comedy', which they entitled
Le Rival au berceau, delighting the artist and concluding with him 'offering
bouquets to the young actresses'.[74] During another visit Degas led three
guests in an 'impromptu entertainment … on the green lawns and pathways
in front of the château', when he 'danced' a minuet with Hortense.[75] This
event was not only photographed but knowingly acted out for the camera's
benefit in a sequence of at least seven 'frames' (fig. 78).[76] Unmistakable
in these photographs are the exaggerated gestures and body language
of melodrama, familiar from the Vaudeville stage and from early filmed
entertainments 'in the manner of Méliès', as one author has proposed.[77]
The decision by Degas and his fellow-actors to 'film' themselves in this mode
– albeit with a still camera – was surely a nod to the latest sensation in the
capital. More than a decade later, around 1915, Degas again found himself
in novel territory when he was visited at his Paris apartment by a renowned
representative of the film industry, the director Sacha Guitry. Asked by Guitry
if he could film him for a forthcoming documentary about senior cultural
figures, *Ceux de chez nous*, the elderly Degas replied, 'I have absolutely
nothing to say to you!' and closed his door.[78] Guitry then positioned himself
and his equipment on the boulevard outside, where a crowd gathered;
after a wait, the white-bearded and almost blind artist emerged, unaware
that he was being captured for a few poignant seconds by Guitry's camera
(fig. 79).[79]

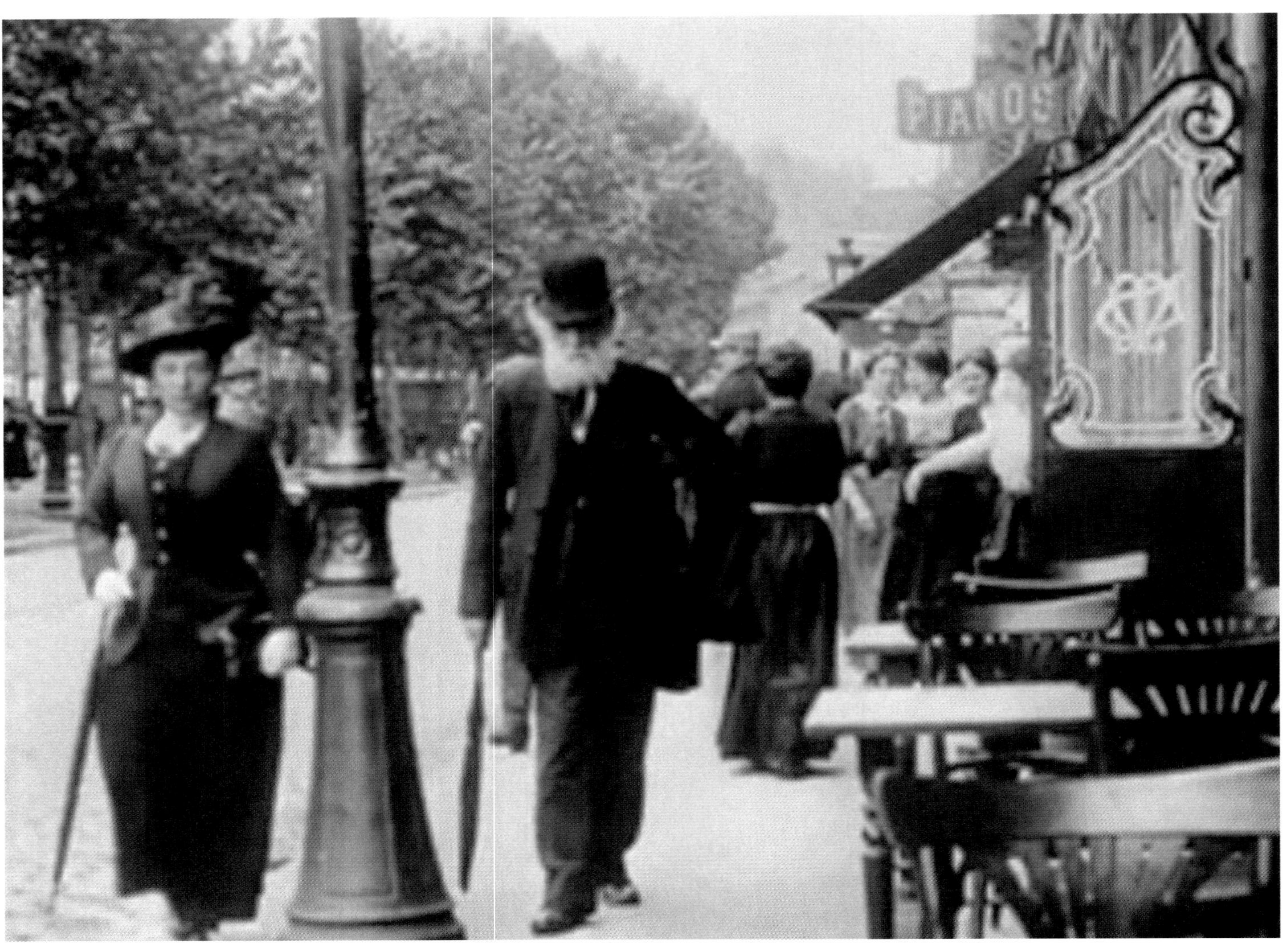

Fig. 79 *Sacha Guitry*, Ceux de chez nous, 1914–15. Film still

If these two cases add further to the sense of film and photography
as ubiquitous presences in Degas's surroundings, they also reflect the
challenges presented by these media to more familiar visual forms at the
end of the century. Cameras were now taken everywhere and used for frivolous
as well as epoch-changing purposes, and even film had become portable and
more technically versatile. Although Claretie was already envisaging filmed
performances of operas – and presumably the ballets that accompanied them
– the technology of most still cameras remained inadequate to the challenge
of recording transient events on the contemporary stage. Despite this limitation,
the Opéra management continued its dutiful practice of photographing
current productions under whatever light was available, even though the
resulting prints showed cast and décor as almost indecipherable grey blurs
(cats 107, 108). Boulevard theatres fared little better; some otherwise
remarkable shots of the popular dancer Loïe Fuller, shown in the midst
of her celebrated act with a swirling robe, managed to focus on the stage but
reduced her figure to a pale ghost (cat. 109). The survival of such imperfect,

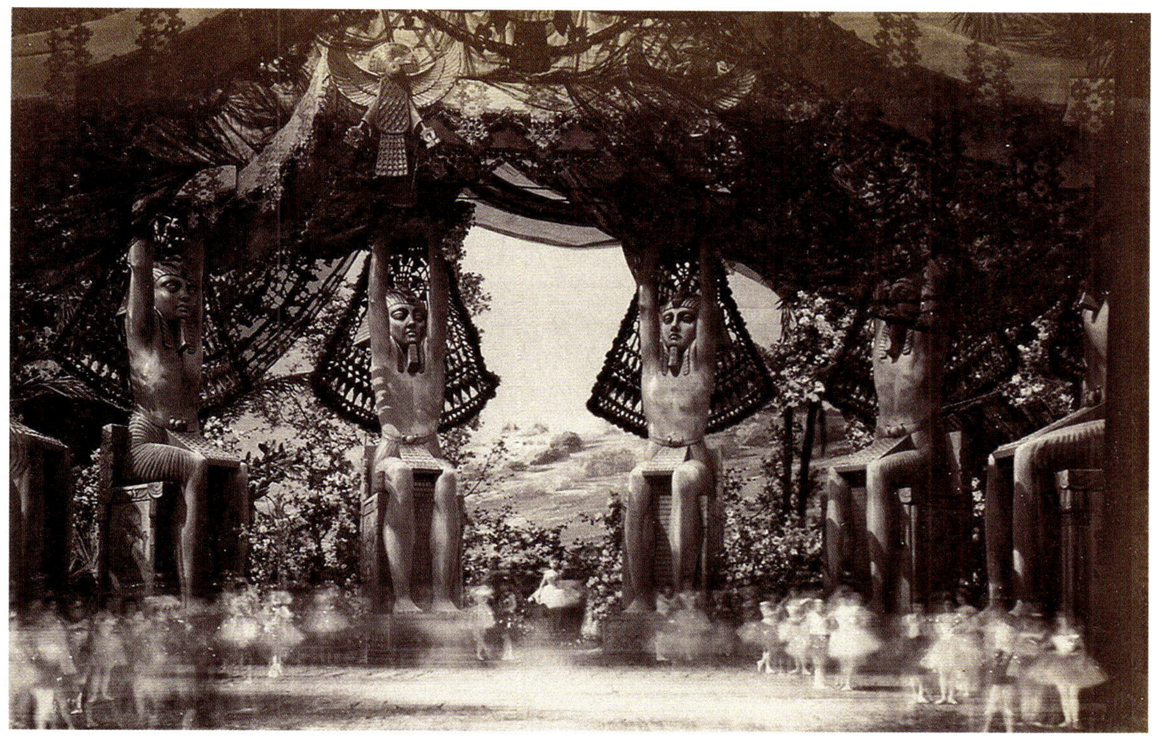

107
Unknown photographer
**Paris Opera Production
of 'Thaïs', Act 3, Scene 2**
1894
Photograph, 12.5 x 19 cm
Bibliothèque nationale de
France, Paris. Bibliothèque-
musée de l'Opéra

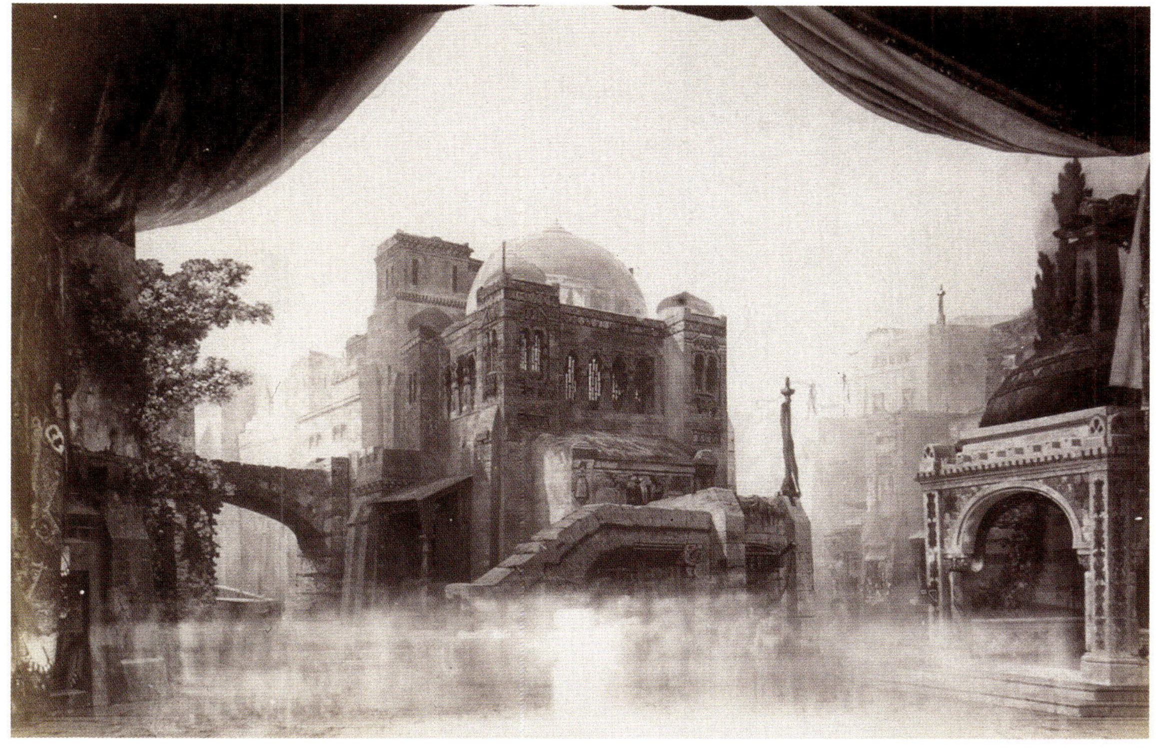

108
Unknown photographer
**Paris Opera Production
of 'Thaïs', Act 1, Scene 2**
1894
Photograph, 12.5 x 19 cm
Bibliothèque nationale de
France, Paris. Bibliothèque-
musée de l'Opéra

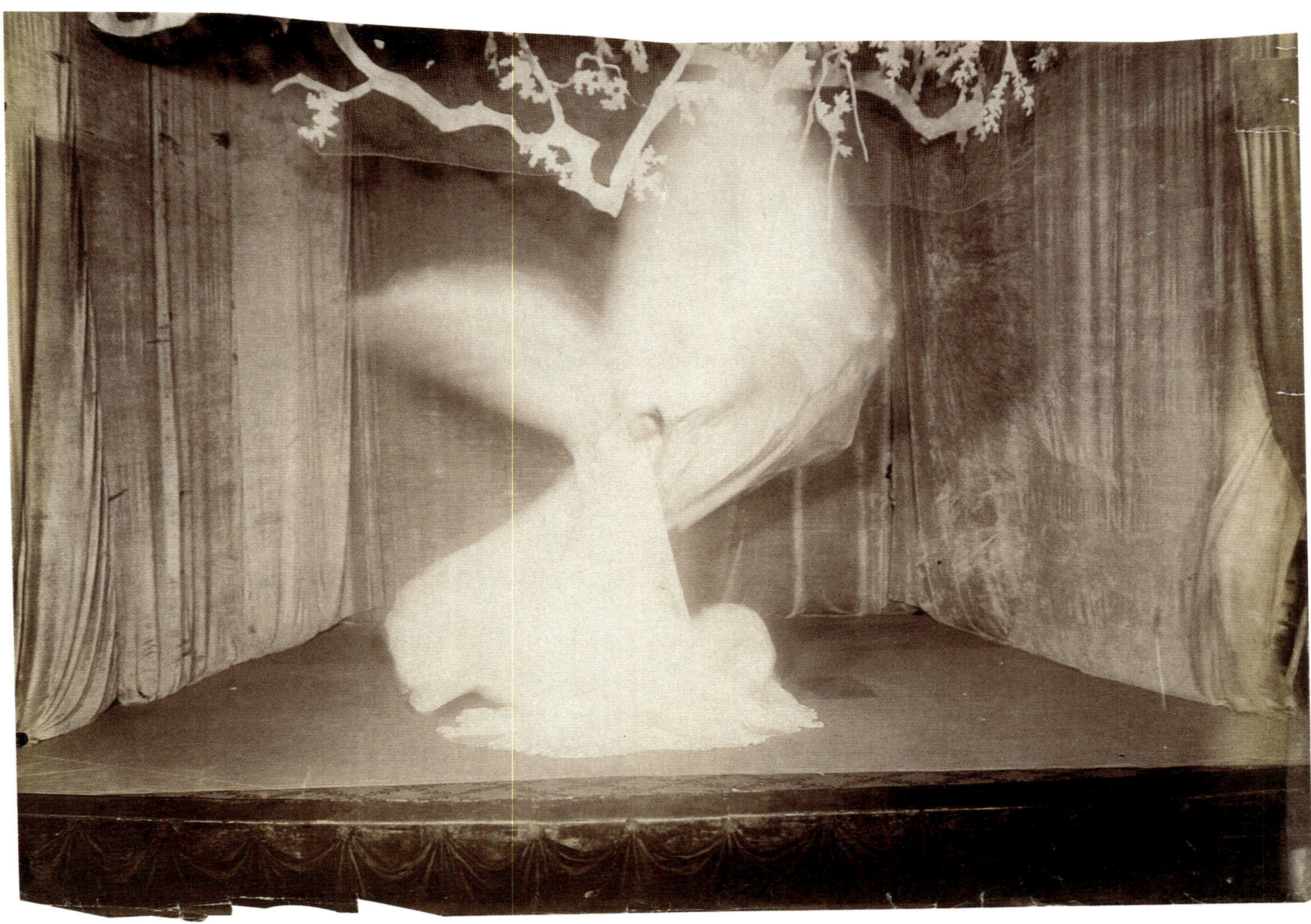

109

Unknown photographer
**Loïe Fuller Dancing in a Scene
from a Production Presented by
the Sada Yacco Japanese Theatre
Company at the Théâtre de
l'Athenée, Paris**
1901
Photograph,
20.5 x 28.7 cm
Bibliothèque nationale de
France, Paris. Département
estampes et photographies

sequentially linked prints may itself point to a world fixated on movement and film. The Lumière brothers also tackled a Loïe imitator in the late 1890s (fig. 80), documenting her moving figure effectively, but apparently obliged to film her on a crude outdoor 'stage' lit by daylight. That same year an ambitious commercial photographer in San Franscisco, Isaiah West Taber, took pictures of Fuller in flailing mid-action, again resulting in a series of 'frames' that recall those of a Lumière or Edison film (cat. 110), albeit of a much higher quality. Unlike his contemporaries in Paris, Taber was clearly equipped with a source of bright light and a camera that could 'freeze' her famously ballooning outfit. Even amateurs, it seems, could aspire to considerable clarity by this date; one image in an album of family photographs associated with Eugène Rouart, the son of Degas's close friend Henry, probably shows the performance of Eugène's sister-in-law Christine Lerolle in 'a robe lent by Loïe Fuller' herself (cat. 111).[80] Christine had been photographed by Degas in an atmospheric interior around 1895 (fig. 82), but was now presented in a park or garden setting where she clearly revelled in her voluminous, crisply focused outfit.[81]

Greatly encouraged by the enthusiastic reception of their films in 1895, the Lumière brothers – and soon their imitators and rivals – rapidly expanded the repertoire. Dancers were a favourite subject almost from the beginning, their innate vitality embodying the potential of the new medium to move

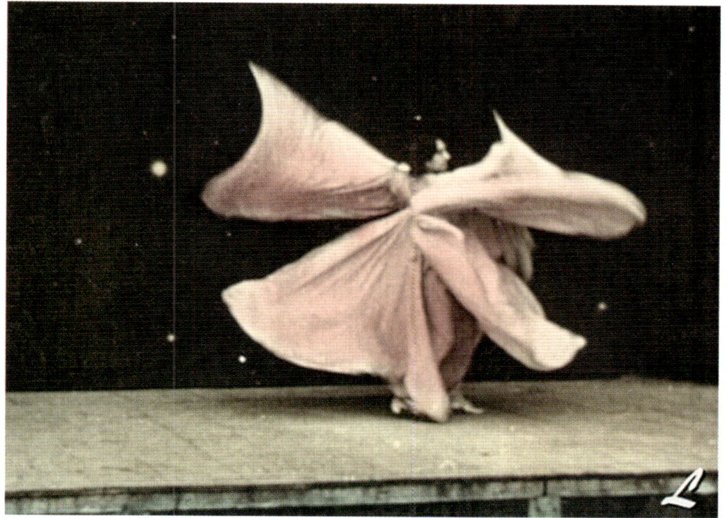

Fig. 80 *Lumière brothers*, Danse serpentine II, 1897–99. Film still

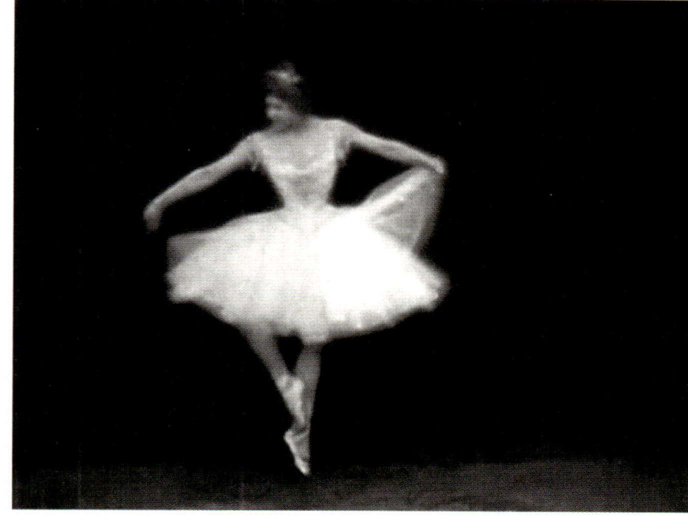

Fig. 81 *Paul Nadar*, Carlotta Zambelli, excerpt from 'Montage Paul Nadar', 1896. Film still. Cinémathèque française, Paris

beyond photography as well as the traditional arts. Sequences of cabaret dancers, 'ballerinas' in Vaudeville acts and various types of informal dancing soon came to the nation's screens, and were quickly joined by short films of celebrated figures from the Paris Opéra itself (fig. 81). These included the glamorous *première danseuse* of her generation, Carlotta Zambelli, who is shown on film performing a short variation for the camera, as well as a succession of other dancers familiar to Degas who had previously been depicted in his pastels and paintings.[82] Among them were Suzanne and Blanche Mante, known to the artist since childhood, when he represented the sisters with their mother in two superb pastels; the renowned Rosita Mauri, the subject of a portrait by Degas made a decade earlier; and the glamorous young star Cléo de Mérode, who claimed in her memoirs that she had formerly modelled for Degas 'several afternoons a week'.[83] Other types of dancer were also filmed, notably the exotic and ethnic varieties that attracted widespread interest at international exhibitions and increasingly in Parisian places of entertainment. Troupes from Russia were a case in point, boosted by the 'Russophilia' that swept the country in the aftermath of the state visit of the Tsar to the French capital in 1896. The distinctive costumes and dancing styles of these performers soon appeared in magazines and on several metropolitan stages, and were briefly noted the following year in Henri de Soria's *Histoire pittoresque de la danse* (fig. 83).[84] At least two short films of Russian dancers in full costume were produced by the Lumière brothers, one showing a single figure and another consisting of a forty-five-second sequence of three women and three men performing on a simple stage with musicians in the foreground, while a similar turn was filmed by Paul Nadar, son of the famous photographer (fig. 85).[85]

Much mystery has formerly surrounded Degas's own pictures of Russian dancers, which were first noted in his studio by Julie Manet on 1 July 1899, but are otherwise little documented.[86] Comprising more than a dozen pastels and drawings, some of them densely worked and of substantial size, they collectively represented one of the last great inventions of his career. Between

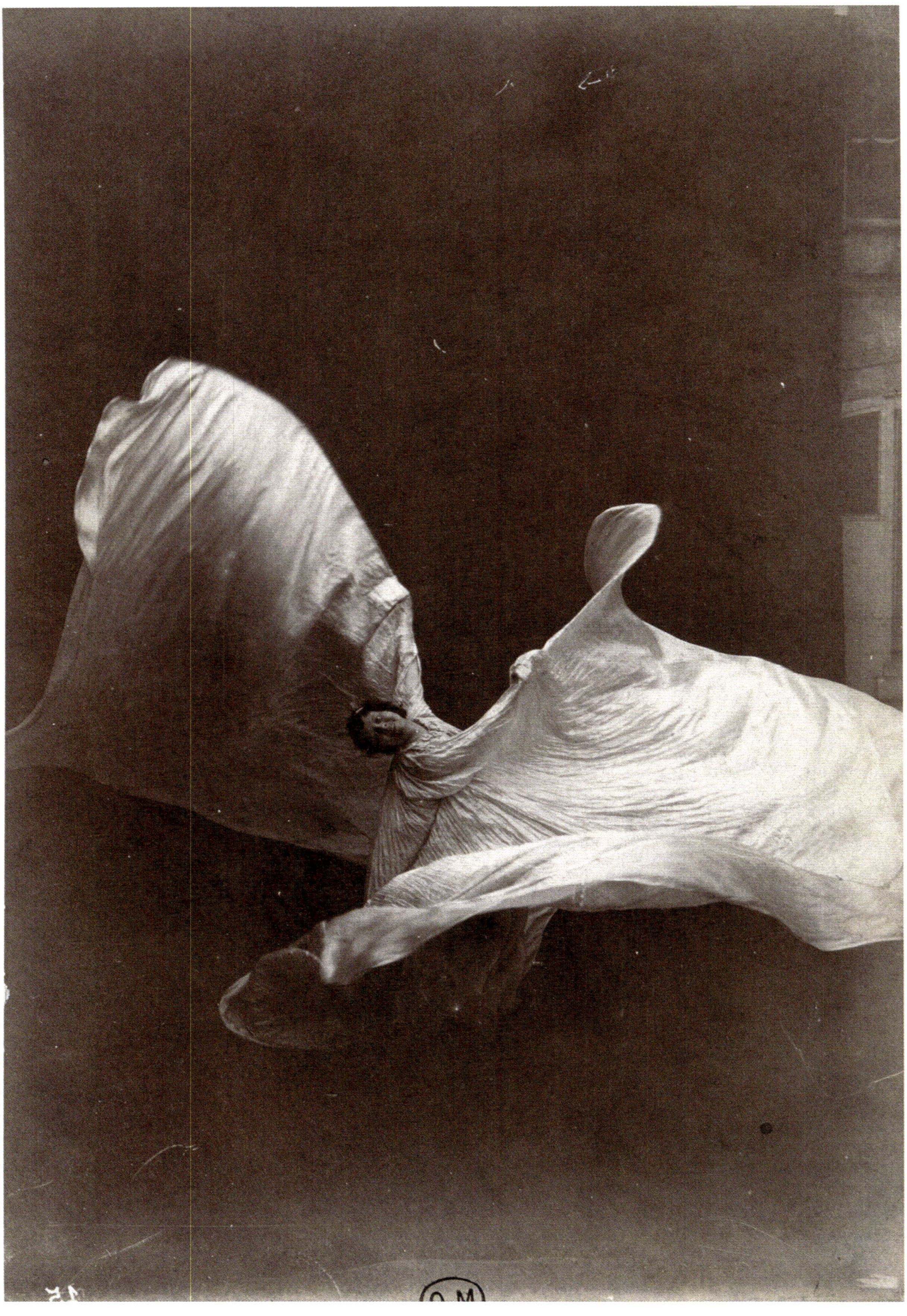

110

Isaiah West Taber
**Loïe Fuller Dancing
with Her Robe**
1897
Aristotype pasted
onto board,
16.7 x 11.3 cm
Musée d'Orsay, Paris

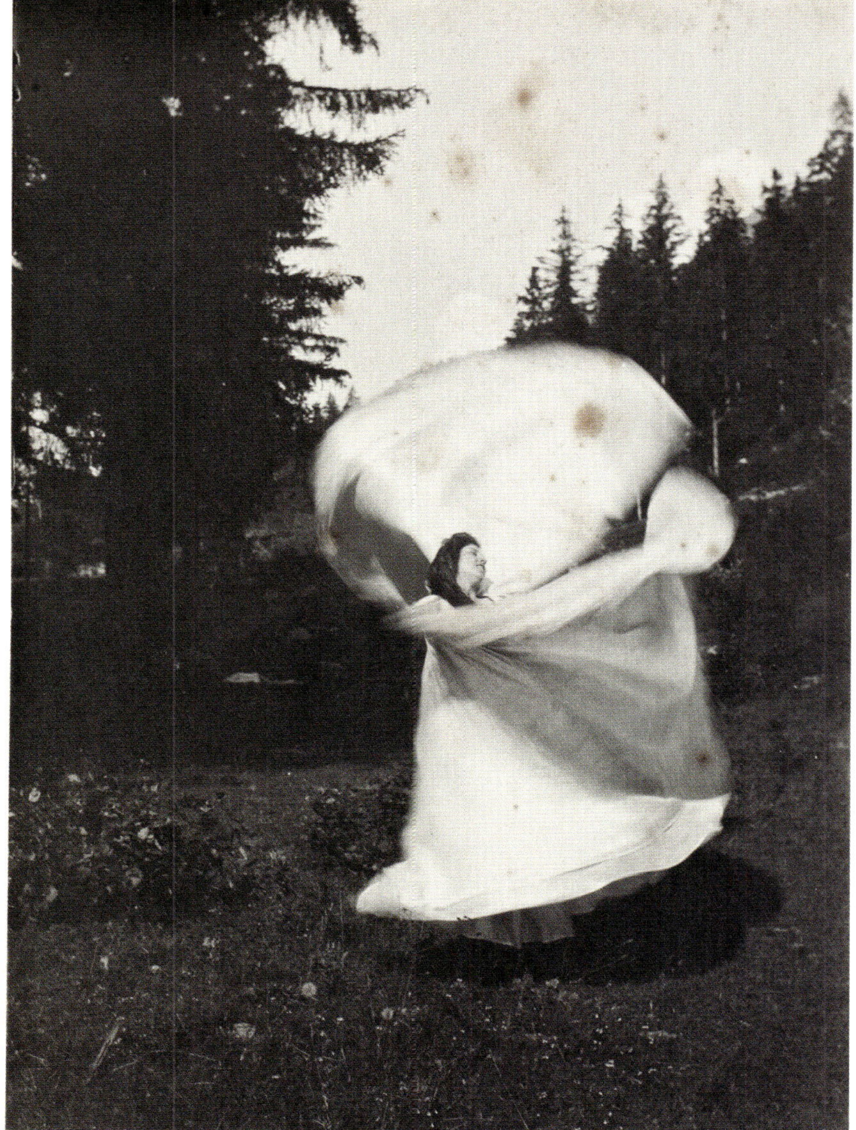

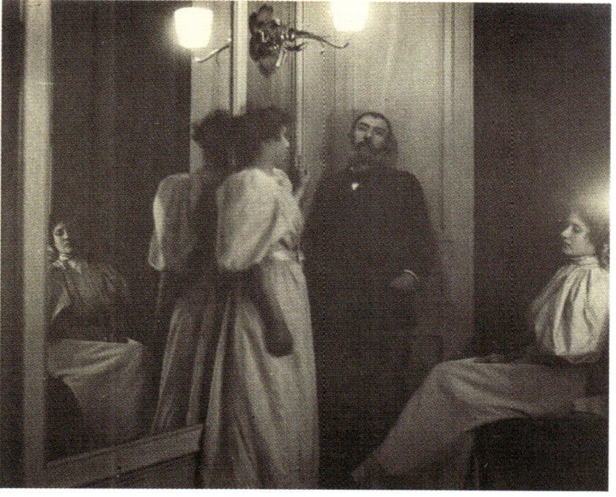

Fig. 82 **Portrait in the Mirror of the Painter Henry Lerolle and His Two Daughters, Yvonne and Christine**, 1895–96. Gelatin silverprint. Musée d'Orsay, Paris

111

Unknown photographer
Christine (?) Lerolle, from the Personal Photograph Album of the Lerolle and Rouart Families, no. 2
1898
Silverprint,
12.5 x 18 cm
Musée d'Orsay, Paris

one and three female performers are shown in each work, all clad in colourful costumes and executing highly energetic steps. Degas never visited Russia and could at best have watched pale imitations of such dancing in ballet productions, where folk steps were always highly stylised.[87] Diligent research by Lisa R. Bixenstine, however, has revealed that numerous troupes of such dancers could be seen in Paris in the late 1890s, when they performed on stages at the Moulin Rouge in 1896, at the Folies-Bergères in 1897, and at the Casino de Paris that same year, as well as at other less celebrated venues.[88] Further insights into Degas's pastels and their context are provided by the Lumière films of Russian dancers. A short black-and-white sequence of this kind reveals that the women of one such company were wearing calf-length boots, pale blouses and dark skirts, and had flowers and long ribbons in their hair. Their dancing and that of the entire group was vigorous and involved much turning within the ensemble, as well as the characteristic jumps, kicks and high-stepping associated with the Russian – or here, more strictly,

Ukrainian – tradition. All these details correspond extremely closely with the pastels made by Degas and seem to indicate direct contact between the artist and dancers from this region. The simplest explanation for the resemblance may be that the Lumière films had spread the reputation of these spectacular dancers in Paris and encouraged wide interest in their performances. Filmed either when one such troupe was visiting the city or conceivably during the Lumières' travels abroad, which took them to Leningrad, Ukrainian entertainers were widely regarded as the epitome of Russian folk dancing, with deep roots in regional culture and even its pre-Christian rituals.[89] Inspired by seeing dancers of this kind live and perhaps on film, Degas evidently sought out a Ukrainian troupe and arranged to draw at least one of the female members, whose poses were then duplicated and reversed as he contrived his pastel compositions. Degas may even have met them locally: Bixenstine identifies one group in 1897 at the Brasserie des Martyrs in Montmartre, a bar and restaurant frequented by artists and writers that was situated on the Rue des Martyrs (fig. 84), close to Degas's apartment and studio.[90]

An almost wild vivacity pervades the pastels of Russian dancers made by Degas, a highly distinctive form of movement that is surely more extreme than in any of his pictures of conventional ballerinas. Indeed the visceral quality of Ukrainian dancing was perhaps responsible for attracting him to their performances, at a time when historians insisted on tracing the roots of ballet back to Greco-Roman and more primitive dance forms. For De Soria, dance appeared 'in the first ages of humanity and among the most savage peoples', while Gaston Vuillier in his 1898 *La Danse* dated its inception 'to the very moment of the creation' and went on to discuss such modern regional descendants as the Spanish fandango and Breton 'countryside' dancing.[91] The open-air setting of the traditional Ukrainian dance is repeatedly emphasised in Degas's pastels, in which he freely improvised rustic backgrounds as he had recently conjured up hillsides, lakes and flower-strewn meadows in a series of landscapes he exhibited in 1892.[92] In the study from Berwick-upon-Tweed (cat. 112), a grassy field or hillside surrounds the two exotically clad figures, whose energy is evoked in looping charcoal lines that zigzag across the composition. Broadly indicating the facial features of the dancers, the artist built the larger scene in blocks of complementary warm red and subdued yellow-green, boldly signing the work in this relatively unpolished state before selling it to Vollard. On a slightly larger sheet, Degas reversed the composition in a pastel that now belongs to the National Gallery, London (cat. 113), adding an extra figure to the foreground and revising his colour palette. Heavier accumulations of pastel now indicate richly textured fabrics, braided and beribboned hair and clusters of yellow, red and blue flowers around the women's heads, as well as the dense textures of their rural surroundings. Repeated strokes of colour have given this work and its companions a physical presence that emphasises Degas's commitment to the series, built up from streaks and flourishes of pastel that underscore the near-frenzy of the women's performance. The horizontal composition entitled simply *Russian Dancers* (cat. 114) was also left unsigned but had clearly reached an advanced state of refinement, evident in its exquisitely modulated surface, rich detail and subtly understated internal rhythms. Arguably the masterpiece of the series, this sumptuous picture is distinctly less frenetic and more fully realised

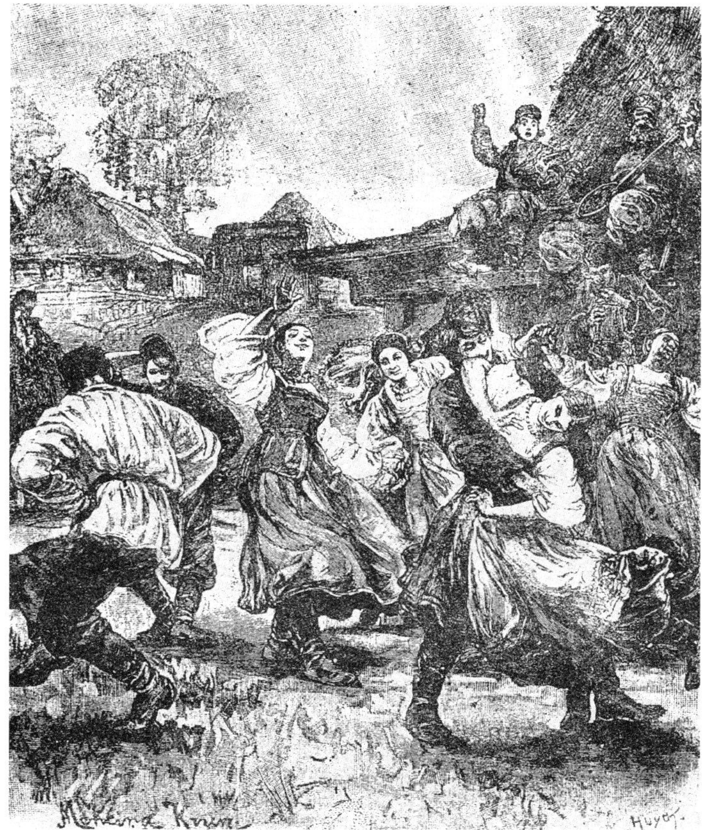

Fig. 83 *Henri de Soria*, Histoire pittoresque
de la danse, Paris, 1897, p. 255

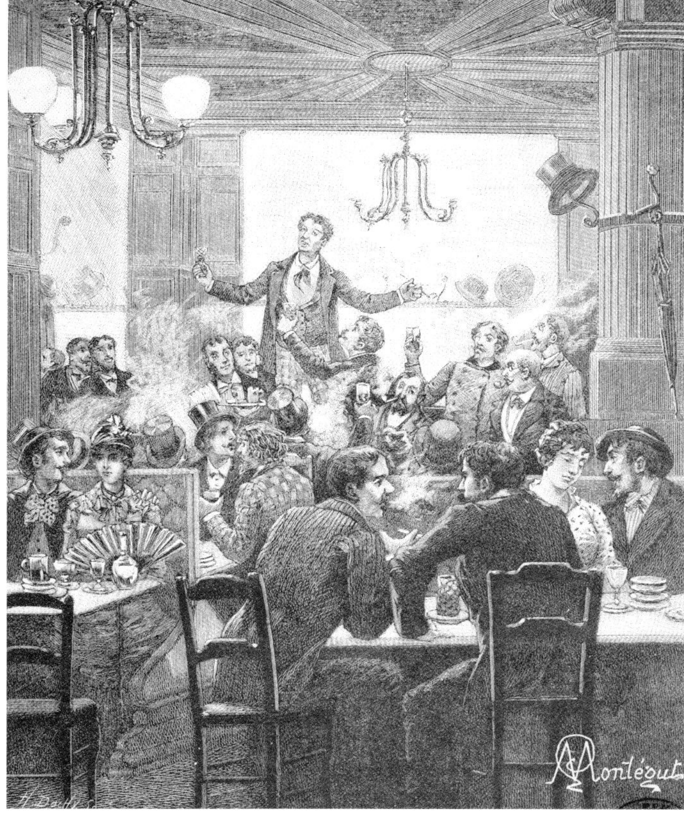

Fig. 84 *M. de Montegut*, Brasserie des Martyrs, from Alphonse
Daudet, Les Trentes Ans de Paris, Marpon et Flammarion, Paris,
1883. Bibliothèque nationale de France, Paris

as a rural scene, even incorporating a simple cottage at upper left and what appears to be dense foliage overhead. Here the pastel has been applied with more finely controlled marks and superimposed touches, building a crust of subtly variegated colour that almost defies description. A certain delicacy also characterises the foreground dancers, as they point their toes and seem to advance in demure fashion towards the viewer. In their lush pasture, the three gaily bedecked women might be celebrating a plentiful harvest and the changing of the seasons in the traditional manner, rather than performing for an audience at the Brasserie des Martyrs, for a fascinated artist in his studio, or for a modern film camera.

In several fundamental respects, the *Russian Dancer* series was the exception that proved the rule in Degas's late career. Made when both his health and his eyesight were said to be failing, they demonstrate with great vividness his ability to launch a new and unexpected theme, one that he pursued with vigour and resolved on an ambitious scale. Many of these pictures were signed by the artist and clearly regarded as finished, several passing to Vollard and in time to his more adventurous clients. Yet all these works stood apart from Degas's former *œuvre*, first as depictions of dancers unconnected with the ballet and second as statements about a new mode of animation that was both primeval and aggressively modern. Perhaps linking them in his mind with the historic beginnings of dance – a more primitive

112

Russian Dancers
c. 1895
Charcoal and pastel
on tracing paper,
65 x 44.5 cm
Berwick Museum
and Art Gallery

113

Russian Dancers
c. 1899
Pastel and charcoal
on tracing paper laid
onto millboard,
73 x 59.1 cm
The National Gallery, London.
Presented by the Sara Lee
Corporation, Chicago, through
the American Friends of the
National Gallery, London, 1998

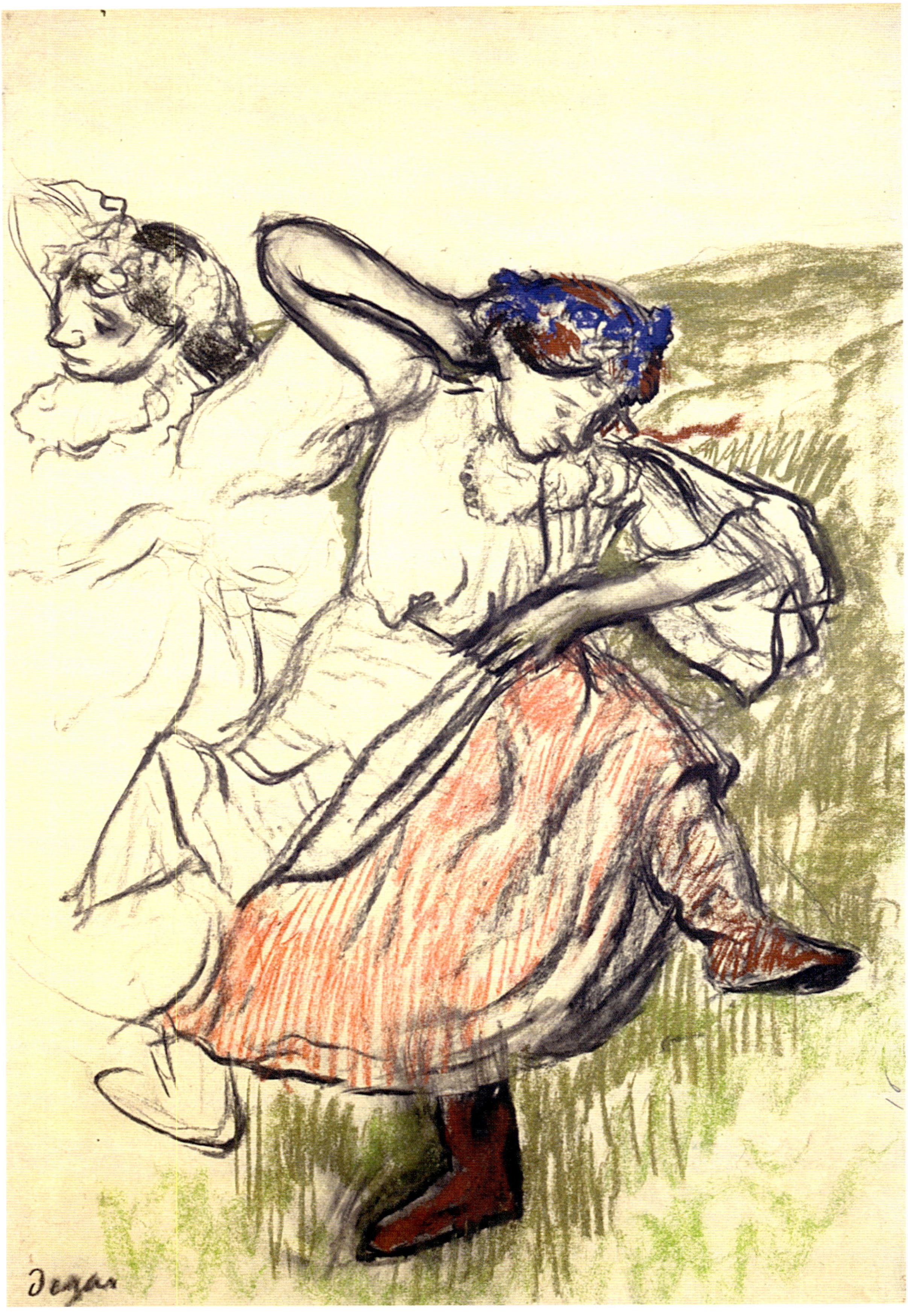

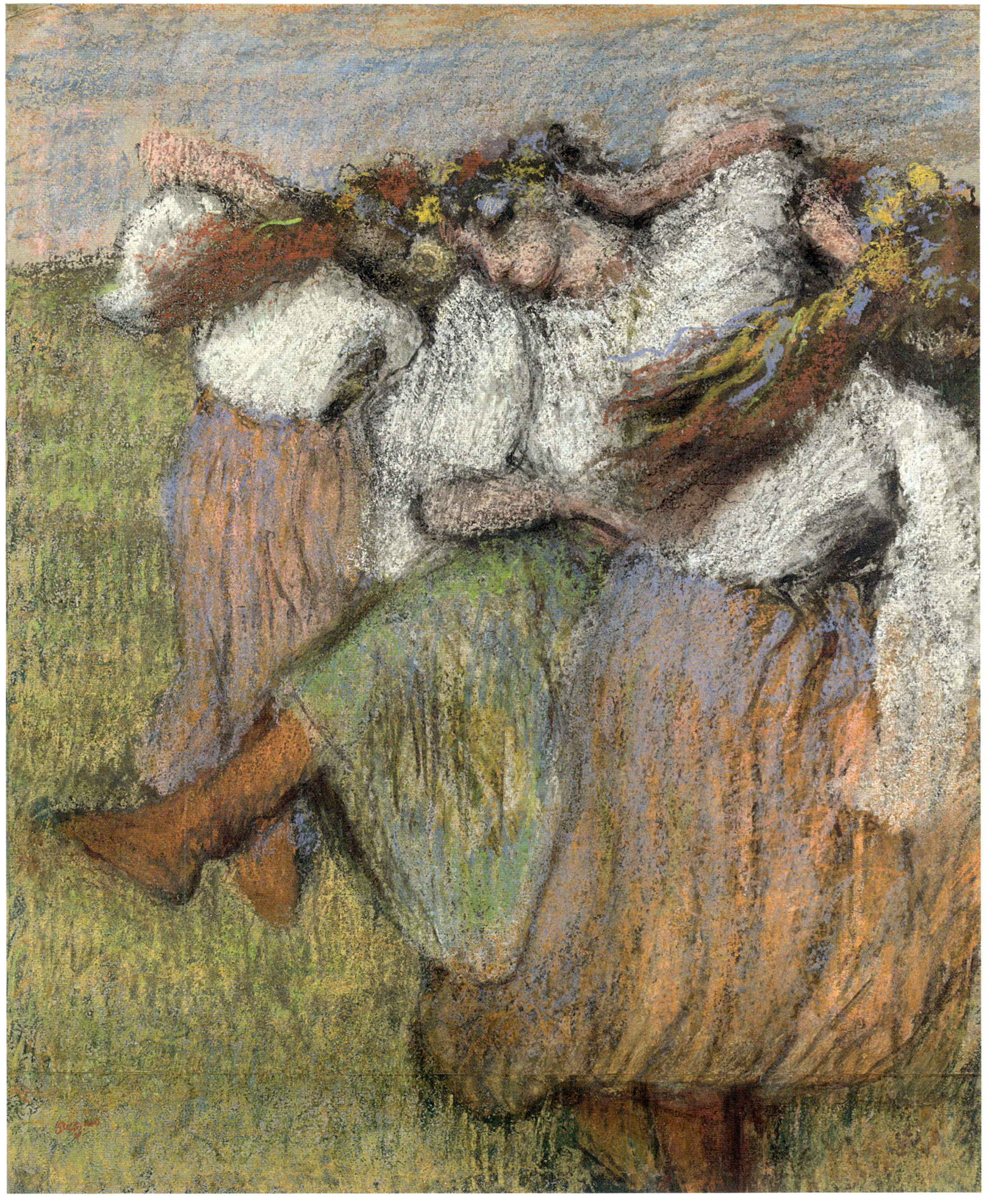

Russian Dancers
c. 1899
Charcoal and pastel
on machine-made
tracing paper,
57 x 75 cm
Private collection

Fig. 85 *Paul Nadar*, Danse Russe, excerpt from 'Montage
Paul Nadar', 1896. Film still. Cinémathèque française, Paris

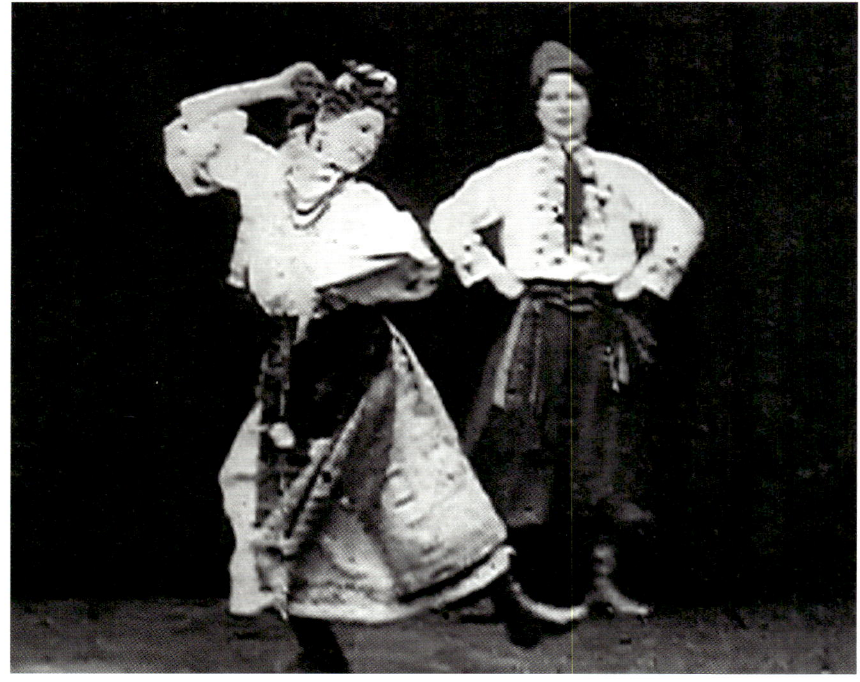

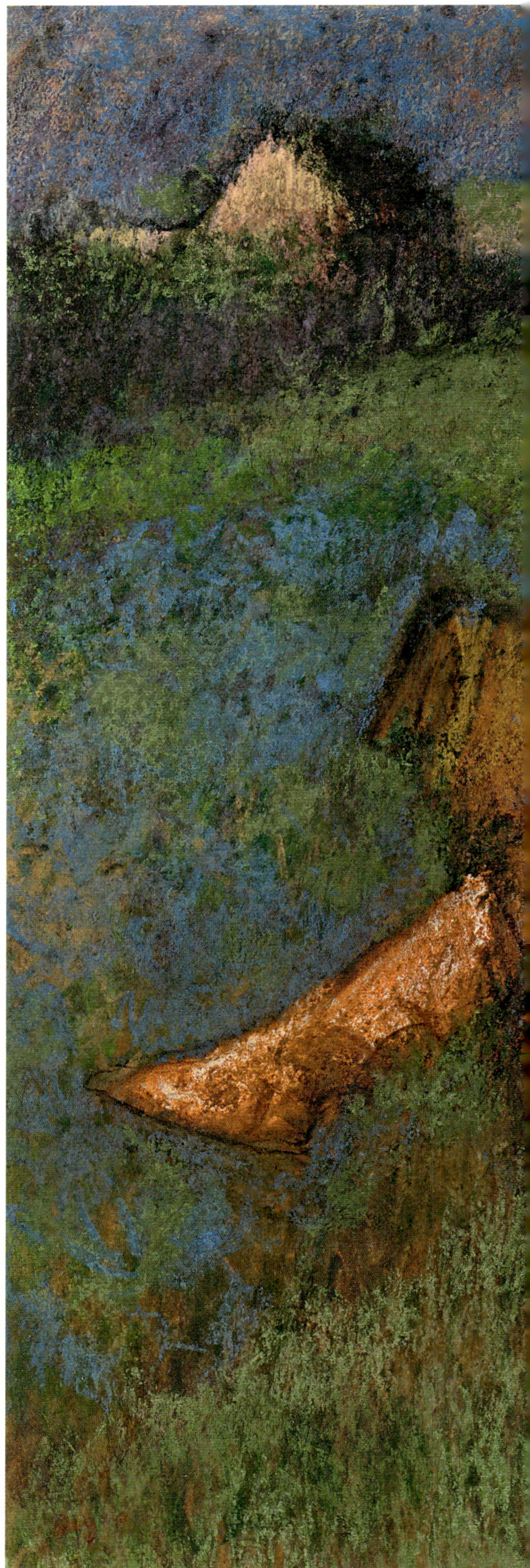

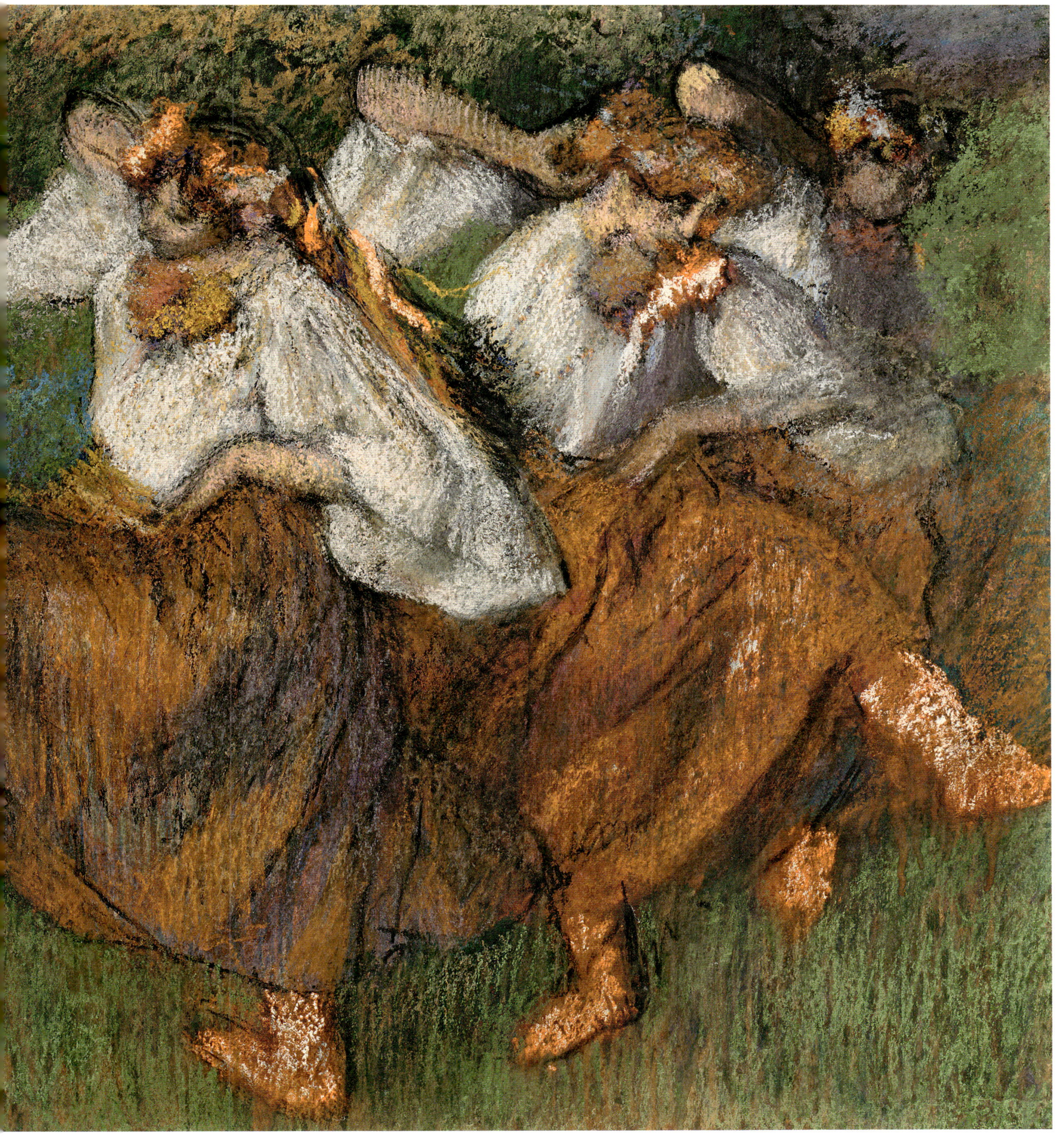

**Dancer Leaning
on a Pillar**
c. 1895–98
Charcoal on paper,
69 x 53 cm
Museum Folkwang,
Essen

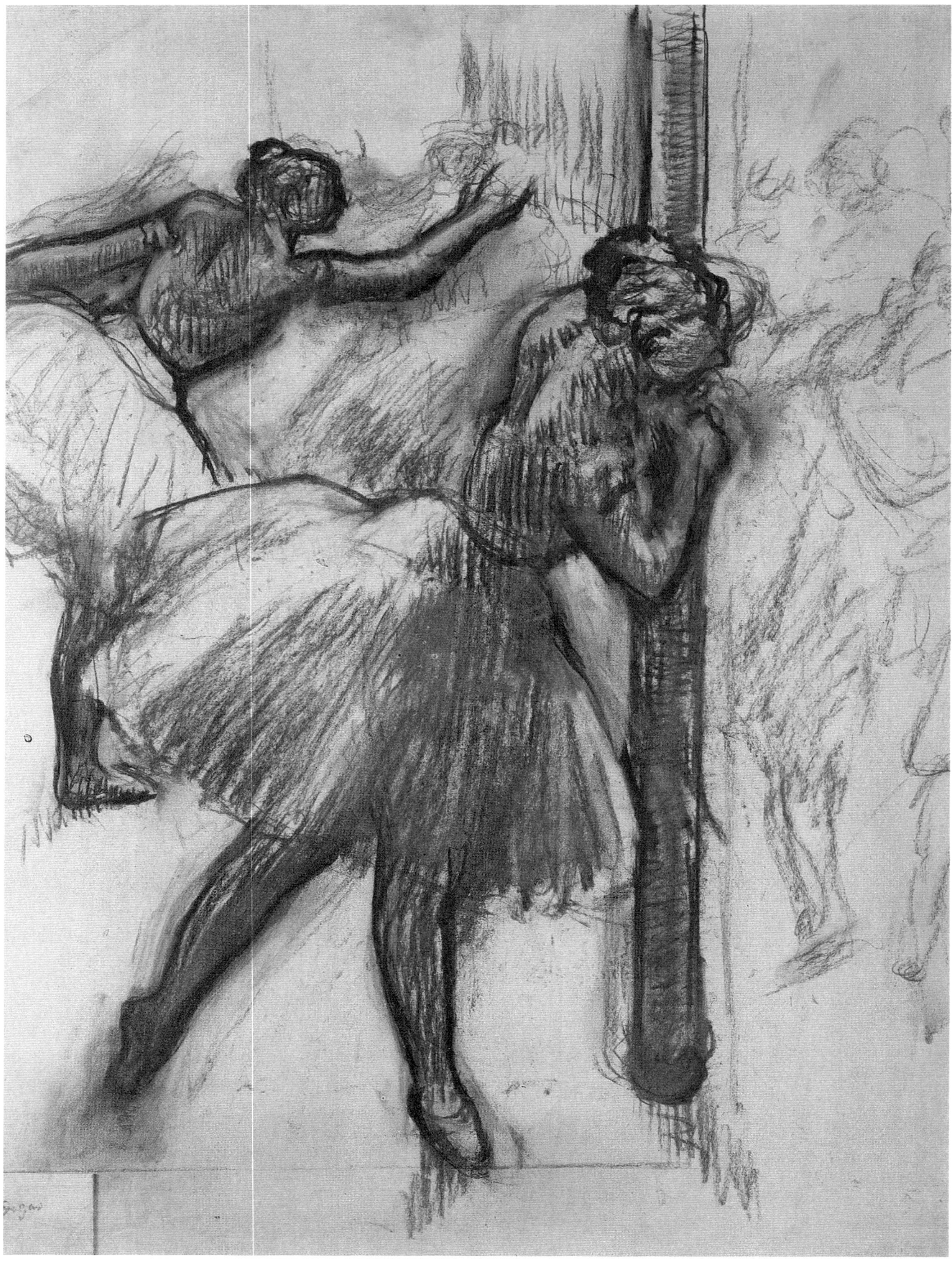

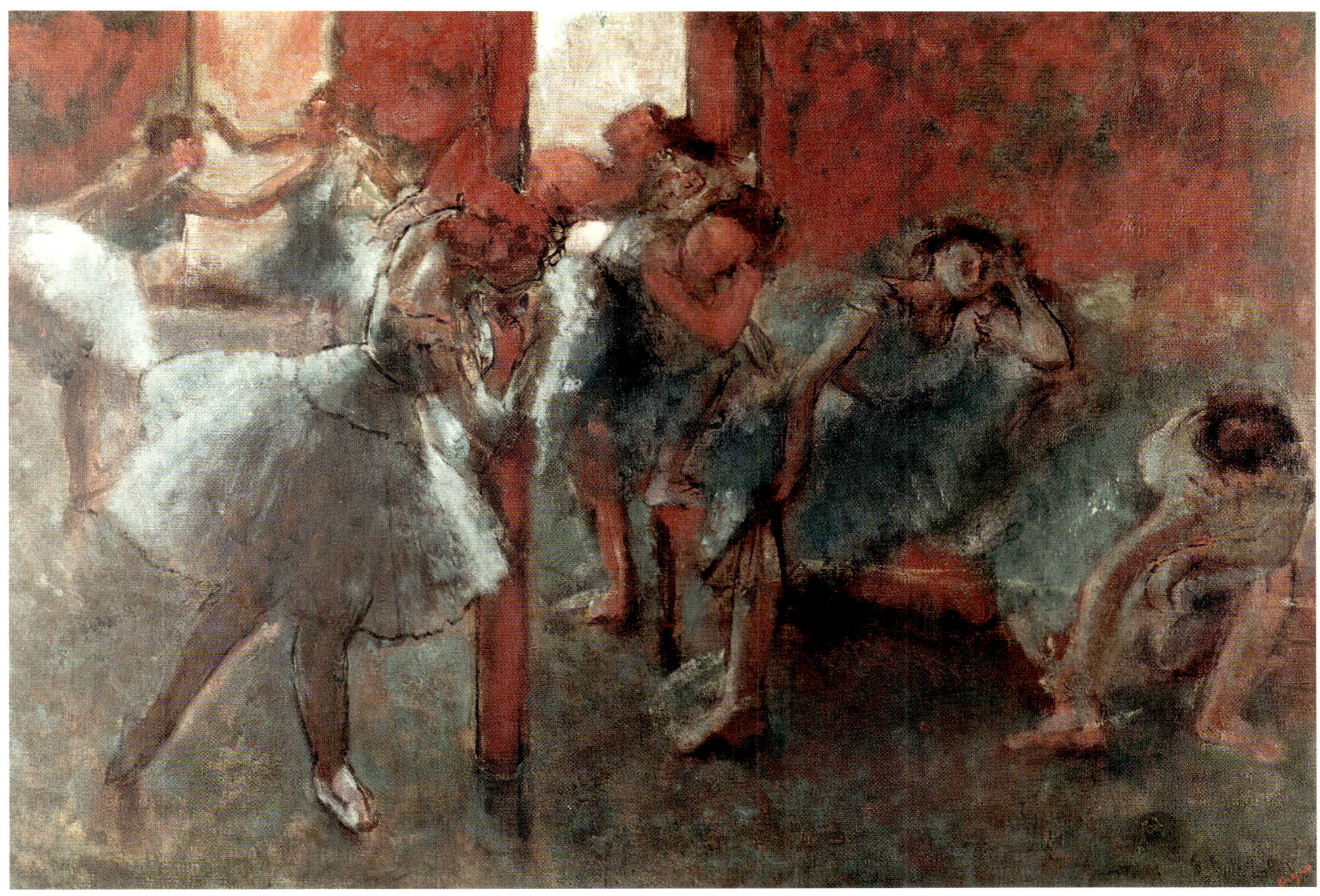

Fig. 86 **Dancers at a Rehearsal**, *c.* 1895–98. Oil on canvas, 70.5 x 100.5 cm.
Von der Heydt-Museum, Wuppertal

'movement of the Greeks' – most of the *Russian Dancers* pastels seemed to
challenge the disciplined serenity of ballet as Degas had known it for almost
four decades. Well-intentioned attempts were formerly made to link these
works with the arrival in Paris of Sergei Diaghilev's Ballets Russes, although
the historical record clearly precludes this.[93] More factually based and perhaps
equally engaging is the possibility that this briefly adopted subject had a link
with the medium of film, suggesting that Degas – like Claretie – was imagining
new dimensions to stage performance and to art itself as the 1890s came
to an end. In practice, Degas's advancing age gradually circumscribed his
activities and focused his life on the Montmartre studio and apartment,
where he worked incessantly and received visits from a loyal circle of friends
and younger admirers, and from the models who still formed the basis of his
creative life.

In Degas's ballet pictures from the turn of the century, some no doubt
developed alongside his pastels of Ukrainian dancers, he pushed further and
more vigorously at familiar themes and devised new variants to extend the
potential of his materials. Drawing still retained its prime role, both as an

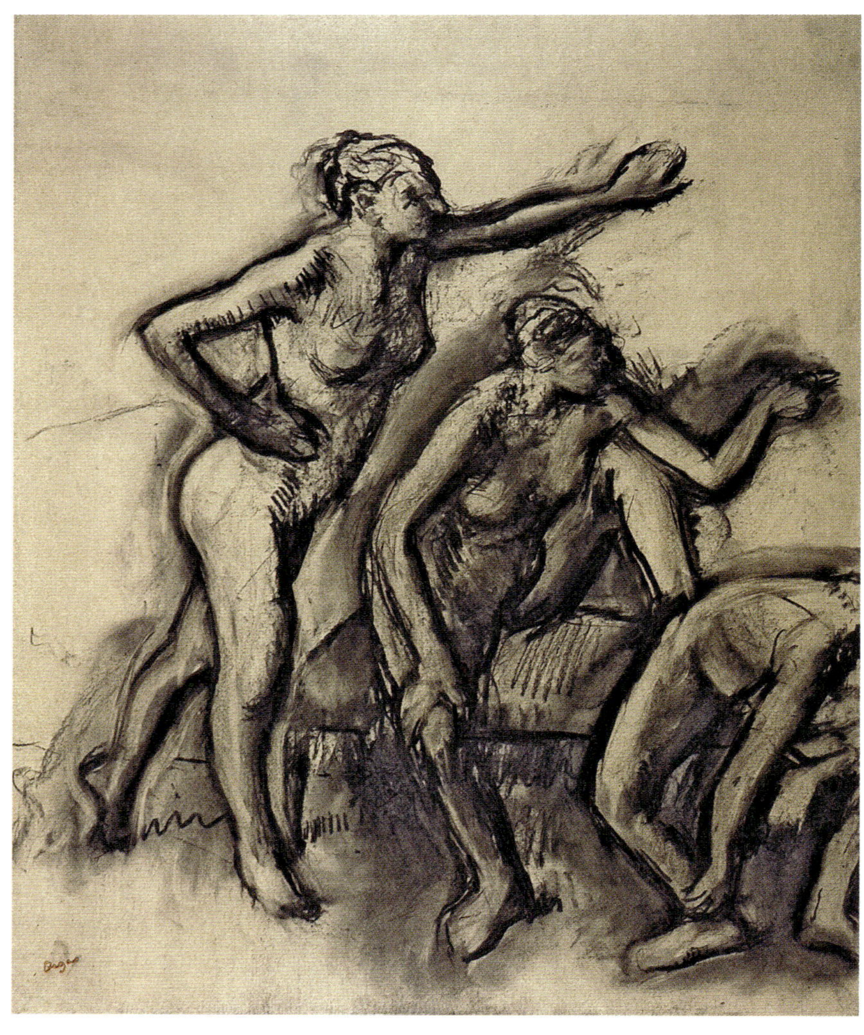

Fig. 87 **Group of Dancers**, *c.* 1897–1901. Charcoal on tracing paper, 77.2 x 63.2 cm. Arkansas Art Center, Little Rock

initial approach to the dancer-model's body and increasingly as a way
of combining line and colour in a single act. This was the period when the
teenage Paul Valéry had his first conversations with Degas, some of them in his
studio, where the artist told his patient listener that 'drawing is not the same
as form, it is a way of seeing form', and insisted over dinner with Mallarmé that
'a man is only an artist at certain moments, by an effort of will'.[94] The majestic
Dancer Leaning on a Pillar (cat. 115) probably emerged from this phase, its
subject dating back to earlier decades while its breadth of draughtsmanship
pointed forward to new audacities. It belongs with many such studies for
a group of late frieze-like canvases and related pictures that visibly fused
draughtsmanship and saturated colours in what was to be a final series
of encounters with this panoramic format (fig. 86).[95] By comparison with the
artist's drawings of the 1870s, the Essen sheet seems coarse, even maladroit,
but the sense of gravity and monumentality that Degas has imparted to the
two principal figures is without precedent in his career. Limbs and torsos
have been repeatedly outlined as if to confirm their palpability and even the

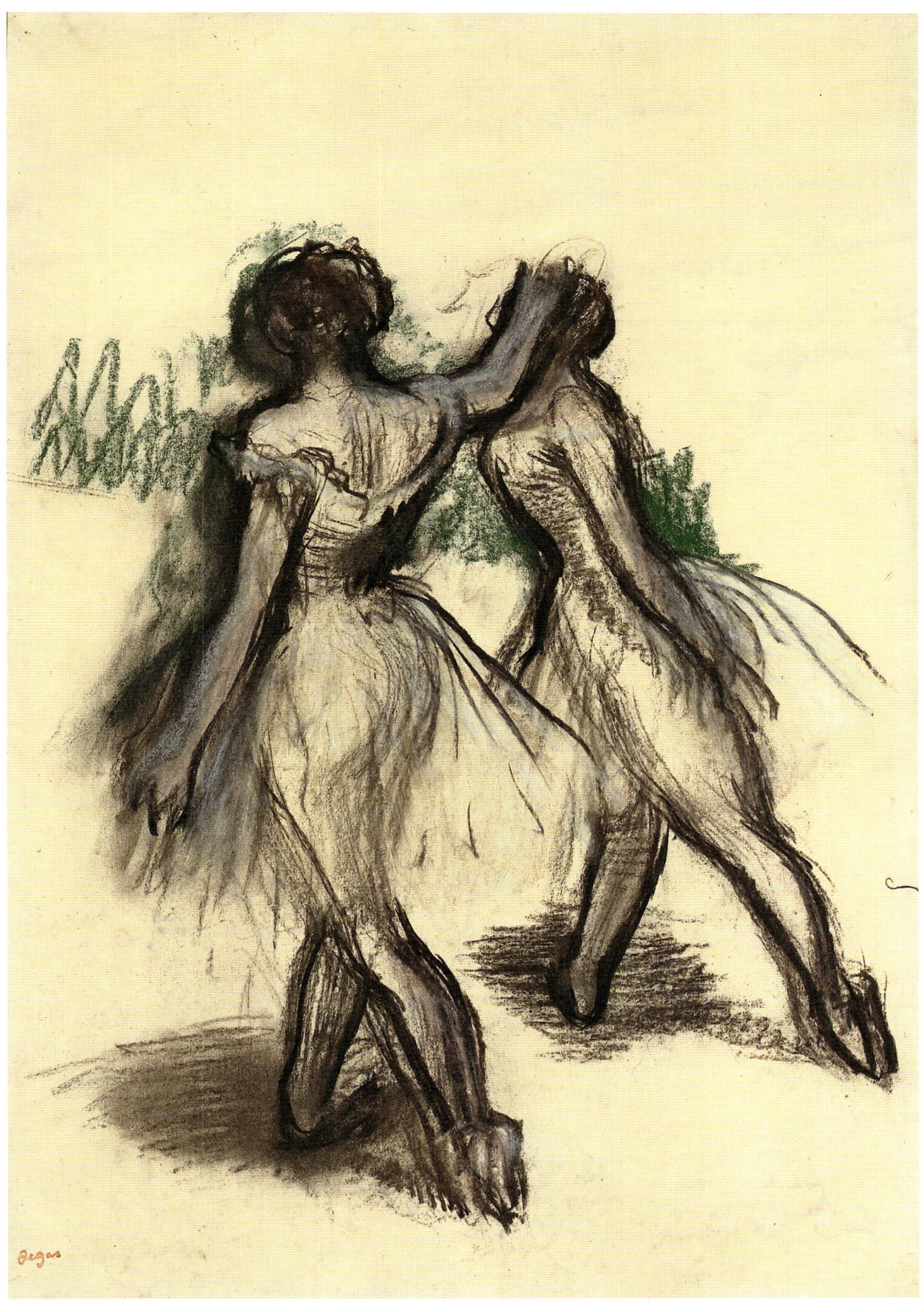

116

Two Dancers
c. 1890–94
Charcoal and pastel
on paper, 58 x 41 cm
Private collection, courtesy
of Galerie Schmit, Paris

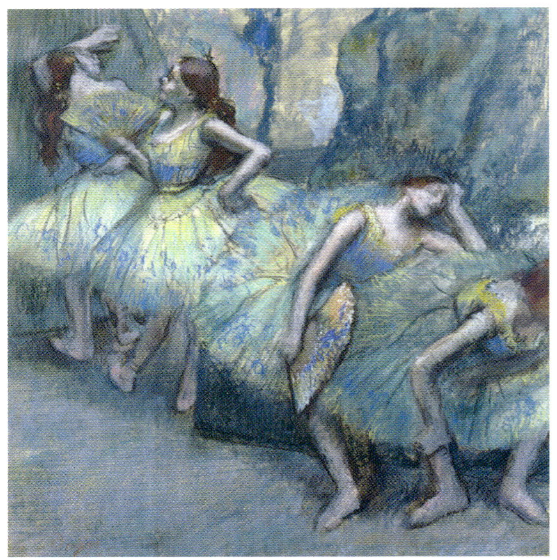

Fig. 88 **Ballet Dancers in the Wings**, 1900. Pastel on paper,
71.1 x 66 cm. Saint Louis Art Museum. Museum Purchase, 24:1935

117

The Red Ballet Skirts
c. 1895–1901
Pastel on tracing paper,
81.3 x 62.2 cm
Lent by Culture and Sport
Glasgow on behalf of Glasgow
City Council. Gifted by
Sir William and Constance,
Lady Burrell, to the City of
Glasgow, 1944

ballerinas' tutus seem to have a tangible, space-occupying mass. Summarising
the twin poles of his art, Degas set the physically active dancer in the distance
against her more sedate companion in the foreground, though the corner-to-
corner diagonal of this latter individual's body also counterposes the vertical
thrust of a pillar. While *Dancer Leaning on a Pillar* is clearly set in the classroom,
the equally forceful *Two Dancers* (cat. 116) implicitly takes place on the stage.
Now following a choreographed pattern, these two individuals and their
movements might seem to represent simplicity itself, especially for an artist
who had been drawing such scenes for several decades. For the eternally restless
and self-critical Degas, however, no such subject could be taken for granted.
Driving himself to draw and re-draw every contour of these dancers' bodies, he
obsessively revisited each form and interval within his emerging composition.
The result is electrifying, the hint of coloured pastel suggesting the tactile,
richly worked oil painting that might have emerged, as well as the masses
of brown and greenish wax in his sculptures from these same years.

On a slightly larger scale, a trio of naked figures – all presumably posed
by the same model – are combined in *Group of Dancers* (fig. 87) to form
another side-to-side progression of lines, masses and spaces. The
sensuousness of charcoal has rarely been so magnificently celebrated as in
this tableau of human flesh, in which drawn, rubbed and partly erased marks
evoke full buttocks and thighs, as well as taut arms and precisely poised feet.
When appropriately clothed in stage costumes, this group reappeared
in several pastels and associated paintings that are located in either the
classroom or the theatre wings (fig. 88), their forward momentum seeming
to direct us to unseen events beyond the picture margin. Degas's frankly
visceral *Group of Dancers* reminds us of the artist's reflection that he had
'too often considered woman as an animal', a confession made to Sickert
in these same years. Yet in its unapologetic, impersonal presentation of nude
figures in action this drawing has a close kinship with the imagery of
Eadweard Muybridge, Etienne-Jules Marey and their peers, whose work was
made in the name of both art and science.[96] Easily perceived as a depiction
of a single model who first stands and sits, then leans forward to grasp her ankle,
the human frieze in the Arkansas sheet also has a purposefulness similar
to Muybridge's photographic panoramas and Marey's chronophotographs.
Despite being evidently stable as posed individuals, each of the three figures
in Degas's drawing contributes to an accelerating momentum that both unifies

Fig. 89 *Eadweard Muybridge*, 'Movements, Female, Getting Out of Bed, Preparing to Kneel',
plate 264 of Animal Locomotion, 1887. George Eastman House, Rochester, New York

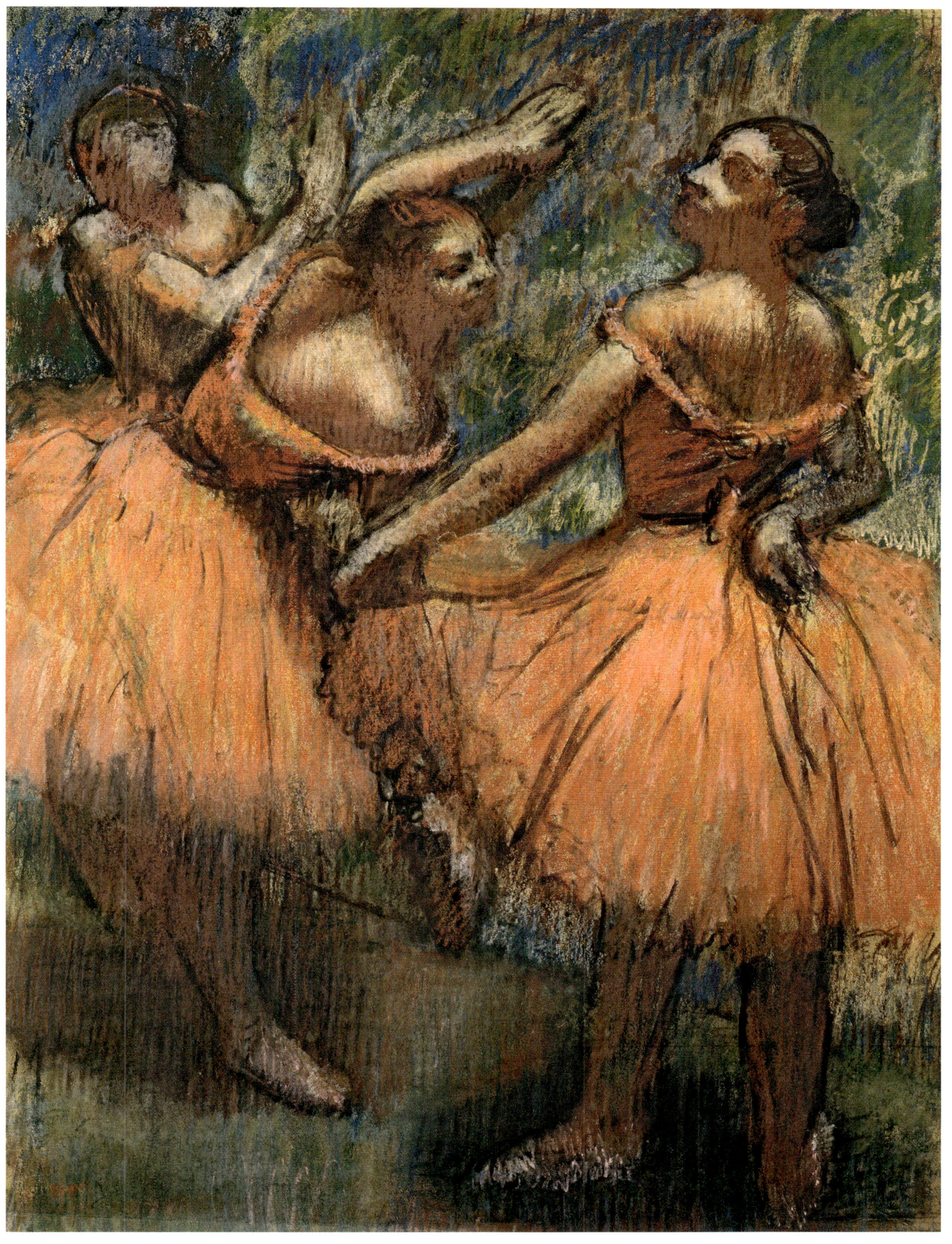

them and propels the group forward; so convincing is this trajectory that our attention is directed to the right and perhaps to other, unseen, companions. Comparable sequences of drawings and sheets with only single figures also lay behind virtually all Degas's late ballet scenes in pastel and in oil on canvas at this later period. Literally dozens of such studies can be related to *Dancers* in the Saint Louis Museum of Art, one of Degas's most ambitious and resolved statements of this kind, which he signed with a flourish at lower left. Not identical in its human cast to the drawing from Arkansas, this gently interwoven group of seasoned ballerinas has a similarly implied progression across the picture, here more securely anchored by the standing figure. Now a new element has also been added to the dynamic life of these women, in a succession of gentle turns by each of the three dancers around their vertical axes, and a counter-move by the right-hand figure as she leans out toward the viewer. Most or all of these features can be found in Muybridge's photographic sequences, such as that which tracks a single naked female who wheels around to sit on a bed (fig. 89). Whether Degas was still working from a copy of *Animal Locomotion* or simply contriving his own variants along Muybridge-like lines we can only guess, although it is hard not to see his great *Dancers* as a lingering homage to the English photographer.

Degas's own photographs of a ballerina-model taken around 1895 continued to inform certain of his most elaborated compositions at this period. The three variants of a statuesque woman in the Burrell Collection's *The Red Ballet Skirts* (cat. 117), for example, are close kin to the figure photographed several times in his studio, with her distinctively strong shoulders, slender arms and pert facial features. The raised arm with which the central dancer in this work supports herself on the scenery and the up-tilted faces of her colleagues also recall the photographs, as does the vertical light source that illuminates lifted features and billowing tutus, leaving torsos and legs in partial shadow. Coincidentally or not, even the warm hues of the artist's glass plates are echoed in the Burrell scene. Both photographed images and richly coloured pastel are notionally set in the wings, where a dancer was temporarily free to stretch and prepare herself for the rigours of the stage or recover from her earlier exertions. Each of the figures in *The Red Ballet Skirts* fits one of these descriptions, though Degas hardly insists on their professional roles or their physical plight. As in so many of these late dance pictures his focus seems to be on the corporeal reality of the models, expressed in vigorously articulated forms and masses, and in their muscular actions and gravitational relationships with their surroundings. Even more extreme in this respect, it can be argued, is the resonant and mysterious *Dancers* from the Princeton University Art Museum, which was probably made at the turn of the century (cat. 118). Set backstage with a glimpse of scenery at left, this pastel tells us nothing about the identities of the three ballerinas portrayed or the production that might be underway. Here the viewer is thrust up against a single dancer, whose head and upturned elbow identify her with a pose in one of Degas's photographs, now modified as she scratches her back with one hand and attends to her hair with the other. Yet these curious actions are almost forgotten as we absorb the striations of light on the model's body and the exceptionally dense palette of pastel colours that embrace deep blues and purples, mossy greens and salmon pinks, and hints of lilac and silver. Profoundly distinct from the lucid structure of the Burrell

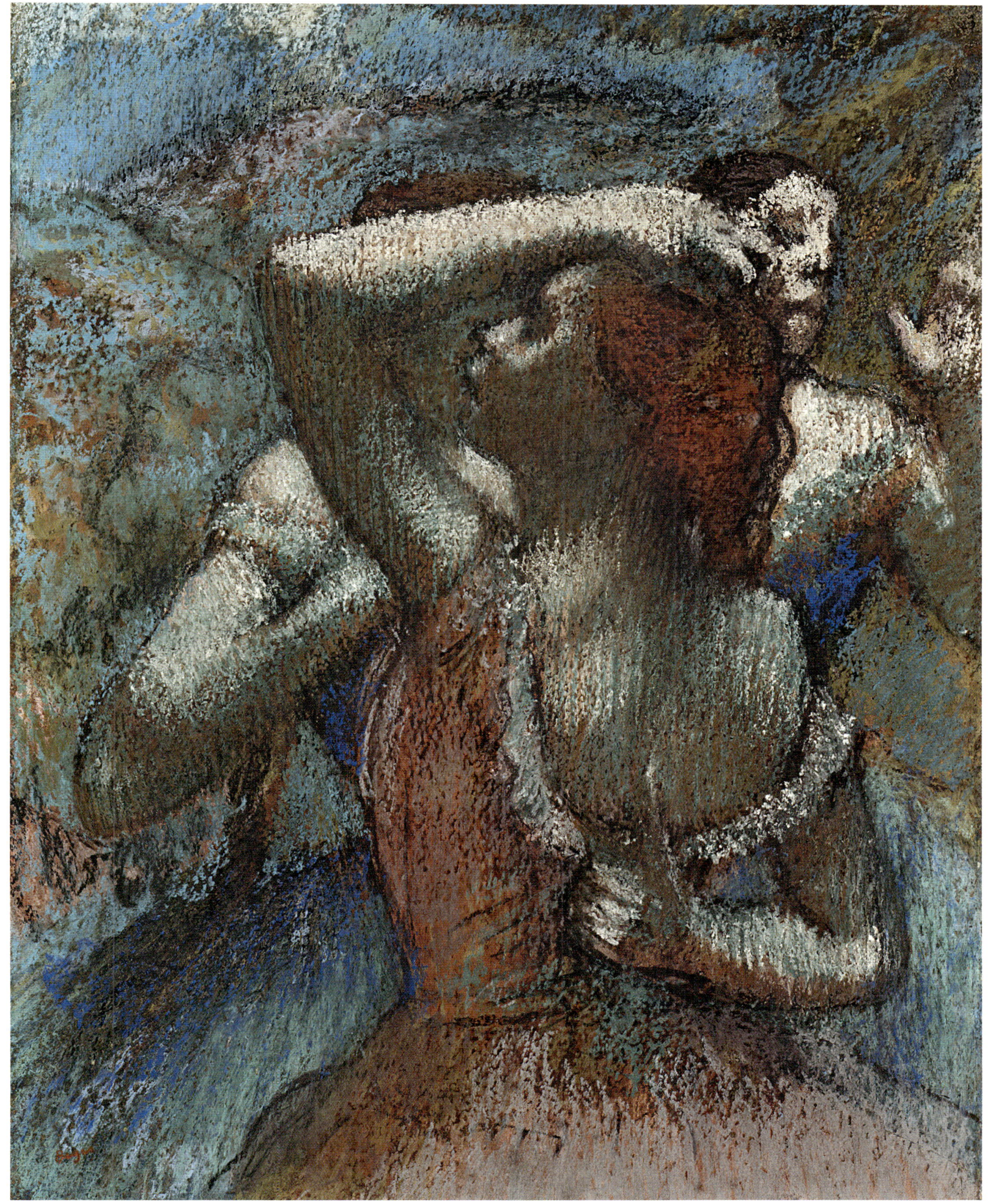

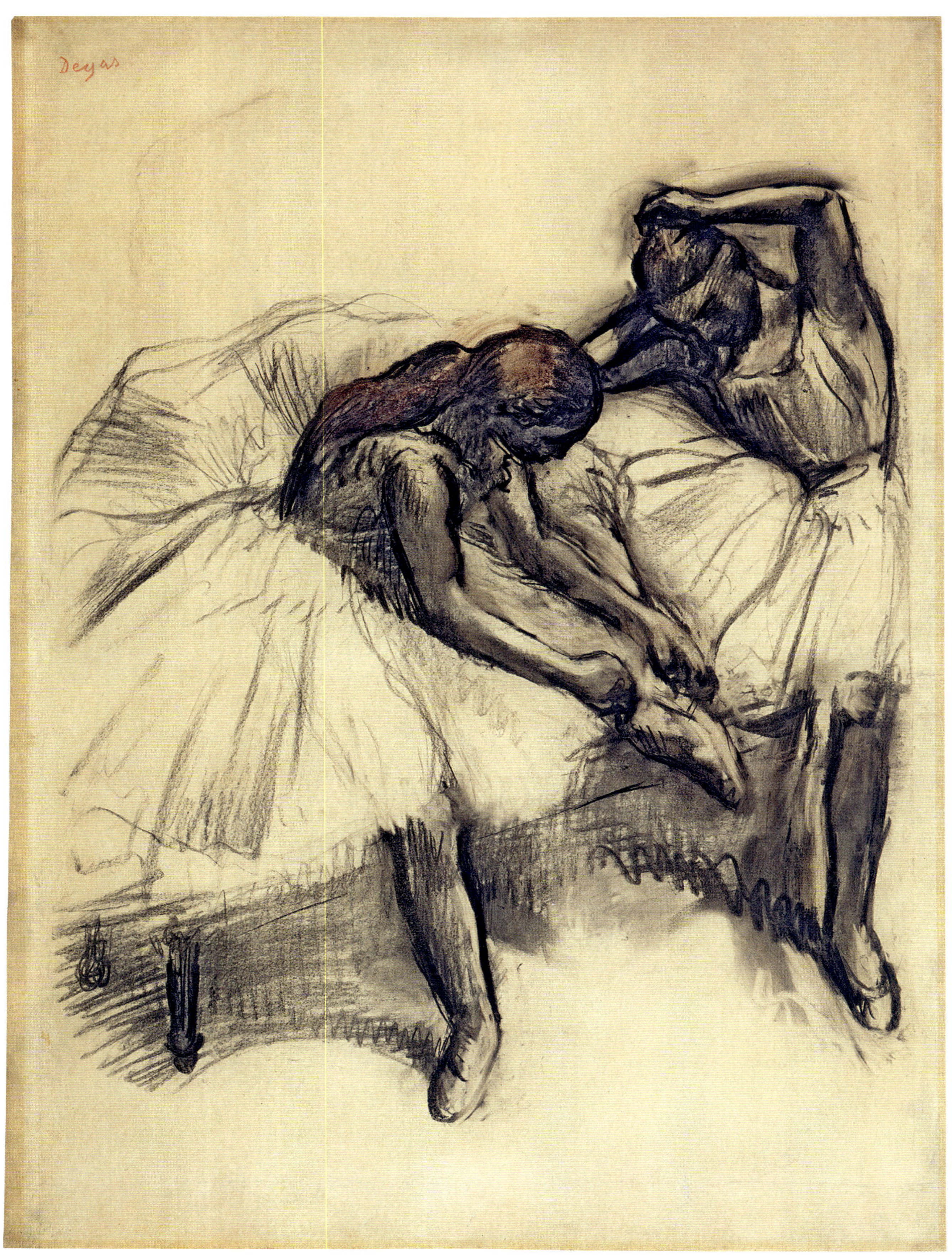
Degas

picture, this scene is elusive by comparison, its three figures mysteriously arranged one behind the other and dissolving into the penumbrous depths beyond. Here the scintillating surface and undulating contours of *Dancers* merge with the rhythmic disposition of torsos and limbs, evoking the lyricism of ballet itself as if the picture were infused with choreography. Most narrative possibilities have been abandoned and we are left with a densely layered statement about human presence and defiant sensuality.

For some years Degas had ceased to show groups of new pictures in public, occasionally selling a few to favoured dealers but content to keep the remainder for reference and possible revision. Some admiring critics who attempted to follow his progress had published essays that sensed a new direction, writing noticeably less about such issues as the delicacy of his technique and the precision of observation that had formerly dominated Degas's ballet *œuvre*. Instead there was an emphasis on the roles of 'memory' and of 'perspicacity and reverie', as Gustave Geffroy noted in an essay about the artist: 'shining like jewels in semi-darkness, the girls of the Opéra take on the appearance of divinities of the dance. These modern women are of all times and of all countries, making one think of – but which? – Hindu idols grouped together with arms and legs that seem to multiply, long and supple like creepers.'[97] Often implicit in such texts was a kinship between Degas's late phase and the Symbolist thinking that currently preoccupied many young writers, dramatists, painters and musicians in Paris and elsewhere in Europe. Degas was close at certain periods to some of Symbolism's current exponents, among them Paul Gauguin, Stéphane Mallarmé and Ernest Chausson, yet he also dismissed the movement's more extravagant modes, disapproving on one occasion of 'the need to lose consciousness in front of a lake'.[98] His photography, too, has been associated with Symbolism by a number of modern authors, its emphasis on shadowy interiors and oblique facial expressions in richly furnished interiors reminding them of the work of Eugène Carrière and Odilon Redon.[99] While there are certain affinities of this kind, such interpretations can too easily overlook the proximity of Degas's photographs to the products of his studio at this same period, which remained almost aggressively based on first-hand observation, whether of models, sculptures or his own previous creations. What is unquestionable was that a shift of emphasis occurred, as colour and texture played new and more radical roles in Degas's art and the topicality of his subject-matter became even less prominent. Now occupied almost entirely by representations of female bathers and dancers, he depicted figures who tended to be self-defining and self-sufficient within each composition. In neither case was the model's ostensible task insisted upon, but instead provided a 'pretext' – as he told Vollard – for the artist to pursue their essential identities as living creatures. Movement in various registers continued to preoccupy him until the end, subtly evident in his late reflections on Muybridge and Marey, though less likely to be expressed in athletic postures among his dancers on stage and in the wings.

The thrillingly austere yet unusually grand *Two Dancers* from the Museum of Modern Art (cat. 119) was executed in charcoal on paper in the early years of the twentieth century. Touches of brown pastel in the women's hair are the only hint that Degas may have planned to develop the drawing in colour, instead deciding to sign it with a flourish at top left and sell it to Vollard. Similar drawings lie beneath most of his richly worked pastels, even

119

Two Dancers
c. 1905
Charcoal and pastel on tracing paper, mounted on wove paper, 109.3 x 81.2 cm
The Museum of Modern Art, New York. The William S. Paley Collection

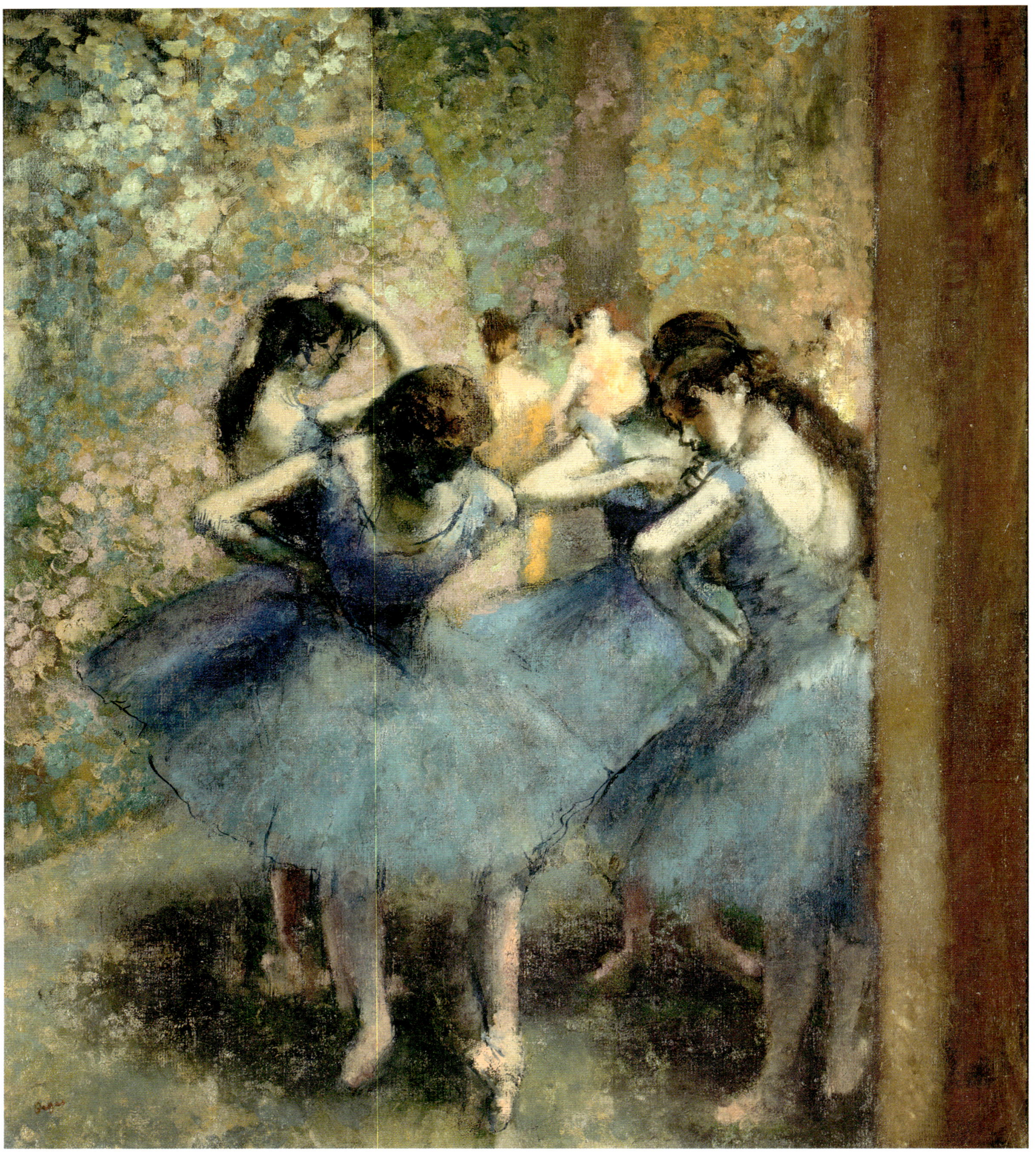

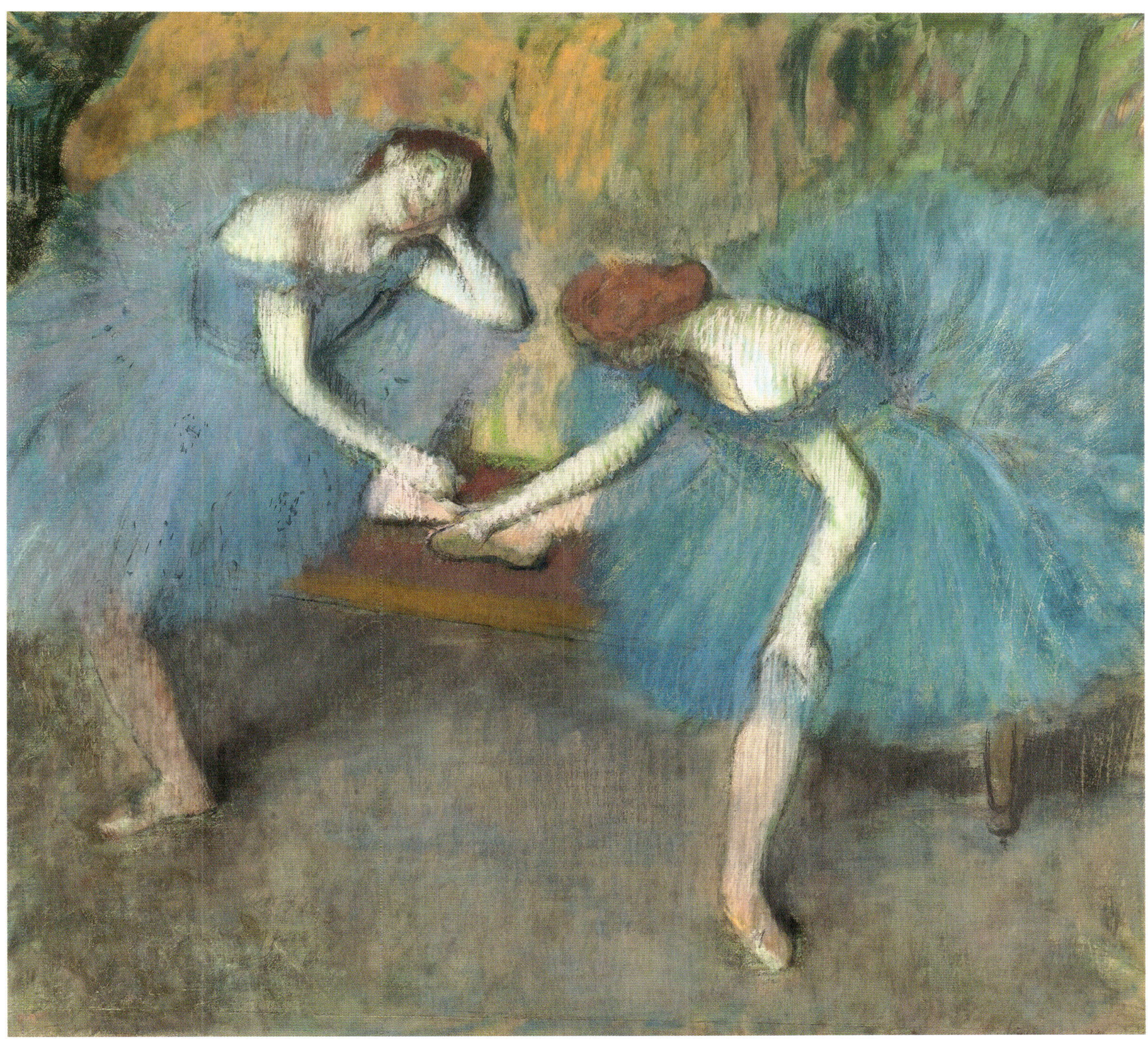

120

Dancers in Blue
c. 1890
Oil on canvas,
85 x 75.5 cm
Musée d'Orsay, Paris.
Gift of Dr and Mrs Albert
Charpentier, 1951

121

Two Dancers Resting
c. 1898
Pastel on beige paper mounted
on canvas, 92 x 103 cm
Musée d'Orsay, Paris.
Bequest of Baronne Eva
Gebhard-Gourgaud, 1965

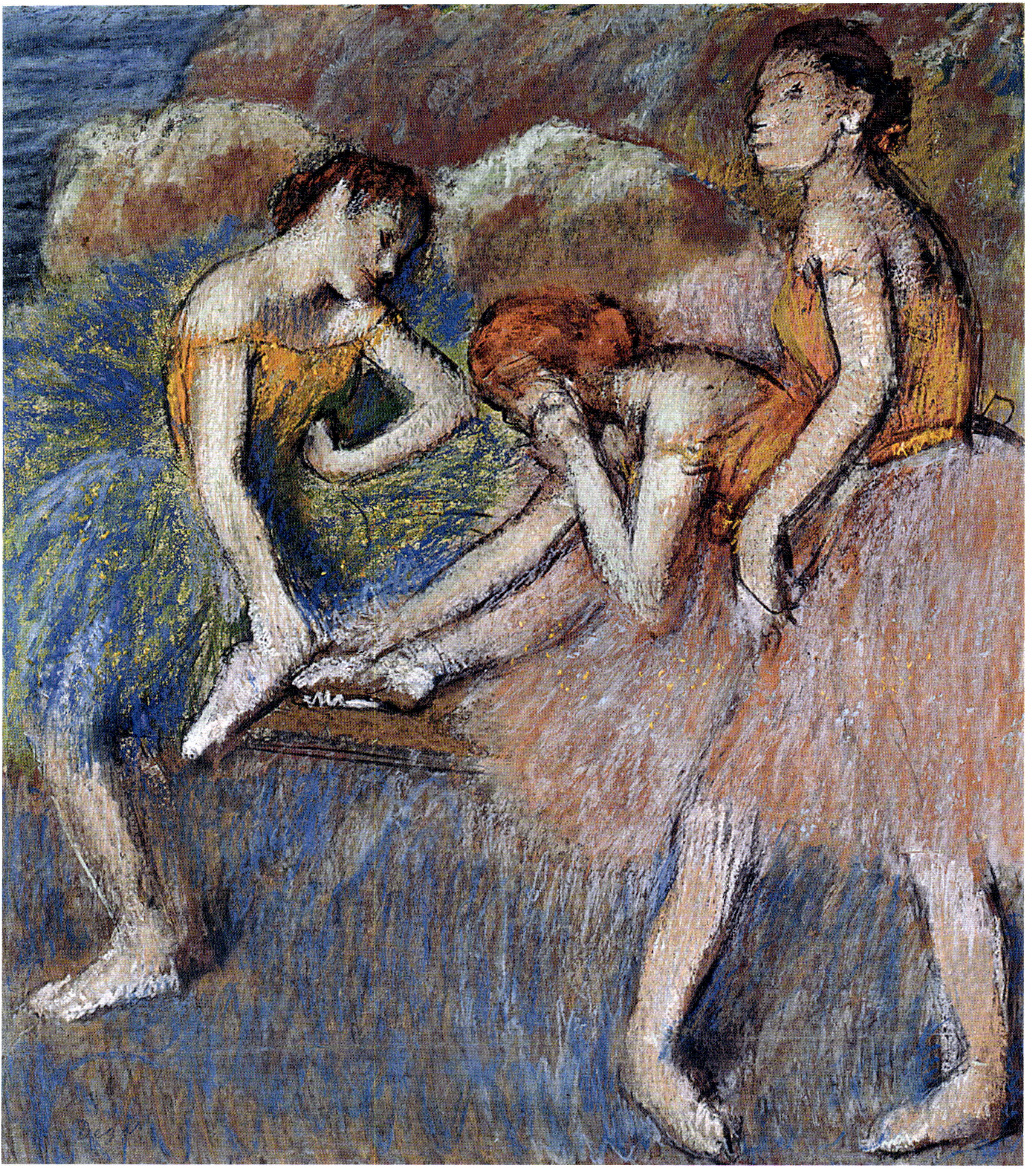

in these last years, sometimes traced from sheet to sheet and thus allowing the artist to generate groups or even entire series of pictures with a broadly common subject. Placed side by side on easels in his studio, such works might have resembled the sequential images of the photographers he had first encountered in the late 1880s, or equally the multiple paintings of *Rouen Cathedral* and scenes of water lilies that Monet was currently exhibiting.[100] Degas's decision to preserve *Two Dancers* in its primal state had other levels of significance, most clearly in its assertion of the continued primacy of drawing and of the human body as the ultimate subject of art. As in many of his definitive late figure compositions, these drawn individuals are visibly animated without being conspicuously active. Firmly seated on the kind of bench normally found in classrooms and in the wings, the two ballerinas nevertheless generate a pattern of competing forces that energises the picture rectangle. Their legs and arms, for example, mutely oppose the diagonal of the bench, the foremost figure thrusting in a contrary direction as her companion tilts backwards and returns the viewer's eye towards the centre. In hundreds of such studies Degas's dancers are rarely found idle, preferring to stretch their limbs, adjust their hair, shoes or costumes, or massage a tired joint. With their professional lives defined by jetées and pirouettes, these anonymous girls retain their vital humanity even when resting; as Marey had insisted thirty years previously, 'Motion is the most apparent characteristic of life.'

Famously telling Sickert that he considered draughtsmanship 'a more fruitful field than that of colour', Degas became an almost shockingly bold colourist in his final pastels and paintings. In the background of *Dancers in Blue* (cat. 120), for example, the artist seems to have used every hue at his disposal to create a scintillating atmosphere for the nervous ballerinas who are about to go on stage. As they stretch and adjust their gauzy costumes in the wings, orange and lemon-yellow figures in the distance face the audience and absorb the brilliant theatrical lighting. Unmistakable here is Degas's use of innovative techniques – stippling and layering of colour, for example – to energise the canvas. Close examination reveals that he also used his fingertips to apply some of this paint, a manœuvre that sounds shockingly anarchic until we recall Degas's reverence for a painter such as Titian, who was reputed to have worked in a similar fashion in his later years. In *Dancers in Blue*, the diagonal rhythms of the dancers' arms bring further vitality to this unusually dynamic composition, which is ultimately contained by the sombre vertical structure at right. The unusually large pastel *Two Dancers Resting* (cat. 121) might almost represent the aftermath of the scene in this painting, as a pair of blue-clad performers relax and recover from their recent exertions in the footlights. Here we see the young women from above, their skirts spread around them in a restful pattern of ovals and lazy curves. Both individuals rub their tired feet, their hands almost touching and thus ensuring that the linear rhythm from lower right to upper left brings unity to the scene. As in *Dancers in Blue* and many other works from the late 1890s, painted and drawn limbs are artfully arranged to energise the design, their contours echoed in billowing tutus and rounded elements of scenery. Unlike the vibrant dotting of colour in the related canvas, *Two Dancers Resting* is built up from the characteristically broad strokes and hatchings of Degas's late pastels, exerting their own quieter life within the picture surface.

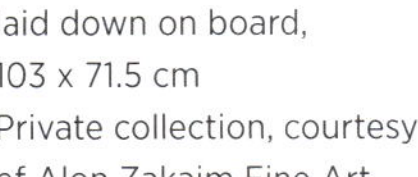

123

Group of Dancers
c. 1905–10
Charcoal on paper
laid down on board,
103 x 71.5 cm
Private collection, courtesy
of Alon Zakaim Fine Art

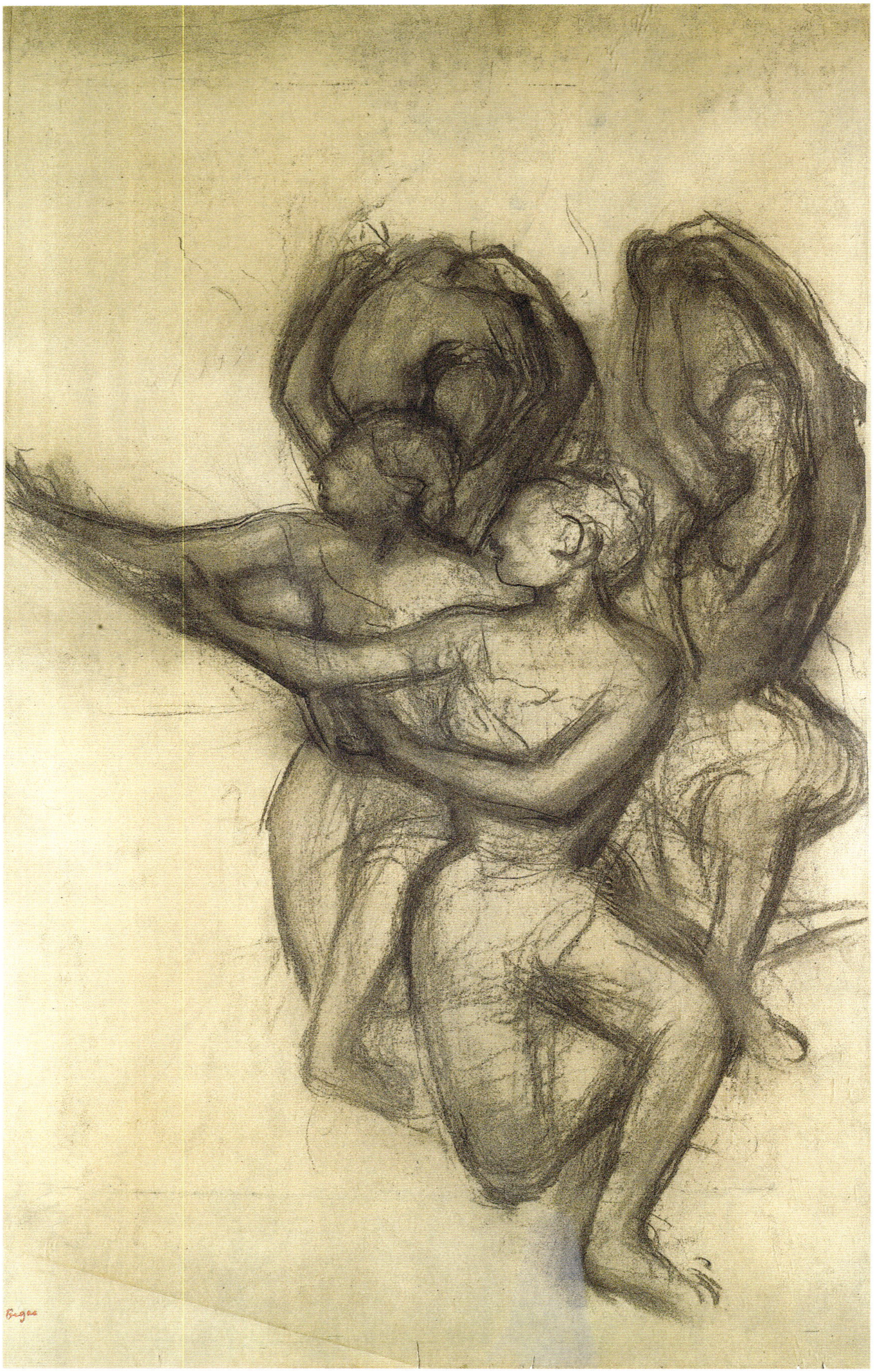

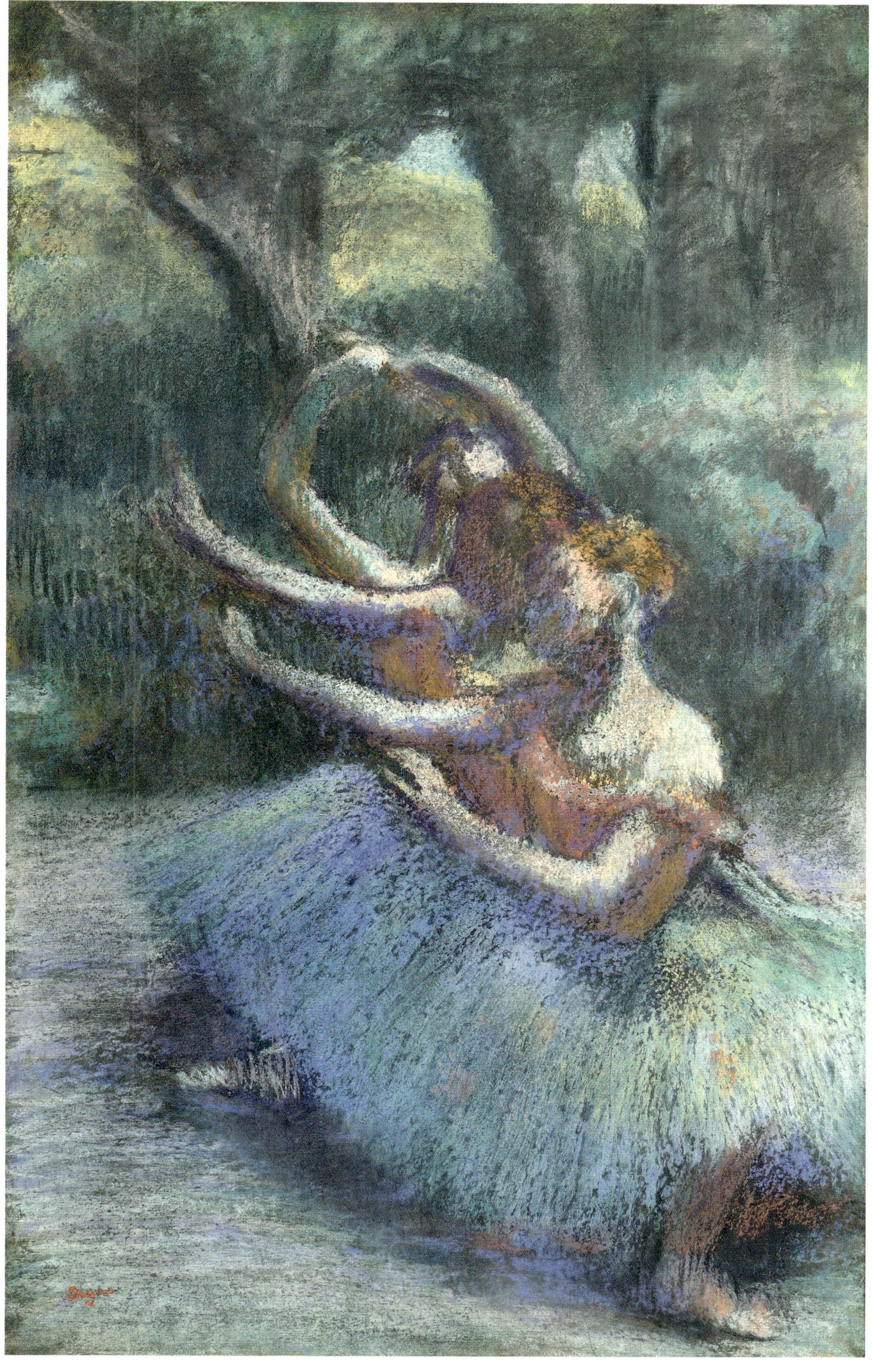

124

**Three Dancers,
Landscape Scenery**
c. 1895–98
Pastel on paper,
82 x 53 cm
Private collection

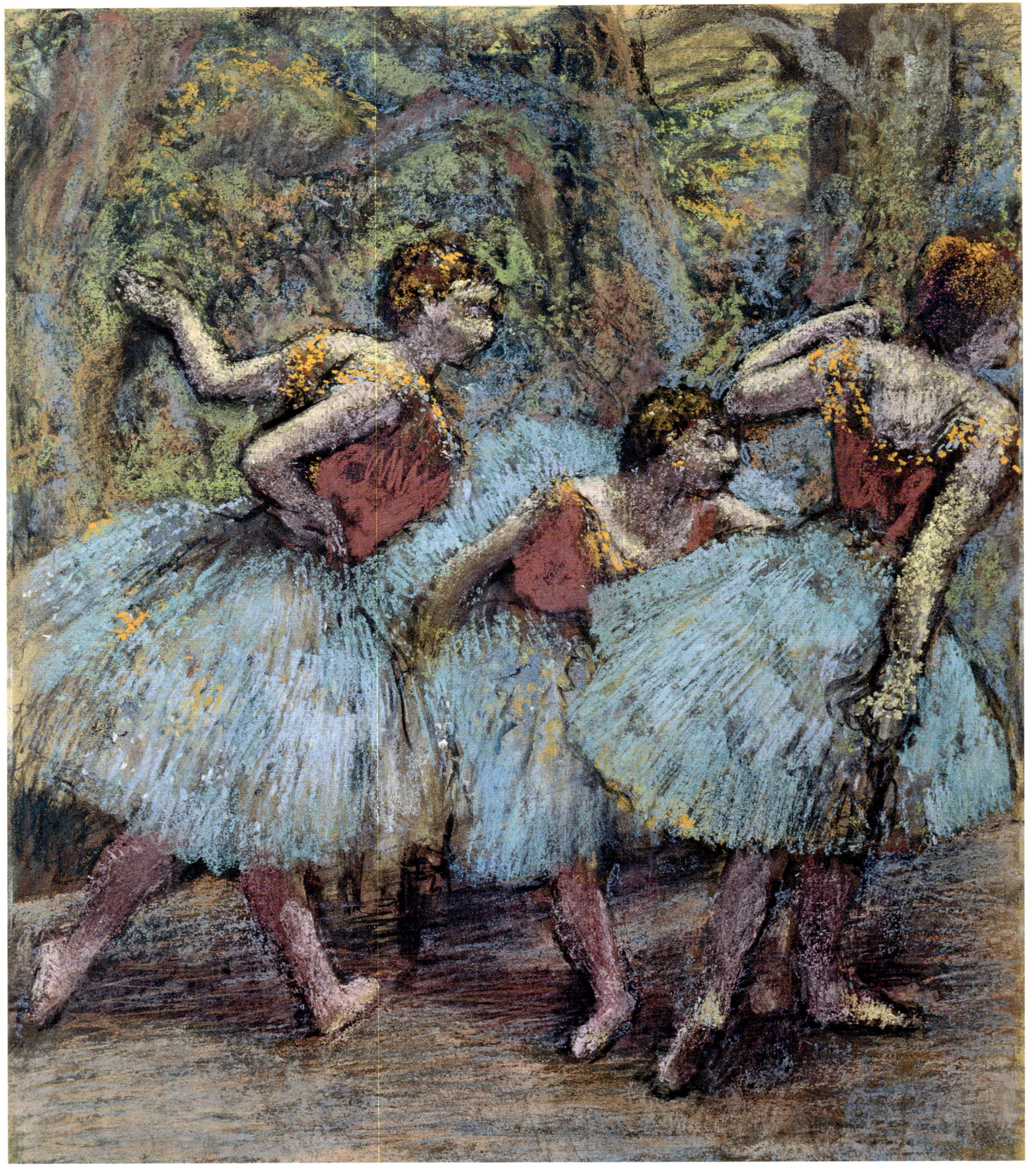

Vivid colour of a different kind dominates *Dancers Resting* (cat. 122), where the central coryphée is the virtual mirror image of her counterpart in the drawing from the Museum of Modern Art, here joined by a single dancer on either side. Again the actions and expressions of these figures are mundane, but in the starkest contrast with *Two Dancers* this picture blazes with hues from across the spectrum. Such vivid colours in juxtaposition inevitably set up chromatic vibrations, animating not just the *dramatis personae* but also the spaces around and between them. This effect is intensified by the artist's distinctive habit of laying strokes of contrasted hue side by side in near-obsessive striations, then sometimes adding counter-strokes over the initial layer in yet further interweavings of colour. Also unmistakable in this work is the progression of forms and planes of variegated hue from foreground to background, inviting our eyes to move past clustered limbs and multicoloured tutus to the pink-yellow stage scenery beyond. This is picture-making of a high order of complexity, rivalling the canvases of the European masters that Degas so fervently admired and was occasionally able to buy in later life from the proceeds of his picture sales; he now owned a battle scene by Delacroix, paintings of saints by El Greco and mythological compositions by Ingres, for example, as well as many hundreds of lesser works and prints by and after his revered predecessors.[101] Showing them reverently to a few friends, Degas was not inclined to discuss these treasures at length but still seems to have regarded them as touchstones of excellence to which he might aspire.

Degas's own persistent ambition and his vestigial attachment to line is again evident in *Group of Dancers* (cat. 123), a work begun in charcoal on paper and subsequently mounted on board. Clearly revisiting a choreographed moment on stage remembered from the past, he drew and re-drew this cluster of elegant ballerinas until their multiple rhythms coalesced into an inevitable-seeming ensemble. Long forgotten is the precision of Ingres, its place taken by a suggestive massing of forms and intermingling of limbs that are clearly captured in movement. Perhaps daunted by the task of developing a work of this scale, Degas chose not to carry the composition further, although something of its swaying, mesmerising character reappeared in the extraordinary *Three Dancers, Landscape Scenery* (cat. 124). In such late scenes of the ballet on stage, it was perhaps the tapestry-like richness of the great Venetian painters that was on Degas's mind. Here a group of spotlit ballerinas perform against a densely coloured, shadowy landscape that offers a view of brightness in the distance. Every detail in this bewitching composition seems to have been richly worked in pastel, from their rustic setting to the bodies and skirts of the dancers and even the stage that surrounds them. An iridescent sheen permeates the lower half of the composition, its vibrancy and lyricism reminding us that such scenes were played out against music from the nearby orchestra. These dancers are all in plié, the foremost figure lowest to the ground and her two companions successively rising in a gentle wave of co-ordinated limbs and echoing profiles. Relying less on fine draughtsmanship, the septuagenarian artist was still preoccupied with the vitality of his subjects and frank in his acknowledgement of the precedence of Marey and Muybridge. Here the continuity of the dancers' actions is spelled out with unusual directness, rhyming with each other but also with the sweep of their tutus and the swaying of trees and foliage.

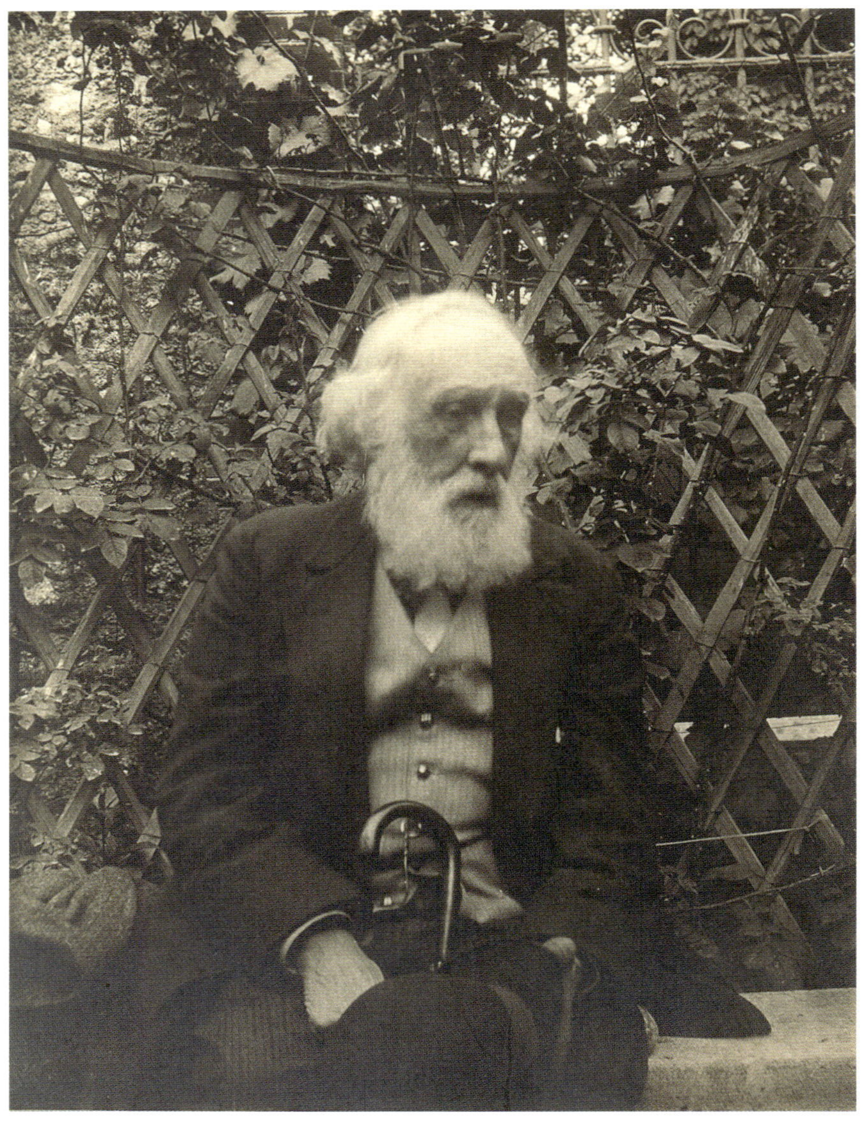

Fig. 90 *Paul-Albert Bartholomé*, Degas in Bartholomé's Garden,
19 March 1912. Silver gelatin print, 22.5 x 17.3 cm. Musée d'Orsay, Paris

Triumphing over almost every technical challenge is *Three Dancers (Blue Skirts, Red Bodices)* from the Beyeler Foundation (cat. 125), one of Degas's most densely enhanced pastels from the early twentieth century. Every square inch of this remarkable picture seems to resonate with complex colour, not just a single hue but accumulated layers of warm and cool tones that allow earlier strata to glow though their accumulated richness. Beneath the bright blues of the dancers' skirts, for example, passages of its complementary colour – orange – add subtly to the whole, not just blending with the upper surface but reverberating chromatically with it. This quality is echoed elsewhere, in the brilliant 'dotting' marks of the pastel stick around the women's shoulders and the repeated striations of blue on the tutus, as well as the horizontal streaks that indicate the stage and the more atmospheric clouds of green, brown and yellow in the leafy background.

Justifying this extravagance is the extraordinary, rhythmic cluster of
ballerinas, mature women rather than girls, who seem to sway from left
to right and yet stay within their allotted spaces. Far from the acrobatic
movement of his early *œuvre*, this solemn lilting in unison is both
particularised and monumental. There is an elegiac quality to such works,
created by an artist who could now look back over four decades of observing
the dance and who was still just as passionate about the inflections of a limb
or the scattering of colour under stage lights.

The effort involved in densely negotiated late masterpieces such as the
Fondation Beyeler pastel inevitably took its toll. Those around Degas knew
that his energy was fading. Photographed in the open air around 1908 by his
longstanding friend, the sculptor Paul-Albert Bartholomé (fig. 90), the artist
seems frail and distracted. Yet letters and other documents of this period
make it clear that he still spent time in his studio: 'Here I am again, back
at drawing and pastel,' he told Alexis Rouart, mentioning in another note
that he wanted 'to do sculpture'.[102] Though he showed little concern with the
subject, serious interest in Degas's art was gathering momentum in Europe
and America, an interest reflected in major exhibitions held in Brussels,
London, Berlin and New York, and in the first retrospective of his work, held
at the Fogg Art Museum in 1912.[103] In this same year, Degas was obliged to
leave his Montmartre apartment and studio, which was due for demolition.
New premises were found for him on the Boulevard de Clichy, where he was
filmed by Sacha Guitry around 1915 and thus entered the vast archive
of historical and visual documentation that was to define the new century.
Photography and film were now part of many avant-garde movements of the
day, as was a continuing fascination with the human body in action and the
artist's instinctive need to render it in palpable form. Even in his extremity,
the man who could claim to have pioneered such activities and become the
first truly major artist to engage directly and creatively with photography
could not escape the medium that had inspired and sometimes infuriated
him. A haphazard, film-like sequence of amateur photographs shows Degas
as an invalid some time before his death in September 1917 (fig. 91), while
one of the items found in his studio soon afterwards is said to have been
'a large camera'.[104]

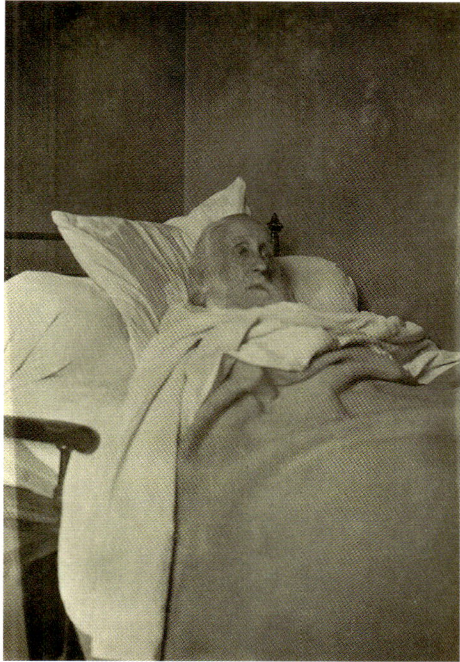

Fig. 91 *Jeanne Fèvre*, **Degas in Old Age in
Bed**, *c.* 1915. Silver gelatin print, 13 x 8.9 cm.
Musée d'Orsay, Paris

SOME DOCUMENTED LINKS BETWEEN DEGAS AND PHOTOGRAPHY

1834	Degas born in Paris.
1839	First announcement of the daguerreotype process.
1851	Collodion glass-plate negative process introduced.
c. 1855–60	Earliest surviving photograph of Degas.[1]
c. 1860	Three photographs of Degas 'posing at a photographer's'.[2]
c. 1862	Three carte-de-visite photographs of Degas.[3]
c. 1859–64	Notebook drawing 'signed' by Degas, 'Disdéri photog'.[4]
c. 1859–64	Two photographs stuck in a Degas notebook.[5]
c. 1860–65	Photographs of Degas taken in photographers' studios.[6]
c. 1865	Painting by Degas based on a Disdéri photograph of the Princesse de Metternich (fig. 11) and her husband.[7]
1866	Two photographs painted by Degas in the background of his *The Collector of Prints* (Metropolitan Museum of Art, New York).[8]
1867–68	Photographs used in the making of Degas's portrait of the dancer Eugenie Fiocre (see fig. 5).[9]
1872	René De Gas plans to have a 'large photograph' taken of Degas's painting *Dance Class at the Opéra* (Musée d'Orsay, Paris).[10]
1872	In a letter from New Orleans, Degas writes: 'Instantaneousness is photography, nothing more.'[11]
1872–73	Carte-de-visite photograph of Degas in New Orleans.[12]
1872–74	Degas inscribes a drawing of a dark-suited man 'Bonnard, photographe'.[13]
1873	The destroyed Paris Opéra building photographed by Degas's friend Louis-Amédée Mante.[14]
1874	The studio of the photographer Nadar used for the first Impressionist exhibition.[15]
Unknown date	Degas's assessment of Nadar: 'faux-peintre … faux-tographe'.[16]
1874	Degas uses a carte-de-visite portrait when painting the figure of Jules Perrot in *The Rehearsal*.[17]

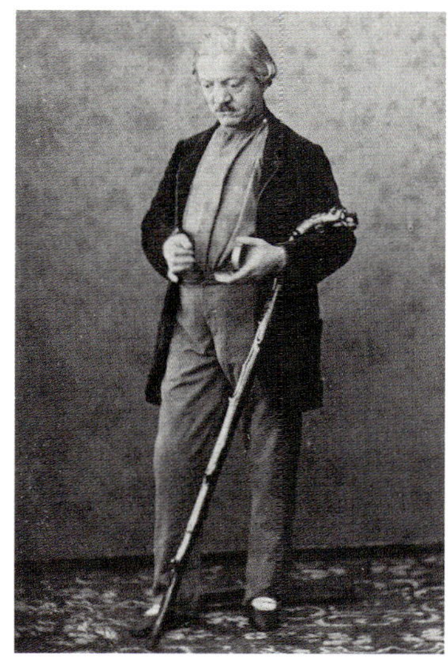

G. Bergamasco, Jules Perrot, *c.* 1860.
Carte-de-visite photograph, 9 x 5 cm.
Private collection

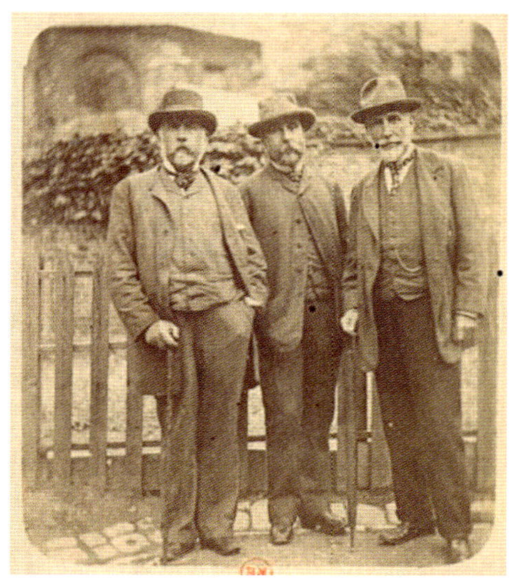

Walter Barnes, Edgar Degas, Ludovic Halévy and Albert-
Boulanger-Cavé at Dieppe, 1885. Photograph, 9 x 7 cm.
Bibliothèque nationale de France, Paris

1874–75	René De Gas photographs Degas's painting *Dance Class* (Metropolitan Museum of Art, New York).[18]
1876	At the second Impressionist Exhibition, a critic refers to a Degas picture of *Dancers* as 'a photograph'.[19]
1876	Jules Claretie mentions seeing 'the almost unique collection of photographs of the works of Monsieur Degas' at the dealer Deschamps in London.[20]
1876	Degas moves to a new apartment, with 'a glass roof, as in a photographer's studio'.[21]
1876	Degas writes to the singer Jean-Baptiste Faure: 'remind Mérante about the photographs he offered me yesterday. I am eager to see them and to work out what I can make of this dancer's talent'.[22]
1878	In the journal *La Nature*, some of Eadweard Muybridge's 'instantaneous photographs' make their first appearance in France.[23]
1879	Degas exhibits his painting *Dancer Posing for a Photograph* (cat. 4) in Paris.[24]
c. 1880	In a letter to Pissarro, Degas refers to the collodion process for processing photographs.[25]
1881	Muybridge presents his high-speed photographs at Marey's Paris home, in the presence of many scientists and artists; the event is soon repeated in the studio of the prominent painter Ernest Meissonier.[26]
1882	Marey publishes several articles with illustrations of his own instantaneous photographs.[27]
c. 1884	Degas's portrait of Mary Cassatt shows her with a handful of photographs or playing cards.[28]
1885	Photographs of Degas and friends at Dieppe are taken by the English photographer Walter Barnes, some apparently arranged by Degas.[29]
c. 1885	Degas photographed outdoors with members of the Halévy family.[30]
c. 1885	Degas sends three photographs to Walter Sickert via Ludovic Halévy.[31]
Mid-1880s	Photographs made of two unfinished paintings by Degas of women ironing.[32]
1886	Degas writes to the socialite and amateur photographer Hortense Howland.[33]

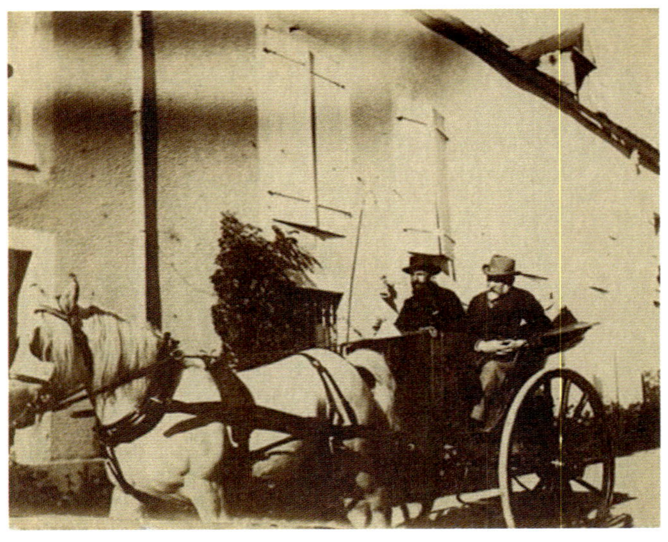

Unknown photographer, Degas and His Friend Bartholomé
on a Trip through Burgundy, 1890. Albumen print,
8.8 x 10.7 cm. Musée d'Orsay, Paris

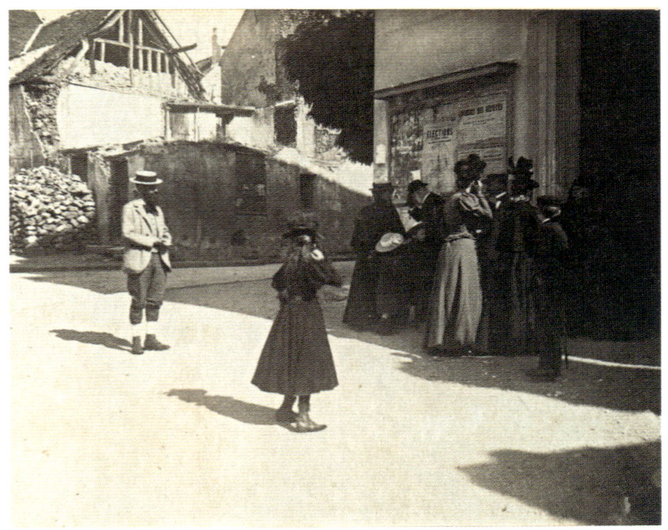

Street Scene, c. 1895–96. Gelatin silver print, 29.1 x 39.8
cm. Museum of Modern Art, New York. Gift of Paul
F. Walter, acc. no. 208.1989

1887–88	Degas photographed alongside Mme Howland.[34]
1887	Publication of Muybridge's *Animal Locomotion*, from which Degas made drawings of horses and female nudes.[35]
1889	Marey displays his photographs and sculptures of figures and animals in motion at the Paris Exposition Universelle.[36]
1889	Degas is photographed on the street by Giuseppe Primoli (fig. 58).[37]
1889	Degas writes good-naturedly to Primoli about the photograph of him leaving a urinal.[38]
1890	Photographs of Degas arriving at Diénay in Burgundy taken by Georges Jeanniot or Charles de Meixmoron.[39]
1890	Photograph of Degas painting in a field by Charles de Meixmoron.[40]
1895	Degas acquires his first camera.[41]
1895	The Italian painter Federico Zandomeneghi mentions that Degas photographed him 'last winter'.[42]

1895	Degas sends a camera and accessories to his sister Marguerite in Buenos Aires.[43]
1895	Writing during a stay at Mont Dore in August, Degas mentions portrait photographs he has taken, spoiled plates, a new camera, experiments with enlargements, and attempts to photograph 'almost at night'.[44]
c. 1895	Two photographs of landscapes at St-Valéry-sur-Somme and two of figures in the street attributed to Degas.[45]
1895	Referring to a photograph of his nephew, Degas insists that 'the truth is never ugly'.[46]
1895	Daniel Halévy notes that Degas has had several photography sessions at their Paris home during the autumn.[47]
1895	Degas photographs Stéphane Mallarmé and Pierre-Auguste Renoir (cat. 96).[48]
1895	Films by the Lumière brothers are shown for the first time in Paris.
1895–96	Degas photographs himself with various friends, including the painter Jacques-Emile Blanche (cat. 95) and the composer Ernest Chausson.[49]

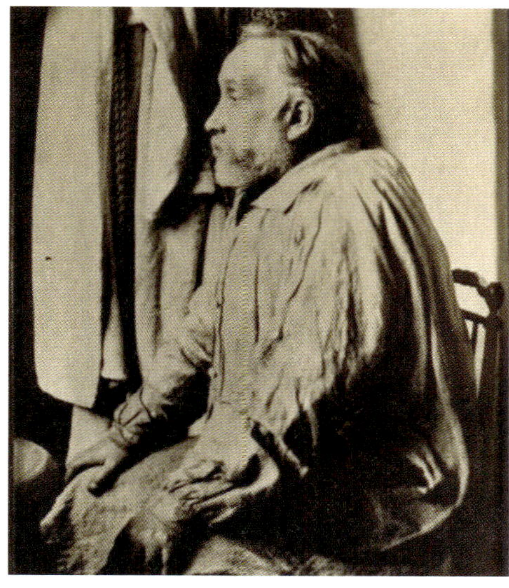

Self-portrait in the Studio, *c.* 1896? Photograph, 8 x 5 cm. Bibliothèque nationale de France, Paris

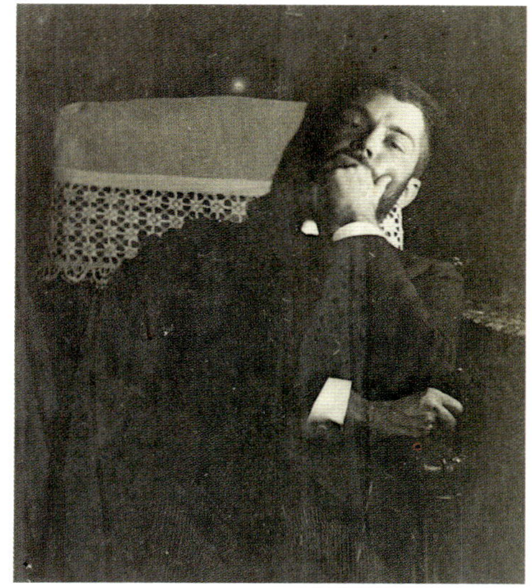

Daniel Halévy, 1895. Gelatin silver print from glass negative, 40 x 28.7 cm. Metropolitan Museum of Art, New York. Purchase: The Horace W. Goldsmith Foundation Gift through Joyce and Robert Menschel, 1998, inv. no. 1998.56

c. 1895–96	Degas takes three photographs of a ballet dancer.[50]
1895–96 onwards	Variants of the photographed dancers appear in many of Degas's pictures.
1895–96	Two photographs of female nudes may date from this period or earlier, one of them inspiring a group of pastels and paintings.[51]
1895–96	Photographs of friends and self-portraits taken by Degas in his apartment, also showing part of his collection.[52]
Unknown date	Stéphane Mallarmé writes a short poem about a photograph of him taken by Degas.[53]
1896	Display of some of Degas's recent photographs at Tasset et Lhote in Montmartre.[54]
1896	Writing of a photograph of his recently deceased sister, Degas says that he cannot look at it without weeping; he has had the photograph enlarged but is opposed to retouching it.[55]
1896	In a letter to Henri Haro, Degas mentions 're-photographing the little Ingres'.[56]
1896	Degas shows some of his enlarged portrait photographs to friends.[57]
Late 1890s?	Degas and friends at Ménil-Hubert photograph themselves as if in a 'film' sequence (fig. 78).[58]
1897	In an interview with Thiébault-Sisson, Degas recalls the first appearance of photographs by Marey.[59]
c. 1900	Photograph of Degas and his niece at Valéry-sur-Somme taken by René De Gas.[60]
1901	Degas takes a photograph of Claudie Léouzon le Duc.[61]
1912	Degas photographed outdoors in old age by Albert Bartholomé (fig. 90).[62]
1914–15	Degas filmed very briefly and against his will by Sacha Guitry, for his film *Ceux de chez nous* (fig. 79).[63]
c. 1915	Series of photographs of Degas in bed some time before his death (fig. 91).[64]

259

ENDNOTES

INTRODUCTION

1 Solange Vernois, 'L'Esthetique du mouvement et ses polémiques au XIXe siècle', in Beaune 1991.

CHAPTER 1

1 Baudelaire 1961, p. 505.
2 Goncourt 1956, vol. 2, p. 967.
3 Baudelaire 1961, p. 505.
4 Sickert 1917, p. 185; and Moore 1918, p. 64.
5 Burty, Chesneau and Carjat, in Berson 1996, vol. 1, pp. 10, 19 and 15 respectively.
6 Berson 1996, vol. 1, p. 5, and vol. 2, p. 7.
7 Drumont, in Berson 1996, vol. 1, p. 21.
8 *La République française* [Philippe Burty], in Berson 1996, vol. 1, p. 37.
9 *La République française* [Philippe Burty], in Berson 1996, vol. 1, p. 37.
10 Claretie writing as 'Ariste' in Berson 1996, vol. 1, p. 9.
11 Chesneau, in Berson 1996, vol. 1, p. 19.
12 L.82, L.94; Baudelaire 1961, pp. 1152–90.
13 Emile Zola, 'Mon Salon', *L'Evénement illustré*, 9 June 1868, in Zola 1991, pp. 220–21. For the most comprehensive analysis of *Mlle Fiocre in the Ballet 'La Source'*, see Dumas 1988; see also Paris 1988, pp. 133–35; and Detroit 2002, pp. 196–98.
14 *Le Monde Artiste*, 17 November 1866, p. 1.
15 Nb. 22, p. 5.
16 Manchester 1987, pp. 60–61; Wells 1964, pp. 17, 29.
17 See cats 32, 33, 39, 40, 45, 46; fig. 40.
18 Mérode 1985, p. 54; Browse 1949, p. 55, note 2; and Guest 1976, p. 136.
19 Guérin 1947, p. 236, recalled in a letter from Poujaud to Guérin.
20 Detroit 2002, p. 81.
21 Detroit 2002, p. 165.
22 See Detroit 2002, pp. 158–60.
23 Baudelaire 1961, p. 1035.
24 For other cartes de visite see Janis 1984, p. 460, and Musée d'Orsay PHO 1992 10 24.
25 See McCauley 1994.

26 First discussed in Rewald 1937; see also Scharf 1968, pp. 187–88; and National Gallery 2004, pp. 62–67.
27 See Minervino and Lassaigne 1974, nos 212 and 212a; see also Detroit 2002, pp. 196–98.
28 See, for example, Musée d'Orsay, PHO 1991 8 and PHO 1994 9 1.
29 Lemoisne 1946–49, vol. 1, p. 62.
30 Guérin 1947, pp. 18–19, 22.
31 See Lemoisne 1946–47, vol. 1, p. 71; and Reff 2006, p. 50.
32 See Claretie 1876; our thanks are due to Theodore Reff for drawing our attention to this text.
33 Guérin 1947, p. 44.
34 Janis 1984, p. 463.
35 The posthumous inventory for Degas's apartment refers to several albums, framed photographs and other related material that all seem to have been concerned with architecture. We are most grateful to Theodore Reff for this information.
36 In the catalogue of the fourth Impressionist exhibition in 1879, Degas's own title for this work was *Danseuse posant chez un photographe*; see Berson 1996, p. 205 (no. 72); see also Paris 1988, p. 244.
37 For Mante's activities as a professional photographer, see Millet 1979; for Bonnard, see Reff 1974, pp. 11, 33.
38 Vente III: 338.2.
39 Detroit 2002, p. 209.
40 See, for example, Adice 1859, Duval 1875, Bernay 1890 and Charbonnel 1899.
41 For the pastel, see L.421; for examples of frieze paintings, see cats 32, 33, 39, 40, 45, 46; fig. 40.
42 See Berson 1996, vol. 1, p. 198.
43 Goncourt 1956, vol. 2, p. 968.
44 See, for example, J.207, J.208 and J.223.
45 See Berson 1996, vol. 1, p. 118, where it is proposed that *The Rehearsal* was no. 38 in the 1877 exhibition.
46 Claretie, 'L.G.' and Jacques, in Berson 1996, vol. 1, pp. 141, 148 and 156 respectively.
47 Chevalier and Claretie, in Berson 1996, vol. 1, pp. 139 and 148.

48 Baudelaire 1961, p. 1160.
49 Duranty, in San Francisco 1986, p. 45.
50 Nb. 30, pp. 205, 204 and 208 respectively.
51 See, for example, J.30, J.33, J.37 and J.269.
52 See Clark 1984, p. 75; Varnedoe 1990, pp. 43–53.
53 See, for example, J.24, J.29, J.208, J.209 and J.260.
54 L.408; see Paris 1988, pp. 277–78.
55 Guérin 1947, pp. 74–75.
56 See Loyrette 1989A; and Detroit 2002, pp. 22 and 106.
57 For Degas's dance-related submissions to the Impressionist exhibitions, see Berson 1996, vol. 2, pp. 7, 34–36, 72–74, 109–12 and 147–48. He did not participate in the 1882 exhibition, and in 1886 ballet subjects were absent from his display.
58 Berson 1996, vol. 1, p. 19.
59 For this work, see Paris 1988, pp. 171–73 and 269–70; and Detroit 2002, pp. 52–57.
60 See Loyrette 1989A, pp. 59–63.
61 Nb. 24, pp. 7, 9–11, 13, 15–17 and 19–21.
62 New York 1993A, p. 203.
63 For Hill's and Sickert's acquisitions of dance works by Degas, see Pickvance 1962, 1963A and 1963B; for *The Green Dancers* (L.572), see Paris 1988, pp. 354–56.
64 Lemoisne 1946–49, vol. 1, p. 1.
65 See Paris 1988, pp. 225–26.
66 L.493.
67 See Detroit 2002, pp. 95–105.
68 See Kendall 1988, pp. 187–90.
69 Berson 1996, vol. 2, pp. 111–12.
70 See Buerger and Shapiro 1981.
71 Guérin 1947, p. 57.
72 L.796; see Richard Thomson, 'Notes on Degas's Sense of Humour', in Kendall et al. 1985, pp. 11–12; and Paris 1988, pp. 442–43.
73 See Heilbrun 1989, pp. 161–63.
74 Guérin 1947, p. 110.

CHAPTER 2

1   Nb. 30, p. 65.
2   Cited in Paris 1988, p. 55.
3   Baudelaire 1961, pp. 1163 and 1035.
4   Nb. 30, pp. 210 and 65.
5   For the genesis of the *Little Dancer*, see Paris 1988, pp. 342–45; and Omaha 1998.
6   Kahane et al. 1998, pp. 53–60.
7   De Mont, Trianon and Enault, in Berson 1996, vol. 1, pp. 339, 361 and 368.
8   'C.E.' and Mantz, in Berson 1996, vol. 1, pp. 337 and 358.
9   Huysmans and de Villars, in Berson 1996, vol. 1, pp. 349 and 371.
10 De Charry, Mantz and Huysmans, in Berson 1966, vol. 1, pp. 333, 349 and 358.
11 See Bertall, 'C.E.', Huysmans, Mantz and de Villars, in Berson 1996, vol. 1, pp. 330, 336, 349, 358 and 371; and Comtesse Louise and Trianon in the same volume, pp. 356 and 368.
12 Claretie and Comtesse Louise, in Berson 1996, vol. 1, p. 335, note 1, and p. 356.
13 Manz, in Berson 1996, vol. 1, p. 338.
14 Manchester 1987, pp. 82–85; for a similar study, see Nb. 2, p. 63.
15 Washington 1984, p. 68. Marie's name (spelled 'Van Gutten') and address also appear in Nb. 34, p. 4; see also Paris 1988, p. 342.
16 L.599 and Vente III: 369.
17 Communicated by the dance historian Sandra Noll Hammond.
18 The possibility that this device prompted Gérôme himself to exploit multiple viewpoints of his sculptures in his own 'series' of paintings of the model is cited in Lafont-Couturier 1998, p. 89.
19 They are all between 46 and 48 cm high.
20 See for example Druick and Zegers 1988; Druick 1989; Callen 1995, pp. 1–31; and Omaha 1998, pp. 3–25 and 45–75.
21 Montucci 1863A, p. 401.
22 Parville 1863, p. 1; Gautier 1864A, p. 3.
23 Saint-Victor 1866, p. 2; and Danicourt 1864, p. 446. For a summary of the contemporary reception of photosculpture see Gall 1997, paragraphs 9–17 and 28–35, and Drost 1985, pp. 118–21 and 125.
24 For a description of the building, see Gautier 1864A, p. 5.
25 Accounts of the time required to produce a photosculpture vary: Gautier (1864A, pp. 6–7) suggested that it took 'a little longer' than taking a photograph; Tissandier (1874, p. 207) reported a few days; and Parville (1863, p. 1) specified 48 hours.
26 Precedents for this system are noted in Soubieszek 1980, pp. 624–27.
27 Buerger 1978, p. 21; see also Soubieszek 1980, p. 629.
28 See, for example, Moigno 1861; Figuier 1862; Parville 1863; Benfield 1864; and Danicourt 1864.
29 See Gautier 1864B; Hermant 1864; Bernard 1866; and Vauvert 1866.
30 See Paris 1988, p. 56. Willème's sculptures were displayed in a previous exhibition at the Palais d'Industrie in Paris in 1863; see Drost 1985, p. 117.
31 Parville 1863 and Tissandier 1874, p. 209.
32 R.VII and R.II respectively.
33 Soubieszek 1980, pp. 617–18 and 629.
34 Saint-Edmé 1864, p. 147.
35 Tissandier 1874, p. 209.
36 For photosculpture's rise and decline in popularity, see Drost 1985, pp. 120–21.
37 See Los Angeles 1999, p. 73.
38 See Drost 1985, fig. 1.
39 See Guest 1953, pp. 75–79; and Pitou 1990, vol. 2, pp. 927–30.
40 Gautier 1864B, p. 396; see also Saint-Victor 1866, p. 2.
41 Sevin 1975, p. 36.
42 All measure approximately 40 x 90 cm, a format that was not standard with many suppliers of the period; see Callen 1982, p. 59; London 2004, pp. 45–46.
43 See Manchester 1987, pp. 86–89; Washington 1984, pp. 85–86 and 104–07.
44 Vollard 1978, pp. 76–77; for Degas's scheme to paint 'a portrait of a family in a frieze', see Nb. 18, pp. 123 and 204.
45 Huysmans, in Berson 1996, vol. 1, p. 291.
46 For a subtle discussion of these pictures, see Meller 1988–93, part 2, p. 262, in which the author likens the frieze format to a musical stave.
47 See, for example, L.502, L.503, L.596, L.597, L.597bis, L.761 and L.764 and BR.111.
48 Fruitema and Zoetmulder 1981, pp. 44 and 46; Bonn 1993, pp. 154–56; and Oettermann 1997, pp. 164 and 170.
49 Oettermann 1997, p. 158.
50 See Oettermann 1997, p. 170.
51 Fruitema and Zoetmulder 1981, pp. 22 and 44–46; and Oettermann 1997, p. 171.
52 For Degas's interest in books on this subject, see Reff 1976, vol. 1, p. 154.
53 See Janis 1984, p. 463.
54 We are indebted to the meticulous research into the photograph and its site by Thomas Yanul.
55 Shapero 2007, pp. 10 and 28.
56 Nb. 30, pp. 196 and 210.
57 See Brettell and McCullagh 1984, pp. 61–62.
58 D. Halévy 1995, p. 114.

CHAPTER 3

1   Guérin 1947, p. 117.
2   Huysmans, in Berson 1996, vol. 1, pp. 290–92.
3   Huysmans, in Berson 1996, vol. 1, p. 292.
4   Huysmans, in Berson 1996, vol. 1, p. 291.
5   Flor, Cardon and Huysmans, in Berson 1996, vol. 1, pp. 280, 271 and 290 respectively.
6   Huysmans, in Berson 1996, vol. 1, p. 292.
7   Huysmans, in Berson 1996, vol. 1, p. 292.
8   Baldick 2006, p. 94.
9   Moore 1918, p. 64; Sickert 1917, p. 185.
10 See Reff 1976; Druick and Zegers 1988; Glens Falls 2009; Kendall 2009.
11 See Chapter Two.
12 L.758.
13 See, for example, Detroit 2002, p. 147, fig. 162.
14 See Reff 1976, Chapter Four.
15 Moore 1890, p. 423; and Valéry 1960, p. 6.
16 Vente III: 139.3 and Vente III: 137.4.
17 This uncatalogued drawing was sold at the Hôtel des Ventes de Saumur on 26 March 1995 (lot 19).
18 Dagognet 1987, p. 24.
19 Ephrussi, in Berson 1996, vol. 1, p. 278.
20 See L.70, L.82, L.94 and L.124.
21 See New York 1993B, Chapter Three; and Washington 1998.
22 Duranty 1876, p. 45. For examples of such works, see L.368, L.419, J.1, J.209, J.217 and J.265.
23 See Detroit 2002, especially Chapter One.
24 Fillonneau, Blémont and Blavet, in Berson 1996, vol. 1, pp. 146, 63 and 62 respectively.
25 See Druick and Zegers 1988; Callen 1995; and Kendall 2009.
26 For Degas's education, see Loyrette 1989B, pp. 20–29.
27 See Loyrette 1989B, pp. 21, 28–29, 182 and 260–62; Paris 2004; Kendall 2009, pp. 306 and 313.
28 See Nb. 21, p. 4, and Nb. 23, p. 44; see also Druick and Zegers 1988, pp. 205–06; Callen 1995, pp. 22 and 105; and Kendall 2009, pp. 302–08.
29 Nb. 31, p. 81.
30 Marey 1878A; for a detailed bibliography, see Braun 1992, pp. 425–37.
31 Marey 1874, p. 27; for other early publications, see Braun 1992, pp. 425–28.
32 Marey 1878A, part 2, p. 289.
33 Tissandier 1878; Marey 1878B.
34 Suggested in Paris 1988, p. 386; see also p. 459.
35 See Muybridge n.d., pp. 64–95.
36 Hendricks 1975, p. 141; *The Athenaeum*, 18 March 1882, in Muybridge n.d., p. 77.
37 Marey 1873; Marey 1874.
38 Braun 1992, p. 45; Muybridge's endorsement of this event is implicit in Muybridge n.d., p. 47.
39 Braun 1992, p. 6.
40 Braun 1992, p. 6; Emmanuel 1896A and Emmanuel 1896B.
41 Dagognet 1987, p. 24.
42 Marey 1878A, part 1, p. 273.
43 Marey 1878A, part 2, p. 291.

44 Tissandier 1878, p. 23.
45 Philadelphia 2001, pp. 38–40 and 242–44.
46 *The Californian*, 1880, in Muybridge n.d., p. 50.
47 *Le Globe*, 27 November 1881 (incorrectly recorded as 'September' by Muybridge), in Muybridge n.d., p. 68.
48 Meunier 1881.
49 Haas 1976, p. 116.
50 *Family Herald*, 19 November 1881, and *American Register*, 3 December 1881, in Muybridge n.d., pp. 69 and 70, respectively.
51 Wolff 1881.
52 *American Register*, 3 December 1881, in Muybridge n.d., p. 70.
53 Lyons 1993, pp. 258–61.
54 *Galignani's Messenger*, 30 November 1881, in Muybridge n.d., p. 70.
55 *American Register*, 3 December 1881, in Muybridge n.d., p. 70.
56 Pencil copies of equestrian paintings by Meissonier can be found in Degas's notebooks; see Nb. 20, pp. 29 and 31; Nb. 22, pp. 123 and 127; and Nb. 23, p. 41. Degas's admiration for Meissonier's sculpture is reported in Valéry 1960, p. 42.
57 D. Halévy 1995, p. 111; Valéry 1960, p. 98.
58 For Gérôme, see Jeanniot 1933, part 1, pp. 171–72; for Detaille, see D. Halévy 1995, p. 111, and Valéry 1960, p. 69.
59 Claretie, in Berson 1996, vol. 1, p. 335.
60 Claretie, in Berson 1996, vol. 1, pp. 335 and 273.
61 *Le Globe*, 27 November 1881, in Muybridge n.d., p. 68, and Wolff 1881.
62 *Le Globe*, 27 November 1881, in Muybridge n.d., p. 69.
63 *Galignani's Messenger*, 30 November 1881, and *American Register*, 3 December 1881, in Muybridge n.d., p. 70.
64 For Meissonier and photography, see Lyons 1993, pp. 258–61.
65 See Duranty 1876, especially pp. 39–41.
66 Mantz, in Berson 1996, vol. 1, p. 358; 'Our Lady Correspondent', in Flint 1984, p. 43; and Trianon, in Berson 1996, vol. 1, p. 368.
67 Marta Braun, 'Animal Locomotion', in Washington 2010, pp. 271–83, p. 271.
68 Muybridge 1887, plates 196, 393 and 478.
69 Herbert et al. 2004, pp. 125–30.
70 Royal Academy of Arts Archive: RAA/SEC/6/40/1.
71 Royal Academy of Arts Archive: RAA/SEC/4/3/19 and RAA/SEC/6/40/2.
72 In Campbell, Kendall et al. 2009, p. 223, the original wax *Study of a Mustang* is identified as the earliest of Degas's surviving sculptures and dated to '1859–1860'.
73 See, for example, cat. 106; see also London 1996, pp. 254–75.
74 See Pingeot and Horvat 1991, pp. 151–93.
75 Thiébault-Sisson 1921.

76 Braun 1992, p. 54.
77 Marey 1882A and Marey 1882B.
78 Marey 1884.
79 Texts and photographs on this subject are in Marey 1887–89.
80 See Scharf 1962, Scharf 1968 and Coke 1972.
81 See Campbell, Kendall et al. 2009, p. 258–66.
82 Among many examples is the close link between plate 227 from *Animal Locomotion* and two Degas pastels, listed as 1097 and 1098 in the Lemoisne catalogue raisonné.
83 Paris 1977, p. 7.
84 For the waxes and bronzes of these works, see Campbell, Kendall et al. 2009, pp. 326–69, 354–57 and 358–61.
85 See, for example, L.653, L.654 and L.1131.
86 Muybridge 1887, plates 369 and 370.
87 An extensive bibliography can be found in Braun 1992, pp. 425–37.
88 Didi-Huberman and Mannoni 2004, p. 30.
89 See Braun 1992, pp. 138–42; Beaune 1995, pp. 128–29.
90 Didi-Huberman and Mannoni 2004, p. 31.
91 See also Chapter Four, p. 201.
92 See Braun 1992, p. 136.
93 Beaune 1991, pp. 134–36; see also Paris 2008.
94 See Paris 2008, p. 452.
95 For an incident of this kind involving Walter Sickert, see Chapter Four, pp. 215–18.
96 See, for example, London 1996, pp. 112–13.

CHAPTER 4

1 Guérin 1947, p. 117.
2 Fevre 1949, p. 93.
3 Fevre 1949, p. 105.
4 For the photographs by Hortense Howland, see Heilbrun 1989, pp. 163–66; for the Halévys' participation in Degas's photographic projects, see D. Halévy 1995, pp. 140 and 147–50.
5 New York 1998, p. 50, note 58.
6 We are most grateful to Françoise Heilbrun for drawing our attention to these new acquisitions.
7 See, for example, Terrasse 1983, nos 48–50, 55; Heilbrun 1989, p. 172; New York 1998, p. 139.
8 Newhall 1963, pp. 63–64.
9 D. Halévy 1995, pp. 179–80.
10 Guérin 1947, pp. 195–96.
11 Valéry 1960, p. 40.
12 D. Halévy 1995, p. 140.
13 D. Halévy 1995, pp. 149–50; the 1966 translation used here includes a minor error, reading 'morning' for 'evening' in the original French text.

14 For Primoli's photographs, see Paris 1984, figs 312, 319–20. For other photographs of Degas on relaxed occasions, see those by Hortense Howland in New York 1998, figs 3 and 52, and three by Albert Bartholomé in the Musée d'Orsay: PHO 1994 1, PHO 1994 8 and PHO 1994 45.
15 See New York 1993B, pp. 179–81.
16 T.40–46; Paris 1988, fig. 282.
17 See New York 1998, nos 23, 24 and 32.
18 Paris 1988, p. 535.
19 See New York 1998, nos 11 and 12.
20 See Newhall 1963, p. 64, and Paris 1988, p. 22.
21 See New York 1998, no. 1-37.
22 Bailly-Herzberg 1988, p. 63; Sickert 1917, p. 184.
23 Valéry 1960, pp. 69 and 70.
24 See Reff 1998, p. 79.
25 Reff 1968, p. 91. In Paris 1988, p. 569, the possibility that the dancer photographs were created as early as the 1870s is considered.
26 See New York 1998, nos 59 and 60.
27 Guérin 1947, p. 199.
28 New York 1998, p. 44.
29 See New York 1998, nos 42–44.
30 See Braun 1992, p. 434.
31 Marey 1894, pp. 104–07.
32 Marey 1894, p. 165.
33 Marey 1894, p. 181.
34 See Emmanuel 1896A and 1896B.
35 Emmanuel 1896A, p.(v).
36 Emmanuel 1896B, pp. 291 and 293.
37 Herbert et al 2004, p. 46, *Woman Dancing (Fancy)* (Kingston Museum, EM 6295) and *Woman, Fan Dance* (Kingston Museum, EM 6306-6310); p. 105, *Grecian Girl Dancing* (no. 34) and *A Couple Waltzing* (Kingston Museum, no. 35).
38 Solnit 2003, p. 228.
39 Muybridge 1887, plates 187–89 and 191–94 are entitled *Dancing (Fancy)*. For the identity of the woman in these works, see Haas 1976, p. 149; Herbert et al. 2004, p. 29; and Braun 2010, p. 208.
40 Muybridge 1887, plates 369 and 370.
41 See Detroit 2002, pp. 234–57.
42 See entries for these productions in Wolff 1962, Pitou 1990 and Wild 1987.
43 Valéry 1960, p. 41.
44 The scene may relate to the first act of Wagner's opera *Tannhäuser*, which famously featured groups of dancers crossing the stage with their arms raised; see Guest 1953, p. 43.
45 For Degas's late pastel technique, see London 1996, pp. 89–105.
46 Vollard 1986, p. 89.
47 Valéry 1960, p. 19.
48 Lafond 1918–19, p. 114; Havemeyer 1961, p. 255.
49 Guérin 1947, pp. 226 and 229.
50 Duret 1894, p. 205.

51 Duret 1894, p. 206.
52 Duret 1894, p. 208.
53 Detroit 2002, pp. 224–29.
54 Guérin 1947, p. 206; see also London 1996, p. 170.
55 See, for example, Michel 1919, pp. 461 and 630, but also p. 468.
56 See R.XXXIV and L.XVI; see also Campbell, Kendall et al. 2009, p. 301. For related works on paper, see L.689–91, RS.53 and RS.54, Vente IV: 257a and Vente IV: 257b, and Nb. 37, p. 5; see also Detroit 2002, p. 174.
57 See London 1996, pp. 33–34.
58 R.LXVI.
59 Sickert 1917, p. 185; in the variant account in Sickert 1923, p. 6, the artist specified that the work was 'Grand Arabesque, deuxième temps' (cat. 86) (R.XXXVI).
60 See London 1996, pp. 77–87 and 99.
61 L.653, L.654 and L.1131.
62 See Haas 1976, p. 117; Herbert et al. 2004, pp. 109–10.
63 Marey 1874, p. 137.
64 See Solnit 2003, pp. 228–31.
65 Braun 1992, pp. 150–51.
66 Jeanniot 1933, part 1, p. 174. In a letter of August 1889, Degas suggested that Albert Bartholomé should see 'the water railway at the Invalides' that was part of the Exposition Universelle; see Guérin 1947, p. 138.
67 Anon., Le Radical, 30 December 1895, in Banda and Moure 2008, pp. 39–40; see also Borgé 2004, Chapters Three and Four.
68 Anon., La Poste, 30 December 1895, in Banda and Moure 2008, p. 41.
69 These and many other parallels are illustrated in Lyons 2005.
70 Duranty 1876, p. 45.
71 Claretie 1896, p. 43.
72 Claretie 1896, p. 43.
73 Lemoisne 1946–49, vol. 1, p. 155.
74 Barazzetti 1936, part 1, p. 3.
75 Barazzetti 1936, part 3, p. 2.
76 See T.40–45 and Lemoisne 1946–49, plate opposite p. 154, ill. 'c'. Two outdoor portraits of Degas were also taken on this occasion; see T.46 and ill. 'a' in the plate cited here. The resemblance of the sequence to a 'film' was noted in Hoctin 1960, p. 38.
77 Pénault 1990, p. 7.
78 Fevre 1949, p. 142.
79 Vollard 1986, p. 86; for a more detailed account, see Guitry 1979, pp. 121–24.
80 Paris 2004, p. 68.
81 See New York 1998, no. 32a, and an uncatalogued photograph in the Musée d'Orsay, accession no. PHO 2004 4.
82 For Zambelli, see Gaumont-Pathé 0000GB 00951 BOB 1/ 159392.

83 See Gaumont Pathé 0000GPIM 00024/275545, 0000GPRIM 00018/275539, 0000GPRIM 00016/275537. For Mérode, see Detroit 2002, pp. 244 and 251.
84 Soria 1897, p. 255–56.
85 Lumière nos 113, 1091; for the Nadar film see Gaumont-Pathé 0000UPRIM 00007 and Paul Nadar, Programme Nadar – 1896, excerpt: 'Danse Russe', Cinémathèque française, posted online at http://www.europafilmtreasures.eu/ fiche_technique.htm?ID=311.
86 See Manet 1979, p. 238.
87 In 1893, for example, Fête Russe was mounted at the Paris Opéra and Léo Delibes's opera Kassya premiered at the Opéra-Comique.
88 Bixenstine 1987, pp. 114–23.
89 Bixenstine 1987, pp. 113 and 150.
90 Bixenstine 1987, p. 117.
91 Soria 1897, p. 6; Vuillier 1898, pp. 2 and 207.
92 New York 1993B, Chapters Six and Seven.
93 Bixenstine 1987, pp. 103–34.
94 Valéry 1960, pp. 8 and 84.
95 See for example, L.1200 and L.1394.
96 Sickert 1917, p. 185.
97 Geffroy 1894, p. 173; see also DeVonyar and Kendall 2007, p. 33.
98 Sickert 1947, p. 150.
99 See, for example, Roosa 1982 and Childs 2000.
100 For Degas's approach to 'series', see London 1996, pp. 103–04.
101 See Ives et al. 1997.
102 Guérin 1947, pp. 226–27.
103 See Paris 1988, p. 611, and London 1996, pp. 294–95.
104 New York 1998, p. 51, note 131.

SOME DOCUMENTED LINKS BETWEEN DEGAS AND PHOTOGRAPHY

1 Paris 1988, p. 34.
2 Reproduced in L'Amour de l'Art, July 1931: see Lemoisne 1946–49, vol. 1, p. 217; Paris 1988, pp. 34, 104; New York 1998, p. 60.
3 Lemoisne 1946–49, vol. 1, pp. 62, 217.
4 Reff 1985, Notebook 18, p. 31.
5 Reff 1985, Notebook 18, pp. 100, 103.
6 Paris 1988, p. 104; Lemoisne 1946–49, vol. 1, p. 217.
7 L.89; see Scharf 1968, pp. 187–88.
8 L.138.
9 Dumas 1988, p. 27; Detroit 2002, pp. 197–98.
10 For a similar photograph, see Reff 2006, p. 50. For other photographs taken of Degas's pictures, see the collection of the Musée d'Orsay.
11 Guérin 1947, p. 22.

12 Lemoisne 1946–49, vol. 1, p. 62.
13 Reff 1974, pp. 11, 33.
14 Detroit 2002, p. 81; see figs 6 and 7 in the present volume.
15 See fig. 2.
16 See Chapter Two, note 41.
17 See Paris 1988, pp. 239–40.
18 Reff 2006, p. 50.
19 Berson 1996, vol. 1, p. 70.
20 Claretie 1876.
21 Paris 1988, p. 214.
22 Guérin 1947, p. 44.
23 Tissandier 1878.
24 Berson 1996, vol. 1, p. 205.
25 Guérin 1947, p. 57.
26 See Chapter Three.
27 See Marey 1882A and Marey 1882B.
28 L.796.
29 New York 1998, pp. 18–19, 60–63; Providence 2005, pp. 6–8, 48–50, 57.
30 Providence 2005, p. 13.
31 Guérin 1949, p. 108.
32 New York 1998, pp. 38–40.
33 Reff 1969, p. 288.
34 New York 1998, pp. 20, 64.
35 Muybridge 1887.
36 Braun 1992, p. 189.
37 London 1996, p. 16; New York 1998, pp. 61 and 65.
38 Paris 1988, p. 392.
39 New York 1993B, pp. 148, 155.
40 New York 1993B, p. 180.
41 Guérin 1949, pp. 195–96; Newhall 1963.
42 New York 1998, p. 20.
43 Fevre 1949, pp. 91–94.
44 Newhall 1963.
45 New York 1998, nos 34–37.
46 Fevre 1949, p. 104.
47 D. Halévy 1995, pp. 139–40.
48 Valéry 1960, pp. 40–41.
49 New York 1998, no. 6b; Terrasse 1983, p. 10.
50 New York 1998, nos 42–44.
51 New York 1998, nos 40–41.
52 New York 1998, nos 3, 19–25.
53 Paris 1988, p. 540.
54 Reff 1998.
55 Fevre 1949, p. 105.
56 Reff 1968, p. 91.
57 D. Halévy 1960, p. 100.
58 Terrasse 1983, pp. 84–87, and Lemoisne 1946–49, vol. 1, p. 154 (see also p. 219, where they are dated 'vers 1903').
59 Thiébault-Sisson 1921.
60 Paris 1988, p. 492.
61 New York 1998, no. 33.
62 Paris 1988, p. 496; dated '1915' in Lemoisne 1946–49, vol. 1, p. 220.
63 See Chapter Four, pp. 223–24.
64 Collection of the Musée d'Orsay, Paris; see London 1996, p. 55.

BIBLIOGRAPHY AND SOURCES

Adhémar and Cachin 1974
Jean Adhémar and Françoise Cachin, *Degas: The Complete Etchings, Lithographs and Monotypes*, London, 1974

Adice 1859
G. Leopold Adice, *Théorie de la gymnastique de la Danse Théâtrale*, Paris, 1859

Bailly-Herzberg 1988
Janine Bailly-Herzberg (ed.), *Correspondance de Camille Pissarro, III: 1891–1894*, Paris, 1988

Baldick 2006
Robert Baldick, *The Life of J.-K. Huysmans*, London, 2006; first edition, Oxford, 1955

Banda and Moure 2008
Daniel Banda and José Moure (eds), *Le Cinéma: naissance d'un art; premiers écrits, 1895–1920*, Paris, 2008

Barazzetti 1936
S. Barazzetti, 'Degas et ses amis Valpinçon', *Beaux-Arts*, part 1, 190, 21 August 1936, pp. 1–4; part 2, 191, 4 September 1936, pp. 1–2; part 3, 192, 28 September 1936, pp. 1–2

Baudelaire 1961
Charles Baudelaire, *Œuvres complètes*, Claude Pichois (ed.), Paris, 1961

Beaumont 1949
Cyril Beaumont, *The Complete Book of Ballets*, London, 1949

Beaune 1991
Marion Leuba et al., *La Passion du mouvement au XIXe siècle: Hommage à Etienne-Jules Marey*, exh. cat., Chapelle de l'Oratoire, Beaune, 1991

Beaune 1995
Marion Leuba, *Marey: pionnier de la synthèse du mouvement*, exh. cat., Musée Marey, Beaune, 1995

Benfield 1864
T. Benfield, 'Revue photographique', *Le Scientifique: journals des sciences pures et appliques*, 6, 185, 15 September 1864, pp. 796–800

Bernard 1866
Léo de Bernard, 'La Photosculpture', *Le Monde illustré*, 19, 505, 15 December 1866, p. 399

Bernay 1890
Berthe Bernay, *La Danse au théâtre*, Paris, 1890

Berson 1996
Ruth Berson (ed.), *The New Painting, Impressionism, 1874–1886*, 2 vols, San Francisco, 1996

Bixenstine 1987
Lisa R. Bixenstine, *Edgar Degas's 'Russian Dancers' Series (1897–1899): Their Dating, Pastel Techniques, and Their Content within His Late Period 1885–1908*, PhD dissertation, Ohio State University, 1987

Blasis 1830
Carlo Blasis, *The Code of Terpsichore; The Art of Dancing: Comprising Its Theory and Practice and a History of Its Rise and Progress, from the Earliest Times...*, translated by R. Barton, London, 1830; reprinted New York, 1976

Boggs 1962
Jean Sutherland Boggs, *Portraits by Degas*, Berkeley, 1962

Bonn 1993
Marie-Louise van Plessen and Ulrich Giersch, *Sehsucht: das Panorama als Massenunterhaltung des 19. Jahrhunderts*, exh. cat., Kunst- und Ausstellungshalle der Bundesrepublik Deutschland, Bonn, 1993

Borgé 2004
Guy and Marjorie Borgé, *Les Lumières: Antoine, Auguste, Louis et les autres. L'invention du cinéma, les autochromes*, Lyons, 2004

Brame and Reff 1984
Philippe Brame and Theodore Reff, *Degas et son œuvre: A Supplement*, New York, 1984

Braun 1992
Marta Braun, *Picturing Time: The Work of Etienne-Jules Marey (1830–1904)*, Chicago, 1992

Braun 2010
Marta Braun, 'Animal Locomotion', in Washington 2010, pp. 271–83

Brettell and McCullagh 1984
Richard R. Brettell and Suzanne Folds McCullagh, *Degas in the Art Institute of Chicago*, Chicago, 1984

Browse 1949
Lillian Browse, *Degas Dancers*, London, 1949

Brussels 1994
Benoît Peeters, *Les Métamorphoses de Nadar*, exh. cat., Botanique, Centre Culture de la Communauté Française, Brussels, 1994–95

Buerger 1978
Janet Buerger, 'Degas's Solarised and Negative Photographs: A Look at Unorthodox Classicism', *Image*, 21, 2, June 1978, pp. 17–23

Buerger and Shapiro 1981
Janet Buerger and Barbara Stern Shapiro, 'A Note on Degas's Use of Daguerreotype Plates', *Print Collector's Newsletter*, September/October 1981, pp. 103–06

Callen 1982
Anthea Callen, *Techniques of the Impressionists*, London, 1982

Callen 1995
Anthea Callen, *The Spectacular Body*,
New Haven and London, 1995

Cambridge 2009
Diana Donald and Jane Munro (eds), *Endless Forms: Charles Darwin, Natural Science and the Visual Arts*, exh. cat., Fitzwilliam Museum, Cambridge, and Yale Center for British Art, New Haven, 2009

Campbell, Kendall et al. 2009
Sara Campbell (ed.) and Richard Kendall, with Daphne S. Barbour and Shelley G. Sturman, *Degas in the Norton Simon Museum: Nineteenth-century Art, Volume II*, Pasadena, 2009

Charbonnel 1899
Raoul Charbonnel, *La Danse. Comment on dansait, comment on danse*, Paris, 1899

Childs 2000
Elizabeth Childs, 'Habits of the Eye: Degas, Photography, and Modes of Vision', in Dallas 2000, pp. 68–87

Claretie 1876
Jules Claretie, 'Revue théâtrale', *La Presse*, 26 June 1876, pp. 1–2

Claretie 1896
Jules Claretie, 'La Vie à Paris', *Le Temps*, 13 February 1896, p. 2, in Banda and Moure 2008, pp. 42–43

Clark 1984
T. J. Clark, *The Painting of Modern Life: Paris in the Art of Manet and His Followers*, Princeton, 1984

Coke 1972
Van Deren Coke, *The Painter and Photograph, from Delacroix to Warhol*, Albuquerque, 1972

Dagognet 1987
François Dagognet, *Etienne-Jules Marey: le passion de la trace*, Paris, 1987

Dallas 2000
Dorothy Kosinski (ed.), *The Artist and Camera: Degas to Picasso*, exh. cat., Dallas Museum of Art and San Francisco Museum of Modern Art, 2000

Danicourt 1864
Léon Danicourt, 'Science appliqués, conférence de M. l'Abbé Moigno', *Revue des cours scientifique*, 1, 32, 9 July 1864, pp. 442–47

Detroit 2002
Jill DeVonyar and Richard Kendall, *Degas and the Dance*, exh. cat., Detroit Institute of Arts and Philadelphia Museum of Art, 2002–03

DeVonyar 2008
Jill DeVonyar, 'Re-presenting the Dance: Degas's Inheritance and Legacy', in Portland 2008, pp. 199–233

DeVonyar and Kendall 2003
Jill DeVonyar and Richard Kendall, 'The Class of 1881: Degas, Drawing, and the Little Dancer Aged Fourteen', *Master Drawings*, 41, 1, 2003, pp. 151–62

DeVonyar and Kendall 2007
Jill DeVonyar and Richard Kendall, 'Dancers by Edgar Degas', *Princeton Art Museum Review*, 66, 2007, pp. 31–40

Didi-Huberman and Mannoni 2004
Georges Didi-Huberman and Laurent Mannoni, *Mouvements de l'air: Etienne-Jules Marey, photographe des fluids*, Paris, 2004

Drost 1985
Wolfgang Drost, 'La Photosculpture entre art industriel et artisanat, la réussite de François Willème', *Gazette des Beaux-Arts*, 106, October 1985, pp. 113–29

Druick 1989
Douglas Druick, 'La Petite Danseuse et les criminels: Degas moraliste?', in Musée d'Orsay 1989, pp. 225–50

Druick and Zegers 1988
Douglas W. Druick and Peter Zegers, 'Scientific Realism, 1873–1881', in Paris 1988, pp. 197–211

Dumas 1988
Ann Dumas, *Degas's Mlle Fiocre in Context: A Study of 'Portrait de Mlle E. F. à propos du ballet La Source'*, Brooklyn, 1988

Duranty 1876
Edmond Duranty, *The New Painting: Concerning the Group of Artists Exhibiting at the Durand-Ruel Galleries*, Paris, 1876, translated in San Francisco 1986, pp. 37–49

Duret 1894
Théodore Duret, 'Degas', *The Art Journal*, 1894, pp. 204–08

Duval 1875
Georges Duval, *Terpsichore, petit guide à l'usage des amateurs de ballet, par un abonné de l'Opéra [Georges Duval]. Précédé d'une préface de Mlle Rita Sangalli*, Paris, 1875

Emmanuel 1896A
Maurice Emmanuel, *La Danse Grecque antique d'après les monuments figurés*, Paris, 1896; facsimile, Paris and Geneva, 1984

Emmanuel 1896B
Maurice Emmanuel, 'La Danse Grecque antique', *Gazette des Beaux-Arts*, 15, 463, April 1896, pp. 291–308

Fevre 1949
Jeanne Fevre, *Mon oncle Degas*, Geneva, 1949

Figuier 1862
Louis Figuier, 'La Photo-sculpture', *Année scientifique et industrielle*, 6, 1862, pp. 432–34

Flint 1984
Kate Flint, *Impressionists in England: The Critical Response*, London and Boston, 1984

Fruitema and Zoetmulder 1981
Evelyn J. Fruitema and Paul A. Zoetmulder, *The Panorama Phenomenon: Subject of a Permanent Exhibition, Organised on the Occasion of the Centennial of the Mesdag Panorama in the Hague which was inaugurated on the 1st of August 1881; Catalogue in the Shape of an Illustrated Historiography*, The Hague, 1981

Gall 1997
Jean-Luc Gall, 'Photo-sculpture', *Etudes photographiques*, 3, November 1997, posted online 13 November 2002, www.etudesphotographiques.revues.org/index95.html

Gautier 1864A
Théophile Gautier, 'Photosculpture', extract from *Le Moniteur universel*, 4 January 1864

Gautier 1864B
Théophile Gautier, 'Photosculpture,' *Le Monde illustré*, 8, 401, 17 December 1864, p. 398; illustrations pp. 396 and 397

Gautier 1986
Théophile Gautier, *Gautier on Dance*, Ivor Guest (ed.), London, 1986

Geffroy 1894
Gustave Geffroy, 'Degas', *La Vie artistique*, 1894, pp. 147–80

Gerstein 1982
Marc Gerstein, 'Degas's Fans', *Art Bulletin*, 64, 1, March 1982, pp. 105–18

Glens Falls 2009
Jill DeVonyar and Richard Kendall with
Erin B. Coe, *Degas and Music*, exh. cat.,
The Hyde Collection, Glens Falls, N.Y., 2009

Goncourt 1956
Edmond and Jules de Goncourt, *Journal:
Mémoires de la vie littéraire*, 4 vols, Paris,
1956

Guérin 1945
Marcel Guérin (ed.), *Lettres Degas*, Paris, 1945

Guérin 1947
Marcel Guérin (ed.), *Degas Letters*,
trans. Marguerite Kay, Oxford, 1947

Guest 1953
Ivor Guest, *The Ballet of the Second Empire*,
London, 1953

Guest 1966
Ivor Guest, *The Romantic Ballet in Paris*,
Middletown, Conn., 1966

Guest 1976
Ivor Guest, *Le Ballet de l'Opéra de Paris*, Paris,
1976

Guest 1984
Ivor Guest, *Jules Perrot, Master of the
Romantic Ballet*, London, 1984

Guitry 1979
Sacha Guitry, *Le Petit Carnet rouge
et les autres souvenirs inédits*, Paris, 1979

Haas 1976
Robert Bartlett Haas, *Muybridge:
Man in Motion*, Berkeley, 1976

D. Halévy 1932
Daniel Halévy, *Pays parisiens*, Paris, 1932

D. Halévy 1938
Daniel Halévy, 'Souvenirs de famille',
Revue de Musicologie, 19, 68, November 1938,
pp. 129–32

D. Halévy 1960
Daniel Halévy, *Degas parle…*, Paris, 1960

D. Halévy 1966
Daniel Halévy, *My Friend Degas*,
trans. by Mina Curtiss, London, 1966

D. Halévy 1995
Daniel Halévy, *Degas parle*, Paris, 1995

L. Halévy 1883
Ludovic Halévy, *La Famille Cardinal*, Paris,
1883

Havemeyer 1961
Louisine Havemeyer, *Sixteen to Sixty:
Memoirs of a Collector*, New York, 1961

Heilbrun 1989
Françoise Heilbrun, 'Sur les photographies de
Degas', in Musée d'Orsay 1989, pp. 159–80

Heilbrun 2008
Françoise Heilbrun (ed.), *A History of
Photography: The Musée d'Orsay Collection
1839–1925*, Paris, 2008

Hendricks 1975
Gordon Hendricks, *Eadweard Muybridge:
The Father of the Motion Picture*, London, 1975

Herbert 1988
Robert L. Herbert, *Impressionism:
Art, Leisure, and Parisian Society*,
New Haven, 1988

Herbert et al. 2004
Stephen Herbert (ed.) with Marta Braun,
Paul Hill and Anne McCormack, *Eadweard
Muybridge: The Kingston Museum Bequest*,
Hastings, 2004

Hermant 1864
A. Hermant, 'La Photosculpture',
Le Monde illustré, 15, 401, 31 December 1864,
pp. 426–27; illustrations pp. 429 and 432

Heylli 1875
Georges d'Heylli, *Foyers et coulisses:
Histoire anecdotique de tous les théâtres
de Paris. Opéra*, Paris, 1875

Hoctin 1960
Luce Hoctin, 'Degas photographe', *L'Œil*, 65,
May 1960, pp. 36–43

Ives et al. 1997
*The Private Collection of Edgar Degas:
A Summary Catalogue*, Colta Ives,
Susan Alyson Stein and Julie Steiner et al.,
The Metropolitan Museum of Art, New York,
1997–98

Janis 1968
Eugenia Parry Janis, *Degas Monotypes*,
Fogg Art Museum, Cambridge, Mass., 1968

Janis 1984
Eugenia Parry Janis, 'Edgar Degas's
Photographic Theater', in Paris 1984,
pp. 451–86

Jeanniot 1933
Georges Jeanniot, 'Souvenirs de Degas',
Revue Universelle, 55, 14, part 1, 15 October
1933, pp. 152–74; part 2, 1 November 1933,
pp. 280–304

Kahane et al. 1998
Martine Kahane, Delphine Pinasa, Willfride
Piollet and Sara Campbell, 'Enquête sur la
Petite Danseuse de quatorze ans de Degas',
48/14: *La Revue du Musée d'Orsay*, 7,
Autumn 1998, pp. 48–68

Kendall et al. 1985
Richard Kendall (ed.), Anthea Callen,
Anna Gruetzner and Richard Thomson,
Degas, 1834–1984, Manchester, 1985

Kendall 1988
Richard Kendall, 'Degas and the Contingency
of Vision', *Burlington Magazine*, 130,
March 1988, pp. 180–97

Kendall 2009
Richard Kendall, 'Monet and the Monkeys:
The Impressionist Encounter with Darwinism',
in Cambridge 2009, pp. 293–316

Kendall and DeVonyar 2000
Richard Kendall and Jill DeVonyar, 'Degas's
Two Dancers on Stage: The Mozart
Connection', *The British Art Journal*, 2, 2,
Winter 2000/2001, pp. 78–80

Kendall and Pollock 1992
Richard Kendall and Griselda Pollock (eds),
*Dealing with Degas: Representations
of Women and the Politics of Vision*,
London, 1992

Lafond 1918–19
Paul Lafond, *Degas*, 2 vols, Paris, 1918–19

Lafont-Couturier 1998
Héléne Lafont-Couturier, *Gérôme*, Paris, 1998

Lemoisne 1912
Paul-André Lemoisne, *L'Art de notre temps:
Degas*, Paris, 1912

Lemoisne 1946–49
Paul-André Lemoisne, *Degas et son œuvre*,
4 vols, Paris, 1946–49

Lipton 1986
Eunice Lipton, *Looking into Degas: Uneasy
Images of Women and Modern Life*, Berkeley,
1986

London 1996
Richard Kendall, *Degas: Beyond
Impressionism*, exh. cat., National Gallery,
London, and Art Institute of Chicago,
1996–97

London 2004
David Bomford, *Degas: Art in the Making*,
exh. cat., National Gallery, London, 2004-05

Los Angeles 1999
Gordon Baldwin and Judith Keller, *Nadar–Warhol, Paris–New York: Photography and Fame*, exh. cat., J. Paul Getty Museum, Los Angeles, Andy Warhol Museum, Pittsburgh, and Baltimore Museum of Art, 1999–2000

Loyrette 1989A
Henri Loyrette, 'Degas à l'Opéra', in Musée d'Orsay 1989, pp. 46–64

Loyrette 1989B
Henri Loyrette, *Degas*, Paris, 1989

Lyons 1993
Philippe Durey and Constance Cain Hungerford, *Ernest Meissonier: Rétrospective*, exh. cat., Musée des Beaux-Arts, Lyons, 1993

Lyons 2005
Sylvie Ramond (ed.), Richard R. Brettell, Richard Shiff, Françoise Heilbrun et al., *Impressionnisme et naissance du cinématographe*, exh. cat., Musée des Beaux-Arts, Lyons, 2005

Mahalin 1887
Paul Mahalin, *Les Demoiselles de l'Opéra [par] un vieil abonné*, Paris, 1887

Mallarmé 1998
Stéphane Mallarmé, *Ecrits sur l'art / Stéphane Mallarmé: Présentation, notes, bibliographie et chronologie par Michel Draguet*, Paris, 1998

Manchester 1987
Richard Thomson, *The Private Degas*, exh. cat., Whitworth Art Gallery, Manchester, and Fitzwilliam Museum, Cambridge, 1987

Manet 1979
Julie Manet, *Journal (1893–1899)*, Paris, 1979

Manet 1987
Julie Manet, *Growing Up with the Impressionists: The Diary of Julie Manet*, translated and edited with an introduction by Rosalind de Boland Roberts and Jane Roberts, London, 1987

Marey n.d.
Etienne-Jules Marey, *Album: Marey*, unpublished manuscript album, Collège de France, Paris: no. CXII Marey 4D

Marey 1873
Etienne-Jules Marey, *La Machine animale: locomotion terrestre et aérienne*, Paris, 1873

Marey 1874
Etienne-Jules Marey, *Animal Mechanism: A Treatise on Terrestrial and Aerial Locomotion*, London, 1874

Marey 1878A
Etienne-Jules Marey, 'Moteurs animés: Experiences de physiologie graphique', *La Nature*, part 1, 278, 28 September 1878, pp. 273–78; part 2, 279, 5 October 1878, pp. 289–95

Marey 1878B
Etienne-Jules Marey, 'Correspondance', letter to the editor, Gaston Tissandier, *La Nature*, 7, 292, 28 December 1878, p. 54

Marey 1882A
Etienne-Jules Marey, 'Le Fusil photographique', *La Nature*, 464, 22 July 1882, pp. 115–16

Marey 1882B
Etienne-Jules Marey, 'The Photography of Movement', *Scientific American*, 47, 9 September 1882, p. 166

Marey 1882–86
Etienne-Jules Marey, *Station Physiologique, méthodes, installations, et instruments*, unpublished manuscript album, 1882–86, Collège de France, Paris: Institut Marey no. 162

Marey 1884
Etienne-Jules Marey, 'Des Forces utiles dans la locomotion', *Comptes rendues du Congrès Internationale d'hygiène et démographie*, 1884, vol. 1, pp. 110–32

Marey 1886
Etienne-Jules Marey, *Station Physiologique II, Locomotion Humaine*, unpublished manuscript album, 1886, Collège de France, Paris: Institut Marey no. 159

Marey 1887–89
Etienne-Jules Marey, *Station physiologique IV, mélanges, 1887-89*, unpublished manuscript album, Collège de France, Paris

Marey 1888
Etienne-Jules Marey, 'The Mechanism of the Flight of Birds', *Nature*, 37, 1888, pp. 369–74

Marey 1891
Etienne-Jules Marey, 'L'Analyse des mouvements par la photographie', *Paris-Photographe*, 1, 1891, pp. 5–12

Marey 1892
Etienne-Jules Marey, *La Photographie du mouvement*, Paris, 1892

Marey 1893
Etienne-Jules Marey, 'Photographie expérimentale', *Paris-Photographe*, 3, 1893, pp. 95–104

Marey 1894
Etienne-Jules Marey, *Le Mouvement*, Paris, 1894

McCauley 1994
Elizabeth Ann McCauley, *Industrial Madness: Commercial Photography in Paris, 1848-1871*, New Haven, 1994

Meller 1988–93
Marie Kálmán Meller, 'Exercises in and Around Degas's Classrooms', *Burlington Magazine*, part 1, March 1988, pp. 198–215; part 2, April 1990, pp. 253–65; part 3, July 1993, pp. 452–62

Mérode 1985
Cléo de Mérode, *Le Ballet de ma vie*, Paris, 1985

Meunier 1881
Stanislas Meunier, 'Chronique', *La Nature*, 9, 436, 8 October 1881, p. 303

Michel 1919
Alice Michel, 'Degas et son modèle', *Mercure de France*, 16 February 1919, pp. 457–78, 623–39

Millard 1979
Charles W. Millard, *The Sculpture of Edgar Degas*, Princeton, 1979

Millet 1979
Jacqueline Millet, 'La Famille Mante, une trichromie, Degas, l'Opéra', *Gazette des Beaux-Arts*, 94, 1979, pp. 105–12

Minervino and Lassaigne 1974
Fiorella Minervino and Jacques Lassaigne, *Tout l'œuvre peint de Degas*, Paris, 1974

Moigno 1861
François Moigno, 'Photo-Sculpture, Art nouveau imaginé par M. Willème', *Cosmos*, 18, 1861, pp. 547–50

Moigno 1863
François Moigno, 'Nouvelles et faits divers', *Les Mondes: revue hebdomaire des sciences et leurs applications…*, 1, 7, March 1863, pp. 169–76

Monde Artiste 1866
Le Monde Artiste, 17 November 1866

Monneret 1978–79
Sophie Monneret, *L'Impressionisme et son époque: Dictionnaire international*, 2 vols, Paris, 1978–79

Montucci 1863A
Henry Montucci, 'Travaux des académies et sociétés savants…', *Revue contemporaine*, 2, 31, January–February 1863, pp. 385–401

Montucci 1863B
Henry Montucci, 'Travaux des académies et sociétés savants…', *Revue contemporaine*, 2, 67, March–April 1863, pp. 818–19

Moore 1890
George Moore, 'Degas: The Painter of Modern Life', *Magazine of Art*, 13, 1890, pp. 416–25

Moore 1891
George Moore, *Impressions and Opinions*, New York, 1891

Moore 1918
George Moore, 'Memories of Degas', *Burlington Magazine*, 32, 1, part 1, 178, January 1918, pp. 22–29; part 2, 179, February 1918, pp. 63–65

Moreau-Nélaton 1931
Etienne Moreau-Nélaton, 'Deux Heures avec Degas', *L'Amour de l'Art*, 12, July 1931, pp. 267–70

Morisot 1957
Berthe Morisot, *Berthe Morisot Correspondence*, Denis Rouart (ed.), trans. Betty W. Hubbard (1957), with introduction and notes by Kathleen Adler and Tamar Garb, London, 1986

Musée d'Orsay 1989
Musée d'Orsay, *Degas inédit*, Paris, 1989

Muybridge 1881
Eadweard Muybridge, *The Attitudes of Animals in Motion: A Series of Photographs Illustrating the Consecutive Positions Assumed by Animals Performing Various Movements*, Berkeley, California, 1881

Muybridge 1887
Eadweard Muybridge, *Animal Locomotion. An Electro-photographic Investigation of Consecutive Phases of Animal Movements, 1872–1885*, Philadelphia, 1887

Muybridge n.d.
Eadweard Muybridge, *Scrapbook*, unpublished, Muybridge Museum, Kingston-upon-Thames

National Gallery 2004
Art in the Making: Degas, London, 2004

Newhall 1963
Beaumont Newhall, 'Degas, photographe amateur', *Gazette des Beaux-Arts*, 61, 1963, pp. 61–64 (originally published as 'Degas: Amateur Photographer, Eight Unpublished Letters by the Famous Painter Written on a Photographic Vacation', *Image*, 6, June 1956, pp. 124–26)

New York 1993A
Alice Cooney Frelinghuysen et al., *Splendid Legacy: The Havemeyer Collection*, exh. cat., The Metropolitan Museum of Art, New York, 1993

New York 1993B
Richard Kendall, *Degas Landscapes*, exh. cat., Metropolitan Museum of Art, New York and Museum of Fine Arts, Houston, 1993

New York 1997
Ann Dumas, Colta Ives, Susan Alyson Stein and Gary Tinterow, *The Private Collection of Edgar Degas*, exh. cat., The Metropolitan Museum of Art, New York, 1997–98

New York 1998
Malcolm Daniel with Eugenia Parry and Theodore Reff, *Edgar Degas, Photographer*, exh. cat., The Metropolitan Museum of Art, New York, J. Paul Getty Museum, Los Angeles, and Bibliothèque nationale de France, Paris, 1998

Northampton, Mass. 1979
Linda Muehlig, *Degas and the Dance*, exh. cat., Smith College Museum of Art, Northampton, Mass., 1979

Oettermann 1997
Stephan Oettermann, *The Panorama: History of a Mass Medium*, trans. Deborah Lucas Schneider, New York, 1997

Omaha 1998
Richard Kendall with Douglas W. Druick and Arthur Beale, *Degas and the Little Dancer*, exh. cat., Joslyn Art Museum, Omaha, Sterling and Francine Clark Art Institute, Williamstown, and Baltimore Museum of Art, 1998–99

Paris 1977
Michel Frizot, *E. J. Marey 1830–1904: La photographie du mouvement*, exh. cat., Centre national d'art et de culture Georges Pompidou, Musée national d'art moderne, Paris, 1977–78

Paris 1984
Maurice Guillaud et al., *Degas: Form and Space*, exh. cat., Centre Culturel du Marais, Paris, 1984–85

Paris 1988
Jean Sutherland Boggs et al., *Degas*, exh. cat., Galeries Nationales du Grand Palais, Paris, National Gallery of Canada, Ottawa, and Metropolitan Museum of Art, New York, 1988–89

Paris 1995
Maria Morris Hambourg, Françoise Heilbrun and Philippe Néagu, with contributions by Sylvie Aubenas et al., *Nadar*, exh. cat., Musée d'Orsay, Paris, and The Metropolitan Museum of Art, New York, 1995

Paris 2004
Solange Thierry et al., *Au coeur de l'impressionnisme: la famille Rouart*, exh. cat., Musée de la Vie Romantique, Paris, 2004

Paris 2008
Philippe Comar, *Figures du corps: une leçon d'anatomie à l'école des beaux-arts*, exh. cat., Ecole nationale Supérieure des Beaux-Arts, Paris, 2008–09

Parville 1862
Henri de Parville, 'Photographie omnibus', *Causeries scientifiques, découvertes et inventions*, Paris, 1862, pp. 162–63

Parville 1863
Henri de Parville, 'Revue des sciences', *Le Constitutionnel*, 5 April 1863, pp. 1–2

Pénault 1990
Pierre-Jean Pénault, 'Monsieur Degas à la campagne', *Le Pays d'Auge*, 40, 6, June 1990, pp. 3–16

Philadelphia 2001
Darrel Sewell et al., *Thomas Eakins*, exh. cat., Philadelphia Museum of Art, Musée d'Orsay, Paris, and Metropolitan Museum of Art, New York, 2001–02

Pichot 1864
Amédée Pichot, 'Chroniques et Bulletin Bilbiographique', *Revue britannique*, 3, May 1864, pp. 253–60

Pickvance 1962
Ronald Pickvance, 'Henry Hill: An Untypical Victorian Collector', *Apollo*, 76, 10, December 1962, pp. 789–91

Pickvance 1963A
Ronald Pickvance, 'L'Absinthe in England', *Apollo*, 77, 15, May 1963, pp. 395–96

Pickvance 1963B
Ronald Pickvance, 'Degas's Dancers: 1872–1876', *Burlington Magazine*, 105, 723, June 1963, pp. 256–66

Pingeot and Horvat 1991
Ann Pingeot and Frank Horvat,
Degas Sculptures, Paris, 1991

Pitou 1990
Spire Pitou, *The Paris Opéra: An Encyclopedia
of Operas, Ballets, Composers, and
Performers: Growth and Grandeur, 1815–1914*,
2 vols, Westport, Conn., 1990

Portland 2008
Annette Dixon (ed.), *The Dancer: Degas,
Forain, Toulouse-Lautrec*, exh. cat., The
Portland Museum of Art, Portland, 2008

Providence 2005
Maureen O'Brien (ed.), *Edgar Degas, Six
Friends at Dieppe*, exh. cat., Museum of Art,
Rhode Island School of Design, Providence,
2005

Raunay 1931
Jeanne Raunay, 'Degas souvenirs
anecdotiques', *La Revue de France*, part 1, 15
March 1931, pp. 263–82; part 2, 1 April 1931,
pp. 469–83; part 3, 15 April 1931, pp. 619–32

Reed and Shapiro 1984
Sue Welsh Reed and Barbara Stern Shapiro,
Edgar Degas: The Painter as Printmaker,
Boston, 1984

Reff 1968
Theodore Reff, 'Some Unpublished Letters
of Degas', *Art Bulletin*, 50, 1, March 1968,
pp. 87–94

Reff 1969
Theodore Reff, 'More Unpublished Letters
of Degas', *Art Bulletin*, 51, 3, 1969, pp. 281–89

Reff 1974
Theodore Reff, 'Works of Art by Degas
in the Detroit Institute of Arts', *Bulletin of the
Detroit Institute of Arts*, 53, 1, 1974, pp. 2–44

Reff 1976
Theodore Reff, *Degas: The Artist's Mind*,
New York, 1976

Reff 1978
Theodore Reff, 'Edgar Degas
and the Dance', *Arts Magazine*, 53, 3,
November 1978, pp. 145–49

Reff 1985
Theodore Reff, *The Notebooks of
Edgar Degas: A Catalogue of the Thirty-eight
Notebooks in the Bibliothèque Nationale and
Other Collections*, 2 vols, New York, 1985

Reff 1998
Theodore Reff, 'Degas Chez Tasset',
in New York 1993, pp. 75–81

Reff 2006
Theodore Reff, 'Atelier Degas', in
'Art Impressioniste et Moderne', sale
catalogue, Christie's, Paris, Wednesday
24 May 2006, pp. 10–53

Rewald 1937
John Rewald, 'Un Portrait de la Princesse
de Metternich par Edgar Degas', *L'Amour
de l'art*, 18, March 1937, pp. 89–90

Rewald 1944
John Rewald, *Degas's Complete Sculpture*,
London, 1944

Rewald 1990
John Rewald, *Degas's Complete Sculpture:
A Catalogue Raisonné*, London, 1944; revised
edition, San Francisco, 1990

Roberts 1963
Keith Roberts, 'The Date of Degas's *The
Rehearsal* in Glasgow', *Burlington Magazine*,
105, 723, June 1963, pp. 280–81

Roosa 1982
Wayne Roosa, 'Degas's Photographic Portrait
of Renoir and Mallarmé: An Interpretation',
Rutgers Art Review, 3, January 1982, pp. 80–
96

Rouart 1945
Denis Rouart, *Degas: à la récherche
de sa technique*, Paris, 1945

Saint-Edmé 1864
Ernest Saint-Edmé, 'La Photographie en
1864, la photo-sculpture', *Annales de
Conservatoire des arts et métiers*, 5, 1864,
pp. 146–47

Saint Louis 1967
Jean Sutherland Boggs, *Drawings by Degas*,
exh. cat., City Art Museum, Saint Louis,
Philadelphia Museum of Art, and Minneapolis
Society of Fine Arts, 1967

Saint-Marc 2010
Stéphanie de Saint-Marc, *Nadar*, Paris, 2010

Saint-Victor 1866
Paul de Saint-Victor, 'La Photosculpture',
La Presse, 15, January 1866, pp. 1–2

San Francisco 1986
Charles S. Moffett with Ruth Berson, Barbara
Lee Williams and Fronia Wissman, *The New
Painting: Impressionism, 1874–1886*, exh. cat.,
Fine Arts Museum of San Francisco and
National Gallery of Art, Washington DC, 1986

Scharf 1962
Aaron Scharf, 'Painting, Photography and the
Image of Movement', *Burlington Magazine*,
104, May 1962, pp. 185–95

Scharf 1968
Aaron Scharf, *Art and Photography*,
London, 1968

Sevin 1975
Françoise Sevin, 'Degas à travers ses mots',
Gazette des Beaux-Arts, 86, 117, July–August
1975, pp. 18–46

Shapero 2007
Bernard J. Shapero Rare Books, *Vintage
Photographic Panoramas, 1850–1950*, with an
introduction by Roland Belgrave, London,
2007

Sickert 1917
Walter Sickert, 'Degas', *Burlington Magazine*,
31, 176, November 1917, pp. 183–92

Sickert 1923
Walter Sickert, 'The Sculptor of Movement', in
*Catalogue of an Exhibition of the Works in
Sculpture of Edgar Degas*, exh. cat., Leicester
Galleries, London, 1923, pp. 5–8

Sickert 1947
Walter Sickert, *A Free House*, London, 1947

Solnit 2003
Rebecca Solnit, *River of Shadows: Eadweard
Muybridge and the Technological Wild West*,
New York, 2003

Soria 1897
Henri de Soria, *Histoire pittoresque
de la danse*, Paris, 1897

Soubieszek 1980
Robert A. Soubieszek, 'Sculpture as the
Sum of Its Profiles: François Willème and
Photosculpture in France, 1859–1868', *Art
Bulletin*, 62, 4, December 1980, pp. 617–30

Terrasse 1983
Antoine Terrasse, *Degas et la photographie*,
Paris, 1983

Thiébault-Sisson 1921
François Thiébault-Sisson, 'Degas sculpteur
par lui-même', *Le Temps*, 23 May 1921, p. 3

Thomson 1985
Richard Thomson, 'Notes on Degas's Sense
of Humour', in Kendall et al. 1985, pp. 9–19

Tinterow and Norton 1989
Gary Tinterow and Ann Norton, 'Degas aux
expositions impressionistes', in Musée
d'Orsay 1989, pp. 289–351

Tissandier 1874
Gaston Tissandier, *Les Merveilles de la
photographie*, Paris, 1874, pp. 205–10

Tissandier 1878
Gaston Tissandier, 'Les Allures du cheval, représentées par la photographie instantanée', *La Nature*, 289, 14 December 1878, pp. 23–26

Valéry 1960
Paul Valéry, *Degas Danse Dessin*, Paris, 1936; reprinted in *Degas Manet Morisot*, trans. David Paul, New York, 1960

Varnedoe 1990
Kirk Varnedoe, *A Fine Disregard: What Makes Modern Art Modern*, London, 1990

Vauvert 1866
Maxime Vauvert, 'Merveilles de la science', *La Monde illustré*, 19, 505, 15 December 1866, pp. 399

Vente I
Vente Collection I, *Catalogue des tableaux, pastels et dessins par Edgar Degas et provenant de son atelier...*, Paris, 6–8 May 1918

Vente II
Vente Collection II, *Catalogue des tableaux, pastels et dessins par Edgar Degas et provenant de son atelier...*, Paris, 11–13 December 1918

Vente III
Vente Collection III, *Catalogue des tableaux, pastels et dessins par Edgar Degas et provenant de son atelier...*, Paris, 7–9 April 1919

Vente IV
Vente Collection IV, *Catalogue des tableaux, pastels et dessins par Edgar Degas et provenant de son atelier...*, Paris, 2–4 July 1919

Vollard 1924
Ambroise Vollard, *Degas*, Paris, 1924

Vollard 1978
Ambroise Vollard, *Recollections of a Picture Dealer*, New York, 1978; first published Boston, 1936

Vollard 1986
Ambroise Vollard, *Degas: An Intimate Portrait*, New York, 1986; first published New York, 1937

Vuillier 1898
Gaston Vuillier, *La Danse*, Paris, 1898

Washington 1984
George Shackelford, *Degas: The Dancers*, exh. cat., National Gallery, Washington DC, 1984–85

Washington 1998
Jean Sutherland Boggs with Shelley G. Sturman and Kimberly Jones, *Degas at the Races*, exh. cat., National Gallery of Art, Washington DC, 1998

Washington 2010
Philip Brookman with Marta Braun, Andy Grundberg, Corey Keller and Rebecca Solnit, *Helios: Eadweard Muybridge in a Time of Change*, exh. cat., Corcoran Gallery of Art, Washington DC, Tate Britain, London, and San Francisco Museum of Art, 2010–11

Wells 1964
William Wells, 'Degas's Staircase', *Scottish Art Review*, 1964, 9, pp. 14–17, 29–30

Wild 1987
Nicole Wild, *Décors et costumes du XIXe siècle à l'Opéra de Paris*, Paris, 1987

Williamstown 2005
Nancy Mowll Matthews et al., *Moving Pictures: American Art and Early Film, 1880–1910*, exh. cat., Williams College Museum of Art, Williamstown, Reynolds House Museum of American Art, Winston-Salem, and the Phillips Collection, Washington DC, 2005–07

Wolff 1881
Albert Wolff, 'A travers Paris', *Le Figaro*, 27, 331, 27 November 1881, p. 1

Wolff 1962
Stéphane Wolff, *L'Opéra au Palais Garnier (1875–1962)*, Paris, 1962

Zola 1991
Emile Zola, *Ecrits sur l'art*, Jean-Pierre Leduc-Adine (ed.), Paris, 1991

Zurich 1995
Félix Bauman and Marianne Karabelnik (eds), *Degas Portraits*, exh. cat., Kunsthaus, Zurich, and Kunsthalle, Tubingen, 1995

Basel
Fondation Beyeler

Beaune
Musée des Beaux-Arts et Musée Marey

Berwick-upon-Tweed
Berwick Museum and Art Gallery

Mr and Mrs Stephen Bettis

Birmingham
Barber Institute of Fine Arts,
University of Birmingham

Jean Bonna

Bradford
National Media Museum

Broadway
Trinity House

Cambridge
Fitzwilliam Museum

Cambridge, Massachusetts
Harvard Art Museums/Fogg Museum

Chicago
Art Institute of Chicago

Detroit
Detroit Institute of Arts

Essen
Museum Folkwang

Peter and Patricia Findlay

Flint, Michigan
Flint Institute of Arts

Glasgow
Culture and Sport Glasgow on behalf
of Glasgow City Council

Jasper Johns

Kingston
Kingston Museum and Heritage

Collection Jan Krugier

Ms Tzila and Mr Aviel Krugier

Galerie Krugier & Cie, Geneva

Lausanne
Fondation de l'Hermitage
Musée Cantonal des Beaux-Arts

London
British Library
Courtauld Gallery
National Gallery
Natural History Museum
Royal Academy of Arts
Tate
Victoria and Albert Museum

The Honorable Earle I. Mack

Moscow
State Pushkin Museum of Fine Arts

New York
Metropolitan Museum of Art
Museum of Modern Art
Pierpont Morgan Library

Norfolk, Virginia
Chrysler Museum of Art

Norman, Oklahoma
Fred Jones Jr Museum of Art

Notre Dame, Indiana
Snite Museum of Art,
University of Notre Dame

Oxford
Ashmolean Museum

Paris
Bibliothèque-Musée de l'Opéra
Bibliothèque nationale de France
Collège de France
Ecole nationale supérieure des beaux-arts
Musée de l'Assistance Publique
Musée des Arts Décoratifs
Musée d'Orsay

Portland, Oregon
Portland Art Museum

Princeton, New Jersey
Princeton University Art Museum

Providence, Rhode Island
Museum of Art, Rhode Island School
of Design

Rochester, New York
George Eastman House

Rotterdam
Museum Boijmans Van Beuningen

Saint Louis, Missouri
Saint Louis Art Museum

Galerie Schmit

Thomas Gibson Fine Art Ltd

Toledo, Ohio
Toledo Museum of Art

Washington DC
National Gallery of Art

Williamstown, Massachussets
Sterling and Francine Clark Art Institute

Diane B. Wilsey

Thomas G. Yanul

Zurich
Foundation E. G. Bührle Collection

*and others who wish
to remain anonymous*

PHOTOGRAPHIC ACKNOWLEDGEMENTS

Every effort has been made to trace the photographers of works of art reproduced. All works are reproduced with kind permission of the owners. Specific acknowledgements are as follows:

Arkansas Arts Center Foundation Collection. Purchase, Fred W. Allsopp Memorial Acquisition Fund. 1983.010.002: fig. 87
Birmingham, © The Trustees of the Barber Institute of Fine Arts: cat. 79
Bradford, © National Media Museum/SSPL: cats 37, 74
Bremen, Kunstverein, photo Lars Lohrisch: fig. 66
Cambridge, © Fitzwilliam Museum: cats 81, 97
Cambridge, Mass., © President and Fellows of Harvard College: cat. 51; /Katya Kallsen: cat. 7
Chicago, © The Art Institute of Chicago: cats 23, 41, 105
J. C. Couval: cat. 91
Farmington, Connecticut, © Alfred Atmore Pope Collection, Hill-Stead Museum: fig. 38
Florence, © Scala/Art Resource: fig. 51; /The Metropolitan Museum of Art, New York: figs 3, 16, 22, page 259 (right); /Musée d'Orsay, Paris: fig. 4; /2009 Museum Associates/LACMA: fig. 8; /© 2011. Digital image, The Museum of Modern Art, New York: page 258 (right); /The National Gallery, London: fig. 11; /The Philadelphia Museum of Art: fig. 60
Roy Fox: cats 13, 83, 87
Kelvin Freeman: cat. 67
Glasgow, © Culture and Sport Glasgow (Museums): cats 1, 85, 117
Patrick Goetelen: cat. 47
Graham Haber, 2010: cat. 24
Veljko Ilic: cat. 53
Kingston, photo reproduced with kind permission of Kingston Museum and Heritage: cat 68
Pernille Klemp: cat. 44
Lausanne, Musée cantonal des Beaux-Arts de Lausanne/J.-C. Ducret: cat. 80
London, courtesy of Alon Zakaim Fine Art: cat. 123

London, © The Bridgeman Art Library: cats 39, 101, figs 1, 21, page 257 (left); /Brooklyn Museum of Art, New York: fig. 5; /Sterling and Francine Clark Art Institute, Williamstown, Mass.: figs 24, 26; /Dahesh Museum of Art, New York: fig. 28; /private collection/Archives Charmet: fig. 2; private collection/Giraudon: fig. 18; /© Pushkin Museum, Moscow: fig. 65; /Von der Heydt-Museum, Wuppertal/Giraudon: fig. 86
London, © British Library Board: cats 63, 64, 66, 98, figs 52, 72, 73
London, © Christie's Images Limited, 2011: cat. 52, 58
London, © Corbis/Bettmann: fig. 49
London, © Royal Academy of Arts/Prudence Cuming: cats 28, 65.1, 65.2, 69, 72, 75, fig. 48
London, © Tate, 2010: cat. 26
London, © V&A Images/Victoria and Albert Museum: cats 15–17, 35, 36, 70, 71, 88, 89
London and New York, © Trinity House: cat. 54
Los Angeles, © The J. Paul Getty Museum: figs 15, 59
Jean-Louis Losi: cat. 29
Michigan, Tim Thayer, Oak Park: cat. 46
New York, © Christie's Images Limited (2008): cat. 57
New York, courtesy of George Eastman House, International Museum of Photography and Film: figs 19, 54, 89
New York, © 2010. Image copyright The Metropolitan Museum of Art/Art Resource/Scala, Florence: cats 33, 49
New York, © 2010. Digital image/The Museum of Modern Art/Art Resource/Scala: cats 96, 119
New York, photo courtesy of Wildenstein & Co., Inc.: cat. 114
Oslo, The National Museum of Art, Architecture and Design: fig. 29
Oxford, photo © Ashmolean Museum, University of Oxford (WA1937.23, bequeathed by Mrs W. F. R. Weldon, 1937): cat. 106
Paris, Les Arts décoratifs/Laurent Sully Jaulmes – all rights reserved: cat. 30
Paris, © Association frères Lumière: figs 77, 80
Paris, © Bibliothèque nationale de France: cats 3, 5, 14, 31, 107–09, figs 6, 7, 10, 17, 34, 35, 41, 61–64, 78, 84

Paris, Cinémathèque française: figs 76, 81, 85
Paris, © Collège de France, Archives: cats 73, 76, 77, 91, figs 55, 68–71, 90
Paris, © Ecole des Beaux-Arts: fig. 56
Paris, image by permission of the estate of Sacha Guitry: fig. 79
Paris, © F. Marin – APHP: cat. 94
Paris, © RMN (Musée d'Orsay)/Michèle Bellot: cat. 110; /Jean-Gilles Berizzi: fig. 27; /Hervé Lewandowski: cats 104, 120, 121, figs 12, 40, 57, 82, 90, 91, page 258 (left); /Patrice Schmidt: cat. 111; /Jean Schormans: cat. 84, fig. 14
Paris, © RMN (Musée du Louvre. Droits réservés): fig. 23
Pasadena, © 2011 The Norton Simon Foundation: fig. 20
Rochester, courtesy of George Eastman House, International Museum of Photography and Film: cats 27, 34, figs 33, 36, 37
Rome, © Fondazione Primoli: fig. 58
Rotterdam, © Museum Boijmans Van Beuningen: fig. 53
Saint Louis, © Saint Louis Art Museum, Museum Purchase: cat. 78, fig. 88
Peter Schibli: cat. 125
Giorgio Skory: cat. 122
Studio Tom Haartsen: cat. 60
Jim Walker FRPS: cat. 112
Washington, National Gallery of Art: cats 32, 45, figs 25, 30, 67
Bruce M. White: cat. 118
Williamstown, Mass., © Sterling and Francine Clark Art Institute/Michael Agee: cats 86, 95

BENEFACTORS OF THE ROYAL ACADEMY OF ARTS

Richard and Susan Shoylekov
Mrs Amy Jo Spitalier
Bob and Amy Stefanowski
Mr Robert Suss
John Tackaberry
Ms Inna Vainshtock
Mary Wolridge

Patron Donor
Victoria Miro
and others who wish to remain anonymous

TRUSTS AND FOUNDATIONS
American Express Philanthropy
Art Mentor Foundation
The Atlas Fund
The Albert Van den Bergh Charitable Trust
The Bomonty Charitable Trust
The Charlotte Bonham-Carter Charitable Trust
William Brake Charitable Trust
R M Burton 1998 Charitable Trust
C H K Charities Limited
P H G Cadbury Charitable Trust
The Carew Pole Charitable Trust
The Clore Duffield Foundation
John S Cohen Foundation
Ronald H Cordover Family Foundation
The Evan Cornish Foundation
The Sidney and Elizabeth Corob Charitable Trust
Alan Cristea Gallery
The Dovehouse Trust
The Gilbert and Eileen Edgar Foundation
The John Ellerman Foundation
The Eranda Foundation
Lucy Mary Ewing Charitable Trust
The Margery Fish Charity
The Fletcher Priest Trust
The Flow Foundation
The Garfield Weston Foundation
Gatsby Charitable Foundation
The Golden Bottle Trust
The Gordon Foundation
Sue Hammerson Charitable Trust
The Charles Hayward Foundation
Heritage Lottery Fund
The Harold Hyam Wingate Foundation
The Ironmongers' Company
The Emmanuel Kaye Foundation
The Kindersley Foundation
The de Laszlo Foundation
The David Lean Foundation
The Leche Trust
The Leverhulme Trust
The Maccabaeans
The McCorquodale Charitable Trust
The Michael Marks Charitable Trust
The Simon Marks Charitable Trust
The Paul Mellon Centre
The Paul Mellon Estate
The Mercers' Company
Margaret and Richard Merrell Foundation
The Millichope Foundation
The Mondriaan Foundation
The Monument Trust
The Henry Moore Foundation
The Mulberry Trust
The J Y Nelson Charitable Trust
Newby Trust Limited
The Old Broad Street Charity Trust
The Peacock Charitable Trust
The Pennycress Trust
PF Charitable Trust
The Stanley Picker Charitable Trust
The Pidem Fund
The Edith and Ferdinand Porjes Charitable Trust
Mr and Mrs J A Pye's Charitable Settlement
Rayne Foundation
The Reed Foundation
T Rippon & Sons (Holdings) Ltd
Rootstein Hopkins Foundation
The Rose Foundation
Schroder Charity Trust
The Sellars Charitable Trust
The Archie Sherman Charitable Trust
The South Square Trust
Spencer Charitable Trust
Stanley Foundation Limited
Oliver Stanley Charitable Trust
The Steel Charitable Trust
Peter Storrs Trust
Strand Parishes Trust
The Joseph Strong Frazer Trust
The Swan Trust
Thaw Charitable Trust
Sir Jules Thorn Charitable Trust
Tiffany & Co
The Bruce Wake Charity
Celia Walker Art Foundation
Warburg Pincus International LLC
Weinstock Fund
Wilkinson Eyre Architects
The Spencer Wills Trust
The Maurice Wohl Charitable Foundation
The Wolfson Foundation
The Hazel M Wood Charitable Trust
The Worshipful Company of Painter-Stainers

**AMERICAN ASSOCIATES OF
THE ROYAL ACADEMY TRUST**

Burlington House Trust
Mrs James C Slaughter

Benjamin West Society
Mr Francis Finlay
Mrs Deborah Loeb Brice
Mrs Nancy B Negley

Benefactors
Mrs Edmond J Safra
The Hon John C Whitehead

Sponsors
Mrs Drue Heinz Hon DBE
David Hockney CH RA
Mr Arthur L Loeb
Mrs Lucy F McGrath
Mr and Mrs Hamish Maxwell
Mr and Mrs Richard J Miller Jr
Diane A Nixon
Ms Joan Stern
Mr and Mrs Frederick B Whittemore
Dr and Mrs Robert D Wickham

Patrons
Mr and Mrs Steven Ausnit
Mr and Mrs E William Aylward
Mr Donald A Best
Mrs Mildred C Brinn
Mrs Benjamin Coates
Mrs Mary Sharp Cronson
Anne S Davidson
Mrs June Dyson
Mr Jonathan Farkas
Mr and Mrs Lawrence S Friedland
Mr and Mrs Leslie Garfield
Dr Bruce C Horten
The Hon W Eugene Johnston and Mrs Johnston
Mr William W Karatz
Mr and Mrs Wilson Nolen
Lady Renwick
Mr and Mrs Stanley De Forest Scott
Mrs Frederick M Stafford
Ms Louisa Stude Sarofim
Martin J Sullivan OBE
Mr Arthur O Sulzberger
Mr and Mrs Alfred A Taubman
Ms Britt Tidelius
Mr Robert W Wilson

Donors
Mr James C Armstrong
Mr Constantin R Boden
Dr and Mrs Robert Bookchin
Ms Laura Christman and William Rothacker
Alyce Faye Cleese
Lois M Collier
Mr Richard C Colyear
Mr and Mrs Howard Davis
Ms Zita Davisson
Ms Maria Garvey Dowd
Mr Robert H Enslow
Mrs Katherine D Findlay
Mrs Raymond C Foster Jr
Mr and Mrs Gordon P Getty
Mr and Mrs Gustave M Hauser
Mrs Judith Heath
Ms Elaine Kend
Mr and Mrs Nicholas L S Kirkbride
The Hon Samuel K Lessey Jr
Annette Lester
Mr Henry S Lynn Jr
Ms Clare E McKeon
Ms Christine Mainwaring-Samwell
Mrs Charles W Olson III
Cynthia Hazen Polsky and Leon B Polsky
Ms Jane Richards
Mrs Nanette Ross
Mrs Martin Slifka
Mr Albert H Small
Mr Morton I Sosland
Mrs Judith Villard

Corporate and Foundation Support
American Express Foundation
The Blackstone Charitable Foundation
The Brown Foundation
Fortnum & Mason
Gibson, Dunn & Crutcher
The Horace W Goldsmith Foundation
Hauser Foundation
Kress Foundation
Leon Levy Foundation
Loeb Foundation
Henry Luce Foundation
Lynberg & Watkins
Edmond J Safra Philanthropic Foundation
Siezen Foundation
Sony Corporation of America
Starr Foundation
Thaw Charitable Trust

CORPORATE MEMBERS OF THE ROYAL ACADEMY
Launched in 1988, the Royal Academy's Corporate Membership Scheme has proved highly successful. Corporate membership offers benefits for staff, clients and community partners and access to the Academy's facilities and resources. The outstanding support we receive from companies via the scheme is vital to the continuing success of the Academy and we thank all members for their valuable support and continued enthusiasm.

Premier Level Members
A T Kearney
BNY Mellon
Barclays plc
CB Richard Ellis
Christie's
Deutsche Bank AG
FTI Consulting
GlaxoSmithKline plc
Goldman Sachs International
Insight Investment
Jones Lang LaSalle
JTI
KPMG
Lombard Odier Darier Hentsch
Schroders plc
Smith and Williamson

Corporate Members
Abellio
All Nippon Airways
Aon
Apax Partners
AXA Insurance & AXA Investment Managers
Bloomberg LP
BNP Paribas
The Boston Consulting Group UK LLP
British American Tobacco
Capital International Limited
Clifford Chance
Crédit Agricole CIB
Ernst & Young
F & C Asset Management plc
The French Chamber of Commerce
GAM
Generation Investment Management LLP
GKN Aerospace
Greenpark Capital
Heidrick & Struggles
HSBC
Jefferies International
John Lewis Partnership
JP Morgan
Lazard
Lend Lease
Man Group plc
Mizuho International plc
Morgan Stanley
Northern Trust
Pentland Group plc
Rio Tinto
Royal Bank of Scotland
The Royal Society of Chemistry
Slaughter and May
Société Générale
Summit Partners
Tiffany & Co
Timothy Sammons Ltd
Trowers & Hamlins
UBS
Vision Capital Group
Weil, Gotshal & Manges

SUPPORTERS OF PAST EXHIBITIONS
The President and Council of the Royal Academy would like to thank the following supporters and benefactors for their generous contributions towards major exhibitions in the last ten years:

2011
Eyewitness: Hungarian Photography in the Twentieth Century. Brassaï, Capa, Kertész, Moholy-Nagy, Munkácsi
  2009–2013 Season supported by JTI
  Hungarofest
  OTP Bank
243rd Summer Exhibition
  Insight Investment
Premiums and *RA Schools Annual Dinner and Auction*
  Newton Investment Management
Watteau: The Drawings
  2009–2013 Season supported by JTI
  Region Holdings
Modern British Sculpture
  American Express Foundation
  The Henry Moore Foundation
  Hauser & Wirth
  Art Mentor Foundation Lucerne
  Sotheby's
  Blain Southern
  Welcome to Yorkshire: Tourism Partner

2010
GSK Contemporary – Aware: Art Fashion Identity
  GlaxoSmithKline

Pioneering Painters: The Glasgow Boys 1880–1900
Pioneering Painters: The Glasgow Boys 1880–1900
  2009–2013 Season supported by JTI
  Glasgow Museums
Treasures from Budapest: European Masterpieces from Leonardo to Schiele
  OTP Bank
  Villa Budapest
  Daniel Katz Gallery, London
  Travel Partner: Cox & Kings
Sargent and the Sea
  2009–2013 Season supported by JTI
242nd Summer Exhibition
  Insight Investment
Paul Sandby RA: Picturing Britain, A Bicentenary Exhibition
  2009–2013 Season supported by JTI
The Real Van Gogh: The Artist and His Letters
  BNY Mellon
  Hiscox
  Heath Lambert
  Travel Partner: Cox & Kings
  RA Outreach Programme
  Deutsche Bank AG

2009
GSK Contemporary
  GlaxoSmithKline
Wild Thing: Epstein, Gaudier-Brzeska, Gill
  2009–2013 Season supported by JTI
  BNP Paribas
  The Henry Moore Foundation
Anish Kapoor
  JTI
  Richard Chang
  Richard and Victoria Sharp
  Louis Vuitton
  The Henry Moore Foundation
J W Waterhouse: The Modern Pre-Raphaelite
  2009–2013 Season supported by JTI
  Champagne Perrier-Jouët
  GasTerra
  Gasunie
241st Summer Exhibition
  Insight Investment
Kuniyoshi. From the Arthur R. Miller Collection
  2009–2013 Season supported by JTI
  Canon
  Travel partner: Cox & Kings
Premiums and *RA Schools Show*
  Mizuho International plc
RA Outreach Programme
  Deutsche Bank AG

2008
GSK Contemporary
  GlaxoSmithKline
Byzantium 330–1453
  J F Costopoulos Foundation
  A G Leventis Foundation
  Stavros Niarchos Foundation
  Travel Partner: Cox & Kings
Miró, Calder, Giacometti, Braque: Aimé Maeght and His Artists
  BNP Paribas
Vilhelm Hammershøi: The Poetry of Silence
  OAK Foundation Denmark
  Novo Nordisk
240th Summer Exhibition
  Insight Investment
Premiums and *RA Schools Show*
  Mizuho International plc
RA Outreach Programme
  Deutsche Bank AG
From Russia: French and Russian Master Paintings 1870–1925 from Moscow and St Petersburg
  E.ON
  2008 Season supported by Sotheby's

2007
Paul Mellon's Legacy: A Passion for British Art
  The Bank of New York Mellon
Georg Baselitz
  Eurohypo AG
239th Summer Exhibition
  Insight Investment
Impressionists by the Sea
  Farrow & Ball
Premiums and *RA Schools Show*
  Mizuho International plc
RA Outreach Programme
  Deutsche Bank AG
The Unknown Monet
  Bank of America

2006
238th Summer Exhibition
  Insight Investment
Chola: Sacred Bronzes of Southern India
  Travel Partner: Cox & Kings
Premiums and *RA Schools Show*
  Mizuho International plc
RA Outreach Programme
  Deutsche Bank AG
Rodin
  Ernst & Young

2005
China: The Three Emperors, 1662–1795
  Goldman Sachs International

Impressionism Abroad: Boston and French Painting
  Fidelity Foundation
Matisse, His Art and His Textiles: The Fabric of Dreams
  Farrow & Ball
Premiums and *RA Schools Show*
  The Guardian
  Mizuho International plc
Turks: A Journey of a Thousand Years, 600–1600
  Akkök Group of Companies
  Aygaz
  Corus
  Garanti Bank
  Lassa Tyres

2004
236th Summer Exhibition
  A T Kearney
Ancient Art to Post-Impressionism: Masterpieces from the Ny Carlsberg Glyptotek, Copenhagen
  Carlsberg UK Ltd
  Danske Bank
  Novo Nordisk
The Art of Philip Guston (1913–1980)
  American Associates of the Royal Academy Trust
The Art of William Nicholson
  RA Exhibition Patrons Group
Vuillard: From Post-Impressionist to Modern Master
  RA Exhibition Patrons Group

2003
235th Summer Exhibition
  A T Kearney
Ernst Ludwig Kirchner: The Dresden and Berlin Years
  RA Exhibition Patrons Group
Giorgio Armani: A Retrospective
  American Express
  Mercedes-Benz
Illuminating the Renaissance: The Triumph of Flemish Manuscript Painting in Europe
  American Associates of the Royal Academy Trust
  Virginia and Simon Robertson
Masterpieces from Dresden
  ABN AMRO
  Classic FM
Premiums and *RA Schools Show*
  Walker Morris
Pre-Raphaelite and Other Masters: The Andrew Lloyd Webber Collection
  Christie's
  Classic FM
  UBS Wealth Management

2002
234th Summer Exhibition
  A T Kearney
Aztecs
  British American Tobacco
  Mexico Tourism Board
  Pemex
  Virginia and Simon Robertson
Masters of Colour: Derain to Kandinsky. Masterpieces from The Merzbacher Collection
  Classic FM
Premiums and *RA Schools Show*
  Debenhams Retail plc
*RA Outreach Programme**
  Yakult UK Ltd
Return of the Buddha: The Qingzhou Discoveries
  RA Exhibition Patrons Group

* Recipients of a Pairing Scheme Award, managed by Arts + Business. Arts + Business is funded by the Arts Council of England and the Department for Culture, Media and Sport

OTHER SUPPORTERS
Sponsors of events, publications and other items in the past five years:
Carlisle Group plc
Castello di Reschio
Cecilia Chan
Country Life
Guy Dawson
Derwent Valley Holdings plc
Dresdner Kleinwort Wasserstein
Lucy Flemming McGrath
Fosters and Partners
Goldman Sachs International
Gome International
Gucci Group
Hines
IBJ International plc
John Doyle Construction
Harvey and Allison McGrath
Martin Krajewski
Marks & Spencer
Michael Hopkins & Partners
Morgan Stanley Dean Witter
The National Trust
Prada
Radisson Edwardian Hotels
Richard and Ruth Rogers
Rob van Helden
The Wine Studio